GENERAL PRINCIPLES

OF

CRIMINAL LAW

SECOND EDITION

BY

JEROME HALL

DISTINGUISHED SERVICE PROFESSOR OF LAW
INDIANA UNIVERSITY

THE LAWBOOK EXCHANGE, LTD.
Clark, New Jersey

ISBN 9781584774983 (hardcover)
ISBN 9781616191337 (paperback)

Lawbook Exchange edition 2010

The quality of this reprint is equivalent to the quality of the original work.

THE LAWBOOK EXCHANGE, LTD.

33 Terminal Avenue
Clark, New Jersey 07066-1321

*Please see our website for a selection of our other publications
and fine facsimile reprints of classic works of legal history:*
www.lawbookexchange.com

Library of Congress Cataloging-in-Publication Data

Hall, Jerome, 1901-
    General principles of criminal law / by Jerome Hall— 2nd ed.
       p. cm.
    Originally published: 2nd ed. Indianapolis : Bobbs-Merrill Co., c1960.
    Includes bibliographical references and index.
    ISBN 1-58477-498-3 (cloth a& paper)
      I. Criminal law. II. Title: Criminal law. II. Title.

K5018.H35 2005
345—dc22   2004053810

Printed in the United States of America on acid-free paper

GENERAL PRINCIPLES

OF

CRIMINAL LAW

SECOND EDITION

BY

JEROME HALL

DISTINGUISHED SERVICE PROFESSOR OF LAW
INDIANA UNIVERSITY

THE **BOBBS-MERRILL** COMPANY, INC.
A SUBSIDIARY OF HOWARD W. SAMS & CO., INC.
Publishers · INDIANAPOLIS · NEW YORK

To My Wife

PREFACE

This book, first published in 1947, was written to elucidate the basic ideas of criminal law in the light of current knowledge and to organize that law in terms of a definite theory. In the preparation of this edition, I have tried to realize more fully the original intention.

The first edition has been almost completely revised and reorganized, and several new chapters have been added. A large part of the history of criminal attempt and shorter discussions not directly pertinent to the principal subject of the book have been omitted. I have used the earlier publication of certain of my articles to further the analysis of some of the more difficult problems. Chapter 13 includes parts of the article published in 65 Yale Law Journal, chapter 11 appeared in 33 Indiana Law Journal, some passages were published in 100 University of Pennsylvania Law Review, and chapter 8 is a revision of the essay in *Studies in Jurisprudence and Criminal Theory* (1958). I thank the publishers for permission to reprint these excerpts and I greatly appreciate the secretarial and research assistance generously provided by Indiana University.

JEROME HALL

Bloomington, Indiana

PREFACE TO THE FIRST EDITION

Serious thinking in any field of knowledge culminates in a search for and analysis of basic principles that comprise the foundations upon which the entire discipline rests. This book is devoted to an analysis of such principles of criminal law and of the major doctrines of that law. Because the principles of criminal law include many of the ultimate ideas of Western civilization, one might well devote a lifetime to the study of those principles and still regard the results with diffidence. The prospective reader is entitled to know the relevant facts of the present work.

Not long after the publication of *Theft, Law and Society* in 1935, I turned my attention increasingly to the more general problems of criminal law. In 1937, I wrote an article on the principle of legality, which elaborated my report on that subject at the Hague meeting of the International Society of Comparative Law. Next, I engaged in the study of criminal attempt, strict liability, and the interrelations of criminal law and torts. By 1940, I had become persuaded of the great importance of and need for a book dealing with the fundamental principles and doctrines of criminal law and of the possibility that a continuation of my efforts might produce such a work. During the succeeding years, the greater part of my time available for research, subject to the discharge of various other duties, has been devoted to that objective. I have taken advantage of the publication of several of my articles on the above and other problems for use in this book; the prior publication permitted further thought and improvement of the analysis. Thus the parts of the articles included in this book have been revised and in some very important regards they have been greatly modified.

The reader will, of course, form an opinion concerning the kind of analysis that is presented and the methods employed. But it may not be superfluous to note that various problems are discussed in different contexts in the book. This does not involve repetition; it implies that a reading of the writer's entire analysis of those problems requires reference to the Index and to the relevant discussions noted there as well as in the cross-references cited in the footnotes.

I am obliged to my former student, Ruth Smalley, for considerable assistance during the past two years. Not only did she relieve me of the major burden of the routine aspects of the research as well as of the compilation of the index and the checking of proof; she also contributed much valuable criticism and made many helpful suggestions.

I am also obliged to Dean Bernard Gavit for facilitating the research in many ways. Finally, I wish to thank the publishers for permission to reprint from my articles which appeared in the Columbia, Harvard, Pennsylvania, and Yale law reviews, and in *Twentieth Century Sociology* (1945, Philosophical Library).

JEROME HALL

CONTENTS

CHAPTER V

MENS REA: (3) THE THEORY OF NON-MORAL PENAL LIABILITY

CHAPTER VI

CRIMINAL CONDUCT—THE EXTERNAL MANIFESTATION OF MENS REA

CHAPTER VII

HARM

CHAPTER VIII

CAUSATION

CHAPTER I

CRIMINAL LAW THEORY

IN an inclusive sense, "theory" signifies the knowledge of a subject, acquired without any practical objectives in view; and it is especially concerned with the ultimate ideas which comprise the foundation of a science or social discipline. "A theory" has a much narrower reference, for example, the kinetic-molecular theory of matter. In this sense, a theory is a definite conceptual scheme which correlates many otherwise disconnected bits of knowledge.[1] While a scientific theory is directly valid in relation to the empirical laws it explains, these, in turn, are verified by their correspondence with fact. Significance, simplicity, and suggestivity in research determine preference among competing theories.

The above observations also apply in a general way to descriptive theories of criminal law, although their verification and significance depend upon additional, normative factors. A theory of criminal law is constructed of a set of ideas by reference to which every penal law can be significantly "placed," and thus explained.[2] This, indeed, is the gist of explanation in any field — the location of data in the

[1] " . . . by 'theory' one understands an explicit formulation of determinate relations between a set of variables, in terms of which a fairly extensive class of empirically ascertainable regularities (or laws) can be explained (always provided that suitable boundary conditions for the application of the theory are supplied). . . ." Nagel, *Symposium: Problems of Concept and Theory Formation in the Social Sciences,* pub. in Science, Language, and Human Rights 46 (1952).

[2] The rules of penal law are elucidated by being related to more general propositions, which are organized in terms of a theory of penal law.

context of a theory.[3] In sum, the most important functions of a theory of criminal law are to elucidate certain basic ideas and organize the criminal laws, thereby greatly increasing the significance of criminal law.

A theory of penal law (briefly, penal theory or criminal theory) should be tested by the significance of its explanation of existing penal law, and the scholar's primary vocation is to increase that knowledge. If he foregoes the rigors of that task because of his desire to reform the law, the results are bound to be problematical. Both theory and reform are obviously important, but the two should not be confused nor should theory be depreciated in the name of humanitarianism. The only sound procedure is to cleave persistently to the single-minded goal of elucidating the existing penal law, asking only — which theory will maximize our understanding of that law? It also happens, however, as the writer has elsewhere shown,[4] that a rigorous adherence to theoretical inquiry inevitably uncovers areas where reforms are needed. When these discoveries are thus made, as by-products of research, the proposed reforms are apt to be defensible. In any case, the subject matter of the theory presented in this book is the existing criminal law — the existing penal codes, statutes and decisions.

It ought to be more widely recognized how extremely difficult it is to exclude one's values from the construction of his theory of penal law; indeed, much of the diversity of existing theories, unsuspected when only their far-ranging superstructures are considered, results from conflicting valuations, e.g. those regarding negligence and punishment. Perhaps, the most that should be expected is that such

---

[3] "A fact or law is explained only when a sufficient knowledge of the system to which it belongs is reached to enable one to interpret the fact or law in terms of that system, and as one of the actual members of that coherent and orderly whole." Robinson, The Principles of Reasoning 291 (1947). "We are said to *explain*, when a conjunction of elements or features in the real, whose connexion is not intelligible from a consideration of themselves, is made clear through connexions shown between them and others." Joseph, An Introduction to Logic 502 (2nd ed. 1916).

[4] Theft, Law and Society (2nd ed. 1952).

"preferences" and their implications be articulated. Accordingly, the writer believes it will be helpful if some of the postulates of the present work are noted at the outset.

In the theory presented in this book, *mens rea* is defined to exclude negligence and, of course, the quite innocent conduct that is subjected to strict liability. It seems evident that this narrow definition of *mens rea* has many advantages. For example, it makes possible the precise definition of the relevant, probably most important, principle of penal law, with similar far-ranging consequences for the definition of many crimes. For the reference of that definition is to definite states of awareness — intentionality and recklessness — and the corresponding conduct is clearly voluntary in the sense of being end-directed or end-hazarded, *i.e.* as to certain proscribed harms.

In contrast to this, current "penal law" holds that negligent behavior may give rise to penal liability. The consequences for theories built upon that preference are considerable and unfortunate. In the first place, it is necessary, on that premise, to define *mens rea* and the corresponding "fault" or "guilt" in wide terms which include the inadvertence of negligent behavior. This not only clouds the meaning of *mens rea* and penal harm, it also greatly obscures the causal problem in penal law; and other complications result from using "*mens rea*" to denote very diverse states of mind. For example, if dubious findings that certain persons "could" have acted carefully are also admitted within the scope of *mens rea*, is it not likely that both "*mens rea*" and "guilt" denote such different states of mind, conduct and behavior as to be very imprecise tools of analysis, perhaps in some cases, a mere formality? We shall discuss this question in later chapters.

The writer's preference in the above regard, expressed in a narrowly defined concept of *mens rea*, also implies positively that normal adults who voluntarily commit certain harms ought to be punished. What needs to be stressed, however, is the even stronger negative implication of this definition. Since the punishment of a human being is a very serious matter, any doubt regarding the appropriateness of penal liability should be resolved by narrowing its scope. Accordingly, if one is uncertain whether negligent persons should be subjected to punishment, that doubt ought to be resolved in the indicated way. Non-punitive sanctions which modern law abundantly provides may also be more effective.

Another major preference, reflected in the writer's theory, is firm adherence to a rigorous principle of legality. The protection of the individual from the heavy punitive hand of public officials, the equality of treatment which must also be included in any cogent view of justice, the certainty of legal processes, which is the condition of any knowledge of law — these and other precious values depend on precise legality — the "rule of law." Where the conditions of penal liability are vague, the principle of legality is proportionately weakened. Since it can have no greater vitality and precision than its contents allow, the inclusion of widely diverse states of mind, conduct, behavior and harm takes an inevitable toll. So, too, while even verbal insistence upon guilt may be laudatory, the inclusion, in the definition of crimes, of motives and other uncertainties regarding the competence of inadvertent or ignorant harm-doers greatly weakens legality. To weaken that basic principle seriously and, at the same time, to insist that a higher ethics requires that or, what comes to the same thing, to insist that such an ethics requires certain decisions regarding guilt, the effect of which dilutes legality because of the vagueness of the decisions, is hardly a satisfactory solution of difficult problems.

It must, of course, be granted that some aspects of any theory of criminal law require that difficult decisions be made. How to maintain rigorous legality and at the same time deal justly with extreme cases which barely oppose the central purpose of the relevant laws, how to preserve that legality and also individualize punishment by taking many subtle, personal factors into account raise perennial problems for judges and administrators as well as for theorists. Again, some persons who intentionally or recklessly commit forbidden harms, and are thus within the writer's definition of *mens rea*, have, for one reason or another, different values than those represented in the current penal law. Are there nevertheless valid grounds for subjecting them to its onerous sanctions? These difficult problems, which no theory of criminal law may avoid, will be discussed in later chapters. The present purpose is to call attention to important aspects of criminal theory which are the source of considerable misunderstanding. All scholars agree, of course, that it is important to advance the science of criminal law as far and as rapidly as possible; and this involves standards which are quite different from that concerning the ethics of punishment. But it is pertinent to ask whether the restriction of criminal conduct to intentional and reckless harm-doing does not also result in greater clarity and in a higher degree of congruence between the theory and the relevant data. The precise definition of the other basic concepts, which this facilitates, also furthers the progress of criminal theory.

Finally, it should be noted that although the theory presented in this book is for the most part expressed in terms of traditional psychology, that does not in the writer's view depend upon, nor, on the other hand, does it oppose, a metaphysics of the "will" or "mind." Its psychology rests rather upon certain common experiences, *e.g.* that of self-direction towards various ends. Where such terms as "will," "volition," "intention," "motive" and so on are employed, they refer to the indicated experiences, especially those characterizing human actions.[5] So, too, it is hoped, the use of traditional terms regarding moral culpability will not be assumed to imply the acceptance of dogmatic or classical views of personal responsibility or any disinclination to take advantage of available knowledge to improve the penal law and its administration especially as regards harm-doers who suffer from more or less serious impairment.

THE PROGRESS OF THE PROFESSIONAL LITERATURE

Criminal theory originated in ancient cultures, notably in

[5] *Cf.* Mayo, *Is There a Case for the General Will?* pub. in Philosophy, Politics and Society 92 (Laslett ed. 1956).

Plato's dialogues. For example, in his *Laws* Plato discusses mental disease and intoxication, intentional and negligent harm-doing, criminal attempts, differences between tortious and penal liability, and so on. Nor is it surprising that there is also a large literature of theological speculation regarding crime and punishment, *e.g.* the medieval discussions of *mens rea* and *versari in re illicita*.[6]

In the professional literature of Anglo-American criminal law from the thirteenth century onwards, this interest in the fundamental ideas of criminal law increases progressively. Bracton, "the crown and flower of English medieval jurisprudence," is the first important writer in this field. The terms he employed to designate specific crimes are, for the most part, still extant: robbers, burglars, thieves, forgers, treason, conspirators, sedition, homicide, breaking the peace, mayhem, assault, arson, larceny, abortion, false imprisonment. A few have become obsolete, *e.g.* outlaws, cattle-lifters, clippers-of-coin, hiding treasure-trove. His "falsifier" has been subdivided; his "harbourers" have become accessories after the fact or receivers of stolen goods; "murder" is no longer the secret killing it was in his day. These and many other terms were carefully detailed.

But we find hardly any classification of crimes in Bracton's *Legibus* or in the later medieval treatises. The lines of analysis were procedural; distinctions among treason, felony and misdemeanor were made with a direct eye to that end.[7] Bracton's treatise was, of course, far in advance of Anglo-Saxon thought reflected in mere collections of completely isolated rules. Bracton juxtaposed the rules defining types of crime and he analyzed some of their elementary concepts. There are also occasional significant generalizations;[8] but these were restricted to a specific offense (homi-

---

[6] Gand, De L'Intention en Droit Pénal 7-9 (1911).

[7] *Concerning the Crown* is the second treatise of Bracton's Book III, vol. II, which is entitled "Of Actions" (Twiss ed. 1879).

[8] As when he states "a crime has not been contracted, unless the will of hurting has intervened, and the will and the purpose distinguish the misdeed, and a theft is never at all committed without the intention of thieving. And according to what may be said of an infant or a madman, when the innocence of design protects the one, and the imbecility

cide). No attempt was made to apply them generally;[9] indeed, a salient feature of his treatise is the lack of any organization of the field.

Hale's *Pleas of the Crown* provided the first great peak in the English professional literature of the criminal law.[10] His earlier contribution to that branch of law was a small book entitled *Pleas of the Crown, or a Methodical Summary of the Principal Matters Relating to that Subject* (1682). He there divided offenses into those immediately against God (heresy, witchcraft) and those immediately against man, capital and non-capital, the former consisting of treason (high and petit) and felonies against (1) the life of man, (2) the goods (larceny, robbery, piracy), (3) the habitation (burglary, arson) and (4) "protection of Justice." The book is little more than the outline of a contemplated treatise, but it exhibits considerable thought on the classification of crimes. It was precisely this arrangement which Hawkins adopted in his treatise (1716) some twenty years prior to the posthumous publication of Hale's *Pleas of the Crown*. Hawkins recognized the limitations of the earlier works; they were, he said, "far from being compleat Systems." He sought to apply a "clear Method" and to reduce "all the Laws relating to this Subject, under one general

of the act excuses the other." 2 Bracton, De Legibus et Consuetudinibus Angliae 399-401 (Twiss ed. 1879).

[9] *Cf.* his significant analysis of four offenses where, he states, they "are to be considered from seven points of view, the cause, the person, the place, the time, the quality, the quantity, and the event." *Id.* at 157. These, however, were not used as categories for general application, but as brief, specific differentiae of the four crimes he discussed.

[10] Of the intervening works since Bracton, few were more than justices' handbooks. Perhaps the most significant contribution was Lambarde's table of analysis, in which he classified crimes into public and private, then subdivided the former into offenses against the King and those against the Commonwealth, and the latter into crimes against the body, against goods, and against both. Eirenarcha 222-3 (1607). But his discussion is hardly more than a digest of the cases. Staunford has been too summarily dismissed as little more than an annotated Bracton. 5 Reeves, History of English Law 164-5 (1880). As for Coke's Third Institute (1641), *cf.* "A more disorderly mind than Coke's and one less gifted with the power of analysing common words it would be impossible to find." 2 Stephen, History of the Criminal Law of England 206 (1883).

Scheme. . . ."[11] Notwithstanding these laudable aspirations, his plan was modelled so closely after Hale's that much of it seems sheer plagiarism. He devoted the first two pages to mental incapacity and compulsion; beyond that, he confined himself closely to particular statutes and specific rules.

Hale's treatise remains in many ways the greatest accomplishment of any single scholar in the field.[12] For the first time in the professional literature, placed at the very beginning of the treatise, is a detailed discussion of the "general part" of criminal law, including punishments, incapacities (infancy, idiocy, insanity), accident, ignorance of law and of fact, compulsion and necessity. This analysis covers fifty-eight folio pages, and immediately after concluding it, Hale reveals his awareness of its significance: "Having premised these general observations relating to all crimes, that are capital, and their punishments, I shall now descend to consider of capital crimes particularly, and therein first of high treason."[13] His discussion of the particular crimes includes summaries of the arguments of various scholars, presented in a closely reasoned analysis. Throughout he exhibits an exceptional faculty for discovering "the one in the many," e.g. in his opening chapter on homicide, he analyzes first "those considerations, that are applicable as well to murder as to manslaughter."

From our present vantage-point, however, Hale's treatise is marred by his concentration upon particular statutes, specific cases and procedural questions. His "general part" was confined almost entirely to questions of culpability. His discussion of principals and accessories comes near the end

[11] 1 Hawkins, Pleas of the Crown, Preface (1716).

[12] Hale is without doubt one of the greatest scholars in the entire history of the common law. He was one of the first to think in terms of a science of law. See his Analysis of the Law (3rd ed. 1739); excerpts are reprinted in the writer's Readings in Jurisprudence 592-9 (1938). He read widely in science and philosophy "and had the new books, written on those subjects, sent him from all parts . . . he used to recreate himself with philosophy, or the mathematicks; . . . and he used to say, 'No man could be absolutely a master in any profession, without having some skill in other sciences.' " Burnett, The Lives of Sir Matthew Hale, Wilmot and Queen Mary 13-14 (1774).

[13] 1 Hale, Pleas of the Crown 58 (1736).

of the first volume; regarding treason, it is in the middle of his discussion of that offense. Solicitation (incitement) is treated even more in immediate relation to particular offenses rather than as a doctrine having general application. Despite these limitations, it is possible for the first time in the professional literature to recognize a potential *system* of the law of crimes in Hale's *Pleas*.

The next important advance was Blackstone's *Commentaries*. Somewhere between the extremes of Bentham's youthful, almost ruthless disparagement and Sir William Jones' superlatives,[14] the fact is that Blackstone was assuredly a learned scholar, [15] but hardly a very original one. He begins with certain general principles, but they are precisely those which Hale had discussed. Attempt is still treated in relation to certain specific crimes (robbery and larceny), not as a general notion. Nor did he recognize the like relation of solicitation to the specific crimes. Blackstone's chief contributions to criminal theory are his discussion of principals and accessories, his analysis of "crime," in contrast with Hale's brief parenthetical definition, and a detailed classification of crimes.

It is easy to demonstrate, however, that in each of these advances Blackstone borrowed from Grotius, Pufendorf, Domat, Beccaria and Montesquieu. Blackstone's definition of "crime" is a formal one, but in his discussion of *mala in se* and in his earlier definition of "law," he was clearly under the influence of natural law writers. His definition of punishment[16] follows Pufendorf's;[17] and his discussion of the "right to punish" is likewise in the direct line of the seventeenth and eighteenth century natural law writing. Blackstone's classification of crimes is similar to that of Montes-

[14] "His Commentaries are the most correct and beautiful outline that ever was exhibited of any human science." Quoted in Story, Miscellaneous Writings 230 (1835).

[15] In his Discourse on the Study of the Law (1758) he writes of law as "a science" and of "scientific method." *Id.* at 25, 26, 30.

[16] 4 Bl. Comm. * 7 *et seq.*

[17] "Punishment . . . is an evil of suffering inflicted for an evil of doing, or, it is some uneasy evil inflicted by authority, in a compulsive way, upon view of antecedent transgression." Pufendorf, Law of Nature and Nations bk. 8, ch. 3, 763 (4th ed. 1729).

quieu[18] and Pufendorf,[19] and is almost identical with Domat's.[20] The advance in systematization, however, was substantial; and even Bentham had a word of praise for Blackstone's classification.[21] Indeed, whatever one may think of Blackstone's originality, there is no question but that, building on Hale and the above Continental writers, he left the criminal law of England not only better organized than he found it but also in a state which, for the most part, is even now generally accepted.[22]

Of the more important later treatises, East's (1803) was limited entirely to specific offenses. As regards criminal theory, he thus represented a retrogression. Russell (1819) merely followed Blackstone as regards general concepts, but he displayed modernity in relegating "crimes against religion" to three pages in the latter part of the book. Gabbett (Dublin, 1835) also followed Blackstone closely, as did a number of early American works on the criminal law of various states.

A full report of the principal modern advances in English criminal theory would take detailed account of those made in jurisprudence by Bentham and Austin, and of their further elucidation in the professional literature of criminal law by Stephen and Kenny. The contributions of these scholars comprise much of current criminal theory, and we shall have many occasions in the following chapters to discuss them. What can be said here is that most of the principal concepts of current criminal theory were analyzed in the work of the above writers. There was clear recognition

[18] 1 Montesquieu, The Spirit of Laws 201-4 (Nugent trans. 5th ed. 1793).

[19] Pufendorf, *op. cit. supra* note 17, at 782.

[20] See 5 Domat, Le Droit Public Suite Les Lois Civiles Dans Leur Ordre Naturel 192-3 (1697). A direct bit of evidence of Blackstone's aping the French writers is his "Crimes against the Public Police."

[21] A Fragment on Government or, a Comment on the Commentaries xli (1823).

[22] "Since the publication of Blackstone's *Commentaries* hardly any work has been published in England upon the Criminal Law which aims at being more than a book of practice, and books of practice on Criminal Law are simply compilations of extracts from text-writers, and reports arranged with greater or less skill—usually with almost none. . . ." 2 Stephen, H. Cr. L. 218-19 (1883).

of the difference between general and specific conceptions as well as substantial correspondence in this regard with nineteenth century Continental criminal theory. Some of the general notions, *e.g.* legality, were largely assumed or commented on briefly by the English writers, and the like neglect of "causation" is indicated in the fact that Stephen, in his *Digest,* treated it only in connection with homicide.[23] There was hardly any analysis of "concurrence" or of "harm" incorporated into extant penal theory, despite Bentham's elaborate exposition of "pains" and Austin's discussion of "injuries."

In the United States, two major treatises on the criminal law were published in the past century. Wharton (1st ed. 1846), modelled after Chitty, Archbold and Burn, was concerned principally with pleading, practice and evidence. It was a practitioner's manual and a digest of cases. Bishop's treatise (1st ed. 1856) was the first major American contribution to criminal theory. It consisted of two large volumes, the first of which was devoted entirely to general problems, although much of it was concerned with the interpretation of statutes. The second volume dealt with the specific offenses. In the preface to his third edition (1865), Bishop stated that he had planned the first volume as a text for schools, the second was for practitioners; actually he mingled both divisions of the criminal law throughout the entire work. Wharton's 8th edition (1880) was a radically new revision, representing his effort to achieve a systematic treatise.[24] Holmes' *The Common Law* (1881) contributed many brilliant insights and acute analysis of basic issues, and it will be discussed in later chapters.

Without in the least depreciating the important contributions of the past century, indeed in order only to set the task for current scholarship, it must be noted that the major shortcoming of the nineteenth century professional litera-

---

[23] Stephen, A Digest of the Criminal Law 138 (1877). The term does not appear in the Index of his History of the Criminal Law.

[24] See his Preface to the 8th edition for an illuminating statement of his progressively increasing insight into the general problems of criminal law.

ture on criminal law, both Anglo-American and Continental, was the lack of system. Although there were valuable general insights and many searching analyses, it can hardly be said, if one has in mind the criteria discussed above, that there was any theory of criminal law. Bentham and his disciples had a social, ethical theory about criminal law, expressed mainly in terms of utility, rather than a theory of criminal law. Indeed, concentration on punishment was typical of the eighteenth and nineteenth century European treatises on criminal law and the continuing influence of that is apparent even in the current literature, *e.g.* Garraud's discussion of the general part of the penal code.

In this century there has been considerable refinement of basic conceptions and principles. Political upheavals have stimulated numerous studies, especially of legality ("rule of law") and of the moral basis of penal liability. The advance of physical science and the philosophy of science encouraged legal scholars to explore "causation" and other difficult notions. So, too, the impact of psychiatry has given rise to a vast literature on guilt and responsibility. The task of present scholarship is to incorporate this progress in a valid theory of criminal law.

For the reasons indicated at the beginning of this chapter, the degree of systematization of a discipline is the prime index of the state of knowledge of its subject matter. As was also noted above, important advances in that direction have been achieved. Progress toward systematization resulted from discovering that crimes can be decomposed, *i.e.* analyzed into several elementary "material" (essential) ideas; then, that certain ideas are common to two or more offenses. These served as unifying agents, bringing together, *c.g.* murder and manslaughter, robbery, larceny and assault, and, on a larger canvas, crimes against the person, against property, and so on. It was next perceived that certain generalizations applied to all the specific prescriptions. These became the "general part" of the criminal law, and the rules were placed in the "special part" of penal codes. There was also considerable elucidation of the fundamental principles upon which the entire structure of the criminal law rests. Beyond all that, however, there remains the present paramount challenge of inclusive systematization, disclosing the interrelations of the various parts of penal law — in short, the construction of a coherent theory of that law.

In Continental Europe, criminal theory has been cultivated much more intensively than elsewhere, but there, too, the orientation has been practical rather than scientific. Instead of being the subject matter of theory, the penal code has occupied the driver's seat, directing theory to make sense of every provision that had the formal markings of penal law. This has impeded scientific progress. For while it is true that a code to some extent reflects scientific theory, it is also true that there are inevitable gaps between them. Interests and political pressures, accidents and historical conventions have greatly influenced the codes; and inevitably these set arbitrary limitations on theories which took their directions from the code. Even if every provision in a penal code were sound, the fact remains that it is intended to guide the general public as well as lawyers and judges in the solution of practical problems. Accordingly, subjects which a scientific theory would treat in a certain way are located quite differently in a code.

Equally serious has been the influence of criminal procedure upon theories of substantive criminal law. Obviously, the prosecution should not, *e.g.* be required to prove all the material elements that determine penal liability in all cases; it can only be expected in first instance to make out a *prima facie* case that suffices for the particular situation. The respective burdens and the logic of proof, as well as canons of orderly procedure, dominate the judicial inquiry. This also determines the meaning of *"corpus delicti."*[25] So, too, it is usual and expedient that there be a presumption of sanity; and there are other essential aspects of crime which,

[25] That the origin of this (*Tatbestand*) is procedural is indicated in Feuerbach's treatment of it in the procedural part of his Lehrbuch des peinlichen Rechts 524-25, 527 (6th ed. 1818). *Corpus delicti* is discussed *infra*, chapter 7 at notes 48-54.

from a procedural viewpoint, are thought of only as defenses.

Finally, and most unfortunate so far as criminal theory is concerned, is the fact that *everything* included in the so-called "Penal Code" and all other laws whose sanctions sound in terms of "punishment" have been assumed to be penal law. The theorist, proceeding in this practical perspective, assumes that his theory must take account of all these laws. This, of course, would be defensible, indeed necessary, were the purpose a practical one since a litigant may be subjected to any of the State's commands. But when the practical need determines the subject matter of scientific inquiry, the result is the inclusion, within the accepted field of penal law, of such greatly disparate data as to render the discovery of significant theory impossible.[26] It goes without saying that in the long run the soundest attainment of practical objectives also suffers proportionately when penal theory is thus restricted.

A major unfortunate consequence, so far as criminal theory is concerned, is that orientation towards practice and procedure has induced scientifically untenable bifurcations, *e.g.* the separation of excuse and justification from a supposed complete definition of the specific crimes.[27] It has produced other unresolved antinomies in extant criminal theory, such as dubious distinctions of formal from substantive crimes, emphasis upon empirically insignificant generalizations such as control of the criminal proceeding by the sovereign, zealous efforts to combine negligence and conscious harm-doing within a single conception of "fault," and so on.

OUTLINE OF A THEORY OF PENAL LAW

In a scientific and normative perspective, criminal theory takes quite different directions. Since this theory is both descriptive and systematic, it requires a unified substantive subject matter, and that need functions as a definite prin-

[26] Hall, Studies in Jurisprudence and Criminal Theory, ch. 1 (1958).
[27] This is discussed *infra*, chapter 7 beginning at note 55.

ciple of selection among verbally or practically designated "penal" laws. Such a theory is therefore not directed by the "penal code"; it is directed towards that code. Since the theory is descriptive, normative and scientifically oriented, it selects "penal laws" which exhibit common characteristics by virtue of their reference to certain classes of conduct and harm.

By adhering to common empirical-normative references the theorist gathers together penal laws which are often widely separated or indiscriminately lumped together; and, as stated, he also excludes many so-called "penal laws" from the field of penal law. Transcending the practical logic and criteria of codes and procedure, descriptive theory seeks to provide an organized body of knowledge that is no less helpful to the practitioner than it is valid for the scholar. Among the advantages of proceeding in this fashion are not only the avoidance of the current difficulties, noted above, but also the possibility of constructing a system of ideas which comprise the structural side of a science of criminal law.

With these observations in mind, let us glance briefly at some European penal codes. The French Codes of 1791[28] and 1810[29] were drafted by practicing lawyers and judges, motivated largely by the humanitarian movement associated especially with the work of Beccaria and Voltaire and therefore concentrated on punishment and the abuse of official discretion. However commendable the motivation and the political progress reflected in this penal law, it can hardly be claimed that these codes were the products of scientific analysis or construction. The general part of the earlier code consisted mainly of provisions concerning punishment, proscription, minority, attempt and complicity. The Code of 1810 amplified these prescriptions and emphasized the principle of legality. It greatly influenced penal codification throughout Europe.

[28] Remy, Les Principes Généraux du Code Pénal de 1791 (Thèse, Paris, 1910).
[29] Sabatier, *Napoléon et les Codes Criminel*, 34 Rev. Pen. et Dr. Pen. 905 (Paris, 1910).

The general part of the European and derivative codes continues to exhibit the influence of practical considerations rather than that of scientific construction. The best evidence of this is its indiscriminate character. Article 4 of the French Code, the principle of legality, is found almost everywhere in the general part of the current codes.[30] Provisions concerning punishment and correction bulk large and various conditions of exculpation, *e.g.* infancy and insanity, are included. In the Austrian Penal Code, the first article prescribes *mens rea (dolus* and *culpa)* and there follow the exculpatory conditions of insanity, infancy, error and ignorance, and also provisions concerning complicity, attempt, etc. The general part of the Bulgarian Code includes the provision that a culpable act must be either intentional or negligent (Art. 4); and a similar provision (Art. 26) is found in the general part of the Greek Code, except that negligence is punishable only exceptionally and then by specific provision. The general part of the Hungarian Code defines "intentionality" (Art. 12). The new Yugoslav Code contains similar provisions (Art. 7) and also a provision to the effect that a crime may be committed either by action or omission (Art. 13). There are many provisions regarding jurisdiction — the limits of application in time and space, and also concerning the proscription of prosecution.

In sum, the general part of current penal codes includes provisions concerning: (1) legality, (2) jurisdiction, (3) punishment and correction, (4) defenses allocated to excuse and justification, (5) action and omission, (6) attempt and complicity and (7) *mens rea (dolus* and *culpa)*. The guiding influence has been the applicability of these provisions to the Special Part.[31] Current European criminal theory also emphasizes subjective and objective aspects of criminal infractions and while that allows a degree of or-

[30] See generally, for this and the following references, Ancel and Marx, Les Codes Pénaux Européens (3 vols. Paris, 1957-58).

[31] Some provisions, *e.g.* that concerning self-defense (Swiss Code, Art. 33), apply only to certain crimes.

dering, it falls far short of reflecting a theory which brings the various parts of penal law into a coherent unity.

It is submitted, moreover, that the above noted provisions are "general" for different reasons, and not in the same sense. Not only does the "general part" include provisions of very different formal types, these provisions also serve very different functions. A descriptive theory makes it possible to distinguish these propositions and to recognize their respective functions as well as their relations to each other.

The first step in this direction is the recognition that penal law consists of three principal types of proposition or, more specifically, from the perspective of scientific construction all criminal law can be stated in terms of three types of proposition, each of which serves important distinctive functions. The narrowest and most numerous of these — "rules" — comprise the specific part of penal codes and, in conjunction with the doctrines, they define particular crimes and fix the respective punishments and treatment. At the other extreme, at the apex, are the widest generalizations, namely, the "principles" of penal law; and intermediately are propositions more general than the rules but lacking the extensiveness of the principles; and these are here termed the "doctrines" of penal law.[32] It thus appears that the propositions presently located in the general part of current criminal codes consist of doctrines and principles and other generally applicable "norms," e.g. those concerning jurisdiction and statutes of limitations which, while they have general application, are not derived from the rules and doctrines of substantive law.

More important than the formal structure of the above three types of proposition is their functional difference. The doctrines of penal law concern insanity, infancy, intoxication, mistake, coercion, necessity, attempt, conspiracy, solicitation and complicity. The doctrines thus express the common "material" (legally essential) parts of

---

[32] Civilian lawyers will note that "doctrine" does not refer to theory or scholarly writing, but is given a special meaning.

the definitions of the specific crimes, while the rules (the Special Part) state what is distinctive about each crime. If, *e.g.* it is desired to know how larceny differs from arson or rape, the rules provide the answers. But the rules do not exhaust the definition of those crimes; *e.g.* if the defendant was insane when he caused an injury, no crime was committed by him. Thus, the doctrines are essential in the definition of the various crimes.

The principles of criminal law consist of seven ultimate notions expressing: (1) *mens rea,* (2) act (effort), (3) the "concurrence" (fusion) of *mens rea* and act, (4) harm, (5) causation, (6) punishment and (7) legality. These principles can be allocated to three conceptions: law, crime and punishment. The combined meaning of the principles can be stated in a single generalization: *the harm forbidden in a penal law must be imputed to any normal adult who voluntarily commits it with criminal intent, and such a person must be subjected to the legally prescribed punishment.* Criminal theory is largely concerned with the elucidation of this generalization.

It will be noted that the principles of criminal law, excepting those that concern "punishment" and "legality," refer to essential elements of "crime," and this is a fair index of the relative complexity of that conception. The meaning of "punishment" will be explored at various places in this book but it may be noted here, that to be understood, it must be thought of in relation to the principles defining "crime," the chief implication being that punishment has a moral connotation.

That the principles are wider, "higher-level" generalizations than the doctrines is evident by reference to their respective contents, *e.g. mens rea* or causation, on the one hand, as compared with insanity or mistake, on the other. Secondly, the principles may be viewed as standing outside the penal law, *i.e.* that law is fully stated when the doctrines are added to the rules (the Special Part). Since the principles are derived from the total body of propositions comprising the rules and the doctrines, they may also be viewed as the ultimate norms of the penal law. While the doctrines state essential general "material" elements of crimes, the principles, by incorporating what is common in the doctrines and the rules, provide a complete general definition of crime.

More problematical is the relation of the rules (Special Part) to the doctrines of criminal law. The fact that most of the doctrines concern unusual or abnormal states of mind or situations has encouraged the treatment of the rules as complete definitions of the specific crimes, and of the doctrines as defenses. In addition, the form of the specific rules is unqualified, and they seem to state complete definitions, *e.g.* larceny is the taking, *animo furandi*, etc. But despite the apparent completeness of the rules, it is submitted that they are neither autonomous nor complete. For, in the first place, it is certain that if the defendant was an infant or insane or mistaken as to a material fact, etc., he did not commit any crime. This cannot be ignored in a coherent criminal theory. Secondly, the affirmative normal conditions of criminal conduct, *e.g.* sanity, sobriety, maturity, freedom and so on are not determined by the rules but by the doctrines. In any case where a pertinent question is raised, the specific definitions must be determined by adding the relevant doctrine to the rules in issue. It follows that the rules do not completely define the specific crimes, and that only after the doctrines have been added to the rules has the penal law, *i.e.* the definitions of all the specific crimes, been fully stated. The form of doing this is, *e.g.*: one who sets fire to a dwelling-house, not being insane, intoxicated, an infant, coerced, etc., commits arson, and is to be punished thus and so. This may be stated affirmatively: a sane, sober adult, acting freely, etc., who sets fire, etc. But in either statement the doctrines are essential.

It is relatively easy to perceive the necessary role of the doctrines concerning the harm, in the definition of specific crimes. For the rules, as ordinarily stated, say nothing about attempts, solicitations or conspiracies to commit the specified harms; hence, it is evident that the relevant doctrines must be added to the rules to define those specific crimes. This, however, is no less true of the doctrines concerning *mens rea*. For example, the *mens rea* in larceny is specified as *animus furandi* and an insane man who intentionally takes another's chattel does not commit larceny because he lacks the required *animus furandi*. The meaning of *animus furandi* and, thus, of larceny can only be determined after it is qualified by the doctrines of insanity, mistake, intoxication, infancy, and so on. What is true of harm and *mens rea* applies also to the act. In sum, in every material respect, rules require the qualification of doctrines in order that complete definitions of crimes be provided.

We come to closer grips with the relationship of doctrines to rules when we consider the plea of "not guilty," where the defendant raises no "exceptional" defense but simply denies the charge. A conviction in such cases seems to rest wholly on the Special Part, thus apparently confirming the supposition that the rules state complete definitions of the specific crimes. But for reasons noted above, the rationale of procedure cannot determine the substantive definition of crimes. Procedure, we must remember, is oriented towards practical objectives, in the attainment of which requirements regarding burdens, assumptions, the logic of proof, the order of debate and other useful canons are necessary and decisive. It is untenable, however, to transpose procedural criteria and canons to the definition of substantive penal laws. In substantive theory, *all* penal law that is relevant to the definition of specific crimes — doctrines no less than rules — must be considered.

The fact that the doctrines referred to in terms of "justification" and "excuse" are ignored in pleas of alibi and other simple "not guilty" pleas does not imply that the rules comprising the Special Part are autonomous and sufficient definitions or that the doctrines are a sort of condition subsequent which annuls pre-determined criminality. To maintain this when alibi and other simple "not guilty" pleas are involved would be inconsistent with the recognition of the meaning and role of the doctrines concerning, *e.g.* insanity, necessity and attempt in the definition of specific crimes.

One test of the validity of a theory is that of its coherence. We shall later discuss in some detail the assumption that the rules in the Special Part state complete definitions of crimes and that justification and excuse may be treated apart from these definitions.[33] We may note here that when the issue is that of alibi or other simple "not guilty" plea, questions of excuse and justification are procedurally irrelevant.[34]

It is submitted that the theory which satisfies the various requirements is that (1) the rules provide essential criteria of specific crimes that are not included in the doctrines, but that (2) the rules do not completely define the specific crimes. The rules provide definitions of the "normal" criminal conduct of "normal" persons committing specified harms in "normal" situations. But not only is it untenable to assume that the meaning of "normal" is known, we are also explicitly barred from making that assumption in many situations, *e.g.* where justification or excuse is pleaded or when attempt is in issue. "Normality," in the above statement, may be considered only a receptacle; or, if it has or is given substantive meaning, it remains the fact that what it means must be determined by incorporation of the relevant doctrines in their affirmative significance. In sum, a *complete* definition of specific crimes must *always* include the doctrines. In insanity, necessity, attempt, etc., this is explicitly recognized in the procedural context. In alibi and other simple "not guilty" pleas, the defendant, by waiving

[33] See chapter 7 at note 55ff.

[34] This, however, does not support the thesis that the rules play no part whatever in the definition of "voluntary," *i.e.* that "voluntary" means *only* that the exculpatory doctrines—insanity, infancy, coercion and so on—are excluded. *Cf.* Ryle, The Concept of Mind 62-74 (1949). First, there is the common, indubitable experience of intending and of deliberate action in which one is conscious of effort. Second, the principle of legality also bars the above thesis because, in that view, there is no legal norm upon which penal liability may be based. The rules must therefore perform an essential function in the definition of specific crimes. Finally, the doctrines are palpably incomplete, referring only to certain personal characteristics or to special external situations. They do not, *e.g.* include the verbs employed in the rules, which connote action. See Sheldon, God and Polarity: A Synthesis of Philosophies 28-36 (1954), and Aristotle, Ethics, III, 1111a 15-25.

the "exceptional" defenses, admits that he is a normal person and that the situation in issue was a normal one.[35] In effect, from the viewpoint of criminal theory, he is admitting that if he is convicted, the terms of the rules are to be given the meaning required by the doctrines in their affirmative significance. If he is found guilty, legality is also satisfied because the rules, thus qualified or interpreted, are complete definitions. He is guilty not because no exculpatory doctrine applies but because the rules, qualified by the affirmative meaning of the doctrines, include his case.

Nor is it helpful to maintain that the rules are "formally" complete definitions of the specific crimes. That view has encouraged untenable bifurcation exhibited, *e.g.* in the current use of "justification" and "excuse."[36] It results in inconsistency when attention is concentrated upon alibi, etc. And, in the end, since descriptive definition is inevitable, the doctrines are in fact joined to the rules to provide definitions of the specific crimes. In addition to avoiding the indicated limitations, the significance of the proposed solution is expressed in the consequent systematization of the penal law.

In the theory delineated above, the principles of criminal law are the ultimate basis of elucidation. They may be viewed: (1) as "high-level" concepts, (2) as the most general norms of criminal law and (3) as general descriptions comprising propositions of a science of criminal law. The concepts, it will be recalled, are legality, *mens rea*, act (effort), the fusion ("concurrence") of *mens rea* and act, harm, causation and punishment. One important function of penal theory is to analyze the criminal law in terms of these concepts. Second, since the principles are derived from the union of rules and doctrines, they, like the subject matter from which they were abstracted, may be stated as legal norms. This is the use that judges make of the principles

---

[35] The common law meaning of a plea of "not guilty" is not here involved but, instead, the logic of the plea, which is more fully illustrated in modern criminal procedure requiring, *e.g.* that insanity be specially pleaded.

[36] See *infra* chapter 7 beginning at note 55.

in writing their opinions. For example, in a case where the
defendant stood by, watching his friend commit a homicide,
a court reversed the conviction on the ground that there
must be an act to incur penal liability.[37] In this view, the
principles are the authoritative maximum norms of criminal
law. Finally, the use of the principles as descriptive generalizations will be discussed in a later chapter,[38] but it may be
noted here that there is an important difference between
the legal and the scientific meaning of "principle," *i.e.* between the most general legal norms and the most general
descriptions comprising a science of criminal law.

A descriptive theory of criminal law consists of propositions having empirical-normative reference. A simple figure
representing this has three main foci: penal theory, penal
law, and the facts in the external world to which penal law
directly, and theory, indirectly and more generally, refer.
In other words, penal theory is about penal laws which have
immediate descriptive-normative reference that is expressed ultimately in terms of certain principles. A due regard
for scientific methods may suggest that the empirical-
normative references of the theory be employed first to
select only those penal laws which define the major crimes,
i.e. the area of "penal law" which practically everyone
agrees is penal law. Later, all other laws, including most
of the presently designated "misdemeanors" of all legal
systems, which conform to the criteria specified in the
theory, are included in the field of penal law. It is these
"really" penal laws which comprise the subject matter of
descriptive criminal theory.[39]

If we visualize the subject matter of penal theory in terms
of the principles of criminal law, a representative figure
includes, at one extreme, certain conduct and, at the other
extreme, a harm, and these polarities are causally interrelated—all three parts of the figure being qualified by the
principles of legality and punishment. This figure represents

[37] "It is plainly not the law that one can be guilty of murder, without
overt act. . . ." Anderson v. State, 91 P. 2d 794, 798 (Okl. 1939).
[38] See chapter 16.
[39] Hall, *op. cit. supra* note 26, chapter 1.

a unified means-end situation. It is impossible therefore to make sense of any part of it isolated from the other parts of it. In such an action-situation, the conduct phase must be viewed as a means *in relation to* certain ends, *i.e.* the proscribed harm. So, also, of the harms. As ends sought, they are intelligible only when related in a teleologically causal way to their cognate means, *i.e.* to certain conduct. The rules and doctrines of the penal law, which substantively (empirically and normatively) accord with the descriptive theory here employed, refer directly and in less extensive generalizations to the indicated three divisions of the described means-end situation.

It follows that the principles of criminal law qualify each other in the above indicated way. For example, the death of a human being or the destruction of a house by fire, although a loss, disvalue or harm in some sense, regardless of how it was caused, is not a *legal harm* unless it was caused in certain ways by human beings whose conduct embodies a certain state of mind, all of which are legally proscribed. When a proscribed harm is thus defined by reference to the proscribed conduct, it accumulates meaning as part of an intelligible, unified social situation. The harm, of course, differs from the conduct; nor does the one "swallow" the other. The meaning of each is, however, derived contextually, and this is expressed *e.g.* in the principle of harm. So, too, criminal conduct takes its meaning from its relationship to, *i.e.* its authorship of, a forbidden harm. Finally, causality, interpreted in this contextual way, must differ in meaning from the "causation" to which a physical scientist refers. If, *e.g.* a nurse innocently gives poison to her patient, it may certainly be said in a medical sense that she caused his death. Equally, one who knows the potion is poisonous and administers it also causes the death in that sense, *i.e.* the guilty knowledge is ignored as irrelevant. This meaning of "causality" is distinguished from the state of mind of the actor, which is allocated to *mens rea*. To draw and explicate such distinctions is a principal task of analysis.

But in a descriptive theory of penal law, causality, no less than conduct and harm, has a relational meaning, indicated above. In this sense, the nurse's innocent behavior was not the cause of the patient's death since she did not cause his death in the teleological (means-end) sense of the term.[40] This is also the perspective of legal interpretation oriented towards liability, elucidating "legal cause." Concretely, a criminal is a *legal cause* in the sense that he was the author of a forbidden harm—and that implies that he knew what he was doing; hence *mens rea* is an essential reference of this meaning.[41] When courts hold that certain conduct was not the "legal cause" of a harm, despite the fact that it was both a necessary and substantial (adequate, sufficient) cause of it, and the stated reason is that the conduct did not express the required *mens rea,* they are, accordingly, defining and elucidating the normative, legal principle of causation. The analyst, intent on drawing mutually exclusive distinctions, may allocate the *mens rea* or its purely cognitive aspect to a subjective factor concerning the actor's "culpability." While he distinguishes elements which comprise the legal notion of causation, the judicial decisions establish the authoritative meaning of the principle as a legal norm.

The principle of legality is in some ways the most fundamental of all the principles. It qualifies the meaning of both crime and punishment, and is thus presupposed in all of criminal theory—except, of course, where it is itself the subject of inquiry. It should therefore be remembered that when a legal writer speaks only of harm, conduct, punishment and so on, his discussion is probably elliptical. What he probably means to say is legally proscribed conduct, legally proscribed harm, legally prescribed punishment, and so on.

---

[40] See chapter 8, *infra. Cf.* the classical thesis that behavior in and through ignorance is not voluntary. Aristotle, Eth. Bk. III, 1, 1110b, 17-23.

[41] A *mens rea* finds expression, first, in certain conduct and that, in turn, qualifies the meaning of "causing" a proscribed harm. This is discussed in chapter 8.

Just as the doctrines of attempt, solicitation, conspiracy and complicity are especially significant in relation to the principle of harm, so does the principle of *mens rea* subsume various other doctrines of criminal law, obviously, *e.g.* those on insanity and infancy. It represents the summation of all the narrow *mentes reae* stated in the rules, qualified by all the relevant doctrines. The like reference of the other principles of criminal law to doctrines and the rules has a corresponding significance. This interrelationship of the rules, doctrines and principles, discussed above, implies that the meaning of each is dependent on the meaning of the others. To understand the specific crimes thoroughly, it is therefore essential to know the relevant principles. So, likewise is it true, viewing the matter from the other side, that an adequate understanding of the principles necessitates the study of their incidence in the particulars, the specific crimes, defined in the rules, qualified by the doctrines.

A descriptive-normative theory of criminal law is thus concerned with certain types of proposition which it distinguishes as the rules, doctrines and principles of criminal law, and which it interrelates to comprise a system of penal law. It elucidates the respective empirical meanings and functions of the principles, doctrines and rules. But the relationship of the criminal law to fact does not exhaust the meaning of that branch of law. For just as the penal law denotes certain facts (the words of the rules and doctrines are unintelligible apart from those references) so, equally, does that law express certain ethical principles. If one is interested in the full range of criminal theory, analysis of its ethical rationale is unavoidable; indeed, as will appear, that is essential to an understanding of what the criminal law means. An important function of criminal theory is to articulate this so-called penal "policy" and to subject it to sustained criticism. In sum, penal theory systematizes and elucidates the structure, factual meaning and ethical rationale of penal law.

Principles

CHAPTER II

LEGALITY—*NULLA POENA SINE LEGE*

IN a very wide sense, the principle of legality—the "rule of law"—refers to and requires not only a body of legal precepts but also supporting institutions, procedures, and values.[1] Many writers on the subject stress the procedural connotations of the principle, especially the fairness of the trial and the independence of the judiciary. Rather less emphasized in the general legal literature than might be expected is the historic meaning of the principle of legality as a definite limitation on the power of the State.[2] This is the central meaning of the principle in penal law.

The principle of legality is, first of all, a summation of the form of all the penal laws, of what distinguishes them as positive laws from all other rules; and it qualifies and is presupposed by everything else in penal theory. In a formal sense, a positive law may be regarded as *any* command of the State. There is no logical reason why a penal law must be specific, *e.g.* the Sovereign's command may be to "punish socially dangerous conduct by any sanction which the judge

---

[1] The "rule of law" includes: "1. That body of legal precepts governing, 2. those institutions vested with appropriate legal power, and 3. those legal procedures by which those precepts may be applied by those institutions — which together are designed to effect the protection of essential interests of individuals guaranteed by our society through limitations on the authority of the State." The Rule of Law in the United States 19 (A. B. A. Committee Rep't, pub. by Intn'l Comm. of Jurists, 1958). See also *id.* at 10 and 85; Government Under Law (Sutherland, ed. 1956); and Hamsun, *La notion de légalité dans les pays occidentaux*, Rev. Int. Dr. Comp. No. 1 (1958).

[2] Goodhart, *Rule of Law and Absolute Sovereignty*, 106 U. Pa. L. Rev. 943 (1958).

deems proper." An important distinction must therefore be drawn between the principle of legality viewed as a formal requirement[3] and the meaning of the actual principle in Western culture, perhaps especially in Anglo-American experience.

In the penal law of most European countries and the United States the principle of legality is the very antithesis of the above extremely wide command. Its meaning can be ascertained by reference to its operation as a definite idea in Western legal history. *The essence of this principle of legality is limitation on penalization by the State's officials, effected by the prescription and application of specific rules.*[4] That is the actual meaning of the principle of legality so far as the criminal law is concerned. In Europe, this principle is usually called *nulla poena sine lege.*

Its meaning is expressed in several ways.[5] In a narrow connotation, centered on *poena*, it concerns the sanctions of penal laws: no person may be punished except in pursuance of a statute which prescribes a penalty. Employed narrowly as *nullum crimen sine lege,* the principle means that no conduct may be held criminal unless it is precisely described in a penal law. In order that there be no doubt regarding the meaning of the principle, it has two important corollaries: penal statutes must be strictly construed, and they must not be given retroactive effect.

ORIGINS

Certain European writers have maintained that, despite the Latinity of the phrase, *nulla poena sine lege* is not of Roman origin[6] but was born in eighteenth century Liberal-

---

[3] *Supra* p. 25.

[4] Permanent Court of International Justice, Series A/B, No. 65 at 53, 56 (Advisory Opinion, 1935).

[5] Roux, Cours de Droit Criminel Francais 16 (1927); 1 Garraud, Droit Pénal Francais §137, 292 (3rd ed. 1913). A scholarly detailed discussion is by de la Morandiere, De La Regle Nulla Poena Sine Lege (1910).

[6] Schottlaender, Die geschichtliche Entwicklung des Satzes: Nulla poena sine lege, Heft 132, Strafrechtliche Abhandlungen 1 (1911); Matzke, Juristische Wochenschrift, 7 July, 1934; Klee, *Strafe ohne*

ism. The matter, however, is not so simple. A few threads
of evidence are sufficiently clear to refute that all-too-facile
history even though they do not reveal an unbroken line
of development.[7] It is also true that the "extraordinary"
offenses of Roman jurisprudence suggest unlimited authority. But side by side with *extraordinaria judicia* there was
also definite insistence on the prescription of both offense
and penalty. As regards first offenders, magisterial discretion probably joined an appeal to the populace to provide
specific decisions which, in the course of time, defined "ordinary" offenses in prescribed rules.[8] There is also evidence
that although specified penalties could be mitigated, they
could not be increased.[9] Certainly, as to Roman citizens and
in the ordinary course of administration, there were long
periods when prescribed penalties had to be strictly adhered
to.[10] This was rigorously applied by Sulla who insisted that
for certain crimes, both offense and penalty be exactly described in the statute upon which accusations were

---

geschriebenes Gesetz, D. J. Z. 641-643 (1934); Drost, Das Ermessen
des Strafrichters 80 ff. (1930).

[7] Strachan-Davidson states Mommsen was guilty of overstatement
when he wrote: "The criminal law begins when the arbitrary will of
him who wields the power to punish and the right of judgment has
limits placed on it by the law of the State or by custom as strong as
law. . . . The law establishes a corresponding satisfaction for each
crime. . . . From that time forth there is in Rome no crime without
a criminal law, no criminal procedure without a law of procedure, no
punishment without a law of punishment." "This," states Strachan-
Davidson, "is indeed an ideal; but I believe that it is impossible to
fix the Valerian law or any other enactment as the date from which
the ideal is realized." 1 Strachan-Davidson, Problems of the Roman
Criminal Law 103-104 (1912).

[8] *Id.* at 108.

[9] D. 42. 48. 19. 155 (2); D. 50. 17.

[10] D. 50. 16. 131 provides: *"Poena non irrogatur, nisi quae quaque
lege vel quo alio jure specialiter huic delicto imposita est."* 11 Scott,
The Civil Law 278 (1932). (". . . a penalty is not inflicted unless it is
expressly imposed by law, or by some other authority.") See also D.
50. 16. 244; ". . . an appeal cannot be taken from a penalty, for where
anyone is convicted of an offense, the penalty for it is fixed, and must
be paid at once. . . ."
"Hence, the difference between these things becomes apparent, because certain penalties are prescribed for certain illegal acts; but this
is not the case with fines, as the judge has power to impose any fine
he pleases, unless the amount which he may impose is fixed by law."
Id. at 296.

brought.[11] The prohibition of the retroactivity of penal laws was also well known and followed under Sulla; long before that it appears to have been approved by the ancient Greeks.[12] Under Augustus, several penal laws were declared to be non-retroactive, although not until 440 A. D. was it so enacted.[13] Thus the principle of legality had a vague and checkered ancient history. But clouded as that history is in the ambiguities of sporadic expression, *extraordinaria judicia*, appeals to the populace, and such wide powers as those of the Principate, it is nonetheless certain that the principle of legality prevailed during long periods in the Roman criminal law.[14]

We shall not inquire into the ramifications of the principle in the Middle Ages[15] nor whether the penalization in canon law of "offenses against conscience" barred its application to the major wrongs.[16] The medieval doctrine of the primacy of law was deeply rooted[17] until challenged in its theological aspect by the rise of the modern State. On the other hand, one must not read into ancient or medieval phrases those special meanings which the principle acquired in the revolutionary eighteenth century. So, too, those who find the origin of the present significance of *nulla poena sine lege* in the Magna Carta[18] are on unsettled territory

[11] See Schottlaender, *op. cit. supra* note 6, at 9, 10.

[12] 2 Vinogradoff, Outlines of Historical Jurisprudence 139, 140 (1922).

[13] Schottlaender, *op. cit. supra* note 6, at 16 ff; see also *"Nemo potest mutare consilium suum in alterius iniuriam."* D. 50. 17. 75. Code 1. 14. 7. For a summary of this history see Dash v. Van Kleeck, 7 Johns. 477, 3 Am. Dec. 291, 309 (N. Y. 1811).

[14] See Levy, *Statute and Judge in Roman Criminal Law*, 13 Wash. L. Rev. 291 (1938).

[15] See 3 Carlyle, A History of Mediaeval Political Theory in the West 35 ff. (1928).

[16] See Petroncelli, *Il principio della non retroattivita delle leggi in diritto canonico*, 29 Pubblicazioni Della Universita Cattolica Del Sacro Cuore (1931).

[17] "Medieval Doctrine, while it was truly medieval, never surrendered the thought that Law is by its origin of equal rank with the State and does not depend upon the State for its existence." Gierke, Political Theories of the Middle Ages 74 (trans. Maitland, 1900).

[18] See Mezger, Strafecht 77 (1949).

even though it is probable that the *"lex terrae"* of the famous 39th clause did mean more than procedural guarantees. It seems actually to have been both a procedural and a substantive limitation on the royal prerogative.[19]

In English history, the principle of legality is prominent from the promulgation of the Charter of Henry the First, and it was reiterated in the Constitution of Clarendon. Magna Carta is, however, the great symbol of the sociopolitical forces that established the supremacy of the rule of law in England.[20] In Bracton it found colorful expression.[21] The principle was strengthened in important petitions and bills of rights.[22] The rise of Parliament played an important part;[23] indeed it was parliamentary influence which transformed what might in only a very vague style be termed *nulla poena sine lege* into a definite approximation to the principle. For with regular legislation came the distinctive techniques of statutory construction of penal

[19] "The struggle was waged to secure trial in properly constituted courts of justice and in accordance with established law. The latter requirement would apply equally to substantive rules as far as they existed, and to procedure. . . ." Vinogradoff, in Magna Carta Commemoration Essays 85 (1917); see also Powicke, *id.* at 121; McKechnie, Magna Carta 379, 380, 394 (2nd ed. 1914); McIlwain, High Court of Parliament 55 (1910).

[20] Over five hundred years ago, Fortescue wrote: "In such a Constitution, under such [humane] laws, every man may live safely and securely." Regarding the origin of concern for the individual: *"Indeed, one would much rather that twenty guilty persons should escape the punishment of death, than that one innocent person should be condemned and suffer capitally."* De Laudibus Legum Angliae ch. 27, at 93 (trans. Gregor, 1874).

[21] "The king ought not to be under any man, but under God and under the law, because the law makes him king. . . . he is no king if his will rules and not the law." Quoted by Pollock, Essays in Jurisprudence and Ethics 213 (1882).

[22] See the Resolution of March 29, 1628 passed by the House, quoted by Pollock *id.* at 225, and the Petition of Grievances of Commons to James I, 1610, quoted *id.* at 221.

[23] *Cf.* Sir Robert Phillips: ". . . the Right of the Subject is thus bulwarked by the law of the kingdom. . . ." ". . . I can live although another without title be put to live with me; nay, I can live, although I pay Excises and Impositions for more than I do: but to have my Liberty, which is the soul of my life, taken from me by power, and to be pent up in a gaol without remedy by law, and this to be so adjudged to perish in gaol; O improvident ancestors! O unwise forefathers! to be so curious in providing for the quiet possession of our

statutes by the courts, which also characterize the Continental significance of the principle of legality.[24]

But England ran far in advance of the Continent in imposing law upon government. The Prussian Code of 1721 provided that offenses which were not enumerated in the territorial code nor forbidden by the imperial law should be judged *"ex aequo et bono,"* except that the more difficult cases should be personally decided by the king. The Bavarian Code of 1751 directed that cases not provided for by the Code should be decided *"ex aequitate et analogia juris,"* and the Austrian Code of 1769 contained a similar provision.[25]

Even before the French Revolution,[26] however, the movement for codification had advanced some of the technical

---

lands and liberties of parliament, and to neglect our persons and bodies, and to let them die in prison, and that *durante bene placito*, remediless. If this be law, why do we talk of our Liberties?"

Coke: ". . . it is against law, that men should be committed, and no cause shewed . . . it is not I, Edward Coke, that speaks it, but the Records that speaks it; we have a national appropriate Law to this nation. . . ."

"Then the House of Commons came to the following Resolutions: Resolved. '1. That no Freeman ought to be detained or kept in prison, or otherwise restrained by the command of the king or privy council, or any other, unless some cause of the commitment, detainer, or restraint be expressed, for which by law he ought to be committed, detained, or restrained.' " Proceedings in Parliament Relating to Liberty of the Subject, 3 How. St. Tr. 65, 66, 78, and 82 (1627-1628).

[24] ". . . the Civill Law ceasing, Crimes cease. . . ." Hobbes, Leviathan 152 (1651).

"A penal law then, shall not be extended . . . by construction. The law of England does not allow of constructive offences, or of arbitrary punishments. No man incurs a penalty unless the act which subjects him to it, is clearly both within the spirit and the letter of the statute imposing such penalty. 'If these rules are violated,' said Best, C. J., in the case of Fletcher v. Lord Sondes [3 Bingham 580], 'the fate of accused persons is decided by the arbitrary discretion of judges, and not by the express authority of the laws.' " Dwarris, A General Treatise on Statutes 247 (1873). *Cf.* 2 Bentham, Works 512-513 (Bowring ed. 1843).

[25] See Schottlaender, *op. cit. supra* note 6, at 43-44. Affinity with the German law of June, 1935, is apparent. See note 60 *infra*.

[26] "The main thesis of this work [Essay of Globig and Huster on Criminal Legislation (1783)] was the need of a code which contained a complete and plain formulation of the criminal law. . . ." von Bar, A History of Continental Criminal Law 248 (1916).

The Constitutio Bambergensis, Arts. 125-126 (1507), prohibited inferior courts from applying customary penal law and also prohibited

ideas underlying *nulla poena.* Indeed, it was in the Code of
the Austrian monarch, Joseph II (1787), that specific prohibition of judicial legislation first entered modern Continental criminal law.[27] The English tradition of the rule of
law,[28] translated by eighteenth century French philosophers
into terms expressive of the revolutionary ideology, joined
the Continental movement for codification to provide
nulla poena with its particular current meanings. We must
remember, too, that in revolutionary France the thesis of
judicial severity and arbitrariness in the *ancien régime* was,
rightly or wrongly, almost unquestioned. It coincided with
and facilitated the rise to power of the legislature.[29] La-
fayette, who participated actively in the Revolutionary Assembly of 1789, proposed the drafting of a Declaration of
the Rights of Man—his inspiration coming, it is said, from
the Virginia Declaration. On August 26, 1789, the famous
Déclaration appeared, containing in its eighth article the
provision: *"Null ne peut être puni qu'en vertu d'une loi*

---

analogy by inferior justices. See Schottlaender, *op. cit. supra* note 6,
at 36-37.

[27] See von Bar, *op. cit. supra* note 26, at 252.

[28] The American Declaration of Independence complained that the
king "has made judges dependent on his will alone for the tenure of
their offices, and the amount and payment of their salaries"; and the
American Colonies generally had asserted the English tradition guar-
anteeing against conviction for any crime except by the law of the
land. *Cf.* ". . . William Penn, in the preface to the plan of government
prepared for Pennsylvania, in 1682, declared that any government is
free to the people under it, *where the laws rule, and the people are a
party to those laws.*" 2 Kent, Commentaries 4n. (a) (1896); *cf.* New
York Act of 13 May, 1691; Mass. Const. of 1780, Art. 12.

"No man's life shall be taken away; no man's honour and good name
shall be stained; no man's person shall be arrested, restrained, ban-
ished, dismembered, nor any ways punished; no man shall be deprived
of his wife or children; no man's goods or estate shall be taken away
from him, nor any ways endamaged; under colour of law, or counten-
ance of authority, unless it be by virtue or equity of some express law,
established by the general court, and sufficiently published, or in case
of the defect of a law in any particular case, by some clear and plain
rule of the word of God." Laws of Mass. 1672, at 1; 1702, at 1; 1750,
at 1; 1784, at 1.265; 1795, at 1. So cited and quoted in State v. Dan-
forth, 3 Conn. 112, 118 (1819).

[29] See M. Bergasse's address in the Assemblée Nationale, quoted in
2 Buckey et Roux, Histoire Parlementaire de la Révolution Francaise
284.

établie et promulguée antérieurement au délit et légalement appliquée." The *Déclaration* fixed the prevailing meanings of *nulla poena* not only as a basic constitutional safeguard of the individual against oppressive government but also as a cardinal principle of penal law. The principle was restated in the French Constitution of September 3, 1791; it was not repeated in the *Code Pénal* of 1791, although the Military Code of that year did contain it.[30] It reappeared in the French Code of 1810, thence to remain practically unchanged.[31] The *Code Pénal* of 1810 became the model of almost the entire European continent. Its provision of the principle of legality was incorporated in the Bavarian Code by Feuerbach in 1813. But it was not until 1850 that it appeared in the Prussian Constitution, nor until 1851 in the Prussian Code;[32] and not until 1870 in the Reich Code. It was omitted from the Reich constitutions of 1849 and 1871, although it was included in most of the federal state constitutions—Bavaria's as early as 1818, Wurtenberg's in 1819.[33]

Feuerbach is generally credited with the formulation of the principle in its current terms. His *Lehrbuch des peinlichen Rechts* first appeared in 1801—at the peak of liberal revolutionary reform, at the zenith of Classicism. He enunciated three basic maxims:[34] *nulla poena sine lege, nulla poena sine crimine, nullum crimen sine poena legali.* His integration of the prevailing political liberalism with penal policy was simple enough: only one who violates the liberty guaranteed by the social contract and safeguarded by penal

[30] Pt. 1, arts. 1 and 2.

[31] The present article 4 of the Code Pénal provides: *"Nulle contravention, nul délit, nul crime, ne peuvent être punis de peines qui n'étaient pas prononcées par la loi avent qu'ils fussent commis."*

[32] The Prussian Code of 1794 (Intro. § 87) provided that "acts and omissions which are not prohibited by the laws cannot be regarded as crimes." But "laws" here included Natural Law. Schottlaender, *op. cit. supra* note 6, at 49.

[33] Prohibition of analogy was included in the *Projects* for German Penal Codes in 1909, 1913, 1919, and 1925. See Ackermann, Das Analogieverbot im Geltenden und zukunftigen Strafrecht, Heft 348, Strafrechtliche Abhandlungen (1934).

[34] Lehrbuch des peinlichen Rechts, par. 24 (1801).

law commits a crime.[35] Since all potential offenders cannot be known in advance and physically controlled, he argued that deterrence must be effected psychologically, by threat. Like Bentham,[36] he insisted on strict adherence to the statute. He rejected analogy completely; indeed, his theory of the judicial function would, by present standards, be regarded as extremely narrow. But his central insight into the value of legality was very apt. Indeed, Feuerbach is among the most eminent of those who made the principle of legality one of the enduring ideas of Western civilization.

NULLUM CRIMEN SINE LEGE

Most of the moot questions about the principle of legality concern the requirement of specific definition of criminal conduct in penal laws. The relevant issues go to the heart of the ethics of criminal law, the function of adjudication and the character of constitutional government. In the Continental European literature, "legal analogy" in penal law is condemned and contrasted with valid "interpretation." In the common law tradition, the relevant distinctions are judicial legislation (the Continental "legal analogy"), liberal ("extensive") interpretation, and strict interpretation. In most European codes and in the common law of crimes, the principle of legality has meant strict interpretation of penal statutes. This excludes liberal interpretation and, *a fortiori*, judicial legislation.

It is debatable to what extent the above distinctions are operative in the judicial process, especially at the periphery of the legal definitions. One's judgment in that regard depends on his opinion concerning the role of the concept in problem-solving and the effect of the canons of interpretation on judicial attitudes. Certainly, the common assumption

---

[35] *Id.* at par. 28.

[36] Bentham had written: "Hence the first law with which a great code ought to be begun, should be a general law of liberty — a law which should restrain delegated powers, and limit their exercise to certain particular occasions, for certain specific causes." 1 Works 576 (Bowring ed. 1843). *Cf.* 2 Bentham, Works 512.

in the innumerable debates on *nullum crimen*, namely, that it is of paramount importance in the judicial process, is evident. Indeed, if that assumption is rejected, the alternative is the very improbable thesis that the rule of law is a myth and that discussing it is irrational.

Analogy, Ambiguity and Vagueness

The principal issue in the vast polemical literature on the principle of legality concerns "analogy."[37] Analogy is, strictly speaking, a likeness of relation. But the term has a more popular connotation to which legal reasoning more closely adheres. To illustrate what is commonly termed "reasoning by analogy": two phenomena resemble each other in certain features which are regarded not as accidental but as essential, and the similarities are deemed to preponderate over the differences. A proposition is known to be true of one of the phenomena; it is asserted by "analogy" to be true of the other. Reasoning by analogy is not applied to things which are practically identical; such reasoning is applied only when it is admitted that significant differences exist. Thus, it being granted that rule R was correctly applied to the X situation, then Y situation is subsumed under R by analogy if Y resembles X in a number of particulars whose joint significance, not numerical superiority, outweighs that of the known differences. The same rule is thus applied to both situations.

But suppose the differences between the two situations are so important as to make improper the subsumption of X and Y under the same rule even though both situations also have important common characteristics. This was the kind of problem which became extremely important on the Continent in the recent past. It raised questions which transcended criminal law and involved all constitutional government. It marked the front line of intellectual warfare in bitter national and international polemics.

We may begin our analysis with the elementary insight that no two cases are identical; yet all cases have *some*

---

[37] See Levi, An Introduction to Legal Reasoning (1949).

common characteristic. Upon the level of generality selected to determine the criteria of likeness or dissimilarity depends the outcome. Hence it is clear that there are no limits whatever which the analogical method cannot reach. Just as every similarity in two factual situations strengthens an analogy, so differences, as they mount, diminish it. Any two situations, facts or events have some similarities, some differences. How can one decide which preponderate? In consequence, there is an inevitable competition among analogies. A new situation has some characteristics in common with those admittedly included under statute A, but other characteristics are like those admittedly included under statute B. Which statute shall govern the present adjudication? "Analogy," in sum, refers to a method of reasoning employed to derive answers to such questions. It can function upon any level of generality to produce any desired result; hence, the central issue concerns the proper "girth" of analogy in penal law. The question to be discussed is: What is the significance of *nullum crimen sine lege* in the determination of this issue?

The definition of that principle stated above, *i.e.* its meaning in Western legal history, suggests both a legislative and a judicial requirement. With reference to the latter, the gist of the answer to the above question, provided in the following discussion, is that the principle of legality requires judges to take a certain attitude towards penal laws, especially to avoid the derivation of wide meanings which express the general policy of a statute and to adhere, instead, to the well-established meaning of its words. Nonetheless, the opposition sometimes supposed to exist between the *ratio verborum* and the *ratio legis* is untenable because the meaning of the words cannot be apprehended unless careful attention is given to the purpose of the law. Since the principle of legality cannot require what is impossible, its intention is not the neglect of the policy of a statute but the limitation of the range of that policy by the actual meaning of the words in the statute.

While laws have "objective" meaning in the sense of contrast with merely individual opinion or preference, the canons—literal or ordinary interpretation, strict interpretation, liberal interpretation, and "legal analogy" (judicial legislation)—must also be given operative meanings, *i.e.* as *functional determinants of the judge's interpretive attitudes.*[38] Although objective differences in fact and meaning are very numerous, the four above indicated attitudes towards the interpretation of statutes are probably all that can actually be maintained even by experts. More specifically as regards penal statutes, this implies:

(a) A "sufficiently" clear meaning exists, which is sometimes designated the "literal," "genuine," or "normal" meaning of the words. The judge must apply this penal law just as fully as he must apply clear private law. *Nullum crimen* in the sense of strict interpretation is irrelevant.

(b) A liberal interpretation of ambiguous words would hold the conduct in issue within the statute; but the canon of strict interpretation of penal statutes requires the judge to select the narrower meaning which exculpates the accused.

(c) In countries where the principle of legality is nonexistent, the judges are required not only to interpret penal statutes liberally but also to enact penal law under certain conditions. This is the antithesis of *nulla poena sine lege*.

The canon of construction of penal statutes, required by the principle of legality,[39] includes several species of interpretation, the common result of which is to favor the defendant. One of these is to adhere to the ordinary meaning of the words instead of to the meaning induced from the general purpose or "legislative intention" of the statute.[40]

[38] *Cf.* ". . . we are driven, in the end, to the unsatisfying conclusion that the whole matter ultimately turns on impalpable and indefinable elements of judicial spirit or attitude." Allen, Law in the Making 503 (5th ed. 1951).

[39] For certain exceptions discussed in the earliest English work on statutory interpretation see, A Discourse upon the Exposicion & Understanding of Statutes 156 ff. (Thorne ed. 1942).

[40] ". . . the statute should not be extended to aircraft, simply because it may seem to us that a similar policy applies. . . ." Holmes,

Another is to adhere to the narrower meaning of ambiguous words established in usage or legal precedent. Still another is to invalidate vague statutes. Again, a conservative view of grammar is frequently reflected in the attitude of strict interpretation.

Suppose, *e.g.* that under a larceny statute forbidding the taking of property, etc., the defendant is charged with making criminal use of machinery.[41] It is generally agreed that "property" must be interpreted in conformity with past decisions; but it is also necessary, in accord with *stare decisis*, to extend those decisions beyond the particular facts in the respective cases, *i.e.* to derive their *ratio decidendi*. In the relevant cases, "property" has been uniformly limited to corporeal personal property. Accordingly, the use of machinery is excluded from the meaning of "property," despite the "principle" or purpose of the statute which embraces the misappropriation of any property. Here, strict interpretation adheres to the narrower meaning of "property" authoritatively established in the case-law on larceny.

In a Virginia case,[42] the court set aside a conviction of the statutory charge of "disorderly conduct on a bus" because it held buses were not included in the terms of the statute which specified car, train or caboose. "On principle" all types of public transportation were within the purpose of the legislation; but the court adhered to the ordinary meaning of the above words in the statute, and that meaning did not include bus. There could hardly be a case which more definitely indicated the invalidity of the unqualified thesis that penal statutes should be interpreted to carry out the "legislative intention."[43] In penal law, the range of that

---

J., in McBoyle v. United States, 283 U. S. 25, 27, 75 L. Ed. 816, 51 S. Ct. 340 (1931). See text *infra* at note 51.

[41] People v. Ashworth, 220 App. Div. 498, 222 N. Y. Supp. 24 (1927).

[42] Lewis v. Commonwealth, 184 Va. 69, 34 S. E. 2d 389 (1945). So, also, held in Akron Trans. Co. v. Glander, 99 N. E. 2d 493 (Ohio, 1951), involving a tax on a franchise.

[43] It is worth noting that at the next session of the Virginia legislature the code was amended to include "omnibus or other public

purpose must be limited by the actual meaning of the words.

In the United States this view of "strict construction" has been greatly influenced by the distinction drawn by Chief Justice Marshall in *Wiltberger*: "To determine that a case is within the intention of a statute, its language must authorize us to say so. It would be dangerous, indeed, to carry the principle, that a case which is within the reason or mischief of a statute, is within its provisions, so far as to punish a crime not enumerated in the statute, because it is of equal atrocity, or of kindred character, with those which are enumerated."[44] As stated, this does not imply that the purpose or policy of a penal statute may be ignored. But it is one thing to determine the meaning of words by reference to the purpose of a statute, and quite another to expand the ordinary meaning of a word, *e.g.* of "car" or "train" in the above case, and thus induce "any vehicle used for public transportation," as might well be suggested by the purpose or policy of the statute. In other words, the logic ("extension") of the purpose of a statute must be restricted by the established ordinary meaning of the words or by the meaning authoritatively established in past decisions, *e.g.* "property."

What, then, is the significance of judicial observations which seem to support a different thesis? For example, in 1863 Chief Baron Pollock remarked that, "The distinction between a strict construction and a more free one has, no doubt, in modern times almost disappeared, and the question now is: What is the true construction of a statute?"[45] In the same case Baron Bramwell quoted approvingly the statement in Sedgwick's *Statutory Law*, that "penal provisions, like all others, are to be fairly construed according to the legislative intent as expressed in the enactment. . . ."[46]

---

conveyance." This act was interpreted in Taylor v. Commonwealth, 187 Va. 214, 46 S. E. 2d 384 (1948).

[44] United States v. Wiltberger, 5 Wheat. 76, 96 (1820).

[45] Attorney General v. Sillem (1863), 2 H. and C. 431, 159 Eng. Rep. 178, at 214.

[46] *Id.* at 159 Eng. Rep. at 223.

Many American statutes purport to abolish "strict construction" and to substitute "true," "genuine," "normal" construction.

Such opinions and statutes have been made the basis of
two lines of argument: (1) that they abolished strict construction. But even when this was plainly stated to be the
legislature's intention, the courts in those states continued
to interpret penal statutes strictly.[47] And (2) the above
judicial comments suggested a theory which allows a place
for both "true, normal construction" and for strict construction. Specifically, the position is that penal statutes are to
be read initially in a normal, genuine way, *i.e.* just as are
civil statutes, but if, in the course of such reading, a judge
comes upon an ambiguous word, he must interpret it
"strictly," *i.e.* in its narrow sense, favoring the accused.
This solution has much to recommend it; and when more is
known about statutory interpretation, it may even turn out
to be the most tenable of the various competing theories.

But the problems of statutory construction are more complicated than the above theory seems to recognize, at least
in the United States and probably in other countries where
courts are authorized to invalidate legislation on constitutional grounds. Whether the problems of statutory interpretation are essentially different where judges lack that
authority and must accept all parliamentary enactments
as valid may be doubted. In the United States, at any rate,
a distinction is drawn between vague penal statutes and
merely ambiguous ones. Only the former are declared violative of "due process" and void;[48] but it is possible to give
ambiguous statutes their narrower meaning and allow them

[47] *Infra* p. 48.
[48] The standard laid down in Connally v. General Constr. Co., 269
U. S. 385, 391, 70 L. Ed. 322, 46 S. Ct. 126 (1926) is: "whether or
not the vagueness is of such a character 'that men of common intelligence must necessarily guess at its meaning.' " Quoted in Winters
v. New York, 333 U. S. 507 at 518, 92 L. Ed. 840, 68 S. Ct. 53 (1948).
It is evident that this standard itself raises difficult questions of interpretation. It should also be borne in mind that many of the cases
decided by the United States Supreme Court involve the Bill of Rights
and therefore result in decisions which may not be typical of the

to remain valid in the consequent restricted sense. This implies that there is a definitely ascertainable difference between ambiguity and vagueness and also that strict construction, as defined above, is relevant only to ambiguous statutes, not to vague ones.

In *Lanzetta,*[49] the leading American case of invalidation on the ground of vagueness, a New Jersey statute made it a felony for any person "not engaged in any lawful occupation," who had previously been convicted of a crime, to be "known to be a member of any gang" and so on. In upholding the validity of this statute in an earlier case, the New Jersey Supreme Court had emphasized "the evident aim of this provision" and that "the word [gang] is to be given a meaning consistent with the general object of the statute." Lanzetta had been convicted before the above New Jersey decision had been rendered, and was therefore not bound by it. But the United States Supreme Court found, in addition, that the New Jersey statute must be judged on its own terms, and that the above New Jersey decision did not cure the statute of its vagueness. For "gang" is a very vague word, including, *e.g.* a gang of workmen; and "known to be" a member also raised doubts. The Supreme Court held that the terms of the statute "are so vague, indefinite and uncertain that it must be condemned as repugnant to the due process clause of the Fourteenth Amendment." Not a word was said in the decision regarding the strict construction of penal statutes. Again, in *Winters,* which involved a statute forbidding the distribution of publications devoted to "deeds of bloodshed, lust or crime" and so on, instead of reading the statute in a "normal," "genuine" way, the Supreme Court said: "The standard of certainty in statutes punishing for offenses is higher than in those depending primarily upon civil sanction for enforcement."[50]

---

common law interpretations by State courts in cases involving ordinary crimes. *Cf.* the cases cited *infra* at note 50.

[49] Lanzetta et al. v. State of New Jersey, 306 U. S. 451, 83 L. Ed. 888, 59 S. Ct. 618 (1939).

[50] Winters v. New York, 333 U. S. 507, 515, 92 L. Ed. 840, 68 S. Ct.

On the other hand, *McBoyle*[51] concerned an ambiguous statute. The defendant had been convicted of the inter-state transportation of a stolen airplane, the statute providing that "motor vehicle" shall include automobile, truck, motorcycle and so on, "or any other self-propelled vehicle not designed for running on rails." Although the latter clause might suffice as a proper dictionary meaning of "airplane," well within the purpose of the statute, the Supreme Court reversed the conviction on the ground that an airplane was not within the ordinary meaning of the above words. However, the statute, the National Motor Vehicle Theft Act, remained a valid law in the given narrower sense. So, too, in the later case of *Evans*,[52] the Supreme Court upheld a district court's dismissal of a prosecution for harboring an alien illegally in the country, on the ground that it was ambiguous whether the penalty clause directly attached to the words forbidding the illegal bringing in of aliens also applied to illegally harboring them, both types of conduct having been forbidden in the statute's defining clause. Here, the Supreme Court took a conservative view of grammatical construction.

We need not here decide whether vagueness and ambiguity can be reduced to a single genus or property of language.[53] At least in a relative sense, some words, *e.g.* "liberty" and "progress" are very general and vague while others, *e.g.* "bed" and "ripe" are narrow and ambiguous.[54] The legal test is whether, after the decision of the

---

53 (1948), and see the cases there cited. *Cf.* United States v. Petrillo, 332 U. S. 1, 91 L. Ed. 1877, 67 S. Ct. 1538 (1947) where the Court upheld (5-3) the constitutionality of a statute making it unlawful to coerce the licensee of a radio station to employ more persons than the number "needed . . . to perform actual services."

51 McBoyle v. United States, 283 U. S. 25, 75 L. Ed. 816, 51 S. Ct. 340 (1931).

52 United States v. Evans, 333 U. S. 483, 92 L. Ed. 823, 68 S. Ct. 634 (1948).

53 *E.g.* in every case of ambiguity the court excludes and thus invalidates a possible meaning which the prosecution, at least, believed was valid.

54 The latter examples are discussed by Holloway, Language and Intelligence 139-142 (1951).

instant case, the statute in question is "sufficiently" clear and precise to satisfy "due process." It is unlikely that "gang," *e.g.* could in a single decision be rendered sufficiently definite to satisfy the constitutional requirement; that term is therefore vague. On the other hand, a clause concerning the age of the defendant, which may mean that he must be "over 18" either at the time he committed previous larcenies or at the time of the present prosecution can be rendered quite definite by excluding the latter meaning.[55] This is therefore an instance of mere ambiguity. Finally, as appears in the above cases, the corollary of the principle of legality which concerns interpretation includes more than the strict construction of ambiguous statutes, in the sense of the American distinction. It also prohibits vague ones.

The above decisions seem to cast doubt upon the rather facile theory previously stated (that judges read penal statutes in a "normal," "genuine" way and then, if they come upon an ambiguity, they must adopt the narrower meaning). This does not meet the test of the courts' actual interpretation of penal statutes, nor would it do so even if vagueness were added to ambiguity in the statement of the theory. For, as was seen in *Lanzetta* and as was stated explicitly in *Winters,* (and this applies also to the Virginia bus case and *McBoyle*) the courts did not read those penal statutes, even initially, in the same way that they read non-penal ones. If they had, they would probably have found some of the legislative purposes quite clear and the words reasonably suited to carrying them out. The judges can hardly dismiss even from an initial reading of a penal statute the insistent direction that they must be guided not by the unqualified purpose but, as Holmes said in *McBoyle*, by what the words "evoke in the common mind." Moreover, since the defense invariably calls the judges' attention to either ambiguous or vague provisions or to both, it is more than dubious that judges read penal statutes in two different ways—first, "normally," as though they were reading a civil statute, and then if they

[55] People v. Lund, 382 Ill. 213, 46 N. E. 2d 929 (1943).

come upon an ambiguity or vagueness in that mode, interpret it favorably to the defendant.

No doubt, much importance must be given to the critical words of distinguished judges and scholars, *e.g.* that courts are not to read penal statutes in an extreme way, hunting difficulties. But these statements must be compatible with the decisions discussed above. It is suggested that the above observations of Baron Pollock and many other English and American judges[56] must be understood as a caveat not to be carried away by the argument of defense counsel or the canons of construction to a highly refined realm of linguistic nicety which could result in the nullification of any penal statute. It is in this sense that judges are admonished to avoid the attitude of the proverbial lawyer "fired with a passion to pervert the plain meaning of words." Language cannot be used to describe human conduct with the precision that is available to a physicist or chemist dealing with inanimate data. Having that in mind, the purpose of a statute, stated with "sufficient" clarity and precision, ought to be given full effect by the courts. Subject to that necessary qualification, strict construction prevails and seems to be viewed alike in the United States and in England, at least as regards serious crimes.[57]

[56] "The rule of strict construction does not, indeed, require or sanction that suspicious scrutiny of the words . . . which characterize the judicial interpretation of affidavits in support of *ex parte* applications or of magistrates' convictions, where the ambiguity goes to the jurisdiction." Maxwell, The Interpretation of Statutes 263 (10th ed. 1953).
"We agree to all the generalities about not supplying criminal laws with what they omit, but there is no canon against using common sense in construing laws as saying what they obviously mean. . . ." Holmes, J., in S. S. Kresge Co. v. Ward, 279 U. S. 337, 339, 73 L. Ed. 722, 49 S. Ct. 336 (1929). *Cf.* Holmes, J., in the McBoyle case, *supra* note 40.

[57] "The court . . . must not strain the words on any notion that . . . the thing is so clearly within the mischief that it must have been intended to be included. . . ." The Gauntlet, (1872) 4 C. P. 184, 191. See also Remmington v. Larchin, (1921) 3 K. B. 404 and Rex v. Chapman, (1931) 2 K. B. 606. In London and N. E. v. Berriman, (1946) A. C. 313, the court approved the rule that, "If there is a reasonable interpretation which will avoid the penalty in any particular case, we must adopt that construction." But *cf.* Williams, Criminal Law 447 (1953). A writer on Scottish criminal law states

It must be confessed, however, that we are still far from having very substantial knowledge of the actual process of statutory interpretation. Not only is "scientific" knowledge, even in a very wide sense, unavailable. There are, instead, unusually serious difficulties in the way of an investigator, *e.g.* the assumptions that when judges say they are interpreting "strictly" or "liberally," that is both decisive and accurate; that the many canons of statutory interpretation, reiterated in countless decisions and accumulated in the treatises, are the most significant avenues to an understanding of the problem or, indeed, that they are more helpful than hazardous to that end; and, finally, and most regrettable, is the assumption that the differences in interpretation are meaningful apart from the factual-normative contexts in which they are expressed. The temptation in these circumstances is to take a completely negative attitude regarding practically everything that has been written about statutory interpretation, to stigmatize it as wholly subjective, ideological and otherwise untrustworthy.

But there are problems of great importance that must be met here and now and by aid of whatever knowledge of statutory interpretation is available. There are, *e.g.* valuable insights to be gleaned from historical investigation. Thus, we know that the strict construction of penal statutes played an extraordinary role in the eighteenth century when a humanitarian ideology propagated by Beccaria, Romilly, Howard, Buxton and others rose against severe, indiscrimi-

---

"that penal statutes should be strictly construed . . . has long been one of our rules for the interpretation of statutes." Elliott, *Nulla Poena Sine Lege*, 1 (n. s.) Jur. Rev. 22 (1956).

If a penal statute is vague, it violates "due process." Gorin v. United States, 312 U. S. 19, 85 L. Ed. 488, 61 S. Ct. 429 (1941) citing United States v. Cohen Grocery Co., 255 U. S. 81, 89, 65 L. Ed. 516, 41 S. Ct. 298 (1921), Lanzetta v. New Jersey, 306 U. S. 451, 83 L. Ed. 888, 59 S. Ct. 618 (1939) and other cases, at 26-27.

See also, note 24 *supra*; Farwell, L. J., in Baylis v. Bishop of London, (1913) 1 Ch. 127, 137; Scrutton, L. J., in Harnett v. Fisher, (1927) 1 K. B. 402, 424: "This Court sits to administer the law; not to make new law if there are cases not provided for." Allen *op. cit. supra* note 38 gives several examples where, though judges heartily disapproved a rule of law, they felt themselves "powerless to change the rule."

nate penalization. Statutes which were quite clear in their meaning were completely distorted. "Strict construction" then was any interpretation, however fantastic, which saved minor offenders from the capital penalty. This movement and its significance with reference to the interpretation of penal statutes have been discussed elsewhere at length.[58] What seems to have been rather definitely established is that statutory interpretation is a relative process in the sense that it changes and must be appraised in relation to time, facts, sanctions, and ideals.

Recognition of the maximum possible certainty of meaning in relation to the various problems and types of fact would seem to be the next step towards enlightenment regarding statutory interpretation. Throughout the criminal law there are numerous specific concepts which elicit reasonably uniform responses in their application, even though the results depend not only upon the legal rules but also upon non-legal institutions, common ideas, and standards born of recurrent experience in a particular culture. The principle of legality enjoins the judge to remain anchored to the authoritatively established and the ordinary meaning of the words and to resolve his doubts in favor of the accused. That attitude is rendered workable by the objective characteristics of social fact, language and case-law. The officials' training provides additional assurance of uniformity. There is available a vast body of experience, not least that of past interpretations exhibited in many decisions. There are the inertia of the language institution and the slowness of change in moral ideas. Although these by no means entirely exclude uncertainty and divergence in results, yet in all probability they exert considerable influence in preserving the principle of legality as opposed to liberal ("extensive") interpretation and deliberate, judicial law-making (so-called "legal analogy"). The principle of legality can do no more than implement the attainment of the maximum possible certainty resulting from the operation of specific rules in a social milieu. It means no less.

[58] Hall, Theft, Law and Society, especially ch. 4 (2nd ed. 1952).

An important bit of evidence of the vitality of the principle of legality is that, despite American legislative efforts
to eliminate strict interpretation and to have penal statutes
construed like civil ones, and excepting certain procedural or
formal matters and sexual crimes, strict interpretation continues to prevail in American penal law. This might seem a
rather curious situation to those unfamiliar with the common law tradition regarding crimes since it amounts to a
refusal by the courts to accept the proffered enlargement of
their powers. There could hardly be any better evidence of
the enduring strength of the principle of legality.[59]

Divergence from the Principle of Legality

Since the meaning of words must be determined analogi-
cally if *stare decisis* is to function, the problem of statutory
interpretation rests finally upon the crucial differences
among "analogies." What these are may be seen when we
distinguish the necessary use of analogy from that required
by the laws adopted in Russia in 1922 and 1926 and in Germany in 1935.[60] The necessary use of analogy, especially by

[59] See L. Hall, *Strict or Liberal Construction of Penal Statutes*,
48 Harv. L. Rev. 748, 754-756 (1935). Roux, *op. cit. supra* note 5,
at 84; 1 Garraud, *op. cit. supra* note 5, art. 146 at 303. Rex v. Halliday, (1917) A. C. 260, 274.
  "Arkansas was the first American jurisdiction to require in general
a liberal construction of its penal statutes." Bond, *Constitutional Law
—Vagueness in the Definition of a Crime*, 7 Ark. L. Rev. 136 (1953).
But the decisions do not seem to reflect any change in statutory interpretation. See *Ex parte* Jackson, 45 Ark. 158, 163, 164 (1885) and
State v. Bryant, 219 Ark. 313, 241 S. W. 2d 473 (1951).
  In Louisiana, the new penal code purported to reject strict interpretation and to adopt what was assumed to be the civil law canon of
"genuine interpretation." But *cf.* Donnedieu de Vabres, Traité Élémentaire de Droit Criminel 68. In State v. Vallery et al., 212 La. 1095,
34 S. 2d 329 (1948), the Louisiana Supreme Court refused to "assume
legislative functions" and the decision and the results reached reveal
no influence of the new provision regarding interpretation. But *cf.*
State v. Powell, 212 Or. 684, 321 P. 2d 333, 337 (1958).
  [60] The German Act of June 28, 1935, provided: "Any person who
commits an act which the law declares to be punishable or which is
deserving of penalty according to the fundamental conceptions of a
penal law and sound popular feeling, shall be punished. If there is
no penal law directly covering an act it shall be punished under the
law of which the fundamental conception applies most nearly to the
said act."
The Russian Penal Code of 1926 provided:
II—6. "A crime is any socially dangerous act or omission which

Anglo-American judges, is a process that is so minute in the changes effected as to be hardly perceptible. Excepting occasional leaps that undoubtedly occur, it reflects the day-by-day growth of criminal law which, for the most part, keeps pace with change in the language institution itself. It has thus amounted largely to an all-but-unnoticed bringing up-to-date of old terms so that, filled with new content, they referred more adequately to the changed conditions. When American judges speak of expanding criminal law by "analogy," they certainly do not mean the so-called "legal analogy," the deliberate law-making, avowed and apparent to all, which was required in the Russian and German innovations. They do not mean liberal interpretation. They are speaking of necessary analogy,[61] limited by the traditional judicial function to apply, not to make, law, and restricted by the canon of strict construction illustrated in a vast number of definite cases. In sum, they are speaking of the minimal, "normal" expansion of past decisions which is necessary in the maintenance of any system of law.

This does not imply acceptance of the eighteenth century dogma which sought to limit the judicial function to a mechanical application of the "legislative intention" expressed in the statute. This Continental prohibition of any "interpretation," its insistence on the literal application of the words in the statutes, may have had ideological effect; it was naive irrelevance so far as the actual process of adjudication is concerned. Only infrequently are the intentions of

---

threatens the foundations of the Soviet political structure and that system of law which has been established by the Workers' and Peasants' Government for the period of transition to a Communist structure."

II—10. "In cases where the Criminal Code makes no direct reference -to particular forms of crime, punishment or other measures of social protection are applied in accordance with those Articles of the Criminal Code which deal with crimes most closely approximating, in gravity, and in kind, to the crimes actually committed. . . ." The Penal Code of the R. S. F. S. R. (1934).

61 Cf. "It is characteristic that leading English and American treatises on statutory construction do not even refer in their indices to the term 'analogy,' and the few cases in which the terms of a statute have received an extended application beyond their possible literal meaning, are clearly exceptional or anomalous. . . ." Freund, *Interpretation of Statutes*, 65 U. of Pa. L. Rev. 207, 227 (1917).

a large group of legislators determinable with precision. Rarer yet will these intentions or even those of the majority be uniform or specific. With passage of time, difficulties mount. Although conditions arise which the legislators could not possibly have had in mind, the judges were told to abstain from any interpretation whatever. That is plain fiction.

But the invalidity of the eighteenth century dogma of statutory interpretation does not minimize the significance of the above noted twentieth century abandonment of *nullum crimen sine lege*. To appreciate that, one need only contrast interpretation rigorously limited by the objective meaning of language, ordinary speech, authoritatively determined meanings and the other factors noted above with deliberate legislation by judges motivated to convict and punish, on vague ideological grounds, persons whose conduct was legal.

On the technical side of the question, it is apparent from decisions of the *Reichsgericht*, during the period when it still included judges of the older regime, that the 1935 German law enjoining "legal analogy" gave the trial judges an opportunity to escape the labor of diligent research and study of the penal code, encouraging easy resort to "principle" and the "sound feelings of the people." It is equally clear that these judges expanded statutes to include conduct which the legislature intended to leave unpunished.[62] But it is especially significant that "legal analogy" was apparently little resorted to in Germany despite the Act of June 28, 1935[63] and the repressive policy of the government. A fair inference is that the penal law did not have the wide gaps which were dramatized as hindrances to "substantial justice."

Substantial justice rarely suffers from lack of laws. By comparison with lack of discovery of criminal conduct, lack of detection, lack of complaint, and inefficiency in adminis-

---

[62] *E.g.* incest although the act was not consummated; homosexuality by women; acts criminal within the jurisdiction, but committed outside the jurisdiction when they were not criminal. See Frankfurter Zeitung, June 24, 1936; R. G. 27/3/36 Deutsche Justiz, 1936, 774; R. G. 18/2/36, Deutsche Justiz, 1936, 609.

[63] The Act is set forth in note 60 *supra*.

tration, the failure to punish the guilty resulting from gaps in the penal law is an almost trivial defect. Since the opponents of legality were very astute individuals, it is highly probable that they sought objectives other than substantial justice for the occasional enemy who could not be eliminated "according to law." The injunction to employ "legal analogy" had its maximum effect in stimulating a repressive attitude not only in the interpretation of laws but also in the finding of facts, and not merely in marginal cases but also in prosecutions which were well within the confines of accepted penal law.[64] There was, of course, no injunction to allow the morally innocent to escape; only the command to widen the net of punishability.

When repression was sought, the argument supporting abandonment of legality ran in terms of "Society versus the criminal."[65] If what people thought Lombroso said were only true! If "the criminal" actually stood apart, marked like the leper, there might conceivably be some justification for reversion to uncontrolled primitive justice. The supposition that "the criminal" is not only perfectly well known but that he is thus known in advance of trial, is, in the light of the facts, as fantastic as it is ominous. The principle of legality signifies that only after a thorough inquiry directed by rational procedure and aided by the long experience crystallized in precise rules of criminal law can defensible judgments be reached regarding the dangerousness of any one. Even then innocent persons are sometimes convicted.[66] On the other hand, it is inevitable that in any legal system a few malefactors are permitted to escape—that is the price

[64] *Cf.* "There is nothing more dangerous than the common axiom: *the Spirit of the laws is to be considered.* To adopt this is to give way to the torrent of opinions. . . . The spirit of the laws will then be the result of the good, or bad logic of the judge; and this will depend on his good or bad digestion; on the violence of his passions; on the rank, and condition of the accused, or on his connections with the judge; and on all those little circumstances, which change the appearance of objects in the fluctuating mind of man." Beccaria, Essay on Crimes and Punishments 14, 15 (1770). *Cf.* Montesquieu, Spirit of Laws bk. XI, ch. VI (1748).

[65] See Radin, *Enemies of Society*, 27 J. Crim. L. 328 (1936).

[66] Borchard, Convicting the Innocent (1932).

paid for the larger benefits conferred by conformity to the principle of legality. But the legislature usually intervenes soon afterwards.[67]

Failure to comprehend the more complex methods by which Anglo-American case-law implements the principle of legality caused certain European criminologists to assert, in defense of the above innovations, that *nullum crimen* did not exist in England or America. In a sense this is a narrow literal truth; but actually, as intended by these writers, it is quite fallacious. The principle of legality as developed on the Continent premises inclusive penal codification. In many American states which have substituted inclusive collections of statutes for the common law of crimes, a rather accurate parallel can be drawn. The qualifications would run along lines suggested by distinctive techniques of adjudication, the reference to many detailed precedents and the differences resulting from required reliance upon the case-law to define common law terms which were listed but not defined by the statutes.[68] In perhaps a majority of the American states, as in England, despite the large and constantly increasing volume of statutes, there exists a residuum of common law which makes *nullum crimen* in its literal, Continental sense, to that extent irrelevant. But instead of a code, there is a vast body of case-law which defines criminal conduct. It is highly probable that this renders the principle of legality much more effective than does the generality of codes, especially where the relevant case-law is scant.

If one wishes to find parallels in English legal history to the above noted Continental abandonment of *nulla poena*, he needs to look backward some hundreds of years. The ancient prerogative of the Crown, exercised in the issuance of numerous decrees, and the powers of the Council operated without regular legal restraint. For almost two hundred years the Court of Star Chamber had very wide jurisdiction and "it punisheth errors creeping into the Commonwealth,

---

[67] See *supra* note 43.

[68] State v. De Wolfe, 67 Neb. 321, 93 N. W. 746 (1903); *In re* Greene, 52 F. 104 (C. C. W. Ohio, 1892).

which otherwise might prove dangerous and infectious diseases . . . although no positive law or continued custom of common law giveth warrant to it."[69] But the Star Chamber was abolished in 1641. Since then the rule of law has reigned almost wholly unchallenged as regards the criminal law.

The above qualification is required especially by the law regarding certain misdemeanors. In recent years it has been forgotten that from 1660 to 1860 the courts, without the authority of specific precedent, frequently held criminal conduct that was *contra bonos mores* which, so it was said, "outraged public decency."[70] There are scattered instances of courts continuing this practice even after 1860.[71] But the shock produced by *Manley*,[72] which involved an interference with police services, indicates how rarely English courts have exercised this discretionary power even regarding minor offenses. And *Manley* has been strongly disapproved in a later decision which recommended reversal by the House of Lords.[73] So, too, while at first glance it might seem that under such generalities as *"contra bonos mores"* there would be almost unlimited discretion,[74] an examination of relevant American cases indicates that a strong legal tradition imposes definite limitations on the range of such penal statutes.[75] An area of relative vagueness probably does exist there; and it is understandable that some departure from

---

[69] Hudson, quoted in 1 Holdsworth, H. E. L. 504 (7th ed. 1956).

[70] 4 Bl. Comm. 65; 1 Hawkins, P. C. ch. 5, §4 (8th ed. 1824) ; 1 East, P. C. chs. 1, 3, 4 (1716).

[71] Reg. v. Stephenson, (1884) 13 Q. B. 331.

[72] Rex v. Manley, (1933) 1 K. B. 529. The defendant falsely stated that she had been robbed, thus causing police officers to make an investigation to discover the offender. She was convicted of effecting "a public mischief." So, too, Commonwealth v. Mochan, 177 Pa. Super. 454, 110 A. 2d 788 (1955). But *cf.* State v. Musser, 118 Utah 537, 223 P. 2d 193 (1950). And see Stallybrass, *Public Mischief*, 49 L. Q. Rev. 183 (1933) ; Jackson, *Common Law Misdemeanors*, 6 Camb. L. J. 193 (1937).

[73] Reg. v. Newland & others, (1954) 1 Q. B. 158, 167-68, (1953) 2 All E. R. 1067. But *cf.* Reg. v. Bailey (1956) N. I. 16, and Coutts, *Effecting a Public Mischief*, 21 J. Cr. L. 60 (1957).

[74] See Schinnerer, *Analogie und Rechtsschopfung*, 55 Zeitschrift fur Strafrechtswissenschaft, Heft 6 at 771 (1936). See *Note*, 25 Brooklyn L. Rev. 46-73 (1958).

[75] See § 675 (present § 43) of the New York Penal Code. There

the principle of legality should be tolerated where the penalty is slight.

Again, *nullum crimen sine lege* was hardly ever closely followed as regards juveniles, vagabonds, mendicants, and other persons "without visible means of support." Since a mode of life includes many acts, it cannot be assumed that the relevant rules are wholly empty of content or that the principles of conduct and legality have been completely abandoned in these instances. It must be granted, however, that there is a long tradition regarding the penalization of such classes of persons which developed with little realization of the challenge to basic principle.[76]

But the totality of these offenses, where relatively little effort has been devoted to frame specific definitions of the relevant criminal conduct, comprises but a small segment of the criminal law. The case-law is precise, the penal statutes have typically been specific, and there is the detailed implementation of a bulky volume of precedents where strict interpretation is applied and illustrated.[77] There are other potent, though more subtle, non-technical forces affecting the common law adjudication of criminal cases, which have been noted above. Indeed, it seems evident that defensible ethical principles, expressed in clear

---

are two important limitations: the statute is confined to misdemeanors; and the vast majority of misdemeanors are specifically described in the Code. Finally, as to the relatively small area provided for by § 43, the judges have imposed numerous restrictions. See People v. Baylinson, 211 App. Div. 40, 43, 206 N. Y. Supp. 804, 807 (1st Dep't 1924); People v. Tylkoff, 212 N. Y. 197, 105 N. E. 835 (1914); People v. Burke, 243 App. Div. 83, 84, 276 N. Y. Supp. 402, 404 (1st Dep't 1934), *aff'd without opinion*, 267 N. Y. 571, 196 N. E. 585 (1935); People v. Ward, 148 Misc. 94, 96, 266 N. Y. Supp. 466, 468 (Ct. Sar. 1933); *In re* Farley, 143 N. Y. Supp. 305 (Sup. Ct. 1913); People v. Helmes, 144 Misc. 695, 259 N. Y. Supp. 911 (Ct. Chen. 1932).

76 See Lacey, *Vagrancy and Other Crimes of Personal Condition*, 66 Harv. L. Rev. 1203 (1953). *Cf.* Perkins, 9 Hast. L. J. 237 (1958).

77 See *Note*, 47 Col. L. Rev. 624-5 (1947). As regards children, "sexual psychopaths" and others, it will be noted that "in theory" they are not criminals. Hence, *nullum crimen sine lege*, is not strictly applicable. However, see Paulsen, *Fairness to the Juvenile Offender*, 41 Minn. L. Rev. 547 (1957).

precise rules of law and supported by popular attitudes and official tradition, provide more effective guarantees of individual security and freedom from arbitrary penalization than can result from any merely verbal expression of *nulla poena sine lege* in a constitution or formal Bill of Rights.

TREATMENT OF OFFENDERS — *NULLA POENA SINE LEGE*

It is often not recognized that there is an inevitable incompatibility between the principle of legality and complete exculpation even in marginal cases where very good motivation combines with a minimum of the proscribed harm, *e.g.* a tragic case of euthanasia. The fact is that we cannot have it both ways. If we agree that it is preferable to have a legal system with the attendant guarantees against official abuse, then we are bound to accept the limitations of any such system and recognize that mitigation, not exculpation, is the relevant recourse in meritorious cases.

This is especially pertinent to *nulla poena sine lege* in its particular reference to punishment. Indeterminate sentence, probation, suspended sentence, nominal sentence, waiver of felonies on pleas to misdemeanors, compromise, modified sentence, "good time" laws, parole and pardon have almost completely transformed eighteenth century law and penological ideas. But despite this flexibility of the sanctions of current penal law, attacks on the retention of any limitation, *e.g.* that of maximum sentences, continue to be pressed,[78] although their number and acerbity diminished very sharply after the penological enlightenment disseminated by the twentieth century dictatorships.

It is easy to imagine why some proposed solutions of difficult problems took the form of urging the retention of *nullum crimen* but abandonment of *nulla poena*, for it is the former which protects the mass of respectable citizens, while the latter, which bars complete individualization of "treatment," affects only proven criminals. But if anything can be done to any convicted person, the guarantee of legality

---

[78] *E.g.* Menninger, *Verdict Guilty—Now What?* 219 Harper's Mag. at 62 (1959).

has in fact vanished entirely. It might be rare, *e.g.* that a murderer escaped punishment while habitual thieves and sexual offenders languished in prison because the experts were not convinced that they were "cured." But those possibilities must be recalled when it is urged even with the greatest altruism that legal restraints on official power be wholly eliminated.

The current issue can be indicated most briefly by reference to demands being made in the United States, notably, at present, by psychiatrists, for the complete elimination of prescribed penalties. The judge, it is argued, should be confined entirely to the conduct of the trial; his participation should end when a verdict is reached. Sentences, we are informed, should be wholly indeterminate; "treatment," if any is necessary, should be given by an administrative board of experts who have ample opportunity to study the offender and, presumably, considerable knowledge concerning rehabilitation. In addition, the argument occasionally extends to advocacy of the entire elimination of the requirement that there be any definite criminal conduct, *i.e.* of *nullum crimen* as well as *nulla poena.* "Anti-social" persons would in some sort of proceeding be declared "dangerous" and placed in the hands of experts, to be dealt with as they determined in accordance with their views or knowledge of psychiatry and sociology.

This is the thesis of the Positivist School, first developed on the European Continent.[79] It was given a very illuminating application by twentieth century Neo-Positivists who accepted the strictures on the legal limitation of official power and substituted not enlightenment and benevolence, but calculated cruelty—all in the unimpeachable cause of "social defense."[80] That is one vitally important reason why the issues raised in proposals to abandon the principle of legality cannot be resolved merely because it is claimed that

[79] See *infra* chapter 16.
[80] Cantor, *Prison Reform in Germany—1933*, 25 J. Crim. L. 89 (1934).

experts should be authorized to determine who are criminals and what shall be done with them. There is, in sum, an irreducible incompatibility between the uncontrolled exercise of such great powers and the values implicit in the common law of crimes. In this field, if in any, it is necessary also to insist that reform have some fair relation to fact and that it should be based on the actual state of current knowledge. Especially should it be remembered that *nulla poena* represents the peak of all the values expressed in criminal law, indeed, what is done to criminals is an index of the quality of a civilization. Hence, whatever shortcomings the Classical School had, it is to their abiding credit that they urged not only *nullum crimen sine lege* but also, and even more, that they insisted on *nulla poena sine lege.*

Criminologists, unschooled in the history and value of criminal law, assumed that the discretion exercised by an administrative board would be "wise and good." Unfortunately, history recorded other eventualities—and in places where "scientific criminology" reached its highest peak. On the other hand, it is impossible, in the abstract, to condemn or to praise every departure from legality as regards the treatment of criminals. Accordingly, among the questions to be asked the current critics of legality are: Are wise, informed judges, experts and administrators available and in sufficient number? Is "treatment" really humane or does that, as well as "social defense," sometimes and in some places mean harsh punishment, long imprisonment, and the "tyranny of experts"? Is there really available a body of knowledge which permits the discovery of dangerous persons in advance of any criminal conduct by them or that demonstrably shows whether they have been "cured" or are still dangerous? If so, where is it published or recorded? These are the issues which should check propaganda and guide penal theory. They raise the insistent question, whether present efforts should not be devoted to improvement of the already far-ranging administration of the law, instead of to its abandonment.[61]

[61] See McIlwain, *Government by Law*, 14 For. Affairs 185 (1936).

In this regard, it is noteworthy that the program of the new European "social defense" movement upholds the principle of legality.[82] Critics have questioned the compatibility of that avowal with the extensive program to individualize treatment, enlarge the authority of experts and so on. Some of the proposals of the new "social defense" school have long been in vogue in the United States and other countries where legality is also rigorously implemented. Thus, it is only when critical points are reached and particular issues and cases are considered that one can evaluate the program of this movement.[83] While, in general, one applauds the sound individualization of treatment and feasible programs of crime prevention and rehabilitation, it should also be remembered that the rule of law, especially as regards crime and punishment, is the greatest achievement of Western political experience.

That is the reason why the various meanings of the principle of legality have been carefully articulated in many countries. These meanings have the common characteristic of insistence on clear, definite legal prescription. *Nullum crimen* and *nulla poena* specify that requirement regarding the two vitally important questions: who is a criminal? and, assuming that a criminal has been legally designated, what may be done to him? The rule of strict interpretation implements that purpose. Still another form of assurance was taken out — the prohibition of retroactive penal law.

NON-RETROACTIVITY

The prohibition of retroactivity expresses the essential temporal condition of the principle of legality: the required criminal law must have existed when the conduct in issue

---

[82] Besson et Ancel, La Prévention des Infractions contre la Vie Humaine et L'Intégreté de la Personne (2 vols. Paris, 1956).

[83] See the thoughtful essay by Professor P. Nuvolone, *Le principe de la légalité et les principes de la défense sociale,* (n. s.) Rev. sci. crim. et dr. pen. comp. 231 (1956), in which he suggests that individualization of treatment can largely be achieved by incorporating in the penal law certain classifications of offenders, *e.g.* by reference to first offenders, simple recidivists, habitual and professional, on the one side, and passion, violence, fraud, and sexual offenders, on the other.

occurred. As was seen above, this dates from the ancient Greeks, and there has probably been no more widely held value-judgment in the entire history of human thought than the condemnation of retroactive penal law. In the United States the guaranty was regarded as of such importance by the Fathers of the Constitution that it was stipulated in the original draft,[84] well in advance of the adoption of the Bill of Rights.

But the history of that least challenged phase of the principle of legality is far from showing a solid line of unbroken acceptance;[85] and even English history is not without a number of instances of *ex post facto* legislation, some for very serious offenses.[86] But these had to do with political cases which arose during turbulent Stuart times. They are suggestive of the use of the coercive legal apparatus during crises and before constitutional government is firmly established. No express constitutional provision forbids retroactivity in England, as does the American Constitution. But the bias against such penal legislation is deeply embedded in the common law.[87] The handful of formally retroactive English public laws,[88] excepting the Stuart instances, seems

[84] U. S. Const. Art. I, §9 cl. 3 and §10 cl. 1. Chancellor Kent traced the history of *ex post facto* in Dash v. Van Kleeck, 7 Johns. 477 (N. Y. 1811).

[85] Examples of *ex post facto* legislation in Nazi Germany were the lex van der Lubbe, the punishment of Communists regardless of prohibitions in the Weimar constitution, and the homicide of Roehm and his associates. Each of the above was subsequently declared "legal."

[86] The King v. Thurston (1663), 1 Lev. 91, 83 Eng. Rep. 312; for other instances collected, see Calder v. Bull, 3 Dall. 386, 1 L. Ed. 648 (1798).

[87] Even Bentham wrote: "This is one of the noblest characteristics of the English tribunals: they have generally followed the declared will of the legislator with scrupulous fidelity, or have directed themselves as far as possible by previous judgments. . . . This rigid observance of the laws may have had some inconveniences in an incomplete system, but it is the true spirit of liberty which inspires the English with so much horror for what is called an *ex post facto* law." 1 Works 326 (Bowring ed. 1843). See Allen, *op. cit. supra* note 38, at 445; Phillips v. Eyre, (1870) L. R. 6 Q. B. 1, 23; Reg. v. Griffiths, (1891) 2 Q. B. 145, 148. But see *Ex parte* Clinton (1845) 6 How. St. Tr. (n. s.) 1105, 1107.

[88] See Allen, *op. cit. supra* note 38, at 440ff.

to have been intended to relieve an individual or a group from an unjust hardship.[89]

The leading American case on this subject is *Calder v. Bull*[90] which held four types of penal enactment violative of the *ex post facto* provision: "1st. Every law that makes an action done before the passing of the law, and which was innocent when done, criminal; and punishes such action. 2d. Every law that aggravates a crime, or makes it greater than it was, when committed. 3d. Every law that changes the punishment, and inflicts a greater punishment, than the law annexed to the crime, when committed. 4th. Every law that alters the legal rules of evidence, and receives less, or different testimony, than the law required at the time of the commission of the offense, in order to convict the offender." Later decisions widened the area of constitutional guarantee to include laws which retroactively require certain qualifications for office, not justifiable as a proper exercise of the "police power;" laws which impose a pecuniary penalty for an act which, when committed, was not subject to that liability; and laws which retroactively deprive a person of his right to follow a certain vocation.[91] Although the *ex post facto* provision in the United States Constitution has avowedly been limited to penal legislation, there is reason to think that, in addition, very important judicial decisions which, *e.g.* reverse prior decisions that declared penal statutes unconstitutional, must not be given retroactive effect.[92]

[89] *Ibid.* The American colonies early provided against retroactivity. As to substantive law, the problem has rarely been raised in the Supreme Court. See Cummings v. Missouri, 71 U. S. 277, 18 L. Ed. 356 (1867) and *Ex parte* Garland, 71 U. S. 333, 18 L. Ed. 366 (1867), both outgrowths of post Civil War legislation. On the problem generally, see Smead, *The Rule Against Retroactive Legislation: A Basic Principle of Jurisprudence*, 20 Minn. L. Rev. 775 (1936), and Field, *Ex Post Facto in the Constitution*, 20 Mich. L. Rev. 3 (1921).

[90] 3 Dall. 386, 1 L. Ed. 648 (1798).

[91] Cooley, Constitutional Limitations 545 (8th ed. 1927).

[92] State v. O'Neil, 147 Iowa 513, 126 N. W. 454 (1910) and see *infra* chapter 11. It has also been held that an indeterminate sentence law, supplanting the concurrent definite-term provision, was invalid since it might result in a longer term of imprisonment. State v.

It is true, of course, that in a literal sense all case-law, including judicial interpretations of statutes or codes, operates retroactively. For despite the traditional theory of pre-existing, all-inclusive law, the fact is that there are many gaps; and it is the subsequent decision which reaches back into time and places the authoritative stamp of criminality upon the prior conduct. But such "retroactivity" is an essential aspect of any legal system. The important thing, therefore, is not the invalidity of a literal interpretation of the traditional theory in this regard but the actual quality of the adjudication. Specifically, is a decision retroactive only in the above unavoidable way or is it also unexpected and indefensible by reference to the law which had been expressed prior to the conduct in issue? In the vast majority of cases, it is very probable, in advance of adjudication, that certain conduct will be held criminal. But there are exceptions. Especially in a long stretch of legal history, there are cases, landmarks in every system, where the courts have plainly made a new law[93] which was given retroactive effect. In any event, the inevitability of a slight, "normal" degree of retroactivity in judicial decision provides no ground for tolerating it in its obvious manifestations.

Underlying the revulsion against retroactivity of penal laws are certain definite values: It is unjust that what was legal when done should subsequently be held criminal, that what was punishable by a certain sanction when committed, should later be punished more severely, or that procedural changes should be applied retrospectively to an accused person's disadvantage. There would be hardly any dissent from this evaluation when the conduct in issue was moral or involved only slight immorality. But why should not the

---

Fisher, 126 W. Va. 117, 27 S. E. 2d 581 (1943). This raises questions regarding subsequently enacted measures of "social defense," *e.g.* offenders often prefer definite sentences to prison to uncertain allegedly corrective ones. That a subsequently enacted law permitting evidence of the convicted person's previous criminal record in the pre-sentence hearing does not violate the *ex post facto* provision, held in Ward v. California, 269 F. 2d 906 (C. C. A. 9th, 1959).

[93] See, *e.g.* the writer's discussion of the Carrier's case in Theft, Law and Society, ch. 1 (2nd ed. 1952).

very immoral perpetrator of a serious harm be punished by reliance on a subsequently enacted law? Why not in such cases increase an existing penalty to one that is proportionate or facilitate the process of conviction by changing the rules of procedure? Does not "substantial justice" require affirmative replies to these questions?

A few years ago European apologists of retroactivity ridiculed the notion that a potential law-breaker is entitled to notice of the penalty he may incur. Although they wished "to strike terror into the hearts of criminals,"[94] they argued that experience and observation amply demonstrate that penal laws do not deter, and that it is a vestige of a rationalistic age to believe that the prospective offender will weigh the advantage of his crime against the evil of his punishment. Yet criminals who give no heed to any possible punishment were elsewhere said by these same criminologists to be so expert in the law that they cannily operated in areas just beyond the reaches of the statute.[95] These inconsistencies were not as irrational as might be supposed. For, given the objectives of eliminating "undesirables" and of maintaining, also, the semblance of legality, the methods employed would be: first, utilize existing laws so far as possible, implying support of deterrence; and, in addition, where there cannot be the slightest pretense of legality because no existing law is remotely relevant, defend *ex post facto* law on the ground of "substantial justice" — here any deterrent effect of law must obviously be depreciated.

Not unrelated to the above position has been the insistence by criminologists and psychiatrists in democratic countries that criminal conduct should be ignored and that punishment or, as they prefer, "treatment" should depend entirely on the dangerousness of the "offender." Since this would wholly eliminate the principle of legality, the relative time of the occurrence of the "anti-social" conduct would become

[94] See Frank, quoted by Cantor, *supra* note 80, at 84, 88.

[95] Frank, quoted by Preuss, *Punishment by Analogy in National Socialist Penal Law*, 26 J. Crim. L. 847, 848 (1936).

irrelevant. This position therefore extends far beyond the challenge to non-retroactivity; and its wider implications will be discussed in later chapters.[96]

Among the reasons alleged for opposing retroactive penal laws, the injustice of the punishment is sometimes based on the ground that people should be forewarned that they will be punished if they do certain acts. But there are serious limitations on the persuasiveness of this explanation of non-retroactivity, which will become apparent in the later discussion of the doctrine of *ignorantia juris*. It may be suggested here that since the lack of knowledge of the law is irrelevant as regards the major crimes, the rationale of *ignorantia juris* and, thus, of the congruent principle of legality (specifically, non-retroactivity) cannot be the unfairness of punishment because of lack of notice. The rationale of non-retroactivity, it is submitted, is opposition to the lawless infliction of suffering, aggravated by the fact that this is done by public officials claiming authority to inflict that "punishment." The revulsion against this use of unfettered power by officials far transcends the significance of the complaint of unfairness because of lack of notice.[97] Such a complaint, if made in behalf of an offender who had committed a serious harm, might evoke little sympathy. But when the "official" action is seen to undermine the foundations of constitutional government, quite a different valuation is attached to the enforcement of an *ex post facto* penal law. In sum, non-retroactivity is a corollary of the principle of legality.

There is a further point to be noted regarding the above hypothetical case, where it was assumed that the conduct in question was grossly immoral. In fact, however, this is often a moot question, and conduct which falls outside the proliferation of modern penal laws is not apt to arouse public condemnation. Who is to decide that the conduct in issue was immoral or grossly immoral, so as to justify

[96] *Infra* chapter 13 at note 12. Also see "Criminology" in the Index.
[97] See *infra* chapter 11 on *error juris*.

retroactive penal law on that ground? Merely to raise this question reveals the function of non-retroactivity as an essential implication of the principle of legality. For it is precisely the extra-legal determination of the vitally important questions — who is a criminal? and what may his punishment be? — that the principle bars. To allow the State to impose heavy personal deprivations even for admittedly grossly harmful conduct that is outside the reach of existing penal laws would therefore circumvent the central purpose of the principle of legality. Indeed, to do that in reliance upon a retroactive enactment would amount to a hypocritical use of "law," more grievous than a direct attack on legality. Since legal systems are less than perfect, some malefactors inevitably fall beyond the reaches of existing legal control. The tolerated escape of these offenders is an index of the rationale and the vigor of the principle of legality.

POLITICS AND PENAL POLICY

In a theoretical discussion, practical political questions are usually irrelevant. In penal law, however, policy plays an important role even in the interpretation of statutes; and penal policy is closely connected with political policy. Attention should at least be directed to this problem.

In democratic countries the political significance of criminal law had been almost forgotten when the impact of twentieth century dictatorship, with its unvaried immediate seizure of the punitive legal apparatus, revived a startled realization of the dependence of civil liberty on criminal law. By a sure and unconscionable instinct, the forces of repression cut straight to the heart of the traditional institution — the principle of legality.

But neither the principle of legality nor the departures from it can be explained simply in terms of democratic theory or constitutional government. For when one finds that Denmark some years ago departed from the principle, that Italy in her 1930 Code reaffirmed it, including non-retroactivity, that Poland did likewise, that Germany abandoned the principle in 1935, and that in Russia, which discarded it entirely in 1922 and 1926, it has recently been reaffirmed, it must be concluded that the identification of the principle of legality with democratic constitutional government is invalid. It would, however, be equally fallacious to think that the principle of legality is not an essential aspect of free constitutional government.[98] What is indicated, instead, is something more complex than either of these, namely, that the principle is a necessary, but not a sufficient, condition of such government and, also, that it can and does serve the purposes of non-democratic forms of government.

In Germany, the judge had been freed from "slavish adherence to the statute" long before 1935.[99] Applying the penal law under pressure of a completely centralized government, itself the creature of economic and moral collapse, he found ready-made the theory of so-called "scientific" criminology. The law of June, 1935 was but one of numerous legal and constitutional changes which characterized the Nazi regime. They become comprehensible only when placed in the context of the sustaining ideology. In Italy, the dominant philosophy did not stress the opposition of Community and law, and the Code of 1930 was adopted some years after the Fascist revolution. Stability of government joined a strong legal tradition. The setting up of special tribunals to hear political offenses in disregard of constitutional law[1] and the broad definition of some crimes,[2] together with the turning-over of the chief interests of the

[98] *Supra* note 81. "Thus, we can say that although the rule of law is not by itself a guarantor of freedom, nevertheless its existence is a prerequisite if such freedom is to be established." Goodhart, *The Rule of Law and Absolute Sovereignty*, 106 U. of Pa. L. Rev. 943 (1958).

[99] The 1927 draft of a German Penal Code had already incorporated many of the views of the Positivist School. Gerland, *The German Draft Penal Code and its Place in the History of Penal Law*, 11 J. Comp. Leg. & Int. L. 28 ff. (1929).

[1] Cantor, *The Fascist Political Prisoners*, 27 J. Crim. L. 169 (1936); Fraenkel, The Dual State (1941).

[2] *E.g.* Art. 282: "Whoever commits an offense against the honor or

State to administrative boards, no doubt facilitated retention of the principle of legality in the ordinary run of offenses.[3]

The German Act of June, 1935 was conservative by comparison with the Russian Penal Code of 1926. There, all "socially dangerous" behavior was made punishable, and the standards of dangerousness were the objectives of the revolution. But there has subsequently been a long series of changes in Soviet law, apparently including definite tendencies to return to legality,[4] which make it difficult to generalize with reference to the entire period.[5] The early Soviet view of law represented a phase of revolutionary propaganda. Lenin announced that the Communist dictatorship is "a dictatorship untrammelled by any law, an absolute rule, a power that is based directly on violence. . . ."[6] This was the typical Marxist ideological attack upon law as an instrument of the ruling class, with its boast that a classless society would have no need of it.[7] Yet Lenin himself retreated from this position. The fourteenth Congress of the Communist Party demanded a return to legality.[8] Others argued that non-legality was bad for the peasants. The Code of Criminal Procedure contained guarantees against illegal arrest, although the special police were not to be hampered by judicial review. There have been drastic repudiations of Marxist legal philosophers accompanied by the rise of a huge powerful State and emphatic avowals by the enlightened legal philosophers that legality serves the national interest.

---

prestige of the Head of Government shall be punished with penal servitude from one to five years."

[3] See generally Steiner, *The Fascist Conception of Law*, 36 Col. L. Rev. 1267 (1936).

[4] Hazard, *Soviet Textbooks on Laws*, 31 Slav. & E. Eur. Rev. 215-216 (1943).

[5] Berman, *Principles of Soviet Criminal Law*, 56 Yale L. J. 803, 810-12 (1947), and Hazard, *Soviet Commentators Re-Evaluate the Policies of Criminal Law*, 55 Col. L. Rev. 773-77 (1955).

[6] Quoted in Mirkine-Guetzévitch, *The Public Law System of the Sovietic Dictatorship*, 12 J. Comp. Leg. & Int. L. 248, 250 (1930).

[7] See Dobrin, *Soviet Jurisprudence and Socialism*, 52 L. Q. Rev. 402 (1936).

[8] Mirkine-Guetzévitch, *supra* note 6, at 249.

Even as regards the treatment of juveniles, the Russians abandoned their former theory and resort to admittedly punitive measures.[9]

The German law of 1935 was terminated by the American occupation, and the new German Code in its first paragraph provides: "An act is punishable only when the law prohibiting it was in force prior to the act." Similar provisions are also included in the new codes of Communist countries, *e.g.* that of Yugoslavia (Art. 2). Article 3 of the 1958 Russian draft of "Basic Principles" of a new penal code[10] seems to revoke "legal analogy" (judicial legislation), and Section 6 forbids retroactive penal legislation. But it is uncertain not only whether the principle of legality will be enacted but also what meaning will be given it,[11] especially in the area of political offenses. These, of course, are crucial questions.

Several common traits characterize these revolutionary authoritarian movements whether they abrogated or retained the principle of legality. Special police are exempt from any legal controls — they arrest, try, execute, and exile without restraint. Appeal is limited or non-existent. Special tribunals for the trial of political offenders may be depended upon to effectuate the will of the government. There is sweeping abrogation of constitutional guarantees. And all of this is rationalized and sustained by relentless all-embracing "thought control" which is used by the leaders to implement their political aims. The salient feature of authoritarian political theory in its attack on legality consisted in the subordination of the individual to The Community or The People and, in any case, to The Party. In

[9] Berman, *Juvenile Delinquency, the Family and the Court in the Soviet Union*, 42 Am. J. Soc. 682 (1937); Hazard, *supra* note 4, and Hazard, Law and Social Change in the U. S. S. R. 105, 108 (1953).

[10] The "Basic Principles" are published in The Federal Criminal Law of the Soviet Union, in the series, Law in Eastern Europe (Ed. Szirmai, 1959).

[11] "The 1958 draft 'basis' is not as open in its condemnation of the analogy principle as one might have expected, given the desire of Soviet lawyers to eliminate it." Hazard, *Soviet Codifiers Release the First Drafts*, 8 Amer. J. Comp. L. 75 (1959).

short, during those revolutions, law, especially criminal law, was a party weapon.

But societal needs soon transcend the transitory critical conditions, and numerous situations exist or arise which cannot be dealt with by reference to revolutionary ideals. Non-political situations affecting ordinary inter-personal relations and the family give rise to different needs and perspectives. Quite apart from the reaches of political dogma, specific issues may be decided by law or arbitrarily. The uniformity, regularity and stability which characterize law recommend legality to autocratic states no less than to democracies. Indeed, as Sulla long ago perceived, there is even greater reason why authoritarians should prefer legality since, for them, order is paramount, a point that did not escape Italian and Hungarian commentators, for example, in their pre-war arguments for retention of *nulla poena sine lege*.[12]

The fuller, more usual significance of the curtailment of the principle of legality can be grasped when one takes into account the fact that Denmark departed to some extent from it. The motivation was undoubtedly good, namely, to use the resources of the community humanely and more effectively; but even that slight departure from legality has been criticized by Danish scholars.[13] It is in the light of this aspect of the problem that one can understand the sweeping inroads of positivist criminology in liberal countries. That the abolition of *nulla poena sine lege* took place first in the treatment of juveniles is also significant as an index to the motivation behind the movement for individualization in democratic countries. But the hazardous possibilities of this are now all-too-apparent — the abolition of *nulla poena sine lege* may result not in the humane use of science but in harsh repression and stupidity. The retention of the principle of legality by almost all the liberal states, indeed, the

[12] *Special Reports* written by Professors Racz and Delitala for the International Congress of Comparative Law, Hague, 1937.

[13] See Mueller, *Criminal Theory*, 34 Indiana L. J. 227-8 and footnote 98 (1959), citing Hurwitz and Marcus.

LEGALITY — NULLA POENA SINE LEGE 69

movement to extend it to juvenile delinquency,[14] remains of paramount significance.

[14] The *Special Report* of Aimée Racine to the International Congress of Comparative Law, Hague, 1937, at 23, discusses the insistence of a group of Belgian scholars and lawyers that the juvenile is entitled to at least as much legal protection as the adult.

And see *In re* Smith, 326 P. 2d 835 (Okl. 1958) and United States v. Dickerson, 168 F. Supp. 899 (D. C. 1958); but *cf. In re* Holmes, 379 Pa. 599, 109 A. 2d 523 (1954); and Paulsen, *op. cit. supra* note 77.

CHAPTER III

MENS REA: (1) THE OBJECTIVE MEANING OF THE PRINCIPLE

THE PROBLEM OF DEFINING *MENS REA*

THE principle of *mens rea* is the ultimate evaluation of criminal conduct and, because of that, it is deeply involved in theories of punishment, mental disease, negligence, strict liability and other current issues. Its paramount role in penal theory also results from the fact that *mens rea* is the fusion ("concurrence") of the elementary functions of intelligence and volition. "Only" its projection into reality, its actualization in the external world, is required to form criminal conduct, and that complex subject needs and receives the maximum attention in the professional literature. If any distinction is to be drawn *inter pares*, the crown, therefore, must surely go to the principle of *mens rea*.

This, of course, presupposes that one is not generalizing over all "penal laws." In that all-embracing reach, one can only say something to the effect that *mens rea* is the mental state exhibited in any conduct or behavior which violates any "penal law." This, however, says very little about any *mens rea*. Indeed, where "penal laws" proscribe negligent harm-doing and behavior "at peril," the above sort of definition is a formality which may mislead by suggesting that nothing more can be said in defining *mens rea*. But if one attends to the judicial opinions and to the persistent efforts of scholars to solve relevant problems, it is evident, despite such formulations as the above, that *mens rea* is intended to refer to actual distinctive states of mind. That is certainly the meaning of the term in the ancient maxim, *actus non facit reum nisi mens sit rea;* and the connotation "blameworthy" has played a great role in the history of penal law. In that history, *mens rea* is meaningful in relation to harm-doing, and to characterize *mens rea* as "evil mind" or "evil will" makes sense only if actual harm, sought or hazarded, is held in view.

Many contemporary writers avoid any normative characterization of *mens rea* because there are areas of modern "penal law" where it is very doubtful, and others where it is certainly not true, that what is forbidden is harmful or that the intention to bring it about is immoral. "In the old cases," wrote the late Professor Stallybrass, "*mens rea* did involve moral blame, and did mean a guilty mind. . . ." As regards modern penal law, however, he approves Justice Shearman's statement in a 1925 case, that, "The true translation to my mind of *mens rea* is . . . 'The intention to do the act which is made penal by the statute, or by common law.'"[1] Justice Devlin has recently stated the current view very aptly: "*Mens rea,*" he said, "consists of two elements. It consists first of all of the intent to do an act, and secondly of the knowledge of the circumstances that makes that act a criminal offence."[2] Because he recognized the need to exclude at least some states of mind from the definition of *mens rea*, it is especially instructive to observe Professor Sayre's procedure in this regard. He asked: "[W]hat state of mind must be proved to convict?" "How can this 'general *mens rea*' be defined?"[3] And he

---

[1] Stallybrass, in The Modern Approach to Criminal Law 406 (Ed. Radzinowicz and Turner, 1945).

[2] Devlin, *Statutory Offences*, 4 J. of Soc. Pub. Teachers of L. 213 (1958). The terms "knowledge," "circumstances" and "makes," taken together, may have been intended by Justice Devlin to have normative significance. *Cf.* "I think it is clear that the criminal law as we know it is based upon moral principle." Devlin, *Enforcement of Morals*, 45 Proc. Brit. Acad. (1959).

Cf. "It is this so-called guilty knowledge which represents the true meaning of *mens rea* as a blameworthy state of mind." Edwards, *Mens Rea* in Statutory Offences 250 (1955).

[3] Sayre, *The Present Signification of Mens Rea in the Criminal Law*, pub. in Harvard Legal Essays 411 (1934).

answered: "By the phrase 'general *mens rea*' is meant the criminal intent necessary to convict normal adults acting without compulsion for a crime other than a public welfare offense which is not based upon negligence and does not require any particular form of specific intent." This was a beginning towards a descriptive definition of *mens rea*, but it can hardly be said to provide one.

It is not suggested that the above definitions are invalid in any "absolute" sense. Since the practitioner is bound to take account of *all* "penal laws," his definition is necessarily a formal one. From that practical viewpoint, *i.e.* with reference to *all* "penal laws," the above current definitions, which omit any substantive characterization of *mens rea*, are the only possible ones. What is suggested, however, is that, for reasons discussed in the first chapter, the utility of the formal, practical definition depends on its support by penal theory. Moreover, descriptive, normative knowledge of *mens rea* not only influences the practitioners in their work, despite formal definitions; it also provides the foundation upon which enlightened practice of law must rest. For, if lawyers are to deal effectively with the problematical areas of "penal law," it is necessary that they have a clear, definite knowledge of *mens rea* in the admitted area of serious harm-doing and indubitable penal law. If a valid descriptive definition of *mens rea* is derived there, it is possible to view the marginal problems from a solid vantage-point and to recognize the instances of expediency and error elsewhere in the "penal law."

What is quite clear about the traditional meaning of "*mens rea*," from its origin in St. Augustine's adaptation of Seneca[4] to current discussions, is its moral connotation expressed in terms of "evil mind" or "evil will" by the early writers, and in terms of "guilt" or "moral culpability" by modern ones. As was suggested above, two factors determine the meaning of *mens rea*—an actual harm and the mental state of the actor who voluntarily commits it. Current professional literature has emphasized the latter,

---

[4] See *infra* note 33.

the so-called "subjective" aspect of the principle of *mens rea* in its reference to the defendant who caused a proscribed harm. What has escaped adequate attention is that, as is evident at least as regards the more serious crimes, an actual harm, a social disvalue, was committed.

The solution of the *mens rea* problem is difficult, but not especially because of the vagueness, of "guilt," which one might elucidate on the premise that a "sufficient" degree of individual freedom warrants the evaluation of human actions. Nor do the new psychologies exclude such evaluation, even when they alter one's factual estimates at various critical points. What raises especially complex problems for the legal scholar is that he must validate his conclusions by reference to a vast number of existing laws. In addition, the general problem is not encountered in case-law systems. Only particular facets of it are met there—special pleas, detailed definitions, narrow inquiries and specific rules. To discover some unity in this vast disarray of particulars, through which the essential components of *mens rea* can be discerned, is not an easy task.

We can learn a great deal regarding the solution of this problem by considering the difficulties which beset the leading scholar of the common law of crimes in the last century. Although he dealt with a traditionally moral concept, Stephen, writing, as did Holmes, in the heyday of legal positivism, could not accept the view that crime implied immorality. Thus, he started his inquiry on the premise: *"Actus non facit reum nisi mens sit rea* . . . is frequently though ignorantly supposed to mean that there cannot be such a thing as legal guilt where there is no moral guilt, which is obviously untrue, as there is always a possibility of a conflict between law and morals."[5] This greatly influenced his interpretation of *mens rea* and, at the same time, posed an insoluble problem—how to make sense of an ethical principle in non-ethical law.

[5] 2 Stephen, A History of the Criminal Law of England 94-95 (1883).

The present disorganization of Anglo-American criminal theory is due in large measure to the fact that Stephen formulated the problem of *mens rea* in the above way. It is due also, perhaps even more, to Holmes' theory of criminal liability, which will be discussed later. Specifically, Stephen maintained that *actus non facit reum nisi mens sit rea* implies wrongly that "no act is a crime which is done from laudable motives, in other words, that immorality is essential to crime." It is also misleading, he insisted, because, "It naturally suggests that, apart from all particular definitions of crimes, such a thing exists as a 'mens rea,' or 'guilty mind,' which is always expressly or by implication involved in every definition." "This," he said, "is obviously not the case, for the mental elements of different crimes differ widely," *e.g.* murder, theft, rape, receiving stolen goods. "In some cases (manslaughter by negligence) it denotes mere inattention." In his *Tolson* opinion he also said: "Of course it would be competent to the legislature to define a crime in such a way as to make the existence of any state of mind immaterial." Accordingly, he concluded: "It appears confusing to call so many dissimilar states of mind by one name."[6] "There is no one such state of mind. . . . The truth is that the maxim about 'mens rea' means no more than that the definition of all or nearly all crimes contains not only an outward and visible element, but a mental element, varying according to the different nature of different crimes. . . . and therefore the expression itself is unmeaning."[7]

In this country, Stephen's views were fortified in a detailed analysis of *mens rea* by Professor Sayre.[8] Turning from

[6] Queen v. Tolson (1889), 23 Q. B. 168, 185, 186, 189. Stephen also wrote: " . . . as all crimes (except crimes of omission) must be voluntary actions, intention is a constituent element of all criminal acts." 2 H. Cr. L. 112. Apparently, Stephen did not identify intention with *mens rea*. It should also be noted that strict liability had been applied to a serious crime in Reg. v. Prince (1875), 13 Cox C. C. 138, discussed *infra* ch. 11 at note 45.

[7] Stephen, *op. cit. supra* note 5, at 95.

[8] Sayre, *Mens Rea*, 45 Harv. L. Rev. 974 (1932).

Bishop's vague insight into the meaning of *mens rea*,[9] Sayre adopted Stephen's position, though not without the misgiving suggested above, which he never resolved. Besides the influence of Stephen, there was also, by the time Sayre wrote, a huge structure of strict liability that had been incorporated into "penal law." And there was the almost overwhelming authority of Holmes, whose theory of objective liability challenged any ethical view of penal law. Sayre was thus led to believe "it is quite futile to seek to discover the meaning of *mens rea* by any common principle of universal application running alike through all the cases."[10] "A *mens rea*," he said, "does not mean a single precise state of mind which must be proved as a prerequisite for all criminality. *Mens rea*, chameleon-like, takes on different colors in different surroundings."[11] Almost in Stephen's words, he concluded, "The truth is that there is no single precise state of mind common to all crime. . . . The old conception of *mens rea* must be discarded, and in its place must be substituted the new conception of *mentes reae*."[12]

Nonetheless, and indicative of the inner conflict in his views, he also asserted: "The *mens rea* is as vitally necessary for true crime, therefore, as understanding is necessary for goodness."[13] The growth of strict liability "bears no promise of a time when a *mens rea* will cease to be a general prerequisite of criminal guilt."[14] Sayre noted the theory of certain modern writers "that criminality depends upon behavior, and only behavior,"[15] and he rejected this, insisting on the importance of the mental element. Yet he was unable to solve "the baffling problem of exactly what constitutes the necessary *mens rea*";[16] nor could he over-

[9] 1 Bishop, Criminal Law §§287, 290 (9th ed. 1923).
[10] *Supra* note 8, at 1021-1022; and *cf. op. cit. supra* note 3, at 404.
[11] *Id.* at 402.
[12] *Id.* at 404.
[13] *Id.* at 410.
[14] *Id.* at 405.
[15] *Id.* at 400.
[16] *Id.* at 411.

come the other difficulties Stephen raised. He thought that in early law *"mens rea* doubtless meant little more than a general immorality of motive;" and he was certain that *"mens rea* today means something quite different from immorality of motive." He believed that it means "a particular kind of intent . . . a *criminal* intent, that is, the intent to commit a crime . . . to do that which, whether the defendant knew it or not, constitutes a breach of the criminal law."[17] After stating that "generalizations cannot be made," he concluded that "one thing is clear. . . . A criminal intent is still a cardinal element of crime. . . ."[18]

The foregoing summary of the position held by these distinguished scholars has until recently represented the state of criminal theory regarding this principal notion of penal law. It is important to explore the issues they raised, especially those concerning the diversity of criminal states of mind, penal liability imposed for negligent behavior, and strict liability. It is also necessary to determine whether a descriptive definition of *mens rea* can be validated, in first instance, by reference to the major crimes, where actual *mentes reae* are undoubtedly required. And, before reaching final conclusions, it will be helpful to take account of Holmes' theory of objective liability.

To facilitate following the course of this discussion, an outline of a pertinent means-end situation may be suggestive. The most common of human experiences is the direction of conduct toward the attainment of goals. Such conduct involves (a) an end sought; (b) deliberate functioning to reach that end, which manifests the *intentionality* of the conduct; and (c) the reasons or grounds for the end-seeking, *i.e.* its *motivation*. The ethical distinction relevant to such action is that between "good" and "right," and their opposites. This distinction is very old; it is probably the

---

[17] *Id.* at 412. Restating this, he wrote: "The 'general *mens rea,'* therefore, means the intent to commit some act which would constitute a crime if the surrounding circumstances were such as the defendant honestly believed them to be and as a reasonable man in the defendant's position would have believed them to be." *Id.* at 417, note 42.

[18] *Id.* at 414.

most important one in ethics and, as will appear, it is fundamental in penal liability.[19] If we examine a person's conduct with a view to assessing its moral significance, we can distinguish these two basic components, *e.g.* a man who gives property to an orphan asylum does right, but if he did that because he hated his heirs, his motive was bad. On the other hand, a motive may be good, although the act done is wrong, *e.g.* Jean Valjean. Finally, a good motive may coincide with a right act—which, of course, represents the ideal.

It must be emphasized that the distinction between goodness (or badness) of motive and the rightness (or wrongness) of what is done does not imply an actual bifurcation in the relevant conduct. Every act that is morally significant is motivated as well as intentional. We are, in fact, concerned with a unified process, a course of action which always, at every step and at each moment involves both motive and intentionality. This is true even though it may also be true that motive precedes intention. If we do not recognize this or if we lose sight of it, we are apt to relegate motive to a prior and concluded area or, for some other reason, we are apt to concentrate on one of the essential components of action.[20] In sum, the above distinction is analytical. It implies the necessity of viewing morally significant conduct from two perspectives, *i.e.* with reference to the goodness or badness of the motive and the rightness ("fitness") or wrongness of what was done. Keeping the above in mind, we may turn to a more critical examination of the theories of our distinguished predecessors regarding *mens rea*.

MENS REA IN MEDIEVAL LAW

It will be helpful to consider, first, certain phases of the history of the principle, especially to test Sayre's thesis that

---

[19] *Cf.* " . . . the most important points . . . are thought to be the circumstances of the action and its end." Ethics, Bk. III, 1111a, 18. See also, notes 39 and 53 *infra*. An excellent modern presentation is Ross, Foundations of Ethics (1939).

[20] See *infra* pp. 100-102.

in early law *"mens rea* doubtless meant little more than a general immorality of motive."[21] Whatever reservations one should exercise regarding theories of neatly separated stages of legal evolution, it is probable that early law reflected little sensitivity about the moral fault of persons who caused serious harms. But the theory that Anglo-Saxon law was wholly disinterested in whether an injury was committed intentionally, by negligence or accidentally[22] is a gross oversimplification.[23] Certainly, at least from Aethelred on, Anglo-Saxon law distinguished intentional harm from accident.[24] A doom of Canute specified: "if anyone does anything unintentionally, the case is entirely different from that of one who acts deliberately."[25] There probably was not complete exculpation in the former case, but this was soon regularly established. The dooms make it abundantly clear that there was also a rough proportion of offenses and penalties, and at times they are even enlightened by an incisive thrust in this regard that seems quite modern.[26]

It is certain, however, that throughout this period of early law there was very slight concern with a harm-doer's

---

[21] Sayre, *op. cit. supra* note 3, at 411-12.

[22] 2 Holdsworth, H. E. L. 51-53 (3rd ed. 1923).

[23] For a correction of that opinion, see Winfield, *The Myth of Absolute Liability*, 42 L. Q. Rev. 37 (1926). Writing of the late Anglo-Saxon period, he states: ". . . there was a rough appreciation of the distinction between intention, inadvertence, and inevitable accident." *Id.* at 42. *Cf.* Exodus, xxi, 13, and Laws of Alfred, No. 36, 1 Thorpe, Ancient Laws and Institutes of England 85 (1840). *Cf.* ". . . the primitive Germanic law . . . did not even distinguish, in its earlier phases, between accidental and intentional injuries." Wigmore, *Responsibility for Tortious Acts: Its History*, pub. in 3 Select Essays in Anglo-American Legal History 475 (1909).

[24] "And if it happens that a man commits a misdeed, involuntarily or unintentionally, and likewise he who is an involuntary agent in his misdeed should always be entitled to clemency and to better terms, owing to the fact that he acted as an involuntary agent." VI Aethelred, cap. 52 No. 1, pub. in Robertson, The Laws of the Kings of England from Edmund to Henry I 107 (1925).

[25] Canute, cap. 68 No. 3, *ibid.*; *cf.* 1 Thorpe, Ancient Laws and Institutes of England 329 (1840). A similar doom was II Canute, cap. 69, *id.* at 413. *Cf.* Numbers, 35: 20-24, and Plato, Laws IX, 862a, 865a.

[26] "But every deed shall be carefully distinguished and judgment meted out in proportion to the offense." VI Aethelred, cap. 10, No. 1 in *op. cit. supra* note 24, at 95.

motive. One receives from the dooms the definite impression
that such an inquiry would have seemed irrelevant. The
chief line of development of which we can be reasonably
confident was from the distinction between deliberate
wrong-doing and accident[27] to more careful analysis of
the former, *i.e.* of criminal intent. Thus, by the time of
Edward I the incapacities resulting from infancy and insanity were recognized as defenses. By the reign of the
third Edward, coercion was a defense in certain cases of
treason; and it had become settled that in order to hold
the owner of an animal criminally liable for injuries done
by it, his knowledge of its ferocity must be shown.[28] Self-
defense was likewise becoming recognized as a regular
ground of exculpation, though a pardon was required.[29]
The ideas and the language employed in the creation of
these defenses were relevant to the identification of purposive conduct, to the "what" of the act, not the "why"
of it. The corresponding interpretations of *mens rea* were
made without appreciation of the underlying principles.
But in the later medieval period, it is otherwise. With
Bracton, there is explicit formulation of what is involved,
though not yet systematic treatment.

The *mens rea* formula had been recited in the *Leges
Henrici*, and we have been taught by Pollock and Maitland
that "the original source is S. Augustinus . . ."[30] who, in
a discussion of perjury, said that one who believed he was
telling an untruth perjured himself even though in fact he
was mistaken and his statement was true. In that context
he said: *"ream linguam non facit, nisi mens rea."*[31] There
are many Biblical expressions[32] that might have suggested
the formula, and such influence on medieval law was not

[27] See Case 114 (1212), 1 Selden Society, Select Pleas of the Crown
67 (1887).
[28] Holdsworth, *supra* note 22, at 372-373.
[29] 2 Bracton, Legibus f. 134 (Twiss ed. 1879).
[30] 2 H. E. L. 476 note 5 (2nd ed. 1898).
[31] 38 Augustini Episcopi, Tom. Q. 973 (Migne ed. 1841).
[32] *E.g.* St. Mark, ch. 7.

inconsiderable. But there is a direct source of the formula in the letters of Seneca, who wrote: *"Actio recta non erit, nisi recta fuerit voluntas...."*[33] St. Augustine seems to have done little more than restate a particular application of this in terms of wrong rather than right, although it is no doubt true that he was its likely point of dissemination among medieval legal scholars.

While Bracton must be interpreted in the light of the above development, it is apparent why Professor Sayre was led to ascribe an essential role to motive in his treatise on the medieval criminal law. For there are a number of passages in Bracton which can be interpreted as giving motive that significance, *e.g.* he calls a slaying homicide "if it be done from malignity."[34] But the context concerns sin "on account of corrupt intentions;" it must be remembered that his treatise was far from being devoted entirely to law.[35] There is also Bracton's exculpation of an accidental homicide on the ground that ". . . he slew a man without any meditation of hatred. . . ."[36] There are many more passages where he includes both intention and motive in his analysis, as, when writing of homicide, he points out that it is, "With intention, as if anyone with certain knowledge and with a premeditated assault, through anger or hatred, or for the cause of gain, wickedly . . . has slain a person."[37] He writes likewise of arson by "malicious design."[38]

These references to motivation are not surprising in a thirteenth century legal treatise. The dual aspect of morality, discussed above, was probably well known; indeed,

[33] 3 Epistles of Seneca 92 l. 57 (Loeb Classical Lib. 1925).

[34] See *supra* note 29, at f. 120b.

[35] Bracton is "an untrustworthy guide to the legal notions of his English contemporaries whenever he ventures beyond a mere description of what, as a matter of fact, was done in courts of law." 1 Maitland, Collected Papers 314 (1911).

[36] See *supra* note 29, at f. 120b.

[37] *Id.* at f. 121.

[38] *Id.* at f. 146b.

it had been clearly expressed by St. Anselm.[39] But such direct, unequivocal passages as "the will and the purpose distinguish the misdeed,"[40] taken in their context, indicate that Bracton was distinguishing criminal conduct from accident, rather than discussing its motivation, and he was doing that in the very terms which, since his time, have characterized the meaning of *"mens rea."*[41] In any case, it is clear that Bracton's occasional reference to motivation cannot support the assertion that he regarded it as a material element of criminal conduct. Most crimes are stimulated by bad motives. It would therefore be only natural for him to refer to that. Finally, his emphasis on intention, noted above, is strengthened by the principal passage in which he states his general view in terms directly relevant to criminal law.[42]

Although the *mens rea* maxim appeared in the *Leges Henrici,* it does not seem to have been used by Bracton. *Voluntas nocendi, animo* and *maleficio* are his terms. Equivalent Norman French is employed in the *Mirror* where it is said " . . . there can be no crime or sin without a corrupt will. . . ."[43] Coke's familiar use of the phrase

[39] "For just as what it willed must be considered, so too must it be seen why it willed. . . . Wherefore every will has a *what* and a *why* . . . ." St. Anselm, *Dialogue on Truth,* pub. in Selections from Medieval Philosophers 176 (McKeon ed. 1929). *Cf.* 2 Aquinas, Summa, Q. 7, Art. 4, 244 (Pegis ed. 1944).

[40] *Supra* note 29, at 136b.

[41] Sayre translated the text of the above as "the desire and purpose distinguish evil-doing." *Supra* note 8, at 985. But "voluntas" meant will or intent, not "desire." Sayre's translation made it easier for him to accept the view that bad "motive was the material meaning of *mens rea* until modern times."

[42] "But wrongs may be said to be all things, which are not in accordance with right. . . . Likewise in those cases, we must consider with what intention or with what will a thing is done. . . . For take away the will, and every act will be indifferent, for your meaning imposes a name upon your act, and a crime is not committed unless a guilty intention intercede, nor is a theft committed unless with the intention to steal." *Op. cit. supra* note 29, at f. 101b. *Cf.* the early 14th century case where a landlord was sentenced to be "hung" for taking his tenant's corn because the rent was in arrears, *i.e.* despite the motive. Y. B. 33-35 Edw. I. (R. S. 502, 1304-06) translated by Sayre, *supra* note 8, at 987 note 49.

[43] The Mirror of Justices 138 (Selden Society ed. 1893).

indicates that the terminology had by his time become common. The formula was used by him[44] to mean "intent," specifically in larceny, "intent to steal."[45] The first systematic treatment of *mens rea* was provided by Hale. He posited penal liability on the "two great faculties, understanding and liberty of will."[46] Hale joins two of the words commonly used by Bracton to express the relevant phrase: *ex animi intentione*[47] which, like his predecessors, he contrasts with accident. There is no penal liability for acting "without intention of any bodily harm to any person."[48] "Malice in fact" has become "a deliberate intention of doing some corporal harm to the person of another."[49] The only instance of any discussion of motive by Hale concerns larceny in extreme necessity of hunger or clothing, and here he repudiates that as a defense, noting, however, that the judge is empowered to reprieve and the king may pardon.[50] Hale epitomized his analysis of criminal intent thus: "The consent of the will is that, which renders human actions either commendable or culpable. . . ."[51] It is rather

[44] Third Institute 6, 107 (1641).

[45] Sayre believed that Coke's interpretation of *mens rea* shows that it "had already undergone a revolutionary change in meaning. . . . It is used, not with its old connotation of moral guilt, but with reference to a precise intent at a given time." *Supra* note 8, at 999-1000. The fallacy of this view is evident on reference to the text above.

[46] 1 Hale, P. C. 14 (1736). ". . . where there is no will to commit an offense, there can be no . . . just reason to incur the penalty. . . ." *Id.* at 15.

[47] *Id.* at 38.

[48] *Id.* at 39.

[49] *Id.* at 451.

[50] The jurors present that John of Wangeford arrested Richard Baldry of Whaddon and his wife Matilda, on suspicion of theft, and handed them over into the custody of the township of Whaddon, and they were imprisoned in the jail of that same town for six days, and afterwards the townsmen took them to the County Court of Cambridgeshire. And they escaped from the custody of the same town. Hence judgment of escape on the aforesaid township of Whaddon. And the jurors say that they are not suspected of anything other than stealing bread during the great famine. Hence they may return if they wish. They had no chattels. (Assize Roll 82, m. 27 r. (Cambridge Eyre, 1260)). See also *id.* m. 34 v.; Assize Roll 632, m. 89 v. (Northamptonshire Eyre, 1330); Bracton's Notebook, Cases 1723 and 1725 (Common Bench, 1226).

[51] *Op. cit. supra* note 46, at 14-15.

clear that *mens rea* meant the intention to do a wrong act, with concomitant knowledge of the material facts.

No question of the materiality of motive arose until there was recognition of the fact that a good motive may be coupled with a wrong action. This is what one would expect not only from the long established view of the immateriality of motive but also because a consideration of motives requires and indicates a much more advanced level of ethical criticism than is involved in appraisals based only on the fact that a harm was inflicted intentionally, not by accident.[52]

Accordingly, if one were to generalize, not regarding *mens rea* alone, but regarding the whole of moral culpability, a tenable assertion would be that the trend has been from the complete neglect of motive to its recognition as essential, not in the substantive law, but to a just administration of that law. So, too, confining ourselves to *mens rea*, a defensible generalization is that its meaning has changed concomitantly with the development of the various ideas and doctrines elucidating it, *e.g.* its distinction from accident and negligence, and the evolution of the law on insanity, necessity, coercion, mistake, etc. In sum, the essential meaning of *mens rea, i.e.* that represented in the *intentional doing of a morally wrong act,* implying concomitant knowledge of the material facts, has persisted for centuries. But, as indicated, its meaning has changed progressively with the advance of the criminal law and of morals in general. The most important aspects of this evolution of *mens rea* are discussed in the chapters of this book concerned with the relevant doctrines.

MOTIVE AND INTENTION

The problems discussed above concern the recognition of a *principle* of *mens rea* and the traditional emphasis upon intention as the essence of that criminal state of mind.

[52] " . . . it marks a great advance in morality when men do begin to attach importance to motives and are not guided exclusively in their praise or blame, by the 'external' nature of the act done or by its consequences." Moore, Ethics 183 (1912).

Holmes, Stephen and Sayre distinguished intention from motive along rather traditional lines;[53] and if they did not always exclude motive from, and associate intention with, *mens rea*, it was because negligence, the *mentes reae* and strict liability seemed to bar the way. The elucidation of *"mens rea"* was further and more seriously complicated by Salmond's adoption of a purely intellectual connotation of "motive," with the result that the traditional, legal meaning of *mens rea* was greatly confused.

Motive, for Austin, is a wish (volition or desire) ;[54] and volitions are those desires which result in immediate bodily movements. A motive is a desire that precedes a volition,[55] and this is the meaning of a *"motive* determining the will."[56] Desires[57] are thus viewed as occurring in a chronological series—a prior motive causing the immediate motive which in turn causes a volition.[58]

Of primary importance is that Austin distinguished motives as "springs of action" which "urge" from intention—a "state of understanding." He said, "The intention is the aim of the act, of which the motive is the spring."[59] He applied this distinction to the common law definition of murder, which he criticized because of its confusion of motive ("malice") with intention.[60] All that the law requires is that the killing be intentional.[61]

---

[53] Stephen, *op. cit. supra* note 5, at 110-111.

[54] " . . . and every wish is a pain which affects a man's *self*, and which urges him to seek relief, by attaining the object wished." 1 Austin, Lectures on Jurisprudence 168n. (4th ed. 1879).

[55] *Id.* at 428.

[56] *Id.* at 432.

[57] "Desire" is synonymous. *Id.* at 424, 428, 431.

[58] Austin had also discussed "motive" in the context of his ethical philosophy. *Id.* at 164-65, 168n. He speaks there of self-regarding motives, *e.g.* love of reputation (vanity) and the desire of subsistence and, also, of unselfish motives, *e.g.* religion and benevolence. He notes that even bad motives may result in social good as when a man works out of a desire of subsistence. So, too, he refers to idealistic tyrannicides whose motives were pure and benevolent but who nevertheless harmed the "general good." *Id.* at 165.

[59] *Id.* at 165.

[60] *Id.* at 355.

[61] *Ibid.* Although Austin spoke of an ulterior "purpose," it is clear

Salmond unfortunately adopted a different meaning of "motive" which, while it had and continues to have some support in usage, resulted in confusing it with intention. He first follows Austin in speaking of motive in terms of desire:[62] D desires an evil to S for the sake of an ulterior desire (resulting good to himself). "He *intends* the attainment of this ulterior object no less than he intends the wrongful act itself."[63] Salmond then states that intentions are divisible into immediate intentions and ulterior intentions. The former "relates to the wrongful act itself;[64] the latter . . . relates to the object . . . for the sake of which the act is done."[65] For example, a thief's immediate intention is to appropriate another's property, and his ulterior intention is to buy food or pay a debt. Salmond applied the marginal meaning of "motive" to the latter: "The ulterior intent," he said, "is the *motive* of the act."[66] The immediate intent is "coincident with the wrongful act itself; the ulterior intent or motive is that part of the total intent which lies outside the boundaries of the wrongful act." Thus, for Salmond, "ulterior intent" and "motive" are synonyms.[67]

Salmond's views have had considerable influence in this country, and an American writer on criminal law agreed: "In reality motive is a species of intent."[68] Another

---

that he meant that in his sense of a motive, *i.e.* a desire or wish. *Id.* at 428.

[62] Salmond, Jurisprudence 397 (7th ed. 1924).

[63] *Ibid.*

[64] For Salmond, "act" included consequences. See *infra* chapter 6 at note 10.

[65] *Id.* at 398.

[66] *Ibid.*

[67] This usage finds some support in current philosophy, *e.g.* "I call a motive forward-looking if it is an intention." Anscombe, *Intention*, 57 Arist. Soc. Proc. (n. s.) 328 (1956-57). This is contrasted with "backward-looking" motives, *e.g.* revenge, gratitude, pity. See Anscombe, Intention (1957).

It is not the writer's purpose to evaluate the various meanings of "motive," and the criticism of Salmond's usage is based upon the prevailing meaning of the word in criminal law, expressed in countless decisions holding that motive is not a material element of a crime. This is further supported, in the writer's view, by the fact that the "forward-looking motive" which Salmond adopts is also acknowledged by him to be an intention.

[68] Hitchler, The Law of Crimes 87 (1939).

scholar, summarizing and, in the main, also following Salmond, concluded that "in many cases whether a crime has been committed will depend upon the motive. . . ."[69] In support of this, he said: "If one kills merely for revenge or in order to obtain property, the crime of murder is committed; if, on the other hand, the killing is done in the due execution of a sentence of death upon a convicted criminal, or, under proper circumstances, for the prevention of felony or in defense of oneself, the homicide is lawful."[70] Other writers have added other "exceptions,"[71] but a criticism of the above instances will be sufficient to expose the underlying difficulty.

If we apply the usual distinction between intention and motive to the crimes which Salmond and his followers asserted are exceptional, the consequence is clear. In criminal attempts, the purpose to effect a particular harm is not a motive; it is part of the plan, it implies intention. We do not know what the actor is doing in any sense relevant to criminal law, until we know, e.g. that his purpose is to poison someone or to set a certain house on fire. He may have other plans, but that is not relevant to the substantive crime and enough is known regarding his intention to interpret his act as a criminal attempt. On the other hand, the motives (in the usual sense) may be very diverse: the victim may be a relative, dying in intense pain, and a desire to relieve him may have impelled the attempt to kill; again, the motive may have been revenge or avarice. Not the motive, but the intention can be inferred from the criminal action. In burglary, the intention to commit a crime—not an intention ("motive") beyond that—is likewise an essential part of the

[69] Cook, *Act, Intention, and Motive in the Criminal Law*, 26 Yale L. J. 645, 661 (1917).

[70] After implying that motive is material in the above cases, Professor Cook continued: "If so, it would follow that although there may exist all the external circumstances which would justify one in killing to prevent felony or in self-defense, he would still be guilty of murder, if he should kill solely for revenge and not with the motive (desire and intention) to save his life or to stop the commission of the felony." *Id.* at 662.

[71] Hitchler, *op. cit. supra* note 68, at 87-90; also Hitchler, *Motive as an Essential Element of Crime*, 35 Dick. L. Rev. 105 (1931).

material intent. Until we know that the intruder intends to commit a crime we cannot distinguish his breaking and entry from a non-criminal breaking and entry. The breaking may have been in order to enter, the entry in order to steal, the stealing in order to get money to buy things, the buying of things to effect other objectives. But it does not aid analysis to designate the various subsequent intentions or the final "ulterior" one a "motive."

That an intention is beyond or "ulterior" to the scope of legal relevance does not transform it into a motive in the generally accepted legal sense of the term. Nor is analysis aided by confusing an established meaning of (irrelevant) "motive" with a marginal meaning of "motive" which is also confused with the established meaning of "intention" that is material. Some parts of a plan of action do not proceed far enough to be criminal (e.g. preparation); while others extend beyond the commission of the harm which constitutes the crime and are irrelevant for that reason. Action directed toward the commission of a crime may involve many goals which succeed one another in a long series. For example, D plans to (a) buy a gun (b) and bullets (c) practice target shooting (d) break a window in X's home (e) enter (f) kill X (g) inherit X's money (h) use it to buy a newspaper (i) enhance his prestige and (n) so on and on, culminating in his ultimate vision of "the good life." All of these goals may have been consciously in D's mind. His actions directed to the attainment of those ends are intentional ones. But his intending all those goals is not relevant to criminal law, which is concerned only with the voluntary commission of certain more or less narrowly described harms.

With reference to killing "for revenge or in order to obtain property" in contrast to killing in execution of a legal sentence or to prevent a felony or in self-defense, the first thing that needs to be said is that the former situations are criminal whereas the latter are legal. As regards lawful conduct there is no point in asking whether intention, motive or both are material. We are confined to criminal conduct if we wish to determine what facts are material in criminal law. Secondly, as shown above, motive in the sense of ulterior intention beyond the penal harm, in issue, is irrelevant. Finally, if the above writer meant to assert that all the above situations are alike except as regards the motives, in the usual sense, it can readily be shown that he was mistaken. For hardly any part of penal law is more definitely settled than that motive is irrelevant.[72] If the deceased was advancing on the defendant with drawn knife, saying, "I'm going to kill you," and safe escape was impossible, it makes not the slightest difference whether the defendant hated his assailant or whether the assailant was his son whom he loved beyond measure.[73] The above distinguished commentator was perhaps misled by occasional, misplaced judicial stress on motive in loosely formulated instructions.[74] Their correct import is not, *e.g.* that hatred or revenge supersedes the apparent necessity of the measures taken in self-defense but rather that the solution of the question—was it self-defense or an unnecessary killing?—is sometimes aided by considering the motives of the accused.[75] The contrast of a killing "merely for revenge" with one in execution of a capital sentence again confuses legal with criminal conduct. It is tautological to assert that in legal behavior the acts done are not criminal. If the duly authorized executioner rose from a sickbed to give himself the pleasure of killing his hated enemy, the convicted man, that would not have the slightest effect on the legality of his conduct. On the other hand, if someone paid him the same sum of money to kill an innocent,

[72] State v. Logan, 344 Mo. 351, 126 S. W. 2d 256, 122 A. L. R. 417, 425 (1939).

[73] "Whenever the circumstances of the killing would not amount to murder, the proof even of express malice will not make it so. One may harbor the most intense hatred toward another; he may court an opportunity to take his life; may rejoice while he is imbruing his hands in his heart's blood; and yet, if, to save his own life, the facts showed that he was fully justified in slaying his adversary, his malice shall not be taken into account." Golden v. Georgia, 25 Ga. 527, 532 (1858). Similarly, if an order is justified by a lawful purpose, it is not rendered illegal by a bad motive in the mind of the officer issuing it. Isbrandt-sen-Moller Co. Inc. v. United States, 300 U. S. 139, 145, 81 L. Ed. 562, 57 S. Ct. 407 (1937).

[74] Wright v. State, 30 Ga. 325, 327 (1860).

[75] People v. Williams, 32 Cal. 280 (1867).

i.e. non-convicted, person on the same scaffold, the homicide would be criminal even though he wanted to contribute the money to charity and even though the victim was a notorious offender. The material difference in these cases does not concern motivation. It concerns the intentional doing of an act that is forbidden in penal law.[76]

Thus it must be concluded that Salmond and his followers also obscured the meaning of *mens rea*. In a formal way they recognized the difference between asking *what* a person did, *i.e.* to ascertain whether he acted, and *why* he acted that way. But they did not adhere to the ordinary and legal difference between these ideas. For when they asked "why did a person do a particular act"? they proceeded to answer it in terms of an objective which he sought, an intention oriented towards the future, a purpose, which they called "motive." The ambiguity of "why" implemented their predilection.

"Motive" may also mean cause, in a scientific sense;[77] and this is the meaning psychiatrists prefer. But the ordinary, traditional and legal meaning of "motive" is the reason

---

[76] Libel is the most important exception to the rule that motive is irrelevant. In many states truth, alone, is not a defense; it must also be shown that the end was justifiable and the motive good. See *Note*, 19 A. L. R. 1505 (1922). The reasons for this exceptional rule have not been thoroughly investigated. See generally, Leflar, *The Social Utility of the Criminal Law of Defamation*, 34 Tex. L. Rev. 984, 991 (1956).

Under the prevailing rule, if the libel is false, good motivation is no defense. Commonwealth v. Snelling, 15 Pick. 337 (Mass. 1834). The materiality of motivation is thus presently limited to the publication of truthful statements: one cannot publish truthful defamation unless one acts from good motives. See State v. Burnham, 9 N. H. 34 (1937); *cf.* People v. Doss, 318 Ill. App. 387, 48 N. E. 2d 213, aff'd 384 Ill. 400, 51 N. E. 2d 517 (1943) and Reg. v. Newman (1852), 1 Dears. C. C. 85, 169 Eng. Rep. 647.

The other major crime which involves similar questions is criminal conspiracy. See United States v. Reading Co., 226 U. S. 324, 357, 57 L. Ed. 243, 33 S. Ct. 90 (1911); Swift & Co. v. United States, 196 U. S. 375, 396, 49 L. Ed. 518, 25 S. Ct. 276 (1905) and *infra* note 90.

[77] The psychiatric view of motive as a cause of behavior is to be contrasted with the ethical-legal view of motive as a reason for action. See Psychoanalysis, Scientific Method and Philosophy (Hook ed. 1959). In the legal view, there is no compulsion or necessity in the action of normal persons. Action is motivated in the sense that there is a reason for it.

or ground of any given conduct.[78] The reference of "motive," in this sense, is to the actor, whereas intention is directed outside him.[79] It is doubtful whether one is responsible for his motives; but the crucial point for legal purposes is that action involves a choice. The motive may be good or bad[80] but, in either case, it is distinguished from the intentionality of the action.[81]

Despite this preponderant meaning, there are many cases, in addition to those on libel and conspiracy,[82] where motive seems to have been held a material element of *mens rea*. In *McSorley*,[83] *e.g.* the defendant, a member of the Pennsylvania Turnpike Commission, was convicted of "misfeasance in office" in that he assigned the use of an automobile and a chauffeur to a former member of the Commission at a cost to it of $2,800. The Superior Court held that "the Commonwealth had the duty to prove the act complained of *and* that the defendant acted from a corrupt motive."[84] The above facts were proved except those establishing a "corrupt motive." In illustrating the meaning of "motive or reason," the court referred to "a benefit or gain to the defendant, his political party, his relatives, his friends, or the hope thereof ...."[85] It rejected the authority of an earlier Pennsylvania

---

[78] See Baker v. State, 120 Wis. 135, 97 N. W. 566, 570 (1903); Bates v. Commonwealth, 189 Ky. 727, 225 S. W. 1085 (1920).

[79] " . . . intention . . . refers to the objective effect which the lawbreaker contrives to produce on others by his act or omission, and that motive refers to the subjective effect and its accompanying emotion which he desires to produce on himself." Norwood East, *Murder from the Point of View of the Psychiatrist*, 3 The Med.-Leg. and Crim. Rev. 69-70 (1935).

[80] *Cf.* Warren, Dictionary of Psychology (1934). It is not necessary, in the present context, to distinguish motive as desire (Austin's usage) from motive as ground or reason, since all of this must be distinguished from intention.

[81] See Troland, Human Motivation 5 (1928); State v. Santino, 186 S. W. 976 (Mo. 1916); Williams v. State, 113 Neb. 606, 204 N. W. 64 (1925), and Kessler v. Indianapolis, 199 Ind. 420, 157 N. E. 547 (1927) for cogent distinctions between motive and intention.

[82] See notes 76 *supra* and 90 *infra*.

[83] Commonwealth v. McSorley, 189 Pa. Super. 223, 150 A. 2d 570 (1959).

[84] *Id.* at 573.

[85] *Id.* at 575.

case,[86] where more than 9,000 persons were employed prior to an election, most of whom did no highway work but, instead, worked in the political campaign. "The motive shown there was to win an election through the padding of the payroll."[87] In the instant case, however, the defendant testified that his motive was to secure the advice of the former Commissioner regarding important problems concerning the turnpike. The court reversed the conviction and discharged the defendant, holding: "The expenditure of $2,800 of the Commission's money to secure advice on a hundred million dollar project from one with experience nowhere else available, negatives a finding of criminal intent or corrupt motive."[88] In such cases it is clear, despite the occasional reference to "intent," that the court did treat motive as a material element.

What should be noted, however, regarding *McSorley* and similar cases is that they were essentially cases of misappropriation where knowledge of illegality is part of the relevant *mens rea*. The "padding" of the payroll in the case referred to above was a misappropriation because the defendant knew he was making illegal use of funds. Apparently, the expenditure of $2,800 by McSorley for expert advice was not a misappropriation of funds. On the other hand, had McSorley given $2,800 of the Commission's money to the Red Cross, no matter how worthy his motive, there would have been a misappropriation. In other words, the decision can be stated in terms of intention to misappropriate, excluding motive as irrelevant to the definition of *mens rea*, without, of course, excluding evidence of motive that is relevant to the proof of criminal intention. In sum, the technique of restating such cases in conformity with the principle of *mens rea* is to articulate the relevant criminal

[86] Commonwealth v. Brownmiller, 141 Pa. Super. 107, 14 A. 2d 907 (1940).

[87] See *supra* note 83 at 575.

[88] *Id.* at 574.

intention and state the decision in terms of that. This, unfortunately, has not always been done by the courts.[89]

In some cases of conspiracy where knowledge of illegality is part of the relevant *mens rea*, the language of the decisions is also in terms of "corrupt motive," but it is again clear that this is often the evidentiary basis upon which the material knowledge of the law is determined. The logic of inferring corrupt motive from knowledge of the illegality may be doubted, but many of these decisions can be restated in terms of *mens rea* based upon knowledge of the law.[90]

In sum, motive in penal law is distinguished from intention (*mens rea*) and from the scientific sense of "cause." The former distinction is clarified if ulterior intention is ascribed to an objective or end, while motive retains its personal subjective meaning as a ground or reason of action. This is the distinction emphasized above.[91]   That an action

[89] In Laws v. The State, 26 Tex. Cr. R. 643 (1888), D killed deceased who had just committed a theft at night. A statute made a homicide justifiable when committed for the purpose of preventing theft at night. Held: "If the killing was upon malice, and not to prevent a theft or the consequences of a theft, it would not be justified under the statute, although a theft by night was actually being committed by the deceased at the time he was killed." *Id.* at 655. The conviction of second degree murder was reversed on the ground of the trial court's failure to define "night time." This case is sometimes cited to support the proposition that motive is a material element in a crime. Perkins Criminal Law 723 (1957). However, the statements relied upon were dicta. No citations in support were given.

In Alsup v. State, 120 Tex. Cr. R. 310, 49 S. W. 2d 749 (1932) it was charged that D, wishing to collect a reward offered for killing a bank robber, persuaded two men to rob a bank, then appeared when the robbery was in progress, and killed them. The court said: "If the killing of Tate was upon malice and not to prevent him from fleeing with property taken from the bank, although Tate might have been actually fleeing with such property at the time he was killed, appellant would be guilty of murder." *Id.* at 312, citing the Laws case *supra.* Conviction was reversed on other grounds.

[90] Commonwealth v. Gormley, 77 Pa. Super. Ct. 298 (1921). But *cf.* U. S. v. Moore, 173 F. 122 (1909), State v. Scarlet, 91 N. J. L. 343, 102 A. 162 (1917) and Morris v. State, 97 Ga. App. 762, 104 S. E. 2d 483 (1958), where knowledge of the illegality being proved, it was held that "corrupt motive" was thereby established.

[91] "Money and power, when men seek them, are objectives; ambition, greed, envy, jealousy, are clearly not objectives, but motives. Objective externalizes itself in action, is the completion or culmination of a series of activities; motive is at best only inferred, is not externalized. Therefore the same objective may be attributable to any one or any combination of a considerable variety of motives. Motive is an

was motivated excludes accident and negligence and implies intention. An intention is thus descriptive of a mode of conduct that is contrasted with accident and inadvertent movement. A motive answers the question why, neither in terms of causation nor in those of a further ulterior objective, but in terms that give a reason which is the subject of an ethical appraisal. For when we ask questions about a person's motives, we are asking for data relevant to evaluation of his character or at least of the morality of a particular act. Given a motive, a relevant intention can be inferred. But the converse does not apply, *i.e.* one may be positive that certain conduct was intentional without knowing any motive for it. All of this conforms to the preponderant ethical-legal meaning of motive and to its exclusion from the scope of *mens rea*.

MENS REA AND PERSONAL GUILT

Moral culpability, *i.e.* personal guilt, includes both *mens rea* and motivation. For example, D kills T; all agree that what he did is morally wrong. But the appraisal of D's moral culpability must also take account of his motive: was D acting from cupidity, knowing he was named the chief beneficiary of T's will? Or was the motive his love for his sick wife who needed an operation? Just as we cannot pass an adequate moral judgment if we know only what harm has been committed but not the motive for committing it, so, too, we cannot properly estimate conduct solely on the basis of its motivation—we need to know also what was done. It is necessary to unite these judgments in a single evaluation to determine the moral culpability of the actor.

Difficult problems concern harms perpetrated from laudable motives, *e.g.* theft of food for a hungry family, actions inspired by religious convictions,[92] certain cases of eutha-

---

aspect of the personality of the agent, not something that he does or achieves. When we attribute motives to any person we make the often dubious assumption that we know his hidden feelings and desires." MacIver, Social Causation 17-18 (1942).

[92] Commonwealth v. Has, 122 Mass. 40 (1877); Reynolds v. United States, 98 U. S. 145, 25 L. Ed. 244, 310 S. Ct. 595 (1878); State v. Hershberger, 150 N. E. 2d 671, 676 (Ohio, Juvenile Ct. 1958).

nasia,[93] some political crimes, and the like.[94] The relevant moral judgment implied in the penal law is absolute: no matter how good the actor's motive, since he voluntarily (*mens rea*) committed a penal harm he is to some degree morally culpable—"sufficiently" so to warrant at least control under probation.[95] The legal restriction of the *substantive* law to that aspect of the actor's guilt has not been understood by criminologists and psychiatrists who assert that the law is not interested in an offender's motives; but it also raises serious questions for lawyers.

Even if it is granted that a point is reached in some cases where no harm was committed, nay, that a benefit was conferred, *e.g.* in the assassination of a brutal tyrant, such marginal cases cannot be made the sound basis for incorporating motive as an essential element in the definition of crimes. Instead, it should be recognized that the preservation of the objective meaning of the principle of *mens rea* as well as of the attendant principle of legality has its price. For it is impossible to forbid any class of harms without including rare marginal instances where a maximum of good motivation combines with the minimum of the proscribed harm, or even no harm at all, so that the final estimate is that the value protected by the rule was not impaired in that instance. When cases involving this type of problem recur, *e.g.* infanticide by mothers shortly after birth, which were formerly within the definition of murder, it is possible to construct a new crime by defining a separate class in

---

[93] See Earengey, *Voluntary Euthanasia*, 8 Med.-Leg. & Crim. Rev. 91 (1940); Williams, The Sanctity of Life and the Criminal Law 311-350 (1957). *Cf.* Kamisar, *Some Non-Religious Views Against Proposed "Mercy-Killing" Legislation*, 42 Minn. L. Rev. 969 (1958).

[94] Reg. v. Booth (1872), 12 Cox C. C. 231; People v. Kirby, 2 Parker Cr. R. 28 (N. Y. 1823); Smith v. Commonwealth, 100 Pa. 324 (1882); Knowles v. United States, 170 F. 409 (C. C. A. 8th, 1909); Reg. v. Sharpe (1857), 7 Cox C. C. 214; People v. Molineux, 168 N. Y. 264, 61 N. E. 286 (1901); People ex rel. Hegeman v. Corrigan, 195 N. Y. 1, 87 N. E. 792, 796 (1909). One of the best judicial opinions concerning the relation of good motivation to criminal behavior is by Cockburn, J., in Reg. v. Hicklin (1868), 11 Cox C. C. 19, 3 Q. B. 360, 371-373.

[95] See *infra* note 97 and chapter 5 at note 63.

terms which accord with the objective meaning of *mens rea*
and harm, *i.e.* in terms which do not refer to motivation.
The exercise of official discretion even to the point of foregoing prosecution or suspending sentence, *e.g.* as regards a
Jean Valjean, is the "safety valve" which preserves the
principles of *mens rea* and legality in the vast majority of
cases. What needs emphasis is that there is an extremely
important difference between the preservation of the legality
and ethical significance of the principle of *mens rea* by
allocating questions of motivation to administration and the
depreciation of both penal law and its ethical significance
by making the relevant rules vague, if motive is made
material.[96]

Despite the doubts raised by marginal cases, the logic
of the substantive law excludes the possibility that there can
ever be a violation of a penal law that is not a legal harm.
The parallel ethical rationale implies equally that there can
never be such action that is not immoral.[97] Legal liability
in the marginal cases does not therefore imply that the penal
law is amoral, that it seeks mere outward conformity. It
implies that it is based on an objective ethics, expressed in
the principle of *mens rea* and, accordingly, that conscience
may err.[98] The premise is that the morality of a sound body
of penal law is objective in the sense that it may be validly
opposed to individual opinion.[99] In extreme cases of im-

[96] The German Criminal Code, sec. 211, makes bad motive a material element of murder, and among those listed as "bad," are
"vulgar motives." This might seem to have the advantage of avoiding
extremely unfortunate sentences for murder, *e.g.* where an abandoned
mistress, hurt and jealous, kills her lover. The difficulty in some
countries, however, results from the sole provision of the maximum
penalty for murder, with reliance upon the Executive to set that
aside. In contrast, in Illinois, *e.g.* where, also, there are no degrees
of murder, the range of punishment extends from 14 years imprisonment to the capital penalty.

[97] But see chapter 11 *infra* for qualification of this regarding
certain petty offenses. *Cf.* R. v. Bourne (1938), 3 All E. R. 615, concerning a doctor who performed an abortion on a young girl who had
been raped.

[98] See Ross, Foundations of Ethics 165 (1939); *cf.* the 7th Rep.
of H.M. Comm'rs of Cr. L. 29 (1843).

[99] The writer is indebted to a letter from Justice J. C. de Wet,

paired conscience, the M'Naghten Rules exclude liability; and in many others, where the motives were good, mitigation makes its greatest appeal.

Holmes emphasized the fact that penal law disregards the defendant's ethical insensitivity and lack of education; and we shall later discuss his theory.[1] It may be noted here, that in view of the simple valuations expressed in penal law, these factors should not be exaggerated—it does not require a college education or extraordinary sensitivity to understand that it is wrong to kill, rape or rob. Recent anthropological studies stressing universal values regarding homicide, treason, incest, theft and so on are also relevant. At the same time, one who defends the objective morality of the modern principle of *mens rea* must postulate a sound, spontaneously constructed penal law, the product of experience and inquiry functioning freely over many centuries; and this premise encounters difficulty in some parts of every actual legal system.

There are cases which trouble those who are concerned that actual guilt be the essential condition of penal liability. Sometimes organic disabilities are evident and there are other impairments which are not fully recognized in current' legal rules, *e.g.* regarding addiction to alcohol and narcotics. Cultural differences sometimes engender attitudes which strongly oppose those represented in the penal law. For example, in certain Latin-American countries the sexual mores of the dominant minority are imposed by penal law upon the Indian population which for centuries approved the conduct that the code condemns as a serious crime. A neighborhood group of delinquents who respect each other's possessions and may be courageous and self-sacrificing, think it is quite proper, perhaps praiseworthy, to take property from the automobiles of the "rich." So, too, occasional

---

South Africa, for insight regarding the pathetic situation of superstitious natives subjected to penal law that is foreign to them.

For an interesting discussion of such a Canadian case, Rex v. Sinnisiak (unreported), see Keedy, *A Remarkable Murder Trial*, 100 U. of Pa. L. Rev. 48 (1951), where a death sentence was commuted and the prisoners were released by order of the Governor.

[1] Holmes' theory is discussed *infra*, chapter 5.

visitors from other countries find in some important respects a different criminal code. There are Mormons in the United States who believe they are obeying a divine injunction as well as an onerous social obligation when they contract multiple marriages. There are other religious minorities, *e.g.* Jehovah Witnesses and Christian Scientists, who also encounter difficulty with prevalent opinion and penal law. There are conscientious objectors and political rebels. And, finally, we must recall the ethically insensitive, thoughtless persons, Shaw's "sick consciences," sometimes members of criminal or juvenile gangs, who often do not share the values of the majority. In sum, there are undoubtedly many cases of violence, theft, bigamy, political subversion and so on, where the offenders acted in accordance with their conscience.

With reference to some of these offenders, it is pertinent to observe that penal law has an educational function to perform. But if it be granted that some of these offenders are not only well motivated but also enlightened, what can be done in their behalf that is compatible with the preservation of legality? Occasionally, a court takes cognizance of the standards of the community from which the defendant comes, as did an English court in *Wilson v. Inyang;*[2] but while this can always be done in fixing the sentence, its recognition as a defense in substantive law would raise serious difficulties. A radical solution of the problem of justice in such cases might suggest the abandonment of the entire penal law. If that is excluded, there is no escape from the alternative that a functioning legal order must cleave to the objective meaning of the principle of *mens rea* (the constant premise being a sound, freely constructed penal law) ; and this undoubtedly falls far short of perfect justice. Mitigation is, of course, very much in order in such cases, but full exculpation would not only contradict the values of penal law; it would also undermine the foundation of a legal order. This is the difficult problem which confronts officials who wish to preserve legality and also dispense justice. The

[2] (1951) 2 K. B. 799, 2 All E. R. 237. *Cf. supra* notes 92-97.

tensions are insistent and they sometimes lead to the enactment of provisions which are at odds with the principle of legality.

This is the tendency of provisions to the effect that if a negligent or an ignorant harm-doer "could" have acted with due care or "could" have known he was at fault, the conditions of just punishment are satisfied. In support of these provisions it is urged that they apply the test of actual fault, *i.e.* they exculpate if the defendant lacked such competence. But this is a very dubious claim, and it may well be the case that, instead of achieving that result, the actual effect is the imposition of a verbally disguised objective liability, aggravated by the concomitant depreciation of legality. If the requirement is competence to know the law, the ethical force of such provisions is illusory. For example, if sitting on a park bench is punishable by ten years' imprisonment, can it be successfully maintained that the fact that an offender could have discovered that there was such a law justifies the punishment or indeed any liability? With reference to Muslims, Mormons, Christian Scientists, Jehovah Witnesses and political and other rebels, what is pertinent is not that they could have known the law but that they espouse a different code of morals. So, too, it does not seem persuasive to argue that they "could" have known what was ethically right.

"Capacity," as that is determined by officials interpreting such vague provisions as that noted above, probably means the competence to form correct valuations, which are assumed to be those represented in the penal code. If that assumption is sound, it is only the intrusion of substantive incompatibility when sanctions are imposed because an offender "could" have known and so on, or when there is exculpation on the ground that, though normal, he "could not" have known, etc. What is compatible with objectively moral penal law is the enforcement of it, mitigated by discretion and the occasional use of the "safety valve" to effect complete exculpation. The fact that this must be the over-all conclusion does not exclude the most enlightened individualization that is compatible with legality, *e.g.* the definition of crimes to reflect objective differences such as first offenders and habitual ones, a wide choice of sanctions, and the humane administration of penal-correctional institutions.

The need to exclude motive from the scope of *mens rea* may be further seen in the consequences of a contrary rule. Suppose it were enacted that criminal conduct required proof not only of the intentional or reckless doing of a forbidden act but also of a bad motive. The result would be that the judge and jury would hear evidence about *why* the defendant did the act; and they would be required to find not only what his motives actually were but also to evaluate them. Now, although motives are not always the dark unknowables they are sometimes believed to be, it is also true that it is often very difficult and sometimes impossible to discover them—a criminal sometimes refuses to talk and nothing may be known about him. Even in the usual run of less difficult cases, a detailed case-history of the defendant's past life may be needed if reliable knowledge of his motivation is to be discovered. In some cases, a very long time would be required to complete the investigation; in others the results would be quite negative— the true motivation is sometimes concealed from the actor himself who rationalizes his conduct in terms of what he mistakenly believes his motives were. But suppose that in a majority of the cases, the motives could be established with reasonable assurance. The equally difficult task remains— to evaluate them. In doing this, the actor's own estimate could hardly be accepted even if he had undoubtedly followed his conscience—unless one is prepared to hold that every fanatic has *carte blanche* to wreak whatever harm he wishes to inflict.[3] Moreover, if

---

[3] Statements are sometimes made, usually by way of dicta, to the effect that *mens rea* requires consciousness of wrong-doing: "The unanimity with which they [Courts] have adhered to the central thought that wrong-doing must be conscious to be criminal. . . ." Jackson, J., in Morissette v. United States, 342 U. S. 246, 252, 96 L. Ed. 288, 72 S. Ct. at 244 (1952). "The element of conscious wrong-doing, the guilty mind accompanying the guilty act. . . ." Cardozo, J., in Tenement House Department of City of New York v. McDevitt, 215 N. Y. 160, 168, 109 N. E. 88, 90 (1915). "Such legislation dispenses with the conventional requirement for criminal conduct—awareness of some wrongdoing." Frankfurter, J., in United States v. Dotterweich, 320 U. S.

a court could exculpate because it found that the harm-doer's motives were good, it would also be empowered to refuse exculpation because it thought his motives bad. These are among the reasons for excluding motive from the definition of *mens rea* and holding it not essential in criminal conduct.

It is equally important to emphasize that in the administration of modern penal law, motivation is of very great importance. To appreciate the significance of that, we must first note the modernity of this development. We have already seen that, apart from larceny of food in extreme necessity, motives were hardly considered by Hale. Even two centuries later we find in a forgery case decided in 1809, the matter-of-fact assertion that the defendants "were all indigent and, many of them, very distressed persons, who were tempted to engage in this criminal practice, by the necessities of the moment, and by the persuasion of the wholesale dealers. . . ." Nonetheless, they were all hanged.[4] Apart from larceny of food, the sporadic mercy of the Crown, and the probable tempering of harsh law by the jury, the recognition of motivation in the administration of the criminal law coincides with the rise of probation, suspended sentence, parole, and the like.[5] The same development is

---

277, 281, 88 L. Ed. 48, 64 S. Ct. 134 (1943). He also referred to "consciousness of wrongdoing" in Lambert v. California, 355 U. S. 225, 231, 2 L. Ed. 2d 228, 78 S. Ct. 240 (1957).

These statements are not entirely free of ambiguity since "conscious wrongdoing" may mean consciously doing the forbidden acts with knowledge of the material facts, but without consciousness of their being morally wrong. It should also be added that the courts in the above cases were dealing with instances of strict liability. In that context, overstatement of the principle of *mens rea* by judges who support that current law is understandable.

In many cases where *mens rea* was a material element and thus directly in issue, the courts have made it abundantly clear that consciousness of the immorality of the conduct is not included in *mens rea*. See *e.g.* Reynolds v. United States, 98 U. S. 145, 162, 166-167, 25 L. Ed. 244, 310 S. Ct. 595 (1878). The prevailing view of *mens rea* is stated by Justice Devlin, in the text *supra* at note 2. See Cockburn, J., in Reg. v. Hicklin (1869), 11 Cox C. C. 19, 3 Q. B. 360, 371-373.

[4] The King v. Holden and Others (1809), 2 Leach 1020, 168 Eng. Rep. 607.

[5] *Cf.* Sayre's argument that, ". . . under the older view, when the object of criminal administration was conceived to be the awarding of punishment in accordance with moral deserts," (*op. cit. supra* note 8 at

apparent in the European countries whose penal codes provide for determination of the sentence in accordance with "extenuating" and "aggravating" circumstances.[6]

For the reasons stated above, the determination and evaluation of the motives of criminal conduct are allocated to administration and, in the first instance, to judicial discretion in the selection of a proper sentence from penalties ranging from suspended sentence and probation to severe maximum punishment.[7] The institutions to which offenders may be committed vary considerably; and in many of them treatment is individualized. Not only the motivation of the particular crime but also the total personality of the offender must be studied,[8] and pre-sentence investigation is now re-

---

1018) a parent who refused to summon a doctor for his very sick child, because of religious conviction, was exculpated. With the shift to the modern viewpoint, he states, they reached "a directly opposite conclusion." In support, he relies upon Reg. v. Wagstaff (1868), 10 Cox C. C. 530. But this is surely reading much into Justice Willes' opinion. The question concerned "the gross and culpable negligence" of parents resulting in the death of a child. Willes stressed the consequence of withholding food, regardless of any belief. "There was," he said, "a very great difference between neglecting a child in respect to food, with regard to which there could be but one opinion, and neglect of medical treatment, as to which there might be many opinions." *Id.* at 533. The exculpation was by way of a jury's verdict. The next year the duty to provide medical help was prescribed by statute. 31 & 32 Vict., ch. 137, §37 (1869), and Queen v. Downs (1875), 13 Cox C. C. 111 was decided accordingly. These cases and the statute do not support Sayre's thesis of a trend from motive to objective liability, but indicate increased sensitivity to a parent's duty to take care of his children.

[6] Ploscowe, *An Examination of Some Dispositions Relating to Motive and Character in Modern European Penal Codes*, 21 J. Crim. L. & Criminal, 26 (1930).

[7] Darling, J.: "Before passing sentence the judge considered the appellant's motives; the Court is of opinion that he had a perfect right to consider motives, whether they were good or bad. There is no legal ground for saying that a judge may only consider motives if he decides that they were good motives. He should consider both, and award a severe or lenient sentence according to the category in which he places them." The sentence was reduced from life imprisonment to 10 years. Rex v. Bright (1916), 12 Cr. App. R. 69, 71.

In the United States, the major development in this regard has been the pre-sentence hearing based upon the report of probation officers and the court's own investigation. This is the current practice in most Federal courts and in many state courts. See Rule 32, Rules of Criminal Procedure for the District Courts of the United States (1946); People v. McWilliams, 348 Ill. 333, 180 N.E. 832 (1932).

[8] Salleilles, *op. cit. supra* note 79, at 242-3; note 7 *supra.*

quired in Federal courts unless a judge prefers to dispense with it. The questions are later considered by various boards and administrative personnel, and at different times. Accordingly, the final significance of the totality of substantive penal rules *and* their administration is sometimes almost complete exculpation. The jury's verdict can effect that, and there must also be a large number of cases where State's attorneys, regardless of what substantive law was involved, deliberately forego prosecution because the harms committed were actually minor ones and the motives were very laudable. In sum, although motivation is carefully considered in modern criminal law systems, the preservation of the objective meaning of the principle of *mens rea* and of legality requires that motive be excluded from the definition of criminal conduct. A sound division of relevant functions implements the consequent allocation of the issues concerning culpability—*mens rea* to the substantive legal, and motive to the administrative, discretionary phases of the process of adjudication.

It is also pertinent to recall that the meaning of *mens rea* from its very inception until the present time has changed in important ways. There persists, of course, the early insight into the difference between voluntary harm-doing and accident. This insight has been clarified and greatly deepened—to distinguish a child's "intending"[9] from an adult's, and the psychotic's and grossly intoxicated person's impaired "intention" from that of normal, sober persons. So, too, clarification of the doctrines concerning behavior in ignorance or mistake of fact and conduct under extreme duress has modified and greatly increased our understanding of *mens rea*. These refinements of the principle of *mens rea* have, of course, led to a much nicer determination of penal liability than was possible or desired in early law, shown, *e.g.* in the evolution of the felony-murder, misdemeanor-manslaughter rule;[10] and its recent termination in England

___

[9] Kean, *History of Criminal Liability of Children*, 53 L. Q. Rev. 364 (1937).

[10] See the Index.

is a logical consequence of this tendency.[11] Indeed, the progress of the principle of *mens rea* has probably been the most important factor in the construction of the modern penal law. There is no reason to believe that the principle has reached a final resting point, and the meaning of *mens rea* will undoubtedly continue to be refined.

We may terminate this preliminary discussion of *mens rea* by indicating the conclusions reached above. The common error in the position taken by Stephen and Sayre, it is suggested with great respect, consisted in their failure to appreciate the significance of the general characteristics of the many specific criminal intents.[12] Because the *mens rea* of each crime differs from that of the others, they were led to espouse a nominalist fallacy. For the fact that the *mens rea* of murder differs from that of robbery, *e.g.* is not inconsistent with the presence of a common, "essential" characteristic, expressed in the voluntary doing of a morally wrong act, just as the fact that every individual is in some ways unique is not inconsistent with the fact that in certain very important respects all human beings are essentially alike. It is precisely the function of the principles of criminal law to stipulate what is common in all crimes. To substitute *"mentes reae"* for the singular term, as Sayre suggested, ignores the genus of the various criminal states of mind, the principle and, in its larger import, the systematization of the penal law. On the other hand, if there is a principle of *mens rea*, we are in possession of an extremely valuable generalization, by reference to which we are able to organize a very large number of rules and doctrines.

[11] Homicide Act, 1957, 5 and 6 Eliz. 2, ch. 11; R. v. Vickers, (1957) 2 All E. R. 741.

[12] This criticism of Stephen is expressed in Professor J. W. C. Turner's article, *The Mental Element in Crimes at Common Law*, 6 Camb. L. J. 31, 38 (1936), reprinted in, The Modern Approach to Criminal Law 195, 205 (Ed. Radzinowicz and Turner, 1945). *Cf.* "Stephen's problem was one of nominalism. The *mens rea* concept is a general one. . . ." Harno, *Some Significant Developments in Criminal Law and Procedure in the Last Century*, 42 J. Crim. L. and Criminol. 428 (1951).

In sum: (1) the professional literature, especially beginning with Hale, distinguished *mens rea* from motive. *Mens rea*, a fusion of cognition and volition, is the mental state expressed in the *voluntary* commission of a proscribed harm. (2) The exclusion of motive, as not essential in *mens rea*, does not deny the importance of motive in determining the culpability ("guilt") of the defendant. Instead, the reason for doing that is the necessity to preserve the objectivity of the principle of *mens rea* and the principle of legality, *i.e.* to signify some degree of culpability regardless of how good the motive was. Thus questions of motivation and mitigating circumstances are allocated to administration which can explore such issues thoroughly. (3) Implied in the above conclusions is that the principle of *mens rea* must be given an objective ethical meaning—the premise being that actual harms (disvalues) are proscribed. Accordingly, neither the offender's conscience nor the personal code of ethics of the judge or the jury can be substituted for the ethics of the penal law. The insistence that guilt should be personal must be interpreted to accord with the paramount value of the objectivity of the principle of *mens rea*.

CHAPTER IV

MENS REA: (2) INTENTION, RECKLESSNESS AND NEGLIGENCE

WE must remember, when we review the halting efforts of generations of judges and scholars to elucidate the meaning of *"mens rea,"* that they were concerned with ultimate functions of personality — thinking and willing. The traditional psychology, originating with the Greek philosophers, was neatly summarized by Hale: "Man," he said, "is naturally endowed with these two great faculties, understanding and liberty of will . . . the liberty or choice of the will presupposeth an act of the understanding to know the thing or action chosen by the will. . . ."[1] Psychology, however, has its special history, and we find Austin engaged a century and a half ago in the de-reification of "the will" and the use of ordinary language to describe that "fancied something," that "imaginary being."[2] A century after that, John Dewey counselled that one should avoid nouns in referring to the "two great faculties" and speak, *e.g.* of " 'conscious' as an adjective of some acts," not of "consciousness."[3] More recently the perennial issues have been revived by Professor Gilbert Ryle who seeks to banish the "Ghost in the Machine" and substitute the logical implications of certain propositions, which resemble criminal pleas,

---

[1] 1 Hale, P. C. 14, 15 (1736).

[2] 1 Austin, Lectures on Jurisprudence 428, 431 (4th ed. 1879). *Cf.* " . . . hearing, seeing . . . remembering, imagining, thinking, judging, reasoning, are not inventions of the psychologist . . . acts performed by every normal human being, they are everyday common-sense distinctions." Dewey, Philosophy and Civilization 257 (1931).

[3] *Id.* at 260.

for the ancient "myths."[4] Such iconoclasm, however, finds little favor among philosophers who are unwilling to surrender the badge of their vocation;[5] and this seems, also, the inevitable position of those who, dealing with legally significant action, can find criminality or one crime rather than another one only by reference to different states of mind.

The "subjective" reference of *mens rea* is to the mind of a person bent on legally proscribed harm-doing. We cannot see these mental functions, nor can the most sensitive instruments record their operation. It seems likely that the first method of describing and explaining them was to point to and thus (illicitly!) call the *attention* of others to events and experiences which obviously excluded the relevant conscious mental states. Accidents, *e.g.* are patently antithetical to intention, and overwhelming physical forces, tossing ships and houses hither and yon, also exclude any resulting bodily movements from the category of (voluntary) conduct. From the recognition that any man's body, moved by natural forces, was a mere object, it was not a great step to the exclusion of the mental states of feeble-minded and psychotic persons from the sphere of *mens rea*. "Where there is a total defect of the understanding, there is no free act of the will in the choice of things or actions."[6] The relevant meaning is communicated in the expressions that there was no intention, choice or "movement of the will." There was only behavior, the physical motion of material bodies, like that of sticks and waves. It is not difficult to imagine why negligent harm-doing was not, in early times, similarly excluded from the range of *mens rea:* For there was no outside operative force there, nor any serious mental disease; instead, the harm-doer was probably doing *something* intentionally.

The various steps in the enlargement of the principle of *mens rea* by the method of exclusion are recorded in the

---

[4] Ryle, The Concept of Mind (1949).

[5] *E.g.* several papers in 48 J. of Philos. 257-301 (1951).

[6] Hale, *op. cit. supra* note 1, at 15.

history of the doctrines of penal law, viewed procedurally as defenses. They imply, as Hale stated, that the will "presupposeth understanding." It may therefore be suggested that *mens rea* does not include foresight of consequences in a restricted sense, but that it connotes the full co-presence of relevant knowledge.[7] It includes no less than what the M'Naghten Rule stipulates regarding the mental capacity of a normal adult, hence "foresight of consequences" can only be a summary reference to the wide ambit of the mental functions implied in understanding the nature and quality of the relevant conduct.[8]

Gross intoxication raised more difficult problems than did accident, psychosis and infancy.[9] Since the intelligence of a very drunken person is as clouded as a psychotic's and his control equally impaired, he would seem likewise unable to entertain a criminal intention (*mens rea*).[10] The meaning of *mens rea*, in its subjective reference, was further advanced by the recognition of still other doctrines which it subsumes. In mistake, *e.g.* knowledge of the material facts is just as absent as it is in the case of feeble-minded persons and psychotics, and the accompanying intention is not a *mens rea*.[11] In sum, the first methods of defining *"mens rea"* were those of exclusion by pointing

[7] Turner, *The Mental Element in Crimes at Common Law*, pub. in the Modern Approach to Criminal Law 195, 205 (Ed. Radzinowicz and Turner, 1945). *Cf.* Justice Devlin, chapter 3 *supra*, at note 2.

[8] Many courts interpret the M'Naghten Rules in terms of understanding the consequences of an act. See *infra* chapter 13.

[9] See chapter 14 *infra*.

[10] It would seem therefore, if the present rules on inebriate homicide are defended, that the position must be maintained that there is a great difference between the mind of the gross inebriate *at the time of the killing* and that of the insane person—or some other adequate locus and ground of liability must be found. "To hold otherwise would be to say that a man may freely indulge himself in liquor in the same hope that it will not affect his driving, and if it later develops that ensuing intoxication causes dangerous and reckless driving resulting in death, his unconsciousness or involuntariness at that time would relieve him from prosecution under the statute. His awareness of a condition which he knows may produce such consequences as here, and his disregard of the consequences, renders him liable for culpable negligence as the courts below have properly held." People v. Decina, 2 N. Y. 2d 133, 138 N. E. 2d 799 (1956).

[11] See chapter 11 *infra*.

to and then elucidating situations where, in any recognized sense of the term, there was no *intention* by the defendant to commit the harm in issue or where his intelligence was so greatly impaired that there was no criminal intention.

Accompanying the method of explanation by exclusion there must always have been the experience of normal understanding and volition, implicit in the judgment of the triers, and equally important. For the meaning of *mens rea* cannot be determined solely by the method of excluding it from the minds of certain persons, because that merely expresses its negation. It was essential, therefore, that there be a relevant affirmative conception, *i.e.* "normality," by reference to which *mens rea* could be described. This, in time, became recognized as a composite of the common features of the *mentes reae* of the specific rules, qualified by the affirmative implications of the relevant doctrines. But the passage from the method of exclusion, by pointing to specific instances, to the elucidation of the exclusionary doctrines, and thence to the critical construction of the relevant affirmative concepts marked great advances.

THE BASIC CONCEPTS

Among those who contributed most to the critical reexamination of the concepts of the legally relevant mental states was John Austin. For Austin, as we have seen, volitions are desires which are immediately followed by bodily movements. But, in his view, "an intention is not a volition;"[12] hence intentions are not desires. Instead, an intention is an expectation: "To *expect* any of its [an act's] *consequences*, is to *intend* those consequences," but "an *intended* consequence is not always *desired;*"[13] so too, "the party who wills [desires] the act, may not expect the consequence."[14] Thus, finally, "intention does not imply will."[15]

---

[12] Austin, *op. cit. supra* note 2, at 423.

[13] *Id.* at 433-434. "To desire the *act* [bodily movement] is to *will* it. To *expect* any of its *consequences* is to *intend* those consequences." *Ibid.*

[14] *Ibid.* and at 436.

[15] *Id.* at 434.

In order to grasp Austin's meaning more fully it is necessary (1) to distinguish an act from its consequences, (2) treat intention as purely cognitive, *i.e.* expectation,[16] which is always directed towards the act and may or may not also be directed towards its consequence, and (3) interpret desire in its ordinary meaning as an emotion or feeling. In sum, according to Austin, while a person wills (desires) and intends (expects) his act,[17] he does not will and he may or may not intend (expect) the consequence. Austin's criticism of those who employed "will" and "intention" synonymously conformed to his distinctions.

These terms, in the course of their long history, have accumulated many meanings and any criticism of a scholar's use of them should make due allowance. It seems clear, however, at least from the perspective of penal theory, that serious exception must be taken to Austin's view of volition as a desire,[18] and to his restriction of intention to cognition. It is important to distinguish volition from desire because volition, in a sense other than the ordinary meaning of "desire," is essential in the characterization of "act," while desire is not. Austin himself allocated volition to act, recognizing that volition is the desire which, on that account, must be distinguished from all other desires. But if volition is exceptional in the extremely important determination of "act," the definition of it should take account

---

[16] " . . . the *intention,* or state of his understanding at the instant of action, regarding the effects or tendency of his acts. . . . " *Id.* at 165. Austin's definition of "act" and "consequences" is discussed *infra,* chapter 6.

[17] "When I will an act, I expect or intend the *act.* . . . " *Id.* at 434. "The act itself is intended as well as willed." *Ibid. Cf.* "Whoever wills the end, wills also (so far as reason decides his conduct) the means in his power which are indispensably necessary thereto." Kant, Critique of Practical Reason 34 (Abbott ed. 1883). It would seem even more persuasive that one who wills the means also wills the end. But *cf.* Austin in the text below.

[18] *Cf.* "Further, even when the mind does command and thought bids us pursue or avoid something, sometimes no movement is produced; we act in accordance with desire, as in the case of moral weakness." Aristotle, On the Soul Bk. III, ch. 9, 433a.

of that. Again, we experience many desires which come and go without any encouragement from us, while, on the other hand, when we act, we set ourselves to achieve a goal. It seems both warranted and necessary, therefore, to allocate desire to the realm of feeling, emotion or even motive, and to treat volition as distinct from that. To say, as did Austin, that volition is only a species of desire, clouds the analysis of criminal law problems.

Equally questionable is Austin's view of intention. Salmond criticized this on the rather obvious ground that one may intend to achieve such a difficult or remote goal that he does not expect to succeed. To this, it may be answered that Austin's "expectation" can be diluted, without essential alteration, to the point of meaning only anticipation of the possibility of occurrence. Thus, a sane person would not expect to hit the moon with a bullet shot; he would not try to achieve a goal unless he thought there was some possibility of success. The knowledge of that possibility is, perhaps, in Austin's view, the expectation that is the essence of his meaning of intention.

The difficulty in Austin's meaning, even in this favorable interpretation, lies elsewhere, namely, in the fact that for him, intention is a state of pure thought — expectation. While he closely associated intention with volition as regards the act, he held that "intention does not imply will," *i.e.* that the two functions are actually separate. This is inconsistent with the legally recognized meaning of *mens rea* as the fusion of volition and thought. It also leads to the curious result that, in Austin's terms, the death of a murderer's victim would only be expected by him, not desired. Perhaps even more serious was the bifurcation of act and consequences, resulting from the failure to treat them in a means-end relation. But *mens rea*, not merely its cognitive side ("expectation"), must be related to the proscribed harm. Finally, almost the only constant in the long history of the term is that *mens rea* includes an intention, a "movement of the will." Indeed, the classical synonym of *mens rea* is "evil will;" and that valuation placed the emphasis on the precise relevant meaning which escaped Austin.

On the other hand, despite the current authority of distinguished scholars, it is respectfully submitted that Austin's exclusion of desire from the definition of "intention" is sound. The direct origin of the current use of "desire" to define "intention" was Salmond's treatise; and Salmond accepted Holmes' definition of intention as "foresight that certain consequences will follow from an act, and the wish for those consequences working as a motive which induces the act."[19] In Salmond's terms: "Intention is the foresight of a desired issue, however improbable. . . ."[20] It must be noted, however, that Salmond's "desire" was quite different from Austin's, which conformed to ordinary usage. Thus, Salmond argues, if one desires an end, he desires the means to that end "though in themselves those means may be indifferent or even objects of aversion."[21]

Salmond's definition of "intention" partly in terms of "desire" was adopted by several scholars perhaps because of its empirical connotation or because it seemed necessary in distinguishing intention from recklessness, *i.e.* in the former, the actor *desires* the occurrence of the harm, while the reckless actor does not desire it. As to this, it may be said directly that the reckless actor desires to increase the risk of causing a proscribed harm and thus desires it, although to a lesser extent. There are other, more important reasons for questioning Salmond's usage. First, in its well-established meaning, "desire" connotes feeling or emotion,[22] the satisfaction of which is pleasurable. In

---

[19] Holmes, The Common Law 53 (1881), quoted by Salmond, Jurisprudence 393 (7th ed. 1924). *Cf.* " . . . if the conduct described crossed the line, the fact that he desired to keep within it will not help him." Holmes, J., in Horning v. District of Columbia, 254 U. S. 135, 137, 65 L. Ed. 185, 41 S. Ct. 53 (1920).

[20] Salmond, *id*, at 394. As was noted in the text, *supra*, Salmond argued that, "Intention does not necessarily involve *expectation*. I may intend a result which I well know to be extremely improbable." *Ibid.*

[21] *Id.* at 395.

[22] Stroud, Mens Rea 3-4 (1914).

that sense it is possible to act against one's strongest desire—self-preservation.[23] The hero who sacrifices himself so that his comrades may escape death does so because he chooses the path of duty and he suppresses even his desire to survive. Only verbal complications result if it is insisted that the hero desired death. If an escaping felon drives over his friend who is standing in the way of his automobile, one can hardly accept the view that in the ordinary sense, he desired his friend's death.

On the other hand, the inclusion of Salmond's special meaning of "desire" into the definition of "intention" has an important advantage over Austin's view of intention. For by approximating the meaning of "volition," "desire" qualifies "intention" in a way that approximates, perhaps is identical with, its traditional meaning, stated above. If "desire" is shorn of its ordinary connotation of feeling or emotion, it may refer to a decision, choice, resolution, *i.e.* the traditional meaning of "intention."

But if that was Salmond's meaning, it can be expressed without importing the ambiguity of "desire," and in terms which are ethically significant and thus relevant to *mens rea*. In stating the difference between intention and recklessness, one need only use words which have ethical and intellectual connotations but not emotional ones. In intention, the actor chooses, decides, resolves to bring a proscribed harm into being, he consciously employs means to that end. The reckless person makes no such decision, resolution, choice. But while he has not made that drastic decision, he has made an ominous one. He has chosen to increase the existing chances that a proscribed harm will occur.

For the reasons noted above, it will perhaps be agreed that if "intention" and "recklessness" can be defined equally well or better without employing "desire," both the law of economy and the difficulties noted above suggest that that be done. What should be noted finally, is that the definition

---

[23] Ewing, *Can We Act Against Our Strongest Desire?* 44 Monist 126 (1934).

of ultimate terms has limited possibilities. When the bottom
of the psychological kit is reached and the concepts found
there (cognition and volition) are stated in terms of intention and recklessness, one may substitute various synonyms,
but whether the use of them helps very much is problematical. One can, however, facilitate whatever elucidation is
possible by avoiding the use of vague or ambiguous words.[24]

"Intention," defined in terms of decision, resolution or
choice, has reference to a definite goal, a proscribed harm;
and in its initial state, it is pointed towards the future
attainment of that objective since some time, however brief,
must elapse between the decision to produce the harm and
the actual production of it. Another meaning of "intention"
is inferred from end-seeking conduct in the very process of
its movement towards the forbidden goal. This conduct is
described as "intentional," and from it the prior *mens rea*
(criminal intention) is also inferred. A third meaning of
"intention" is purpose; and this is implied in both of the
above meanings. Whether a person has reached a decision
or is consciously moving to implement it, he has a purpose,
end or goal in view. Since "purpose," however, sometimes
means motive,[25] it is desirable to use other words to signify
this connotation of "intention." The persuasiveness of these
distinctions must rest finally upon introspection and experience. Their importance will be discussed later[26] when we
consider the difference between an internal *mens rea* and

---

[24] *Cf.* "The confusion caused by speaking of intention in terms of
desire will now be dispelled, it is hoped, by the recent case of Lang
v. Lang. . . . " Gotlieb, *Intention and Knowing the Nature and Quality of an Act*, 19 Mod. L. Rev. 270 (1956). In Lang v. Lang (1954),
3 W. L. R. 762, Lord Porter said, "If the husband knows the probable
result of his acts and persists in them . . . that is enough, however
passionately he may desire or request that she should remain. His
intention is to act as he did, whatever the consequences, though he
may hope and desire that they will not produce their probable effect."
So, too, Justice Devlin, *Criminal Responsibility and Punishment*
(1954) Cr. L. Rev. 666-7.

[25] "*That part* of the intent of an act for the sake of which it is
adopted, we call its *purpose*. Sometimes the word 'motive' is used in
the sense here given to 'purpose'." Lewis, An Analysis of Knowledge
and Valuation 367 (1946).

[26] See chapter 6 at 179.

the *mens rea* that is expressed in the conduct which causes a proscribed harm.

It was suggested in the preceding chapter, that the concepts of penal theory refer to means-end (conduct-harm) situations. Such a teleological construction excludes negligence, and it is therefore necessary for the purpose of enlarging the range of discussion that the figure be altered to include a wider causal connection between conduct *or behavior* and harm. In pursuance of this purpose, we may distinguish the two extremes in the relevant legally significant mental states — intention and negligence. We have discussed the former, emphasizing that the actor seeks the proscribed harm not in the sense that he desires it, but in the sense that he has chosen it, he has decided to bring it into being. The forbidden end is "in his mind" as he moves toward its attainment.

At the other extreme, negligence implies inadvertence, *i.e.* that the defendant was completely unaware of the dangerousness of his behavior although actually it was unreasonably increasing the risk of the occurrence of an injury. There has been considerable debate on the question whether negligence is a state of mind and much of the controversy thereon turns on questions of terminology.[27] If "state of mind" denotes an active process, inadvertence is excluded. On the other hand, it is essential to take account of the defendant's state of mind in describing negligence since it means not only that the behavior in question fell below a certain objective standard but also that it was not intentional or reckless. Since conduct implies an end that is sought or hazarded, it is evident that a homicide or a battery is not voluntarily effected by negligent behavior. Errors are sometimes made because, in the negligent commission of a harm, the defendant is also acting intentionally,

---

[27] Some writers hold that negligence is a condition of mind, and as such, is opposed to wrongful intention, *e.g.* Bigelow, Salmond, Wharton, Thompson, and Barrows. Others maintain that negligence is solely a form of behavior, *e.g.* Terry and Pollock. "Negligence neither is nor involves . . . any . . . mental characteristic, quality, state or process." Edgerton, *Negligence, Inadvertence, and Indifference*, 39 Harv. L. Rev. 849, 852 (1926).

e.g. he is driving an automobile. But the fact that his conduct was intentional in that respect is no warrant for characterizing it as voluntary with reference to the commission of a harm caused inadvertently.

Between the extremes of intentionality and negligence lies recklessness. Recklessness is like the former in that the actor is conscious of a forbidden harm, he realizes that his conduct increases the risk of its occurrence, and he has decided to create that risk.[28] It is thus a form of intentional harm-doing in that it, too, is volitional in a wrong direction. But, as noted, recklessness differs from intention in that the actor does not seek to attain the harm; he has not chosen it, has not decided or resolved that it shall occur. Instead, he believes that the harm will not occur or, in an aggravated form of recklessness, he is indifferent whether it does or does not occur. That he deliberately increased the risk does not alter the essential fact that he did not intend to produce the harm.[29] On the other hand, it will be recalled, recklessness resembles negligence in that both include an unreasonable increase in the risk of harm; both fall below the standard of "due care."

A problem that presents some difficulty in the maintenance of these distinctions concerns deliberate action in a situation known to be dangerous. For example, the driver of an automobile sees another car approaching rapidly on a crossroad or he sees a train bearing down on him. He is thus aware of a dangerous situation. But it does not follow that any conduct on his part which increases the danger is reckless. In the solution of such problems, it is essential to separate the question: Was due care used?, from the

---

[28] It "must . . . indicate an attitude of mental indifference to obvious risks." Eve, J., in Hudston v. Viney (1921), 1 Ch. 98, 104. See Austin, *op. cit. supra* note 2, at 440-442; 7th Rep. of H. M. Comm'rs of Cr. L. 25-26 (1843).

[29] On the other hand, recklessness should not be confused with intention in situations where the actor does intend to effect an injury, but is indifferent as to which particular person will be hurt. That a killing thus effected was intentional and murder was held in Smith v. State, 124 Ga. 213, 52 S. E. 329 (1905) and People v. Stein, 137 P. 271 (D. C. Cal. 1913).

question: If due care was not used, was the actor reckless or inadvertent *in that regard*? The situation may have been fraught with such danger that any action whatever would be risky, perhaps very risky, to others. The nature of the defendant's conduct would need to be judged in relation to that kind of situation. If he unreasonably increased the already high risk of harm, did he do so *knowing* that he was adding to the existing risk or was he only clumsy, excited or uninformed?

Since inadvertence connotes the complete absence of awareness, it seems doubtful that there can be degrees of negligence. But the notion of degrees of negligence is recognized in the law of various jurisdictions and it refers to degrees of risk, objectively appraised. It implies, *e.g.* that the careless handling of a loaded revolver is a higher degree of negligence than the careless handling of a lawn mower.[30] In any event, what is pertinent in penal theory is that no degree of negligence, however great it may be deemed to be, can ever be recklessness. Since recklessness connotes awareness while negligence excludes awareness, it follows that, like life and death, where the one is, the other is not. No matter how difficult it may be in particular cases to determine whether the defendant was reckless or negligent, there is a hard impenetrable wall that separates them.

Recklessness, everyone agrees, is within the scope of penal law; hence it may also be important to distinguish degrees of recklessness, *i.e.* differences in the degrees of risk that are consciously taken. In business transactions that is commonly recognized, and one knows when he buys a government bond, "blue chip" stock, and shares in a prospective oil well that he is taking progressively greater risks. Degrees of recklessness are recognized in European penal law,[31] and that is helpful especially in explaining certain

---

[30] The preponderance of American authority holds that the above situations are correctly analyzed in terms of a single standard of negligence, *i.e.* ordinary due care in handling a pistol requires a different sort of behavior than does due care in using a lawn mower.

[31] *E.g.* the distinction between *dolus eventualis* and *bewusste Fahrlässigkeit* ("conscious negligence"). Mezger, Strafrecht 341, 350

differences between manslaughter and second degree murder.[32] It should be added, as was suggested above, that even very risky conduct must be distinguished from intentional conduct. One either intends to commit a harm or he does not intend to commit it and the fact that he was very reckless does not imply intentionality.

The three states of mind defined above — there may be more if one thinks different degrees of recklessness comprise essentially different mental states — represent all the types of mental state that are considered relevant to penal liability. That they are not arbitrarily constructed or restricted can be verified by reference to their persistence over many centuries in advanced legal systems, the unavailability of other categories that are legally significant, and their utility in explaining and ordering the rules of law. They are accordingly the basic mental concepts relevant to an inquiry regarding the "subjective" or personal aspect of the principle of *mens rea*, its reference to the offender's mind.

OPERATIVE FACTS, EVIDENCE, AND REASONABLENESS

The concepts discussed above must be distinguished from the proof of their existence in any particular case. A theory which is sometimes put forward as both scientific and adequate is that the operative facts, *i.e.* those connoting the above concepts, are established solely by reference to "objective risk." In accordance with this theory, the degree of risk must be determined quite apart from the defendant's intention to produce a proscribed harm. In every case which is considered in court, an injury has been caused (or that is claimed). So far as the objective behavior and other external data are judged retrospectively, they were therefore 100 per cent risky. Since the theory of objective risk is asserted as a descriptive generalization,

(1949); Welzel, Deutsches Strafrecht 61 (1958); Schönke-Schröder, Strafgesetzbuch-Kommentar, S. 59, Anm. IV, 2, X, 4 (8th ed.).

[32] *Cf.* the distinction of manslaughter by automobile from second-degree murder, in Commonwealth v. Malone, 354 Pa. 180, 47 A. 2d 445 (1946), a homicide committed in playing "Russian Poker."

it must, if valid, function as a prediction, applied prior to the occurrence of proscribed harms. This raises the decisive question: Can the required *mens rea* be correctly ascertained by reference only to the observable facts existing at the time the harm occurred? It is submitted that here also the theory of objective risk is untenable. For, while it is often true that an intentional act is more dangerous than a reckless or negligent one, that is by no means always true.

An intention to attain a particular objective is a definite mental state; its meaning does not change because the evidence which establishes it varies from case to case. This is obscured in the theory of objective risk. It is said there that when the objective risk is very great, intention is inferable; when it is less probable, recklessness is involved; and when it is unreasonable but still less probable, there is negligence. There is an important element of truth in these assertions, but they are also very misleading. They are valid insofar as they amount simply to another way of asserting that we cannot directly apprehend the states of others' minds and must rely on observable data to know them, and that in the interpretation of such data, the degree of risk supports an inference as to intention, recklessness or negligence. The theory is fallacious, however, in confusing a mental state with the proof of its existence and, also, in implying that the risk suggested by the immediate behavior and situation is the only, or decisive, way of establishing the relevant mental state.

In fact, however, an intention can be established by evidence that is entirely unrelated to the objective risk reflected in the immediate external facts of the relevant situation, *e.g.* by a confession. Moreover, in some cases the immediate external data may be quite remote from the actor's state of mind, *e.g.* he puts harmless powder in a cup of coffee, thinking it is poison, and hands it to his intended victim. Again, the probability of causing a particular harm may be very slight, one chance in a thousand. Yet, the harm, effected through a freak combination of circumstances, may have been committed intentionally; indeed, it has been suggested that the very improbability of success, *i.e.* the slightness of the objective risk, emphasizes the intensity of the effort.[33] For example, a famished man, seeing an officer with a bag of food, attacks him though he realizes that the chances of overpowering him are very small. Or a person, seeing his deadly enemy 200 yards away, shoots him with an arrow under circumstances where there is very little probability of success; but a gust of wind, a quick movement by the victim, etc., do result in the harm. So, too, of many criminal attempts. The intention in such cases obviously exists and it cannot be established by inference from the objective risk, determined immediately prior to the act. It must be ascertained in other ways and, notwithstanding the theory, the likelihood that such recourse is the usual method of determining mental states is supported by reference to the proof actually relied on in most trials.

If we distinguish the legally material state of mind, viewed, *e.g.* as an image of the proscribed goal in the actor's mind, from the evidence of its existence, the problem becomes simple. All sorts of evidence, including the relation of the parties, significant statements regardless of the time they were uttered, and especially evidence of motivation that may hark back many years before the harm was committed, are relevant to establish the existence of the intention.[34] These data are interpreted in the light of experience, *e.g.* that a sane person does not intentionally kill a human being without some reason. The absence of a motive excludes (voluntary) conduct; but there are undoubtedly situations where the immediate facts are the only known ones and they are so persuasive that they allow no other inference than that the defendant intended to effect the harm in question.

[33] von Bar, quoted by Griffon, De L'Intention en Droit Pénal 109 (1911).

[34] "The evidences of such a malice must arise from external circumstances discovering that inward intention, as lying in wait, menacings antecedent, former grudges, deliberate compassings, and the like, which are various according to variety of circumstances." Hale, *op. cit. supra* note 1, at 451.

Recklessness, no less than intention, includes a distinctive state of awareness. To ascertain whether recklessness existed, we must determine the actor's knowledge of the facts and his estimate of his conduct with reference to the increase of risk. In the determination of these questions, the introduction of the "reasonable man" is not a substitute for the defendant's awareness that his conduct increased the risk of harm any more than it is a substitute for the determination of intention, where that is material. It is a *method* used to determine those operative facts[35] in the minds of normal persons. The method should not be confused with the fact to be determined. Its limitations often raise doubts concerning the correctness of the fact-finding. But this does not in the least alter the material issue — unless it is determined that the defendant knew he was increasing the risk of harm, it cannot be defensibly held that he acted recklessly. Since intention differs from recklessness in the essential ways noted above, the facts on which each is rested are also different.

As regards negligence, both the proof of it and the standard of care by reference to which it is determined are objective. But that does not exhaust all that is essential in negligent behavior. The fact that nothing is asserted or proved concerning intention to harm or awareness of increased risk obscures the fact that their non-existence is essential to, and is presupposed in, the finding that the harm was inadvertent. Negligence, too, can be established by evidence unrelated to the objective risk of the immediate behavior, *e.g.* the fact that the victim was the defendant's child would tend to prove the lack of voluntary harm-doing, just as the fact that the defendant had made certain threats against the victim would point in the opposite direction.

The confusion of the material mental state with the proof of its presence has been greatest in the case-law on recklessness. This is the combined result of misinterpretation of the "reasonable man" test and the failure to recognize the distinctive, subjective character of recklessness. Thus,

35 See *infra* pp. 155, 162-63.

the jury is frequently instructed to find either that the defendant was aware of the fact that he was increasing the risk of harm *or* that a reasonable man in the defendant's situation *would have been aware* of that.[36] The second clause would be defensible if it could be interpreted to mean that the method of discovering the actual state of mind is the use of the "reasonable man" test; it would then be merely an awkward description of a necessary method of inquiry. The likelihood, however, is that the disjunctive was intended to mean what it directly implies, namely, that even though the defendant was not aware of the fact that he was unduly increasing the risk of harm, he was nonetheless reckless if the "reasonable man" would have known the risk.[37] This is plainly opposed to the meaning of recklessness which has been widely recognized since Austin.[38] In effect, it holds that even though certain persons were only negligent, they are nonetheless to be held reckless. It submerges recklessness in negligence in such a fashion as to perpetuate the presently confused analysis of these concepts.[39]

The jury needs to be informed that to find a defendant reckless they must find that his conduct fell below the standard of "due care" *and* that the defendant knew he was increasing the risk of harm; and that they are warranted in so finding if they find that a reasonable man in the given situation would have been aware of it — unless they also find that the defendant, though not insane, did not for some reason, *e.g.* defective sight or hearing or excitement, realize that he was increasing the risk of harm.

---

[36] See, *e.g.* Moreland, A Rationale of Criminal Negligence 9, 27, 31-34, 144-147 (1944); and A. L. I. Restatement, Torts § 500 (1934).

[37] "In order that the actor's conduct may be reckless, it is not necessary that he himself recognize it as being extremely dangerous. . . . It is enough that he knows or has reason to know of circumstances which would bring home to the realization of the ordinary, reasonable man the highly dangerous character of his conduct." A. L. I. Restatement, Torts § 500 (c) (1934). *Cf.* Commonwealth v. Pierce, 138 Mass. 165 (1884), quoted *infra*, notes 72 and 74.

[38] See Austin, *op. cit. supra* note 2, at 440-442.

[39] See chapter 11 *infra* regarding this problem in connection with ignorance of fact.

THE CASE-LAW

The progressive exclusion of negligence from the meaning of *mens rea* has been overlooked in recent years because, with the advent of the automobile,[40] negligence became both conspicuous and exceedingly harmful. In addition, the failure precisely to articulate the principle of *mens rea* has clouded adjudication. It is probable that early law reflected a cruder evaluation, penalizing negligence in homicide cases where instinctual drives and public attitudes operated without the inhibitions that were elsewhere imposed. From Bracton[41] to Blackstone,[42] as well as in the intermediate case-law, various phrases appear to support the view that negligent harm-doers were punishable.[43] But an examination of the facts in the cases raises serious questions; and the likelihood is that at least from the seventeenth century on, if not from the very beginning of the common law, negligent harm was generally not criminal. The doubt is almost wholly restricted to homicide; where the negligent behavior violated all standards of decent performance, the grievous consequences probably caused the normal penal bounds to be extended.

Hull's Case[44] is the leading seventeenth century decision. It concerned a death caused by a laborer's throwing a piece of timber which struck a co-worker. Although the opinion is not entirely free of ambiguity, it indicated that recklessness was material in manslaughter.[45] By the nineteenth century, English penal law rather plainly required reck-

---

[40] *Cf.* Lord Atkin in Andrews v. Director of Public Prosecutions (1937), 26 Cr. App. R. 34, 47-48.

[41] 2 Legibus 278 (Twiss ed. 1879); Mirror, ch. 4, 16.

[42] 4 Bl. Comm. 192.

[43] "Expressions will be found which indicate that to cause death by any lack of due care will amount to manslaughter, but as manners softened and the law became more humane a narrower criterion appeared." Atkin, J., in Andrews v. Director of Public Prosecutions, *supra* note 40 at 46.

[44] (1664) Kelyng 40, 84 Eng. Rep. 1072.

[45] This is implied in the hypothetical case posed: "where a man shoots an arrow or gun into a market-place full of people . . . in common presumption his intention was to do mischief. . . ." *Id.* at 1073.

lessness, described as "the grossest ignorance or the most criminal inattention."[46] In the early part of that century, the principle was still confused by the application of a more rigorous rule to the homicide of pedestrians by drivers of horses and carts — here the opinions run definitely in terms of "negligence."[47] If the jury thought the defendant "acted carelessly and negligently, they would pronounce him guilty of manslaughter."[48] Even in the middle of the century, in such a case, Earle, J., directed the jury that "a party neglecting ordinary caution, and, by reason of that neglect, causing the death of another, is guilty of manslaughter."[49] But these decisions seem to have been restricted to drivers of horses and carts (the counterpart of current automobile cases) and, possibly, to the abuse of firearms.[50] Against them must be set *Hull's Case* and a number of cases where medical men were charged with manslaughter. In 1874, in the trial of an attendant in an asylum, charged with manslaughter of a patient, Lush, J., charged the jury in terms of "gross carelessness": the defendant is not liable "if you think it inadvertence not amounting to culpability."[51] His statement of the distinction is unclear by present standards, but it is significant in its explicit exclusion of negligence.[52] In that same year the rule was definitely formulated: "Mere negligence will not do, there must be wicked negligence, that is, negligence so great, that you must be of opinion that the

[46] Rex v. Williamson (1807), 3 C. & P. 635, 172 Eng. Rep. 579.

[47] Knight's Case (1828), 1 Lew. C. C. 168, 168 Eng. Rep. 1000. *Cf.* "A. drives his cart carelessly, and it runs over a child in the street, if A. had seen the child, and yet drives on upon him, it is murder; but if he saw not the child, yet it is manslaughter. . . . " Hale, *op. cit. supra* note 1, at 476.

[48] Rex v. Grout (1834), 6 C. & P. 629, 630, 172 Eng. Rep. 1394, 1395.

[49] Queen v. Dalloway (1847), 2 Cox C. C. 273.

[50] See Rampton's Case (1664), Kelyng 41, 84 Eng. Rep. 1073.

[51] Reg. v. Finney (1874), 12 Cox C. C. 625, 626.

[52] That Lush, J. had recklessness rather clearly in mind is shown in his statement: "Now, if the prisoner, seeing that the man was in the bath, had knowingly turned on the tap and turned on the hot instead of the cold water, I should have said there was gross negligence. . . . " *Ibid.*

prisoner had a wicked mind, in the sense that she was reckless and careless whether the creature died or not."[53]

What rises to prominence in the later case-law is not any serious doubt regarding the relevant principle, but the inability of the judges to express the difference between recklessness and negligence clearly and their delay in adopting apt terms even after the essential differences had been articulated. For many years they relied on adjectives qualifying "negligence" to carry their meaning; and they continued to do this long after the adjectives were regarded as mere "vituperative epithets."[54] Nor has so-called "criminal negligence" been clarified by judicial efforts to distinguish it from civil negligence. The opinions run in terms of "wanton and wilful negligence," "gross negligence," and more illuminating yet, "that degree of negligence that is more than the negligence required to impose tort liability." The apex of this infelicity is "wilful, wanton negligence," which suggests a triple contradiction —"negligence" implying inadvertence; "wilful," intention; and "wanton," recklessness.[55]

A signal effort to formulate the rule correctly was made in 1925 by Chief Justice Hewart in a case involving a death in childbirth.[56] The Chief Justice stated the issues precisely in terms of a comparison between civil and criminal negligence. He seems to have fully understood the essential difference between recklessness and negligence,[57] using both terms and specifying that ". . . there is a difference in kind between the negligence which gives a right to compensation and the negligence which is a crime."[58] Since

---

[53] Brett, J., in Reg. v. Nicholls (1874), 13 Cox C. C. 75, 76.

[54] Baron Rolfe in Wilson v. Brett (1843), 11 M. & W. 113, 115-116.

[55] The language difficulty was discussed by Bailhache, J., in Tinline v. White Cross Ins. (1921), 3 K. B. 327, at 330.

[56] Rex v. Bateman (1925), 19 Cr. App. R. 8.

[57] "There must be *mens rea*." *Id.* at 11. " . . . showed such disregard for the life and safety of others as to amount to a crime against the State and conduct deserving punishment." *Id.* at 13.

[58] *Id.* at 16. The recency in some jurisdictions of the requirement of recklessness in manslaughter by use of automobile may be seen from the effect of the Bateman Case on Canadian decisions. McCarthy

the ideas and the corresponding rules are essentially different, it would seem necessary to employ different terms to express them. Unfortunately, the distinguished jurist continued to speak of "negligence" in describing recklessness; it is not surprising that he failed to provide an adequate explication of its meaning.[59]

In 1937, English judges were still speaking of recklessness as "a degree of negligence which far transcends [civil] negligence. . . ."[60] In that year, the leading English decision on this subject was rendered by the House of Lords in a case of manslaughter by automobile.[61] Lord Atkin, who delivered the opinion, was critical of the current descriptions of "criminal negligence," including that of Chief Justice Hewart in the above case. In distinguishing between "degrees of negligence," he found neither *mens rea* nor "the ideas of crime and punishment" helpful. Although, throughout his opinion "degrees of negligence" is reiterated,[62] he nonetheless aptly concluded that, "Probably of all the epithets that can be applied 'recklessness' most nearly covers the case."[63] But the opinion did not advance beyond Lord Hewart's insight that there is a difference "in kind;" nor did it provide a clear explication of recklessness.[64]

---

v. The King (1921), 59 D. L. R. 206 applied the rule of ordinary care. But in Rex v. Greisman (1926), 4 D. L. R. 738, decided shortly after the Bateman Case, recklessness was required, the court recognizing that: "To constitute crime there must be a certain moral quality carried into the act before it becomes culpable." *Id.* at 743.

[59] Yet he said: "It is desirable that, as far as possible, the explanation of criminal negligence to a jury should not be a mere question of epithets." "It is, in a sense, a question of degree, and it is for the jury to draw the line, but there is a difference in kind between the negligence which gives a right to compensation and the negligence which is a crime." Rex v. Bateman (1925), 19 Cr. App. R. at 16.

[60] Rex v. Leach (1937), 1 All E. R. 319, 322.

[61] Andrews v. Director of Public Prosecutions (1937), 26 Cr. App. R. 34.

[62] "For purposes of the criminal law there are degrees of negligence, and a very high degree of negligence is required. . . ." *Id.* at 47.

[63] *Ibid.*

[64] Indeed it was confused by criticism of that term as ". . . probably not all-embracing," since it " . . . suggests an indifference to risk, whereas the accused may have appreciated the risk and intended to

The American decisions reveal a parallel development. There is the like effort to articulate the basis on which "criminal negligence" is justifiably treated as satisfying the principle of *mens rea*. Even in some very early cases, emphasis was placed on "obstinate, wilful rashness;"[65] "gross negligence," it was said, involves an "act done wilfully . . . the known effect of which, under the circumstances, must be to endanger life."[66] That negligence did not suffice was recognized in the judicial reaction to an early nineteenth century Federal statute making any act of "misconduct, negligence or inattention" on the part of persons engaged in steamboat navigation which caused death, involuntary manslaughter. The statute was declared a departure from "the common law, and the statutes of all the states of the Union."[67] Nonetheless, the same confusion, noted above, precluded a clear enunciation of the meaning of "recklessness." The relation of awareness of increased danger to "gross heedlessness and incautionness"[68] was not clarified, and there was also a tendency to treat knowledge of the danger as the equivalent of intention.[69] The cases reveal insights into the dual aspect of recklessness; but these were obscured by indiscriminate references to negligence and recklessness[70] and by such

---

avoid it and yet shown such a high degree of negligence in the means adopted to avoid the risk as would justify a conviction." *Id.* at 48. See Dean, *Manslaughter and Dangerous Driving*, 53 L. Q. Rev. 380 (1937).

[65] "The death of a man, killed by voluntarily following a medical prescription, cannot be adjudged felony in the party prescribing, unless he, however ignorant of medical science in general, had so much knowledge, or probable information of the fatal tendency of the prescription, that it may be reasonably presumed by the jury to be the effect of obstinate, wilful rashness, at the least, and not of an honest intention and expectation to cure." Commonwealth v. Thompson, 6 Mass. 134, 140 (1809), citing Hale, P. C. 429; followed in Rice v. State, 8 Mo. 403, 405 (1844) and State v. Schulz, 55 Ia. 628 (1881).

[66] United States v. Freeman, 25 Fed. Cas. No. 15,162, at 1211 (D. Mass. 1827).

[67] United States v. Warner, 28 Fed. Cas. No. 16,643, at 407 (1848).

[68] Ann v. The State, 11 Humph. 159, 164, 30 Tenn. 159 (1850).

[69] Lee v. State, 1 Cold. 62, 66, 41 Tenn. 62 (1860).

[70] ". . . if they believe that said accidental shooting and killing was the result alone of the recklessly careless use of a loaded, deadly

expressions as "a careless and reckless manner,"[71] "reckless negligence,"[72] and "reckless carelessness."[73] Nor, for reasons stated above, was analysis clarified by Holmes' theory that recklessness must be determined from "the degree of danger attending the act."[74]

The chief advance represented in the more recent American cases, just as in the English decisions, is a wider appreciation of the distinctive character of recklessness and, thus, of the principle of *mens rea*. But improvement in language habits is a very slow process even for those who presumably are experts in elucidating the precise meaning of words. Many courts continue to speak of "culpable negligence"[75] and to inform juries that it denotes a "higher degree of negligence than is required to establish civil. liability."[76] " 'A long distance separates the negligence which renders one criminally liable from that which establishes

---

pistol by defendant, they should, notwithstanding the accident, find defendant guilty of manslaughter." Chrystal v. Commonwealth, 72 Ky. 669, 671, 672 (1873).

[71] State v. Hardie, 47 Ia. 647, 649 (1878). The gun cases are complicated by the fact that many involve an assault; this shifts the case toward "the commission of an unlawful act" category.

[72] In Commonwealth v. Pierce, 138 Mass. 165 (1884), the jury was instructed that on a charge of manslaughter, "it is not necessary to show an evil intent;" and that, "if by gross and reckless negligence he caused the death, he is guilty of culpable homicide. . . ." *Id.* at 174.

[73] York v. Commonwealth, 82 Ky. 360, 365 (1884).

[74] Commonwealth v. Pierce, 138 Mass. 165 (1884). In sustaining the conviction, Holmes said: ". . . recklessness in a moral sense means a certain state of consciousness with reference to the consequence of one's acts . . . it is understood to depend on the actual condition of the individual's mind with regard to consequences, as distinguished from mere knowledge of present or past facts or circumstances from which some one or everybody else might be led to anticipate or apprehend them if the supposed act were done." *Id.* at 175. " . . . it is clear, in the light of admitted principle . . . that the recklessness of the criminal no less than that of the civil law must be tested by what we have called an external standard." *Id.* at 177-178. The standard selected was "the degree of danger attending" the act. *Id.* at 178.
Thirty-five years later, Holmes wrote: "But, when words are used exactly, a deed is not done with intent to produce a consequence unless that consequence is the aim of the deed." Abrams et al. v. United States, 250 U. S. 616, 627, 63 L. Ed. 1173, 40 S. Ct. 17 (1919).

[75] People v. Angelo, 219 App. Div. 646, 221 N. Y. Supp. 47, 49 (1927).

[76] Chandler v. State, 146 P. 2d 598, 603 (Okl. 1944).

civil liability.' "[77] It seems, however, to have become rather widely recognized that "The word 'culpable,' in the phrase 'culpable negligence,' is something more than a mere epithet;"[78] " 'that the issue they [the jury] have to try is not negligence or no negligence, but felony or no felony;' "[79] and that "In defining common-law manslaughter it should not be necessary to fill instructions with 'epithets.' The term 'reckless' is not an epithet, but a descriptive adjective. . . . [Criminal] negligence is not merely conduct which fails to conform to the familiar, common standard, the conduct of a reasonable man under like circumstances. . . . To be reckless, conduct must be such as to evince disregard of or indifference to consequences, under circumstances involving danger to life or safety of others, although no harm was intended."[80]

It is apparent from the above survey of the case-law that its common link with negligence is the chief reason for the prevalent confusion of "recklessness," *e.g.* the assertions that it is a sort of negligence, that it is gross negligence and the like. Actually, recklessness is no more a degree of negligence than is intention. *Awareness* of increasing the danger separates it completely from the genus of negligence. It would be far more defensible to assert that recklessness is a lesser degree of intention; but that, too, is imprecise. If the essential differences discussed above were borne in mind, judges would no more talk of recklessness as "a degree of negligence" than they now speak of intention as a degree of negligence.

Despite the prevalent awkwardness in describing recklessness, it is nonetheless evident that negligence has long been regarded with suspicion in the common law of crimes and that it has been progressively excluded from penal

[77] People v. Bearden, 290 N. Y. 478, 483, 49 N. E. 2d 785, 788 (1943).
[78] ". . . it suggests or indicates some such meaning as criminal. . . ." People v. Angelo, 219 App. Div. 646, 221 N. Y. Supp. 47, 49 (1927).
[79] State v. Custer, 129 Kan. 381, 392, 282 P. 1071, 67 A. L. R. 909, 917 (1929) quoting Rex v. Bateman (1925), 19 Cr. App. R. 8, 16.
[80] *Id.* at 395; 67 A. L. R. at 920 (1929). Judge Burch's opinion is a carefully supported analysis of the meaning of "culpable negligence."

liability.[81] For example, as was stated in 1942 by the English Court of Criminal Appeal: "Negligence, everybody agrees, in the sense of a mere want of ordinary care, is not enough to justify conviction by a jury on a charge of manslaughter."[82]

When early law distinguished voluntary harm-doing from misadventure, it remained for a long period content if the former were involved in any manner that could be related to the actual harm. The rule was that a person who intentionally caused any injury should be responsible for any resultant harm, however unforeseeable or accidental that might be. The felony-murder, misdemeanor-manslaughter rules rose to check the range of this rationalization of penal liability as regards criminal homicide; and the ancient formulas, *mala in se—mala prohibita,* provided ready pegs on which to rest these important limitations. It became established that the defendant must have intended to commit a harm that was legally proscribed and that his liability for the homicide would to some substantial extent be determined by reference to the gravity of the harm he intended to commit. The next step was to restrict such penal liability by requiring the offender to be reckless with reference to the death caused by him in the commission of a crime. Thus the progress of criminal law in the last century reached the point of almost eliminating the felony-murder, misdemeanor-manslaughter rules, and this has been achieved in the 1957 English Homicide Act.[83] This promising de-

---

[81] The extent to which this has been carried may be seen in Akerele v. The King (1943), L. R. A. C. 255, reversing the conviction of a doctor whose treatment caused the death of ten children. But *cf.* the conviction for reckless misrepresentation in relation to rationing which was affirmed although the trial judge found that the defendants "who made them, either from inattentiveness or from carelessness, really did not address their minds to the question whether they were true or false." Williams Brothers v. Cloote (1944), 60 T. L. R. 270, 272.

[82] Rex v. Bonnyman (1942), 28 Cr. App. R. 131, 134. While reiterating a preference for the term "recklessness" as regards penal liability, the court nonetheless persisted in describing it as "a special or high degree of negligence. . . ." *Id.* at 136. *Cf.* "Negligence, to become criminal, must be reckless or wanton. . . ." People v. Lynn, 385 Ill. 165, 52 N. E. 2d 166, at 168 (1943).

[83] 5 Eliz. 2, ch. 11 (1957).

velopment was, however, interrupted and in some states[84] even reversed; in the United States, the common law rules and analogies drawn from them remain very much alive.[85] The consequence is that negligence and even chance occurrences enter into the determination of penal liability. In a few states, homicide committed by the negligent operation of an automobile is manslaughter.[86] This, of course, cannot be reconciled with the dominant and, it is believed, sound meaning of the principle of *mens rea*.

For the reasons suggested above, negligence also remains a potent factor in the law of homicide in the prevalent interpretation of "recklessness." In *Young*,[87] the defendant was driving her automobile behind a streetcar which she was trying to pass, when a boy stepped from the car, was struck and killed by the impact of the automobile. The court held that, while the defendant may have been negligent, she was not reckless within the meaning of the statute.[88] The crucial fact was that the defendant did not

[84] See *infra* chapter 8 at notes 77-84.

[85] See *infra* chapter 14 at notes 86-92.

[86] In 1921, Michigan enacted a statute creating the separate offense of negligent homicide committed in operating a vehicle "at an immoderate rate of speed or in a careless, reckless, or negligent manner, but not wilfully or wantonly." Early interpretations of the statute, referring to the legislative purpose of creating a lesser offense than involuntary manslaughter, found that "To do this it eliminated as necessary elements . . . negligence classed as wanton or wilful. Included in these terms is gross negligence. So that, in the enactment of the statute, there is expressly eliminated as elements of the crime all negligence of such character as to evidence a criminal intent; and . . . gross negligence was of that character." People v. Campbell, 237 Mich. 424, 428, 212 N. W. 97, 99 (1927). In a later case, a conviction for manslaughter was reversed on the ground that the evidence presented a "case of negligent homicide for the jury . . . based on . . . ordinary negligence." People v. Orr, 243 Mich. 300, 307, 220 N. W. 777, 779 (1928). In a later case, a Michigan court held the defendant guilty on the ground that "he was negligent in trying to drive a car when a man of ordinary prudence would have known it was not safe for him to do so." People v. Robinson, 253 Mich. 507, 235 N. W. 236, 237 (1931). *Cf.* "Under this statute, a finding that the accused was guilty of ordinary negligence supports a conviction." State v. Ramser, 17 Wash. 2d 581, 136 P. 2d 1013, 1015 (1943). See State v. Bolsinger, 21 N. W. 2d 480 (Minn. 1946).

[87] 20 Cal. 2d 832, 129 P. 2d 353 (1942).

[88] The court accepted the definition of "recklessness" of the A. L. I. Restatement on Torts, *supra* note 37.

see the boy until he stepped on the fender of her automobile. The opinion which applied the correct rule was, however, weakened by the court's statement: "This is not a case where defendant had an opportunity to see the deceased for some distance but still continued on her course. . . ."

In *Welansky*,[89] a conviction of manslaughter was affirmed under circumstances which raise a serious question regarding the prevalent judicial interpretation of "recklessness." The defendant was the owner of a popular Boston night club which, after a football game on a certain Saturday night, was crowded to the bursting point. An electric light bulb in one corner of the room had been turned off by a patron seated there, and the bar boy, sent to turn it on, lit a match in order to see the bulb. Artificial decorations became ignited, the fire spread so rapidly that in a few moments the entire place was ablaze, and panic followed. Two doors, barred by clothing racks, could not be opened, the revolving door was jammed, and other exits became impassable. Many persons lost their lives. At the time of this tragic fire, the owner of the club was a patient in a hospital.

The court held that the standard of reckless conduct "is at once subjective and objective. . . ." As to knowledge of the facts, the test is subjective; but with reference to the estimate of danger, the test is objective: "Knowing facts that would cause a reasonable man to know the danger is equivalent to knowing the danger . . . even if a particular defendant is so stupid [or] so heedless . . . that in fact he did not realize the grave danger, he cannot escape the imputation of wanton or reckless conduct . . . if an ordinary normal man under the same circumstances would have realized the gravity of the danger."

The distinction drawn between knowledge of the facts and estimate of the danger seems initially persuasive, and it may also survive critical examination. But there is considerable vagueness in the above opinion regarding these criteria.[90] If Welansky had actually anticipated that a

[89] 316 Mass. 383, 398-99, 55 N. E. 2d 902, 910 (1944).
[90] In some cases, knowledge of the facts and estimate of the danger

patron, desiring a dark corner of the premises, would turn off an electric light bulb, that a fire might start and spread with tremendous speed, that many persons would become panic-stricken and killed, etc., etc., he would certainly have taken action to prevent a tragedy such as that which occurred. No claim was made that Welansky was not a normal person. Yet the imputation to him of what the jury decided "the reasonable man" would estimate the danger to be implies either that he actually did know the danger, which implication is excluded or, as the decision holds, that negligence in estimating danger is sufficient to support penal liability at least for manslaughter.

It is not intended to minimize the difficulties met in adjudication by both judges and jurors. In *Murray, e.g.* the defendant, who had been drinking heavily, drove his automobile in such a way that he literally ran down a pedestrian who was wearing a light colored suit while crossing a well-lighted boulevard in Los Angeles. The evidence showed that the pedestrian was plainly visible for thirty to forty yards; and the case was distinguished from *Young,* noted above, on the ground that here there was "an opportunity to see the victim . . . for some distance. . . ."[91] In *Young,* the fact that the defendant did not see the deceased in time to prevent the homicide was decisive. In *Murray,* the court relied on the above statement in the *Young* opinion, with the result that the objective test of liability was also applied to knowledge of the facts. This would appear to be a retrogression, if not from *Young,* certainly from *Welansky,* which required awareness of the facts.

---

can hardly be distinguished. For example, if an automobile going 50 m. p. h., with neither brakes nor steering wheel functioning, is headed towards a stationary object 100 yards away, knowledge of the facts can hardly be distinguished from the estimate of the danger of collision. But if there is an element of uncertainty regarding a future event — and that is the reference of increased risk inherent in recklessness — the distinction seems tenable. The validity of the rule which imposes an objective test regarding the estimate of danger is, of course, a different question.

[91] People v. Murray, 136 P. 2d 389, 392 (D. C. Cal. 1943).

An Indiana case[92] further illustrates the psychological grip of objective liability when the defendant violates elementary standards of safety and kills someone. In this case, a road was under repair, necessitating a halt in traffic at a certain point and a single line of traffic for a short distance. For six miles from that point, signs had been erected warning that repairs were being made. At the place of single-lane traffic, twenty cars had stopped and there was a long unobstructed view, in full daylight, of the last car, in which the deceased was riding. The defendant, driving 50 to 60 m.p.h., collided with that automobile, causing the death. In replying to the claim that the information failed to allege that the defendant knew the facts or knew of any danger, the court emphasized the conditions—broad daylight, a level dry road, unobscured vision for 1600 feet, and so on. It held that the defendant "must have been aware" of the danger. But the stated rule of liability was objective: "It is sufficient that the actor realizes, or should realize, that there is a strong probability that such harm may result."[93]

If one may venture a rather wide generalization, it seems that negligence, where definitely recognized, has not often been penalized at common law and that, with few exceptions, the remaining vestiges of it survive largely because they are concealed in other issues. The most plausible explanation of this evolution is that the common law of crimes has tended to conform to the meaning of *mens rea* expressed in (voluntary) conduct.

THE ETHICAL RATIONALE

The distinctions concerning intention, recklessness and negligence, discussed above, are warranted on ethical grounds. The relevant ethical principle expressed in terms of *mens rea*, that penal liability should be limited to the voluntary (intentional or reckless) commission of harms

---

[92] Beeman v. State, 115 N. E. 2d 919 (1953).

[93] *Id.* at 923. See the pointed remarks of Devlin, J. in Roper v. Taylor's General Garages Ltd. (1951) 2 T. I. R. 284.

forbidden by penal law, represents not only the perennial view of moral culpability, but also the plain man's
morality.[94] It is a necessary principle if punishment is
to be distinguished from other sanctions.[95] It facilitates
the systematization of the penal law; and, more fully than
competing generalizations, it accords with the moral import
of the judicial decisions concerning laws which almost
everyone agrees are criminal laws.

The application of this ethical rationale to intentional
harm-doing is obvious. Intention implies some degree of premeditation; hence the maximum culpability is represented
in the intentional commission of a harm—assuming that the
other variables, including motivation, are "constant." As
regards recklessness, it is equally evident that harms thus
effected signify less culpability than do the "same" harms
committed intentionally because recklessness indicates a
lesser participation or commitment of the self in the production of the harm.

As has already been seen, these simple evaluations are not
fully or consistently implemented in the penal law. Although
recklessness is potentially applicable to all crimes, if only
because of its relation to action in known ignorance of fact,
little use has been made of this. In exceptional instances,
e.g. perjury, a sound policy might exclude recklessness from
the relevant *mens rea*, while, on the other hand, the variety
of criminal homicides and criminal fraud readily permits
implementation of the distinction. In some cases of criminal
homicide, however, verdicts of murder have been affirmed
on the ground that a high degree of recklessness is the "legal
equivalent" of intention.[96] This has also been held in criminal assault.[97] The penal law is indiscriminate in this regard. At the same time, as regards many other crimes, only
their intentional commission is charged; and this seems to
err in the opposite direction by allowing reckless harm-doers

[94] See Bradley, Ethical Studies, Essay 1 (1876).
[95] See *infra* chapter 9.
[96] Commonwealth v. Sostilio, 325 Mass. 143, 89 N. E. 2d 510 (1949).
[97] See dissent in Brimhall v. State, 31 Ariz. 522, 255 P. 165 (1927).

to escape entirely. If "reckless larceny," "reckless rape" and so on are excluded from penal liability "on principle," the retention of negligent harm-doing within that liability seems obviously fallacious.

Despite the evolution of judicial decision in the direction of excluding negligence, scholars in the field are still far from having reached a consensus on this subject.[98] Some believe that persons who lacked the capacity to act with due care (though not insane) should be exculpated. Others limit that position by the stipulation that the sub-ordinary (not insane) person must have done the best he could.[99] But a standard implies adequacy; and in the case of an individual with less than ordinary skill, it would be extremely difficult to derive a "personal standard" by which to apply the above proposal. In any case, both of the above proposals assume that negligence is sometimes properly within the scope of penal law; and the present moot issue extends far beyond that to the total exclusion of negligence, regardless of the negligent harm-doer's competence.

Perhaps the strongest argument in favor of the penalization of at least some negligent harm-doers is that: "Negligence denotes a lack of due solicitude . . . ,"[1] "*une attitude absolument anti-sociale*;"[2] and this implies that punishment

---

[98] Here again, Holmes' and Stephen's influence is apparent. Stephen said: "In some cases it [*mens rea*] denotes mere inattention." Queen v. Tolson (1889), L. R. 23 Q. B. 168, 185. Also, see 2 H. Cr. L. 95, 122-23 (1883), where he writes of "homicide by negligence," and 3 H. Cr. L. 11 (1883).

The like position is defended by Professor A. Goodhart, English Law and the Moral Law 85-86 (1953). Negligence is included as a basis of penal liability in Sec. 2.02, A. L. I. Model Penal Code, Tent. Draft No. 4 (1955). The supporting reasons are stated, *id.* at 126-27.

[99] This is implied by Pound, An Introduction to the Philosophy of Law 178 (1922). Professor Keedy's assertion that that is the present rule in criminal law (*Ignorance and Mistake in the Criminal Law*, 22 Harv. L. Rev. 85 (1908)) does not seem to be supported by the cases. *Cf. Note*, 12 Harv. L. Rev. 428, 429 (1899).

[1] Aquinas, Summa II-III, Q. 54, Art. 1. "According to the canons a penalty is inflicted on those who cause death unintentionally, through doing something unlawful, or failing to take sufficient care." *Id.* at II-II, Q. 64, Art. 8. *Cf.* "The law has no cognizance of unintentional offences." Plato, Apology of Socrates, 26a.

[2] Schmidt, Faute Civile et Faute Pénale 97 (1928). So, also, writes Brunhes, L'Imprudence devant la Loi Pénale 47 (1932).

is deserved in these cases. Again, it is likewise argued that when a duty is violated by persons *able* to conform to it, their conduct is morally culpable[3]—a phase of the maxim, *non scire quod scire debemus et possumus culpa est.* The most frequent argument supporting the punishment of negligent persons stresses deterrence.

The thesis that inadvertent damage reflects a moral fault is difficult to accept. In tort law, the typical rationale is that, "as between the innocent victim and the wrongdoer" (note the weighting of the issue in terms suggesting moral culpability) the latter should bear the loss. It is usual to stop with some such assertion, but the difficulties really begin at that point. For that appears to concede that the policy merely represents a choice of the lesser of two evils. If reparation for damage caused inadvertently cannot be justified on its merits, negligent harms are like natural forces, and the damages should lie where they fall. From this viewpoint, the existing tort law on negligence imposes strict liability, a tax on incompetence.[4] For many an escape is offered by insurance—the injured person is compensated but the loss is distributed over a wide field—hence both the monetary judgment against a particular person and his lack of culpability are of minor consequence.

The sentiment that one who negligently causes damage should repair the loss, though questionable on ethical grounds,[5] is supported by the expectation that normal persons will carry on their activities with decent competence.

---

[3] Moore, Ethics 14 (1944); The Philosophy of Moore 180 (Schilpp ed. 1942).

[4] In an interesting discussion of civil liability, Salmond argues that "compensation is not a rational end of the administration of justice," but he draws the non sequitur that "Compensation, therefore, . . . must be supported as being a species of punishment." Immediately after that he asserts that "the principle of punishment demands that there shall be liability where, and only where, there is fault; that of compensation . . . requires liability . . . irrespective of any fault. . . ." Salmond, Essays in Jurisprudence and Legal History 128, 129, 132 (1891).

[5] "It is quite true that negligence does not depend upon moral fault; it is equally true that it does not depend upon fault even in a legal sense." Seavey, *Negligence — Subjective or Objective?* 41 Harv. L. Rev. 1, 27-28 (1927).

So, too, the consequent attitudes sustain the tort rules of liability for negligent behavior.[6] The public conscience is salved by contrasting punishment with compensation; as the French put it, the tort judgment is directed not against the person, but only represents *"une perte á un patrimoine."* But none of the arguments noted above justify *punishment* for harms caused inadvertently.

It is alleged, however, that punishment stimulates care, that it deters negligent behavior. Yet this is contradicted in the usual infliction of very light sentences, even for homicide.[7] If punishment actually deterred negligence, the thing to do would be to inflict very severe penalties—the heavier the sanction, the greater the deterrence. There is, moreover, an additional difficulty in this regard. The deterrent theory must justify punishment for inadvertence quite apart from, and in addition to, its justification of punishment for recklessness. But deterrence rests on rationalist tenets, *i.e.* that a potential offender weighs the advantage of his course of conduct against the evil of the sanction, and refrains on grounds of self-interest. Neither that premise nor the facts apply to negligent harm-doers. Yet the advocates of the deterrent theory seem to believe that the punishment of inadvertent harm-doers will somehow condition potentially inadvertent harm-doers beyond and in addition to the influence effected by the punishment of reckless offenders. But what reason is there to believe that there is any such "carry-over?"[8] Finally, as to the negligent individuals who are themselves punished, it may be suggested that both the slightness of the punishment and its unrelatedness to the causes of the inadvertence and inefficiency render it very unlikely that any correction whatever results. The entire thesis seems to rest on the deterrent effect of the frequent, immediate, on-the-spot disciplining of children for their

---

[6] Salmond, *op. cit. supra* note 4, at 412.

[7] "The normal sentence for involuntary manslaughter is reputed to be six months' imprisonment." Kenny, Outlines of Criminal Law 141, note 5 (1936). And see Michael and Wechsler, Criminal Law and Its Administration 1276, note 15 (1940).

[8] See *infra* chapter 11 at note 42.

mistakes by their parents. But the conditions regarding the punishment of adult inadvertent harm-doers are quite different in every respect.

The more persuasive argument in favor of punishing some negligent harm-doers approximates, if it does not fully rest upon, a traditional ethical ground—the insensitivity of these harm-doers to the rights of other persons. In the preceding chapter it was concluded that ethically insensitive actors should be subjected to penal liability regardless of the fact that they followed their conscience, the ground being that the objective ethical principle of *mens rea* is paramount. Our present concern is to consider whether the negligent harm-doer is in that same class of person.

There are several reasons to answer this question in the negative. First, in the complex character of present industrial society, where the negligent handling of machines, especially automobiles, causes many injuries, the thesis that ethical insensitivity is the underlying factor is not persuasive. For example, a very large number of the deaths caused by negligently driven automobiles occur in collisions. Despite the currency of "the death instinct," self-preservation is still deeply rooted, and if it did not stimulate careful driving, it is even less likely that insensitivity to the interests of other persons did cause the careless driving. It seems much more probable that a dull mind, slow reactions, awkwardness and other ethically irrelevant facts were the underlying cause. Second, the insensitivity which one ascribes to certain inadvertent harm-doers (assuming that it is not merely imagined) has very deep roots. It has become part of the "structure of personality" which had its origin in childhood and in a vast number of subsequent experiences. In other words, even if such insensitivity had its origin in many immoral acts, the personality pattern has become fixed in the adult. His present attitudes are not matters of choice; hence there is no warrant for punishing him on the suggested traditional moral ground. Third, as was suggested above, there is no evidence that the sporadic punishment characteristic of criminal law administration will sensitize thoughtless individuals to the rights of other persons. Even if the psychological premise were sound, the legal apparatus cannot assure such a close association between negligence and pain as to provide any support for the use of punishment on this ground.

Fourth, a legal sanction ought to be proportionate to other legal sanctions; hence, especially if the asserted basis of punishment is an ethical one, the punishment for reckless misconduct should be greater than that for negligence. But the causes of negligence may be so deeply rooted in the personality structure of the inadvertent harm-doer as to require a great deal of punishment to alter his habits—assuming that punishment has any such effect. This, however, would contradict the limits set by the punishment of reckless misconduct. The usual Continental codal provision for much reduced punishment for specified harms caused negligently is only an incongruous makeshift when appraised with reference to the avowed purposes of justice and correction. Fifth, on the assumption that there is no evidence one way or the other regarding the deterrence of negligent harm-doers by punishment or the threat of punishment, it is submitted that the issue should be resolved against the use of punishment and in favor of non-punitive sanctions. Finally, one must especially bear in mind that there is no challenge to the ethics of penal law in the behavior of negligent harm-doers. "Ethical insensitivity" to others' interests is either a misleading metaphor or it implies a lack of awareness of ethical values; in any case, the inadvertent harm-doer did not flout those values.

The situation is greatly altered when we confront the intentional or reckless harm-doer. Here, we deal with the voluntary offender, and that makes a very great difference. But the instant question is more difficult, namely, having excluded inadvertent harm-doers, even the alleged "ethically insensitive" ones, from penal liability, is it consistent to include violators who acted in conformity with their conscience?

This problem concerns offenders who, though they acted, were not, in the light of their own consciences, intentional *harm-doers*. They did, however, consciously commit what are regarded by the community as major harms. One must be wary here of the metaphor, "sick conscience," for the fact is that we are not discussing sick people such as psychotic or feeble-minded persons; and we are discussing the simple values of penal law concerning major crimes. It is in this context that the (conscious) conduct of minorities, uneducated persons and fanatics must be sharply contrasted with mere inadvertence. Voluntarily doing what is proscribed as a serious harm in a rational penal code *challenges* the community's sound values. The offender, whether he be unlettered or a genius, has consciously done what the community in its freely evolved penal law has emphatically condemned as a felony or serious misdemeanor—and he now seeks exculpation. On what ground? On the alleged ground that what he did was right or, at the minimum, that although, *e.g.* he assaulted a member of a despised race or burned his house, he did not know it was wrong to do that. Both pleas must be rejected by reference to the objective meaning of the principle of *mens rea* and the necessary conditions of a legal order, epitomized in the principle of legality. In some measure, however mitigated, it must be made clear that sane adults who consciously commit such harms act immorally and in violation of the law. If this represents a loss of value in some extreme cases, that is the inevitable consequence of the preservation of greater values in an imperfect world.

In some imagined state of anarchy, the theorist, allocating to himself the powers of Omniscience, may wish to probe the issues further, and in a glow of magnanimity (at others' expense!) exclude such harmful conduct from the scope of the ideal code. The above discussion rests upon the premises of an actual society, a functioning legal order, and the responsibility to take appropriate action to preserve the values of the community expressed in a rational penal law. In defending this position, it will have been noted, one must meet the arguments of those who would continue to punish negligent harm-doers and, on the other hand, of those who, like some psychiatrists, would not punish even the most deliberate homicide, regardless of the competence of the offender. The ground for rejecting both of these positions is the conscious functioning mind of normal human beings, including that of normal criminals; and that is expressed in penal law when *mens rea* is restricted to intentionality and recklessness.

But just as it should not be forgotten that tort liability remains available to shift economic losses and that other non-punitive sanctions may be quite apt, so must it also be remembered that education, presupposing voluntary attendance and cooperation, is always defensible. Corrective treatment, to be effective, would require careful study of the various types of negligence and of their causes. This would involve differentiation in terms of physical defects, ignorance, bad judgment, lack of experience, timidity, excitability, fatigue, and so on.[9] The consequent educational services would alter the present restrictive choice between punishment and the complete lack of any social influence; and this might secure complete acceptance of the view that negligence should no longer be a ground of penal liability.

CONCEPTUAL PROBLEMS AND TERMINOLOGY

In the past century, the major handicap in the way of elucidating *"mens rea"* was the failure to distinguish the principle of *mens rea* from the *mentes reae* specified in the rules of penal law. Considerable progress has been made by scholars of penal law to transcend that difficulty, especially as regards the subjective reference of *mens rea* to intention and recklessness.[10] But there remains a lack of appreciation of the significance of the principle of *mens rea* as an organizational idea. This includes not only its formal relation to the rules and doctrines but also its objective ethical meaning derived from its dual reference—to the proscribed harms

9 See Schmidt, *op. cit. supra* note 2, at 103.

10 Professor J. W. C. Turner's essay, *op. cit. supra* note 7, was a major achievement in this regard. See, also, Stroud, Mens Rea 15 (1914).

(disvalues) and to the above noted mental states of the persons who voluntarily commit those harms. Other current difficulties regarding *mens rea* concern problems of terminology, especially "constructive intent," "transferred intent," "specific intent" and "general intent."

The current confusion resulting from diverse uses of "general intent" is aggravated by dubious efforts to differentiate that from "specific intent." Each crime, as Stephen pointed out, has its distinctive *mens rea, e.g.* intending to have forced intercourse, intending to break and enter a dwelling-house and to commit a crime there, intending to inflict a battery, and so on. It is evident that there must be as many *mentes reae* as there are crimes. And whatever else may be said about an intention, an essential characteristic of it is that it is directed towards a definite end. To assert therefore that an intention is "specific" is to employ a superfluous term just as if one were to speak of a "voluntary act." It follows also that if some intentions are to be distinguished from others, the criteria selected to do that must be coherent with the specificity of all intentions. This provides one guide to a critical reading and improvement of current professional discourse in terms of "general intent" and "specific intent." Insofar as these terms are used to refer to actual intentions, both of them are unfortunate, and the adjectives should be discontinued.

As is usual with such literally inapt expressions, however, there are substantive difficulties which bar any easy reform of the above terminology. For example, it is often assumed that there is a difference between an intention to kill J. Q. Jones and the mental state of one who shoots into a room so full of persons that the shot is practically certain to hit someone. The latter state of mind is said to be a "general intent," and convictions are affirmed on the ground that assault and battery and criminal homicide do not require "specific intents." This artifice could be avoided by holding that what is material in criminal homicide is not J. Q. Jones but "any human being." Both the substantive problem and that of a congruent terminology become more complicated when the facts evidence not an intentional killing, but a reckless one. In such cases, "general intent" is sometimes used to refer to recklessness or to include recklessness; and this is confusing because it is necessary to accommodate this meaning with the psychological specificity of intention noted above, the difference between intention and recklessness, and the use of "general intent" to designate the principle of *mens rea.*[11]

Underlying much of the above difficulty is the thesis that some statutes specify several qualifications on the relevant *mens rea, e.g.* criminal fraud and burglary, and that the cumulative effect is a very specific *mens rea.* If that were all that was involved, the problem could be solved by substituting analysis in terms of more or less specificity among *mentes reae* for that in terms of "specific" and "general intents."

But the more serious difficulty is the assumption that some crimes require only a "general intent" in the sense that the *mens rea* is fully expressed in the defendant's immediate commission of the material facts of the relevant crime;[12] while other crimes require specific intentions, *i.e. mentes reae*, which can be established only by proof *aliunde.* For example, rape is said to require only a "general intent" while burglary is said to require a "specific intent."[13] In fact, as was noted above, the actual intention in rape is as specific as can be imagined; but we are to consider now the alleged evidentiary difference by reference to which the above terminology is defended. In burglary, it is said, proof of the

---

[11] "[W]e shall find that some of the specific offenses call for a corresponding form of evil in the intent, others demand only evil in general, and still others are constituted only when two different evil intents combine." 1 Bishop, Criminal Law § 291a at 195 (1923). See note 13 *infra.*

[12] In Rex v. Steane (1947), K. B. 997, Goddard, C. J. said: "In many offenses it is unnecessary to allege any particular intent. The commonest case is in larceny where the prisoner is simply charged with stealing." *Id.* at 1004. But it was acknowledged that the prisoner may introduce evidence that he did not intend to steal. *Id.* at 1004-5.

[13] See *Note*, 55 Col. L. Rev. 1214 (1955); Walden v. State, 156 S. W. 2d 385, 387 (Tenn. 1941); People v. Fruci, 67 N. Y. S. 2d 512, 188 Misc. 384 (1947); 22 C. J. S. Crim. L. Sec. 32 at 91.

breaking and entry is not sufficient; they must also be shown to have been done with the intention to commit a felony, and that requires proof *aliunde*. In rape, on the other hand, it is assumed that the act of forced intercourse expresses the required *mens rea*. But if the person who broke and entered is sober, has a kit of tools with him, and so on, there is no more need for evidence *aliunde* to establish his criminal intention than there is in forced intercourse. What is pertinent is the fact that the person who broke and entered may be able to establish by evidence *aliunde* that he had no intention to commit a felony, *e.g.* he had permission to do what he did or he was a neighbor who mistook a near-by door for his own, and so on. But precisely the same applies to any charge of rape. What, *e.g.* looks like an obvious case of rape may turn out to be a mere assault and battery because the perpetrator is the long-lost unrecognized husband of the woman, or the parties may have consummated a legal marriage which the woman later decided was illegal.

The above problem involves a confusion of procedural concepts with those of substantive penal theory, and it has wide ramifications which are discussed elsewhere in this book.[14] It may be noted here that no immediate external situation, however criminal it appears to be, can of itself preclude the possibility that the relevant *mens rea* was lacking; and evidence *aliunde* is always admissible in that regard. Accordingly, the above ground for the use of "general intent" and "specific intent" is not valid because crimes are not distinguishable by reference to evidence *aliunde*.

As was suggested above, "general intent" is sometimes employed not as descriptive of any particular *mens rea* but, instead, to refer to the principle of *mens rea*. It is a way of saying that the principle of *mens rea* is satisfied, *e.g.* where D shoots at J. Q. Jones and hits X. More fully, what is intended to be said is not that the actual intention in D's mind was "general"—the plain fact is that he intended to shoot J. Q. Jones—but that that (specific) intention satisfied

[14] This is discussed *infra* chapter 7 at notes 65-68.

the principle of *mens rea* regardless of the fact that it was
not actually achieved. It is in this context that "transferred
intent" is also used. This expression has the advantage of
suggesting that the term does not refer to any actual intention and that, instead, it connotes a policy which, applied to
the above situation, holds D to the same liability to which
he would have been subjected had he intended to shoot the
person who was actually shot. Unfortunately, however, the
fictitious term inhibits relevant questions, *e.g.* instead of the
present rules, should D be held guilty of an attempt to kill
the person shot at and of manslaughter of the person
actually killed? It is hoped that the above brief discussion
of questions of terminology, involved in the further elucidation of the principle of *mens rea*, will suffice to delineate an
important problem.

CHAPTER V

MENS REA: (3) THE THEORY OF NON-MORAL PENAL LIABILITY

THE position reached in the two preceding chapters is that: (1) The principle of *mens rea* is the ultimate summation of the moral judgments expressed in the proscription of the voluntary (intentional or reckless) commission of numerous social harms; and (2) it implies the personal guilt of normal adult offenders. It was also submitted that both the offender's *mens rea* and his motives must be considered in appraising his moral culpability. But it was maintained—on the premise of a freely constructed and therefore sound penal law which proscribes actual harms (disvalues)—that since the offender's motives do not affect his *mens rea*, he is culpable to some degree no matter how good his motives were. It was also recognized that there are marginal cases involving conscience, religious faith or cultural differences, which give rise to difficult questions and serious tensions; and it was concluded that the preservation of the principles of *mens rea* and legality requires that questions of motivation be assigned to administration, not incorporated into the substantive definition of crimes. The second of the above chapters[1] discussed the "subjective" reference of "*mens rea*"—to the offenders' actual mental states. Attention was especially focused on the intentionality and recklessness expressed in the voluntary commission of proscribed harms; and the reasons for excluding negligence from the scope of *mens rea* were set out.

[1] See chapter 4.

In the present chapter, the conclusions reached above are applied to various rules and doctrines of current penal law, especially those at odds with the above position. The problem of non-moral penal liability to be considered in this chapter is not that involved in the current formal definition of *mens rea*, which was previously discussed. Nor shall we be concerned here with strict penal liability imposed for the innocent violation of "public welfare" and other laws. Here, we are to consider a more fundamental question regarding the nature of penal liability for any crime, including the traditional felonies. This was the challenge raised by Justice Oliver Wendell Holmes in *The Common Law*.[2] That Holmes' discussion, consisting of a series of analyses of various specific problems,[3] is penetrating and subtle is almost gratuitous to observe.[4] Indeed, any inquiry concerning *mens rea*, regardless of how it terminates, is bound to profit from a careful consideration of Holmes' theory.

HOLMES' THEORY

Holmes' study of liability in early law led him to conclude that it was built on vengeance which "imports a feeling of blame, and an opinion . . . that a wrong has been done." It was, moreover, confined to intentional harm-doing—"even a dog distinguishes between being stumbled over and being

[2] There is much in Holmes' work which supports a very different ethical theory than that of The Common Law. See Hall, Studies in Jurisprudence and Criminal Theory 141, note 26 (1958) and note 13 *infra*.

[3] It is rather significant that later writers on tort-crime interrelations do not discuss Holmes and do not cite him. Most of the major contributions on this subject are by English writers — Stephen, Kenny, Allen and Winfield. But there are also important essays by American scholars, *e.g.* Ames, *Law and Morals* (1908) in Selected Essays on the Law of Torts (1924), who likewise did not refer to Holmes.

[4] It is impossible to assess the extent of Holmes' influence on the acceptance of "objective liability." But that it has been considerable is indicated by numerous bits of evidence. Thus Professor J. W. C. Turner makes certain relevant observations regarding criminal liability and moral standards, and he cites Stroud. Turner, *The Mental Element in Crimes at Common Law*, 6 Camb. L. J. 31, 35 (1936); Stroud relied on Holmes. Stroud, Mens Rea 10 (1914). *Cf.* Sidgwick, The Elements of Politics 115 (1919).

kicked."[5] He knew of no satisfactory evidence of liability for "accidental consequences." On the contrary, he insisted, "Our system of private liability for the consequences of a man's own acts . . . started from the notion of actual intent and actual personal culpability."[6] The striking fact is not so much that later research contradicts this,[7] but that Holmes also argued with particular emphasis that present criminal law has repudiated this "primitive" rationale and rests no longer on moral culpability but on an objective non-moral foundation. Thus it would seem, in Holmes' analysis, though not in his evaluation, the history of criminal law represents a devolution, a regression from liability based on moral blame to one resting on non-moral criteria. The concluding words of his first lecture announce his thesis for contemporary law—he intends to prove that "while the terminology of morals is still retained, the law . . . by the very necessity of its nature, is continually transmuting those moral standards into external and objective ones, from which the actual guilt of the party concerned is wholly eliminated."

The first clue to understanding Holmes' theory of liability is suggested by his postulate that "the secret root from which the law draws all the juices of life . . . [is] of course, considerations of what is expedient for the community concerned."[8] The criminal law is but a specific instance that supports this generalization. Whereas vengeance "takes an

---

[5] The Common Law 3 (1881). *Cf.* his later assertion, "The hatred for anything giving us pain . . . which leads even civilized man to kick a door when it pinches his finger. . . ." *Id.* at 11.

[6] *Id.* at 4.

[7] "The church, even before the conquest, had been urging that the objective rules of liability which formed the Anglo-Saxon law of crime and tort ought to be modified in accordance with subtler ideas of moral guilt. . . ." Plucknett, *Roman Law and English Common Law*, 3 U. Toronto L. J. 43 (1939).

"As criminal law develops, it moreover scrutinizes more closely the mental condition of offenders. . . ." Kenny, Outlines of Criminal Law 27 (15th ed. 1936).

Ames, *supra* note 3, at 3. See generally, Wigmore, *Responsibility For Tortious Acts: Its History*, in 3 Select Essays in Anglo-American Legal History 479 (1909).

[8] The Common Law 35.

internal standard, not an objective or external one, and condemns its victim by that,"[9] modern law has eliminated "actual guilt." Holmes concedes that vengeance still operates in modern society, but it "does not cover the whole ground."[10] The scientific requirement is a general theory, valid for the entire criminal law. Hence, *e.g.* he rejects reformation out of hand, since that theory requires no punishment whatever or very early release in cases where recidivism is extremely unlikely and, also, at the opposite extreme, where the offender is incurable. Choosing, therefore, between retribution and deterrence, Holmes upholds the latter, "the preventive theory." The utilitarian ground of his rejection of a moral basis for penal liability is apparent.

For example, when he asserts that "No society has ever admitted that it could not sacrifice individual welfare to its own existence,"[11] he supports that as a valid ethical position. When he speaks of conscription, he implies that its justification is axiomatic, and it does not occur to him that the purpose of the war can make any difference in that judgment. As Holmes proceeds to elucidate "expediency," he sometimes displays a surprising and, occasionally, a shocking insensitivity, *e.g.* his reiterated approval of a "justifiable self-preference," of the conduct of a man on a plank in a sea, who thrusts off anyone who lays hold of it, and of killing an innocent person on the ground that the alternative was one's own death. He assumes rather than establishes the answer to numerous other difficult problems in his assertion that, "When the state finds itself in a similar position, it does the same thing."[12] This was the rather blunt utilitarianism which he espoused with occasional but nonetheless highly significant waverings that at times ran into sheer inconsistency.[13]

[9] *Id.* at 40.
[10] *Id.* at 42.
[11] *Id.* at 43.
[12] *Id.* at 44.
[13] In 1871, he wrote: "A culpable state of mind is an element in most wrongs; and negligence and wilfulness, into which negligence shades

Holmes' purpose was to establish the validity of his theory by reference to the penal law. He stressed the disregard of "the personal peculiarities of the individuals concerned."[14] "If the punishment stood on the moral grounds which are proposed for it, the first thing to be considered would be those limitations in the capacity for choosing rightly which arise from abnormal instincts, want of education, lack of intelligence, and all other defects which are most marked in the criminal classes."[15] Not only is this not done but, on the contrary, "the law does undoubtedly treat the individual as a means to an end, and uses him as a tool to increase the general welfare at his own expense. It has been suggested above, that this course is perfectly proper. . . ."[16]

The validity of his theory was, he thought, established by the following rules and doctrines of penal law:

1. "[E]ven the deliberate taking of life will not be punished when it is the only way of saving one's own."[17] 2. Ignorance of the law is no defense.[18] 3. The law "take[s] no account of incapacities unless . . . infancy or madness." This shows that "the tests of liability are external, and independent of the degree of evil in the particular person's motives or intentions."[19] 4. With reference to the rules on

---

away, express the more common of these states." Review of Campbell, The Law of Negligence, 5 Am. L. Rev. 536 (1871).

In The Common Law, his clearest expression of the contradiction of his objective theory is on page 50 in the passage beginning "It is not intended to deny that criminal liability as well as civil, is founded on blameworthiness." See, especially, Holmes' support of subjective liability in Silsbee v. Webber, 171 Mass. 378, 50 N. E. 555 (1898).

There are numerous other passages that, if they do not contradict his chief argument, certainly call for explicit reconciliation, e.g. Holmes did not explain the "exceptional" rules where the tests are "subjective," (see The Common Law 66-74) in relation to his general theory that the law by its very nature, must be external. Cf. Commonwealth v. Ryan, 155 Mass. 523, 30 N. E. 364 (1892), and Abrams et al. v. United States, 250 U. S. 616, 627, 63 L. Ed. 1173, 40 S. Ct. 17 (1919).

14 Supra note 8, at 45.

15 Ibid.

16 Id. at 46-47.

17 Id. at 47.

18 Id. at 47-48.

19 Id. at 50.

provocation to homicide, "the law decides on general considerations what provocations are sufficient."[20]

The key terms in his theory of both tort and criminal liability are "external" and "objective," which Holmes uses synonymously. He means by them two utterly different things. Holmes sometimes means that the data relied upon to form conclusions regarding mental states are observable. But, for Holmes, the terms mean also, and more frequently, that the test of liability is "external" or "objective" in the sense that it ignores facts relevant to culpability.

In discussing the difference between murder and manslaughter, he states that the law has adopted "external tests,"[21] such as the weapons used and the length of time between the provocation and the act. "Tests" seem to refer to the evidentiary data from which such mental states as intention and premeditation are inferred. Here, it seems, Holmes is insisting that mental states can be known only from external evidence.

Holmes' other meaning, namely, that the standard of *liability* is "external" or "objective" is employed much more frequently and insistently. The conclusion of his first lecture, it may be recalled, asserted that the law "is continually transmuting those moral standards into external or objective ones, from which the actual guilt of the party concerned is wholly eliminated."[22] "[T]he tests of liability are external, and independent of the degree of evil in the particular person's motives or intentions."[23] The law "is wholly indifferent to the internal phenomena of conscience."[24] He notes the liability in arson for remote consequences "whether they were actually intended or not."[25] In discussing provocation, he stresses "the objective nature of legal stand-

20 *Id.* at 61.
21 *Id.* at 62.
22 *Id.* at 38.
23 *Id.* at 50.
24 *Id.* at 110.
25 *Id.* at 65.
26 *Id.* at 61.

ards."[26] Even malice aforethought does not mean "a state of the defendant's mind. . . . It is, in truth, . . . like . . . negligence. . . ."[27]

An initial appraisal of Holmes' thesis might suppose that Holmes rejected mentalist psychology, that he was a forerunner of behaviorist jurisprudence. But it is perfectly clear that Holmes not only recognized the existence of mental states, but that he also employed such common terms as intention, motive and consciousness in traditionally accepted ways. This is further evidenced by his discussion of those phases of criminal law where he admitted that actual *mentes reae* are recognized and referred to in the rules. Thus in certain cases of attempt and in crimes such as the purchase of counterfeit dies, "the law goes on a new principle, different from that governing most substantive crimes"[28]— which presumably comprises a standard of actual guilt. So, too, in larceny, actual *animus furandi* is required—not "because the law is more anxious not to put a man in prison for stealing unless he is actually wicked, than it is not to hang him for killing another,"[29] but because "the intent is an index to the external event which probably would have happened" [30] (permanent deprivation of property). Again, in burglary, actual intent is required[31] because it, too, "is an index to the probability of certain future acts which the law seeks to prevent."[32] And Holmes conceded, further, that "the question of knowledge is a question of the actual condition of the defendant's consciousness."[33]

THE "REASONABLE MAN" AS METHOD
AND AS STANDARD OF LIABILITY

Since it is thus clear that Holmes recognized the existence of mental states, his principal thesis concerns the link between the two meanings of "external." Holmes' argument

[27] *Id.* at 62.
[28] *Id.* at 67.
[29] *Id.* at 72.
[30] *Ibid.*
[31] *Id.* at 74.
[32] *Ibid.*
[33] *Id.* at 56; also *cf.* 62.

that legal judgments necessarily rest on external phenomena and that the substantive test of liability, with rare exceptions, is also "external" seems to imply that there is a *necessary* connection between them. This is suggested, *e.g.* by the closing words of his first lecture.[34] A fair inference from some of his statements is that because rational findings of mental states necessarily rest on external evidence, *therefore* the test of liability must also be external. As noted, this inference is partially contradicted in Holmes' discussion of the "exceptions" concerning attempt, larceny, and so on. But the difficulties raised by these rules[35] dissolved in Holmes' conviction that the criminal law is non-moral, that expediency is its *ultima ratio.*

With regard to the question of evidence of other persons' minds, it is hardly necessary to emphasize that Holmes' discussion represents the reassertion of an ancient truth. It found elaborate expression in medieval thought where the importance of what went on in a man's "heart" was paramount: "Now man, the framer of human law, is competent to judge only of outward acts; because *man seeth those things that appear,* according to 1 Kings xvi. 7: while God alone, the framer of the Divine law, is competent to judge of the inward movements of wills. . . ."[36] This is reminis-

---

[34] *Id.* at 38, quoted in the text *supra.* This conclusion of the first lecture raises the following dilemma: if, as Holmes argues, the nature of law necessitates external standards and eliminates actual guilt, then early "law," which he holds was subjective, is not law; if the nature of law does not necessitate external standards, objective liability is not inevitable.

[35] "To argue that intent is discoverable only through behavior, and is therefore not so vital as represented to be, is a flagrant *ignoratio elenchi* for the *issue before us is not the means of discovery but the object to be discovered;* and the very fact that the one is an indicator of the other amply proves which is the more significant of the two." Roback, Behaviorism and Psychology 132 (1923). See 3 Holdsworth, H. E. L. 374-75 (1937); Stephen, General View of the Criminal Law of England 75-76 (1863).

[36] St. Thomas Aquinas, Summa Theologica, II-I, Q. 100, Art. 9. (8 Dominican Fathers' translation 138.) But St. Thomas elsewhere states that since some men are "prone to vice, and not easily amenable to words, it was necessary for such to be restrained from evil by force and fear, in order that, at least, they might desist from evildoing. . . ." *Id.* at Q. 95, Art. 1 reprinted in Hall, Readings in Jurisprudence 36-37 (1938). This implies that man can judge of the rela-

cent of a famous legal aphorism which has come to us from the end of the medieval period in Justice Brian's remark that, "The thought of man shall not be tried, for the devil himself knoweth not the thought of man."[37] But Justice Brian was refusing to apply a legal sanction in the absence of any conduct; he did not hold that *mens rea* cannot be reliably known. The traditional adherence of the common law to this common sense realism received a pithy reformulation by Justice Bowen one year after the publication of Holmes' *The Common Law,* in his observation that "the state of a man's mind is as much a fact as the state of his digestion."[38]

Holmes hardly discussed the epistemology of the traditional theory regarding knowledge of others' minds, but preferred to rest on what he regarded as "the very necessity of its [law's] nature" and the deliberate policy of the law — to maintain only an outward conformity to the rules. The two questions — the knowledge of others' mental states and the test of liability — are, of course, interdependent. Only if it is possible to know the actual state of others' minds can the rules refer to that. If such knowledge is available, we may then determine when the rules of liability have actual reference to mental states and are therefore "subjective," and when, if ever, they do not do that, but impose, instead, an "objective standard."

The epistemological problem is extremely difficult if it is treated in a rigorously logical fashion;[39] but if one recognizes the necessity to rely upon a degree of faith — such as underlies the acceptance of any empirical induction — the question becomes relatively simple. Human conduct that is associated causally (teleologically) with certain

---

tion of conduct to evil, that decisions based solely on what is external can be supported as rational evaluations of human conduct. Summa II-II, Q. 60, Art. 2. *Cf.* Michael and Wechsler, *A Rationale of the Law of Homicide,* 37 Col. L. Rev. 710-711 (1937).

[37] 2 Pollock & Maitland, The History of English Law 474 (2nd ed. 1923).

[38] Edington v. Fitzmaurice (1882), L. R. 29 Ch. Div. 459, 483.

[39] *E.g.* Alexander, *Other People's Experiences,* 51 Proc. Arist. Soc. (n. s.) 25 (1951).

harms proscribed by law is labelled "intentional" by triers of the material facts on the basis of their experience and knowledge of certain external data and the need to make sense of those events and actions. In the deliberate suiting of means to attain ends, "intention" designates a distinctive and essential aspect of such action. Given certain facts, we *must*, on the basis of our experience in a given culture, introspection, and the instant facts, conclude that any and every rational human being in those circumstances did or did not *intend* the results. Consequently, on the level of the elementary mental processes embodied in the adaptation of ordinary means to attain common ends, all rational human beings, and thus the defendant — barring mental or physical defects or other exceptional disability — may properly be said to have acted intentionally under circumstances where any normal one of them could be said to have acted intentionally. That is the rationale of the "reasonable man" test used as a *method of inquiry*.[40]

As stated, Holmes accepted the traditional view regarding the knowledge of other persons' states of mind. Others, notably the late Judge Jerome Frank, have seriously questioned the reliability of such knowledge, arguing that there is great disparity between findings regarding mental states and the actual mental states;[41] but Holmes did not press that viewpoint. He accepted the traditional legal theory that, although the validity of fact-finding, involving bias, faulty memory, perjury, etc., may be questioned, nonetheless, in the vast majority of the cases, the relevant external facts are "sufficiently" established; hence, the probabilities are high that the inference drawn from them in the above indicated way, *i.e.* by use of the "reasonable man" method, fits the mental state of the particular normal defendant on trial.

There is, to be sure, a very important lesson to be learned from the questions Holmes raised. If the criminal law is to

[40] See pp. 120-21, 162-63.
[41] See Frank, Courts on Trial (1949).

be administered humanely, officials must be ever conscious of the possibility of error which led medieval inquisitors to insist on nothing less than confession. It constitutes a permanent limitation on all claims to knowledge of other persons' minds. This is supported by the insight that language is frequently employed not as a vehicle to communicate facts but as a mask, deliberately to conceal or disguise them. There are also the marginal instances previously noted, where cultural differences, inexperience or some unknown ailment may effect a wide disparity between the judgments of the triers and the actual mental states. But, in the writer's opinion, the inevitable limitations on such knowledge do not support the dogmatic view that in the vast majority of findings, based on rational methods of investigation, there is no reasonably accurate correspondence.

In any case, it is sufficient for the present argument that Holmes did not rest his theory upon that so-called "skeptical" position. This, indeed, is what makes his theory so very interesting. He acknowledged that mental states can be discovered and, in the face of that, he maintained that this knowledge is irrelevant in modern penal law, and properly so! In sum, his theory challenges the ethics of penal law, not its epistemology.[42]

In the light of the above conclusion regarding knowledge of mental states, the distinctive phase of Holmes' theory — asserting the non-moral basis of modern penal law — may be more closely examined. As was suggested above, Holmes' theory of objective liability was the product of a Utilitarianism which held expediency not only the sole objective of all law but also a defensible, adequate one. He was thus close kin to Bentham and Austin. None of them saw any distinctive quality in criminal conduct; therefore, none felt the need for any justification of punishment in terms other than that of the utility of the sanction. But while Bentham and Austin were simply disinterested in exploring the pos-

---

[42] Holmes' position must also be distinguished from positivist theories of ethics. See *supra* note 2.

sibility that criminal harms were intrinsically immoral, Holmes grappled with the widely accepted ethical rationale of modern criminal law and deliberately repudiated it. In Holmes, formal and procedural criteria received less emphasis than in Austin, but his advocacy of expediency is more pronounced. He thus brought to the earlier Utilitarianism the full tide of modern social positivism, the biological version predominating.[43]

While Holmes was encouraging the acceptance of objective penal liability in this country, the leading contemporary English scholar of the criminal law was pursuing a different course. Stephen's *General View of the Criminal Law of England* had preceded Holmes' *The Common Law* by nineteen years and received the latter's careful attention; his *History of the Criminal Law* followed Holmes' book by two years. In the earlier work, Stephen distinguished the "popular" from the legal meaning of crime. In the former sense, a crime "means an act which is both forbidden by law and revolting to the moral sentiments of society."[44] In the latter, crimes are merely "acts forbidden by the law under pain of punishment."[45] The discussion shifts between these poles but, on the whole, it is clear that Stephen preferred the former. In the earlier book, he asserted that "the administration of criminal justice is based upon morality. . . . It is, therefore, absolutely necessary that legal definitions of crimes should be based upon moral distinctions. . . ."[46] His analysis of punishment in the *History* considerably re-enforced this position. It consists largely of a refutation of "[s]ome modern writers of eminence . . . [who] have been in the habit of regarding criminal law as being entirely

[43] In the writer's view, the greatest error regarding Holmes is to treat him as a systematic philosopher. In fact there were several Holmeses. The interpretation given in the text above expresses various aspects of the earlier Holmes, the legal scientist and historian. *Cf.* Fisch, *Justice Holmes, The Prediction Theory of Law, and Pragmatism*, 39 J. of Philos. 85 (1942); Wiener, Founders of American Pragmatism (1948).

[44] Stephen, A General View of the Criminal Law of England 3 (1863). Also, 1 H. Cr. L. 5 (1883).

[45] Stephen, *op. cit. supra* note 44, at 4. *Cf.* 1 H. Cr. L. 1.

[46] *Op. cit. supra* note 44, at 82. But *cf. id.* at 6.

independent of morality;"[47] and his discussion of criminal responsibility strongly supported his view.[48] Thus, while Stephen's interpretation of *mens rea* handicapped efforts to organize the criminal law, he was too thoroughly grounded in its principles to be misled by the theory of his brilliant American confrère.

THE CURRENT LAW

An appreciation of the ethical rationale of the principles of penal law places the entire question in a cogent perspective. It becomes possible then to appraise the ethical significance of "intention," "recklessness," and "negligence" with reference to penal liability, as was suggested in the preceding chapter. It is necessary, nextly, to consider the doctrines noted above, upon which Holmes particularly relied to sustain the full sweep of his theory. It may be first noted that in trying to refute the broad thesis that objective liability reigns everywhere in criminal law, one may be tempted to support an equally general, contradictory position. In the writer's view, however, the most defensible position, stated broadly, is that while the principles of the criminal law are potentially founded on moral culpability, some of the rules and doctrines, *as presently interpreted*, are not merely amoral, they are definitely invalid on moral grounds. This, of course, contaminates the current meaning of some of the principles since they are derived from the rules and doctrines. It is therefore not easy to describe the quality of current penal law in a single generalization, and

---

[47] 2 H. Cr. L. 79.

[48] *Id.* at 94-123.

A major difficulty involved in comparing Holmes and Stephen lies in the ambiguity of "morality." In both writers it sometimes means moral attitudes, mores or public opinion, and at other times it means moral principles. That Holmes recognized the distinction is apparent from his well-known observation that "The first requirement of a sound body of law is, that it should correspond with the actual feelings of the community, whether right or wrong." The Common Law 41 (1881). There is considerable agreement between Holmes and Stephen as to the correspondence of the criminal law and moral attitudes — both as to the fact of such general correspondence in the existing law and as to the desirability of that. The chief difference between them is that stated in the text.

we may better proceed to the consideration of the issues which Holmes raised.

Insofar as Holmes relied on the doctrines of necessity and *ignorantia juris*, it will be shown that his analysis was, at best, very inadequate. The general conclusion of his discussion of those doctrines, namely, that "public policy sacrifices the individual to the general good" was unwarranted; indeed, it was hardly relevant, as will be seen later.[49] Nor can it be doubted that the distinctions of modern penal law in terms of intention, recklessness and negligence, and the emphasis in many crimes, *e.g.* receiving stolen property and criminal fraud, on the defendant's personal knowledge, not only refer to actual mental states but that they also represent relevant ethical valuations. We may also immediately recognize a tacit admission in Holmes' statement that the law "takes no account of incapacities" short of infancy or madness, namely, that the law does recognize those incapacities. If expediency were the sole ground of criminal liability, would any such exception be allowed? Infants and insane persons are sometimes more destructive than sane adults. But their lack of normal mental capacity, *i.e.* the absence of an essential requirement of moral culpability, not expediency, accounts for their exculpation from penal liability.

Holmes' theory also ignores the necessary structure of modern rules of law, *i.e.* the necessity to rely on broad generalization [50] or, more specifically, it does not take account of relevant mitigating factors. Thus, while it is true that liability extends to the full range of the proscription, there are many degrees of liability within those limits. The avenues to the determination of degrees of guilt are provided not only by laws on parole, probation, suspended sentence and the like but also by the minimum-maximum penalties, reference to "first offender," "passion," and the like, written into the defining laws themselves. The clear implication of such far-ranging diverse sanctions for the

---

[49] See chapters 11 and 12 *infra*.
[50] Plato, Statesman 295.

same offense and of the different factual references is that individual differences, inhering in the particular personality, understanding, and situation are to be considered. The reasons for doubting the validity of Holmes' reliance upon the doctrines he cited in support of his theory will be discussed more fully in later chapters.

On the other hand, it must be recognized that Holmes' thesis that objective liability is imposed in important segments of penal law was quite correct, *e.g.* negligence, including current equivalent interpretations of "recklessness," and rules on provocation which ignore the defendant's actual state of mind as well as his individual limitations. As Holmes also pointed out, those rules permit no diminution of liability even in situations which provoke "reasonable" men, *i.e.* words alone are conclusively presumed not to constitute legal provocation. A few states and Britain have excluded this rule as unfair and it is also not unlikely that a study of the sentences and of the punishment actually administered in the other states would reveal considerable mitigation in such cases. Equally difficult to justify is the rule that provocation must be "reasonable." The same problem is presented with regard to "cooling time" which, again, is measured by the external standard of a "reasonable man." A related situation which Holmes did not discuss, is the requirement in the law of homicide, self-defense, and elsewhere, that ignorance or mistake of fact must be "reasonable."

Several striking cases reveal the invalidity of objective liability to support a finding of murder when the defendants were obviously defective "marginal normal" persons. The leading case in this country is *Fisher v. United States*[51] where the defendant, a dull-witted, obviously impaired person, who was a janitor in a library, killed the librarian under provocative circumstances. The killing took some minutes to complete, enough, *i.e.* for a "reasonable man" to have realized the dangerous nature of his conduct. The defense introduced substantial medical testimony not to

[51] 328 U. S. 463, 90 L. Ed. 1382, 66 S. Ct. 1318 (1946).

establish insanity, but such deterioration of personality as to exclude the premeditation required in first degree murder. The objective test of liability barred the way and the conviction of first degree murder was affirmed.[52]

Perhaps the corresponding English case is *Regina v. Ward*[53] where the defendant "admittedly a man of subnormal intelligence," after working hard all day and aggravated by stomach pains and ulcer, in a fit of anger violently shook the "always crying" child of his mistress, causing death. Counsel for the defendant argued that the objective test, then recognized regarding provocation, should not be applied here, where the issue was whether the defendant realized the serious nature of his act. Lord Goddard, however, in a very brief opinion, firmly supported objective liability: ". . . if the jury come to the conclusion that any reasonable person, that is to say, a person who cannot set up a plea of insanity, must have known . . . then that amounts to murder in law. . . ."[54] A commentator has remarked that this rule "leads to the odd result that a man may be hanged for being stupid, and not because he intended to kill."[55]

With reference to the current law on mistake, legal provocation and "cooling time," it should be noted that we

[52] Reform of the law has not been advanced in this country by its being urged in terms of "partial responsibility." In the writer's view, this is, at best, an awkward way of stating the subjective test of liability, and recognition of that would have far-reaching consequences. See *infra* chapter 13.

[53] Reg. v. Ward (1956), 1 Q. B. 351.

[54] *Id.* at 356. See also, Bedder v. Director of Public Prosecutions (1954), 2 All E. R. 801 where in the House of Lords the objective test was affirmed with reference to "provocation." Lord Simonds: "It was urged on your Lordships that the hypotetical reasonable man must be confronted with all the same circumstances as the accused . . . But this makes nonsense of the test. Its purpose is to invite the jury to consider the act of the accused by reference to a certain standard or norm of conduct and with this object the "reasonable" or the "average" or the "normal" man is invoked. If the reasonable man is then deprived in whole or in part of his reason, or the normal man endowed with abnormal characteristics, the test ceases to have any value." *Id.* at 804. But *cf.* Wilson v. Inyang (1951), 2 K. B. 799, 2 All E. R. 237, and Edwards, *Provocation and the Reasonable Man,* Crim. L. Rev. at 900 (1954).

[55] 72 L. Q. Rev. 167 (1956).

deal with persons who admittedly caused major harms. In the provocation cases, the issue is whether the crime is murder or manslaughter — the defendant admits a culpable homicide. In mistake of fact, the defendant admits commission of a harm, usually a major one, and he seeks exculpation by asserting a privilege, *e.g.* of self-defense, which is normally available to persons who are actually attacked. In these cases, the import of the law in most American states is that when a person intentionally inflicts a serious injury, he takes a great risk. Even less does a hot-tempered person who kills a human being, or an admitted offender who nourishes even a "reasonable" provocation for an unusually long time stimulate any strong desire to mete out justice.[56] Yet, on reflection, it must be recognized that the rules in these respects fall short of the moral standards generally prevailing in modern criminal law. They are understandable as emotional attitudes but they are ethically indefensible. And as regards negligence, even the above rationalizations cannot be invoked in penal law.[57] In the above instances, the criminal law in varying degrees imposes objective liability.

Unfortunately, Holmes' theory was not confined to those segments of the criminal law. Since, as we have seen, intentionality and motivation comprise the two essential components of any valid judgment of moral culpability, the exclusion of both of them from modern criminal law left only objective liability. The intriguing point in Holmes' theory is that instead of being profoundly disturbed by objective punitive liability, he embraced the "unmorality" of modern penal law *con amore*. The plain implications of the present analysis, especially the two preceding chapters, are, on the contrary, not only that the largest part of modern penal law is founded on moral principles but also and

---

[56] "It would seem to follow from your proposition [defendant's counsel's, that the defendant was of defective mental balance, though not insane] that a bad-tempered man would be entitled to a verdict of manslaughter where a good-tempered one would be liable to be convicted of murder." Avory, J., in The King v. Lesbini (1914), 3 K. B. 1118.

[57] *Supra* pp. 137-39.

equally that rules and doctrines which impose punitive sanctions despite the lack of culpability are unsound.

SUMMARY

"Objective" *liability* is not to be confused with the appraisal of the external evidence ("reasonable man" method) that must be relied upon to discover other persons' mental states.[58] In contrast to that, the "subjective" reference of the principle of *mens rea* connotes the personal guilt (moral culpability) of the defendant because it takes his actual state of mind as the basis for determining his liability. "Objective" liability ignores the defendant's actual state of mind and holds him liable to the standard of the "reasonable man." Such liability must also be contrasted with the objective ethical meaning of the principle of *mens rea* which normally implies personal guilt and, as will be further submitted shortly, also rests upon defensible ethical grounds even when it prevails over an individual's contradictory values, *i.e.* his conscience. The limitation of *mens rea* to intentionality and recklessness supports the ethics of personal guilt.

It was previously submitted that neither a defendant's personal ethics nor that of his group should supplant the objective meaning of the principle of *mens rea*. In this regard Holmes' perception of the objectivity of the penal law was quite sound. But the valid ground of this, it is suggested with great respect, is not expediency but the correctness of the community's freely derived values, as expressed in penal law, and also the concomitant necessity to preserve the principle of legality. This underlines one of the major differences between Holmes' theory and that presented in this book. In Holmes' theory, whenever penal law does not take account of subjective factors, it imposes non-moral, "objective" liability; and he approved this on grounds of expediency. In the writer's view, a sharp distinction must first be drawn between a defendant's factual knowledge (his ignorance or mistake of fact) and his ethical appraisal. As to the former,

[58] See *supra* pp. 120-21, 155.

Holmes' theory seems hardly relevant.   Factual mistake and ignorance should be recognized throughout penal law as a ground for exculpation; and where it is not recognized, that is to be regretted.

As to the latter, Holmes' theory would imply, *e.g.* that the imposition of penal liability upon a fanatic who followed his conscience was non-moral liability.   In the writer's view, the maintenance of the objective meaning of the principle of *mens rea* in the imposition of penal liability in such cases is not an instance of non-moral liability.   Instead, it signifies the paramount value of the principle of *mens rea* and the consequent sacrifice of the lesser value, exemplified in the marginal cases where an enlightened conscience is in advance of the community's values.   In most of the relevant cases, conscience is in error.   Not only fanatics but also many normal offenders rationalize their actions — their situations were "exceptional."   If they take the property of a corporation, the owners are rich and the taker's needs and virtues overbalance the loss to the stockholders.   Even in murder, perhaps especially there, since most murders occur in very intimate relationships, rationalization runs high.   One may grant the appeal of any conscientious offender in the tribunal of Judgment Day, when everything about his id, libido, unconscious motives and temptations as well as all the contributing limitations of society are fully known and perfectly appraised, and still insist that a human legal order, if it is to exist at all, must set its morals, expressed in penal law, above the wayward conscience of any individual.   This entails that consciousness of wrong-doing is not essential in *mens rea*.[59]   Especially in the light of the fallibility of any individual's judgment, *mens rea* must be given objective meaning — no man's or group's conscience can supersede the conscience of the community as that is expressed in its penal law.   This implies that actual fault must in marginal cases be subordinated to the objective meaning of the principle of *mens rea* and the conditions necessary to the maintenance of legality.

[59] See *supra* pp. 99-100, footnote 3.

The proper sphere of subjective liability, *i.e.* actual guilt, therefore concerns the whole vast dimension of fact — whether the defendant had a serious mental disease or was intoxicated, was actually provoked,[60] whether, despite the passage of reasonable time, he was actually in a passion when he killed and, certainly not least, whether he actually knew the material facts. What penal law now does to a large extent (and what it should do throughout its total range) is to make liability depend upon the actual state of the defendant's mind regarding the relevant facts. By reference to the vast majority of the cases *vis à vis* current penal law, this phase of subjective liability is far more important than the liability involved in an occasional challenge to the community's values that is both conscientious and enlightened.

Accordingly, as will be discussed later,[61] legal recognition of ignorance or mistake of fact, regardless of its unreasonableness, involves no contradiction of the ethics of the penal law. In the current law, in cases involving recklessness, as we have seen,[62] it is held that while actual knowledge of the material facts is required, *i.e.* the test of liability is "subjective" as to that, the estimate of the dangerousness of the situation must be treated objectively — if the "reasonable man" would have recognized the danger, that binds the defendant and he cannot show that, in fact, he was not aware of it. A similar question is raised regarding the omission of parents to summon medical assistance when their children are very sick. In these cases, the issue is heightened when the parents were intelligent persons who were doing the best they could to restore their children's health. They merely made the (criminal!) mistake of doubting medical science.[63] At any rate, they did not

---

[60] This is observed in second degree murder.

[61] *Infra* chapter 11 at note 25.

[62] Commonwealth v. Welansky, 316 Mass. 383, 55 N. E. 2d 902 (1944), discussed *supra* at 131.

[63] It is noteworthy that health statutes in most states exempt persons from various requirements on account of religion. There have been very few prosecutions for manslaughter, based on omission to summon a doctor, and no recent convictions known to the writer.

challenge the community's values, expressed in its penal law since there was no intention to kill or injure any human being and there was no conscious risk-taking in that direction. There was a factual mistake regarding a danger or, conceivably, greater factual knowledge than the medical man could or would provide. If this kind of ignorance or mistake of fact is not recognized as a defense, it must be on grounds other than that of incompatibility with the principle of *mens rea.*

The recommended restriction of the objectivity of penal liability to the ethical meaning of *mens rea,* to exclude contradictory values, would encounter considerable difficulty in the trial of certain cases. For example, there is a type of avowed factual ignorance in homicide cases where the defendants stoutly insist that it never occurred to them that shooting into a room occupied by several persons might have fatal results. Or, if they admit shooting at someone, they insist that they were excellent marksmen and intended only a minor flesh wound, not the death that followed. In many of these cases, the triers of the facts do not believe the defendants. In many other cases of alleged recklessness, the reported facts seem to support the plea that the defendant simply gave no thought to any possible danger.[64] In reading some of the reports, one can hardly escape the conclusion that the reason for adhering to the objective standard was not the difficulty of the fact-finding regarding the defendant's actual state of mind, but that the community would be outraged if someone who, *e.g.* had caused a number of deaths, escaped punishment. What the defendants did was so offensive to the triers, that they convicted. This is the irrational side of penal law; and the theorist can only elucidate the problem.

It should, of course, be borne in mind that since most defendants are "reasonable" men, both the objective method of fact-finding and the objective standard of liability function accurately and justly in most cases. In other words,

[64] See *supra* pp. 130-33.

although the defendant is directly and verbally held to the objective standard of liability, that standard in most cases also fits the defendant's actual ("subjective") state of mind. Again, given knowledge of the material facts, the determination of intentionality rests upon a subjective standard of liability because in the vast majority of simple means-end situations which comprise the relevant crimes, if any sane, sober adult ("reasonable man") would have intended the harm, it is very probable that the defendant actually intended it. In the usual run of cases, no question in that regard is even raised. But we must also remember that there are more complicated facts where insensitive persons may be reckless but not intentional homicides, and still others where the defendants were dull-witted but not actually reckless. This problem of the "marginal-normal" defendant is a very serious one since penal justice is not to be measured only by its statistical performance.

Yet, in current law, as we have seen, an objective standard of liability is imposed despite the requirement of recklessness; and many mistakes of fact, especially in homicide, assault and self-defense, must be "reasonable." Ordinary negligence still incurs liability in some corners of penal law, the felony-murder, misdemeanor-manslaughter rules are still law in almost all the United States, and there is the vast array of rules and regulations where strict penal liability is imposed. In homicide, defendants are held to the standard of "the reasonable man" as regards legal provocation and "cooling time;" and regardless of the fact that the defendant was mistaken or confused by alcohol or in a passion and so on, he is held criminally liable or criminally liable for a more serious crime than his actual mental state warrants. In other crimes, *e.g.* receiving stolen property, the test of liability in some states is not based upon the defendant's belief that the property was stolen.

The policy advocated in the above discussion is that actual guilt, not the standard of the "reasonable man," should be the test of penal liability. But (a) this test should not be subordinated to the "conscience" of offenders opposed to the major values of sound penal law; and (b) the subjective test should not be carried to a point where the principle of legality is undermined, *e.g.* by making motives material. This policy accords with the main thrust of the common law of crimes, and that is being further advanced, *e.g.* in the recent abolition of constructive homicide in Britain and in current tendencies regarding strict liability, that are revitalizing the principle of *mens rea.* Many subtle factors would enter into the implementation of this policy in various countries, *e.g.* the diverse standards of legality in different cultures,[65] which in some instances influence scholars to tolerate or perhaps even approve what others, including the writer, would regard as a very vague principle of legality.

If the validity of the suggested policy is granted "in principle," the only remaining issue concerns its feasibility. Is "marginal normality," *i.e.* the diminished competence of violators who are neither insane nor up to the standard of the "reasonable man," so difficult to determine in a courtroom that we are perforce obliged to retain objective liability even in penal law? The fact is, as has been suggested above, that actual mental states are constantly being determined in court at the present time. That a person was or was not actually in a state of passion when he killed, that the buyer of stolen goods actually believed they were stolen, that a confidence man knew he was misrepresenting or knew that he had no knowledge of the facts, that a defendant was grossly intoxicated or insane and is not malingering, how a "reasonable man" would have felt or acted and what he would have known or believed — these and many other difficult questions of fact are now adjudicated.[66] Since no one to the writer's knowledge is urging the abandonment

---

[65] Hall, *supra* note 2, at 111.

[66] "The instruction is in error also in stating that it must appear that the danger to the defendant was such that a reasonable person, under the same circumstances, would have been induced to believe, etc. The jury are not to determine what a reasonable man would have been induced to believe, but, what did the defendant at the time and under the circumstances, acting as a reasonable man, believe?" People v. Duncan, 315 Ill. 106, 112, 145 N. E. 810, 812 (1924). *Cf.* State v. Cope, 67 N. E. 2d 912 (Ohio, 1946).

of this law and practice, it may be assumed that by and large the results are satisfactory. Indeed, on the merits of the question, there is no apparent reason why it should be more difficult to discover whether persons like Fisher[67] and Ward[68] actually realized the seriousness of their conduct than it is to discover whether "the reasonable man" would have realized that. Without challenging the validity and necessity of "the reasonable man" standard as a method of inquiry, its use for that purpose does not warrant the continued exclusion of the above indicated areas from the general practice of determining actual mental states and fixing penal liability by reference to that. In the outrageous "depraved heart" homicides, some courts seemed eager to apply the test of "the reasonable man." Unfortunately, "righteous indignation" and sound penal policy do not always coincide; and it must be recognized, however regrettably, that the rule of subjective guilt, even within the above indicated limits, will largely remain an ideal.

Nonetheless, the path of penal theory is clear. The presumption should, of course, be that in the absence of a plea of insanity, the defendant is a "reasonable man." But just as is now the practice in many jurisdictions in cases of fraud, receiving stolen property and so on, the defendant would, under the suggested policy, be permitted to introduce evidence showing that in fact he did not know or realize, etc. As suggested, this will not eradicate the objective test entirely so far as factual questions are concerned, not only because the jury will be influenced by irrational factors but also because, in appraising the evidence of the defendant's actual state of mind, they will read into that their own experience of normal conduct and understanding. Yet, it can hardly be doubted that in many cases, the instructions given the jury, concerning the test they are to apply, have considerable influence. For example, in *Ward*, the jury, after three hours of considering their verdict, requested further instruction. The judge repeated his instruction con-

---

[67] *Supra* at 160.
[68] (1956) 1 Q. B. 351, *supra* at 161.

cerning "a reasonable being" and the jury quickly returned a verdict of murder.[69]

In view of the uncertainties which encumber fact-finding in this area and also because of the almost inevitable repugnance which a crassly indifferent harm-doer stimulates, one must be realistic about the prediction of changes that would follow a thorough-going rule of subjective liability as to factual questions, especially in the homicide cases. In the vast majority of the cases, nothing is said about any individual peculiarity which might entitle the defendant to special consideration. In those cases, a sound instruction would at least alert the jury to the "operative" facts, the actual mental state, whose existence they are required to determine; it might also check an inclination to convict on emotional grounds. And for a small minority of persons like Ward and Fisher, a thorough-going rule of subjective liability regarding the relevant *mens rea* would open the door to fair and otherwise defensible adjudication. Limited only by the ethical meaning of the principle of *mens rea* and the correlative preservation of the principle of legality, penal liability should be subjective.

[69] *Id.* at 353.

CHAPTER VI

CRIMINAL CONDUCT—THE EXTERNAL MANIFESTATION OF *MENS REA*

THE BASIC CONCEPTS

CRIMINAL conduct is described in terms of certain psychological concepts, *e.g.* thinking and acting; and relevant principles of criminal law provide the basic criteria for the analysis of that conduct. These traditional terms express the common sense "living psychology" of criminal law which, of course, has been influenced by the contemporary professional psychologies.[1] It will also be recalled that the meaning of each principle of criminal law is qualified by its relation to the other principles of criminal law;[2] and once crime is thus defined, *i.e.* by reference to the principles, certain conduct is within the scope of criminal theory. This conduct is the subject of the present chapter.

Many problems concerning the concepts and terms employed in the analysis of criminal conduct were discussed by Austin and Salmond, and their views have had considerable influence. Both use the term "act," but in very different senses. For Austin, an act is an expected movement which immediately follows a wish (volition) for that movement, *i.e.* an act is a voluntary movement; hence, to speak

---

[1] "That this same '*will*' is just nothing at all, has been proved (in my opinion) beyond controversy by the late Dr. Brown: Who has also expelled from the region of entities, those fancied beings called '*powers*' of which this imaginary '*will*' is one." 1 Austin, Lectures on Jurisprudence 424 (4th ed. 1879). *Cf.* 1 Locke, Essay Concerning Human Understanding, Bk. 2, ch. 21, sec. 5, 363-364 (1854).

[2] See chapter 1 *supra* and chapter 7 *infra*.

of a "voluntary act" is to use a superfluous adjective.[3] Austin sharply distinguished act from consequences. He states the case of a shooting and restricts "act" to "the muscular motions by which I raise the weapon; point it at your head or body, and pull the trigger."[4] "The contact of the flint and steel, the ignition of the powder, the flight of the ball . . . the wound and subsequent death . . ."[5] are the consequences of this act. It is noteworthy that Austin only mentions circumstances. "[E]very act," he says, "is . . . also attended by *concomitants*, which are styled its *circumstances*."[6] Literally interpreted, this implies that act does not include circumstances; in any case, we may infer that means employed by the actor are "circumstances,"[7] and even fingers used to lift a book are "a mean or instrument." Austin's very narrow definition of "act" was adopted by Holmes[8] and, in effect, in the American Law Institute's Torts Restatement.[9]

At the opposite extreme is Salmond's very wide definition. For him, "act" includes (1) the offender's bodily movements or omissions *and* (2) the accompanying circumstances *and* (3) the consequences.[10] Referring also to a shooting, he states that the circumstances include the facts that "the rifle is loaded and in working order, and that the person

[3] A volition, in Austin's meaning, is the *only* kind of wish which is immediately followed by the expected movement.

[4] *Op. cit. supra* note 1, at 427.

[5] *Ibid.*

[6] *Id.* at 433.

[7] *Id.* at 425.

[8] The Common Law 91 (1881).

[9] "The word 'act' includes only the external manifestation of the actor's will. It does not include any of the effects of such manifestation no matter how direct, immediate and intended . . . if the actor intentionally strikes another, the act is only the movement of the actor's hand and not the contact with the other's body immediately established thereby." Restatement, Torts § 2, comment *c* (1934). This is adopted in the A. L. I. Model Criminal Code, Tent. Draft No. 4 at 122 (1955). *Cf.* Welzel, Das Deutsche Strafrecht 28 (2nd ed. 1949); Maurach, Deutsches Strafrecht, Allgemeiner Teil 195 (1954).

[10] Salmond, Jurisprudence 383 (7th ed. 1924). *Cf.* Mezger, Strafrecht, Lehrbuch 95 (3rd ed. 1949).

killed is in the line of fire."[11] Consequences include "the fall of the trigger, the explosion of the powder, the discharge of the bullet, its passage through the body of the man killed, and his death,"[12] which is practically identical with Austin's consequences. But, as stated, for Salmond, circumstances and consequences as well as the actor's bodily movements or omissions are all included in "act." The pertinent question is whether "act" should be narrowly circumscribed, in Austin's direction, or widely defined in the manner of Salmond. Related to this is the question whether "circumstance" has an independent legally material status.[13]

That these issues are not merely verbal becomes clear when one considers the place of negligent behavior in the above definitions. For Austin, intention and volition "are inseparably connected" in an act.[14] But negligence implies the absence of both of them[15] and, thus, of any act.[16]

The contrast in Salmond's discussion is striking. For him, although an "act is an event subject to the control of the will, . . . it is not essential that this control should be actually exercised."[17] And "if the will is dormant, the act is unintentional. . . ."[18] Salmond rejects Austin's narrow definition of "act" because, "Intention is not a necessary condition of legal liability, and therefore cannot be an essential element in those acts which produce such liability."[19] Thus, whatever one may think of the logic of this

[11] *Ibid.*

[12] *Ibid.*

[13] This question is discussed *infra* chapter 7.

[14] *Op. cit. supra* note 1, at 427. But *cf.* chapter 4 *supra* at notes 12-15.

[15] In negligence and "heedlessness," "the party is inadvertent." *Id.* at 440.

[16] *Id.* at 427. So, too, "events which are not *willed* are not *acts.*" *Id.* at 432.

[17] *Op. cit. supra* note 10, at 382.

[18] *Id.* at 383. He resolves any doubt regarding his definition by stating, "If I am negligent . . . and kill someone . . . I am criminally liable for manslaughter. . . . " *Id.* at 386.

[19] *Id.* at 382. The difference cannot be explained by the supposition that Austin, in his analysis of "act," had penal liability in mind, while

rejection of Austin's position, it is clear that in Salmond's view some acts are "unintentional;" they are "not the result of any determination of the will."[20] That raises the question, in addition to those noted above, whether "act" should be restricted to voluntary movements or defined more widely to include negligent, *i.e.* inadvertent, behavior.

This question also involves omissions. Austin first held that an omission, unlike a forbearance, "is not the consequence of an act of the will but of that state of the mind which is styled 'negligence,' and implies the absence of will and intention."[21] Thus "act" excluded negligent omissions. Then Austin encountered difficulties precisely at the point which has given rise to the greatest problem concerning "act," namely, that posed by (voluntary) forbearance. He first recognized "internal acts" as imperceptible "determinations of the will;"[22] and he said, "A Forbearance is a determination of the will, *not* to do some given external act."[23] It is "the *not* doing it *in consequence of a determination of the will.*"[24]

Later, however, Austin abandoned this traditional view of "internal act" which, he decided, needlessly obscured the subject.[25] Since he had restricted volition to wishes immediately followed by bodily movements, he was led to conclude that, " 'To will a forbearance' (or 'to will the absence or negation of an act') is a flat contradiction in terms." "It follows from the nature of volitions, that *forbearances* from acts are not *willed,* but *intended.*"[26] "When I forbear from an act," he conceded, "I *will.* But I will an

Salmond had only civil liability or both penal and civil liability in mind. Salmond's text, *e.g.* at 380, where he specifies that negligence is included in *mens rea*, excludes this supposition. Both writers apparently had only criminal law in view.

20 *Ibid.*

21 *Op. cit. supra* note 1, at 377.

22 *Id.* at 376.

23 *Id.* at 377.

24 *Ibid.*

25 "The term 'volitions,' or the term 'determinations of the will,' sufficiently denotes the objects to which I applied the term '*internal acts*'. . . . " *Id.* at 433.

26 *Id.* at 437.

act *other* than that from which I forbear . . . I *intend* [expect] the forbearance."[27] He illustrates this by noting that if, instead of keeping an appointment, he goes to the theater, he intends the forbearance, but does not will it.[28] The outcome was that by failing, finally, to hold that forbearance was volitional, he was unable to provide a common criterion of criminal conduct.

This, Salmond quickly detected. He criticizes the restriction of "act" to overt movements on the ground that that leaves us "without a name for the genus." In his view, there are both "negative acts" and "internal acts." But his inclusion of negligent movements and omissions within "act" also leaves us without an actual genus and only subsumes quite different data under a single term. There are other questionable aspects of Salmond's use of "act:" "To think is an internal act; to speak is an external act. To work out an arithmetical problem in one's head is an act of the mind. . . ."[29] This obliterates a distinction between cognition and volition which, as will appear, is important to observe in legal analysis. The widely divergent meanings of "act" expressed by Austin and Salmond have permeated the Anglo-American professional literature, and the consequent ambiguities raise serious obstacles in the analysis of problems and the construction of criminal theory.

To state the problem in relation to current law, we begin with the usual case of overt bodily movements such as occur in most crimes and, following Austin and Holmes, have no difficulty in allocating them to "act." Then we proceed to solicitation and, influenced perhaps by behaviorist psychology as well as the decisions, we extend "act" to include the talking.[30] Mere possession, *e.g.* of stolen

---

[27] *Ibid.* " . . . an intention is not a volition. . . . " *Id.* at 423. It will be recalled, *supra* at 110-111, that the writer's view of intention differs sharply from Austin's conception.

[28] *Id.* at 437.

[29] *Op. cit. supra* note 10, at 381-82.

[30] It has long been established that talking is a form of conduct and may be criminal, as in solicitation to commit a crime, *e.g.* The

goods, gives rise to serious questions. And, finally, there are many crimes where, in ordinary parlance, the defendant did nothing. These data, all of them legally material, are not included in the definition that "act" means *only* external voluntary muscular movement, as Holmes suggested.[31]

The restriction of "act" to overt movement was probably first suggested by a doctrine of political ideology—that distinguishing law from morals. The older writers had treated the requirement of an act in connection with treason statutes which ran in terms of merely "compassing or imagining;" the principle was established that "men were not to be tried for their thoughts." The early date of its enunciation,[32] when there was hardly any theory of criminal law, is additional proof that this was not employed as a scientific generalization. Moreover, the consequent use of "negative act" which this stimulated, increases the difficulties of penal theory. It not only suggests that there are pertinent substantive differences, but it also involves moot issues of penal liability, *e.g.* regarding negligence. It thus obscures the fact that no relevant principle has been expressed. In sum, the problem for current criminal theory is: Which terms and concepts best accord with the existing penal law and also take significant, coherent account of the various material facts indicated above, *i.e.* overt movement, talk, possession and omission?

The problem is to overcome the limitations, especially the ambiguities, that abound in current usage: First, "act" (or "action," which is sometimes used as a synonym) is often associated particularly or wholly with overtness, *i.e.* with observable movements, whereas what is needed is a concept which also includes voluntary omissions (forbearances). Secondly, "act" is sometimes employed to mean voluntary movements, or to mean voluntary movements and their con-

---

King v. Higgins (1801), K. B., 2 East 5, 102 Eng. Rep. 269, obtaining property by false pretenses and many political offenses.

[31] "An act is always a voluntary muscular contraction, and nothing else." Holmes, *supra* note 8.

[32] Hales v. Petit (1562), 1 Plowd. 253, 259, 259a, 75 Eng. Rep. 387, 397.

sequences or, still again, to mean voluntary and involuntary movements,[33] the concomitant circumstances and the consequences. And, finally, "act" is frequently identified with "conduct."[34] Analysis is obviously handicapped by such ambiguity and diverse terminology. It is therefore necessary either to discontinue the use of "act" entirely or, if one prefers, to define it in precise, analytically helpful terms. At this point of the discussion, the writer prefers the first, more drastic solution. Later, if an apt concept is precisely delineated, one may prefer to employ the term "act" in that sense.

Accordingly, to state directly one of the principal conclusions reached, it is suggested that "effort" be employed, at least initially, to refer to both overt voluntary movement and (voluntary) forbearance. Let us note first, the reasons for preferring "effort"[35] to certain competing concepts other than "act." "Behavior" is not helpful in the elucidation of penal liability because it has a mechanistic connotation. What is needed is a term which distinguishes mere bodily movements, caused, *e.g.* by an outside physical force or exhibited in an epileptic seizure, as well as negligent movements from *voluntary* movements and forbearances. "Behavior" should be used to designate the inadvertent movements and omissions.

This also implies that "behavior" should not be used as a synonym of "conduct." The use of "conduct" has been approved by legal writers, at least since Bentham,[36] for another reason. Unlike "act," it does not emphasize overtness; hence it may well be used to include (voluntary) forbearance. But the fact to be emphasized here is that "conduct" also has a well established wider meaning which includes manifested effort ("act") and an accompanying conscious mental state. That is the meaning that can be

[33] Perkins, Criminal Law 514 (1957).

[34] See *infra* p. 178.

[35] Holmes spoke of "inward effort." *Supra* note 8, at 54; and T. Parsons speaks of " . . . the energy or 'effort' factor of action processes. . . . " Parsons, The Social System 4 (1951).

[36] Bentham, A Fragment on Government xliv, n. (1823).

put to good use in constructing the legal definition of criminal conduct; and it also avoids the common practice of using "act" and "conduct" as synonyms. This usage is unfortunate, even if it is difficult to avoid, because it is often necessary to distinguish the volitional side of conduct, the effort, from its cognitive side; and apt terms are required to do that.[37]

In the above discussion of "act" the writer has criticized Salmond's very wide definition because of the inclusion of negligent behavior; and his failure to distinguish, in his terms, muscular movement from consequences will be discussed later.[38]

It is equally important to emphasize that the implied preference for Austin's and Holmes' view of "act" is intended only *vis à vis* Salmond's definition. Actually, the Austin-Holmes' definition, which would separate the muscular movement even from the means employed, errs in the opposite direction. That extremely narrow meaning of "act" is also at odds with ordinary usage; and no aid to analysis or theory, apparent to the writer, is served by it. Indeed, it seems, unfortunately, to have stimulated essays supporting the view that circumstances occupy an independent status.[39]

On the other hand, the inclusion of the means in the meaning of "act," although an improvement upon Austin's definiton, leaves troublesome questions unanswered. The principal difficulty is that there is no natural point of fact in situations relevant to criminal law, where act can be separated from effect. Both the current difficulty and the solution of this problem, it is suggested, are determined by the fact that penal law is concerned with means-end situations; hence, it is impossible to isolate the one from the other or to draw a line and have act or conduct (means) [40]

---

[37] *E.g.* in analysis of "control" in mental disease, the case where A is pushed against X and the problem of coercion.

[38] See chapter 7.

[39] *Ibid.*

[40] "Conduct" and "act" are distinguished in the text immediately following. As will appear, "act" (manifested effort) has a narrower meaning than "conduct" which means the manifestation of the entire relevant *mens rea*.

on one side of it and effect (end) on the other. For the essence of a means-end situation is precisely that means can be defined *only by reference to end*, and end, *only by reference to means*. The means precedes the end; and it also seems evident to common sense that the conduct causes the effect, and not vice versa.[41] The major point, as stated, is that the definition of either must refer to the other.[42]

In order to elucidate "conduct" as a term of penal theory, we must next recall that *mens rea* itself includes a volitional element which is distinguishable from the concomitant thinking or knowing. We must, therefore, also distinguish the volitional character (the effort) of the intention from the further effort that is required to incur criminal liability. The effort represented in the former is the traditional "internal movement of the will." The additional effort required in criminal liability is *manifested effort* which actualizes the *mens rea* in the external world, *i.e.* in conduct, causing a proscribed harm. In sum, *mens rea* includes the state of knowing or believing, with reference to the material facts and, also, the internal effort of intention, while criminal conduct is *mens rea* manifested by a further effort evidenced in the production of a penal harm.[43]

Criminal conduct is also described in terms of the principle of concurrence. Its function is to distinguish *criminal* conduct from innocent conduct by making it quite clear that the former expresses a *mens rea*. The principle of concurrence therefore emphasizes the *fusion* ("concurrence") of the essential elements, *i.e.* of the *mens rea* and the additional effort that manifests the *mens rea* in criminal conduct. The internal *mens rea*, held in check, is by that extra effort externalized. The floodgates are removed and the internal *mens rea* is expressed in conduct. It is manifested by an effort of the same genus as, but additional to, the effort already functioning in the intention of the *mens rea*. The additional effort may be viewed as the projection

---

[41] See *infra* chapter 8.
[42] See *infra* chapter 7.
[43] *Cf.* Holland, The Elements of Jurisprudence 107 (12th ed. 1917).

forward into conduct of the already existent action-thought of *mens rea*.

In the analysis of both *mens rea* and criminal conduct, the mental functions to be distinguished are cognition and volition. Thinking is contemplative, wide-ranging and not essentially purposive, *e.g.* there is idle curiosity. Effort, on the other hand, is narrow, specific and externally directed, *i.e.* effort is end-seeking or end-hazarding. It may be directed to a present purpose, *e.g.* listening to a dull lecture or it may, while internal, be directed towards a future goal. In all its aspects, effort is positive and operative; and this suggests that there is no such thing as a negative effort and that "negative act," in a sense other than voluntary forbearance, is fictitious. Effort brings one into contact with the external world which is discovered in the resistance met, and this develops an awareness of one's self.

However difficult it may be to describe and analyze criminal conduct adequately, the salient fact to be kept in view is that a *mens rea* does not incur penal liability despite the fact that *mens rea* is not merely thinking. As stated, it includes at least the psychic effort of an intention (decision, resolution) to effect a proscribed harm. This effort is clearly distinguishable from the thinking and knowing which are also included in *mens rea*, *e.g.* the knowledge of certain facts in criminal fraud and receiving stolen property. The volitional aspect of *mens rea* has a time-ticket imposed on its actualization; its emergence into external reality must follow its incidence, if only by a few moments. What is required to incur penal liability is that the *mens rea* be thus manifested in criminal conduct.

THE LOGIC OF THE CASE-LAW

Since criminal conduct is the actualization of *mens rea*, analysis of that conduct must begin with *mens rea*. The logic of the case-law can therefore be specified as follows: (1) If cognition is lacking, there is no *mens rea*, and that is the end of the matter. (2) If cognition has functioned, but there is no internal effort, *i.e.* no intention, *mens rea* is lacking for that reason; and that is likewise the end of the matter. (3) If there was a *mens rea, i.e.* a fusion of cognitive functions with the internal effort of intention, analysis centers on the actualization of the *mens rea*. The occurrence of a proscribed harm caused by the defendant is the condition of the actualization of the *mens rea*, the principal qualification being the attempt doctrine regarding preparation. (4) Finally, as a corollary of the preceding category, there may be a *mens rea* and also prior or subsequent effort by the defendant which caused some sort of injury. But there was no criminal conduct because "concurrence" was lacking, *i.e.* the relevant *mens rea* was not expressed in the defendant's conduct.

We have been discussing effort as a function of volition and an essential component of criminal conduct. Many legal problems turn on the meaning of "volition," usually expressed in the adjective, "voluntary," and a large part of this book, especially the discussion of the doctrines relevant to *mens rea* (coercion, necessity, mistake, etc.), will be devoted to the elucidation of that term. That *mens rea* is a condition (the internal state) of the required manifested effort is implied in cases where an epileptic seizure occurred just prior to the commission of the harm in issue;[44] and the same problem is raised where a somnambulist or a person having a nightmare has committed a harm.[45] In the absence of cognition there may be movement or behavior, but there is no *effort*, internal or external. On the other hand, awareness alone, "cognition," does not render a movement voluntary, *e.g.* one may be pushed by someone or blown by a tornado and know perfectly well that he is moving and will collide with another person, but that does not make the movement voluntary. Such behavior represents no effort *by* the moving person, *i.e.* as Aristotle put it, the principle of movement is not *in him*. Typically, there-fore, in the first class of cases noted above, where death was

[44] People v. Freeman, 61 Cal. App. 2d 110, 142 P. 2d 435 (1943). People v. Decina, 2 N. Y. 2d 133, 138 N. E. 2d 799 (1956) ; 43 Cornell L. Q. 117 (1957).

[45] R. v. Dhlamini, 1955 (1) S. A. 120 (T).

caused during an epileptic seizure[46] or somnambulism, earlier criminal conduct is sought, upon which penal liability may be rested.[47] If that is excluded, judicial analysis in such cases proceeds from the lack of *mens rea* because of the absence of either cognition or volition or both of them, to the legal characterization of the external movement and situation, *i.e.* to the conclusion that there was no criminal conduct and no penal harm.

While, as seen, the absence of *mens rea* excludes manifested effort ("act") and therefore, criminal conduct, there may be a *mens rea* that was not manifested; indeed, this must happen very frequently—whenever a prospective offender abandons his criminal intention. In the case of certain young men who went to a public dance, one of them, armed with a revolver, engaged in a fight, shot and killed someone and was duly convicted of the homicide. Then, his companions were indicted as accessories before-the-fact. But the prosecution failed to prove that any assistance or encouragement was given prior to or accompanying the homicide. The defendants were present, they saw what was happening and they undoubtedly favored their friend's cause. They may have intended to assist him or even to kill the deceased, themselves. Nonetheless, they were held not guilty because "a mere mental assent to or acquiescence in the commission of a crime by one who did not procure or advise its perpetration, who takes no part therein, gives no counsel and utters no word of encouragement to the perpetrator, however wrong morally, does not in law constitute such a person a participant in the crime."[48]

[46] State v. Gooze, 14 N. J. Super. 277, 81 A. 2d 811 (1951); People v. Decina, *supra* note 44. See *infra* chapter 14.

[47] People v. Higgins, 5 N. Y. 2d 607, 159 N. E. 2d 179 (1959); Edwards, *Automatism and Criminal Responsibility*, 21 Mod. L. Rev. 375 (1958).

[48] Anderson v. State, 66 Okl. Cr. 291, 91 P. 2d 794 (1939), quoting from Moore et al. v. State, 4 Okl. Cr. 212, 111 P. 822, 824 (1910). In a leading Indiana case, the court said that one cannot be guilty of murder "who by neither word or gesture has done anything to contribute to the commission of the homicide nor to assist, encourage, or evince approval of it at or before the fact. . . . " Clem v. State, 33 Ind. 418, 432 (1870).

In *Levering,*[49] the only witness against the defendant, charged with the murder of his wife, had been informed by him of his homicidal intention and had seen him administer poison to the deceased. The issue was whether this witness was an accomplice whose testimony therefore required corroboration. This was decided in the negative on the ground that an accomplice "must do something; must take some part; must perform some act, or owe some duty to the person in danger that makes it incumbent upon him to prevent the commission of the crime."[50]

In such cases as *Anderson* and *Levering,* which recall comments by Brian, J., Blackstone and other classical writers,[51] there was no question of negligence, accident, intoxication, insanity, coercion, etc. The defendant was a normal person in a normal condition, and he understood what was going on. Nor, as is suggested in some of the classical texts, is there merely a practical reason for exculpation, namely, that it is impossible for any mortal to know another person's mind. There may be a voluntary confession or other equally persuasive evidence, *e.g.* in many cases of preparation to commit a crime there is not the slightest doubt regarding the *mens rea.* The decisive factor in this type of case is that it is not necessary to settle the question of *mens rea.* For even on the assumption that there was a *mens rea,* a material element is lacking, namely, the effort of manifesting the *mens rea* in the external world (beyond the stage of preparation).

In sum, *mens rea* includes relevant cognition, *i.e.* knowledge of the material facts, and an internal effort, "movement of the will;" and the additionally required manifested effort ("act") must be established by relevant evidence, different from and beyond that which establishes the *mens rea.* This evidence consists of the occurrence of a legally proscribed harm under conditions which make it

---

[49] Levering v. Commonwealth, 132 Ky. 666, 117 S. W. 253 (1909).
[50] *Id.* at 677, 257.
[51] "The thought of man is not triable. . . . " Y. B. (1477) P. 17 E. 4. 2a pl. 2. *Cf.* Bl. Com. Bk. IV, 21.

imputable to the offender. What was previously his internal *mens rea* became, through an additional effort, manifested in criminal conduct which caused the harm. That additional effort, judged in relation to the harm, is the manifested effort of criminal conduct.[52] As has already been suggested above, that manifested effort, which includes voluntary overt movement and, as will appear, voluntary forbearance, may be termed an "act."[53]

One of the persistent difficulties handicapping the analysis of relevant problems is the confusion of "act" in an ordinary sense with the technical meaning of that term. This is reflected in diverse uses of "act" which is extremely difficult to avoid. A current suggestion to clarify the case-law is to the effect that there are degrees of *mens rea,* ranging from "full *mens rea*" to some modicum of it; and, as was indicated in the preceding discussion, this would presumably affect the meaning of "act" and "conduct." While this suggestion provides helpful initial insight, considerable study is required to test and implement it, if it is validated.

This is not easily done by reference to the cases. For example, if an act is a function of volition, there is no act if the volition did not function. But the adjective "wilfully" is sometimes used, especially in strict liability regulations, merely to exclude completely unconscious movement;[54] and despite the defendant's innocence, it is nonetheless said in the decisions that he acted because he "intended" to do what he did. Again, where the defendant innocently shipped misbranded articles from his establishment, that is said to be an act, although he did not know they were misbranded.[55] This usage raises serious difficulties because it is interpreted to mean that the defendant acted with some sort of "diminished *mens rea.*" In fact,

---

[52] " . . . one should accentuate the distinction between the act of will in the sense of choice and the act of will in the sense of voluntary activity and the control of conduct." Moore, The Driving Forces of Human Nature and Their Adjustment 325 (1948).

[53] "Internal act" refers to the "movement of the will" accompanied by an internal physical effort. See the text *infra* at note 99.

[54] See Edwards, *Mens Rea* in Statutory Offenses (1955).

[55] See *infra* chapters 10 and 15 at note 52.

for reasons to be discussed later,[56] such innocent conduct lies beyond the range of penal law. There are other uncertainties which confuse the meaning of "act" within the sphere of penal law, *e.g.* it is said that the defendant acted when he killed the man whom he mistakenly thought was about to shoot him. Certainly, it is customary to say that a person acted in ignorance of the facts. On the other hand, this is inconsistent with the assumption that knowledge of the relevant facts is necessary to the exercise of volition, *i.e.* to the existence of an act. Nor can this use of "act" be lightly dismissed, for it is compatible with a sound doctrine of *ignorantia facti* and the rule of liability regarding, *e.g.* movements in an epileptic seizure. This indicates that the above question regarding the meaning of "act" is far from being merely verbal. There is also a problem regarding coercion because, although that seems antithetical to (voluntary) action, some harms committed under coercion are criminal. One may hardly expect that a consistent set of terms, which took precise account of the various distinctions, would be quickly adopted and uniformly employed. But a step towards the solution of this problem might start with the postulate that "act," as a legal term, be taken to imply knowledge of the material facts.

THE PRINCIPLE OF CONCURRENCE

The remaining step in the above indicated stages of analysis of criminal conduct concerns situations where there was a *mens rea* and an act and, also, a harm of some sort, but still no penal liability because an additional material element was missing, namely, the fusion of the legally material thought and effort in conduct, which Anglo-American criminal law designates as "concurrence."[57] The principle of

---

[56] *Cf.* Aristotle, Eth. III, 1, 1110b 17-23; III, 5, 1113b.

[57] "Intelligence and will act and react on one another, or rather, since even to say this is to reify them too much, the whole man, in virtue of certain judgements which he has made and certain desiderative tendencies which he has, both judges that a certain end is the most worth pursuing, and decides to pursue it." Ross, Foundations of Ethics 194 (1939).

See also, chapter 14 *infra*, on intoxication. In Sabens v. United

concurrence requires that the *mens rea* (the internal fusion of thought and effort) coalesce with the additional manifested effort ("act"), that they function externally as a unit to comprise criminal conduct. As was previously stated, this is a way of making certain that the defendant's conduct was criminal, *i.e.* that his conduct actually expressed a *mens rea*.

For example, last week D decided to kill X. Today, they are both climbing an Alpine mountain, D's foot slips and injures X, the climber below, who loses his hold and falls to his death; and D's evil intention is discovered. The principle of concurrence bars the addition of the *mens rea* to the physical movement to effect a mechanical "sum" of criminal conduct. This is anything but a technicality. Instead, the requirement of the integration or "concurrence" of *mens rea* and manifested effort ("act") prescribes an essential quality of morally significant conduct—the conduct met in life-situations, which causes *criminal* harms.[58] Thus, the function of the principle of concurrence—analogous to that of legality in its corollaries, *ex post facto* and the strict construction of penal statutes—is to make it quite clear that criminal *conduct*, not thinking or movement or both of them unrelated to each other, is required to incur criminal liability.

In the light of the significance of this principle,[59] the relevant case-law can be placed in a proper perspective. Many of the reported cases concern crimes against property. There are cases where the defendant, thinking he had a legal right to do so, took a chattel, later discovered he had made a mistake, and then converted it. It is uniformly held that the taking and asportation were not larceny since there was

---

States, 40 App. D. C. 440, 441 (1913), where the trial judge instructed the jury that a verdict of first degree murder could be returned if they found that the defendant formed the intention to kill and in pursuance of that design "voluntarily made himself drunk for the purpose of nerving himself for the accomplishment of the design" etc., the conviction of first degree murder was reversed.

[58] See chapter 8 *infra*.

[59] " . . . liability becomes a voluntary deliberate acknowledgment that deeds are our own, that their consequences come from us." Dewey, Human Nature and Conduct 316 (1930).

no *animus furandi* at that time;[60] nor is the later conversion larceny, despite the concomitant *mens rea*, since there was no trespass to possession at that time. Larceny by bailee and embezzlement were invented to make that conduct criminal, *i.e.* laws were formulated in terms of that concurrence.

In the expansion of the law of larceny, the principle of concurrence influenced the invention of other ideas to cope with new social problems. Thus, "breaking bulk," applied in the *Carrier's Case,*[61] rendered it possible to find both a "trespass" to possession and also its concurrence with the *mens rea.* Similarly, the invention of the notion of custody, distinguished from that of possession, made it possible to find not only that a subsequent conversion by a servant was a trespass, but also that it concurred with the required *mens rea.*[62] And the invention of "continuing trespass" and its application to cases where a taking was intentional but not criminal, made it possible to find the concurrence of a subsequent *animus furandi* with the required act.[63]

While it is evident that the principle of concurrence was not strictly observed in some of the above decisions, it is also true that the main function it is designed to perform, stated above, and the ethical import of the principle were preserved. As *White,*[64] *e.g.* shows, there is very little, if any, social or moral difference between simple larceny and a wilful, though non-criminal trespass followed by a conversion with criminal intention. In other similar cases, there was also, somewhere along the line, the concurrence of a

---

[60] Wilson v. State, 96 Ark. 148, 131 S. W. 336 (1910), King v. State, 15 Ala. App. 67, 72 S. 552 (1916). Ransom v. State, 22 Conn. 153 (1852) concerned a finder of lost property as did Brewer v. State, 93 Ark. 479, 125 S. W. 127 (1910).

[61] Hall, Theft, Law and Society ch. 1 (2nd ed. 1952).

[62] Holbrook v. State, 107 Ala. 154, 18 S. 109 (1895).

[63] *Cf.* Wilson v. State, *supra* note 60, where the original trespass was innocent and the principle of concurrence barred larceny, and Commonwealth v. James White and another, 11 Cush. 483 (Mass. 1853) where the original trespass was wilful, but not criminal, and the court invoked "continuing trespass" to find the "concurrence" in the subsequent conversion with criminal intent.

[64] *Ibid.*

mens rea with a wrongful act. In most of these cases, the judicial problem was technical and verbal—to subsume such harmful conduct within the established definitions of specific crimes without impairment of the principles of penal liability. In the process of doing this, there was undoubtedly some expansion of the scope of the principle of concurrence and *pro tanto* of that of legality. But this did not violate the central purpose of the principle of concurrence, not to impose criminal liability for harmful, but morally innocent, behavior by locating a prior or subsequent *mens rea* and "transferring" that to the behavior.

Considerations similar to those which **enlarged the principle** of concurrence in the above cases of crimes against property influenced the decision of certain homicide cases. In *United States v. Van Schaick et al.*[65] many passengers on a boat were drowned, and one cause of the great loss of life was the defectiveness of the lifebelts. In a prosecution for manslaughter against the captain and the owners of the boat, the fact that the latter were not on the boat (or, by hypothesis, that the captain himself was absent) when it sank was held irrelevant. "The nature of the offense," said the court, "precluded a single act of the company or master . . . The duty [to use due care for the safety of the passengers] was continuing."[66] It was held that the culpable forbearance "continued" up to the time the harm occurred.

In such cases there is no need to resort to a fiction of "continuing" forbearance in order to satisfy the principle of concurrence; indeed, this tends to obscure its meaning. If an offender intentionally or recklessly created a dangerous situation which later causes a proscribed harm, liability attaches to his conduct, *i.e.* to the "concurrence" of the *mens rea* and the manifested effort ("act"), not to that of the *mens rea* and the harm. The fact that a proscribed harm is an essential condition of the criminal conduct does not alter

[65] 134 F. 592, 604 (1904).
[66] *Ibid.*

the material components of the conduct or the reference of the principle of concurrence to it.[67]

In one of those rare cases which greatly stimulate academic disputation, a medical student, after an affair with a young lady who became pregnant, gave her a large dose of cocaine in the state of Ohio, intending to kill her then and there. Later, he transported what he believed was her dead body into Kentucky, where he performed a decapitation. The medical evidence established that the young woman was actually alive in Kentucky until the decapitation. Despite the Kentucky court's acceptance of the fact that the defendant believed she was dead when he performed the decapitation, he was held guilty of murder in that state.[68] He was certainly guilty of an attempt to murder in Ohio. But the mistake of fact in Kentucky excluded the *mens rea* of criminal homicide there; and the court's reliance upon the defendant's homicidal intention in Ohio was clearly violative of the principle of concurrence.[69] Unlike the larceny cases, discussed above, where there was both continuing illegal possession and the *animus furandi* at the time of the conversion, in the above homicide case there was no intention to kill or injure a human being at the time of the decapitation. The Kentucky court apparently believed that since the defendant set out intentionally to kill and since he did, in fact, kill, the failure of the cocaine to do that in Ohio was unimportant. But the fact remains that the *mens rea* did not concur with the actual killing. The departure from the principle of concurrence in this case can only mean that the conduct required by the law of criminal homicide was nonexistent.

Some rather dubious decisions have also been rendered in cases where the defendant committed a battery on someone and, after rendering him *hors de combat*, took his property. This has been held robbery despite the fact that there was

[67] *Cf.* setting a time-bomb which explodes some hours later.

[68] Jackson v. Commonwealth, 100 Ky. 239, 38 S. W. 422 and 1091 (1896).

[69] So held in a similar Indian case. *In re* Palani Goudan, 26 Madras L. T. R. 68, discussed in *Note*, 33 Harv. L. Rev. 611 (1920).

no *animus furandi* until after the battery.[70] There are also questionable decisions in cases where the facts occurred in the reverse order, *i.e.* a larceny first, then the use of force to retain possession.[71] The pertinent question is whether liability for battery and larceny from the person should not be substituted for those holdings. As regards burglary, it seems to be well-established that the intention to commit a crime must exist both at the time of the breaking and at the time of the entry.[72] The efforts of prosecutors to establish concurrence by invoking the tort rule of trespass *ab initio*, so that a legal entry would be found criminal because of the defendant's subsequent misconduct, have been unsuccessful.[73] So, too, an employer who later ratifies his agent's criminal conduct does not share his penal liability.[74] Thus, the principle of concurrence implements an ultimate postulate of penal policy—a person is criminally responsible for his own conduct, not for the conduct of others.

OMISSIONS

In the light of the above discussion of criminal conduct, we may consider the current theory and case-law on criminal omissions. Among the most important influences on the Anglo-American law on this subject was the work of Macaulay, and the sponsorship of his views by Stephen supplied the guinea-stamp of unquestioned validity. At the time he drafted the *Notes on the Indian Penal Code*,[75] Macaulay was undoubtedly familiar with Bentham's challenge to extend the "rules of beneficence:" "In particular, in cases where the person is in danger, why should it not be made the duty of every man to save another from mis-

[70] People v. Jordan, 303 Ill. 316, 135 N. E. 729 (1922); Turner v. State, 198 S. W. 2d 890 (Tex. 1946).

[71] *Cf.* People v. Jones, 290 Ill. 603, 125 N. E. 256 (1919) and Thompson v. State, 24 Ala. App. 300, 134 S. 679 (1931). But *cf.* Mason v. Com., 200 Va. 253, 105 S. E. 2d 149 (1958).

[72] Colbert v. State, 91 Ga. 705, 17 S. E. 840 (1893); Conrad v. State, 154 Tex. Crim. R. 624, 230 S. W. 2d 225 (1950); Rex v. Smith (1820), 168 Eng. Rep. 874.

[73] State v. Moore, 12 N. H. 42 (1841).

[74] Morse v. State, 6 Conn. 9 (1825).

[75] 7 Lord Macaulay's Works 413 (Trevelyan ed. 1873).

chief, when it can be done without prejudicing himself
. . . ?"[76] Bentham supported his proposal by persuasive
hypothetical cases: a woman's headdress catches fire; a
drunken man falls into a puddle; a man with a lighted candle
is going into a room where gunpowder is scattered about—
in each case someone is present who can easily prevent the
harm without the slightest danger to himself. "Who is
there," asked Bentham, "that in any of these cases would
think punishment misapplied?"[77] These views greatly impressed Bentham's American disciple, Livingston; in the
latter's *Draft Code*, it was made a criminal homicide to omit
saving a person's life if that could have been done "without
personal danger or pecuniary loss."[78]

Macaulay rejected those proposals. As regards the rich
man who "omitted to relieve a beggar" though death was
the certain result, and the surgeon who refused to make a
journey to perform an operation although he was the only
qualified person, he thought that the ground for rejecting
penalization was obvious. He believed it equally clear that
a jailer who intentionally caused his prisoner's death by
failing to supply him with food was guilty of murder. The
basis of these beliefs is implied in his discussion—the moral
obligation in the first type of case is vague. Would it bind
another beggar who had some food? Would it require the
rich man to donate a very substantial sum? Would the
summoned doctor have to pay his own traveling expenses?
With reference to warning a traveller of a flood, would one
be required to go fifty or a hundred yards, a mile, ten miles?
"What is the precise amount of trouble and inconvenience
which he is to endure?" He thus derived a program and a
rationale: "We must grant impunity to the vast majority
of those omissions which a benevolent morality would pronounce reprehensible, and must content ourselves with pun-

[76] Introduction to the Principles of Morals and Legislation ch. 17,
§ 19 at 323 (1879). See also, 1 Bentham, Works 164 (1859).

[77] *Id.* at 323, note 1. *Cf.* 2 Bracton, Legibus 281 (Twiss ed. 1879).

[78] Quoted by Macaulay, *op. cit. supra* note 75, at 494. Livingston's
Code, Art. 484-485. A similar provision was proposed by Appleton,
L'Abstention Fautive, Rev. Trim. 604 (1912).

ishing such omissions only when they are distinguished from the rest by some circumstances which mark them out as peculiarly fit objects of penal legislation."[79] That differentia was to be found, he said, by reference to positive law. Certain omissions were to be criminal "provided that such omissions were on other grounds, illegal. An omission is illegal . . . if it be an offence, if it be a breach of some direction of law, or if it be such a wrong as would be a good ground for a civil action."[80]

At the time Macaulay presented his theory, the English criminal law had by a curious coincidence arrived at almost the same rationale.[81] It may be briefly summarized. There are a few relevant remarks in the treatises[82] and in two or three eighteenth century cases involving masters' failure to supply their apprentices with food and decent shelter.[83] In one of these,[84] Justice Lawrence referred to the "duty to provide the apprentice with sufficient food and nourishment." The problem was discussed more fully by the entire bench in a similar case in 1802.[85] The court held it a misdemeanor "to refuse or neglect to provide sufficient food, bedding, etc. to any infant of tender years . . . (whether such infant were child, apprentice, or servant), whom a man was obliged by duty or contract to provide for. . . ." These cases involved a relationship where a legal duty to act was definitely recognized. In 1826, the limiting implication of the rule was expressed in a case where the sister and brothers of a feeble-minded adult, who lived with them, were charged with neglecting to supply him with sufficient food, clothes, etc. The court, in exculpating the defendants,

---

[79] *Id.* at 496-497.

[80] *Id.* at 495. See his illustrations *ibid.*

[81] "The Indian Penal Code may be described as the criminal law of England freed from all technicalities and superfluities. . . . " 3 Stephen, H. Cr. L. 300 (1883).

[82] 2 Hawkins, P. C., ch. 29, § 10 (8th ed. 1824).

[83] The King v. Self (1776), 1 Leach 136, 168 Eng. Rep. 170.

[84] R. v. Squire, Ms. (1799), quoted in 1 Russell on Crimes 460, note 41 (11th ed. 1958).

[85] Rex v. Friend (1802), Russ. & Ry. 20, 168 Eng. Rep. 662.

held that "omission, without a [legal] duty, will not create an indictable offence."[86] This was the state of English law when Macaulay penned his *Notes*. Later cases amplified but did not essentially modify the rules thus established.[87] Stephen agreed that "the thing omitted is one which it is a legal duty to do."[88] This rationale of criminal omissions has been reiterated in countless decisions[89] and in many textbooks.[90]

It requires only brief scrutiny, however, to disclose the superficiality of that theory. The assertion that an omission is criminal if there is a legal duty to act, or that an omission is not criminal unless there is a legal duty to act is a mere tautology if "legal duty" means a duty imposed by criminal law. The same is true of all crimes—it is not criminal to do any overt act unless the penal law forbids its being done, *e.g.* to speak rudely or to waste food and clothing is not criminal because there is no (penal) legal duty to refrain from such acts. Thus the above theory of criminal omissions is no more than a reference to the principle of legality —*nulla poena sine lege*. It is misleading because the emphasis on omissions conveys the notion that they rest on a distinctive basis as regards legal duty.

On the other hand, if "legal duty" to act refers to a duty imposed by private law, the above, still current theory is fallacious. This is obvious if it is intended to mean that whenever a civil law requires the doing of an overt act, failure to do it is criminal. If the theory is taken to mean that an omission is not criminal unless a legal duty is also imposed by civil law, *i.e.* that every criminal omission in-

[86] Rex v. Smith (1826), 2 C. & P. 448, 457, 172 Eng. Rep. 203, 207.

[87] See Kirchheimer, *Criminal Omissions*, 55 Harv. L. Rev. 615, 621-628 (1942), and Perkins, *Negative Acts in Criminal Law*, 22 Iowa L. Rev. 659 (1937).

[88] 3 H. Cr. L. 10 (1883); Digest 152-157 (4th ed. 1887).

[89] "It is the omission or negligent discharge of legal duties only which come within the sphere of judicial cognizance." Union Pacific Ry. v. Cappier, 66 Kan. 649, 72 P. 281, 282 (1903).

[90] One of the first to maintain and elaborate this doctrine was Feuerbach. His views are summarized by Gand, Du Délit de Commission par Omission 17 (1900).

cludes the breach of a private law, that view is equally fallacious. Failure to file a tax return, to keep a road in repair, and to perform official duties are common instances of the lack of any relevant private legal duty. Indeed, the earliest instances of criminal omissions were completely unrelated to private law. They concerned legal duties to go without delay "in pursuit of thieves," appear in court, pay tithes, announce the object of the journey when going to market, the observance of religious festivals,[91] the baptism of sick persons by priests, rendering military services, attendance at certain assemblies, repair of bridges, raising and taking part in the hue and cry, [92] preventing a felony or apprehending the felon,[93] misprision of felony, and so on.[94] Thus it cannot be maintained that the breach of a private legal duty is an essential element of criminal omissions. The relationship of certain rules of private law to the criminal law is sometimes one of reference by the latter to the former. The penal law may then mean that it is forbidden to omit doing certain acts which are defined in the private law. This does not imply that the penal law is enforcing private law, but only that the latter proscriptions are also penal laws. The conclusion of the above discussion must, therefore, be that, so far as the principle of legality is concerned, there is nothing distinctive about criminal omissions.

[91] The above Anglo-Saxon dooms are found in Robertson, The Laws of the Kings of England from Edmund to Henry I, 17, 19, 29-31, 35 (1925).

[92] For citations, see Winfield, *The Myth of Absolute Liability*, 42 L. Q. Rev. 42-43 (1926).

[93] 2 Hawkins, P. C. § 10 (8th ed. 1824).

[94] Roman law punished: failure to prevent a crime when it was possible to do so; the soldier who did not aid his captain, taken prisoner by the enemy; the slave who did not defend his master from attack; the husband who permitted the prostitution of his wife; the son who did not reveal the trap which his brother was laying for their father. It punished the judge who refused to decide a case more severely than one who decided wrongly. Gand, *op. cit. supra* note 90, at 40-41.

For various omissions penalized in the French law, see the Code Pénal, Arts. 312, 319, 346, 347, 471, 475. Decisions of the Cour de Cassation are discussed by Appleton, *op. cit. supra* note 78, at 596.

Can criminal omissions be distinguished from overt criminal conduct by reference to some other significant criterion, *e.g.* as regards causation? Consider the case of a husband who, having decided to kill his wife, discovers on an outing that his wife's foot is caught in a railroad track; and although he sees or hears an on-coming train, he does nothing to extricate her. If the required *mens rea* is to be inferred, he must know the facts relevant to her danger—that she is caught in the tracks and that a train is approaching. But that knowledge is not enough to incur penal liability, *e.g.* the husband may be a helpless paralytic who is unable to do anything to prevent his wife's death. Given the necessary competence and, thus, the relevant *mens rea* (*i.e.* the above factual knowledge and the intention to let her be killed) and also the death of the wife from the impact of the train, the defendant's forbearance is criminal. The problem to be considered is whether criminal omissions, *i.e.* forbearances, differ from overt criminal conduct as regards their causal relation to the harm in issue.

Since "causing" the proscribed harm involves a principle of penal law, the objection that an omission cannot cause such an effect is, if valid, a crucial one. This position has sometimes been urged in opposition to such reforms as those proposed by Bentham. Its proponents assert, *e.g.* that one who passes by a drowning child whom he might easily have saved, does not thereby *cause* the child's death—that was the effect of immersion in water. So, too, of all the instances cited by Bentham—the onlooker was not the cause of the burning or the drowning or the explosion.

But if the meaning of "cause" employed in the above argument were applied to universally recognized criminal omissions, penal liability could not be justified there; actually it is not even doubted. For example, if a husband sees his wife standing in the way of an on-coming train, or a father sees his infant immersed in the bathtub and, being able to do so, he fails to act, no one doubts his penal liability on the ground that the train in the one case, the water in the other, caused the death.

It is therefore evident that penal liability is not imposed for causing a harm in the sense that is relevant *only* to the movement of inanimate things. If "cause" is restricted to that meaning, it is apparent that there is no difference in that regard between the situation where a stranger stands by while a child drowns and that where the child's father stands by. The father is liable whereas the stranger is not liable although the physical facts and the chain of physical causation are identical in both cases. This indicates that physical causation, alone, does not determine liability.[95] There must also be something else; and in criminal omissions that element is illegal inaction, one might say, wrongly allowing the forces of physical causation to operate when one, bound by law, could have altered certain of their consequences, *i.e.* precisely the human factor. For, while it is true that a forbearance alone cannot kill anyone or do anything else in the world (an external force is required to do that, *e.g.* in the above case, the moving train) what is legally material is that the intended harm was permitted to occur. The moving train is, in legal effect, part of the external means employed by the husband. In sum, "legal causation" has a teleological significance that distinguishes it from mechanical causation;[96] and some goals may be attained by forbearance.

The failure to include manifested forbearances in the same class with overt efforts has been encouraged by a misinterpretation of the typical overt conduct, by which the vast majority of crimes is committed, as the *sole* cause of the relevant harms. But if an offender shoots and kills someone or drowns someone, although his overt efforts are in law the "necessary and substantial cause," they are not in fact the entire cause of the death. The mass of the speeding bullet, the water, the characteristics of the biological organism, etc., etc., all enter into the substantial cause of the death. What needs to be stressed is that they do not form part of the *legal* cause to any greater extent than does the

[95] See *infra* chapter 8.
[96] See *infra* and chapter 7.

speeding train in the case of the omission stated above. So, too, if overt effort is singled out as *the* legal cause, (voluntary) forbearance may with equal reason be given that same significance. If the above were borne in mind, together with the character of human end-seeking, the tendency to treat the problem of causation in criminal forbearances as *sui generis* would terminate.

In overt efforts, the defendant initiates the subjection of his victim to certain physical forces or he initiates the aggravation of already operative forces, *e.g.* a disease. In forbearance, he does not initiate the occurrence of the harm, but he permits current forces to take a toll which he could prevent. In both, there is use of, there is "cooperation with," those external forces, and although a difference in culpability and punishment may be indicated, there is no essential difference in conduct or causation.

The traditional theory of volition holds that a *mens rea* represents a psychical movement of the will which is sufficient to support the imputation of the resulting harm to the defendant. In this view, unlike Austin's, there is, accordingly, a common genus in overt efforts and forbearances, namely, the functioning of the will. In both views, there is a temporal interval between the incidence of the effort of the *mens rea* and the later manifested effort.

But it seems to the writer that a *mens rea* pointed towards the future differs significantly from an actually manifested, externally operative *mens rea*. It is the difference between intending not to lift a finger on a future occasion and intentionally not lifting one here and now in the present crucial moment. The occurrence of a proscribed harm is an essential condition of the manifested effort. But the meaning of "manifested effort" is not exhausted in the occurrence of a proscribed harm. For, once that effort is thus recognized, it must be further analyzed and described in the ways noted above, *e.g.* by reference to the preceding *mens rea*.[97]

---

[97] *Cf.* " . . . we mean by it ["an action"] originating, causing, or bringing about the existence of something, viz some new state of an existing thing or substance or, more shortly, causing a change of state

In the traditional psychology, the psychical, imperceptible movement of the will is distinguished from physical effort; and the degree of willing is measured by the extent of its subjection to, or expression of, intelligence. From the relevant ethical viewpoint, the imperceptible movement of a human will, expressing an intention (decision) to produce a proscribed harm, is the decisive factor. This includes forbearance which expresses a *mens rea* and, in a pertinent teleological sense, causes a harm.[98]

At the same time, however, there are persuasive grounds for narrowing, indeed, completely closing, the gap which the traditional theory allows between overt efforts and forbearances by restricting the latter to psychical functions or, at least, by not distinguishing manifested forbearance from the "movement of the will." To sit in a chair, in the above hypothetical case, was staying away from the railroad tracks at the crucial time, and that involved physical effort. There is, *e.g.* the evident experience of muscular effort under considerable provocation, hence the terms "exercise" restraint, "control" yourself, etc. are not mere metaphors. This physical effort in forbearance may even be perceptible in the tensing of muscles, "holding one's self back."[99] This suggests a correction of both the traditional view of (voluntary) forbearance as merely psychical and of Austin's thesis that the relevant "act" consists not of the forbearance, but of overtly doing something other than what the defendant was legally obliged to do, *e.g.* going to the theater.

In European criminal theory, a distinction is drawn between direct omissions and indirect omissions.[1] The former

---

of some existing thing." Prichard, *Duty and Ignorance of Fact*, pub. in Proc. Brit. Acad. 68 (1932).

[98] See *infra* chapter 8.

[99] The New York Times, February 20, 1959 reports the findings of Sir John Carew Eccles, an Australian physiologist, under the heading, "Nerves Held Able to Alter Muscles." Sir John's findings are that "nerve cells can alter the structure and function of muscles to which they are attached . . . that one biological system (a nerve) can 'talk' to another system (a muscle) to cause a controlled change with biological meaning for a living organism."

[1] Kirchheimer, *supra* note 87, at 620.

are usually minor offenses, *e.g.* omission to file a tax return or to register at a new place of residence; and these are also called "real" omissions.[2] The latter, *"commission par omission,"* sometimes called constructive or "unreal" omissions, concern more serious crimes, *e.g.* a homicide caused by a criminal forbearance. The above distinction is also accepted on the ground that in the direct omissions, *mens rea* is not required, while it is required in *commission par omission*. But these legal requirements do not depend upon any difference in types of conduct; in addition, strict liability is not confined to omissions, *e.g.* overt violations of the food and drug act, sale of liquor to minors, and so on.

The second confusion engendered by the above distinction concerns the principle of harm, *i.e.* direct omission is referred to so-called "formal" crimes, such as the failure of a subpoenaed person to appear as a witness, failure to comply with multiple dwelling laws, etc. The supposition here is that no harm occurs but, as will be submitted later,[3] this is untenable. In any event, the notion of "formal harm," assuming its validity, is by no means peculiar to omissions, *e.g.* overt criminal attempts, forgery, perjury and so on. Finally, it is sometimes asserted that direct omissions can be committed by anyone, *e.g.* anyone may be summoned to appear as a witness, while only persons in special relations, a parent or the captain of a ship, can commit an indirect omission. But there are numerous special regulations which require affirmative acts only of persons in particular businesses—only they must file certain reports, maintain certain safety appliances, etc., while, on the other hand, many persons are exempt from paying taxes. Nor is there any *legal* reason why anyone who can, *e.g.* supply food to a hungry person, may not be subjected to penal liability for not doing that. In sum, theories based on the assumption that direct omissions are different from so-called "indirect" ones cloud

[2] *Cf.* Mezger, Strafrecht 131, Schoenke, Strafgesetzbuch 26-27, Maurach, Deutsches Strafrecht, Allgemeiner Teil 245.

[3] See chapter 7.

analysis of the relevant problems which require elucidation, finally, in terms of the principles of criminal law.

The author of a recent article[4] argues that there is a very important difference between crimes of commission and those of omission, namely, that while *mens rea* is quite useful as regards the former (there, intention and recklessness are "ice-cutting concepts"), it is not useful or even relevant in criminal omissions. The alleged reason is that "with omissions, the great difficulty is that the mind of the offender may not be addressed at all to the enjoined conduct, if he is unaware of the duty to act."[5] The illustration offered in support of the above view concerns a legal prohibition against placing garbage cans on the sidewalk, and ". . . one can hardly place such a can on the sidewalk without knowing that he is doing it."[6] As that and the other illustrative cases reveal, the author had in mind petty offenses regarding which it is widely agreed that knowledge of the relevant rule of law is essential to the finding of *mens rea*; and that also seems to be the author's premise. But he came to the general conclusion that the doctrine of *ignorantia juris* "ought to have no application in the field of criminal omissions."[7]

The untenability of this view is evident or, at least, its generality must be questioned on reference to serious criminal omissions, *e.g.* homicides committed by forbearance. On the other hand, the above argument regarding knowledge of the rules is equally applicable to overt petty offenses, *e.g.* a prohibition against parking an automobile at certain places or during a certain time. The fact that the defendant intentionally makes certain overt movements does not *ipso facto* establish *mens rea* even if (merely because) they are the ground of strict liability. The decisive test of the validity of the assertion that criminal omissions are distinctive is its

[4] Hughes, *Criminal Omissions*, 67 Yale L. J. 590 (1958).

[5] *Id.* at 600-601.

[6] But as regards crimes of omission, if one is "quite unaware of the existence of the rule, in what sense can he be said to have been addressing his mind at all to the conduct required of him by law?" *Ibid.*

[7] *Id.* at 602.

application to crimes of equal gravity, *e.g.* a death caused by the intentional omission (forbearance) of a husband or father to render assistance to his wife or child, on the one hand, and an overt killing by such a person, on the other. The doctrine of *ignorantia juris* clearly applies in both cases. Conversely, in petty offenses making it criminal, *e.g.* to place a garbage can on the sidewalk and to omit sweeping a sidewalk, knowledge of the rules is essential to the presence of *mens rea*.

The difficulties actually met in cases of omission are of quite a different order, *e.g.* they sometimes complicate, without altering, the problem of causation. In overt criminal conduct, the harm usually occurs immediately after the defendant's conduct. But in criminal omissions, the harm much more frequently happens a substantial time after the initial forbearance.[8] Accordingly, it must be concluded that, while the above and perhaps evidentiary difficulties may be greater in some crimes of omission,[9] in no essential legal regard do those crimes differ from crimes of commission.[10] The principle of legality applies equally to both, and there is no essential difference so far as act, *mens rea* or causation is concerned. Just as in overt conduct, penal liability for forbearance requires intentional or reckless harm-doing. Here, too, the relevant corollary is that inadvertent omissions lie outside the bounds of penal liability.

Case-Law on Omissions

Unfortunately, the decisions on criminal omissions do not conform to the common rationale of criminal forbearance and overtly committed crimes. It is perhaps to be expected

---

[8] For example, in Commonwealth v. Welansky, 316 Mass. 383, 55 N. E. 2d 902 (1944), the case of a fire in a Boston night club, the defendant's forbearance continued during a long period of time.

[9] See *supra*, note 65.

[10] Mr. Hughes, *op. cit. supra*, note 4 was apparently led to his position by the views of Ryle and Hart concerning "volition," "intention" and other mentalist terms. See *id.* at 606. But those writers do not restrict their theory to omissions. Mr. Hughes, however, not only recognizes that *mens rea* is quite useful in overt crimes, *id.* at 600, he also approves those writers' complete rejection of conscious mental states as the "Ghost in the Machine," a "spurious unity."

that in the older cases, negligent omissions resulting in death would be subjected to liability for criminal homicide. Thus, on an indictment for murder by omitting to provide necessaries, Justice Patteson charged the jury: "If the prisoner was guilty of wilful neglect, so gross and wilful that you are satisfied he must have contemplated the death of Mrs. Warner, then he will be guilty of murder. If, however, you think only that he was so careless, that her death was occasioned by his negligence, though he did not contemplate it, he will be guilty of manslaughter."[11] This was made quite clear by Maule, J., in a prosecution for manslaughter against a mine worker whose duty it was to regulate the ventilation. The jury was told that the question was "whether, by his omitting to do so, he was guilty of a want of reasonable and ordinary precaution. If . . . a man using reasonable diligence would have had it done . . . you ought to find the prisoner guilty of manslaughter."[12] These decisions hark back to times preceding the firm recognition of the difference between negligence and recklessness.[13] But it also appears that the language of negligence was used indiscriminately with reference to omissions long after the criteria of recklessness were being articulated as regards crimes of commission.[14]

In a significant American case,[15] e.g. the defendant, a switch-tender, failed to adjust certain switches, resulting in a train wreck and the death of a passenger. A conviction for manslaughter was affirmed although the trial judge had

[11] Verdict of manslaughter. Reg. v. Marriott (1838), 8 C. & P. 425, 433, 173 Eng. Rep. 559, 563. Cf. Rex v. Russell (1933), Vict. L. R. 59.

[12] Verdict—Not guilty. Reg. v. Haines (1847), 2 Car. & K. 368, 371, 175 Eng. Rep. 152, 153-4. So, too, in Reg. v. Hughes (1857), 7 Cox C. C. 301, 302, Lord Campbell, C. J., charged: "If the omission was not malicious and arose from negligence only, it is a case of manslaughter."

[13] See supra pp. 122-23.

[14] Discussing homicide by omission, Stephen said, " . . . no one can say how much more, carelessness than is required in order to create a civil liability. . . . It is a matter of degree determined by the view the jury happen to take in each particular case." 3 H. Cr. L. 11 (1883). Cf. supra at 128.

[15] State v. O'Brien, 32 N. J. L. 169 (1867).

refused to instruct the jury that the defendant "could not legally be convicted, unless his will concurred in his omission of duty."[16] But the court also stressed the presence of "culpable or criminal negligence;"[17] hence, it is not clear which rule was applied.[18] In a similar case, the defense was that there was "mere inattention," not criminal negligence. The court held, however, that there was gross and criminal negligence "as the man was paid to keep the gate shut . . . ."[19] More recent decisions treat the problem more adequately,[20] although some cases and treatises continue to confuse the required *mens rea* with negligence[21] and to assume that any "faulty" omission is criminal.

These lapses from the established rationale of the decisions on criminal commission are related to important variations in the facts. Where the defendant was charged with manslaughter of his wife, who died in childbirth, the court soundly insisted that: "One cannot be said in any manner to neglect or refuse to perform a duty unless he has knowledge of the condition of things which require performance at his hands."[22] But quite different language is frequently

[16] *Id.* at 170. "In order to make out against the defendant the lesser offence of manslaughter, it was not necessary that it should appear that the act of omission was wilful or of purpose." *Id.* at 171.

[17] *Id.* at 172.

[18] Professor Perkins interpreted the decision as upholding the conviction of manslaughter if the omission "was a matter of inattention, if the omission amounted to 'criminal negligence'." Perkins, *supra* note 87, at 667 note 25; also Perkins, Criminal Law 514 (1957).

[19] Rex v. Pittwood (1902), 19 T. L. R. 37, 38. The sentence was three weeks' imprisonment for the manslaughter of one person and serious injury to another.

[20] *Supra* 128.

[21] " . . . where the duty of acting exists, negligence . . . will make the defendant responsible. . . . " May, Law of Crimes 24 (4th ed. 1938); *cf.* State v. Benton, 187 A. 609 (Del. 1936). "If the omission is not malicious, and is a mere case of negligence, the parent is perhaps guilty of manslaughter only." State v. Barnes, 141 Tenn. 469, 212 S. W. 100, 101 (1919).

[22] Westrup v. Commonwealth, 123 Ky. 95, 93 S. W. 646, 648 (1906). This sentence is found in State v. Smith, 65 Me. 257, 266 (1876), involving similar facts. There the court, in sustaining a conviction, added: "A criminal intent on the part of a party who has carelessly caused the death of a human being need not be alleged nor proved in order to constitute manslaughter when such death was the result of the neglect of a known duty to the deceased." *Id.* at 267.

used in cases involving homicide in the operation of a railroad train or other dangerous instrumentality. In a case where a train was driven on the wrong track, *e.g.* the defendant pleaded ignorance of that fact. The court held that irrelevant to a conviction for manslaughter, resting its decision on a "special duty" from which it inferred the rule: "the failure to perform the duty even through inattention is gross and culpable, or, in other words, criminal, negligence."[23] In affirming the trial judge's refusal to instruct that the defendant could be convicted only if he went upon the track "knowingly" and with "indifference," the court said: "This means that defendant was [would be] relieved from the duty of using the precaution to learn whether or not the engine was on the right track. In other words, negligent acts of omission would not be punishable."[24]

A duty to perform an overt act, of course, implies a duty to know the relevant facts. But a person may be negligent in failing to inform himself, or his ignorance may be intentional or reckless. The omission to do a required act must be evaluated by reference to these crucial questions. A person who was negligent in the acquisition of knowledge of certain facts might be reckless as regards the omission to do an act if he was aware of his ignorance of the facts. In some of the cases, especially those that involve the operation of trains, it was reasonably assumed that the defendant, knowing the nature of the instrumentality and being able to operate it safely, was aware of the hazard of not knowing relevant facts and of acting accordingly. It was then also assumed that his omission to do the ultimately required act was voluntary, *i.e.* that he actually knew the situation was dangerous.[25] The correct rule was applied where a death was caused by "a most unusual stop" of a train that had never stopped there before and was thus not reasonably

---

[23] State v. Irvine, 126 La. 434, 52 S. 567, 569 (1910).
[24] *Id.* at 572.
[25] This was seen above. Rex v. Pittwood, *op. cit. supra* note 19, at 37; *cf.* State v. Benton, 187 A. 609, 618 (Del. 1936).

expected, the court emphasizing the lack of "any knowledge of the existence of such a train on that night. . . ."[26]

Because recklessness is now generally understood to be required in manslaughter, there must be particular reasons for the lapses that occur in the decisions where omissions are concerned. The explanation is suggested by the fact that almost invariably, in the context of their language in terms of negligence, the judges concentrate upon the duty of the defendant to act. This was noted above,[27] where the court reasoned from the fact that "the man was paid to keep the gate shut" to the conclusion that he was "criminally negligent," *i.e.* that he must have known that his omission was increasing the risk of the proscribed harm. But this should have been found as a matter of fact, and the judges should articulate the requirement and meaning of recklessness in criminal omissions.

The penal law does not require that a person actually know he is under a legal duty to act to prevent serious harms; it requires only that there be such a duty.[28] On the other hand, the penal law does require that the defendant know the facts to which his duty refers as well as the facts which make it necessary to perform the duty. Thus a parent, master or captain would need to know that he was in that respective relation to a certain person or persons (which could usually be assumed) and he would need to know also, *e.g.* that his child was sufficiently ill to require medical care—and that sort of knowledge cannot be assumed.[29] Both of these factual questions are glossed over in many decisions on criminal omissions. At best, they are proportionately imprecise as regards the principle that voluntary misconduct, *i.e.* intentional or reckless harm-doing, must be found in criminal omissions no less than in criminal commissions.

[26] State v. Tankersley, et al., 172 N. C. 955, 90 S. E. 781, 783 (1916).

[27] Rex v. Pittwood, *op. cit supra* note 19, at 37.

[28] For the exceptional situation in certain petty offenses, see *infra* chapter 11.

[29] *Supra* note 8, at 902, 913; also, *supra* note 22, at 646.

POSSESSION

The subtleties of "possession" provide a severe test of the usefulness of any terms and conceptions employed to elucidate criminal conduct. The possession of stolen property or narcotics and the receipt of stolen goods, *e.g.* present situations where there is manifested effort but no overt conduct, at least in the usual sense. The defendant may be in his room when the thief or narcotics peddler enters and places the articles in a certain receptacle. Not a word is spoken, but the defendant knows what is happening, he intends to take possession, and he "takes possession"—in the customary reifying mode of speech. The intention to take possession, implying knowledge of the nature of the commodity and of other facts which make the possession illegal, *i.e.* the *mens rea*, is distinguishable from the relevant manifested effort shown in the actual taking of possession. That is more easily apprehended in cases where there was a substantial interval of time between the *mens rea* and the taking possession, and also overt effort in doing that. For example, last month the defendant agreed with a narcotics peddler regarding delivery and paid him in advance or in other ways showed his intention to take possession. Later, when a messenger arrives with the package of narcotics, he holds out his hand and receives it or he directs the messenger to place it in a particular receptacle. In such cases of overt conduct, taking possession is easily distinguished from the *mens rea*. In the first situation above, where the messenger simply placed the package in a drawer, etc., the defendant's forbearance is manifested in more subtle ways such as remaining in physical proximity to the narcotics. It can hardly be doubted that an entirely new situation exists at the termination of the transaction since the defendant now *has* narcotics in an external sense, and he brought that about by doing something more than deciding to take possession of the drug.

In many of the cases involving illegal possession, the judicial opinions discuss only the defendant's knowledge of the material facts, and nothing is said about any act by him.

For example, in *Gory*,[30] the defendant, a prisoner in a county jail, was charged with illegally possessing marijuana in a box where he kept personal articles. The defendant pleaded ignorance of the presence of the drug, and the conviction was reversed for failure to establish his knowledge of that. It was necessary to prove "physical control with the intent to exercise such control;" and "knowledge of the *existence* of the object" is essential to such control. As was suggested above, the logic of these decisions is (a) since there is no knowledge of the material facts there is no *mens rea* and (b) since there is no *mens rea* there can be no *manifested* effort (act).[31]

"Possession" raises other difficult problems, and some of the decisions spin an intricate web to conform to the relevant legal principles. In *Hudson*,[32] *e.g.* the defendant received a letter containing a check from a public agency, intended for another similarly named person. At an unspecified later time he opened the letter and converted the check. It was held that the critical point in the case, determining the defendant's taking *animo furandi* was when he knew the relevant facts and decided to convert the check. An earlier opinion by Lord Coleridge was cited, holding that "when he knew what he had got, that same instant he stole it." In a recent similar case Goddard, C. J. noted that, "The whole essence of the case depends on when a man can be said to take the particular articles he is charged with stealing."[33] This was found to rest upon the defendant's knowledge and his intention to convert. Thus, *mens rea* is the critical factor in these cases in determining the fact and time of the act of taking. It is undoubtedly possible to simplify the law on this difficult subject; but reforms that avoid the current technicalities regarding which particular property crime was committed will not supplant the need for analysis in terms of the relevant principles of criminal law.

[30] People v. Gory, 28 Cal. 2d 450, 170 P. 2d 433 (1946).
[31] *Cf.* Aristotle, *op. cit. supra* note 55.
[32] (1943) 1 K. B. 458, 29 Cr. App. R. 65. See Kerr, *The Time of Criminal Intent in Larceny*, 66 L. Q. Rev. 174 (1950).
[33] Russell v. Smith (1957), 2 All E. R. 796, 797.

POLICY OF CRIMINAL OMISSIONS

While there is no legally significant difference between criminal omissions and criminal commissions, there are important non-legal ones. For example, there is often a difference in the degree of moral culpability between actively committing a criminal harm and passively allowing one to occur. A parent who beats his child arouses more resentment than does his voluntary omission to provide necessaries. Many persons who could never bring themselves to take overt steps to harm certain individuals would feel quite content to "leave them to their fates" should they fall into dangerous situations. And as regards the scope of legal duty, which Macaulay discussed, it is still the fact that affirmative aid to strangers is regarded as outside the sphere of duty. Whatever religion and ethics teach, the prevailing attitudes draw sharp distinctions between overt action and passivity.[34] The legislature cannot ignore these mores, nor should it implement them beyond necessary limits.[35]

The prevailing policy may be briefly indicated. Someone ought to call a doctor to care for a very sick child, and the

---

[34] Certain other theories have been advanced concerning criminal omissions. Thus it has been maintained that the basis of liability is not an omission but a prior overt act, *e.g.* a good swimmer promises a poor one that he will stand by; a nurse promises to attend a sick person. In these instances, it is said, the wrong lay in the prior overt act, not in any subsequent omission. But that theory is clearly untenable. The prior overt acts were commendable. Moreover they were not the causes of the subsequent harm—the patient died not because the nurse promised to be present but because she was not present. Related to the above theory is that criminal omissions uniformly represent either reliance on some person or expectation of aid. But these views, though not without significance, do not explain the rules. Thus, an infant can hardly be said to rely upon anyone who has not actually cared for it. As for "expectation," although its vagueness leaves much to be desired, it may be granted that if that notion is extended to characterize a community attitude it is a relevant social factor in accounting for the case-law.

[35] For a discussion of the following outrageous cases of omissions which were held not criminal in France: a servant knew about numerous attempts by a wife to kill her husband and did nothing; a man pleaded for his life, but by-standers did nothing to restrain the murder. *Cf.* Connaughty v. State, 1 Wis. 143 (1853); a brother knew that his sister was locked up in a dungeon for long periods with no air or light; an innkeeper refused to take in a sick traveller; a doctor refused to attend a sick person; a pharmacist refused to supply medi-

child's parents usually know that is their particular duty.[36]
Someone ought to show the danger signal to avoid a railroad
collision; a certain employee knows that is his special obligation. An aged person should be looked after; one who
assumed that obligation by entering into a contract or, in
certain situations, by taking charge of such a person knows
he is under a particular obligation in that regard. A sick
man should receive medical care; the doctor who takes the
case knows he is the doctor depended on. The implied
rationale is that the situation must be such that there is a
moral obligation to do a certain act and the obligation must
rest on particular persons.[37]

That this has been operative as an influence on the judges
seems probable from an examination of the cases. Thus a
comparison of *Smith* (1826)[38] with *Instan* (1893)[39] reveals
both the difficulty, indeed the impossibility, of distinguishing
them on the avowed basis of "contract" and, also, the persuasiveness of the above suggested explanation. In the
earlier case, the father's will required the defendants to pay
an annual stipend to their feeble-minded brother. He was
living in the same house, and it could easily have been inferred that they had him in charge. Yet the defendants were
held not legally bound to look after him. But at the end of
the century, in *Instan*, the judges were willing to construct
a legal undertaking by a niece to look after her helpless
aunt, from the fact that she was living with, and was being
supported by, the aunt.[40] So, too, as regards the duty of a
railroad guard to the general public. No such duty was

---

cine; one who saw a house beginning to burn and passed on, see
Cohin, L'Abstention Fautive, 197-200 (1929). But later legislation
has greatly altered this. See note 50 *infra*.

[36] Reg. v. Senior (1898), 19 Cox C. C. 219.

[37] See Perkins, *supra* note 87, at 670.

[38] (1826) 2 C. & P. 448, 172 Eng. Rep. 203.

[39] (1893) 1 Q. B. 450, 451.

[40] It has been held that one insured against fire owed a duty to
extinguish a fire which started accidentally, and that if he failed to
do so with intent to collect the insurance, he was guilty of a criminal
offense. Commonwealth v. Cali, 247 Mass. 20, 141 N. E. 510 (1923).

found in 1869[41] but it was readily discovered in 1902.[42] The ground stated in support of the penal liability imposed in the above cases would hardly bear scrutiny if a contract action were involved.[43] It was little more than a rationalization of the judges' belief that the situations were such as to impose definite moral obligations upon particular persons to do certain acts. This was stated in so many words in *Instan* by Justice Coleridge: "The prisoner was under a moral obligation to the deceased from which arose a legal duty towards her. . . ."[44]

Although this hypothesis seems persuasive, it is also evident that it is not a sufficient explanation of the case-law. For example, an expert swimmer might be the only person to see a child drowning. He would know that he was the only one who could rescue the child, and he should certainly feel obliged to save him. How can such a situation be differentiated from one identical with it—except that the by-stander is the child's father? Although there may be a difference in degree, most persons would probably agree that there is no essential difference in the nature or specificity of the moral obligation or of its incidence. The essential difference, it is suggested, inheres not in moral obligation, but in the mores, in the public attitudes regarding the respective parties; and these, in turn, are influenced by the relationship of the parties to the child. Thus, the reason the stranger who refuses food to a hungry child escapes any liability while the latter's father might be guilty of a criminal homicide is that, despite avowals, we have not reached the point of really believing that everyone is morally obliged to be his brother's keeper; or, at least, that is not believed sufficiently to be given implementation by the criminal law.

[41] Reg. v. Smith (1869), 11 Cox C. C. 210.

[42] Rex v. Pittwood, *op. cit. supra* note 19, at 37. *Cf.* the earlier like American decision where it was held: "He owed a personal duty not only to his employers, but to the public." State v. O'Brien, *supra* note 15, at 172.

[43] *Cf. Comment*, 11 B. U. L. Rev. 273 (1931).

[44] (1893) 1 Q. B. 450, 454. See, also, Rex v. Gibbins and Proctor (1918), 13 Cr. App. R. 134. These cases would seem to overrule Reg. v. Shepherd (1862), 9 Cox C. C. 123, where a mother was held not

Beginnings have been made to require strangers to render assistance in certain situations,[45] *e.g.* statutes imposing a duty on motorists and railroad employees to aid persons injured by them, the Federal statute requiring the master of a vessel to render assistance "to every person who is found at sea in danger of being lost," under penalty of fine and/or imprisonment not exceeding two years,[46] the duty imposed on owners of certain public places with reference to the presence of children,[47] the duty to install safety devices for the protection of employees and public invitees,[48] the duty to aid an employee in an emergency,[49] and various others. Most of these instances concern relationships other than the traditional ones or the express assumption of certain duties. But Anglo-American law still lags behind that of Continental European and other legal systems where it is now well established that one who, without danger to himself, intentionally fails to assist a helpless person, is subjected to penal liability. Many of the defendants are doctors, hospital officials and other individuals selected by "circumstances" as the particular persons who ought to render help.[50]

---

bound to summon a midwife to attend her daughter who was eighteen and "emancipated." *Cf.* People v. Beardsley, 150 Mich. 206, 113 N. W. 1128 (1907) and Terr. v. Manton, 7 Mont. 162, 14 P. 637, 19 P. 387 (1888).

[45] In this connection, it is noteworthy that where penal codes proscribe omissions by "strangers" to the victim, the penalties are small. *E.g.* Soviet Penal Code, § § 163 and 164; Dutch Penal Code Art. 450.

[46] 37 Stat. 242 (1912), 46 U. S. C. § 728 (1926), FCA 46 § 728.

[47] State v. Sobelman, 199 Minn. 232, 271 N. W. 484 (1937).

[48] Commonwealth v. Welansky, 316 Mass. 383, 55 N. E. 2d 902 (1944).

[49] Reg. v. Brown (Can. 1893), 1 Terr. L. Rep. 475.

[50] Summaries of these decisions are published in Rev. Sci. Crim. et Dr. Pen. (Paris) ; and see Hughes, *op. cit. supra* note 4, at 631-636.

CHAPTER VII

HARM

THERE are many practical problems in the solution of which criminal conduct[1] must be distinguished from its effect, *e.g.* in determining the jurisdiction of a trial court, where the "act" occurred in one state and the effect of it in another. There are difficult questions involving double jeopardy where it is necessary to distinguish a single "act" (conduct) from several consequences. Other important questions arise, at least in the United States, concerning the reasonableness of legislation in the light of the "police power;" and in passing on the constitutionality of such statutes the courts consider the nature of the proscribed effects.[2] Evidently, sound penal policy in legislation and also in the interpretation of statutes requires careful study of

[1] See *supra* chapter 6. Conduct was there distinguished from act.

[2] Statutes prohibiting schools from teaching a foreign language to young children in order to promote "civic development" were held unconstitutional in Meyer v. State of Nebraska, 262 U. S. 390, 67 L. Ed. 1042, 43 S. Ct. 625 (1923) and in Bartels v. State of Iowa, 262 U. S. 404, 67 L. Ed. 1047, 43 S. Ct. 628 (1923), Holmes, J. dissenting. An ordinance making it an offense to associate with thieves and prostitutes was held an improper interference with individual freedom "upon the mere ground of correcting the morals of the person concerned. . . . But if such person so associates with a design or intent to aid, abet . . . prohibitory legislation may well be applied, not to correct the evil consequences which such association may bring on the individual, but to protect society from actual or anticipated breaches of law." City of St. Louis v. Fitz, 53 Mo. 582, 585-86 (1873).
A law making it illegal to possess any hide of any cow, etc., from which the brand has been obliterated was held unconstitutional in Park v. State, 42 Nev. 386, 178 P. 389 (1919). So, too, of an act giving the occupant of a lower berth in a sleeping car control of the upper berth, if unoccupied. State v. Redmon, 134 Wis. 89, 114 N. W. 137 (1907). In this case it was said that the pertinent inquiries are. Does a danger exist? Is it of sufficient magnitude? Does it concern

the proscribed harms.[3] But the principal reason for distinguishing act, conduct, harm and so on is that the solution of legal problems depends upon the precise analysis of every important aspect of a crime, and that requires the use of cogent conceptions.

ROLE OF "HARM" IN PENAL THEORY

It should, indeed, evoke little wonder that "harm" is a central notion of penal theory. "The problem of evil" is deeply imbedded in the human drama, and the proscribed harms have played the major role in it. It was passionate reaction against grievous wrongs which long ago set into motion the course of legal history that culminated in modern penal law; and any thorough discussion of that law can hardly exaggerate the significance of those stimuli.

In penal theory, harm is the focal point between criminal conduct on the one side, and the punitive sanction, on the other. In relation to criminal conduct, harm is essential as the relevant effect, the end sought. Without an effect or end, it is impossible to have a cause or means, and everything in penal law associated with causation and imputation would be superfluous. So, too, as will appear in a later chapter, harm is equally necessary in the elucidation of punishment. This connection is analogous to that between criminal conduct and harm except, of course, that the conduct of officials inflicting privations upon criminals has a very different legal and ethical significance. Harm, in sum, is the fulcrum between criminal conduct and the punitive sanction; and the elucidation of these interrelationships is a principal task of penal theory.

It is the relation of harm to criminal conduct, *i.e.* to conduct expressing a *mens rea*, that merits particular attention. Since the principle of *mens rea* has ethical significance, the

---

the public? Does the proposed measure tend to remove it? Is the restraint in proportion to the danger?

In People v. Johnson, 6 N. Y. 2d 549, 161 N. E. 2d 9 (1959), the harm concerned "loitering in or about any school building or grounds without written consent."

[3] R. v. Cunningham, (1957) 2 Q. B. 396.

plain inference is that the end sought or hazarded is a harm, a social disvalue. It may be possible to arrive at a parallel result by defining "harm" in terms of deviation from public attitudes.[4] Without discussing their respective merits or their combined significance,[5] both of these descriptive theories may be contrasted with that represented in much of the professional literature on penal law.

It is said or implied there that many crimes are not harmful, indeed, that some of them, *e.g.* criminal attempts, the possession of burglar's tools or counterfeit money, have no effect whatever; and, also, that legislatures forbid all sorts of consequences, some of which may be ethically neutral or even good. The corollaries are that harm is not essential in penal law and that "harm" can mean no more than the effect of any proscribed behavior or conduct. This raises a problem which we have previously discussed; and it need only be added that on that premise, there is no possibility of acquiring any knowledge of penal effects. In that formal perspective, the effect of any criminal conduct is only an "X."[6] In practice, however, it is impossible to restrict the meaning of "effect" in that way, as any lawyer who has participated in a criminal trial will aver.

Academic formalism in penal theory — which is quite different than the language lawyers are sometimes required to speak — was more defensible in Austin's time than it is now.[7] The greatly increased consensus regarding the exclusion of negligence and constructive homicide (the felony-murder, misdemeanor-manslaughter rules) and a similar view of strict liability reveal the principal thrust of current theory. But the former perspective persists in conditioning theory; hence it may be asked, if formalism suffices, what is the basis for excluding negligence and strict liability from

---

[4] See Durkheim, Division of Labor in Society (trans. Simpson, 1933).

[5] Hall, Living Law of Democratic Society, ch. 3 (1949).

[6] See chapter 3 at note 2.

[7] But *cf.* the reference to "injurious events" by Clark, An Analysis of Criminal Liability 12 (1880).

penal liability, for insistence on the restriction of *ignorantia juris,* and so on? If the factual-normative characteristics of *mens rea* and proscribed harm are so distinctive and important as to provide substantial support for such proposals, it seems evident that those qualities also determine the scope of significant penal theory. "Theories are nets cast to catch what we call 'the world': to rationalize, to explain, and to master it."[8] In some fields, the consequent knowledge represents the difference between modern science and primitive lore.

Certainly, there is nothing formal about being robbed or killed, and in early societies criminal law was for the most part limited to the proscription of such observable injuries. But in a more advanced view, a harm is a negation, a disvalue, the lack of a natural condition, and the like. Thus, harm implies the existence of values, interests or natural conditions.

There are many theories of value, which legal systems have been said to reflect and serve, that are also exhibited in classifications ranging from a few all-embracing categories, *e.g.* justice and order, to detailed catalogues such as that of the pleasures listed by Bentham. There are relatively simple schemes classifying values as moral, intellectual, aesthetic and hedonic; intrinsic or instrumental; representing life, health, freedom and property; Jhering's division of the social interests in life, freedom, honor and money; and Pound's classification of social interests in general security, social, domestic and religious institutions, in general morals, social resources, general progress and the individual life.[9] There are Spranger's six basic values: (1) theoretical or intellectual, (2) economic or practical, (3) aesthetic, (4) social, (5) political and (6) religious or mystical.[10] There is the list of Lasswell and McDougal, consisting of power, respect, enlightenment, wealth, well-

---

[8] Popper, The Logic of Scientific Discovery 59 (1959).

[9] Pound, *A Theory of Social Interests,* 15 Proc. Amer. Sociol. Soc. 16 (1921), reprinted in Hall, Readings in Jurisprudence 238-246 (1938).

[10] Mukerjee, The Social Structure of Values 78 (n. d. London).

being, rectitude, skill and affection.[11] Parson's and Shils' list includes (1) body [health], (2) property [usable objects, money], (3) knowledge [facts, theories], (4) beauty [sensory and dramatic patterns], (5) ideology [system of values], (6) affiliation [interpersonal relationship], (7) sex [with reproduction], (8) succorant object [child to be reared], (9) authority [power over others], (10) prestige [reputation], (11) leader [law-giver], (12) nurturant object [supporter], (13) roleship [functional place in group], (14) group [social system taken as a unit].[12] Corresponding classifications of crimes, *i.e.* of disvalues, might be suggested; and it is evident that various philosophical perspectives are implicit in these schemes.

In the sociological theory previously referred to, public attitudes (mores, *représentations collectives*) are regarded as "values" or the equivalent of values; and deviations from them are harms in that sense. In the writer's view, however, while public attitudes are important in determining questions of penal policy, it is necessary to recognize, *e.g.* in the elucidation of *mens rea* and *ignorantia juris*, that attitudes and values are not identical. A particular community's attitudes, no less than an individual's, are sometimes at odds with its values, as is often acknowledged by its more enlightened members. In sum, at least for the purpose of the present discussion, harms are actual disvalues, viewed from the perspectives of realism and sociology.[13]

Criminal harms differ in gravity, first, because of the differential external effect upon the victim and the com-

---

[11] Lasswell and McDougal, *Legal Education and Public Policy*, 52 Yale L. J. 203 (1943); McDougal, *The Comparative Study of Law for Policy Purposes: Value Classification as an Instrument of Democratic World Order*, 61 Yale L. J. 915 (1952).

[12] Parsons and Shils, Toward a General Theory of Action 463-4 (1951).

[13] One of the most detailed discussions of such "evils" was Bentham's and the reader will recall his minute classification and the method he suggested for measuring the relative gravity of the evils by reference to the sensibilities of the victim, the type and extent of the evil, etc. A similar approach was suggested by Ortolan, who divided harms into direct harm to the victim and indirect harm—the insecurity and alarm of others in the community. 1 Ortolan, Eléments de Droit Pénal 434, sec. 956 (1886).

munity, *e.g.* a battery is obviously less serious than a death; and secondly, by reference to the degree of moral culpability of the offender, *e.g.* a death caused by a motorist's reckless driving is a less serious harm than a death caused by a deliberate murderer.[14]

It should be recognized, next, that penal harms, while they refer to, are far from being restricted to, physical injuries. In libel, kidnapping, perjury, political crimes, many sexual offenses and others, there is no physical injury; and in still others, *e.g.* rape, the physical injury may be insignificant. Since it is generally agreed that there are actual harms in these crimes, the notion of "criminal harm" must be stated in terms of intangibles such as harm to institutions, public safety, the autonomy of women, reputation and so on. In short, harm signifies the loss of a value. Regardless of the materiality of any object, its value always involves personal appraisal of, and attitudes towards, that object, *i.e.* people value things; hence the locus of a value or a disvalue is not simply in the thing itself.[15] In addition, penal harm must be defined in relation to conduct expressing *mentes reae*. Penal harm, accordingly, has certain normative-empirical references. It is a complex of fact, valuation and interpersonal relations — not an observable thing or effect, as is sometimes assumed. Only if the incorporeality of penal harm is borne in mind, can the more difficult questions regarding the so-called "inchoate" or "formal" crimes be elucidated.

Apart from any verbal question concerning "crime," it is evident that this problem — whether "inchoate" or "formal" crimes, *e.g.* criminal attempts, solicitation, conspiracy,

---

A formal theory has been presented by Hans Kelsen which excludes any ethical, and all but the minimal factual, significance of effect. In this view, it is pointless to evaluate "delict." This is discussed *infra* chapter 9.

[14] Austin recognized ". . . the important principle, that unlawful intention or inadvertence is a necessary ingredient of injury." 1 Austin, Lectures on Jurisprudence 506 (4th ed. 1879).

[15] "That aspect of an object by virtue of which I care for it is its value." Lee, *Methodology of Value Theory*, pub. in Value—A Cooperative Inquiry 154 (Lepley ed. 1949).

perjury, forgery, possession of burglar's tools, and so on, include any harm — cannot be solved by the weight of authority. Austin, *e.g.* said "attempts are perfectly innocuous" and, he added, "the party is punished, not in respect of the attempt, but in respect of what he intended to do,"[16] which raises interesting questions regarding punishment for merely entertaining a *mens rea*. On the other hand, Edward Livingston said, "... every attempt, although it fail ... of itself, is an injury. ... Moral guilt must be united to injury in order to justify punishment. ..."[17] In recent years, many more writers and judges who have expressed themselves on the subject, have written that criminal attempts are harmful in a substantive sense.[18]

Perhaps the common thought underlying these estimates is that in criminal attempts and other relational crimes the harm consists of apprehension and of a dangerous condition in which the probability of still greater harm is substantially increased. If that is a sound insight, it has far-

[16] *Op. cit. supra* note 14, at 523.

[17] 1 The Complete Works of Edward Livingston on Criminal Jurisprudence 235 (1873).

[18] No exhaustive search of the literature on criminal attempts was made with reference to this point. But among the writers examined, those who expressed themselves on this question made the following relevant statements concerning criminal attempts: "... a disturbance of the social order." May's Law of Crimes 191 (4th ed., Sears and Weihofen, 1938); "... in the ordinary judgment of mankind, and in the consequences to the community, the disturbance of the attempt has been created. ... But the public has not suffered so much, therefore it will not punish him so heavily." 1 Bishop, Criminal Law 530, 552 (9th ed. 1923); "... the *corpus delicti* of a criminal attempt might be stated as a *substantial* but incomplete impairment of some interest. ..." Strahorn, *The Effect of Impossibility on Criminal Attempts*, 78 U. of Pa. L. Rev. 962, 970 (1930). "An attempt ... causes a sufficient social harm to be deemed criminal." Hitchler, *Criminal Attempts*, 43 Dick. L. Rev. 211 (1939); "... societal harm. ..." Curran, *Criminal and Non-Criminal Attempts*, 19 Geo. L. J. 185 and 316 (1930). And see Strahorn, *Preparation for Crime as a Criminal Attempt*, 1 Wash. & Lee L. Rev. 1 (1939).

But *cf.*, "... the act of attempt is not in itself harmful to the state. The crime is a mere shadow of the attempted offense. ..." Beale, *Criminal Attempts*, 16 Harv. L. Rev. 491 (1903). Wharton, in the course of misstating the common law regarding voluntary abandonment of a criminal attempt ("this is a defense"), adds as a reason: "Neither society, nor any private person, has been injured by his act. There is no damage, therefore, to redress." 1 Wharton,

reaching implications because it brings within the orbit of
defensible generalization numerous offenses such as possession of burglar's tools or stolen property.

But if, after attention is called to the intangible character
of all penal harms, to the apprehension created by the commission of "inchoate" crimes, to the fact that increasing
the danger of becoming the victim of a more serious crime
is itself harmful, that without some harm committed, there
is no ground for punishment in a legal order which does not
recognize prevention as a sufficient ground of punishment,
and so on, one still persists in the Austinian view that there
are some types of rationally proscribed conduct which do
not cause any harm, what further steps may be taken to
diminish the area of disagreement and contribute to the
elucidation of this problem?

Two further suggestions may be ventured. Any conduct
has at least two references or dimensions: It originates in
an actor and, to some extent, by the mere fact of its presence, it alters pre-existing conditions, *i.e.* it has some effect.
For example, the taking possession of burglar's tools or
narcotics by persons who intend to use them illegally alters
the previous condition of affairs. The quality of daily
life is impaired by such conduct; and one need only ask
whether he would want to live in a community where attempts to kill and to commit robberies and arsons were
frequent, to indicate that there are harmful effects of such
conduct not only in the apprehension aroused but also in
the increased danger of becoming the victim of a more
serious crime.

This is the externality of the penal harm by reference to
which its correlate, criminal conduct, is distinguished from
merely unethical intentions and unethical actions which are

Criminal Law 307 (12th ed. 1932). This statement seems to have
been omitted in the current edition (Anderson, ed. 1957).

In a case involving an attempt to bribe a public official, the court
said: ". . . the gist of the crime is the danger and injury to the
community at large . . . the state must guard against the tendency
to corrupt as well as against actual corruption, both being alike
dangerous and injurious to the community at large." Davis v. State,
70 Tex. Cr. R. 524, 158 S. W. 288, 289 (1913).

not criminal. "Penal harm" also serves to limit the legal effect of an offender's moral culpability and thus to distinguish the ethics of legal punishment from the purely ethical evaluation of immoral conduct. In sum, criminal conduct is legally significant in relation to a penal harm; and any conduct which actualizes a *mens rea* alters the external world, it has effect. If, nevertheless, certain preparations are not penalized in the common law and other legal systems, the reason is a practical one of policy; in logic and theory a harm has been committed.

But if it is still insisted that there is no harm in the so-called "inchoate" and other offenses, what are the final implications and consequences of that position with reference to penal theory? If we set aside the verbal aspect of the disagreement regarding "harm," the dispute is either like those which arise when different perceptions are experienced, and the disputants can only adduce the supporting testimony of other persons, if that is possible; or, the field of crime is narrowed by the indicated extent, *i.e.* by excluding "inchoate" and "formal" offenses from the field of criminal law, as defined by a set of empirical-normative principles. The principle of harm continues valid and significant within the then recognized, narrowed field of crime and criminal law.

The alternative, simply to assert pragmatic or *ad hoc* judgments concerning harms and to list exceptions, to state, *e.g.* that in some crimes there are harms, but in other crimes there is only conduct and so on, cannot comprise a theory and only adds confusion. For, while the narrowing of a unified field of data, even if that is unwarranted, preserves theory within the narrowed field, the intrusion of exceptions at odds with the conception that is generally applied, destroys theory. A theory applies uniformly within a specified area.[19] That area should be enlarged so far as is compatible with theory, and any theory is always subject to

[19] In the long stretch of legal history, many acts were punishable which now seem matters of superstition or intolerance. Every legal system includes inherited archaisms as well as laws representing the preferences of dominant groups, special interests and mistaken

displacement by a better one, *e.g.* one which has at least equal significance over a wider range of data. But no mere assemblage of occasional uniformities, historical qualifications and practical exceptions can function as a theory. Thus, the most important aspect of the above problem concerns the role, functions, and limitations of any theory of penal law.[20] The practice of law depends upon the knowledge of penal law; and that, in large measure, consists of the empirical-normative knowledge that a descriptive theory represents and advances.

In summary, the principle of harm serves the following purposes:

1. It is essential in distinguishing the ethics of criminal law ("penal policy") from pure ethics.[21]

2. Craftsmanship depends on the availability of precise tools; and the need to resolve the ambiguity of "act" also supports the distinction of harm and conduct.[22] In addition to the analytical gain, there are practical needs that are served, *e.g.* in solving various jurisdictional questions and problems involving double jeopardy.

3. It provides a rational basis for punishment as well as for the differentiation of punishments, *i.e.* in proportion to the gravity of the harm. It is also important in corrective

---

legislative appraisals. Neither these facts, however, nor the fact that blasphemy and witchcraft, *e.g.* were once criminal invalidates a theory of penal law any more than the fact that people were or are sometimes irrational in spending their money invalidates the economic law of maximization of satisfaction at minimum cost. See Hall, Studies in Jurisprudence and Criminal Theory, ch. 1 (1958).

[20] The problem is not altered because "effect" may be employed to include both harms and non-harmful results. This merely avoids the problem of what is significant in penal theory. It also ignores the current frequent "lapses" in texts which avow formal definitions but nonetheless elucidate problems in normative-descriptive terms.

[21] *E.g.* ". . . the aim of the law is not to punish sins, but is to prevent certain external results. . . ." Holmes, J., in Commonwealth v. Kennedy, 170 Mass. 18, 20, 48 N. E. 770 (1897), which concerned a criminal attempt.

[22] In addition to the ambiguity of "act," discussed in ch. 6, see Sayre, *Criminal Attempts*, 41 Harv. L. Rev. 838, note 65 (1928). *Cf.* the comments by Arnold, *Criminal Attempts—the Rise and Fall of an Abstraction*, 40 Yale L. J. 64 (1930).

treatment since an offender's harm-doing must be considered in determining his dangerousness.[23]

4. As the summation of all the specific proscribed harms, the principle of harm functions as an essential organizational construct. Other principles of criminal law, especially those concerning conduct and causation, presuppose that of harm. If harm is excluded, conduct and causation become irrelevant, and the combined result is a great loss in the systematization of the criminal law.

It is possible to elucidate the meaning of "harm" more fully by considering certain related notions, namely *actus reus, corpus delicti*, justification, excuse, circumstances, and tort.

"ACTUS REUS"

Terminology is extremely important in any science, and if progress is to be made in penal theory, painstaking care should be devoted to this subject. It is with this in view that the writer voices his concern that *"actus reus"* is finding currency both in England and in the United States. That term was not employed in the older classical treatises or by Stephen, Holmes or Bishop. It seems, in fact, to have been introduced in this century by Kenny,[24] and was employed several times in the 12th edition of his *Outlines of Criminal Law* in the sense of result, *e.g.* "the commission of an *actus reus*."[25] Kenny, however, continued to write of "the natural consequences of the criminal acts themselves"[26] and, as will appear, he also introduced considerable con-

[23] The "sexual psychopath" laws which, in a few American states, allow incarceration without any prior conviction are widely criticized. This indicates the function of a definite harm even in non-penal contexts, to determine dangerousness.

[24] I am indebted for this information to Professor J. W. C. Turner, the editor of Kenny's Outlines of Criminal Law, who writes in a letter dated 16 April 1958, "I have so far been unable to discover any earlier authority for the term than Kenny, who used it in his first edition of the 'Outlines' and had probably been employing it in his lectures for some years before that. I can only *guess* that he coined it for himself."

[25] At 49 (1926).

[26] *Id.* at 9.

fusion when he wrote that "even though there has been an *actus reus* . . . no sufficient *mens rea* preceded it."[27]

In 1930, Professor Stallybrass, writing under the caption of *"Actus Reus,"* discussed not the result of criminal conduct, but "overt act."[28] It is clear, *e.g.* from his reference to a "mere intention unevidenced by an observable act,"[29] that he was interpreting *"actus reus"* as an act, resembling the narrow meaning of Austin and Holmes.[30]

Professor J. W. C. Turner adopted Kenny's definition,[31] stating, "'*actus reus*' will be used to denote *such result of human conduct as the law seeks to prevent.* . . ."[32] This set of terms is often employed in the later editions of Kenny's *Outlines.*[33] Professor Turner fully recognizes that "the *actus reus*, which is the result of conduct . . . must be distinguished from the conduct which produced the result."[34] But he also writes of "activity" which "caused the event;"[35] and as recently as 1958, in the 17th edition of Kenny's *Outlines*, it was necessary to make certain changes lest "act" and "activity" be confused with *"actus reus."*[36] There are also frequent references to "harmful consequences."[37]

[27] *Id.* at 66.
[28] Reprinted in The Modern Approach to Criminal Law 397 (Eds. Radzinowicz and Turner, 1945).
[29] *Ibid.*
[30] See *id.* at 403.
[31] First published in 6 Camb. L. J. 31 (1936); reference here is to its publication in The Modern Approach to Criminal Law 195 (1945).
[32] *Id.* at 196, 197. He employs "consequences" and "deed" as synonyms. *Id.* at 199, 239. He also characterizes the *actus reus* as "harmful." *Id.* at 239.
[33] *Actus*, it is stated, "connotes a 'deed,' a physical result of human conduct," (Kenny's Outlines of Criminal Law 14, 17th ed.) which raises doubts regarding many crimes where the result is intangible, *e.g.* libel, political crimes, sexual offenses, etc.
[34] *Id.* at 15.
[35] *Ibid.*
[36] In the 16th edition (1952), immediately after the caption *"Actus Reus,"* there followed "(a) Act of commission" and "(b) Act of omission." *Id.* at 13, 14.
In the 17th edition, these subheads become "(a) Deed of commission" and "(b) Result of omission." 14, 16 (1958). *Cf.* ". . . the crime is constituted by the event, and not by the activity (or in certain cases as we shall see, by the omission to act) which caused the event." *Id.* at 15.
[37] *Id.* at 16.

Other writers have preferred to adopt Professor Stally-brass' definition of *"actus reus,"* probably because of its formal resemblance to "act."[38] While it is not easy to apprehend any analytical or other advantage which results from the substitution of *actus reus* for proscribed act or conduct or result, so long as it is clear which of these notions[39] is referred to, no serious difficulty is encountered.[40]

Dr. Glanville Williams took a quite different direction, and his discussion of *"actus reus"* raises questions of penal theory which require careful analysis. After referring to the problem of defining "act," especially to Holmes' narrow definition and Salmond's very wide one, he states that, instead of trying to settle this question, he will "make use of the technical term *actus reus* (or its civilian alternative, *corpus delicti*) to express exactly what he means."[41] Accordingly, Dr. Williams states: *"actus reus* means the whole definition of the crime with the exception of the mental element —and it even includes a mental element insofar as that is contained in the definition of an act."[42] He refers to "the muscular contraction regarded as an *actus reus*. . . ;"[43] and then states: "A further step may now be taken. *Actus reus* includes . . . not merely the whole objective situation that has to be proved by the prosecution, but also the absence

---

[38] This is the preference of Professor G.O.W. Mueller, *On Common Law Mens Rea*, 42 Minn. L. Rev. 1053 (1958). It also seems to be the meaning employed by Cross and Jones, An Introduction to Criminal Law 34 (4th ed. 1959). On the other hand, Professor Rollin M. Perkins employs *actus reus* as the deed or result of criminal conduct. Perkins, Criminal Law 653, 723-4 (1957).

[39] See *supra* chapter 6.

[40] In some respects, however, Professor Turner's use of *actus reus* has been questioned. Williams, Criminal Law 19, note 9 (1953).

[41] *Id.* at 16. Dr. Williams, however, continued to employ "act." Accordingly, with reference, *e.g.* to the statement concerning "a mental element in so far as that is contained in the definition of an act," (*id.* at 17) it is necessary to know whether "act" is used in Salmond's sense, which included negligence, or in Austin's which excluded negligence, or in some other sense.

[42] *Id.* at 17

[43] *Id.* at 18.

of any ground of justification or excuse. . . ."[44] Following
that, it is said that this definition of *actus reus* "rather supposes that the situation forbidden by law is something
distinct from the mental element." But, it was added,
"Sometimes this is not true."[45]

Among the questions which arise concerning these statements are the following: (1) Is *actus reus,* as defined above,
the alternative of *corpus delicti?* (2) What is meant by the
exclusion of *mens rea* but the inclusion of the "mental element" of act in the definition of *actus reus?* (3) What are
the interrelations of *mens rea,* justification and excuse, and
actus reus? And (4), what is involved in the statement that
sometimes *mens rea* is not distinct from *actus reus?*

It has long been assumed, both in common law and in
European Continental penal theory, that every crime has a
mental or subjective aspect and an external or objective
aspect.[46] If a writer finds it convenient to use *"actus reus"*
to designate the latter, that is certainly his privilege, and
it may sometimes be useful.[47] However, as will appear,
much more is involved in the above use of *"actus reus."*

In considering the first question noted above, it is clear
that *corpus delicti*[48] serves useful procedural functions. It
is employed most frequently in the United States as part of

[44] *Id.* at 19.
[45] *Id.* at 21.
[46] Typical is Bouzat, Traité de Droit Pénal (1951) which discusses
l'élément légal, l'élément matériel, and l'élément moral.
[47] There is a need for an omnibus notion to include all the material
elements of a crime, but as appears in the very statement of this,
the word "crime" serves that need in the common law countries.
In Continental systems, *"crime"* or an equivalent term means a
serious offense (the ordinary meaning of "felony"). In European
penal theory, therefore, different inclusive terms are used. The
meaning of "crime" will, of course, vary with the theory employed.
For example, in the writer's theory, "crime" is defined in terms of
the seven specified principles, *i.e.* crime, in this sense, is legally
forbidden (voluntary) conduct which (teleologically) causes a proscribed harm, for which the offender is subjected to a punitive
sanction. See chapters 1 and 6.
[48] The problem of *corpus delicti* is related to the problem discussed
supra in chapter 1, *i.e.* the bifurcation of the rules and the exculpatory
doctrines.

the evidentiary rule that there must be proof of the *corpus delicti* before the prosecution introduces the defendant's confession. The purpose is to minimize the weight of a confession and to require collateral evidence to support a conviction. *Corpus delicti* means: "first, the *occurrence* of the specific kind of injury or loss (as, in homicide, a person deceased . . .) ; secondly, somebody's criminality (in contrast, *e.g.* to accident) as the source of the loss, — these two together involving the commission of a crime by *somebody.* . . ."[49] In view of the procedural purpose of the rule, it is not required that the *corpus delicti* be proved beyond a reasonable doubt. That, of course, is the final burden of the prosecution; but the procedural requirement — to lay a proper foundation for the admission of a confession — is satisfied if "only a *prima facie* showing be made that the alleged victim met death by a criminal agency."[50]

Occasionally, *corpus delicti* is used in cases where no confession is involved, to mean *all* the material elements of the crime charged. The corresponding rule of evidence applied to such cases is that the *corpus delicti* must be proved beyond

---

[49] 7 Wigmore, Evidence 401 (3rd ed. 1940). "In the case at bar under either definition, we have ample proof of the *corpus delicti*— the existence of a criminal fact. A dead body is found with a bullet hole . . . ; the body is in a gulch. . . ; there is no weapon. . . ." Ausmus et al. v. People, 47 Colo. 180-1, 107 P. 204, 210 (1910).

"In most cases indeed, evidence of the *corpus delicti* is separable from that identifying the criminal; but in some, it is equally applicable to both." Phipson, The Law of Evidence 137 (9th ed. Burrows, 1952). In cases of tax evasion, *e.g.* it cannot be shown that a crime was probably committed by "criminal agency" without identifying the accused. Smith v. United States, 348 U. S. 147, 99 L. Ed. 192, 75 S. Ct. 194 (1954).

[50] The quotation continues: The *corpus delicti* "need not be established by proof as clear and convincing as is necessary to establish the fact of guilt. . . ." People v. Ogg, 323 P. 2d 117, 123 (Cal. 1958). The "independent evidence must be of such a character that reasonable inferences may be drawn to support a conclusion that a crime of the nature and character charged has been committed by someone." Brown v. State, 154 N. E. 2d 720, 722 (Ind. 1958). The court noted in this case that the degree of proof required to establish the *corpus delicti* cannot be that required to sustain a conviction (proof "beyond a reasonable doubt"). If that were required. "A confession would be of little value in a criminal prosecution if the entire crime first had to be proved . . . by independent evidence. . . ." *Id.* at 728.

a reasonable doubt.[51] In a perjury case, *e.g.* it was held that to establish the *corpus delicti*, it must be proved that the defendant took an oath, etc., before a competent tribunal, in a case where an oath could be lawfully administered, and that he wilfully and so on "states as true any material matter which *he knows* to be false."[52] Accordingly, in another case where all the material facts were established, including the *mens rea,* except that it was not shown that the harm in issue was *caused* by the defendant, the *corpus delicti* was not proved.[53] Thus in neither of the above definitions of *corpus delicti*, nor in any other legally recognized definition known to the writer, does it mean all the material elements of a crime except the *mens rea*. If the above definition of *actus reus* were modified to accord with the recognized meaning of *corpus delicti*, that would remove a gratuitous difficulty but leave the question, why two Latin phrases are employed to perform a procedural function,[54] especially when the newly added one is already ambiguous.

With reference to the second question asked above, and assuming that "act" includes voluntary movement but not inadvertent behavior, what is the meaning of the definition of *"actus reus"* in terms of the entire external situation excluding *mens rea* but including "a mental element insofar as that is contained in the definition of an act?" An "act," in penal theory, implies a *mens rea*. But this, by definition, must be excluded. On the other hand, if it is assumed that the mental element in the designated act is innocent, in what sense can there then be an *actus reus?* This problem may be

---

[51] Tate v. People, 247 P. 2d 665 (Colo. 1952).

[52] People v. Guasti, 243 P. 2d 59, 66 (Cal. Dist. Ct. App. 1952).

[53] In Jones v. State, 151 Tex. Cr. R. 114, 115, 205 S. W. 2d 603 (1947) the defendant shot the deceased, but it was not shown that the death was the result of the shooting. This was also the issue in State v. Meidle, 202 S. W. 2d 79 (Mo. 1947) and in People v. Harrison, 395 Ill. 463, 70 N. E. 2d 596 (1946).

[54] While *"corpus delicti"* serves useful purposes in procedural law, it should not, for reasons stated above and in chapter 1, be incorporated into, or be made the determinant of, analysis of the substantive law. This also applies, of course, to *actus reus* if that is used as a synonym of *corpus delicti*.

further clarified by analysis of the remaining criteria by reference to which *"actus reus"* was defined.

JUSTIFICATION AND EXCUSE

The third question, raised above, concerns justification and excuse. In dealing with this problem, it is necessary to keep in mind the essential character of the situation which penal theory elucidates, namely, that criminal conduct and harm are in a means-end relation. A means implies an end; an end, a means; hence, the elucidation of their meaning requires that each be considered in relation to the other. In other words, any set of facts violative of a penal law comprises a teleological situation which can be described from either extremity, related to the other one.

When, instead of elucidating *"actus reus"* in the context of a means-end situation, a sharp bifurcation is drawn between external situation and *mens rea,* unfortunate conclusions are reached, *e.g.* Dr. Williams' criticism of *Dadson.*[55] There D, an officer, shot at P, who was stealing wood. Later, it was discovered that P had been twice convicted of the offense, and that the instant stealing was therefore a felony. It was held, however, that since D did not know, at the time of the shooting, that P was a felon, he was rightly convicted. Dr. Williams states that the decision "seems hard to reconcile with the requirement of an *actus reus,"* but he concludes not only that "there was no *actus reus"*[56] but also that "the decision in *Dadson* was wrong."[57] The alleged ground rests wholly on the external situation — that P was a felon — and "neither the bad motive nor the ignorance of the arrester can turn the arrest of the felon into an *actus reus."*[58] This untenable position is the result of ignoring *mens rea* in the definition of *actus reus.*[59]

[55] (1850) 2 Den. 35, 169 E. R. 407.
[56] *Op. cit. supra* note 40, at 23.
[57] *Id.* at 25.
[58] *Ibid.*
[59] ". . . the arrest was lawful, because there was no *actus reus."* *Id.* at 23. ". . . he should have had the defence that his conduct was not interdicted by law." *Id.* at 24. Considering the converse of *Dadson, i.e.* where D arrests P reasonably though mistakenly be-

From the very beginning of the modern professional police services in England, the judges have insisted that the
officer's enlarged privilege to arrest must be balanced and
limited by a reasonable belief regarding the external situation, *i.e.* that the arrestee was a felon.[60] Especially, a
privilege to inflict a very serious injury has been rigorously
subjected to limitations designed to protect members of the
public. To allow officers to shoot at people whom they do not
reasonably believe are felons, and then resolve the legality
of that by reference to whether or not the human target
turns out to be a felon would be a risky, intolerable business.[61] The same consideration applies to self-defense to
the extent that the defendant is not privileged if he did not
believe he was in danger, even if it turned out that he
actually was endangered.[62] These rules are well established
and they seem to be quite sound. They imply not that a
pre-existing justification is somehow "cancelled out" by
mens rea but, instead, that there is no justification if there
is a *mens rea*.

Thus, later, when Dr. Williams considers the problem of
criminal attempt, he finds that asking simply whether the

---

lieving he is a felon, Dr. Williams writes: "D is not guilty of a
crime . . . because he has no *mens rea*. . . ." But, he adds, "There is
an *actus reus* because P is in fact not a felon." *Id.* at 23-24.

[60] Hall, *Legal and Social Aspects of Arrest Without a Warrant*, 49
Harv. L. Rev. 566 (1936).

[61] In Collett v. Commonwealth, 296 Ky. 267, 176 S. W. 2d 893, 895-6
(1943), D, a police officer shot and killed the arrestee who was armed
with a revolver which, however, he did not remove from the holster.
D appealed from a conviction of voluntary manslaughter, alleging
that the trial court erred in refusing to instruct that "he had the . . .
additional right, although it did not appear reasonably necessary to
him, to use such force as was actually necessary." In affirming the
conviction, the Court of Appeals of Kentucky held that if the requested
instruction were recognized, "the law of self-defence and apparent
necessity would be stretched beyond all reason . . . although it
may appear from facts later established that the person who has
committed the homicide would himself have been killed . . . had he
not taken the life of his victim, nevertheless, if he was not aware
of those facts and circumstances at the time he committed the homicide, the motive prompting him to kill must necessarily have emanated
from an evil heart, and a wilful intent to commit the crime, and
he cannot be excused from his wilful malicious act by a showing of
circumstances of which he was not aware."

[62] Josey v. United States, 135 F. 2d 809 (C. A. D. C. 1943).

external situation was proscribed by penal law will not do. For there one meets the empty pocket cases and the cases of the administration or taking possession of harmless powders (believed to be poison or narcotics), which are criminal attempts despite the apparent innocence of the external circumstances.[63] He then recognizes that, "This interdependence of act and mind means that neither alone can strictly be characterised as "criminal" or "reus," . . . Act and mind are literally *reus* only in combination."[64] But this leads only to the conclusion that: "An *actus reus*, then, need not be a crime apart from the state of mind."[65] It is respectfully submitted that an *"actus reus"* (if the writer understands the instant meaning of this term) can *never* be a crime apart from the requisite *mens rea*; more precisely, *actus reus* implies *mens rea*.

That *mens rea* is a material element in every crime, *i.e.* that there is a *principle* of *mens rea*, implies that no external situation of itself can be criminal, that there is always the mental side to be considered. In some situations, enough of the mental state is revealed to sustain a very high probability of *mens rea* (this is the relevance of *corpus delicti*) ; while in others, the mental side may be wholly unrevealed. But this does not alter the material elements of a crime; nor, what needs emphasis, does it alter the fact that regardless of how incriminating an external situation may appear to be, it is always possible to prove that there was no *mens rea* or, *per contra*, to show that despite the apparently complete innocence of the external situation, there actually was a *mens rea*, and that the situation was therefore criminal. In support of the first statement are cases where the accused was insane, although no witness of the situation suspected that. In addition, the ramifications of justification and excuse are so considerable that it is possible, no matter how incriminating an external situation seems to be,

---

[63] For further discussion of the problem of the external situation, see *infra* chapter 15.

[64] *Op. cit. supra* note 40 at 494.

[65] *Ibid.*

that in the light of the discovered relevant facts, the injury inflicted was privileged. On the other hand, the "innocent" act of taking possession of harmless powder becomes a criminal attempt to receive narcotics when the prior dealings of the parties are revealed. It follows that the meaning of *"actus reus,"* whatever it might be, should not be varied in relation to the accidents of particular external situations.

In sum, to separate *mens rea* from the remainder of the crime is very hazardous. Once *mens rea* is excluded, the external situation is not the equivalent of *corpus delicti,* so that no procedural need is supplied. More serious is the fact that the separation of *mens rea* from the external aspect of a crime obscures the *necessary* connection between them and encourages the notion that some external situations conclusively express *mens rea* "on their face," while others, *e.g.* the administration of harmless powder, are absolutely legal. But, as noted, this is fallacious in both respects, which is precisely what the classical maxim implies.[66]

We must now consider justification and excuse somewhat more critically. If a prosecutor were to charge a person with handing a coin to a beggar or shaking his fist at a rain cloud or eating dinner or giving a visiting pedagogue a glass of sherry, the case would be quickly and sharply dismissed — *nullum crimen sine lege*! In jurisprudential terms, those acts were "privileged."

If a crime is charged, the procedural task is to determine whether a particular accused person did or did not commit the alleged offense. The procedure is meaningful in relation to the substantive crime in issue. After the prosecution has made out at least a *prima facie* case of every material element of the crime, including the *mens rea,* the accused may defend in one or more of several ways. He may simply plead that he did not do what he is charged with doing, and he may introduce proof of an alibi.

[66] "For take away the will, and every act will be indifferent for your meaning imposes a name upon your act, and a crime is not committed unless a guilty intention intercede. . . ." 2 Bracton, Legibus, f. 101b, p. 127 (Twiss ed. 1879).

But suppose that in some sense of the term, the defendant did "do" what is charged against him. He can say that he did not do it *voluntarily* because, *e.g.* someone pushed him against the prosecuting witness, or he may plead he had an epileptic seizure. In short, he did not act, in the legal sense of "act." He can plead infancy or insanity and, if successful, it is said that the defendant is "excused." In a loose sense, which includes the common law view of "misadventure,"[67] "excuse" might also be applied to the preceding instance (being pushed, etc.). In more precise usage, however, it seems inapt to excuse a man for something he did not do. Again, the phraseology of an ancient doctrine is *ignorantia facti excusat*. This, too, suggests that the locus of excuse is the person of the accused — either he is incompetent or he is a normal adult who, because of a reasonable mistake, was the innocent cause of someone's injury.

"Justification"[68] has been said to include (1) an official's arresting a wanted person or a witness, seizing property, executing a sentence; (2) self-defense; (3) necessity; (4) coercion and (5) consent.[69] What is common in these situations is that no crime was committed because there were special circumstances which made the commission of the injury in question (or what at first seemed to be an injury, *e.g.* consent) a "privilege." Unfortunately, as we have seen, this emphasis on the external situation is sometimes erroneously taken to mean that *mens rea* is irrelevant.

It should also be noted that while the injuries referred to in connection with justification are "privileged," that has

---

[67] At common law, excusable homicide included (a) accidental killing, as where a hatchet flies off and strikes someone, (b) parental correction or official conduct which accidentally caused a death, (c) death of a participant in a lawful contest, and (d) death in reasonable self-defense. The King's pardon was required to "excuse" such homicide. 2 Bishop, Criminal Law 471-3 (9th ed. 1923).

[68] At common law, a justifiable homicide was either one required by law, *e.g.* the execution of a condemned man, or a death caused in prevention of a felony, prevention of a breach of peace, or in arrest or recapture of criminals. Bishop *ibid.* Stephen said the common law distinction of excuse and justification "involves no legal consequences." 3 Stephen H. C. L. 11 (1883).

[69] Stallybrass, *op. cit. supra* note 28, at 427-433.

a narrower range than the same word used at the outset of this discussion, *e.g.* giving money to a charity. The difference is that justification involves the voluntary infliction of an injury. The accused has done something which, under the special conditions, is not a penal harm, but if these conditions were lacking or if the accused was ignorant of their presence, there was a penal harm. It follows that justification rests finally upon the same principle of legality which excludes the above instances of ordinary lawful conduct from the range of penal liability. The logic of justification is the logic of any lawful conduct — *nullum crimen sine lege* is equally relevant. But the relevance of the principle of legality does not imply that justification can be established solely by reference to the external situation. Basing analysis upon justification in its usual procedural reference to the external situation, instead of relying on the relevant principles of criminal law, has led to the difficulties indicated above. It is the principles which are ultimate, not justification.

Excuse and justification are pertinent and useful in procedure,[70] and it may sometimes be convenient to employ them in substantive law. But they are fallacious and misleading when they are applied as notions of substantive penal theory. Some of the supporting reasons have been indicated above and in the first chapter of this book. But the importance of the problem merits further discussion of it.

Let us first examine the questions raised by the late Professor G. L. Radbruch who held there were important differences between justification and excuse.[71] First, he said, there is no right of self-defense against a justifiable act; but there is such a right against a merely excusable one. Second, ignorance or mistake of a fact concerning justification is a defense, but not so of ignorance or mistake relating to an excuse, *e.g.* that the offender believes he is

[70] See *supra* chapter 1.
[71] Radbruch, *Jurisprudence in the Criminal Law*, 18 J. Comp. Leg. and Int'nl L. 218-219 (1936).

insane or is under the age of criminal responsibility. Third, a principal in the second degree and an accessory before the fact are punishable despite the defendant's excuse, but they are not punishable if he was justified. And fourth, civil damages cannot be obtained for a justifiable act, but they are recoverable if the defendant was merely excused.

As regards the third point, Professor Radbruch acknowledged that a normal participant is held penally liable apart from any reliance upon complicity, *i.e.* on the ground that the incompetent individual was merely an instrument. With reference to the fourth point, which Professor Radbruch did not emphasize, it need only be added that the differential civil consequences depend upon civil law; and the fact that an insane person is held civilly liable does not affect penal theory. As regards the first point, it may be questioned whether there is a privilege of self-defense against an insane person, in the usual meaning of that privilege. In the common law of crimes, when deadly force is not involved, the privilege of self-defense includes that of standing one's ground and giving the assailant as good or better than he gives, so long as no disproportionate force is employed.[72] But if one were to be attacked by an insane person there would be no privilege to "carry on." Although blows necessary to ward off an attack would be privileged, there would be a duty to retreat or to terminate the episode, *e.g.* by pinioning the arms of the insane person. So, too, if one were "assaulted" by a child, the privilege of self-defense would surely fall short of that of self-defense against the assault of a normal adult.

Again, it can hardly be shown that anyone who for any reason participates in a justified attack is never penally liable. One who reasonably defends himself or a person being assaulted is justified, but would a third person be exculpated if he inflicted blows on the assailant believing that he was the person being attacked? Finally, Professor

---

[72] ". . . he may repel force by force, and within limits differing with the facts of cases, give back blow for blow." 1 Bishop, Criminal Law 605 (1923), giving numerous citations.

Radbruch's second point seems to be a restatement of the doctrine concerning *ignorantia facti, i.e.* what is relevant is a mistake which excludes *mens rea,* and a mistaken belief in one's legal capacity is not that kind of mistake. Again, the analysis must rest ultimately on the relevant principle of penal law.

The above distinctions drawn between justification and excuse break down completely with reference to coercion. The relevant rules are that the coerced person (under pressure of imminent death or serious injury) is not liable for any injuries he commits, except homicide and, elsewhere, *e.g.* in Canada, for kidnapping, assisting in rape, mayhem, arson and certain other offenses,[73] but that the coercer is always criminally liable for the harm committed by the coerced person.[74]

The allocation of the doctrine of coercion to either excuse or justification meets serious difficulties. If coercion is a form of justification, then, in the usual mode of analysis, the coercer should not be liable; but he is liable. On the other hand, serious difficulties also bar the allocation of coercion to excuse. First, excuse implies complete exculpation, as in insanity and infancy, no matter what harm was committed. But in Anglo-American law the coerced person is guilty of homicide and, in Canada and elsewhere, of that crime or any of the other offenses noted above. Excuse is not applicable in these cases of coercion.

Secondly, the liability of the coerced person for homicide and other serious offenses and the similarity of coercion and necessity indicate that the ground upon which the doctrine of coercion rests is not excuse, but justification. Thus it seems that it is the external situation which is paramount

[73] Canadian Criminal Code, sec. 17.

[74] In R. v. Bourne (1952), 36 Cr. App. R. 125, the coercer was inconsistently held guilty of aiding, while the coerced was excused. *Cf.* Tyler and Price (1838), 8 C. & P. 816; and see the discussion of the Stephenson case in chapter 8 *infra.* In State v. Myers, 7 N. J. 465, 81 A. 2d 710 (1959) D, after severely beating his wife, ordered her to jump into a river. She did, and he stood by while she screamed for help. Held, guilty of murder in the first degree.

since the doctrine of coercion expresses an evaluation with reference to it, which is also that of the doctrine of necessity, namely, the greater value should and may be preserved. If it is a question of the life of the coerced as against a burglary, the latter is privileged; but when it is another's life or kidnapping, etc., there is no such preponderance of value in favor of the coerced person, and he has no defense. But, as noted, the coercer is liable for the harm committed by the coerced person;[75] and this is at odds with the usual interpretation of justification.

If, however, we adhere closely to the relevant law, the most that can be said is that the coerced person is justified in certain situations and that the coercer is nonetheless liable. But, it may be asked, if the coerced person did not commit a crime, how can the coercer be held criminally liable? To this it may be answered that the coercer's liability is not based on complicity, but on a type of causation which is interpreted both realistically and in conformity with the relevant liability.[76]

The basic difficulty, it is submitted, in the current application of excuse and justification to substantive law results primarily from the separation of material components of crimes and their analysis in isolation from each other; and the consequence of this is to attribute ultimate theoretical roles to justification and excuse. But these concepts do not comprise principles of substantive penal law. As was suggested above, the idea of a means-end situation, implying that whenever either criminal conduct or penal harm is absent, the other is also absent, is helpful in avoiding the above fallacies. Other difficulties have resulted from the unwarranted assumption that justification, but not excuse, implies the legality of the inflicted injury. For example, it is not correct to say that a crime was committed by an insane person, but he is excused. Not only is there no *mens rea*, but also, there being no *mens rea*, no proscribed harm

---

[75] This is provided by statute in several American states, *e.g.* Calif. Pen. Code, pt. I, tit. 1, 31; Illinois Statutes, ch. 38, sec. 597.

[76] See *infra* chapter 8 at 270ff.

was committed. It may be awkward to speak of a killing by an insane person as "privileged;" in any case, he cannot commit a crime. Justification and excuse have historical significance, and they are useful in procedure in concentrating attention upon the moot aspect of the cases. So, too, convenience or practical purpose may direct analysis to *mens rea* or to the external situation. But penal theory elucidates penal law systematically and in terms of ultimate notions.

If it is recognized that the principle of legality has equal reference to excuse and justification, and if any crime is envisaged as a means-end situation, implying the necessary interrelated presence of both criminal conduct and proscribed harm — and therefore the impossibility of having either whenever the other is absent — it is possible to analyze the problems of penal law in terms which avoid the above difficulties. If penal theory thus foregoes procedural, historically bound analysis via excuse and justification, it adheres to the principles of substantive penal law — the ultimate notions.

In sum, "excuse" and "justification" refer rather loosely to certain doctrines of substantive penal law, and it is these doctrines which give those two terms whatever substantive legal significance they have. Analysis of the doctrines does not reach ultimate ground until it is expressed in terms of the principles of penal law. It is these principles which are paramount in penal theory. When incompatibilities arise and the analysis of problems encounters such difficulties as those discussed above, it is justification and excuse, not the principles of substantive penal law, which must give way.

CIRCUMSTANCES

A final facet of external situations, which was previously noted in the analysis of "act"[77] and which also seems to be involved in *"actus reus,"* is that of circumstances. Legally relevant conduct presupposes facts, conditions or circum-

[77] See chapter 6, especially 172-173.

stances, *i.e.* an actual world, whichever of these terms is employed to refer to it. In homicide, *e.g.* there are at least two human beings and a lethal instrument which may in-clude any force that can be used to cause death.[78] Many circumstances are often ignored as mere "conditions," *e.g.* in causation,[79] and attention is centered on circumstances which have legal significance. In bigamy, perjury and re-ceiving stolen property, the circumstances include certain legal attributes — that a man be married, or a witness, or that property be stolen. These legal meanings (like "owner-ship") qualify certain material facts and actions; and the composite is treated as factual. A legally relevant circum-stance is one whereby a *mens rea* is consummated or, stated from the other side, whereby a proscribed harm is caused.

All legally relevant circumstances must be allocated to conduct, causation and harm; and the particular allocation to one or the other of these material elements depends on the issue. For example, in assault with a deadly weapon, the use of such a weapon is part of the criminal conduct; being assaulted with such a weapon is part of the specified harm; and, in stating the causal relationship of the use of the weapon to the consequent harm, it is also necessary to refer to the weapon. This is equally true of more subtle situa-tions, *e.g.* in fraud, the defendant uses certain words, pros-pectuses, telephones, and newspapers; the harm is caused by that conduct, and so on. It may seem awkward to speak in this fashion of bigamy or receiving stolen property, but this results only because the relevant circumstances are, like ownership, clothed with legal meanings. In any event, penal statutes cannot list *all* the facts, conditions, circum-stances, instruments, methods, weapons, poisons, etc., by which a homicide or any other crime can be committed. A homicide statute, *e.g.* must therefore be interpreted to in-

---

[78] There are other meanings of "circumstances," *e.g.* that implied in "circumstantial," as contrasted with "direct," evidence, and that concerning the mitigation or aggravation of sentences, which usually extend beyond the orbit of substantive relevance and include matters of motivation which throw light upon the defendant's character.

[79] See chapter 8.

corporate within the proscription against "killing," words which signify "by any means and methods whatever." A similar universal reference is implied in every other penal statute.

It is therefore highly dubious whether one can maintain the distinction made by Professor J. C. Smith between "pure circumstances," which are required by the definition of the crime, and "consequential circumstances," which are required to cause the harm but are "not necessarily required by the definition of the crime."[80] In illustration, Professor Smith states that the definition of murder says nothing about a loaded gun; therefore, loaded gun is not a "pure circumstance" but, since that is necessary in a specific case, to cause death, it is a "consequential circumstance." As was suggested above, however, a loaded gun or any other lethal weapon is implied in the term "kill." In the above terminology, they are "pure circumstances." That circumstance is also necessary and sufficient to cause death; hence, the loaded gun may be allocated to causation, as Professor Smith states. It may also be included in the description of the death, since the description of a penal harm requires that it be related to the pertinent criminal conduct; and sometimes, e.g. death by poison or torture, that has special significance. Again, Professor Smith suggests that on a charge of larceny something in the pocket is a "consequential circumstance."[81] But taking anything of value, etc., is also part of the definition of the crime. It may be allocated to the conduct, as indicated, to the harm, i.e. having something of value taken from, etc., and to the cause, as a necessary condition of the taking, which connects the conduct and the harm.

In his inclusive definition of "act," Salmond gave "circumstances" an apparently independent status on a parity with "bodily activity" and "consequence."[82] Without entering

[80] Smith, *Two Problems in Criminal Attempts*, 70 Harv. L. Rev. 424-25 (1957).
[81] *Id.* at 425.
[82] Salmond, Jurisprudence 383 (7th ed. 1924).

into a detailed critique and translation of these terms in reference to the various relevant theories,[83] it may be stated directly, as was shown above, that circumstances must be allocated to and absorbed in the principles of criminal law and that none of the principles can be allocated or reduced to circumstances. The reason is that it is not circumstances but human conduct and the harm it causes which are material in the legally relevant situations.

In sum, (1) law is relevant to a world of facts, conditions, circumstances. (2) From the whole welter of these circumstances, every law selects those which are "material," hence, circumstances are relevant or irrelevant. Certain corollaries are implied, e.g. in causation, circumstances which are "mere conditions" may be distinguished from necessary and sufficient circumstances. (3) The principles of penal law absorb all that is factually relevant, whether that be termed operative, material facts, conditions or circumstances, and the latter do not absorb the former. This is implied since the principles are derived from penal laws. In a behaviorist scheme the "essential" factors might be reversed. In current penal law, however, it is human conduct which is paramount, while circumstances are, in effect, absorbed in the conduct, the concomitant authorship, and the resulting proscribed harms.

TORT AND PENAL HARM

The position reached in the above discussion is that the proscribed harms, defined by reference to the principles of criminal law, are social disvalues and that this is implied especially by the significance of *mens rea* which, in part, takes its meaning from its relation to harm.

A further step may be taken to analyze penal harm by comparing it with tortious injuries. Modern discussions start with Blackstone whose criteria for comparison of torts and crimes took three directions: a formal legal difference, the nature of the respective harms, and the pur-

---

[83] Salmond's theory is discussed *supra* in chapters 4 and 6.

poses of the two fields of law. Crimes are "in violation of
public law," torts, of private law; crimes are an infringe-
ment of public rights, torts, of civil rights.[84] There is,
nextly, brief but highly significant insistence on the essential difference of the substantive harms. Crimes affect
"the whole community, considered as a community, in its
social aggregate capacity . . . they strike at the very being
of society, which cannot possibly subsist where actions of
this sort are suffered to escape with impunity."[85] On the
other hand, civil injuries are "immaterial to the public."[86]
Thirdly, he reiterated the traditional distinction between
the ends of the two branches of law: redress of the private
injury by way of compensation, and punishment for the
public wrong.[87]

Austin completely rejected Blackstone's theory, arguing
that "the terms 'public' and 'private' may be applied in-
differently to *all* Law."[88] He repudiated the distinction
between torts and crimes on the basis of their respective
tendencies, *i.e.* that the harm of the latter is "more extensive." On the contrary, he asserted, "*All* wrongs [are] in
their *remote* consequences *generally* mischievous. . . ."[89] "*All*
offences affect the community, and *all* offences affect individuals."[90]

Stephen criticized any distinction between torts and
crimes on the basis of morality, asserting "the moral nature of the act has nothing to do with the question . . . there
is no reason why the same act should not belong to both
classes, and many acts do."[91] Kenny reaffirmed Stephen's
view that torts and crimes are not mutually exclusive. "In
the vast majority of cases" crimes are also torts since they

[84] 3 Bl. Comm. 2; 4 Bl. Comm. 5.
[85] 4 *ibid.*
[86] *Ibid.*
[87] *Id.* at 6, 7.
[88] Austin, Lectures on Jurisprudence 416, 517 (4th ed. 1879).
[89] *Id.* at 517.
[90] *Id.* at 417. He qualified this, *id.* at 517.
[91] Stephen, General View of the Criminal Law of England 5, 7
(1863). Stephen had in mind intentional torts. *Id.* at 6.

damage some individual. And he rejected Blackstone's generalization that every crime is also a tort,[92] noting sedition, possession of counterfeit dies, and attempt to commit suicide, in support. Paraphrasing Stephen, Kenny concluded that, "Criminal wrongs and civil wrongs thus are not sharply separated groups of acts; but are often one and the same act as viewed from different standpoints, the difference being not one of nature but only of relation."[93]

This might have been tenable if the word "only" had been omitted; but the inclusion of that word, together with the nature of intentional torts, encouraged the theory that there is no important difference between torts and crimes. The assumption underlying this view is that facts constitute intelligible entities that have significance apart from legal rules or other ideas. Instead, as Whitehead has remarked, fact is "a triumph of the abstract intellect." The relevance of this to Stephen's analysis is illustrated by his observation that it is just as fallacious to distinguish torts from crimes as it is husband from brother. The premise is that "man" refers to a single entity, that it denotes an unchanging natural phenomenon that can have but one meaning. But "man" may mean almost anything, depending upon how we regard him, *i.e.* upon the ideas, including relations, which we employ to direct our scrutiny.

The essential difference as regards the instant problem is that torts almost invariably include actual damage to some person, whereas in crimes, damage is not essential; instead, a social harm, an essential determinant of which is the moral culpability of the actor, supplies the requirement there. It follows that even intentional damage to a particular individual has a different meaning than the intentional commission of a social harm. This leads to the ultimate points of reference, the two elemental, irreducible realities —the individual and the community. The damage requirement in tort law serves to select and limit "the acts" to

[92] 4 Bl. Comm. 5.
[93] Outlines of Criminal Law 22 (15th ed. 1936).

those that damage particular persons. Even apart from the enormous extent of tort law devoted to negligence and strict liability, it follows that *moral culpability is not essential in tort law — immoral conduct is simply one of various ways by which individuals suffer economic damage.* But in penal law, the immorality of the actor's conduct is essential in the determination of the harm, and pecuniary damage is irrelevant.

These conclusions support some of those put forth rather loosely by Blackstone[94] and, in part, reaffirmed by Sir Carleton Allen.[95] Blackstone simply asserted that torts and crimes differ in their "nature or tendencies." Professor Allen significantly specified that at least one essential difference is the moral culpability required for criminal liability. But he also thought that "a wrong does not become two kinds of wrong because it gives rise to two separate legal processes"[96]—a view that seems hardly consistent with his general thesis, but rather reflects the influence of Stephen and Kenny.

In the light of the above suggested difference between penal harms and torts, we may consider the thesis that torts may be as harmful as, or more harmful than, crimes, *e.g.* the negligent operation of a train with much loss of life or the mismanagement of large businesses with vast economic damages, on the one hand, and "stealing a handkerchief," on the other.[97] It is apparent that such argument relies upon accidentals and, even more, that such disparate phenomena are considered as to render valid comparison

[94] ". . . every public offense . . . affects the individual, and it likewise affects the community." 4 Bl. Comm. 5.

[95] Allen, Legal Duties 233-4 (1931). *Cf.* 1 Bishop, Criminal Law § 32 (1923), and Holland, Jurisprudence 328 (1917).

[96] Allen, *id.* at 235-8.

[97] Kenny, *op. cit. supra* note 93, at 6-7, believed that "crimes, taken as a mass" provided much greater and widespread harm than that produced by torts. *Id.* at 5. In general, "this public mischief ought undoubtedly to be made the salient feature." But that criterion, he concluded, is not sufficiently precise. It does not give "the whole thing and the sole thing. . . ." *Id.* at 6. Also, penal actions stood in the way of Blackstone's generalization, since they concerned wrongs admittedly harmful to the entire community, but were nonetheless "civil" wrongs. Kenny also stresses petty police regulations. *Id.* at

impossible. Sound comparisons can be made only if non-essentials are ignored or held identical and some common standard is applicable. This is implied in the legal method of describing and evaluating types of harm regardless of particular factual variations, *e.g.* it is surely valid to hold that robbery is more serious than larceny even though a particular robber took only five dollars while a particular thief took $5,000,000. Again, holding particular "accidental" facts constant, one may compare a death caused by the negligent operation of a train with one caused by a deliberate killing. So, too, the fact that many more lives are lost annually through the negligent driving of automobiles than by intentional homicides of all kinds is irrelevant to the questions: (1) are crimes essentially different from torts? and (2) given the same external aspects of two harms, is one of them more serious than the other because it was caused by immoral conduct?

The significance of the theses enunciated above (that the tort includes economic damage which can be measured in terms of money whereas this is impossible as regards the social harm, and that morally culpable conduct is essential to the latter, the crime, but not in the tort) depends on their verification in the positive law of both fields and on the range of their application. The first supporting data, it will be recalled, were such crimes as sedition, *i.e.* social harms that have no individual incidence. The converse, representing the basic tort principle, may be most readily induced by reference to negligent damage and that in cases of strict liability.

Next, there are significant differences in the two fields among identically labelled wrongs. Thus, obtaining property

---

18-19, 9; and he noted that some acts that arouse indignation—such as corporate negligence and omission to rescue a child when that can easily be done—are not crimes at all. *Id.* at 8. Kenny concluded by accepting Austin's view that there is no valid substantive difference; there is only a difference in procedure, characterized by the state's control of criminal prosecution. His chief point of disagreement with Austin was his re-affirmance of the traditional difference between punishment and compensation. *Id.* at 20. Winfield came to similar conclusions in The Province of the Law of Tort 196-198 (1931).

by false pretenses is committed even though the complainant has sustained no financial loss,[98] but a civil suit for misrepresentation cannot succeed in such circumstances.[99] In libel, too, the distinction between the social harm and the individual damage is registered in the tort requirement that there be publication to a third person whereas prosecution lies if the communication was sent only to the one defamed. This also suggests a likely reconciliation of the presently diverse holdings regarding consent to an injury. An adult might well be permitted to waive any personal damages, *i.e.* his consent would eliminate the tort, but this should not determine the issue in the criminal law. A like significance is indicated by the related doctrines on contributory negligence, participation in a wrong, and condonation, which normally bar civil recovery, but not prosecution.[1] Finally, the differences in the law on assault in the two fields also support the suggested thesis, *e.g.* throwing stones at a blind person is not tortious because no damage is involved; but it is a criminal assault because a social harm is produced. On the other hand, in the case of pointing an unloaded gun, the actor knowing the facts but the victim being reasonably mistaken, the tort requirement is met but the social harm, as defined by the common law of crimes, requires an intent to injure.[2]

It is not implied in the above comparison of torts and penal harms that the two fields of law are mutually exclu-

[98] Miller, Criminal Law 389 (1934).

[99] Harper, Law of Torts § 226 (1933); 1 Harper and James, The Law of Torts, Section 7.15 at 590 (1956).

[1] For an argument that the rules of causation should operate differently in the criminal law and in torts, especially in intentional infliction of serious injuries, see Note, 31 Mich. L. Rev. 659, especially 675 *et seq.* (1933).

[2] Since there is an intent to frighten, there is no theoretical bar to holding the conduct criminal. See Edwards v. State, 4 Ga. App. 849, 62 S. E. 565 (1908). The difficulty in the cases results not from their extension of the *mens rea* in criminal assault to include an intention to frighten, but from the reliance on tort decisions to support the decision of criminal cases. *Cf.* State v. Deso, 110 Vt. 1, 1 A. 2d 710 (1938) and Chapman v. The State, 78 Ala. 463, 56 Am. Rep. 42 (1885).

sive or that the theory suggested above takes account of all of tort and penal law. Punitive damages, penal actions, trespass and nuisance alone exclude any neat coincidence of theory and law. On the criminal law side, wherever objective or strict liability prevails, a similar gap between theory and positive law is evident. The elucidation of "penal harm" in the various ways attempted above can extend no farther than the sustaining theory allows. Its significance, however, is not limited by the fact that the proscription of harms in legal systems is historically conditioned. On the contrary, whatever is known about criminal harms provides the only ground upon which formal, neutral, convenient, fortuitous, and irrational effects can be dealt with in practice.

CHAPTER VIII

CAUSATION

THE principle of causation designates and requires a causal relationship between legally proscribed harms and conduct.[1] That a legally proscribed harm is one of the polarities or relata is certain. But is the other relatum conduct or is it the *mens rea,* anterior to the conduct, which is the cause of the harm?

It seems evident, on reference to the ordinary run of crimes, that something in addition to a *mens rea* is required to produce a criminal harm. There must also be the manifestation of the *mens rea* in the external world;[2] and in most crimes this is observable in the external movements of the offender. This implies that both the *mens rea* and the defendant's external movements are required and that the conduct, thus formed, is the cause of penal harms. As was previously stated,[3] this also applies to criminal omissions (forbearance) ; indeed, they have particular significance in the elucidation of causation in penal law. For while, in a physical sense, an omission cannot of itself produce any external harm, nevertheless in law, as in everyday ethics, under certain conditions, personal forbearance is regarded as making use of external objects and forces. This indicates that "cause" has a distinctive meaning in law, and that is the principal subject of the present chapter. We may terminate the above summary by reaffirming the generalization

[1] *Supra* chapter 6.

[2] See Campbell, *Self-activity and its Modes,* pub. in Contemporary British Philosophy 83 (Lewis, ed. 1956).

[3] See *supra* chapter 6, especially 195-196.

stated above—the polar elements or relata which are required to be in a causal relation are criminal conduct[4] and penal harm.

MEANINGS OF "CAUSE" IN VARIOUS PERSPECTIVES

When it is asserted that conduct and harm must be in a *causal* relationship, what does that signify? It is ancient wisdom that our knowledge of anything consists in our knowing the causes of it. Because Aristotle saw purpose in nature, his theory of four aspects or types of causation[5] —(1) formal, (2) material, (3) final and (4) efficient—is suggestive in the analysis of legal and social problems. To cite his illustrations in the above sequence, the cause of a piece of bronze sculpture includes (1) the idea in the sculptor's mind—the definition of the essentials, (2) the bronze and other materials, (3) the sculptor's objective—a certain work of art, and (4) his molding the raw materials to actualize his idea and achieve his purpose. Although it is hazardous to transfer these meanings, it may be suggested that in terms of modern criminal law, the formal and efficient causes are "operative" in *mens rea* and conduct, while part of the material cause ("circumstances") may be a mere condition and part of it is included in the conduct; or, it may be allocated to the harm. The final cause is either a proscribed harm or it lies outside the legal definition of a crime because it is a motive or an objective beyond that harm.

There are, of course, other meanings of "causation;"[6] indeed, cause is an ultimate notion, deeply characteristic of human thought and expressed even among the most primitive people in their efiort to understand "the way of things." The first insight into the conditions of any adequate analysis of it is, therefore, that the meanings of "cause" must be

---

[4] "Conduct" and "voluntary conduct" are here used as synonyms. Conduct is contrasted with behavior, which is non-voluntary. See *supra* p. 177.

[5] Aristotle, Met. 1013a24-1013b.

[6] Loewenberg, *The Elasticity of the Idea of Causality*, pub. in Causality, 15 Univ. of Calif. Pub. in Philosophy 3 (1932).

related to definite perspectives. Whether the context is that of a philosophy or common sense or science or law or criminal law, there are always and necessarily distinctive questions that are raised; and this must be taken into account if something more than generalities about "cause" are sought. For example, the object of a legal inquiry is not some cause "in general," but "some cause for which the defendant is responsible."[7] The legal perspective thus requires a relevant meaning of "cause," one which is significant in legal liability; and the perspective of criminal law emphasizes a narrower meaning than that, reflecting the distinctive type of liability of that branch of law.

In a factual perspective, which includes that of empirical science, the cause of any given event is the sum of all the necessary conditions of that event, *i.e.* conditions are in no way distinguishable from causes. Indeed, since Hume, philosophers of science have taken an even more inclusive view than that, arguing that there is no *necessary* connection whatever between causes and effects, that there is only the habitual recognition of recurrent patterns, giving rise to descriptions of invariant co-variations which include simultaneous as well as successive changes. This challenges the significance of any effort to distinguish causes from conditions. Cosmologists, interested in the totality of a changing cosmos, also have no need to distinguish causes from conditions. But scientists usually work with a narrower view of cause, one that is crucial in particular experiments.

Common sense often distinguishes cause from condition: While the latter is necessary for the happening of an event, it does not, like a cause, "contribute positively thereto;" for example, a window is a condition, not a cause, of daylight in a room.[8] While it has other perspectives, common

---

[7] Laidlaw v. Sage, 158 N. Y. 73, 52 N. E. 679, 44 L. R. A. 216 (1899).

[8] 2 Coffee, The Science of Logic 62 (1918). The distinction between cause and condition can be traced to Plato: " . . . without bones and muscles . . . I cannot execute my purposes. But to say that I do as I do

sense is apt to focus upon what is interesting, *e.g.* novelty or, in a social context, upon what evokes evaluation; and these are reflected in everyday meanings of "cause."

The legal perspective is largely the inclusive common sense perspective, modified and guided by certain rules of liability. If a motorist drives 100 miles per hour while intoxicated and he collides with another automobile, killing the driver, the existence of the road, the presence of the other automobile, the mining and manufacturing processes that produced the machines, the ancestors of the respective parties and so on are necessary antecedents. But both common sense and law ignore all that as "mere conditions" and they focus on the defendant's excessive speed and his mental condition as the cause.

Again, common sense may share the psychologist's interest in an offender's motivation; while, for a sociologist, "etiology" may mean environmental factors or "differential association," and a biologist might wish to explore the heredity of offenders. But in criminal law "cause" is limited by the references of the rules of penal law, *i.e.* to certain conduct and harms. Accordingly, it is at least imprecise to say that the factual cause of a criminal harm is first determined, then the law is applied to fix liability. If a definite perspective is essential to cogent meaning of the term, relevant law must be employed from the outset to demark those aspects of a situation within which cause-in-fact is determined. The definitions of the various crimes not only select the relevant facts to be considered in the investigation of cause but also, as will be shown later, they participate normatively in the determination of the meaning of causation in penal law.

This does not imply that the issue of causation is identical with that of liability but rather that the narrower issue of causation is limited and in part defined by penal policy.

---

because of them . . . and not from the choice of the best . . . [shows] that they cannot distinguish the cause from the condition. . . ." Phaedo, 99b.

Thus, to take another example, when criminal liability for the death of a human being is in issue, causal relevance does not include the manufacture of guns and bullets. If a bullet was shot into the heart of the deceased, most of the rigorously scientific, *i.e.* in that sense, causal, generalizations of physics and biology are also ignored. What is important is whether the bullet was a substantial factor in the death and whether a particular person intentionally or recklessly shot that bullet into the body of the deceased. If he thus caused the death (*i.e.* substantially and voluntarily) he is criminally liable for the homicide. Accordingly, as will more fully appear, volition functions both as an essential element in legal cause and as an ethical ground of criminal liability (principle of *mens rea*).[9] We may now consider the problem of "legal cause" in more definite terms.

MEANINGS OF "CAUSE" IN THE LEGAL PERSPECTIVE

Of the many meanings of "cause," three are important in law: (1) cause as giving a motive or incentive, (2) cause as means-end action, and (3) cause as invariant co-variation or succession.[10] First, "cause" means giving a person a motive to act—to cause a responsible person to act means to persuade or coerce him to act or to proceed in other ways which foreseeably give him a ground or incentive for action.[11] This type of causation is limited to interpersonal relations and, despite the assumptions made by some sociologists in their discussion of "social control," it must be sharply distinguished from causation in the biological and inanimate realms. In criminal law this meaning of cause is the basis of the liability of an accessory before the fact. It is also operative in fraud, various political crimes, the commission of criminal harms under compulsion, and elsewhere. For example, where the editor of a newspaper advertised obscene literature and photographs, leading to their dis-

---

[9] See generally, Givanovitch, Du Principe de Causalité Efficiente en Droit Pénal (1908).

[10] Collingwood, *On the So-called Idea of Causation*, 38 Proc. Aris. Soc. (n. s.) 85 (1938).

[11] On cause as incentive, see MacIver, Social Causation, ch. 7 (1942).

semination,[12] the causation consisted of influencing the readers of the paper by providing a motive for their purchases.

In its second meaning, "cause" also concerns human action but it refers to the control by human beings, not of other human beings (*i.e.* as persons) but of lesser animals and physical things. One causes light by turning a switch, and an assailant causes an injury or death by shooting someone. This is perhaps the most frequent type of teleological causation—the use of physical means to achieve ends.[13] For example, in a trial for arson, where a picture frame was also burned, Sir Henry Hawkins charged the jury: ". . . if you think that the prisoner set fire to the frame of the picture with a knowledge that in all probability the house itself would thereby be set on fire . . . the prisoner's crime would be that of arson."[14]

The third principal meaning of "cause" is that of recurring pattern, invariable antecedent[15] or invariant order.[16] While common sense shares this scientific view, it also insists that there is a necessary connection between an antecedent and a consequence, if the former is a cause of the latter.[17] In the first two senses, which are teleological, cause is relevant to freedom and practical knowledge rather than to physical movements and theoretical knowledge—the sphere of the third meaning. In the former, cause concerns the human power to alter a situation or prevent the occurrence

[12] The King v. De Marny (1907), 1 K. B. 388, 21 Cox C. C. 371.
[13] Jhering, Law as a Means to an End, ch. 1 (trans. Husik, 1924).
[14] Rex v. Harris and Atkins (1882), 15 Cox C. C. 75, 77.
[15] Mill, A System of Logic, Book III, ch. 8 (1856).
[16] MacIver, *op. cit. supra* note 11.
[17] "The ordinary view of causation goes beyond the regularity view in at least the four following respects: (1) The effect is held to be continuous with, dependent on something in the cause so that the two do not merely happen in regular succession, but are intrinsically connected with each other. (2) The cause is held to explain the effect, to answer not only the question—how?—but the question—why?, so that the demand for causes is primarily a demand for reasons, which implies that there is a logical or quasi-logical connexion between the two such that the cause is at least part of the reason for the effect

of an imminent event. In the latter, human power is irrelevant—causation is a natural process to which human beings can to some degree adjust, but which they cannot alter.

Means-end causation, which is probably the primitive idea of causation, is derived from common experience. There is the experience of the process of reaching a decision, the accompanying tensions and internal effort, external movement in the direction of the desired end and, normally, the occurrence of that end. We say our conduct "caused" that "effect." That seems to be the primary meaning of cause, and it is also its most important one in the criminal law, limited, as by this writer, to certain (voluntary) conduct. For the scientist, on the other hand, cause is merely the way physical bodies move—regularity, invariant co-variation or succession—these are the terms he employs to describe mechanical changes. Thus scientific laws are causal propositions in the sense that they are general descriptions of the co-variation of variables. Cause in this sense is *how* things change in relation to other changes. Whatever the metaphysical position may be, for the scientist there is no going back of this how, this pattern of change, for any deeper explanation than that of scientific cause.[19]

It is evident that both types of causation discussed above —teleological and mechanical—operate in the commission of crimes, including criminal forbearance. Criminal law and most psychologies postulate certain internal states—thinking, intending, feeling, and so on—sometimes assembled as "the self;" and the self is differentiated from the external world, which includes the physical human body. The self— the totality of internal states—cannot effect any change in

and helps to make the occurrence of the latter intelligible. . . . (3) The cause is held actively to produce or determine the effect. . . . (4) Causality involves necessity. If there is a causal law connecting A and B, it is not only the case that B does follow, but that it *must* follow." Ewing, *A Defence of Causality*, 33 Proc. Aris. Soc. (n. s.) 98-99 (1933).

[19] Lundberg, Foundations of Sociology 260 (1939) insists that in social science "a generalized statement of *how* events occur is the only *why* we seek. . . . " This is criticized by MacIver, *op. cit. supra* note 11, at 204-206.

the outer world except by using external means. (As was noted, in criminal forbearance the offender "uses" active external forces by not interfering with certain effects of their operation.) Without implying "dualism," it may be said that the self uses the body and the body uses other instruments upon and against other external objects. These objects, being physical, tend to move in regular patterns, exhibiting the uniformities, the invariant order described in laws of physical causation. Human beings who select certain instruments to achieve their ends, must adapt their conduct to the known ways in which physical changes occur. If a human being cannot survive under water more than three minutes, anyone who wished to kill a person by drowning him would need to use means that kept the victim under water more than three minutes. Since live organisms cannot tolerate strychnine, the object of a poisoner must be the introduction of strychnine into his victim's body. Accordingly, we may expect that *"sine qua non,"* as used in judicial decisions to be discussed later, will refer to the defendant's conduct or to the operation of physical forces or to both.

DIFFERENCES IN CAUSATION IN TORT AND CRIMINAL LAW

Causation raises fewer and simpler problems in criminal law than it does in the law of torts. This, indeed, is self-evident if criminal liability is limited to (voluntary) conduct, while liability for torts encompasses not only such conduct, but also vast areas of inadvertent damage and behavior "at peril." In addition, in tort law the damage or injury may extend to extraordinary lengths[19] and is often very uncertain in its character and dimensions. But criminal harms are definitely described and limited, and injuries other than or beyond those harms are not legally material.[20]

---

[19] ". . . it is frequently held that the defendant is liable for all 'direct' consequences of his negligence, although they were unforeseeable and lay beyond the scope of the risk created. . . . " Prosser, Handbook of the Law of Torts 263 (2nd ed. 1955).

[20] There are, of course, many problems in criminal law concerning the proscribed harms, *e.g.* whether a "human being" has died, whether

CAUSATION   255

The fact that a financial obligation is involved in tort litiga-
tion, while punishment is the criminal sanction, probably
complicates the determination of causal relationships in the
former.

The most significant difference regarding causal problems
in the two fields concerns negligence. In tort law, the lack
of a generally accepted theory of liability for negligence,
attested, *e.g.* in current polemics regarding insurance, has
an especially unfortunate influence upon the elucidation of
problems of tortious causation.[21] Although there is disagreement regarding the penalization of negligent harm-
doing, there is also a very substantial consensus favoring a
definite theory which excludes inadvertence from the scope
of penal law; and, in any event, the reference of the diverse
theories is to a relatively small area of penal law. The
definiteness of causation in the largest, most important part
of penal law and its uncertainty in tort law result from the
fact that, while voluntary harm-doing is in the clearly
marked realm of means-ends, negligent harm-doing is in the
sphere of mechanics — the defendant inadvertently, *i.e.*
fortuitously,[22] moved (or did not move) certain physical
objects. In Kantian terms[23] voluntary action is self-
determination, and one does not look for causes lying back
of that; indeed, reasons are not causes in the sense of being
antecedent determinants. Accordingly, when a harm has
been imputed to a normal actor, on the ground that he
voluntarily committed it, that is a sufficient causal explanation. In contrast, in the realm of mechanics every movement
of physical bodies (including inadvertent movements of
human bodies) is explained in terms of other external
movements or causes. Thus, poor eyesight, inability to judge
speed, awkwardness, and so on are external causes of sub-

---

a certain structure is a "dwelling house," the subject matter of larceny and so on. See chapter 7 *supra*.

[21] "Some rules of conduct, particularly those that are extracted
from the broad notion we call negligence, cover a vague, indefinite
area of risk that escapes all efforts of advance charting." Malone,
Ruminations on Cause-in-Fact, 9 Stanford L. Rev. 73 (1956).

[22] Root v. Topeka Ry. Co., 96 Kan. 694, 153 P. 550 (1915).

[23] Paton, The Categorical Imperative 209 (1948).

standard performance.[24] The salient fact is that inadvertent movements set off other physical movements and so on, which were followed by a more or less remote injury somewhere along the line.

The consequence is that it is often very difficult to discover in specific cases whether a distant harm is actually an instance of a general pattern of mechanical change. In the criminal law, however, purposive conduct is predominant and that kind of causal relationship is spontaneously, almost instinctively, recognized. For example, if D plunges a knife into V's heart and the latter immediately dies, if D gets into V's automobile, starts it and drives off, if he takes money from V at the point of a gun, if he seizes V and forcibly has intercourse with her—in these and the vast majority of situations with which the core of criminal law is concerned, while, of course, cause in the mechanical sense is also operative, there is no problem of causation. The imputation of the harm to the actor is instantaneous and the substantial operation of mechanical cause is so obvious as to exclude any discussion of a problem in that regard. Only in certain cases of homicide, especially where considerable time elapsed between the wounding and the death, does one find discussions of causation comparable in character, but hardly in volume, to what is a commonplace in tort law. In this narrow area of criminal law and in very much of tort law, problems frequently arise because mechanical causation is often extremely difficult to detect and delimit even with the aid of medical and other experts.

In these areas, questions concerning the substantiality or effectiveness of the defendant's conduct or behavior also raise complicated problems for the fact-finders. For example, while it is easy to state definitions of "fatal" and "fatal wound," it is often extremely difficult to predict that a particular wound will cause death or to determine later that it did contribute substantially to it.[25] The authority of a

24 See *supra* pp 114, 167-168.

25 3 Stephen, H. Cr. L. 7; and see Johnson v. State, 236 Ind. 509, 141 N. E. 2d 444 (1957), where a conviction was reversed because it

jury cannot escape the factual uncertainties or transcend
the limitations of medical science; and rules of law, *e.g.* the
burden of proof in a criminal case and that death must have
occurred within a year and a day, can only lessen the guess-
ing. It is essential to distinguish this factual question from
the principle of causation and the principle of *mens rea*,
although, as we shall see, all of these questions are closely
interrelated.

DIRECT CAUSATION IN HOMICIDE

Criminal liability for a homicide is based upon the facts
at the time of the injury and upon the defendant's knowledge of those facts. The subsequent death is, of course, a
material fact; but it is fallacious to assume, because a death
occurred after a battery by the defendant, that he intended
to kill or was reckless in that regard. This would seem
obvious in cases where an apparently minor injury, *i.e.* one
which has slight consequence under normal conditions, was
inflicted. Even in these cases, however, the decisions are
often incompatible with the principles of criminal law. In
some cases where an ordinarily minor battery is followed by
the death of the victim, who was actually in precarious
health, there is no doubt whatever regarding the facts. The
battery itself was definitely not, by normal standards, a
serious one, it accelerated the progress of the disease or
precipitated its fatal efficacy, and the offender was wholly
ignorant of his victim's physical condition, indeed no one in
his position would reasonably have known it. In technical
terms, the battery satisfies the requirement of *sine qua non*,
e.g. "the death of his wife [who had a serious lung disease]
at the time it occurred, would not have happened but for the
assault and battery . . . ;"[26] and it also contributed substantially to the death. But the death was certainly not
caused in the means-end sense of causation. It could not

---

was impossible to determine whether the death was caused by bullet
shots or severe blows, the defendant being charged only with the
former.

[26] Commonwealth v. Fox, 73 Mass. (7 Gray) 587 (1856).

have been voluntarily caused since the defendant believed (reasonably!) that the person he struck was in normal health.

Unfortunately, even in many cases where a valid decision is reached, the relevant principles are not articulated. Thus, in *Couch*[27] the defendant fired several gunshots on a public highway, frightening a pregnant woman and causing her to abort; she died shortly thereafter. Despite the misdemeanor, which the court probably regarded as *malum in se,* a demurrer to the indictment was sustained. This ruling was not explicitly based upon the defendant's ignorance of the deceased's condition; instead, the alleged ground was that the death was not "the natural or the probable consequence of the shooting." But anything that happens is "natural" in a mechanical sense, and the shooting was admittedly the substantial *sine qua non* of the death. *Mens rea* was the limiting principle, qualifying the required kind of causation, and the court may have had that in mind in referring to "probable" consequences. In *Johnson's* case[28] the defendant struck an intoxicated person who later died. The testimony was that the death would not have occurred if the deceased had been sober. An acquittal of manslaughter was directed on the ground that "it was impossible so to apportion the operation of the several causes, as to be able to say with certainty that the death was immediately occasioned by any one of them in particular." Since it was recognized that the battery was a substantial cause, little weight can be attached to the failure to prove that the blow was the "particular" cause. The likelihood is that, just as in *Couch,* a substantial *sine qua non* cause was not recognized as a cause-in-law because of the defendant's state of mind; but there was no clear reliance upon the lack of the requisite *mens rea* or any discussion of the meaning of voluntary homicide. So, too, was it held in a recent case, where the defendant had seized the deceased by the throat

27 32 Ky. L. Rep. 638, 106 S. W. 830 (1908). See *Annotation: Homicide by Fright or Shock,* 47 A. L. R. 2d 1072 (1956).
28 (1827) 1 Lewin 164, 168 Eng. Rep. 999.

and shook him, and the latter, who had very high blood pressure, collapsed and, after paralysis and pneumonia, died. Despite the fact that the choking "contributed to" the cerebral hemorrhage and paralysis, the conviction of manslaughter was reversed on the ground that " 'choking the deceased' was [not] the 'effective agency' in causing his death." It could "not be said with any degree of certainty that the deceased died as the result of any criminal agency."[29] Although the defendant committed a misdemeanor *malum in se* in assaulting the deceased, nothing was said of constructive homicide. Again, the alleged ineffectiveness of physical causation was the dubious ground of the decision rather than the lack of the *mens rea* required in criminal homicide and the lack, therefore, of means-end causation.

In many decisions which impose liability for a criminal homicide where the deceased was in precarious health, the facts show either a shooting[30] or a very violent attack[31] or both such wounding and knowledge of the illness and thus of the risk of very serious injury.[32] In these decisions, assertions that the defendant's "ignorance of the diseased condition" would exclude murder, but not manslaughter, "nor would ignorance on the part of defendant of the diseased physical condition of . . . excuse his acts" are usually dicta which suggest that negligence may support manslaughter. They are not relevant to deaths caused by the infliction of an apparently minor battery by a person wholly ignorant of the precarious health. Where liability for criminal homicide is imposed in this latter type of case it is rested entirely on the misdemeanor-manslaughter rule, as *e.g.* in *Frazier*,[33] where the defendant punched a hemophiliac, and in *Bell*,[34] where the defendant and the deceased

---

[29] Fine v. State, 193 Tenn. 422, 426, 428, 246 S. W. 2d 70 (1952).

[30] In State v. Wilson, 114 La. 398, 38 S. 397 (1905), this was followed by pneumonia.

[31] State v. O'Brien, 81 Ia. 88, 46 N. W. 752 (1890).

[32] Commonwealth v. Fox, *supra* note 26.

[33] State v. Frazier, 339 Mo. 966, 98 S. W. 2d 707 (1936).

[34] State v. Bell, 192 A. 553 (Del. 1937).

engaged in a fist fight. The misdemeanors were declared *mala in se* and the defendants' blows a sufficient *sine qua non* factor. Such holdings have been challenged,[35] and they are glaring examples of the dominance of constructive criminal homicide in the United States.

Except where there is rigid reliance upon constructive homicide, the principle of *mens rea*, though unavowed, functions to exclude liability for homicide in such cases. Thus, the modern decisions have repudiated the law of Hale's day, when, despite the defendant's lack of knowledge of the possibility of serious injury, accelerating death by irritating a disease and even death caused by a slight wound and the injured person's neglect to care for it were held to be criminal homicides.[36] But because the repudiation of the old law is not avowed in terms of the principles which exclude such liability despite the presence of substantial physical causation, the rationale of the decisions is unclear.

Articulation of the principle of *mens rea* and recognition of its limiting function in defining legal causation can clarify judicial decision in this area. What apparently requires emphasis is that only (voluntary) conduct warrants criminal liability; and conduct includes at least knowledge of the risk of harm.[37] That criminal conduct[38] presupposes such knowledge is definitely recognized in the doctrine *ignorantia facti*, which provides a complete defense. The death of the victim of an assault and the dominance of the idea of physical causation inhibit analogous interpretations of the meaning of conduct (cause) in the cases discussed above, while constructive criminal homicide—the felony-murder, misdemeanor-manslaughter rule—continues to supply an easy rationalization of untenable judgments.

[35] Criswell v. State, 151 Tex. Cr. R. 473, 208 S. W. 2d 896 (1948). A Utah statute provides that a homicide committed in a fair fist fight is excusable. Title 103-28.8, U. C. A. (1943).

[36] 1 P. C. 428.

[37] *Cf.* Aristotle, Ethics, Bk. V, 1135a 20-25, and *infra* chapter 11 at note 9.

[38] "I think it is clear that the criminal law as we know it is based upon moral principle." Devlin, *The Enforcement of Morals*, 45 Proc. Brit. Acad. (1959).

We have been considering situations where the defendant's conduct and a certain harm are the only factors involved: The defendant inflicted a wound which was followed by death. His conduct may have been an apparently minor assault which, in fact, was committed on a person in precarious health. Although the battery was certainly a *sine qua non* of the death and also contributed substantially to it, we have seen that, except where the misdemeanor-manslaughter rule was rigidly followed, liability for the homicide was excluded on the actual, if unavowed, ground of the lack of the requisite *mens rea*. While many of these decisions may be based directly on the principle of *mens rea*, that of causation is equally involved since the interrelations of the two are such that the relevant "legal cause" is restricted to means-end causing, *i e.* to causing directed by a *mens rea*. This accords with the established usage of "legal cause," as will more fully appear in the later discussion.

In cases of the voluntary infliction of obviously serious wounds, the decisions rarely distinguish the fatal wounds among them on the basis of any thorough prognosis at the time of the injury. Determination of the factual issue in this regard is probably influenced by the victim's death and the benefit of aftersight. In effect, the statutory provision that in murder there must be an "intent to kill" is liberally interpreted to mean an intent to inflict a serious injury. Yet, the facts in many cases do not show that the offenders intended to inflict a fatal wound. Perhaps the indicated differences are too refined for adjudication and such cases had best be assigned to the discretion of those who impose or modify sentences rather than arbitrarily treated as intentional killings. In any event, it must be acknowledged that on principle, there are gaps between the meaning of the words in the statutes and the facts which are often treated as falling within them.

INTERVENING CAUSE

The problem of causation becomes more involved when the conduct of other persons enters the situation as "inter-

vening causes." While such interventions occupy the entire
terrain of the relevant legal classification, *i.e.* they are intentional, reckless, negligent, or accidental, it will be helpful
to consider them as comprising two principal types:

(1) the defendant fatally injures someone and, subsequently, another person voluntarily or negligently substantially accelerates the death, or a subsequent accident does
that; and

(2) the defendant's conduct motivates other persons
(sometimes the victim) to act, and their conduct is the
immediate cause of a death.

In the first type, where the defendant voluntarily inflicted
a fatal wound, there would, in the absence of the subsequent
independent conduct or event, have been no question regarding the offender's liability for the homicide. But his
liability must be determined by what actually happened, not
by what would have been caused, and by the legal significance of the intervening actor's liability for the homicide.
The liability of both actors is very much affected by the view
that a dying person is a human being, and that an injury
which greatly accelerates his death kills him.

In this type of problem, as stated, the subsequent accelera-
tion of death is caused by the negligent behavior or the
conduct of an independent responsible person or by an accident. Of the first, most of the cases concern negligent
medical care, and a distinction is drawn between negligence
which merely aggravates the original wound, *e.g.* an unskillful operation, and negligence which supplies a new force
which "*sua propria*" accelerates the death, *e.g.* communication of an infectious disease. Only the latter frees the
original offender from liability for criminal homicide.

Most of the negligence cases concern aggravation of the
original wound, and the expression of an exceptional exculpatory rule regarding a new force is therefore apt to be
dictum. In these cases there is a serious stabbing or gunshot
wound, and the defense that negligent surgery accelerated
the death or that competent surgery would have saved the
injured person's life is uniformly rejected. "The underlying

principle is that one who intentionally inflicts a wound calculated to destroy life, and from which death ensues, cannot throw responsibility for the act either upon the carelessness or ignorance of his victim or upon unskillful or improper treatment which aggravated the wound and contributed to his death."[39] Similarly, the negligent failure of the victim to secure medical assistance or competent medical assistance does not exclude liability for criminal homicide.[40]

In *Kane*,[41] the defendant shot a pregnant woman; a miscarriage was followed by septic peritonitis and death. The defense urged that negligent medical and surgical care, not the bullet wounds, was the cause of her death, but this was rejected and a conviction of the homicide was affirmed. The medical care and the operation were "made necessary" by the defendant. "It is only where the death is solely attributable to the secondary agency, and not at all induced by the primary one, that its intervention constitutes a defense. Thus, if the interns at St. Catherine's Hospital had carelessly killed Anna Klein by the negligent administration of a deadly poison, the defendant would not have been liable for her death, though he would still have remained responsible for the assault; but he was liable for killing her, if the jury were satisfied, as they must have been, that, no matter what was done at the hospital, the pistol-shot wounds which he inflicted operated to cause her death."[42]

In *Bush*,[43] on the other hand, a conviction of murder was reversed where a surgeon communicated scarlet fever to the wounded man, who subsequently died. Although the court held that the jury might have found that the bullet wound

---

[39] State v. Tomassi, 137 Conn. 113, 119, 75 A. 2d 67 at 70 (1950). So, too, State v. Gabriella, 163 Ia. 297, 144 N. W. 9 (1913) and Johnson v. State, 64 Fla. 321, 59 S. 894 (1912).

[40] Commonwealth v. Hackett, 84 Mass. (2 Allen) 136 (1861); Embrey v. State, 94 Tex. Cr. R. 591, 251 S. W. 1062 (1923); Reg. v. Holland (1841), 174 Eng. Rep. 313.

[41] 213 N. Y. 260, 107 N. E. 655 (1915).

[42] *Id.* at 657.

[43] Bush v. Commonwealth, 78 Ky. 268 (1880).

alone was not fatal, it emphasized that the scarlet fever was a new factor, *i.e.* it "was not the natural consequence of the wound. . . . If the death was not connected with the wound in the regular chain of causes and consequences, there ought not to be any responsibility."[44] In *Jordan,*[45] the victim of a serious stabbing was taken to a hospital where he died of pneumonia several days later. There was medical testimony to the effect that the wound had almost healed and that the death was caused by pneumonia following the improper administration of an antibiotic and also the excessive injection of certain fluids. The conviction of murder was set aside on the ground that the death did not result from "normal treatment."[46]

Cases of a major accident after a mortal wounding are very rare. In a recent unreported New Jersey case,[47] the victim of a serious stabbing was being carried to a hospital in an ambulance, when a traffic collision occurred. An indictment charging murder was dismissed and a charge of felonious assault was substituted—the alleged reason being the inability of the doctors to determine whether the death was the result of the stabbing or of injuries received in the automobile accident.

[44] *Id.* at 271-72. In Livingston v. The Comomnwealth, 18 Va. 592 (1857), the defendant severely beat the deceased, who became quite ill and died. A doctor testified that a post-mortem examination revealed "sufficient cause of death, without referring it to the beating." *Id.* at 594. A conviction of manslaughter was set aside on the ground that the blow was not a mortal one and that the disease which "supervened" and caused the death was not produced by the beating.

Cf. The trial court's instruction that " . . . if they believed the death resulted from the removal of his appendix, or if they had reasonable doubt as to whether it did or not, they should find the accused not guilty of the homicide alleged, is substantially correct, and suffices for submission of the hypothesis relied upon." State v. Snider, 81 W. Va. 522, 94 S. E. 981 (1918). The judgment was reversed because of a procedural error.

[45] (1956) 40 Cr. App. R. 152.

[46] But *cf.* the Canadian Criminal Code, sec. 197 and Lyons (1949) C. C. C. 351.

The Jordan case is discussed in (1957) Cr. L. Rev. 430, by G. Williams who interprets the opinion to hold that the medical treatment was "grossly improper." See also, Camps and Havard, *Causation in Homicide—A Medical View,* (1957) Cr. L. Rev. 576.

[47] *New York Times,* January 6, 1957.

If a subsequent fatal accident and subsequent negligence which give rise to a new cause of death exclude the first offender's liability for the homicide, it would seem evident that the same result should be reached where there was a subsequent voluntary fatal wounding. What is certain is that the second offender is liable for criminal homicide. "He struck the last blow, and if the deceased had previously received a mortal blow, or whether mortal or not, if the last blow hastened his death, or caused his death by reason of the condition deceased was in when he received the last blow, the defendant would be guilty, if the other elements of murder existed."[48]

The liability of the first offender for the criminal homicide is, however, a moot question. The problem is this—since mortals die but once and inasmuch as the second offender is guilty of the criminal homicide, how can the first offender also be held for the criminal homicide? That he is not liable for the criminal homicide, although, of course, he is guilty of the deadly assault, has been held or asserted in several cases.[49] An opposite decision was rendered in *Lewis*.[50]

In the *Lewis* case, the defendant inflicted a mortal wound on his brother-in-law; the latter soon afterwards cut his own throat and died within five minutes. If the deceased had become insane or if, because of excruciating pain, his suicide had been an instinctive or reflex reaction, his death

---

Cf. cases of the type where the defendant knocked the deceased down and the latter was accidentally killed by a kick from a horse, People v. Rockwell, 39 Mich. 503 (1878), or by a passing automobile, People v. Fowler, 178 Cal. 657, 174 P. 892 (1918). A conviction was upheld in the latter case on the ground that the death was "the natural and probable result of the defendant's conduct in leaving Duree lying helpless and unconscious in a public road, exposed to that danger." *Id.* at 896.

[48] Fisher v. The State, 78 Tenn. 121, 125-26 (10 Lea 150) (1882). So, too, in The People v. Ah Fat, 48 Cal. 61 (1874) and Duque v. State, 56 Tex. Cr. R. 214, 119 S. W. 687 (1909).

[49] State v. Scates, 50 N. C. 409 (1858); Walker v. State, 116 Ga. 537, 42 S. E. 787 (1902), and State v. Wood, 53 Vt. 184 at 186 (1881) where it was pointed out that, "The question does not turn upon the moral aspect of the case." What is decisive is the "consummation of the intent" or the lack of that.

[50] 124 Cal. 551, 57 P. 470 (1899).

would have been imputable to D, as the direct act of D. Those, however, were not the material facts in the *Lewis* case, and we must proceed on the premise that the deceased was a normal, responsible person. It will clarify analysis of this case to assume a somewhat altered set of facts, namely: (1) D inflicts a mortal wound on X as a result of which X would have died ten months later; (2) X cuts a vital artery in his body and (3) dies in five minutes. The difficulties in the way of holding D liable for the homicide of X would have been even more readily perceived if, instead of X's cutting his own throat, Z, his deadly enemy, had done that. In any event, we begin with the certain judgment that Z (or X) is guilty of the homicide of X. This implies that X, though dying, was a human being and that Z voluntarily inflicted a fatal wound on X, *i.e.* one which substantially accelerated X's death.

On what ground then can it be maintained, as the court decided in *Lewis*, that D is guilty of X's homicide? That X would have died within one year and a day as the result of the mortal wound inflicted on him by D does not support this judgment. It is not what would have happened but what did happen that is material, as is evident in many criminal attempts. It may be contended, next, that to free D from liability for the homicide, despite the fact that he inflicted a fatal wound, is to bestow an advantage upon him which he does not deserve. But that also ignores the principle of harm and the fact that inflicting a mortal wound is not homicide, as well as the subsequent independent killing which cannot be imputed to D. Finally, there is the ground emphasized by the court, namely, that X died as the result of two mortal wounds, one of which had been inflicted by D. But the fact that the effect of the first fatal wound continued to the very end of X's life does not support the *Lewis* judgment. That would also have been the fact had the first wound been serious but not fatal; and in that event the first offender would clearly not be guilty of a criminal homicide even if the subsequent voluntarily inflicted wound would not have been fatal except for the victim's weakened condition. In both situations, so long as it is agreed that the second offender (or the deceased) voluntarily killed the deceased, certain rules of legal liability are the decisive factors. At bottom, there is a conflict here between the notion that killing a dying man is a new, sufficient, autonomous cause of his death, and the notion of the continued efficacy of the first fatal wounding. But, it is submitted, the legal principles and the liability of the subsequent actor should prevail over the physical cause of death in determining the issue of legal causation.

Difficulties arose in the *Lewis* case because these principles and rules were not clearly kept in view or because the suicide affected analysis or because the deceased's act, occurring very soon after he was shot by the defendant, was assumed to be simultaneous with the shooting. If, instead of suicide, the later blow had been inflicted by Z, there would probably have been no prosecution of D for the homicide even if X had died within a month. And, as suggested, an interpretation of the *Lewis* decision which would render it consistent with the relevant principles and rules of penal law is that the shooting by the defendant and the cutting by the deceased were simultaneous actions. The facts, however, do not support that interpretation.

Let us assume such a case without the involvement of suicide. D and Z, acting independently, shoot X simultaneously—D through the head, Z through the heart. Both bullets strike at the same moment and X dies instantly. Both D and Z are liable for the homicide. It is often assumed that the liability of such simultaneous actors constitutes an exception to *sine qua non*; but that is untenable. Whether *sine qua non* means merely a necessary condition or whether it means a substantial or sufficient necessary condition, in either case it represents an essential aspect of the principle of causation. But if *sine qua non* is essential in all crimes, there can be no exception concerning simultaneous criminal acts.

In analyzing cases of simultaneous fatal woundings, one must adhere to the facts as well as to the requirement of causal relation. The fact is that both actions caused the death. That either would have caused it in the absence of the other does not imply that neither was in fact a cause. It does not imply that this is an exception to the causal principle. It only signifies that the usual simple application of the "but for" formula is not relevant to this situation, that it would be superficial and misleading to apply it here in a sense carried over from single-cause situations. The fact remains that, although either shot would have been sufficient to cause the harm, both actually caused it; and it is only necessary to find an apt way of stating that in conformity with the principle of causation.

One such way may be suggested. Every specific causal relation implies a causal law, *i.e.* a general description of the co-variation of types or classes of variables.[51] Thus *sine qua non* (or substantial *sine qua non*) designates the entire class of cases within which the instant one falls. It asks—would such harms as the present one have happened except for conduct of the general class of the defendant's conduct? Very similar instances of simultaneous causes, such as those considered above, fall within a single class and causal generalization. It follows that simultaneous instances of the same type or class of causes exemplify *sine qua non* no less than, indeed, better than, does a single instance within that class.

With reference to the type of problem discussed above, it may be concluded, with reservations arising from the

---

[51] Specific events and changes are explained "by being shown to be particular examples of a general law." Campbell, What is Science? 78 (1922). Failure to show that is the reason why driving without a license is not a cause of a death. Commonwealth v. Williams, 133 Pa. Super. 104, 1 A. 2d 812 (1938). *Cf.* " . . . the mere fact that the accused was unlawfully carrying the weapon in question at the time it was accidentally discharged is not, under the circumstances, a material element in the case, for it is manifest that such unlawful act did not, during the scuffle between the parties, render the pistol any more liable to be discharged than though the carrying thereof had been lawful." Potter v. State, 162 Ind. 213, 70 N. E. 129, 131 (1904).

paucity of cases, (a) that a subsequent voluntary fatal wound excludes the original offender's liability for the homicide, (b) that subsequent negligent behavior which sets into operation a new fatal force, *e.g.* a serious infectious disease or obviously improper medical treatment, also excludes the first offender from liability for criminal homicide, but (c) that any other subsequent negligent behavior, no matter how serious, such as a negligently performed operation, leaves the original offender liable for criminal homicide, *i.e.* this does not "break" the chain of causation.

In evaluating these rules, it may be granted that it is often very difficult and sometimes impossible to distinguish among the original offenders in the above situations on grounds of culpability. If only a subsequent *voluntary* fatal wounding excluded the original offender's liability for the homicide, a cynical critic might surmise that "the law" got a "victim," and was thus content to let the first offender off with a lesser punishment. Unfortunately for such criticism, negligence which provides a "new" cause of death also excludes the first offender from liability for the homicide and does not provide a substitute. The solution must lie elsewhere, and it will be found in the principles of harm and causation. The problem is like that encountered in criminal attempts where, also, although the moral culpability of the attemptor is often the same as that of the murderer, the crime and the punishment are very different.[52]

It will, no doubt, have occurred to the reader that the distinction applied in the above negligence-situations is a dubious one. The human body is an organism, and if a person dying from a bullet wound is stricken with scarlet fever or even administered poison, the net effect upon his power to survive may have been no different than if a negligent major operation had been performed. And, although it is easy to recognize the persuasiveness of the existing distinction, that of a "new" force as contrasted with the "same wound merely aggravated," it is nevertheless arbitrary,

[52] See *infra* chapter 15.

since competent medical service in hospitals is usual, to hold that negligence in performing an operation was foreseeable.

If, in fact, the one situation comes pretty much to the other, if fatal wound plus negligent operation is equivalent to fatal wound plus negligently communicated scarlet fever, one needs to face the wider issue—should *any* subsequent negligence, no less than voluntary misconduct, which substantially accelerates death absolve the original offender from liability for the homicide? On principle, it is submitted, an affirmative answer should be given. But it is possible that practical considerations, *e.g.* the hazard of raising many difficult controversies regarding medical service[53] (as compared with the relative ease of establishing a "new" force) should prevail.

CAUSATION BY MOTIVATION

In the first type of causation discussed above—causing in the sense of giving someone an incentive for action—the defendant does not directly commit the harm in issue, but his conduct (including speech) foreseeably motivates another person to commit the harm, for which he is not criminally liable, but which the law imputes to the defendant.

Several situations must be distinguished from this type of causation. There are situations where the harm in question (usually the death of a human being) was not voluntarily committed by the immediate doer; instead it was the direct act of the defendant. For example, where the defendants freed the hands of their psychotic father, who was holding a gun, from the grip of an officer, the parent shot and killed the officer.[54] In these circumstances, the parent was merely the defendants' instrument, just as a child, told by an adult to perform a harmful act, would be the tool of that person. These cases indicate that in the causal relationship being considered, the person who commits the harm imputed to the defendant must be a normal adult.

---

[53] *Cf.* Johnson v. State, *supra* note 39; State v. Gabriella, *supra* note 39; Reg. v. Holland, *supra* note 40. See note 46 *supra*.

[54] Johnson et al. v. State, 142 Ala. 70, 38 S. 182 (1905).

But that fact alone is not sufficient to constitute this type of causal relation. Various other factors define the "independence" or "voluntariness" of the intervening conduct, as is shown, *e.g.* in the classic squib case. In a recent Indiana version[55] the defendant threw a grenade at the feet of one who immediately kicked it some distance away, where it exploded and killed the deceased. This was instinctive or reflex behavior, not the (voluntary) conduct of the person who kicked the grenade, and the death was thus directly caused by the defendant who had thrown it. Similar situations include the case of a boy in a canoe who, to avoid being shot by the defendant, jumped into the water and was drowned;[56] setting fire to a hotel, causing guests to seek an escape which proved fatal;[57] and the case of the wife who jumped from a window to escape a violent attack by her husband.[58] In these situations, although the persons immediately involved were not "mere instruments," their instinctive or reflex behavior was not a "voluntary cause."

Similarly excluded from the type of causation under discussion is an English case, where the defendant, wishing to kill her child, gave a bottle of poison to the person caring for the child, saying it was medicine and should be administered. There, again, since that person was ignorant of the facts, the harm, if committed, would have been the direct act of the defendant.[59]

Another situation which is also excluded is described in a Michigan case[60] where the defendant had knocked the deceased down and a by-stander, without any encouragement, solicitation or agreement whatever by or with the defendant,

---

[55] Madison v. State, 234 Ind. 517, 130 N. E. 2d 35 at 38. (1955).

[56] Letner v. State, 156 Tenn. 68, 299 S. W. 1049 (1927).

[57] Reddick v. Commonwealth, 17 Ky. L. Rep. 1020, 33 S. W. 416 (1895).

[58] Reg. v. Halliday (1889), 61 L. T. R. 701, 702.

[59] The problematical side of this case arises from the fact that the poison was actually given by another child who found the bottle on the mantle-piece. A conviction of murder was affirmed, Reg. v. Michael (1840), 173 Eng. Rep. 867, but this seems invalid since, despite the defendant's intention, the poison was administered accidentally.

[60] People v. Elder et al., 100 Mich. 515, 59 N. W. 237 (1894).

volunteered his assistance in the fight and so violently kicked the prostrate victim that he died. Here, there was a responsible adult who voluntarily committed a serious harm; but whatever motivated him was not caused by the defendant. Accordingly, although one aspect of this situation satisfies the type of causation we shall be exploring, the conduct of the defendant cannot be brought into a legally significant causal relation with it. Besides, the intervening person was criminally liable for the homicide, and we are here concerned with situations where that is not the case.

After the above situations have been distinguished, we may view more precisely what is involved in causing a normal adult voluntarily to commit a proscribed harm by giving him an incentive or motive for doing that. Cases of this type of causation include the accessory before the fact and political crimes involving subversion. But there, again, the immediate actors are guilty of crimes as principals, and we require situations where their conduct was "privileged." More pertinent, therefore, is coercion since the immediate harm-doer (corresponding to the principals in the above situations) is exculpated. But liability is imposed on the coerced person if he commits a homicide or, in some countries, another very serious crime, *i.e.* in that case he acted (voluntarily). As has been previously suggested,[61] a compatible formula might state that the coerced person is relieved of criminal liability for any harm, other than homicide and so on, not because his action there was involuntary or non-voluntary but because a lesser value than his life was at stake, and he was therefore privileged to damage or destroy that value. In this view, *i.e.* that the coerced person acted (voluntarily), causation by motivation is recognized in many situations where, in addition, the immediate actor is not criminally liable, while the harm he committed is imputed to the coercer.

Other pertinent instances are certain cases of influencing or aiding someone to commit suicide. In a Michigan case,[62]

---

[61] See *supra* 235-36.
[62] People v. Roberts, 211 Mich. 187, 178 N. W. 690 (1920).

a man who placed poison at the bedside of his incurably sick wife was held guilty of murder in the first-degree despite the fact that suicide was not criminal in Michigan. The ground of the decision, however, was not that the defendant persuaded his wife to commit suicide, but that he "administered" the poison—the voluntary taking of it by the wife being deemed immaterial. An opposite decision was rendered in a Texas case[63] on the ground that suicide is not criminal and that therefore one who urges or aids a normal adult to commit suicide is not guilty of a crime. In the light of the progress of psychology, including especially the increased awareness of the effectiveness of persistent malevolent pressure on human minds, there is no *a priori* reason why causation by giving an incentive should not receive wider recognition in the criminal law.[64] It is rather significant that, excepting the problematic instance of coercion, the principal area of such recognition has been in cases of suicide of the following type.

In *Stephenson*,[65] the Indiana Supreme Court upheld a conviction of second-degree murder where the defendant kidnapped, assaulted with intent to rape, and seriously injured a young woman who, seizing an opportunity while still a captive, took poison and died. The case, so far as the present inquiry is concerned, is complicated by the court's remark that "taking the poison was not the act of a responsible agent"[66] (although throughout the decision she was regarded as responsible in the accepted legal sense), by the fact that the defendant did not summon medical assistance or release his victim until a substantial time had elapsed after he learned of the poisoning, and also by the fact that he had inflicted such serious injuries upon the body of the deceased that, according to medical testimony, those wounds

[63] Sanders v. State, 54 Tex. Cr. R. 101, 112 S. W. 68 (1908).

[64] *Cf.* Shakespeare's Iago.

[65] Stephenson v. State, 205 Ind. 141, 179 N. E. 633 (1932), 186 N. E. 293 (1933).

[66] *Id.* at 159. The felony-murder rule was also invoked. *Ibid.*

alone might have caused her death. Despite these complications, however, the holding to a significant degree supports the proposition that it is criminal homicide to cause a normal adult to commit suicide by creating a situation so cruel and revolting that death is preferred to unavoidable continued submission.[67] There is also an Italian decision where an abusive husband was held guilty of the manslaughter (*homicide par imprudence*) of his wife on the ground that he made life so unbearable that he "drove" her to poison herself.[68]

These cases[69] suggest that causation by giving a motive for another person's action has been unduly restricted in the past and that the usual unqualified rule that subsequent voluntary conduct breaks the chain of causation should be reexamined. It is true, of course, that the *Stephenson* and the Italian decisions concerned suicide, and that there, as in fraud, the defendant's conduct resulted in harm to the motivated person, *i.e.* they are not cases where the defendant's actions, verbal and overt, motivate someone to injure or kill a third party, as in coercion. On the other hand, in these cases causation by giving a motive is given legal effect, *i.e.* despite the voluntary conduct of the normal adult who directly committed the harm in issue, that harm was imputed to the offender, as his crime. Whatever doubts remain concerning the meaning of (voluntary) conduct, the merely formal preservation of the generally avowed rule regarding the original actor's liability (*e.g.* by merely labelling such intervening conduct "involuntary") will hardly suffice.

Against this background of established and emergent law concerning causation by motivation, we may consider certain

[67] In the Stephenson case, the indictment alleged that the deceased "distracted with the pain and shame so inflicted upon her by said defendants. . . . " *Id.* at 147. Her doctor testified, "She said that she didn't expect to get well; didn't want to get well; that she wanted to die." *Id.* at 162.

[68] Decision of the Court of Appeal of Florence, affirmed by the Cour de Cassation of Italy, January 29, 1918. Noted in 1937 Rev. Sci. Crim. et Dr. Pen. 484.

[69] *Cf.* People v. Goodman, 182 Misc. 585, 44 N. Y. S. 2d 715 (1943).

recent Pennsylvania decisions which suggest that in many situations where recklessness is the relevant *mens rea*, problems which are presently obscured by "proximate causation" can be clarified if viewed as instances of this type of causation. These cases disclose a very wide area of penal law where this type of causation is operative. They also reveal that when an ordinarily required *mens rea* is ignored, as in felony-murder, causal problems in criminal law are not correctly analyzed. Accordingly, although this phase of the Pennsylvania decisions has been substantially corrected in a later case, they are very suggestive in elucidating the distinctive problem of causation in penal law.

The first of the Pennsylvania decisions was the *Moyer* case[70] where, in the course of a robbery at a gasoline station, the attendant was shot and killed. On conviction for first-degree murder, the defendants appealed, claiming that the attendant was killed by a bullet fired by his employer. Although the Court believed that the evidence clearly showed that one of the defendants killed the attendant, it held that even if the owner of the station killed him while resisting the robbery, the conviction of first-degree murder must be affirmed. Conceding that the question "has never before arisen in this Commonwealth,"[71] the court based its decision upon the felony-murder rule and the rule of "proximate causation" as interpreted in the law of torts.[72]

[70] Commonwealth v. Moyer and Byron, 357 Pa. 181, 53 A. 2d 736 (1947).

[71] *Id.* at 741.

[72] " . . . when a felon's attempt to commit robbery or burglary sets in motion a chain of events which were or should have been within his contemplation when the motion was initiated, he should be held responsible for any death which by direct and almost inevitable sequence results from the initial criminal act. . . . 'Every robber or burglar knows that a likely later act in the chain of events he inaugurates will be the use of deadly force against him on the part of the selected victim. For whatever results follow from that natural and legal use of retaliating force, the felon must be held responsible.' " *Id.* at 741-42.

"In the law of *torts*, the individual who unlawfully sets in motion a chain of events which in the natural order of things results in damages to another is held to be responsible for it." *Id.* at 744. "There is no reason why the principle underlying the doctrine of proximate

Two years later in *Almeida*,[73] the *Moyer* decision was applied to a similar situation where a police officer was killed by another officer who was shooting at the defendant. In an extremely long opinion the Court emphasized and reaffirmed the proximate cause principle of tort law,[74] approved Holmes' theory of objective criminal liability[75] and quoted him and Cardozo[76] (from discussions by them which were quite unrelated to criminal law) to the effect that the "welfare of society" warrants judicial legislation. Finding no Pennsylvania authority to support its expansion of the constructive murder statute, the Court cited numerous tort cases, provisions of the American Law Institute's Torts Restatement, and criminal cases which clearly were not precedents, *e.g.* where the defendant made a deadly assault on one who in self-preservation jumped from a window or a boat and was killed, and where train robbers held someone in front of them as a shield, while railroad employees and police were shooting at the robbers.[77]

This expansion of constructive murder—to include the killing of innocent persons by those resisting a robbery—was remarkably extended in 1955 when, in *Bolish*,[78] the defendant was convicted of the first-degree murder of his accomplice who was burned to death in the course of committing statutory arson in a vacant house.[79] The Court held that *Almeida* "is on its facts . . . analogous to the instant

cause as illustrated in the three civil cases just cited should not apply to criminal cases also." *Id.* at 745.

[73] 362 Pa. 596, 68 A. 2d 595 (1949).

[74] "Our decision in the Moyer-Byron case was an application of the long established principle that he whose felonious act is the *proximate cause* of another's death is *criminally* responsible for that death and must answer to society for it exactly as he who is *negligently* the *proximate cause* of another's death is *civilly* responsible for that death and must answer in damages for it." *Id.* at 599-600.

[75] *Id.* at 600. *Cf. supra* chapter 5.

[76] *Id.* at 611.

[77] Although the resistance by the employees and police was relevant, holding someone directly in the line of fire comes very close to shooting him.

[78] 381 Pa. 500, 113 A. 2d 464 (1955).

[79] One judge dissented. The conviction was set aside and a new trial granted because of the improper admission of evidence.

case and in principle . . . directly controlling. . . ."[80] The dissenting Justice, Musmanno, J., believed such an application of constructive first-degree murder was not within the purpose of the statute, he noted that "murder," not "killing," is the statutory term, and he vigorously urged the restriction of the felony-murder rule to the felons' action "in furtherance of the original criminal plan."[81] Instead of expanding criminal law on grounds of "social welfare," Justice Musmanno emphasized the principle of legality and the moral progress of the criminal law.[82]

Five months after *Bolish*, the Court held in *Thomas* (three of the seven judges dissenting) that where two robbers attempt a hold-up and the intended victim kills one of them, the surviving felon is guilty of first-degree murder of his accomplice.[83] "The killing of the co-felon is the natural foreseeable result of the initial act. The robbery was the proximate cause of the death. We can see no sound reason for distinction merely because the one killed was a co-felon."[84] Thus, the existing dogma of the felony-murder rule was compounded to produce curious progeny and to enlarge the established scope of capital punishment.

This reliance, in the above Pennsylvania decisions, upon the "proximate causation" principle of tort law to expand constructive murder is also extremely vulnerable. "Proximate cause" has been subjected to very severe criticism by authorities in the field of torts on the ground that it is a

---

[80] *Id.* at 472. "In reason, logic and principle we can see no valid distinction between those cases and a case where an accomplice is killed while setting fire to a house (or building) or attempting to escape therefrom,—the latter's death is just as readily foreseeable as is the death of an owner who attempts to escape or to rescue lives or property from the building." *Id.* at 474.

[81] *Id.* at 479.

[82] "Whatever Daniel Bolish did, it was not constructive murder and, regardless of the extent of his knavery, he should not suffer death for an act which does not fall within the provisions of the code for murder." *Id.* at 479. "A man who commits arson must be punished for arson and not simply because he is a bad person." *Id.* 481.

[83] 382 Pa. 639, 117 A. 2d 204 (1955). In Commonwealth v. Redline, 391 Pa. 486, 137 A. 2d 472 (1958), the Thomas decision was overruled.

[84] *Id.* at 206.

"puzzling phenomenon"[85] which seriously handicaps the solution of tort problems.[86] In a thoughtful article by a practicing lawyer, it is urged that "lawyers cease the use of the phrases 'proximate causes' and 'proximate effects' . . . [t]he term 'proximate cause' has simply come to mean a cause for which the law will impose liability. Such adopted meaning solves no problems [and] has a tendency to obscure the real ground of liability or non-liability . . . [and] makes for confusion of thought."[87] Although, of course, the Pennsylvania courts were not the first to apply that view of causation to criminal homicide, which seems, indeed, to have been employed by Sir Matthew Hale, the proximate causation of tort law is least persuasive when it is made the basis of an unprecedented expansion of the felony-murder rule.

Instead of amorphous "proximate causation," with its connotations of negligence and strict liability, the problem of causation in the above cases can be readily analyzed if it is recognized as teleological, *i.e.* giving a responsible person a motive for action. In the light of the above discussion of that type of causation, the Pennsylvania cases raise the question, whether the conduct of a person who commits a homicide while resisting a felony may be imputed to the felon. If that question is answered in the affirmative, secondary problems concern the felon's criminal liability (a) if the deceased was an innocent person and (b) if he was the felon's accomplice.

An attempt to rob certainly gives a motive for resistance; moreover, as the Pennsylvania judges emphasized, robbers foresee the probability of such resistance. While it can hardly be said that robbery stimulates resistance in an instinctive or reflex manner, it is certainly true, at least in the United States, that it arouses indignation and, often, active resistance as a rational, though dangerous, response. There is no reason why such foreseeable consequences should

[85] Malone, *op. cit. supra* note 1, at 97.
[86] Prosser, *op. cit. supra* note 19, at 259.
[87] Venable, *Proximate Causes and Effects*, 19 Miss. L. J. 183, 184 (1948).

not be imputed to the robbers; but the precise range of the imputable consequences and the degree of penal liability must be determined by reference to established law.[88] In the absence of a felony-murder rule, there would be liability for the planned felony (robbery or arson in the above cases) or its attempt and liability for deaths recklessly caused, *i.e.* by recklessly giving a motive for resistance. In most states in this country, the upper limit of penal liability would be second-degree murder.

Nor do the felony-murder statutes entail liability in the above cases for murder in the first-degree regardless of whether the deceased was the victim, a by-stander or an accomplice. They do not mean that all deaths caused in resisting a felony, as well as those caused by the felons in furtherance of it, fall within the statutory terms. Causation concerns a relationship, and in criminal law one of the relata is a definitely described harm. Accordingly, not all the foreseeable consequences of voluntary misconduct are legally material. Even tort law does not compensate for all foreseeable injuries to all interests. A man who commits a crime may know that both his victim's and his own family will suffer, perhaps that a death may ensue, but civil liability does not extend to all of the ultimate foreseeable results. In the criminal law the principles of legality, *mens rea,* causation and harm definitely limit the consequences of forbidden conduct to which criminal liability attaches. By reference to these principles, the Pennsylvania court's assumption regarding the relevance of proximate causation is untenable.

Nor does it seem persuasive to ignore the salient fact that the persons killed in the *Bolish* and *Thomas* cases were

---

[88] Mr. Norval Morris, whose criticism of the recent Pennsylvania decisions, 105 U. of Pa. L. Rev. 50 (1956), is in accord with this writer's discussion *supra*, also writes: "The felony-murder rule is thus a rule for establishing the *mens rea* of murder; it is not a rule of causation. . . . " *Id.* at 59. But causation of the teleological type is also involved, *i.e.* to cause in that way means voluntarily to bring about a forbidden end. Thus, the same fiction which in constructive murder assumes *mens rea* to exist where it is non-existent also assumes means-end causation to exist where that is non-existent.

voluntarily present at the scene of danger for felonious purposes. If the surviving felon is guilty of the criminal homicide of his accomplice, it must be shown that he owed a legal duty to him,[89] that he voluntarily violated it, and thereby caused the death in the relevant sense. In the established law on felony-murder, it is quite clear that the legal duty of the felon is limited to the killing of innocent persons, indeed in most states it has been restricted to the killing of such persons by the felon.[90] If it is agreed, as is becoming increasingly recognized,[91] that the constructive felony-murder rule is outmoded, its extension to include even innocent persons killed by those resisting the felony is unwarranted. But if current American statutes bringing such persons within the scope of felony-murder[92] are retained, that provides no support for the expansion of the rule to include the death of felons at the time they were committing the felony.

A recent writer[93] finds the dissenting opinion in *Bolish* inconsistent in holding both that a co-felon is liable "where by his own act he kills a confederate" and also that "the law should not protect the lives of felons and the law-abiding alike." But there are surely important differences between holding a felon liable for intentionally killing his confederate, as when there was a falling-out because of incompetent participation in the felony,[94] and the holding

---

[89] *Contra* to the Bolish decision is People v. Ferlin, 203 Cal. 587, 265 P. 230 (1928).

[90] The principal American case is Commonwealth v. Campbell, 89 Mass. 541 (1863). So held also in Commonwealth v. Moore et al., 121 Ky. 97, 88 S. W. 1085 (1905) and implied in People v. Udwin, 254 N. Y. 255, 172 N. E. 489 (1930).

[91] Report of the British Royal Commission on Capital Punishment 34-35 (1953) and the Homicide Act, 5 and 6 Eliz. 2, ch.11 (1957).

[92] So held in People v. Podolski, 332 Mich. 508, 52 N. W. 2d 201 (1952).

[93] Moesel. *A Survey of Felony Murder*, 28 Temple L. Q. 464 (1955).

[94] People v. Cabaltero, 31 Cal. App. 2d 52, 87 P. 2d 364 (1939). In Rex v. Plummer (1700), Kelyng 105, 84 Eng. Rep. 1103, it was held, on similar facts, that the other co-felons and conspirators, present at the time, were not guilty of the homicide since that act was not within the common design.

that co-felons who voluntarily subject themselves to the risk of resistance by their intended victims do not owe a duty to each other *so far as that risk is concerned.* In criminal law the extent of a duty, *i.e.* of the harms proscribed, depends upon social valuation and experience, with logic in the subsidiary role of developing analogies within established meanings. To hold that a felon has a legal duty to protect his confederate from resistance to the felony by their intended victim and police officers — if that is not merely a device for subjecting a dangerous criminal to the capital penalty — seems rather quixotic and, in any event, the above decisions in that regard were wholly unsupported by legal precedent.

It should, of course, be recognized that some cases of teleological causation involve extremely difficult problems of proof. Even where certain harms were intended, there may be subtleties in such causation which elude practical legal controls and methods of investigation, *e.g.* nefarious forms of suggestion leading to suicide or the commission of crimes. To bring such conduct within the scope of penal law would encourage speculation that is incompatible with a definite principle of legality; and perhaps that is the reason for the modern repudiation of "killing by perjury." The principal purpose of the above analysis of certain situations in terms of causation by giving a motive or incentive is not to urge an extension of present criminal law in directions that weaken legality but rather to suggest a more cogent analysis than that available in terms of "proximate causation" and, finally, to indicate the fuller significance of the principle of causation in penal law.

SUMMARY

Causal problems arise in a context of various legal rules and principles, for example, the principle of harm which excludes irrelevant consequences, rules imposing liability upon subsequent independent actors, and the felony-murder rule. The principle of causation, especially its teleological significance, can be clarified and the analysis of cases facilitated if the types of causation described above[95] are kept in mind. The temptation to exclude *mens rea* from problems of causation arises from over-concentration on mechanical causation, resulting from a failure to appreciate the distinctive meaning of the principle of causation in penal law. This sometimes encourages the view that causation is not a legal problem and that one may therefore, as a legal scholar, ignore it and concern himself with legal liability. But "cause-in-fact" cannot be separated from the principles of penal law because it includes teleological causation, and that involves both the principles and the facts. In other words, since so much of external mechanical causation as a person chooses to employ in the commission of a proscribed harm is imputed to him, cause-in-fact includes certain conduct. The above analysis is therefore to be contrasted not only with the view that policy has nothing to do with the determination of cause-in-law but also with the sharply opposed position that policy is the sole determinant of cause-in-law. Instead, the position defended here is that fact-finding and policy are interrelated in such ways that the factual inquiries are defined and, to a considerable degree, determined by policy. This can be elucidated further by noting, first, the logical stages in an inquiry of legal imputation and, then, the actual process of adjudication.

(1) The *sine qua non* test concerns an essential aspect of the causal principle, *i.e.* unless the defendant's conduct was a *necessary* condition of the harm in issue, he is not liable. It is sometimes stated that the function of this test is only a negative one — to exclude certain persons from liability. But, although it is evident that one whose conduct does not satisfy the above test does not incur liability, more than that is involved. Those included within the meaning of *sine qua non* become candidates for legal liability; and if they are held liable, one reason for that is that their conduct was a *necessary* condition of the harm in issue.

[95] *Supra* 251-54.

(2) But that, alone, does not suffice for legal liability. Two additional qualifications are applied in selection of the types of necessary condition which give rise to legal liability. First, the principle of causation requires that a necessary condition must also contribute effectively, *i.e.* substantially, to the harm in issue. For example, a slight wound may have necessitated going to a doctor or drugstore, and *en route* the slightly injured person was struck by an automobile or shot by his mortal enemy. The slight wound, though a necessary condition of the death, did not contribute substantially to it. "Cause" or "substantial cause" is sometimes used to designate necessary *and effective* conditions.[96]

(3) Finally, the distinctive character of the principle of causation in penal law requires further restriction of cause (*i.e.* substantial or effective causes) and the *residue* is the legal cause. To assert that certain conduct is the legal cause of a penal harm is to assert that it is a type of necessary, substantial cause which includes a relevant *mens rea*, *i.e.* necessary, efficient end-seeking.[97]

Although the above elements in a legal, *i.e.* imputative, inquiry may be distinguished in analysis, actually they do not represent separate inquiries or separate parts of a larger investigation. At every step in the process of adjudication, the legal policy defines and determines the course of the inquiry leading to decisions on each of the above three factors — necessary condition (*sine qua non*), cause (substantial, effective, sufficient), and cause-in-law (legal cause). Not any or all necessary conditions are sought, but only those which are relevant to legal liability. And, as regards the determination of substantial cause, while this involves intuitive perception and experience, as does all fact-finding, it is no less true that policy is also operative there. Why, indeed, should one seek a substantial cause rather than a

---

[96] This usage is not confined to law. *Cf.* "An actual cause, however, is supposed to be a necessary as well as sufficient condition for its effect." Mackay, *Causality and Effectuality*, pub. in Causality, 15 Univ. of Calif. Pub. in Philosophy 132 (1932).

[97] A ". . . legal cause is justly attachable cause." Edgerton, *Legal Cause*, 72 U. of Pa. L. Rev. 211 (1924).

merely necessary condition, if not because substantial causes give rise to a type of liability which expresses the policy of our law? (Some primitive legal systems attached liability to merely necessary conditions.) Policy operates in other ways to determine what is a "substantial cause." From a scientific viewpoint, one necessary condition is as substantial as any other, unless a particular experiment provides a special interest. And where distinctions are drawn between necessary conditions and substantial causes, the meaning of these terms varies in relation to the contexts of the particular inquiries. Thus, a physician making a post-mortem examination of a person who died after loss of blood might find hemophilia the substantial cause of the death and a certain blow merely an accidental condition; or he might say both caused the death. In criminal law, however, the factual inquiry in a homicide case seeks a substantial cause in relation to end-seeking causation by a human actor whose conduct included knowledge of the deceased's condition, *i.e.* in criminal conduct. In sum, a cause-in-law means a cause which is not only a necessary, substantial factor but also one that includes certain conduct which expresses a required *mens rea*.

POLICY AND LEGAL CAUSE

A recent essay by Professor Herbert L. A. Hart and Mr. A. M. Honoré,[98] while principally concerned with the law of torts, raises a very important issue regarding causation in criminal law. Although much of the writer's analysis, set forth in the above pages, fortunately finds support in the Hart-Honoré essay, it would burden this discussion to dwell upon that. It is preferable to try to sharpen our knowledge of causation by considering certain points of difference. It may be noted, however, that the writer fully shares the above authors' view that what is wanted is not "a code for the solution of cases" or "rigid rules" but knowledge of "the general principles involved."

[98] *Causation in the Law*, 72 L. Q. Rev. 58, 260, 398 (1956).

It is obviously important to know exactly what the Hart-Honoré thesis is, and that is not easily discovered despite the authors' efforts to eliminate mysterious and unexplained "metaphorical expressions" and to provide "an elucidation in literal terms." It is possible that the purpose of their analysis was only to eliminate a patent fallacy, *e.g.* that in law the selection of the cause from a number of necessary conditions "can *only* represent a preference for one result rather than another."[99] That that is their avowed purpose is also indicated in the statement that "the view that the distinction between causes and mere conditions is *wholly* without objective or factual warrant is really an exaggeration, and obscures as much as it reveals. . . ."[1] If these sentences are read literally the learned authors appear to be fabricating a target of their own preference. For nothing is more definitely accepted in current legal thought than that a cause is a "substantial factor" in producing the harm in issue, and that that is largely a question of fact.[2] The probability, however, is that Hart and Honoré undertook a much more difficult task than they acknowledge in the above statements, namely, their purpose was to show that policy has nothing to do with the determination of causal questions in law.

That is the stand they take in separating "explanatory inquiry" from "attributive inquiry." In the latter, we are informed, the inquiry starts with two termini — a wrongful act and a harm — and the problem is to determine if there was a causal relation between the two. In explanatory inquiry the starting point is only the harm, and the objective

---

[99] *Id.* at 59, italics added. The authors place that interpretation upon the 1870 essay of N. St. J. Green in 4 American L. Rev. But Green wrote: "The true cause is the whole set of antecedents taken together. . . . But when a cause is to be investigated for any practical purpose, the antecedent which is within the scope of that purpose is singled out and called the cause, to the neglect of the antecedents which are of no importance to the matter in hand." *Id.* at 211.

[1] *Id.* at 60. Italics added.

[2] Dean Leon Green has discussed this in detail in Rationale of Proximate Cause (1927), and see 2 Harper and James, The Law of Torts 1110 (1956) and Prosser, *op. cit. supra* note 19, at 221.

is to find the cause of that. But this asserted difference, it is suggested with deference, is not valid as regards either type of inquiry. In explanatory inquiry, one always requires an hypothesis which includes one or more possible causes, as Poincaré and others have often pointed out;[3] indeed, it is difficult to imagine a scientist searching "in the open" for the cause of a phenomenon. And as regards attribution, the above description is pertinent to the purpose or termination of the inquiry, rather than to the inquiry itself. The assumption that attributive inquiry *starts* with a "wrongful act" oversimplifies a complex process of adjudication in which policy guides the relevant explanatory inquiry in a context of many highly controverted possibilities.

It is also clear that the authors do not wish merely to distinguish the factual explanation of causes from the imputation (attribution) of legal liability; they insist, instead, that the explanatory inquiry proceeds quite apart from any influence of policy. For example, they point out[4] that if we know how a railroad accident happened, we have a causal explanation of it. They then observe that frequently a court will conduct such inquiries, "and, though the object of such causal inquiry is ultimately to determine questions of responsibility, at this stage the inquiry is in a sense theoretical, designed to explain."[5] They illustrate this by describing a case where a workman was injured by a falling pipe, and the issue was whether his injury was caused by the defendant's breach of building regulations. Although the court found that "The cause of its fall . . . is . . . a mystery," judgment was rendered for the plaintiff.

In this case[6] the court was content to find certain simple facts (*i.e.* simple from the viewpoint of an extra-legal explanatory inquiry) namely, that a falling pipe injured a workman and that there was a failure to erect protecting

[3] Hall, Readings in Jurisprudence 687 (1938).
[4] *Op. cit. supra* note 98, at 66.
[5] *Ibid.*
[6] Hughes v. McGoff and Vickers, Ltd. (1955), 1 W. L. R. 416, 2 All E. R. 291.

boards required by the regulation. What was "wholly un-explained" was whether the failure to erect protecting boards was actually a cause of the pipe's falling. While this would have left an ordinary explanatory and a scientific inquiry suspended in doubt, the policy of the law operated to determine the explanatory inquiry conducted by the court. The breach of the safety regulation and the injury being established, a *presumption* in favor of the injured workman was applied to resolve the unexplained mystery regarding the fall of the pipe. Thus, after quoting from earlier decisions: " 'If there is a definite breach of a safety provision . . . and a workman is injured in a way which could result from the breach, the onus of proof shifts onto the employer to show that the breach was not the cause,' "[7] Ashworth, J. concluded, "Not only is it open to me to find that the breach of regulation 24 was a cause of this accident, but I am driven to that conclusion in the absence of any other explanation." One can hardly expect to find clearer examples of the inseparability of the explanatory inquiry from the attributive one or of the influence of the policy of a law upon the relevant explanatory inquiry.

Since the influence of policy upon fact-finding is evident in cases of omission, it is noteworthy that Hart and Honoré view omissions merely as a linguistic problem. "Human conduct," they say, "can be described alternatively in terms of acts or omissions."[8] This may be literally true but it would be extremely awkward or even startling in some situations, *e.g.* to describe in terms of overt action a death caused by a train running over a woman caught in the tracks, while the defendant, her husband, looked on. But the principal point is that if one asks why, in the explanatory inquiry conducted in a courtroom, the mass and motion of the train are treated as if they were part of the husband's conduct — while a doctor or a physicist would ignore the husband entirely in their opinions of the cause of death —

[7] *Id.* at 421.
[8] *Op. cit. supra* note 98, at 268.

an adequate answer can be given only by reference to the definition and direction of the explanatory inquiry by the policy of the legal liability. Apart from that, an explanatory inquiry of criminal forbearances would be aimless or irrelevant.

That there is "factual [and] objective warrant" for the distinction between causes and conditions[9] will be readily granted as regards some perspectives in which those terms are used. The Hart-Honoré theory, however, goes far beyond that. Its authors note that in everyday life we draw the above distinction, e.g. a bent rail is the cause of an accident, while the weight and speed of the train are mere conditions. But it is not only logically possible, it is also factually persuasive that common experience draws the above distinction not because policy is absent there, but precisely because, as regards railroad accidents, policy (evaluation) is the salient feature of the everyday perspective. In other words, with reference to this kind of situation, common sense is very much like the policy of law. It is true, of course, that common sense in non-ethical contexts also distinguishes merely necessary conditions from effective or substantial causes, e.g. sunshine streaming into a room through a window is the "cause" of the light in the room, while the window is a condition of it. But, while common sense, in one of its perspectives, draws the above distinction without influence of policy, can it be assumed that that also occurs in the determination of cause-in-law?

The authors are content to observe that "this distinction [cause and condition] is built into the very structure of our ordinary thought about practical affairs. . . ."[10] They do not seek any reasons for that or associate it with the central

---

[9] *Id.* at 69. The principal difficulty of explaining the meaning of an ultimate notion like "cause" is revealed in the authors' statement, "So '*the* cause' is one condition selected from a complex set of conditions which . . . are together sufficient to *produce* [italics added] the consequence." *Id.* at 72. With reference to the inadequacy of all theories of causation, see Loewenberg, *op. cit. supra* note 6.

[10] *Op. cit. supra* note 98, at 73.

role of problem-solving and evaluation in such affairs. Instead, they argue that common sense distinguishes cause from condition by reference to two criteria — voluntary action and abnormality, *i.e.* a cause may be either free action or an abnormal contingency, while a condition is the negative of these. Although they point out that what is normal "will very often depend on the practical purposes. . . ,"[11] throughout their essay they stress the statistical meaning, *i.e.* "normal" means "usual."[12]

But "normal" has other meanings, and one of them is implicit in any attributive inquiry. Especially in social or legal contexts, norm as standard or value is of at least equal importance in the meaning of "normality" and "abnormality." That a railroad track is bent or that the engineer falls asleep is not abnormal only if it is rare. They are also abnormal in the literal sense of being at variance with accepted standards of railroad operation, just as a common disease would be abnormal by reference to a standard of health. Indeed, under some conditions or in some places a bent rail might be a frequent or even usual occurrence, and nonetheless abnormal.

The influence of policy upon explanatory inquiry might seem to be assumed when the authors, in terminating their discussion of such inquiry, recognize that in human affairs explanation in terms of physical occurrences rarely suffices. What is wanted, in addition, is "explanation in terms of human agency."[13] "We feel that it is not enough to be told that a man died from . . . arsenic . . . and we press on for the more satisfying explanation in terms of human agency. At the common-sense level . . . [that is] an explanation with a special finality. . . ."[14] But even the "special finality" of voluntary conduct does not alter the authors' view of the sheer factuality of explanatory legal inquiry. They do not

[11] *Id.* at 75.

[12] *Cf.* " . . . normal may be either what usually happens or what is normally done by human beings." *Id.* at 78.

[13] *Id.* at 77.

[14] *Ibid.*

consider why human action has such decisive force,[15] nor does the unique role of (voluntary) conduct in the long history of ethics or its central place in the meaning of "cause" in criminal law engage their attention.

An interesting case is then stated. Just as A's cigarette is flickering out in a waste-paper basket, B intentionally pours highly inflammable material into the basket, and the house burns. In that case, we are informed, both "common sense and the law would say that the loss was the consequence of B's action, not of A's."[16] This assumes that "common sense" is univocal.[17] As was noted above, however, common sense includes various perspectives, one of which is a lay view of science.[18] From that common sense perspective, throwing the cigarette into the basket might be regarded as much a cause of the destruction of the house as pouring the inflammable material. So, too, in a common sense normative perspective, if A was a normal adult while B was a child, would A be regarded as not having participated in the cause of the fire?

Although they emphasize the importance of voluntary conduct, Hart and Honoré insist that the finding that the fire in the above case was caused by B, was not in the least influenced by considerations of policy.[19] They argue that regardless of any attitude of approval or disapproval, and even if there is complete indifference, B was *the* cause. "We may or may not wish to punish B or hold him liable, and if we do, he is punished or made liable because he has caused

---

[15] See *supra* chapter 6.

[16] *Op. cit. supra* note 98, at 79.

[17] *Cf.* "The word cause, as used in everyday life, implies *nothing but* regularity of sequence, because *nothing else* is used to verify the propositions in which it occurs." Schlick, *Causality in Everyday Life and in Recent Science*, pub. in Causality, 15 Univ. of Calif. Pub. in Philosophy 101 (1932). *Cf.* Ewing, *supra* note 17.

[18] "Similarly common sense recognizes kinds of events, thunder and wind, life and death, melting and freezing, and so on; all such general terms imply some invariable association. . . ." Campbell, *op. cit. supra* note 51, at 45. See Hobson, The Domain of Natural Science 25, 27-28 (1926).

[19] *Op. cit. supra* note 98, at 79-80.

the disaster and not *vice versa.*"[20] This interesting statement, however, seems hardly relevant to the thesis that policy is excluded if it is found that B was the sole cause of the fire. Even if we approved B's action, we are informed, we would still insist that B was the cause of the fire. This, however, is not persuasive since approval, no less than disapproval, implies policy. We approve or disapprove voluntary actions by reference to their conservation or destruction of recognized values.

But the third possibility—that of complete indifference—raises a serious problem. "If we were quite indifferent . . . if A and B were both members of a gang of thieves and the house was the thieves' den,"[21] still, B was *the* cause of the destruction of the house. Will that assertion bear examination, passing over the ambiguity of the test of "common sense" in this context? For example, a house is property and a value; hence one would disapprove the deliberate destruction of it regardless of its present occupancy. But next, is it actually possible to be quite indifferent regarding any socially important act, *i.e.* any important end-seeking?[22] Finally, if it be assumed that an indifferent attitude (which must be distinguished from disinterested social science) regarding socially important actions is actually possible, what would be the perspective of such a causal thesis? Would we not in that case meet either a scientist who ignored the social significance of the situation and confined himself to its mechanical aspects, or one who had a perverse view of human problems? In a wholly scientific perspective there is no reason for, or basis of, distinction among the necessary conditions of a given change. And why would a creature from another planet, who viewed the human scene with utter indifference, be interested in B's act any more than in A's, when he decided what was the cause of the destruction of a pile of bricks?

[20] *Id.* at 80.
[21] *Ibid.*
[22] *Cf.* Aristotle, Ethics, Bk. V, 1134b 20-22.

In human affairs, conduct is distinguished from inadvertent behavior and especially from accidents. Conduct is distinctive and important because it is in the realm of free choice, self-determination and human control, in a word, it is in the central focus of rational approval and disapproval (*mens rea*). In the absence of any other explanation of the significance of free choice—and one can hardly be satisfied with the statement that the distinction between causes and conditions "is built into the very structure" of our thought— it is not possible to accept the thesis that in practical affairs, valuation has nothing to do with the meaning and finding of causes. Instead, it is submitted with deference, the theory presented above is the more likely one, namely, while policy alone does not distinguish causes from conditions, and although a factual process is included in the determination of that question, nevertheless, policy demarks the limits of relevant factual inquiry and participates in the definition of causes. From a practically infinite array of necessary conditions (*sine qua non*) it selects as "causes" those which are important with reference to "policy," *i.e.* the values expressed in the principles of legal liability, especially that of *mens rea* and its qualification of cause. Thus, imputation in penal law signifies not only that the defendant's conduct was, in fact, the substantial cause of the proscribed harm (the efficiency or adequacy of the necessary conduct), but also that it was end-directed, implying the defendant's *mens rea*.[23] If that is the relationship between relevant explanatory inquiry and the policy of law, it follows that the separation of that kind of inquiry from attributive inquiry is inapt and misleading.[24] In sum, as Collingwood sug-

[23] "But when we say that a man is responsible for an act we usually mean that he is a cause *and* something more or something else. We mean that by virtue of his being a cause he is exposed to an evaluative judgment." MacIver, *op. cit. supra* note 11, at 226.

[24] Writing of attributive inquiry and specifically with reference to the question, "Given this wrongful act (or other designated event) and given this loss or harm, is the latter the consequence of the former?" Hart and Honoré assert " . . . our purpose in asking this question is not to understand what has happened but to determine responsibility." *Op. cit. supra* note 98, at 78.

gested,[25] an attributive inquiry is also a type of explanatory inquiry which finds cause in human conduct, including criminal conduct. This, indeed, is the cause that is especially important in law.

The neglect of policy in the elucidation of legal problems is not a minor affair. For example, Hart and Honoré state that it is "well established" that the presence of "abnormal conditions" at the time of the wrongful conduct in issue does not negative causation.[26] But, as seen above,[27] that generalization does not hold in criminal law, whatever its validity may be in tort law. The cases cited in support include the intentional infliction of a mortal wound upon a dying man. In criminal law, a dying man is as much a human being as is a new-born infant; but if dying is "abnormal," the above generalization lacks significance in criminal law, i.e. it does not refer to the relevant cause, since it does not specify whether the abnormal condition was known or unknown. The authors also apply the above generalization to *Frazier*, where the defendant punched a hemophiliac, not knowing of his precarious health; but they ignore the fact that that decision was rested upon constructive homicide, the misdemeanor-manslaughter rule. The more probable generalization, supported by recent cases, is that it is only where courts rigorously apply that arbitrary rule, that an unknown abnormal condition, existing at the time of the defendant's conduct, does not negative the required kind of causal connection in penal law.

Another of the authors' principal generalizations is: "A free, deliberate and informed human act or omission, intended to produce the consequence which, in fact, ensues, negatives causal connection."[28] This seems dubious even in tort law, e.g. one who neglected to lock a door was held liable for loss of goods stolen by a thief.[29] In criminal law,

[25] *Supra* note 10.
[26] *Op. cit. supra* note 98, at 406.
[27] *Supra* 257-260.
[28] *Op. cit. supra* note 98 at 417.
[29] *Id.* at 413.

the above generalization is incompatible with the rule regarding the accessory before the fact, and with the valid aspects of the *Stephenson*, the Italian, and the Pennsylvania decisions discussed above;[30] and it is not helpful as regards the problem of coercion.[31] Again, the generalization that the "abnormal non-voluntary conduct of a human being" negatives causal connection[32] is very vague, *e.g.* in some situations only negligence which is "extravagant"[33] will do that. Thus, one cannot determine whether the above generalization accords with decisions holding that negligence which does not supply a "new" force but merely aggravates a prior wound does not negative causation,[34] or with other decisions.[35] Finally, there are several generalizations concerning negligence (*e.g.* "an actor is often morally or legally responsible for negligence")[36] which may possibly be valid in tort law but have only very dubious application in criminal law.

In generalizing legal propositions to subsume both tort and criminal law, Hart and Honoré follow in the path of Justice Holmes,[37] except that he employed a definite theory of liability which he defended on utilitarian grounds as valid in both fields. The lack of any theory of liability, *i.e.* policy, which is used in close proximity to analysis of the cases renders it impossible to achieve legally significant generalizations. If policy differs in the two fields of law, that explains important differences in the decisions, *e.g.* regarding negligence. On the other hand, if it is maintained

---

[30] *Supra* pp. 273-281 and *cf.* Hart and Honoré's comment on one of the Pennsylvania decisions, *id.* at 273.

[31] *Id.* at 267.

[32] *Id.* at 417.

[33] *Id.* at 412.

[34] *Cf. supra*, especially R. v. Jordan (1956), 40 Cr. App. R. 152. See note 46, *supra*.

[35] *E.g.* in R. v. Lowe (1850), 3 C. and K. 123, 175 Eng. Rep. 489, an engineer in a colliery was held guilty of manslaughter when a death was caused by the incompetent handling of an engine by an inexperienced boy whom the engineer had left in charge.

[36] *Op. cit. supra* note 98, at 268.

[37] *Supra* chapter 5.

that policy is identical in the two fields, as did Holmes, an articulation of the reasons and especially the testing of that theory in the case-law is needed. Still, again, it may be the case that, although policy differs, it is possible to discover higher categories which unite the two fields significantly. For the reasons indicated above, however, these ultimate notions will express a general policy as, *e.g.* the principles of criminal law do in relation to that field.

The policy of penal law is expressed primarily in the principle of *mens rea*,[38] and its influence in determining the meaning of "cause" in the teleological sense emphasized above—end-seeking conduct—is paramount in the elucidation of relevant legal problems. Penal policy extends beyond that to encompass the requirement of substantial cause, the logic of the principle of harm, implementing the ethic that liability should be limited to the harm actually caused, not extended to that intended or to that which would have happened; and policy also, therefore, takes account of the liability of a subsequent voluntary harm-doer in order to qualify that of an earlier harm-doer. Thus, policy reaches finally to include the entire normative basis of penal liability. In this sense, the policy of penal law is expressed in the generalization that a normal adult who voluntarily commits a proscribed harm should and must be punished as prescribed.

[38] See chapter 3 *supra*.

CHAPTER IX

THE SANCTION — PUNISHMENT

THE principle of punishment generalizes the distinctive character of all the punitive sanctions specified in the rules of criminal law. The sanctions of other legal rules relevant to the broad problem of social protection provide corrective treatment, *e.g.* for juvenile delinquents, alcoholics and drug addicts, or measures of security, *e.g.* the confinement of dangerous psychotics and the isolation of persons having contagious diseases. For the most part, the following discussion will be concerned with punishment.

What this presupposes may be indicated by locating the present discussion in the context of the principal meanings of "responsibility."[1] First, "responsibility" means competence to understand and to conform to relevant moral and legal obligations, *i.e.* that the accused is a normal adult. Second, "responsibility" means authorship, that a particular person *caused* the harm in issue, he is responsible, in that teleological sense, for its occurrence. Third, "responsibility" means accountability, *i.e.* that if he is convicted, having satisfied the first two meanings of "responsibility," he must be subjected to the prescribed sanction—in the present context, punishment.

Although the meaning of punishment and the purposes of punishment may be distinguished, the two are closely interrelated. Ordinarily, one would follow the logical order and discuss first the meaning or nature of punishment, and then

[1] See Moberly, Responsibility (1956).

its justification. The reverse order has been adopted in the following discussion because the justification of punishment concerns its ends and grounds; and the meaning of punishment cannot be understood apart from that knowledge. In addition, the wide perspective which theories of justification delineate provides a framework within which a more precise analysis of the nature of punishment is facilitated.

THE JUSTIFICATION OF PUNISHMENT

In a very thoughtful essay, Professor J. D. Mabbott presents what he calls "a retributive theory of punishment"[2] which, however, rejects the retributive theories of Kant, Hegel and Bradley. Professor Mabbott's theory is "retributive" in the sense that he rejects the utilitarian theories of punishment — deterrence and reformation. He does this mainly because they justify the punishment of innocent persons. For example, the deterrent theory requires only the belief that those punished were guilty; moreover, false publicity, not the actual punishment of guilty persons, suffices to deter. On the other hand, the reformative theory justifies punishing (correcting?) a bad or dangerous man even though he is not a criminal. Professor Mabbott holds, "The only justification for punishing any man is that he has broken a law."[3] This is evidently an expression of the principle of legality.

The author's assertion that his theory is "retributive" has elicited the criticism that: "Surely a punishment which is legally correct may still be unjust . . . ," for example, punishment on the basis of *ex post facto* enactment, punishment where a law requires a morally wrong action, such as ordering an officer to kill or torture civilians, and excessive punishment in relation to the gravity of the offense, such as the death penalty for stealing a loaf of bread.[4] Professor Mabbott does not deal with the issue raised in such cases; as stated, he treats punishment "as a purely legal matter."[5]

---

[2] Mabbott, *Punishment*, 48 Mind (n. s.) 152 (1939).
[3] *Id.* at 158; also see *id.* at 154-157.
[4] Mundle, *Punishment and Desert*, 4 Philos. Quart. 225 (1954).
[5] Mabbott, *supra* note 2, at 154.

The connection on which he insists is that "between punishment and crime, not between punishment and moral or social wrong. . . ."[6]

More important than his use of the term "retributive" are the grounds upon which Dr. Mabbott relies to reject "traditional" retributive theories, namely:

(1) Punishment implies that someone is legally authorized to impose it upon offenders.

(2) No more than do the reformative and deterrent theories can the traditional retributive ones account for the serious objections to retroactive penal legislation.

(3) None of the other theories can account for punishment imposed by an official who disapproves the law which he is enforcing. In Professor Mabbott's theory, the fact that a rule, *i.e.* any rule, was violated makes punishment "proper."[7]

(4) His theory escapes the retributionist's difficulty of measuring moral wrong and equating pain (punishment) with it.[8]

Some of the relevant issues are discussed at length in other parts of this book;[9] nor is it possible here to defend the leading exponents of retributive theories from the criticism leveled against them, except to note that most, if not all, of them assumed the existence of a legal system and presented a retributive theory of punishment on that postu-

---

[6] *Id.* at 155.

[7] *Ibid.* The use of this term instead of "just" or even "justifiable" again indicates that Professor Mabbott's theory is a formal one. "A 'criminal' means a man who has broken a law, not a bad man. . . ." *Id.* at 154. "X has broken a law. Concerning the law, whether it is well-devised or not, I have not asked." *Id.* at 160.
Cf. Quinton, *On Punishment*, pub. in Philosophy, Politics and Society 83 (Laslett ed. 1956).

[8] While Professor Mabbott's theory "escapes" that difficulty, it contributes to the solution of the difficult cases noted above, *e.g.* a capital penalty for stealing a loaf of bread, only by saying: That is the law. *Cf.* "However—and this is the point which Mabbott's account ignores—the duty to obey one's State is not an unconditional duty." Mundle, *op. cit. supra* note 4, at 226. *Cf.* Flew, *"The Justification of Punishment,"* 29 Philosophy 291 (1954).

[9] *E.g.* chapter 2.

late.[10] Apparently, Professor Mabbott proceeded on the assumption that theories in justification of punishment are either utilitarian or retributive; and that since his theory (legality) was not utilitarian, it must be retributive. That, however, is hardly a satisfactory solution, as the above quoted criticism of his theory indicates. The fact is that the theory he espouses is that of formal legality, associated with the school of legal positivism. In any event, it is not a descriptive theory and therefore is not opposed to utilitarian and retributive theories. In other words, a formal theory, *e.g.* insistence on law, if it is to be justified, must find that justification in utilitarian or retributive theories or in both of them. Such justification as legality directly summons, *e.g.* certainty and uniformity, insofar as it is not explicitly resolved into intrinsic and instrumental values, at least presupposes the justification of what the officials do by reference to those theories of ethics.

The difficulty, it is respectfully submitted, which underlies Professor Mabbott's thesis lies in his formulation of the issues.[11] He narrows the choice to law or no law, *i.e.* to the problem of legality, whereas the pertinent issue is that between just law and unjust law.[12] That it is actually impossible to avoid this issue is shown by the fact that Professor Mabbott himself introduces proportionality into his

[10] *Cf.* "Juridical Punishment . . . must in all cases be imposed only because the individual on whom it is inflicted *has committed a Crime.*" Kant, The Philosophy of Law 195 (Hastie, trans. 1887).

[11] Some of the difficulty met in Professor Mabbott's essay seems to reflect Ross' discussion. Ross first rejects retribution on the ground that it requires a perfect assessment of the virtues and pleasures of everyone, which leads him to conclude that "the state has no duty of retributive punishment." Ross, The Right and the Good 60 (1930). Ross states that the alternative is not "a utilitarian view of punishment." The relevant duty, he says, is not to punish moral guilt but "to protect the most fundamental rights of individuals." *Ibid.* It is the failure to respect others' rights which extinguishes a person's own rights and thus makes him a proper subject of punishment. But the voluntary violation of other persons' rights is one way of describing moral guilt; hence it is difficult to see how retributive justice has been excluded. *E.g.* the state "is morally at liberty to injure him as he has injured others. . . ." *Id.* at 61.

[12] *Cf.* Mundle, *op. cit. supra* note 4, at 226.

legal system,[13] which seems hardly consistent with his earlier avowals that he is not interested in the quality of the law.[14]

If the principal issue is not that of merely formal law versus a purely ethical theory, but, instead, just law versus unjust law, there is a ready answer to Professor Mabbott's criticism of other theories of justification. Thus, the objections which he raises against "pure retribution," if they are restated as suggested, are better answered in terms of ethical positive law than they are in terms of merely formal law. The position of the latter is arbitrary as regards retroactive legislation and tautologous as regards the enforcement of a bad law ("because he has no right [*i.e.* legal right] to dispense from punishment"). For, unless a law has some value, is it any criticism of retroactive penal legislation to assert that there was no law at the time of the conduct in issue? The insistence that law exist at that time implies both that punishment is not just except on that condition and also that it is just if that condition is met. But whether it is just then does not depend on the existence of any law, regardless of its content.[15] So, too, the legal duty of officials to enforce bad laws has limits imposed by ethical policy, as both legal history[16] and current practice abundantly attest. In any case, the official "obligation" to apply punitive sanctions cannot be defended or even explained on the sole ground that "that is the law." It rests equally upon the ethical quality of the legal order which must be "basically just," *i.e.* a defensible principle of legality is derived from legal rules that for the most part are substantially just. More directly, legality is not a value to be opposed to or contrasted with intrinsic or instrumental value. It is, in-

---

[13] "But we can grade crimes in a rough scale and penalties in a rough scale, and keep our heaviest penalties for what are socially the most serious wrongs regardless of whether these penalties will reform the criminal or whether they are exactly what deterrence would require." *Op. cit. supra* note 2, at 162.

[14] See *supra* note 7.

[15] See *supra* chapter 2.

[16] Hall, Theft, Law and Society ch. 4 (2nd ed. 1952).

stead, the essential condition of the uniform, sound, effective implementation of any values.

In sum, retributive ethics does not require that a *legal* sanction be applied against one who violated only a moral duty. Nor does the principle of legality, including the rule against retroactive penal legislation, oppose retributive ethics. On the contrary, it supports the principle which requires the moral guilt of those punished and proportions the punishment to the gravity of the harm. So, too, the principle of harm effects limitations which pure ethics, concerned only with subjective guilt, does not require.[17] Thus, apart from exceptional situations concerning civil disobedience in a dictatorship and the grounds invoked in democratic societies for conformity, with freedom to take the legal steps necessary to change unjust or otherwise unsound laws, it is submitted that "the only justification for punishing any man [*i.e.* imposing a legal privation] is" not "that he has broken a law"[18] but that he has broken an ethically valid law.

In Professor Mabbott's view, legislation is wholly a question of utility while adjudication is wholly "retributive," *i.e.* given legislation (only utilitarian considerations, he argues, are relevant to determine that), the only justification of punishment is "retributive."[19] This thesis seems questionable in both of its specifications[20] because legislation is not solely a question of utility; and utility does enter into the determination of the punishment fixed by courts and administrators.[21] Legislators consider questions of

17 See *infra* chapter 15 on criminal attempt.

18 *Supra* note 2, at 158.

19 *Id.* at 161-164.

20 The problem is clouded by the vagueness of "utilitarianism." See Ross, *op. cit. supra* note 11, at 57. In the following discussion, the usual meaning of "retributive" is employed.

21 The above thesis seems to have been suggested by Ross, *op. cit. supra* note 11, at 61-63. But Ross did not insist upon a sharp dichotomy between utilitarian legislation and retributive adjudication, which later writers have urged. *E.g.* he acknowledges that the proportionality of punishment to type of offense, fixed in legislation, is a matter of justice "quite distinct from expediency." *Id.* at 62.

competency and the other defenses, expressed in legal doctrines, as well as the proportionality of proposed sanctions, and so on. The legislative question is not merely whether there should be "a" law but also and principally what should be the contents of the law, what conduct should be made criminal, what sanctions should be fixed. Discussion in the legislature often emphasizes the ethical, retributive issue, *e.g.* the debates in Parliament on recent proposals to suspend the capital penalty.

So, too, as regards adjudication, it is difficult to accept the view that utility is irrelevant on the alleged ground that punishment neither deters nor reforms.[22] The contrary view — that punishment itself, not something additional which accompanies it, influences deterrence and correction — has not only popular support but also that of many philosophers, *e.g.* Plato, and of thoughtful prison wardens. When one considers the very wide range of official choice, extending from suspended sentence and probation to very severe sanctions, as well as the sentences fixed during crime "waves," etc., it seems evident that utilitarian considerations enter into the administration of penal law. In sum, (1) the question whether there should be a legal system cannot profitably be separated from the question, what should be the content of the laws, especially, their moral quality; and (2) the relationship of legislation to adjudication is that of the general to the specific — the judgment only concretizes what is general in the law or, so far as it is legislative, both retributive and utilitarian ethics are involved.

The history of punishment is a dramatic one and it is easy to understand, in the light of the stirring debates in the legislative assemblies, why so much space in the nineteenth century codes was devoted to it, and why scholars

---

[22] "But reform and deterrence are not modifications of the punishment, still less reasons for it." Mabbott, *op. cit. supra* note 2, at 153. *Cf.* Brown, *Does Ought Imply Can?*, 60 Ethics 282-84 (1950). *"There can be no retribution without reformation. . . ."* Hocking, Human Nature and its Remaking 285 (1929).

in the twentieth century still identify themselves with one
or another of the great movements and "schools" which
effected important changes in punishment. In the United
States, the various philosophies of punishment were not
developed as phases of grand political issues, and the lines
were not, therefore, so sharply drawn.

Much of the voluminous writing on punishment reveals
difficulties resulting from the apparently inevitable ambiguity of "punishment," the failure to articulate the postulates
of a theory, and the fact that the problem involves ultimate
"can't helps." Until quite recently this literature has also
been characterized by the advocacy of particularistic justification of punishment—retribution, or deterrence, or correction. If correction is espoused, retribution is damned as a
vestige of man's instinctual past, while deterrence is excluded as ineffective, rationalistic, and even as a cause of
crime. This continues to be the main emphasis of certain
psychiatrists, despite their avowals that there are many
normal criminals and that punishment sustains the conforming individual's "sense of justice." In official circles, on
the other hand, deterrence is vigorously supported as a
necessary and potent defense of social values,[23] and there is
the authority of the summary dismissal of correction by
Holmes. Surviving also, but hardly noticed until recent
years, are theories of retribution[24] which emphasize the justice of punishment.[25] Finally, there is the integrative view

[23] Elmer L. Irey, Former Chief, Enforcement Branch, United States
Treasury, describes the trial and conviction of Ralph Capone for tax
fraud and reports that the next day and every day after that for
several weeks many underworld operators went to the collector's
office "to pay Uncle Sam voluntarily $1,000,000 in taxes . . . [They]
were afraid Uncle Sam would find out." Irey and Slocum, The Tax
Dodgers 35 (1948). *Cf.* "On the other hand, to regard deterrence as
the sole end of the criminal law is a confession either of defeatism or
cynicism." Paton, A Textbook of Jurisprudence 352 (1946).

[24] For a brief discussion distinguishing the retributive theory of
Plato and St. Thomas Aquinas from those of Kant and Hegel, see
Hawkins, *Punishment and Moral Responsibility*, 7 Mod. L. Rev. 205
(1944). *Cf.* Bradley, Ethical Studies, Essay 1 (1876).

[25] After criticizing the defects of mechanical views of retribution,
Morris Cohen wrote: "Despite the foregoing and other limitations of
the retributive theory, it contains an element of truth which only

which is receiving increasingly wide support, in which all types of valid justification—justice, deterrence and reformation, with legality always presupposed—are combined in an inclusive theory.[26] This theory implies, *e.g.* that it is fallacious (a) to ask *only*, "for what end is punishment imposed?" because this automatically excludes the intrinsic value of the relevant moral experience as well as the "vindication" of the law,[27] or (b) to assume that just punishment does not contribute to reformation and deterrence.[28]

In view of the persistent difficulties which envelop this important subject, it may help to delimit the areas of agreement and disagreement if we amplify the above observations in a very simple way. Let $1 =$ rehabilitation, $2 =$ deterrence, and $3 =$ justice. A affirms only 1; B affirms only 2; C affirms only 3; while D affirms 1 and 2 and 3. It should not be difficult to plot the issues involved in various discussions, and thus to articulate the different

---

sentimental foolishness can ignore." Cohen, *Moral Aspects of the Criminal Law*, 49 Yale L. J. 1011 (1940). *Cf.* Cowan, *A Critique of the Moralistic Conception of Criminal Law*, 97 U. of Pa. L. Rev. 502 (1949) and Rooney, *Law Without Justice? The Kelsen and Hall Theories Compared*, 23 Notre Dame L. 140 (1948).

"Most intuitionists would perhaps take the view that there is a fundamental and underivative duty to reward the virtuous and to punish the vicious." Ross, *op. cit. supra* note 11, at 57-58.

[26] Because the ethical validity of a sound body of criminal law is its most important attribute and since this had been greatly neglected, it has been emphasized by the writer. *Cf.* "A third theory, and it is the one which seems to me to come nearest the truth is that there must be an element of retribution or expiation in punishment: but that so long as that element is there, and enough of it is there, there is everything to be said for giving the punishment the shape that is most likely to deter and reform." Asquith, *The Problem of Punishment*, The Listener, May 11, 1950, at 821 (pub. by B. B. C.).

[27] Radin, *Natural Law and Natural Rights*, 59 Yale L. J. 214 (1950), and Coddington, *Problems of Punishment*, 46 Proc. Arist. Soc. (n. s.) 155 (1946).

[28] One of the most interesting changes in the history of ideas is represented in the shift from Plato's axiom that punishment, justly imposed, is always corrective, indeed, that it is a major educational institution, to the axiom of contemporary academic penologists, that punishment never has any beneficial effect. If corrective treatment unavoidably includes a punitive element, the two perspectives are not actually in such complete opposition as the polemics imply.

positions represented in the literature. For example, it will be clear that D, when he adversely criticizes deterrence or correction, cannot be understood to oppose those objectives. If he is consistent, he criticizes only exclusive or excessive claims in their behalf.

On the other hand, A, who espouses rehabilitation, may never inquire whether "corrective treatment" is wholly free of punitive elements or whether it is possible to eliminate retribution entirely, although he also assumes that involuntary incarceration is a necessary condition of correction.[29] Nor does A consider the application of his theory to persons like Professor Webster, the erudite homicide, Whitney, the former Wall Street embezzler, and many other criminals who are very well educated, extremely able and highly successful. Again, what does A say regarding the many thousands of apparently incorrigible minor offenders, such as pickpockets who are unwilling to surrender a skillful art of making an easy living? In the name of "science" or "humanitarianism," would he allow alleged experts to make the pertinent decisions, even to the extent of life imprisonment, uninhibited by "legalistic" control or "moralistic" proportionality? If A would articulate his theory with reference to such questions, he might make an important contribution to the existing knowledge of treatment and punishment.[30]

Some advocates of the theory of correction take a very critical view of "moralistic" theories of punishment.[31] But since this does not prevent them from speaking of "harmful consequences" or relieve them of the need to communicate the meaning of "imprisonment with hard labor" and the like, an already complex problem seems only to be ag-

[29] The new Swedish Protective Code (Sellin ed. 1957) omits the word "punishment" and employs instead "consequence," "sanction" and "measure." Included among the "measures" are fines, imprisonment and imprisonment with hard labor.

[30] See Allen, *Criminal Justice, Legal Values and the Rehabilitative Ideal*, 50 J. Cr. L. Crim. and Pol. Sci. 226 (1959).

[31] *Cf.* Cowan, *op. cit. supra* note 25 and Lewis, *The Humanitarian Theory of Punishment*, 6 Res Judicatae 224, 519 (1953-54).

gravated by the gratuitous addition of verbal problems. In any case, it is difficult to apprehend what is "naive" about the formal public condemnation of normal adults who voluntarily inflict serious injuries on human beings. This "vulgar morality" seems to be at the foundation of the penal law of civilized countries and it is emphasized in the decisions of the courts. Indeed, while polemics against punishment are sometimes carried on without compromise, the courts in those countries are doing very much what the courts in all civilized countries are doing. Within the limits of their authority, they are attending to the gravity of the harm, the personality of the offender, the public interest, the available peno-correctional facilities, and so on. In other words, the courts are not functioning along doctrinaire lines but, instead, they are taking the important considerations into account.

B, the ardent advocate of deterrence, would be shocked by the suggestion that insane persons or petty thieves should be executed or that innocent persons should be punished or that wide publicity should be given to the "execution" of murderers who, in fact, were not punished at all, regardless of any amount of persuasive evidence that criminal conduct would thereby be deterred.[32] The execution of civilian hostages in the last war and the scientific treatment of "public enemies" by experts in dictatorial states seem to have been very effective deterrents. The relevant facts should not be ignored. But if B does not articulate his thinking in relation to these phases of deterrence, he is not apt to recognize that some degree of retribution is required in any legal order he can approve.

So, finally, C, the "pure retributionist," who sees only the intrinsic moral worth of the public condemnation of attacks on human beings, might reflect that from the very beginning of Western thought deterrence has been approved

---

[32] "To achieve the maximum deterrent effect it would be necessary either to impose excessively long sentences or to inflict harsh treatment and impose rigid restrictions and deprivations on the prisoners." MacCormick, *The Prison's Role in Crime Prevention*, 41 J. Cr. L. Crim. and Pol. Sci. 42 (1950).

and the education of corrigible offenders has been urged by many great thinkers. The finest teachings of religion emphasize the forgiveness of transgressors by their victims[33] and that should also temper the administration of criminal law. At the same time, as the retributionist urges, the human cry for justice also makes its demands; and, in addition, the elementary needs of survival require the deterrence of potential harm-doers. We should not shut our eyes to these aspects of the problem and, regardless of social responsibilities, advocate the substitution of *agape* for criminal law no matter how generously we may treat those who have harmed us.[34]

If a theory of punishment took due account of the various problems indicated above, the outlook so far as scientific research is concerned, and consequently also with reference to the administration and reform of penal law, would be greatly altered. Attention could then be directed to carefully formulated, pertinent questions, *e.g.* within the limits set by the principle of legality, in what particular offenses, regarding which types of offender, in relation to what prevalent crime rates, available facilities and so on, should the peno-correctional treatment be determined and adjusted thus and so in order to preserve the maximum intrinsic and instrumental values?[35]

Despite the unusual difficulties which beset the problem of punishment, important progress has been made in recent years in the above direction. For example, it is now

[33] "Criminals may well be called public enemies. But they are men and women. They are entitled to the benefit of the Biblical injunction that we must love our enemies. Perhaps we could come to love them if we made a sacrifice for them." Gausewitz, *Realistic Punishment,* pub. in The Administration of Criminal Justice, Virginia Law Weekly Dicta 47 (1948-49). *Cf.* St. Luke 23-41.

[34] "The effort to make life more decent therefore always involves a struggle against opposing forces. And in this struggle men find hatred as well as love, tonic emotions. Indeed, we must hate evil if we really love the good." Cohen, *supra* note 25, at 1018.

[35] See Coddington, *Problems of Punishment, op. cit. supra* note 27, reprinted in part in Hall, Cases and Readings on Criminal Law and Procedure 99 (1949). *Cf.* generally, Oppenheimer, The Rationale of Punishment (1913).

recognized that the "prevention of crime" and the "protection of society" are ends accepted by everyone, and that the reiteration of such slogans does not solve problems. It seems also to be widely agreed that involuntary incarceration is punishment regardless of the kindness of the administrators or the unexceptionable quality of the treatment program.[36] And although there are unfortunate relapses,[37] only infrequently does one find the punitive sanctions of civilized laws equated with vengeance or other merely emotional reactions or the cruel imposition of suffering as an end in itself.[38] But the most important advance is that the inclusive theory of punishment has been gaining ground in recent years.[39] This has resulted

[36] See the Protective Code (Sellin ed. 1957) and note 29 *supra*. "Experienced penologists do not dismiss the idea of punishment. They recognize the fact that being sent to a prison, however humanely it is operated, is punishment in itself. They know that it is impossible to make a prison so pleasant that the prisoners will not consider their imprisonment punishment." MacCormick, *op. cit. supra* note 32, at 42-43.

[37] ". . . the tradition of legal revenge." Zilboorg, The Psychology of the Criminal Act and Punishment 114 (1954).

[38] The "right" to be punished is not quite the absurd thing that is sometimes assumed, *e.g.* by Quinton, *op. cit. supra* note 7, at 85. There is not only the psychiatric evidence of relief from a burdening sense of guilt, but also the statements of convicted persons, such as: "To punish a man is to treat him as an equal. To be punished *for an offence against rules* is a sane man's right." Macartney, Walls Have Mouths 165, quoted by Mabbott, *op. cit. supra* note 2, at 158. Finally, ". . . prosecuted persons are often anxious to be sentenced to punishment instead of being interned in educative establishments, in mental hospitals or in establishments for the detention of certain abnormal criminals, although these forms of treatment are considered protective measures without a repressive character." Kinberg, *Punishment or Impunity?*, 21 Acta Psych. et Neur. 441-42 (1946).

[39] ". . . no penal philosophy can today be based upon one single idea, be it retribution, prevention or whatever; rather will it be a somewhat dubious mixture of heterogeneous elements, perhaps with one element predominating in the mind of judge A, another in the mind of judge B. Moreover, this hybrid penal philosophy will often have to give way to the stark realities of life: orders to an approved school or probation orders cannot reasonably be made if no vacancies exist in such schools or if the probation officers concerned are already too overworked to look after another case." Mannheim, *Some Aspects of Judicial Sentencing Policy*, 67 Yale L. J. 961, 971-2 (1958).

See the current A. L. I. Model Penal Code, Tent Draft No. 2, sec. 1.02 (2). "Basic considerations of justice demand, moreover, that

largely from the recognition that retribution has an important part in any defensible theory, at least to the extent that punishment should be imposed only on the guilty[40] and that there should be a fair proportion of punishment to the gravity of the harm, even when acknowledgment of that is made in factual terms of "the traditional rating system."[41] Within the above general context of theories in justification of punishment, it is possible more precisely to delineate the distinctive attributes of the punitive sanction.

THE NATURE OF PUNISHMENT

As was suggested above, the nature of punishment is, in part, determined by reference to its purposes and functions. For example, if one purpose of punishment, in the sense of a reason for it, is that an offender deserves to be punished, punishment has a moral significance which is lacking or, at least, is quite different from that where it is viewed only as a painful experience imposed to deter potential offenders. So, too, the latent functions of punishment, e.g. the maintenance of the individual's "sense of justice" and the cohesion of the community's moral attitudes, are additional factors which determine the nature of punishment.

"Punishment" is, of course, a very ambiguous word;[42] but, it is believed, a substantial consensus can be obtained

---

penal law safeguard offenders against excessive, disproportionate or arbitrary punishment, that it afford fair warning of the nature of the sentences that may be imposed upon conviction and that differences among offenders be reflected in the just individualization of their treatment." Id. at 4.

[40] Raphael, Justice and Liberty, 51 Proc. Arist. Soc. (n. s.) 167 (1951) and Shaw, Imprisonment 18 (1924). But cf. Bentham, Rationale of Punishment 3 (1830).

[41] It "is primarily a question of finding that penalty which corresponds to customary standards of punishment." Andenaes, Choice of Punishment, pub. in 2 Scandinavian Studies in Law 59-60 (1958). Cf. " . . . the courts can reasonably interfere only . . . where the punishment proposed is so severe and out of proportion to the offense as to shock public sentiment and violate the judgment of reasonable people." State v. Becker, 3 S. D. 29, 40, 51 N. W. 1018, 1022 (1892).

[42] Even in the legal decisions there is considerable divergence in the

or, at least, the central issues can be drawn by reference to the following suggested characteristics:[43] First, punishment is a privation (evil, pain, disvalue). Second, it is coercive. Third, it is inflicted in the name of the State; it is "authorized." Fourth, punishment presupposes rules, their violation, and a more or less formal determination of that, expressed in a judgment.[44] Fifth, it is inflicted upon an offender who has committed a harm, and this presupposes a set of values by reference to which both the harm and the punishment are ethically significant. Sixth, the extent or type of punishment is in some defended way related to the commission of a harm, *e.g.* proportionately to the gravity of the harm, and aggravated or mitigated by reference to the personality of the offender, his motives and temptation.[45]

It will be noticed that the first three criteria are equally applicable to civil sanctions. The fourth concerns legality, and its significance in penal law differs from that in civil

---

definition of "punishment." *E.g.* in United States v. Lovett, 328 U. S. 303, 316, 90 L. Ed. 1252, 66 S. Ct. 1073 (1946) it was held that "permanent proscription from any opportunity to serve the Government is punishment, and of a most severe type." In Ex parte Garland, 71 U. S. (4 Wall.) 333, 18 L. Ed. 366 (1867), disqualifying persons for the practice of law because of their past conduct was held punishment and a violation of the *ex post facto* provision. See *infra* notes 73 and 74 regarding contempt and deportation.

[43] See Strömberg, *Some Reflections on the Concept of Punishment*, 23 Theoria 71 (1957). For a summary of present American tendencies, which stresses the institutional meaning of punishment, see Jeffery, *The Historical Development of Criminology*, 50 J. Cr. L. Crim. & Pol. Sci. 14-18 (1959) and the citations there given.

[44] *Cf.* "A punishment is an evill inflicted by publique authority on him that hath done or omitted that which is judged by the same authority to be a Transgression of the Law to the end that the will of men may thereby the better be disposed to obedience." Hobbes, Leviathan ch. 28, p. 161. See Givanovitch, *De la notion de la peine*, 27 Rev. Pen. Suisse 360 (1914).

[45] "There is no society where the rule does not exist that the punishment must be proportional to the offense. . . ." Durkheim, The Rules of Sociological Method 73 (Catlin ed. 1938). "The tendency of all conduct codes is to proportion to some extent the severity of the group's reaction to a violator, *i.e.* the punishment, to the severity of injury done to its moral values." Sellin, *The Law and Some Aspects of Criminal Conduct*, pub. in Conference on Aims and Methods of Legal Research 121 (Ed. Conard, 1957).

law, *e.g.* the degree of precision required in penal law, strict interpretation of statutes and the bar on retroactivity. Again, there are important differences in procedure, such as the burden of proof, rules limiting the introduction of confessions, and so on. Non-legal scholars sometimes depreciate this characteristic of punishment, "to vindicate the law," as arbitrary. Without going into the issues thus raised concerning the principle of legality,[46] it may be noted that the above view challenges the predominant meaning of "punishment," which implies the existence of a set of rules and their violation. Even in countries which abandoned the principle of legality some years ago, the "punishment" of persons who committed "anti-social" harms was defended by reference to the violation of an analogous penal law. So, too, those who administer the sanction are authorized officials, *e.g.* the injury inflicted by a mob upon an escaped convicted murderer is not punishment. In sum, punishment is for the transgression of rules; and it is inflicted by legally authorized persons.[47]

With reference to the sixth characteristic of punishment, it may be noted that while there is also a rational relation of compensation to damage, its significance differs in important respects from its analogue in penal law. Some of these differences have been previously suggested in the differentiation of tortious injuries and penal harms. The fuller significance of the differences may be developed in discussion of the fifth attribute of punishment, noted above.

The most pronounced disagreement regarding punishment concerns this criterion, especially, its ethical aspect. Within the correctionist schools, themselves, there is sharp disagreement, certain modern scholars holding that punishment is an unmitigated "absolute" evil, while Plato regarded it as having instrumental value as a necessary cure, no more evil than the bitter medicine which a physician might ad-

[47] Hobbes' Leviathan, ch. 28, reprinted in Vol. 23, Great Books of the Western World 145 (1952).
[46] See *supra* chapter 2.

minister.[48] His views are compatible with St. Thomas
Aquinas' theory of punishment as the privation of a "natural
condition," for again, that is an evil only in a relative
sense. In an "absolute" sense, punishment is good since it
is corrective, deterrent and necessary for the public welfare.[49] There is thus in St. Thomas' theory a very important
difference between the evil of a crime and the evil of
punishment. Stubborn wilfulness, action in disregard of
reason, is the essence of crime; but punishment is imposed
on rational grounds and serves useful purposes.

Bentham views punishment in a very different perspective. For him, it is an empirical question of desire and of
the infliction of sufficient pain to provide an effective
deterrent.[50] He therefore saw no inherent difference between the evil of crimes and that of punishment except
that the latter was "legal;" and he also held it had desirable consequences.[51] Accordingly, for Bentham, the offender's temptation—not his moral culpability or the gravity
of the harm—determined the nature and extent of punishment. "The punishment," he said, "must be more an object
of dread than the offence is an object of desire;"[52] and the

[48] Plato is usually interpreted as a thoroughgoing utilitarian who
stressed the educative influence of punishment but, in fact, he also
espoused a retributive theory. He speaks frequently and favorably of
punishment as "deserved" (Gor. 525; Laws 855), of being "rightly
punished" (Gor. 525) and of "retribution" (id. at 509). In any
case, it is certain that Plato viewed the pain of punishment as both
beneficial and necessary. So, too, Kant, Critique of Practical Reason
148-163 (Abbott ed. 1883).

[49] Retribution is also recognized, e.g. De Malo, Q. 1. Art. 5. ad. 12;
S. T. II II Q. 108, a. 4, I II Q. 21, a. 3; and see Rooney, Lawlessness,
Law and Sanction 43 (1937).

[50] "If hanging a man in effigy, would produce the same salutary
impression of terror upon the minds of the people, it would be folly or
cruelty ever to hang a man in person." Bentham, Rationale of Punishment 29 (1830).

[51] "The same evil done by authority of the law, or in violation of the
law, will constitute a punishment, or an offence. The nature of the
evil is the same, but how different the effect! The offence spreads
alarm; the punishment re-establishes security." Bentham, The Theory
of Legislation 341 (Ogden ed. 1950). "The difference between punishments and offences is not then in their nature, which is, or may be, the
same; ..." Op. cit. supra note 50, at 17.

[52] Bentham, Theory of Legislation 325 (Ogden ed. 1950). Bentham

fact that "temptation diminishes fault" is irrelevant. Thus, it is not sound to ask "whether a penal code be more or less severe. The only question is, whether the severity of the code be necessary or not."[53] Despite his literal and sometimes harsh language, Bentham showed much sensitivity for the welfare of the offender.[54]

Bentham also held that there is no substantive difference between punishment and compensation. All injuries are "offenses," all sanctions are punitive; and they were treated in his penal code.[55] Bentham even said that civil sanctions are sometimes more painful, and therefore more punitive, than criminal ones.[56] For Austin, who in the main adopted Bentham's ethics, the difference between criminal and civil sanctions was only a procedural one, namely, the civil sanction "is enforced at the discretion of the party whose right has been violated" while the criminal sanction "is enforced at the discretion of the Sovereign or State."[57]

Kelsen's discussion of criminal and civil sanctions resembles that of the Utilitarians except that he ignores the

---

goes into great detail and to great extremes in adapting the type of punishment to that of the harm committed. *Op. cit. supra* note 50, at chapter 8 and *cf. id.* at 65 and 68.

[53] Bentham, Theory of Legislation 345 (Ogden ed. 1950). *Cf. op. cit. supra* note 50, at 34 where he urges mitigation if the temptation shows "the absence of confirmed depravity, or the possession of benevolence...." Bentham also advocated individualization adapted to "[a]ge, sex, rank, fortune, and many other circumstances...." Theory of Legislation 327 (Ogden ed.). He preferred punishments which reformed offenders over those that only deterred. Rationale of Punishment 47-8 (1830).

[54] "It ought not to be forgotten, although it has been too frequently forgotten, that the delinquent is a member of the community, as well as any other individual—as well as the party injured himself; and that there is just as much reason for consulting his interest as that of any other.... It may be right [sic!] that the interest of the delinquent should in part be sacrificed to that of the rest of the community; but it never can be right that it should be totally disregarded." Rationale of Punishment 28-29 (1830).

[55] But there is considerable looseness. For example, Bentham discusses punishment separately from compensation and pecuniary satisfaction in relation to theft, peculation and extortion, (Theory of Legislation, 286 Ogden ed. 1950) while he here ignores injuries caused by torts and breach of contract.

[56] But Bentham also said—at least once—that "compensation" must be distinguished from "punishment." The Rationale of Punishment 4 (1830).

[57] 1 Austin, Lectures on Jurisprudence 518 (4th ed. 1879).

possibility of any "desirable consequences." He first states
that civil and criminal sanctions are alike in being coercive;
then, that there is a difference in their purpose, namely,
while criminal law aims at retribution and deterrence,
"civil law aims at reparation." But this, he quickly adds,
is only a "relative" difference, e.g. the fine is like reparation
since both consist of economic deprivations. The civil sanction, however, awards compensation to the plaintiff, while
the criminal one transfers the fine to the community. Again,
he states, this is hardly a significant difference and, concurring with Austin,[58] he notes that both criminal and
civil sanctions deter. He also accepts Austin's view of the
procedural difference. But this, too, states Kelsen, "is of
minor importance." Hence, he concludes, there is only a
"very relative difference between civil and criminal sanction...."[59] This "relativity" must, of course, be interpreted
in the context of Kelsen's naturalistic ethics.[60]

It is significant that writers who find no substantive difference between punishment and compensation also find no
such difference between sanctions and harms. We have
noted this, with a reservation as to consequences, in Bentham's theory. Going far beyond that, Kelsen states that
"the coercive act of the sanction is of exactly the same sort
as the act which it seeks to prevent [namely] ... the delict;
that the sanction against socially injurious behavior is itself
such behavior.... Force is employed to prevent the employment of force in society."[61] That there is no doubt whatever
about the "neutrality" of Kelsen's theory is shown in his
rejection of "the usual assumption" that sanctions are
applied *because* delicts (harms) are committed. That is "not
correct," states Kelsen. "It is a delict *because* it entails a
sanction."[62] In his theory, "there is no other criterion of

[58] *Id.* at 517.

[59] Kelsen, General Theory of Law and State 50-51 (1945).

[60] This is discussed in Hall, Living Law of Democratic Society, ch. 2
(1947).

[61] *Op. cit. supra* note 59, at 21.

[62] *Id.* at 51, italics added.

the delict than the fact that the behavior [delict] is the condition of a sanction."[63] Thus, while natural law philosophers and laymen find important ethical differences between harms and legal sanctions, and utilitarians acknowledge that the two have very different consequences, Kelsen's theory culminates in a formality. Actually, however, Kelsen's insistence on efficacy as a criterion of law and the substantive character of the postulate of his theory (the *grundnorm*) imply an analogous relationship between sanction and delict. The general conclusion to which we are drawn is that for practically all writers, sanctions are meaningful in relation to harms. It follows that if there is an important difference between criminal harms and torts, punishment and compensation are correspondingly different.

Before further consideration of the relation of sanction to harm (always on the premise of legal rules by reference to which harm is a transgression and sanction a prescription), it is necessary to take account of the indicated dissenting view which is espoused by some ardent advocates of rehabilitation, who find no merit whatever in retributive and deterrent theories and characterize punishment simply and solely as the cruel, senseless infliction of suffering.[64] This rejection of any valid relationship of sanction to harm excludes the possibility of finding any rational quality of punishment. It obstructs any effort to distinguish civil from penal sanctions. And it raises other difficulties; for example, it becomes impossible to distinguish the imprisonment of a person for the commission of a crime from the detention of an arrestee or an alien pending deportation.

[63] *Ibid.*
[64] The "fundamental character of [punishment] being a suffering that is a purpose in itself. . . ." Kinberg, *op. cit. supra* note 38, at 438.
Cf. "The essential element in so-called Retributive Punishment is not the infliction of pain or loss on the evil doer, as though that by itself were good, but the assertion of the good will of the community against his evil will. . . . But this action of the community must be painful, because its essential quality is antagonism to the criminal so far as he is criminal." Temple, The Ethics of Penal Action 31 (1934). "No society has ever approved suffering as a good thing in itself." Kluckhohn, pub. in Towards a General Theory of Action 418 (Parsons and Shils Eds. 1951).

But the imprisonment of a witness surely has a very different meaning from that of a felon. So, too, hospitalization of psychotic persons and imprisonment of felons have very different meanings because they are related, respectively, to damage caused by natural forces and to harm deliberately inflicted by normal persons. Unlike punishment, neither educative nor safety measures presuppose culpability; they are not proportioned to the harm committed; and the privation, although intentional, is only a necessity. The recognition of more subtle differences, *e.g.* between very enlightened individualized punishment and corrective treatment depends even more on reference to the respective condition or prior harm which sets the perspective of interpretation.[65]

If we therefore reject polemics which isolate the sanction, and recognize that its interrelatedness with the harm is basic, the relevant problems concern the significance of that relationship. Kelsen's theory offers very little assistance in such an inquiry; and the indiscriminate utilitarian thesis that all harms are evils excludes any substantive differentiation of sanctions. For reasons previously discussed,[66] a penal harm is not merely an illegal pain or the mere "condition" of a sanction. It is also, and much more significantly, an actual disvalue. So, too, the relationship of sanctions to these deviations has social significance which eludes concentration upon the sanctions. We thus return to the central fact regarding sanctions—their relation to relevant harms and, specifically, to the question of any consequent substantive difference between punitive and civil sanctions. The present position is that there are important substantive differences because the respective harms are substantively different and this is reflected in the nature and functions of the corresponding sanctions.

[65] *Cf.* "The Prison Commissioners know that if prisons were made reasonably happy places, and thrown open to volunteers like the army, they might speedily be overcrowded." Shaw, Imprisonment 51 (1924).

There is no real danger "so long as the milder special treatment does not become such a commonplace that the potential criminal can count on it and behave accordingly." Andenaes, *General Prevention— Illusion or Reality?*, 43 J. Cr. L. and Criminol. 176 at 195-196 (1952).

[66] See chapter 7.

In an earlier chapter, the principal ground relied upon to distinguish torts and criminal harms[67] was that the latter, defined in terms of certain principles, connote the actor's moral culpability whereas this is not essential in tortious injuries. This must also characterize the respective sanctions, *i.e.* punishment implies the criminal's moral culpability and is apt (fitting, correct) in light of that, while civil sanctions do not carry this significance but serve instead to discharge certain economic functions. These are the insights which guide the following further discussion of this problem.

With reference to the moot situation which involves voluntary injuries and the thesis that "the same act" is both a tort and a crime, we previously asked, do we really have "the same act" in a legally relevant sense? It was submitted that the thesis that there is "one act" prejudges the meaning of "the act" in a common sense way and ignores the relevant ideational factors. Here we must add that the different sanctions applied to "the act" also alter "its" significance. An intentional harm, viewed from tort law, means one for which it is just or expedient to require reparation; while, viewed from criminal law, it means one where punishment should be imposed upon the offender. To reply that this is "merely" applying different sanctions to "the same act" is to forget that sanctions are essential parts of the respective ideas which give any relevant act its meaning. In sum, one reason why civil injuries differ from penal harms is that they are rationally subjected to different sanctions. Surely, there is little warrant for restricting legal analysis to the external aspects of "acts"? What is paramount is their meaning.

It must follow from the premises here employed, which locate penal harm between conduct and punishment in an interrelated means-end figure, that the penal sanction is also distinctive by virtue of its relation to the penal harm. The salient difference is shown in the fact that punishment

[67] *Ibid.*

focuses primarily on the defendant as a person, while the civil sanction is oriented primarily to the reparation of the victim's economic loss. In other words, the punitive sanction is intimate, while civil sanctions lack that quality. Many persons are, of course, attached to their pocket-books, but the seizure of their property, though personal, falls so far short of the direct, intimate treatment of the person and personality of criminals—the so-called infliction of suffering —as to constitute a very different type of sanction. That is why a criminal cannot substitute another to undergo his punishment, but the reparation of economic damage does not entail any concern with the source of the repairs.[68] In sum, punishment is a coercive deprivation intimately applied to an offender because of his voluntary commission of a harm forbidden by penal law and implying his moral culpability.

There are, of course, other ways of dealing intimately with offenders than that of punishing them. They may, *e.g.* be rewarded or educated. In addition, there are safety measures from which both punishment and education must be distinguished. If a dangerous psychotic is hospitalized or if a normal person who has an infectious disease is quarantined, that, too, is a kind of personal sanction. But there is no such intimate dealing with personality as is found in punishment and correction; and if it were possible to secure immunity without segregation, that would certainly be done. At the same time it should also be recognized that these sanctions are not actually separable. Wisely administered just punishment is educative, while a person

---

[68] Even a fine, viewed as this kind of personal deprivation, is different from money paid to repair damage. But the fine raises various questions. On the one hand, recent statutes providing a very wide range in fines and their administration by reference to the wealth of the defendant reflect its punitive import. So, too, permission to pay fines in installments over a long period of time also accords with its punitive significance. Sellin, The Protective Code—A Swedish Proposal 13 (1957). On the other hand, although an association formed to pay fines would be illegal (*Clubs for Fine Paying*, 84 J. P. 89 (1920), no one really questions where the money comes from. See H. M. Treasury v. Harris (1957), 3 W. L. R. 12, 2 All E. R. 455.

hospitalized because of a communicable disease is deprived of his freedom; indeed, the punitive aspect of the "hospitalization" of psychotics sometimes extends far beyond that.[69] It is, again, becoming rather widely recognized that the rehabilitation of juvenile delinquents also involves painful experiences.[70] But it is nonetheless possible and significant to draw the indicated distinctions among punishment, education and safety measures.

The distinctions suggested above do not wholly conform to current law. There, sanctions are classified as "criminal" and "civil" or "non-criminal" because of the practical interest in the relevant procedures and evidentiary rules which will be applied to the cases, *e.g.* jury trial, presumption of innocence, the State's burden of proof beyond reasonable doubt, etc. So, too, it should be noted that Kelsen's thesis that sanctions determine what are delicts, and not vice versa, is defensible on practical grounds. Since lawyers are concerned with the potential enforcement of *all* positive laws, congruent generalization can only be in terms of formal "conditions" which serve the practical purpose of instructing officials when and what sanctions should be imposed on whom.

From a scientific standpoint, however, what is wanted are valid descriptive generalizations and corresponding

[69] Szasz, *Psychiatry, Ethics, and the Criminal Law*, 58 Col. L. Rev. 183 at 196-97 (1958).

[70] See Allen, *The Borderland of the Criminal Law: Problems of "Socializing" Criminal Justice*, 32 The Social Service Rev. 107, 116 (1958).

Cf. "While the juvenile court law provides that adjudication of a minor to be a ward of the court shall not be deemed to be a conviction of a crime, nevertheless, for all practical purposes, this is a legal fiction, presenting a challenge to credulity and doing violence to reason. . . .

"It is common knowledge that such an adjudication when based upon a charge of committing an act that amounts to a felony, is a blight upon the character of and is a serious impediment to the future of such minor. Let him attempt to enter the armed services of his country or obtain a position of honor and trust and he is immediately confronted with his juvenile court record. And further, as in this case, the minor is taken from his family, deprived of his liberty and confined in a state institution." *In re* Contreras, a minor, 109 Cal. App. 2d 787, 789-790, 241 P. 2d 631, 633 (1952).

theories. Since some enactments are arbitrary, their sanctions are fortuitous. Not the sanctions of all "laws" in the formal practical sense, but only the sanctions of the laws defined in significant descriptive terms, must be selected. Since legal systems include archaisms, anachronisms, irrationalities and fortuitous solutions, it is inevitable that the net cast from a rational-scientific standpoint will collect in its classes sanctions which are treated quite differently in the current law. For example, punitive damages[71] and penalties[72] are found in the civil law of the Anglo-American system. Deportation is treated as a civil sanction even when it is based upon the alien's commission of a serious crime.[73] Contempt proceedings and imprisonment because of disobedience outside the court's presence are treated as "noncriminal" on historical grounds.[74] On the other hand, cur-

[71] Eshelman v. Rawalt, 298 Ill. 192, 131 N. E. 675 (1921). Amer. Oil Co. v. Colonial Oil Co., 130 F. 2d 72 (C. C. A. 4, 1942).

[72] Sherman Act, 26 Stat. 209, 15 U. S. C. § 6, F.C.A. 15 § 6. Helvering v. Mitchell, 303 U. S. 391, 82 L. Ed. 917, 58 S. Ct. 630 (1938); Hepner v. United States, 213 U. S. 103, 53 L. Ed. 720, 29 S. Ct. 474, 27 L. R. A. (n. s.) 739 (1909); Camb. L. J. 16-19 (1955).

[73] The grounds for deportation in the United States statute, 66 Stat. 208, 8 U. S. C. § 1251, F. C. A. 8 § 1251, include illegal entry and other grounds for initial exclusion, conviction of a crime involving moral turpitude, being institutionalized for mental disease, which condition existed prior to entry, and that the alien is likely to become a public charge due to causes existing prior to entry. This suggests three different rationales of deportation: 1) a country's sovereign control of the conditions of entry and stay; 2) therapeutic, safety measure, and 3) punitive.
The prevailing legal authority holds that deportation is not a legal punishment, hence criminal procedure is not required; nor is *ex post facto* applicable. Mahler v. Eby, 264 U. S. 32, 68 L. Ed. 549, 44 S. Ct. 283 (1924). Only an administrative hearing, with appeal, is provided. There have long been strong dissenting opinions to the contrary, *e.g.* Fong Yue Ting v. United States, 149 U. S. 698, 37 L. Ed. 905, 13 S. Ct. 1016 (1893); Galvan v. Press, 347 U. S. 522, 98 L. Ed. 911, 74 S. Ct. 737 (1954). Moreover, in cases which depend upon the prior conviction of a crime, the judge in that trial may recommend that the alien be not deported; in addition, the statutes on deportation are strictly interpreted. Fong Haw Tan v. Phelan, 333 U. S. 6, 92 L. Ed. 433, 68 S. Ct. 374 (1948).
Supporting the view that some deportations are punitive are dissenting opinions in Fong Yue Ting *supra* and Douglas, J. in Harisiades v. Shaughnessy, 342 U. S. 580, 96 L. Ed. 586, 72 S. Ct. 512 (1952).

[74] In "civil contempt" the primary purpose is to compel compliance with a court order, and the defendant is said "to hold the keys to his prison." Such contempt is said to concern non-feasance and private

rent "penal" law includes punitive sanctions for the non-voluntary commission of many harms.[75] All of this is obviously at odds with a descriptive theory of sanctions. Such a theory cuts across presently separated fields of law, *e.g.* to place punitive damages in the class of punishment, and so on. Although there is no escape from this discordance, it does not follow that a scientific classification of sanctions can ignore practical, historically evolved classifications. They are the repository of long experience, and it is by reference to that that the validity of a legal theory is determined. Nor, on the other hand, can lawyers afford to ignore whatever empirical-normative knowledge of sanctions is available. For that knowledge provides the only assured basis for dealing effectively with the practical problems.

SANCTIONS

The above comparison of the sanctions of tort and penal law suggests that additional knowledge could be acquired in a wider study of sanctions. The lines of such inquiry may be briefly indicated with reference to fraud.

A simplified version of the problem of sanctions con-

---

right, while criminal contempt concerns misfeasance and public right. But "The line of demarcation between acts constituting criminal and those constituting civil contempts is very indistinct." 17 C. J. S. *Contempt*, Sec. 5.

"Criminal contempt" is sometimes called "quasi-criminal" because the executive can pardon, there is a requirement of wrong intent, the burden of proof is more onerous (Note, 36 Harv. L. Rev. 617 (1923)), and the statutory basis is, by analogy, required to be "clear and definite." Lynch v. Uhlenhopp (Judge), 248 Ia. 68, 78 N. W. 2d 491 (1956). Nonetheless, the prevailing view is that an act of criminal contempt is not a crime, hence there is no right to indictment or trial by jury. Green v. United States, 356 U. S. 165, 2 L. Ed. 2d 672, 78 S. Ct. 632 (1958) a 5-4 decision. The dissenting opinion (by Black, Justice) said: "In my judgment the distinction between conditional confinement to compel future performance and unconditional imprisonment designed to punish past transgressions is crucial. . . ." *Id.* at 198. "As it may now be punished criminal contempt is manifestly a crime by every relevant test of reason or history. . . . A mandate of the Government has allegedly been violated for which severe punishment, including long prison sentences, may be exacted—punishment aimed at chastising the violator for his disobedience." *Id.* at 201.

[75] See *infra* chapter 10.

cerning fraud involves the criminal law at one extreme, the Federal Trade Commission at the other, and tort law viewed as occupying an intermediate ground. A statement of the bare material facts obliterates empirical nuances that are important in the actual operation of the respective legal controls. Thus many of the cases heard before the Federal Trade Commission include a misrepresentation of fact, scienter, reliance and damage. In theory they fall within the confines of each of the three above legal divisions. This suggests that arbitrary influences or class domination may determine the choice of controls—else why should a businessman be met merely by an order to "cease and desist" when, on the same facts classified as "material" to onerous sanctions, another individual, especially if indigent, would be imprisoned for a substantial term?

But a scrutiny of the fuller situations reveals decisive differences of an order unlike the "legally material." There is, *e.g.* the over-riding influence of the mores which evaluate false commercial advertising and food adulteration quite differently from individual traditional fraud and attempts to poison. These differences are certainly not wholly irrational and, in any event, so long as it is generally conceded that there should not be great gaps between public attitudes and legal controls, though the latter need not always merely reflect the former, such disproportionateness will persist. Other legally "immaterial" facts also influence the selection of sanctions. Financial status, *e.g.* varies considerably even in the revolutionary states. There is little point in suing an irresponsible person even for assault—the penal law is the obvious recourse. But if the assailant is a man of means, substantial damages not only satisfy but are obtainable without risk of the presumption of innocence. Libel, especially by a corporation, even more obviously calls for civil action. If the multiplicity of sanctions is viewed functionally in light of such facts and the probabilities of actual satisfaction, many of the formal inconsistencies fall into a rational frame or become of minor importance.

In addition to reference to the mores and the prospects of actual satisfaction, the use of sanctions may be differentiated from other points of view. A person who has purchased a package of cigarettes in reliance on false advertising is not only disinterested, it would be burdensome for him to take legal proceedings; but multiplied by millions, the damage is very substantial. Again, quite apart from reliance and damage, competitors have interests, indeed the decent conduct of trade should, itself, be protected—and these require suitable types of enforcement. Whether the "person" who commits the wrong is a minor or a corporation also influences the selection of sanctions.

Finally, it must, of course, be recognized that the facts are frequently distinguishable in terms of legal criteria, and even if this alone does not account for the varied treatment of deviators, it is an important factor. Thus, scienter is not required before the Federal Trade Commission, and this is approximated in the courts' departures from the older tort doctrine, especially in intimate vendor-vendee relationships. But as to damage, the Federal Trade Commission and the criminal law are in accord. Perhaps the former deals much more frequently with fraud that has not damaged, not only because it seeks to prevent future harm but also because protection of the consumers' interests requires that they be supplied with what they wanted—even though the substitute is actually better for them. In addition, the competitors' interest requires anticipatory relief. So, too, whereas actual reliance is important in tort and criminal law, it is a matter of minor concern before the Federal Trade Commission—reasonable probability of such reliance, broadly construed, is sufficient. Negligence on the part of the victim is generally irrelevant, but intentionally wrongful participation by him, though significant in torts, affects neither the penal law nor the Federal Trade Commission, which must be guided by other policies. As expected, there is a progressively wider interpretation of the misrepresentation as one proceeds from crime to tort to "unfair or deceptive acts or practices"—the last including, *e.g.* lotteries and unfair discounts. Procedure, taken in the broadest sense, varies considerably in the respective agencies—the purpose of the proceedings, the nature of the wrong and of the sanctions supplying the directing considerations. The variations in fact, doctrine and purpose, indicated above, suggest various approaches to the study of important socio-legal problems which involve comparison of the operation and efficacy of different types of sanction.

STRICT LIABILITY

CERTAIN issues raised by Stephen and others, barring any generalization of *mens rea*, have been dealt with in preceding chapters. The distinction of the principle of *mens rea* from the specific *mentes reae* and the exclusion of negligence from penal law were suggested as solutions of those difficulties as well as the requirement of criminal theory. This is comprised of certain normative-descriptive principles which, until they are supplanted, must provide the premises of any relevant criticism of penal law. This should be borne in mind especially in a discussion of the principal remaining bar to the systematization of the criminal law— the rules of strict penal liability. For unless we remain anchored to the substance of penal law, as defined by valid principles, we lack significant criteria to direct analysis. The need to stress this is suggested by the fact that it is often assumed that wherever statutes and judicial opinions run in *terms* of penal law, the substantive characteristics of penal law are present.[1] But the construction of significant criminal theory, upon which the elucidation of penal law depends, can only be achieved by the persistent observation of verbal and actual differences.

The meaning of "strict liability" is derived by opposing it to liability for "fault." In problems relevant to criminal law, strict liability means liability to punitive sanctions despite the lack of *mens rea*. It is important to avoid confusing strict liability with liability imposed for petty misdemeanors in conformity with the principles of criminal

---

[1] *E.g.* Sayre, *Public Welfare Offenses*, 33 Col. L. Rev. 55, 71 (1933).

law. Statutes sometimes include both types of liability. There is a clause in terms of "knowingly" or "wilfully" doing a certain act, a provision which seems to accord with the principles of penal liability — the fact that the punishment is slight is irrelevant. Then follows a provision omitting the above terms, and usually fixing a lesser penalty. It is this sort of provision that usually comprises strict liability. But "wilfully" and other terms which apparently connote *mens rea,* are often interpreted in ways which actually exclude *mens rea;*[2] and that raises difficult problems of statutory interpretation and penal theory.

On the basis of the discussion in earlier chapters, and especially for the reason stated above, it is clear that whatever sort of liability "strict liability" may be, it is not criminal liability. That is the perspective from which our earlier conclusions require us to approach the instant problem; but regard for the apparent similarity of the sanctions as well as for competent authority and a vast accumulation of supporting case-law requires careful analysis of the established law of strict penal liability.

In contrast to the core of criminal law, the major area of strict liability concerns minor harms. The discussion will center chiefly on these; but it must be noted that in some degree strict liability has been applied in a much greater field than that, *e.g.* the felony-murder, misdemeanor-manslaughter rules, remaining vestiges of negligence, the objective test ("reasonableness") which sometimes results in liability regardless of even capacity to conform, and a number of other major crimes, especially bigamy and sexual offenses,[3] which modern penal theory has not yet uprooted.

---

[2] For a careful, detailed analysis of these and other terms in strict liability statutes, see Edwards, *Mens Rea* in Statutory Offences (1955). See also, Devlin, *Statutory Offences,* 4 J. Soc. Pub. Teachers of L. (n.s.) 206 (1958), Hart, *The Aims of the Criminal Law,* 23 Law and Contemp. Prob. 401 (1958), and Mueller, *Mens Rea and the Law Without It,* 58 W. Va. L. Rev. 34 (1955).

[3] Also: violation of a State banking act—State v. Lindberg, 125 Wash. 51, 215 P. 41 (1923); removal of mortgaged property from the state—Pappas v. State, 135 Tenn. 499, 188 S. W. 52 (1916); *cf.* Bank of New South Wales v. Piper (1897), 13 T. L. R. 413, involving the sale of mortgaged personalty "without the written consent of the

The principal part of our inquiry will be concerned with the relevant criminal theory and the validity of the prevailing law. It will be convenient to examine the case-law first, limiting ourselves largely to those minor offenses that have been styled "public welfare offenses," and to proceed thence to more theoretical considerations.

PUBLIC WELFARE OFFENSES

Slightly more than 100 years ago, an English court held a retail dealer guilty of having adulterated tobacco in his possession despite the fact that he had purchased it in the regular course of trade and neither knew nor had any reason to suspect that it was adulterated. The statute on which the prosecution was brought recited the common practice of using substitutes. It said nothing about knowledge or intent to adulterate the product, or even negligence in discovering the adulteration. Hence it is significant that, in reversing the dismissal of the prosecution by the magistrate in *Woodrow*, Pollock, C. B., said: "So you are here wilfully disobeying the act of Parliament, if you do not take due pains to examine the article in which you deal. . . ."[4] It being noted that this "might require a nice chemical analysis," he replied: "You must get some one to make that nice chemical analysis. . . ."[5] The defendant was "bound to take care. . . . In reality, a prudent man who conducts this business, will take care to guard against the injury he complains of. . . ."[6] Baron Parke added: "It is very true that in particular instances . . . an innocent man may suffer from his want of care in not examining the tobacco . . . but the public

---

mortgagee," which was held not to require intent to defraud; embezzlement (mostly dicta)—Hunter v. State, 158 Tenn. 63, 12 S. W. 2d 361 (1928), 61 A. L. R. 1148, 1153 (1929); fraud—People v. Wahl, 100 P. 2d 550 (1940).

Cf. "It is . . . imprisonment in a penitentiary, which now renders a crime infamous." Brandeis, J., in United States v. Moreland, 258 U. S. 433, 447-48, 66 L. Ed. 700, 42 S. Ct. 368 (1922). And see *In re* Claasen, 140 U. S. 200, 35 L. Ed. 409, 11 S. Ct. 735 (1890).

4 Reg. v. Woodrow (1846), 15 M. & W. 404, 412-13, 153 Eng. Rep. 907, 911.

5 *Ibid.*

6 *Id.* at 912.

inconvenience would be much greater, if in every case the officers were obliged to prove knowledge. They would be very seldom able to do so. The legislature . . . have used very plain words."[7]

A few years later, a Massachusetts court upheld a conviction for selling adulterated milk although, again, the defendant was not at fault. The court emphasized the language of the statute; the fact that the penalty was a fine; the impracticability of requiring proof of knowledge; the importance of protecting the community against the common adulteration of food; and the reasonableness of imposing the risk upon the dealer and thus holding him "absolutely liable."[8] These decisions set the foundations of strict liability which, starting as a minor aberration that was tolerated because it involved only slight sanctions,[9] has since become a mighty structure whose effects, though hardly known, must certainly be very great. The supporting arguments have continued to be precisely those enunciated in the above early cases.

The history of this body of case-law reveals considerable reluctance on the judges' part to concede the irrelevance of *mens rea* and to engage in dubious dogmatics distinguishing "civil penalties" from punitive sanctions, and "public wrong" from crimes. Thus half a century after *Woodrow*,

[7] *Id.* at 913. Earlier decisions and some later ones opposing the above decision are summarized by Sayre, *supra* note 2, at 58 note 10. The history of the cases in which the theory of strict liability was developed is significant in other ways. Thus, the justices who first heard the cases dismissed the complaints in Reg. v. Woodrow, Fitzpatrick v. Kelly, Betts v. Armstead, Pain v. Boughtwood, and Dyke v. Gower. Even Blackburn who handed down the decision in Reg. v. Stephens (1866), L. R. 1 Q. B. 702, expressed doubts as to the omission of any allegation of knowledge in an indictment for nuisance.

[8] Commonwealth v. Farren, 91 Mass. 489 (1864). Earlier American cases imposing strict liability involved the sale of alcoholic beverages and sex crimes, bigamy, adultery, and seduction. For citations and discussion of the early cases, see Sayre, *supra* note 2, at 56-59, 62-66. One of the earliest decisions was Barnes v. State, 19 Conn. 398 (1849).

[9] "There is nothing that need shock any mind in the payment of a small pecuniary penalty by a person who has unwittingly done something detrimental to the public interest." Wills, J., in Reg. v. Tolson (1889), L. R. 23 Q. B. 168, 177.

Wright, J., in quashing a conviction for supplying liquor to a constable on duty, observed, "It is plain that if guilty knowledge is not necessary, no care on the part of the publican could save him from a conviction. ..."[10] But, with rare exceptions, it became definitely established that *mens rea* is not essential in the public welfare offenses, indeed, that even a very high degree of care is irrelevant. Thus a seller of cattle feed was convicted of violating a statute forbidding misrepresentation of the percentage of oil in the product, despite the fact that he had employed a reputable chemist to make the analysis and had even understated the chemist's findings. The limitations that might have been inferred from the remarks of Pollock, C. B., in *Woodrow* were ignored. Alverstone, C. J., only remarked "This is . . . a hard case. . . ."[11] So, too, it has been held that a butcher who innocently and without negligence sold diseased meat violated the statute, and that the provision for imprisonment as one of the sanctions did not alter the irrelevance of *mens rea*.[12] It was suggested that if it required an expert to discover latent imperfections, one who engages in the meat business must incur that expense[13] although, as seen above, liability might be imposed nonetheless.[14]

In the United States there has been a great accumulation of authority, following the early Massachusetts case noted above, including and extending beyond an important Supreme Court decision holding a corporate officer guilty of

---

[10] Sherras v. DeRutzen (1895), 1 Q. B. 918, 922-3. Similarly held as to the sale of liquor to a minor. Faulks v. The People, 39 Mich. 202 (1878). But *cf.* Cappen v. Moore (1898), 2 Q. B. 306, which affirmed an employer's liability despite the fact that his employee had violated express orders.

[11] Laird v. Dobell (1906), 1 K. B. 131, 133.

[12] Hobbs v. Winchester Corp. (1910), 2 K. B. 471.

[13] *Cf.* Groff v. State, 171 Ind. 547, 85 N. E. 769 (1908).

[14] In Rex v. Larsonneur (1933), 24 Cr. App. R. 74, 149 L. T. R. 542, the defendant, ordered deported from England, went to Ireland and was brought back by Irish officers who turned her over to the English police. She was convicted of being an alien found in England to whom permission to land had been refused. The jury's verdict found her guilty "through circumstances beyond her own control." One can only say of the decision that it represents the acme of strict injustice!

shipping misbranded food in interstate commerce, although he had no knowledge of the facts, was not guilty of any fault whatever and, so far as appeared, operated his business in a skillful, careful manner.[15]

Strict liability has expanded so considerably in recent years and in such various forms, that it is impossible to generalize regarding it. Quite apart from the diverse major crimes that have been brought within this sphere, it is difficult to recognize common features in the so-called public welfare offenses. These include, e.g. the sale of narcotics,[16] the sale of adulterated food,[17] the possession or transportation of gambling devices,[18] the transportation of intoxicating liquor,[19] the sale of liquor to habitual drunkards,[20] traffic offenses, violations of building regulations, and a great additional miscellany that can hardly be placed in any classification. The penalty is generally small,[21] but that is also true for violation of countless ordinances, statutes, and regulations which are not subjected to strict liability.

Despite this diversity, it is possible to hazard certain more significant generalizations regarding the public welfare offenses.[22] First, many of the enactments apply not to the general public but only to certain traders, particularly to suppliers of food or drugs and vendors of alcoholic bev-

[15] United States v. Dotterweich, 320 U. S. 277, 88 L. Ed. 48, 64 S. Ct. 134 (1943). For the liability of an employer and sentence to 90 days in jail for the short weight sale by his clerk, see *In re* Marley, 29 Cal. 2d 525, 175 P. 2d 832 (1946); and see generally, Sayre, *Criminal Responsibility for the Acts of Another*, 43 Harv. L. Rev. 689 (1930).

[16] United States v. Balint, 258 U. S. 277, 66 L. Ed. 604, 42 S. Ct. 301 (1922).

[17] Hobbs v. Winchester Corp. (1910), 2 K. B. 471; Commonwealth v. Smith, 103 Mass. 444 (1860); State v. Kelly, 54 Oh. St. 166, 43 N. E. 163 (1896).

[18] People v. Boxer, 24 N. Y. Supp. 2d 628 (1940).

[19] Commonwealth v. Mixer, 207 Mass. 141, 93 N. E. 249 (1910).

[20] Barnes v. The State, 19 Conn. 397 (1849).

[21] But in the Balint case, *supra* note 16, it might have been five years' imprisonment and a substantial fine. *Cf.* Brandeis, J. in note 3 *supra.*

[22] The following remarks may be illustrated by reference to Sayre's tabulations, *supra* note 2, at 73, 84-88.

erages. Others, having more general application as to potential offenders, are restricted to very few activities — the operation of automobiles, safety of highways, hunting, fishing, and various health measures. Next, many of these regulations and the conditions of conforming to them presuppose a continuous activity, such as carrying on a business. This implies that general standards regarding such conduct are important rather than isolated acts. Third, the public welfare enactments are relatively new. They represent relatively recent adaptations to an intricate economy, including an impersonal market. Although analogous control dates at least from the guilds, violations under conditions of trade prevailing in primary groups are more readily recognized as immoral. Thus, fourth, the modern regulations are not strongly supported by the mores. Their occurrence does not arouse the resentment directed at the perpetrators of traditional crimes. Accordingly, although Ross' eloquent denunciation of food adulterers as deliberate large-scale murderers[23] may have much merit, it carries little conviction because sustaining mores are lacking. The escape of such offenders from onerous sanctions attests the impotence of ethics unsupported by public opinion.[24] The above common attributes of large segments of the minor offenses which are subjected to strict liability indicate that this law was constructed to meet new, important social problems; they also help us to understand how strict liability came to be accepted. But they do not provide any justification of penal liability at the present time.

STRICT LIABILITY IN TORTS

In order to understand the significance of strict penal liability more fully, we must place it in the context of its historical development and in relation to the law of torts. For more than half a century, strict liability has occupied the center of interest in a progressively extended polemic

[23] Ross, Sin and Society (1907).
[24] Sutherland raises very important problems in his paper on *White Collar Criminality*, 5 Am. Soc. Rev. 1 (1940), and his White Collar Crime (1949). See also, Clinard, The Black Market (1952).

among legal disputants. The battle has been symbolized by "risk" versus "fault." These notions and their emergence in the distinctive culture of highly industrialized societies designate the chief bases of the dialectics as well as the social import not only of the controversy but also of the major concomitant changes in the positive law itself. The literature on strict liability is voluminous in Europe as well as here.[25] But comparison of such liability in torts and in criminal law has been but little explored, despite the fact that the problem can be clearly understood only in such an investigation.[26]

The chronological development of strict liability in the two fields is highly significant. For, as seen, despite the fact that *malum prohibitum* is an ancient symbol, the deliberate construction of a separate law of "public welfare offenses" dates from the middle of the past century. So, too, despite the highly questionable reliance on nuisance and trespass in *Fletcher v. Rylands*, it is clear that strict liability assumed a prominent role in the law of torts about that same time.[27] The coincidence of strict liability with high industrialization, especially the mechanization consequent on the

[25] For an excellent history, see Bettremieux, Essai Historique et Critique Sur Le Fondement De La Résponsibilité Civile (1921).

[26] The most helpful studies which the writer has seen are Laborde-Lacoste, De La Résponsibilité Pénale Dans Ses Rapports Avec La Résponsibilité Civile et La Résponsibilité Morale (1918). Laborde-Lacoste was a student of Duguit, and his thesis strongly reflects the teacher's views; Schmidt, Faute Civile et Faute Pénale (1928); and Ditte, De La Faute Civile et De La Faute Pénale (1911).

[27] Indeed, much of the English history could be focused on the judicial career of one judge—Blackburn (1859-1886), who wrote the principal opinion not only in Fletcher v. Rylands, but also, in the decisions that extended strict liability in conversion (Hollins v. Fowler (1875), L. R. 7 H. L. 757), and definitely eliminated *mens rea* in the public welfare offenses. Regina v. Stephens (1886), L. R. 1 Q. B. 702; Fitzpatrick v. Kelly (1873), L. R. 8 Q. B. 337. It was Blackburn, too, who wrote the majority opinion in Reg. v. Prince (1875), L. R. 2 C. C. R. 154. The same judge found no difficulty, in another criminal prosecution, in imputing the knowledge of his partner to an admittedly innocent person. Davies v. Harvey (1874), L. R. 9 Q. B. 439. But Blackburn did not live to see the strict liability he fostered firmly established and threatening to swallow much of the law built on "fault"—although Europe did see the first Workmen's Compensation Law (1884) enacted just before his retirement.

Industrial Revolution, has not escaped the attention of many writers, especially on the law of torts. But the relation of this legal development to the broad current of social theory that stimulated and accompanied it has been neglected. These ideological conditions deserve attention.

The Positivism of the last century which drew its direct sources from Gall,[28] Comte,[29] and Bernard,[30] found its warmest advocates among German and Italian criminalists. Uniting a laudable emphasis on facts with a dogma that restricted theory to observable behavior, these writers assailed the citadels of Volition and Responsibility and their corollary, Punishment. In their places rose all-embracing Determinism, enigmatic "Social Accountability" and euphemistic "Treatment." The positivists, consistently with their premises, attacked any distinction of penal from civil law, Ferri asserting that "there is no essential difference"[31] and protesting their "illogical and absolute separation."[32] But while these ideas were widely espoused in intellectual circles, their effect on criminal legislation was conspicuous only as regards the expansion of the so-called public welfare offenses. Traditional ideas of morality and the firm association of punishment with culpability rigorously limited their influence on the major crimes except in the revolutionary states; and even in Russia, as we have seen, the pendulum has for some time moved back toward more traditional theories of punitive justice — even in the area of juvenile delinquency. As regards penal law, French scholars rejected positivism as *"une theorie aussi brutale."*[33]

But in torts, the positivist ideas underlying strict liability attained a signal success[34] — which, alone, suggests that

---

[28] Sur Les Fonctions Du Cerveau; Sur L'Origine Des Qualités Morales 336 ff. (1822).

[29] Cours De Philosophie Positive (1830-42, tr. Martineau, 1893).

[30] Introduction À L'Étude De La Science Experimentale (1865).

[31] Ferri, Criminal Sociology 413 (Smithers ed., 1917).

[32] *Id.* at 511-512. See also Ditte, *op. cit. supra* note 26, at 138.

[33] 1 H. et L. Mazeaud, Traité Théorique et Pratique De La Résponsibilité Civile 74 (1934).

[34] For the influence of the Positivist School on civil responsibility, see Laborde-Lacoste, *op. cit. supra* note 26, at ch. 2.

the problems in the two fields differ greatly. Thus, in France, "carried over to the terrain of civil responsibility, the Italian theory of risk found there the complete success which it failed to achieve in the penal law."[35] Saleilles' essay[36] on accidents (his first professional work was in criminal law) was among the early tracts on that subject, which, together with the legislation on Workmen's Compensation at the end of the last century, won wide acceptance for strict liability in the private law. But the opposition to its spread even there continued vigorously. A distinguished scholar, supporting the traditional "fault" theory, argued that objective risk was immoral since it assumed the inevitability of accidents whereas in the former view, they are preventable.[37] Others contended that strict liability should be applied only where the person who will be compelled to make reparation can be known in advance and can protect himself by insurance.[38] Even Duguit, who vigorously championed the new doctrine, did not propose total elimination of fault; he urged its restriction to individual relationships. Only where the activity is carried on by a group would he substitute objective risk. Here he rejected all considerations of blame and simply asked "Which is the group that ought finally to carry the burden of the risk?"[39] While he recognized that the entire community benefits from activities of the industrial groups, he argued that they profited the latter more abundantly and directly.[40]

These ideas on risk liability in private law have found wide acceptance in all industrialized societies. Although

---

[35] 1 Mazeaud, *op. cit. supra* note 33, at 75-6. Writer's translation.

[36] Les Accidents Du Travail et La Résponsibilité Civile (1897).

[37] Hauriou, cited in Mazeaud, *op. cit. supra* note 33, at 373. Planiol's criticism was much harsher. *Études sur la Responsibilité Civile*, 34 Rev. Crit. 378-9 (1905).

[38] Ripert, Le Régime Democratique et Le Droit Civil Moderne 330 ff. (1936). Ripert's complaint is that "the modern law is no longer concerned with the interests of the actor, but rather with the victim." *Id.* at 331.

[39] Duguit, Les Transformations Generales Du Droit Privé Dupuis Le Code Napoléon 138-139 (1912).

[40] *Id.* at 140.

the trends of controversy and the social legislation may be readily related to the direction of economic change, it is not easy to evaluate these important reforms. All that need be noted here is that the apparent inevitability of accidents in industrial enterprise together with the progress of insurance transforms the relevant ethical questions into policies that are very different from the traditional ones that were apt in a handicraft economy under the control of a few individuals. It seems superficial to identify strict liability in industrial states with primitive rules of action at peril. The contemporary rules represent defensible judgments on the entire situation — the paramount consideration in the modern conditions is that the losses be widely distributed. The legal problems merge into much broader issues of social policy; and it is certainly no foregone conclusion, as is usually assumed, that even the least challenged aspect of strict liability, Workmen's Compensation, functions in the best interests of the workmen,[41] to say nothing of the wider implications of the insurance of incompetency in the motor vehicle and other fields. But practically everyone agrees that many activities are properly subjected to strict liability in private law. The moot issues there concern the extent of that liability, the best means of implementation and the like. Thus, despite Jeremiah Smith's prognostications regarding the "true" subject-matter of torts little more than a quarter of a century ago, strict liability has expanded enormously in private law. The historic examples of trespass, nuisance, wild animals, carriers' and innkeepers' liability have joined more significant developments in conversion, vicarious liability, and liability attached to ownership of an automobile, various hazardous activities, manufacturing, industry, defamation, and the rules on liability for unforeseeable damage

---

[41] " . . . the indemnity assured to the workman—or to his family in case of a fatal accident—is considerably less than the loss sustained." Demogue, *Validity of the Theory of Compensatory Damages*, 27 Yale L. J. 585, 594 (1918). *Cf.* Mass. Jud. Coun. 8th Ann. Rep't. 25 *et seq.* (1932).

to constitute a major division of tort law. The relatively minor inroads of strict liability as regards the major criminal offenses and the criticism of it even in the petty offenses contrast very sharply with its expansion in tort law and its wide approval in that field.

In view of the nature of criminal conduct,[42] there is no avoiding the conclusion that strict liability cannot be brought within the scope of penal law. This has been widely recognized by those who, like Professor Sayre, wish to distinguish "real" criminal law from that of "public welfare offenses."[43] But the conclusions hitherto reached have not usually been antithetical to the continuance of strict liability in areas other than torts. They frequently imply merely differential treatment in the codes and, presumably, an appropriate terminology as well as non-criminal procedure — though these last have not been emphasized. Despite this natural disinclination to challenge a century-old case-law, it is essential to pursue the inquiry to its limits regardless of where the conclusions may lead. Accordingly, since strict liability lies outside the scope of criminal law, we must consider whether it is defensibly retained elsewhere in the corpus juris.

Professor Beale thought such liability was justifiable as a form of private liability, specifically that the relevant damage was a kind of tort, a "public tort." But the untenability of that view is clearly seen by reference to the above discussion. Tort law is almost wholly concerned with actual reparation of economic damage. One can hardly believe that the damage caused by the sale of adulterated food is compensated for by the payment of a few dollars into the public treasury. In tort law, the judgments awarded on the principle of strict liability are substantial,

---

[42] See chapter 6, *supra.*

[43] Gausewitz, *Criminal Law—Reclassification of Certain Offenses as Civil instead of Criminal*, 12 Wis. L. Rev. 365-7 (1937); Perkins, *The Civil Offense*, 100 U. of Pa. L. Rev. 832 (1952); Hart, *op. cit. supra* note 2.

comprising actual reparation of the losses sustained. In trespass and conversion, to be sure, nominal damages are paid—but for merely technical wrongs. Accordingly, this also is an untenable analogy if only because the damage caused by the public welfare offenses is substantial. A tort judgment can be enforced against the defendant's heirs, but this does not seem possible as regards the penalties imposed for the violation of public welfare statutes. These penalties are prescribed; in torts, the damages are unliquidated until fixed by the triers of the facts. Thus it is both confusing and question-begging to assert that the public welfare offenses are a kind of tort. What we have to deal with is not the assessment of damage-judgments but the imposition of small punitive sanctions for faultless behavior that caused substantial damage. Thus strict liability, carrying punitive sanctions, is indefensible either as tort law or as penal law. Can it nonetheless be supported on other grounds?

MALA IN SE—MALA PROHIBITA

The earliest decisions on the so-called public welfare offenses rested solely on practical grounds. Continuing challenges of these necessitated reinforcement by persuasive theory. That was soon thought to be supplied by resort to the distinction, *mala in se—mala prohibita*. That distinction had been employed much earlier in English law in support of the felony-murder doctrine.[44] When the validity of imposing penal sanctions in the absence of *mens rea* was questioned, Blackstone's exposition of the relevant theory[45] was thought

---

[44] Note, 30 Col. L. Rev. 74 (1930).

[45] After identifying *mala in se* with the "laws of nature" and "intrinsically . . . wrong," Blackstone discusses "things in themselves indifferent. . . . These become either right or wrong, just or unjust, duties or misdemeanors, according as the municipal legislator sees proper, for promoting the welfare of the society, and more effectually carrying on the purposes of civil life." 1 Bl. Comm. 55. Later, in amplifying his views, he states that as to *mala in se*, "we are bound in conscience; because we are bound by superior laws, before those human laws were in being. . . ." As to *mala prohibita* these are "without any intermixture of moral guilt . . . conscience is no farther concerned, than by directing a submission to the penalty. . . ." *Id.* at 57-58. "These are naturally no offences at all; but their whole crim-

to be apt. It was applied to "police, health and revenue regulations" in an early Massachusetts case[46] where the defendant was held "bound to know the facts and obey the law, at his peril." *Prince*[47] stressed acts "intrinsically wrong," and in *Tolson*, Wills, J., distinguished a thing "wrong in itself and apart from positive law" from a thing "merely prohibited by statute or by common law."[48] This has been reiterated in many decisions dealing with "public welfare regulations."[49] It was interpreted to support the rule that there need be no *mens rea* in such cases and that even due care is immaterial.

The distinction *mala in se—mala prohibita* reflects an ancient and revered theory that is much older than Fineux and Coke. It is a theory that runs to the very roots of current thought on the instant problem, indeed on petty offenses generally. Many of these offenses have been excluded from the field of criminal conduct on the ground that they are wrong merely by "convention," not by "Nature."[50]

---

inality consists in their disobedience to the supreme power, which has an undoubted right, for the well-being and peace of the community, to make some things unlawful, which are in themselves indifferent."
4 Bl. Comm. 42.

[46] Commonwealth v. Raymond, 97 Mass. 567, 569 (1867).

[47] (1875) L. R. 2 C. C. R. 150, 154.

[48] (1889), L. R. 23 Q. B. 168, 172.

[49] United States v. Balint, *supra* note 16; People v. D'Antonio, 134 N. Y. Supp. 657 (1912); People v. Pavlic, 227 Mich. 562, 199 N. W. 373, 374 (1924).

[50] Representative of the continental position is Carrara, who states that *contraventions* are essentially unlike crimes, that they are violations of law which protect not right, but expediency, and whose sole foundation is utility. 1 Carrara, Programme du Cours de Droit Criminel 83 n. l. (1876). *Cf.* Allen, Legal Duties 237 (1931). One of the best discussions of *leges mere poenales* is Janssen, *Les Lois Pénales*, 50 Nouvelle Rev. Théologique 113, 232, 292 (1923). Janssen holds that such laws are not binding on conscience (this, of course, is quite apart from unjust laws), but that submission to the penalty is binding on conscience. For references to theological arguments opposing his views and asserting that there are no *leges mere poenales* see *id.* at 116, 235, 238. Also Dabin, accepting Janssen's position, argues for a distinction between universal laws and laws that provide means only, *i.e.* of utility. La Philosophie De L'Ordre Juridique Positif 653 *et seq.* (1929).
The distinction thus made between *in se* and *prohibita* has been rejected by several writers, *e.g.* Levitt, *Extent and Functions of the*

But it is impossible to exaggerate the confusion resulting from the courts' use of the above theory as a persuasive mask to gain acceptance for a legalistic ratiocination. The distinction between public welfare offenses and those requiring *mens rea* is only one application of this theory. It has also been used to distinguish statutory from common law offenses, and petty offenses from major crimes. The ground of these distinctions confused analysis of strict liability and provided the necessary condition precedent for its acceptance. The axiom has been that since petty offenses are "conventional" or merely "*mala prohibita*," public welfare offenses do not require any *mens rea*.

It is argued, *e.g.* that traffic laws are mere conventions— the English drive on the left side, we on the right. This is superficially persuasive but, on reflection, it must be recognized that travel in opposite directions simultaneously is an essential condition of modern traffic. The essence of any traffic regulation is the maintenance of order in the flow. This can be achieved in various ways (some streets are one-way drives) but what is not a matter of mere convention is the separation of one-direction traffic from opposite-direction traffic. Similarly, regulations as to stopping at intersections, speed limits, display of lights at night, etc., are arbitrarily designated "conventions." Such laws do not exist in the Sahara, but in modern cities there is need for them; there is as much reason for them in relation to urban conditions, values and objectives as for any law, however traditional. The intentional or reckless omission to remove garbage, to sweep sidewalks, to clear them of ice, or to place safety appliances in factories is culpable, though obviously in a lesser degree than are the traditional felonies. So long as the public good requires any regulation, that regulation is not merely conventional. If another law can fill the same need, this does not mean that either is

Doctrine of Mens Rea, 17 Ill. L. Rev. 587-8 (1922), and Note, 30 Col. L. Rev. 74 (1930). *Cf.* 1 Austin, Lectures on Jurisprudence 501, 590-1 (Campbell, 4th ed. 1879) ; and 1 Bentham, Works 192 (Bowring ed. 1859).

arbitrary. The far greater likelihood is that the two overlap in proscribing the same misconduct.[51]

Again, it is sometimes argued that certain instances of petty offending are clearly not immoral (*e.g.* speeding on an open road), but this argument as to exceptional cases is equally applicable to felonies, *e.g.* tyrannicide or an abortion performed on a young girl who was raped; and what of Jean Valjean? The illustrations can be extended indefinitely.

Next, there is this sort of contention: "yesterday it was illegal to possess alcoholic liquor or gold; today it is legal to possess them. Therefore, such regulations cannot deal with harms which are 'intrinsically wrong,' they must be mere conventions, 'wrong' merely because prohibited by positive law." The corollary of this argument is that acts now called *mala in se* were always *mala in se,* and that they were and are "universally" immoral. But, limiting ourselves to the common law, we know that even "murder" was not in Bracton's day what it is with us. In *Wheatly,*[52] the King's Bench held that one who deliberately delivered less merchandise than he represented was not even to be censured; the judges thought there was nothing wrong in "making another a fool." Until the beginning of the last century, what is now embezzlement was a mere breach of trust. The list can be supplemented considerably. On the other hand, it is possible, indeed necessary, because of similar elements in the laws of various societies, to premise certain common needs, reasoning, moral judgments, etc. The purpose of the present argument is not denial of the community of all humankind but rather insistence that the same mental processes, moral principles and attitudes give rise to different laws when the factual conditions are different. This is "normal," "rational." The import of this as regards petty regulations in modern metropolitan areas is evident.

---

[51] Thus, too, while the limits of a rule may have been arbitrarily drawn in the sense that it might with equal reason have been drawn at other points, this does not mean that the former is indefensible on rational grounds. It may mean only that one choice was as rational as another and was equally suited to the problem in hand.

[52] (1761, K. B.) 1 Black W. 273, 96 Eng. Rep. 151, 152.

We are thus led to appraise the judicial interpretation of the traditional formulae more critically. It runs as follows: Is the forbidden behavior "wrong in itself," *i.e.* would it be immoral entirely apart from and irrespective of its prohibition in positive law, or is it wrong merely because forbidden by positive law? This test, it is submitted, purports to require what, as a matter of fact, is quite impossible to be done. For it assumes that we can eradicate from our value-judgments the centuries-old influence of the positive criminal law. Such a suggested separation of positive law and moral principle also ignores the facts (a) that criminal law is at least as old as ethics; (b) that our ethical principles are in great measure the product of positive law; and (c) that positive law itself provides principles of ethics, indeed, in a great many cases, no extra-legal ethical principle exists. The consequence is that we are required to appraise the petty offenses by reference to the same standards and criteria which are employed to evaluate the major traditional harms. This does not mean that important differences do not exist; but it does mean not only that the judicial reliance upon *mala in se—mala prohibita* in support of strict penal liability[53] is fallacious but also that the theory upon which it rests is highly questionable.

The unfortunate effect of the judicial application of the *mala in se—mala prohibita* doctrine has been the setting up of a rigid dichotomy between traditional harms and the mass of petty misdemeanors which were declared to be amoral. This encouraged the most serious fallacies, namely, the legal theory that *mens rea* is not a material element of these offenses, and that strict liability is therefore justified. The ancient advocates of the classical theory never drew such inferences from the principles underlying the distinction, *mala in se—mala prohibita*. The judges, however,

---

[53] " . . . it is clear that defendant's actions here constituted violations of an offense *malum prohibitum*, and that the necessary elements constituting 'knowingly and wilfully' must be determined accordingly." Riss and Co. Inc. v. United States, 262 F. 2d 245, 249 (C. C. A. 8th, 1958). So, too, Reyes v. United States, 258 F. 2d 774 (C. C. A. 9, 1958).

sought a theory to support penal liability regardless of innocence and care. They read their needs into reverent Latin phrases, and they derived what they wished to discover. Whatever may be said of the ancient theory, it is evident that the judges' application of it is fallacious. If strict liability rests on any rational ground, it must be sought elsewhere than in *"mala prohibita."*[54]

CRITICISM OF PRACTICAL GROUNDS OF STRICT LIABILITY

In appraising the practical arguments that have been made in support of strict liability, little time need be devoted to the emphasis on the slightness of the penalty. Quite apart from the outrageous exceptions met in reference to various major crimes, that explanation is patently apologetic. One can understand how it influenced the judges to ignore established principles; but it is certainly no justification of strict liability. Slight penalties may in some circumstances suggest the need for a simplified procedure and even warrant the removal of procedural safeguards normally insisted on. They cannot be relied on to discard rational penal liability.

More persuasive is the argument that in many of the cases where only the external facts need be proved, it is very probable that there was *mens rea*, *e.g.* the race tout in possession of lottery tickets, of whose character he was "innocent," or the crafty restaurateur in possession of forbidden liquor. In other cases, despite the "at peril" dogma, the courts have required proof of certain knowledge, *e.g.* that a bottle (of liquor) was known to be on the premises and was not simply "planted;" and presumably no court would convict a psychotic person or a somnambulist of any offense.[55] It may accordingly be maintained that, despite the avowals of strict liability, intent and negligence actually

[54] What seems to the writer to be a valid application of that notion is discussed *infra* chapter 11 at note 44.

[55] The Cour de Cassation has held that *force majeure* is also a defense to a charge of violating a *contravention.* Arret du 6 Mar. 1934, Pas. 1934, I. 207.

play some essential part in such offenses. The key to understanding the public welfare offenses, therefore, it may be urged, is that they are designed to catch the willful and the negligent; they are not intended to penalize those who were faultless. But the statutes are so phrased as to include the innocent, and these are caught occasionally as a result of incompetent administration.

But the above arguments are untenable. Beyond indicating that behavior subjected to strict liability is sometimes distinguished from sheer accident, they merely imply that some of the offenses which are declared to be within the scope of strict liability are actually treated as requiring *mens rea*. That offers no justification of strict liability even if *mens rea* is proved. For the argument is plainly a *petitio principii*. It amounts not to any defense of strict liability, but rests instead on the assumption that a wise administration of these statutes avoids their admitted evil.[56] No one would think of maintaining such a position regarding any major crime—*e.g.* a statute which provided that anyone who killed a human being must be held guilty of murder—on the ground that the statute would be enforced only against those who killed with malice aforethought. Nor can the assumption that strict liability is always invoked only against culpable or negligent offenders be admitted on either logical or empirical grounds. There are few facts to support such an optimistic interpretation and numerous cases op-

[56] This was suggested in Hobbs v. Winchester Corp. (1910), 2 K. B. 471. Where a defendant acted without knowledge, "the justices would impose either a reasonable fine or no fine at all," and the magistrate would only inflict "a merely nominal fine," indeed, "under modern legislation . . . he need not even convict at all where there is only a trifling breach of the law. . . ." *Id.* at 481, 485. Unfortunately there is ample reason to believe that this wise counsel is not adhered to. Even more significant is the fact that it should have been necessary to have uttered it. Certainly laws which require such drastic curtailment at the hands of the administrators in order to avoid injustice provide no reason to justify their continuance. See Hart, *op. cit. supra* note 2, at 423-24.

The need for great selectivity in the prosecution of O. P. A. violators, regardless of the wide statutory definition and strict liability, is discussed by Schwartz, *Federal Criminal Jurisdiction and Prosecutors' Discretion*, 13 Law and Contemp. Prob. 83-86 (1948).

pose it. On the other hand, if enforcement is actually directed only against the culpable, there is no warrant for retaining strict liability. The fact that prosecutors often or even usually enforce strict regulations only against culpable offenders does not support strict liability. Instead, it implies that they have the evidence to prove *mens rea* and that the argument of extraordinary difficulty in that regard is unsound.

Another argument in support of strict liability is the claim that it serves as a prod to stimulate increased care and efficiency—even by those who are already careful and efficient. The assumption is that, *e.g.* the officials of a corporation, knowing about strict liability or having it imposed upon them, will take precautionary measures beyond what they would otherwise employ. It seems probable that most persons and businesses within the potential orbit of strict liability can improve their methods of operation. Strict liability is the gadfly which stimulates the greater effort; this redounds to the public good. The objective is unassailable; the sanctions are so slight that there is no serious ground for concern even though the "wrong" persons are occasionally subjected to them—hence criticism of strict liability from the viewpoint of the principles of penal law is merely academic. There is already a consensus that strict liability is not penal law; let us call it "economic law" or "administrative regulation,"[57] if such tagging is preferred. But let us retain it "as is"—that is the ultimate conclusion of the above justification of strict liability.

But that argument, like certain myths, is just too good to be true. It rests wholly on assumptions that have never been established. That there is always room for improvement of business operations is at best a very loose generalization; frequently it is quite fallacious. The cost of operation is one serious limitation. Only "in the abstract" is it possible to employ chemists, bacteriologists, etc., etc., to

[57] Schwenk, *The Administrative Crime, Its Creation and Punishment By Administrative Agencies*, 42 Mich. L. Rev. 51, 85, 86 (1943).

analyze every can of food shipped from all the factories in America. Actually such care and efficiency are incompatible with operating a business at all. Thus an elementary discrimination of what is possible takes the form of what is reasonable—else we merely indulge in exhortation, not actual problem-solving.

If it be conceded that there are margins for improvement of business methods which are reasonably available but not yet tapped, there remains the question: Is strict liability a suitable means to implementation of that end? It need not, of course, be the whole means or the most effective of the various controls. But defense of it surely implies that it has some merit, that it does appreciably increase the social good sufficiently above its various costs to justify its continuance. There are several impelling reasons for doubting this hypothesis.

There is, first, the opinion of highly qualified experts that the present rules are regarded by unscrupulous persons merely "as a license fee for doing an illegitimate business."[58] Such persons are not deterred by the imposition of nominal fines. To let off with a petty fine those who intentionally or recklessly violate such laws as the Pure Food Act is to encourage them to persist in their malevolence; as suggested, it is merely to impose a nominal tax on illegal enterprise.[59] It seems only slightly less probable that the facile practice of imposing such sanctions handicaps the imposition of penalties that are commensurate with the gravity of willful adulteration of food and the like. The legislature is lulled into complacency by "passing a law;" prosecutors are content with the bulge of statistics on "convictions;" and the general public is grossly uninformed. There can hardly be any doubt that strict liability is a futile gesture so far as unscrupulous persons are

[58] Rep. of the Chief of the Food and Drug Administration 4 (1931).
[59] See also Lee, *The Enforcement Provisions of the Food, Drug and Cosmetic Act*, 6 Law and Contemp. Prob. 70 (1939); Chamberlain, Dowling, and Hays, The Judicial Function in Federal Administrative Agencies 91-92 (1942) and Wis. L. Rev. 625 (1956).

concerned, *i.e.* as regards the very ones who are the proper targets of punitive sanctions. Regarding such individuals, it is necessary to put real teeth in the law. Not the least effect would be the elevation of the mores towards a wider appreciation of the gravity of those offenses.

Is it likely that strict liability stimulates care and efficiency on the part of reputable businessmen? That it does so in some cases may be granted, especially perhaps in individually owned businesses where the publicity following a conviction may be far-reaching and possibly disastrous to the future operation of the business.[60] The pertinent question is whether this kind of influence is desirable. Moreover, for large corporations, the probability is that their own standards of service as well as competition for the market are the principal determinants of their business conduct. That they are to any appreciable extent further conditioned by the fear or the imposition of nominal fines is unlikely. Paramount in any realistic appraisal is that the stigma ordinarily attached to a conviction is vitiated by the knowledge that neither moral culpability nor negligence is implied.

In any event, what is not a matter of opinion is that in evaluating the existing law on public welfare offenses, our critical resources are limited—the standards of appraisal must be those applicable generally to the solution of social problems by legal methods. This involves (a) the precise demarcation of objectives, (b) the conduct that must be "controlled" to attain them, and (c) the methods and instrumentalities that are best adapted to function as controls. There are various theories regarding the relationship of law to conduct; prevailing moral ideas and attitudes are among the most important data considered. Underlying relevant theories are certain common premises regarding the occurrence of the evils (harms) that are sought to be prevented. These common notions are expressed in various terms which symbolize the relationship of the human actor

---

[60] Edwards, *op. cit. supra* note 2, at 245.

to the harms, namely: intention, recklessness, negligence, ignorance, and accident. The theories differ in certain respects, but most of them agree that legal control must have some rational relationship to human conduct and, specifically, to the various ways indicated by the above terms in which human beings "cause" the proscribed harms.

It is not very likely that improvement of either business conduct or public opinion is advanced by maintaining an attendant antagonism with the deeply rooted conviction that only the blameworthy should be punished. The arguments advanced elsewhere in this book regarding the deterrence of inadvertent injury are augmented in the present context by the slightness of the sanctions. We have also noted the inefficacy of punitive methods to inform or to develop skill in the careless and the inefficient as well as the probability that a sound corrective law could be applied profitably to such persons who were educable. As regards the sanctions of strict liability, no such likelihood can be discerned. Hence strict liability cannot be justified as a form of corrective law. It seems highly improbable that it represents some new discovery in the methods of legal control, some grand invention of ingenious "social engineers," which rests on novel but nonetheless valid foundations. Penal law implies moral culpability. Corrective law implies that defects exist and that they can be removed. These implications are irrelevant, indeed antithetical, to strict liability. For, since that liability is meaningful only in its complete exclusion of fault, it is patently inconsistent to assert, *e.g.* that a businessman is honest, exercises care and skill, and also, if a misbranded or adulterated package of food somehow, unknown to anyone, is shipped from his establishment, that he should be punished or coercively educated to increase his efficiency.[61]

[61] Professor W. Friedmann supports strict liability on the grounds that this maintains certain standards of conduct and that this "would be seriously impaired if the individual defence of mistake or blamelessness were generally admitted." Friedmann, Law in a Changing Society 199 (1959). However, no evidence was given in support of either of the above assumptions, nor were any reasons advanced to render them

Thus, as one probes for some rational ground of strict liability (outside of torts), it becomes increasingly like the proverbial search in the dark room for the black cat that isn't there. For any attempt to supply a rational base in support of strict liability is itself unsuited to, indeed, is antithetical to, what is sought to be justified. Inasmuch as strict liability means that regardless of lack of intent, recklessness, negligence, the use of superior knowledge and skill, etc., penal liability must nonetheless be imposed, it is impossible to defend strict liability in terms of or by reference to the only criteria that are available to evaluate the influence of legal controls on human conduct. What then remains but the myth that through devious, unknown ways some good results from strict liability in "penal" law?[62] Yet, it is incontestable that myth dies hard, and the legal reformer is sometimes compelled to guide his craft by making concessions to a current irrationality.

An important clue to what is actually the principal support of strict liability is provided by the fact that from the very beginning of the public welfare offenses to the

---

persuasive. *Cf.* the data collected by Sutherland showing that of 70 corporations fined for various infractions, "98 per cent are recidivists." The Sutherland Papers 80 (Cohen, Lindesmith and Schuessler, eds. 1956).

Professor Friedmann, in support of his position, relies upon R. v. St. Margaret's Trust Ltd. And Others (1958), 2 All E. R. 289. In that case, the defendant, operating a finance business, relied on the fraudulent statement of an automobile dealer regarding the amount paid by the purchaser in an installment sale. As a result, the defendant provided more than the permitted proportion, thus violating a regulation passed to check inflation. The finance company was fined five pounds. The plea of innocence, based on the facts and the conduct of the business, was met by the court's statement that "the method of business must be re-arranged so as to give the necessary knowledge." *Id.* at 293. How the fraudulent representations of apparently reputable businessmen could be discovered in ways compatible with the conduct of the finance business was not suggested by the court.

[62] It is significant that the efforts of French scholars to support strict liability take the direction of maintaining that the proscribed harms were actually caused by fault of some sort. Thus Laborde argues that the exclusion of intent still leaves recklessness and negligence to account for the *contraventions*. Laborde, *De L'Élément Moral dans les Infractions Non Intentionalles*, 14 Rev. Crit. 261, 265 (1885). *Cf.* Heitzmann, De La Notion De Contravention, especially at 25 and 45 (1938).

present time, there has been an unvarying insistence on the difficulty of proving *mens rea; e.g.* "to permit such a defense would be to allow every violator to avoid liability merely by pleading lack of knowledge and thus, practically, nullify the statute. . . ."[63] This argument implies that even though *mens rea* exists, it is impossible to prove it, presumably because there are distinctive features in such cases that make this proof peculiarly difficult. But if we appraise the actual situation in this respect, without prejudging it, it is impossible to attach any great weight to that argument. It amounts to no more than a bare assertion or a mere guess. It is obviously at odds with what is actually done in countless prosecutions. Moreover, a glance at the law on various major crimes reveals many situations where serious difficulties must be overcome in proving *mens rea, e.g.* receiving stolen goods, numerous instances where ignorance of fact is a defense, and innumerable statutory provisions where knowledge must be shown.[64] The burden of proof would obviously be lightened, indeed practically eliminated, if there were no need to prove *mens rea.* But even primitive law did not often attach punitive sanctions to harms totally unrelated even to negligence. Many injuries, deaths, and much damage are caused annually by negligence and in accidents. Yet no one proposes to inflict penal sanctions on the sole ground that these harms injure the public interest. Nor has it occurred to anyone to contend that *mens rea* should be eliminated from any common law offense because it is difficult to prove. It has never occurred to anyone to assert that the mere denial by the defendant that he had knowledge, *e.g.* that the goods he purchased were stolen,

---

The like temptation to assume that all violators of public welfare regulations are culpable or at least negligent is constantly revealed in the cases, *e.g.* Reg. v. Woodrow (1846), 15 M. & W. 404, 153 Eng. Rep. 907 and Commonwealth v. Mixer, 207 Mass. 141, 93 N. E. 249 (1910). *Cf.* Bishop, *A Chapter of Blunderings On and Off the Bench, and of their Causes and Remedies,* 4 So. L. Rev. (n. s.) 153 (1878).

[63] Note, 42 Mich. L. Rev. 1103, 1106 (1944).

[64] See United States v. Ausmeier et al., 152 F. 2d 349 (C. C. A. 2d, 1945).

foreclosed the opportunity of proof to the contrary. The fact that minor offenses are involved does not alter the prospects or methods of establishing *mens rea*. Instead, the judges of the facts may be expected to be less hesitant to find such offenders guilty. Nor should it be forgotten that proof of recklessness is sufficient to sustain penal liability; that not only lessens the burden of prosecution, it also conforms to established principles.

This is especially pertinent in the context of current administration, licensing and investigation carried on in the regulation of many businesses. Thus it is a frequent practice in the exercise of these functions for field investigators to lay the foundations for future successful prosecution by establishing knowledge of regulations and of facts regarding the conduct of a business so as to permit the ready inference that there was awareness at least of improper operation, if not actual intent to commit the harm in issue.[65] In short, the likelihood is that the burden of proof of *mens rea* can now be more easily discharged in prosecution of the public welfare offenses than as regards many common law crimes.

A hundred years ago, however, the above current aids to prosecution were lacking; the judges were duly impressed with the difficulties of proof resulting from the sheer volume of the cases and the lack of regulative and fact-finding agencies. It was statistics, not any distinctive feature of these offenses, that suggested the argument that proof of *mens rea* would be onerous and that to insist upon it would nullify the statutes. Judged on its merits, this argument is hardly more than an admission that what ought

[65] In a Wisconsin study, it is emphasized that: "Standard operating procedure calls for the issuance of a warning notice by the field inspector immediately upon discovery of an inadvertently offensive condition or action." Several warnings are given before prosecution is instituted. Remington, Robinson and Zick, *Liability Without Fault Criminal Statutes*, Wis. L. Rev. 625, 653 (1956). A pending bill in the California legislature regarding "quackery" in "cancer cures" empowers a board to issue cease and desist orders, and makes violation of that a misdemeanor. See 11 Stanford L. Rev. 294 (1959) and *supra* note 56.

to be adjudicated is not adjudicated, and a rationalization of that on the ground of necessity. That is the *ratio ultima* of strict liability.

The statistics cannot be disputed: in many jurisdictions the number of these offenses far outweighs all others combined.[66] Nor can it be doubted that if all these cases were contested, the courts could not begin to cope with them. Even a century ago when the volume of such offenses was small by comparison with their present proportions, it was apparent that the judges could not try them. The enunciation of strict liability was a short cut to the avoidance of hearings; it was the major encouragement of pleas of guilt. But any appraisal of such policy-formation a century ago cannot overlook the alternatives actually available at the time. Practically, the choice was full judicial trial (even summary hearings were little developed at the time) or pleas of guilt, *i.e.* a crude administration by the police, prosecutor and magistrate. It is little wonder that the relatively small penalty was persuasive to the point of nullifying basic common law principles. Moreover, the early statutes sometimes authorized officials to forego prosecution in cases where there was no *mens rea*. Even in those circumstances many judicial voices were raised in protest against the erosion of the common law.

PROPOSED SUBSTITUTES FOR STRICT LIABILITY

Any current estimate of strict liability must take account of the vastly improved procedural and administrative facilities that now abound. Summary judicial hearings have been greatly improved; various techniques for arriving at judgments by conference, requiring mere recordation in court are available; administration and administrative law have been greatly improved and expanded in the past quarter of a century. In short, the sole *raison d'être* of strict liability no longer exists—the problem posed by statistics can now be met by available legal institutions.[67] The continued recital

66 Sayre, *supra* note 2. at 69.
67 See, *e.g.* Warren, Traffic Courts (1942).

of the rationalizations of a century ago loses any modicum of persuasiveness when the insistent claims of principle can be satisfied.

The elimination of punitive strict liability would not restrict the inducements made by prosecutors to obtain pleas of guilty to the relevant criminal charges. The general features of contemporary criminal procedure, characterized by the disposal of the greatest part of the business by prosecutors and judges sitting without juries, would obtain here too. The bulk of the problem of protecting the public welfare would be transferred to licensing and administrative agencies,[68] leaving the willful violations to be disposed of by specialized criminal courts or by special procedure. Against these unscrupulous individuals the criminal law, sharpened to allow adequate dealing with crimes that are very serious in modern conditions, would be used much more frequently than in the past. On the other hand, the trial of reputable persons in a criminal court would be discontinued. Instead, sound legislation,[69] inspection, licensing, information,[70] investigation by boards, informal conferences, and publicity would provide much more likely means of influencing legitimate business.

For the incompetents who simply cannot conform to decent standards even after warning, information and counsel by regulatory boards, there is no alternative save to bar them from the pursuit of activities which are harmful to the public—whether that is driving an automobile, sup-

[68] Nat'l. Comm. on Law Observance and Enforcement, Rep. No. 8 (1931).

[69] "A distinguished draftsman of government legislation was once trying to persuade a British department to allow him to re-write a group of confused and overlapping statutes about the adulteration of food and drugs. 'Why?' answered an official playfully, 'we know all about the law inside the department, and the public finds out in the police court?' " Carr, *Ignorance of the Law*, 9 State Government 149, 150 (1936).

[70] "It is believed that more effective compliance with the law may be obtained by showing reputable manufacturers how to bring their products into conformity with its terms than by imposing fines or effecting seizure and confiscations after the violation has been committed." Rep. of the Chief of the Bureau of Chemistry 20 (1926).

plying milk or operating a public bar. It is undoubtedly true
that the penal law functions much less onerously than would
the revocation of a license to do business. But this does not
support the continuance of an anomalous strict "penal"
liability. The community is entitled to protection from inefficient persons who engage in potentially dangerous voca-
tions or activities. They are certainly not restrained or
improved by the perfunctory imposition of petty fines, nor,
for that matter, by much severer penalties. The only proper
recourse in some cases (very few, presumably, by comparison with those who improve their course of business
after notice and assistance are received) must be the termination of the business or other activity. To make that
depend on criminal behavior is to confuse immorality with
inefficiency. To confine revocation of a license to the former
is to ignore a major cause of injury to important social
interests.

In the early stages of the reforms indicated above, serious
difficulties of proof might be met, especially regarding regulations where the relevant conduct is not amenable to
regular inspection. In addition, some violations of public
welfare regulations, even though intentional, are very minor
harms. This indicates not only the defensibility of special
rules of procedure but also periodic changes in procedure.
Specifically, in certain areas a rebuttable presumption that
the harm was done intentionally or recklessly would be both
necessary and defensible.[71] It is noteworthy that this
device has already been employed in recent legislation.[72]

[71] This is suggested by Heitzmann, *op. cit. supra* note 61, at 42.

[72] In certain English legislation, warranties protect the dealer and
reasonable belief in the genuineness of a false warranty is a defense.
The Defence Regulations, No. 1553 (1943). See, also, Pain v. Boughtwood (1890), L. R. 24 Q. B. 363. Proof of innocent ignorance is a
defense in the Food and Drugs Adulteration Act, 1928, 18 & 19 Geo.
V, ch. 31; and see 38 & 39 Vict., ch. 63, § 25 (1875). *Cf.* Churcher v.
Reeves (1942), 1 All E. R. 69. As regards the English Merchandise
Marks Act, 1887, 50 & 51 Vict., ch. 28, although the prosecution need
not prove *mens rea*, the defendant is permitted to establish its non-
existence. The Fertilizers and Feeding Stuffs Act, 1926, 16 & 17 Geo.
V, ch. 45, § 7 (1) provides that reasonable care is a defense.

Finally, there is the practical question of securing the adoption of the proposed legal reforms, and this concerns, initially, the existing mass of precedent on strict liability. The constitutionality of statutes imposing strict liability cannot be discussed here in any detail, but it may be noted that the indicated reform is not nearly as far beyond the reach of the courts as might be assumed.[73] That such a change is something less than utopian is also indicated by the fact that, after many years of troubled acquiescence and despite the volume of relevant case-law, the judicial challenge to strict liability is still heard in England.[74]

In this country, as in England,[75] early decisions recognized non-culpable ignorance as a defense to "public welfare offenses."[76] It is now deemed to be fully established that as regards public welfare statutes and the like, the "power of the legislature . . . to exclude . . . knowledge and due diligence . . . cannot . . . be questioned."[77] The principal authority is *Balint*,[78] a narcotics case, which was explicitly

[73] See Raylin and Tuttle, *Due Process and Punishment*, 20 Mich. L. Rev. 614 (1922).

[74] Thus a distinguished English jurist said: "I myself view with some trepidation any tendency to diminish the importance of the rule as to mens rea which has prevailed in respect of criminal charges. There are cases no doubt where a statute makes it plain that an offence is created without a criminal intention on the part of the person who is charged, but those cases, where the Court is dealing with a question of crime, are to my mind in themselves anomalous; and I should hesitate to increase their number. . . ." Atkin, L. J.. *In re* Niahmond & Ispahani (1921), 2 K. B. 716, 731-2. But *cf.* note 61 *supra.*

[75] Rex v. Dixon (K. B. 1814), 3 M. & S. 11.

[76] Hunter v. State, 38 Tenn. 91 (1858).

[77] Chicago, Burlington & Quincy Ry. v. United States, 220 U. S. 559. 578, 55 L. Ed. 582, 31 S. Ct. 612 (1911).

[78] 258 U. S. 250, 66 L. Ed. 604, 42 S. Ct. 301 (1922). In Nigro v. United States, 4 F. 2d 781 (C. C. A. 8th, 1925) the defendant was charged with having purchased certain narcotics, not in the original packages and marked with counterfeit revenue stamps. The conviction was reversed, the court distinguishing the case from U. S. v. Balint on the ground that the instant case involved the purchase of narcotics, not their sale. The court argued that a seller had an opportunity to protect himself whereas the buyer might find himself in the defendant's situation quite innocently. Nonetheless it is apparent that many of the arguments raised in support of the present defendant apply equally to a seller of narcotics.

based on *Shevlin-Carpenter Co. v. Minnesota.*[79] But that case involved not a public welfare offense but the imposition of punitive damages for an involuntary trespass; and the language in the opinion specifically relied upon in *Balint* was clearly dictum. Without any detailed survey of the cases, it is apparent that serious questioning of the constitutionality of statutes imposing strict liability is far from being precluded.[80]

Two recent Supreme Court cases may well supply a major impetus to the thorough re-examination of the entire problem of strict penal liability. In *Morissette,*[81] the defendant went on government property, used as a practice bombing range, and took three tons of old metal bomb casings which he flattened and sold for $84. Charged with their willful and knowing conversion, he pleaded that he thought the bomb casings had been abandoned. The trial judge refused to al'ow the defense to introduce evidence of innocent intention; there was a conviction and sentence of imprisonment for two months or to pay a fine of $200. The Court of Appeals affirmed, relying on *Balint* and *Behrman,* which also applied strict liability to the possession and sale of narcotics. The Supreme Court reversed the conviction, holding that larceny and related crimes require a *mens rea.*

Lambert v. California[82] held unconstitutional a Los Angeles ordinance making it criminal for a "convicted person" to remain in the city more than five days without registering with the police. Unfortunately, the decision was rested on the dubious ground that ignorance of the law should have been recognized as a defense in this case because the proscribed conduct was an omission.[83] Notwithstanding this

---

[79] 218 U. S. 57, 54 L. Ed. 930, 30 S. Ct. 663 (1910).

[80] Funk v. United States, 290 U. S. 371, 78 L. Ed. 369, 54 S. Ct. 212 (1933), and Patton v. United States, 281 U. S. 276, 74 L. Ed. 854, 50 S. Ct. 253 (1930) set aside centuries of precedent.

[81] 342 U. S. 246, 96 L. Ed. 288, 72 S. Ct. 240 (1952).

[82] 355 U. S. 225, 2 L. Ed. 2d 228, 78 S. Ct. 240 (1957).

[83] But *cf.* Reyes v. United States, *supra* note 53, at 774 which upheld a conviction for failure to register when leaving the United States, having been convicted of violation of a narcotics law, the court dis-

gratuitous restraint, the common tendency of the above decisions is not only to limit the present area of strict penal liability rigorously but also to revitalize the principle of *mens rea* as the basis of criminal liability. Thus it is not without significance that it was said in *Morissette*, " . . . the law on the subject [of strict liability] is neither settled nor static. The conclusion reached in the *Balint* and *Behrman* cases has our approval and adherence for the circumstances to which it was there applied."[84]

On the other hand, strict liability was affirmed within its present limits in *Morissette*, it remained unchallenged in *Lambert*, which obviously avoided the wide implications of the decision, and strict liability seems to have been vigorously supported there in the dissenting opinion of Justice Frankfurter.[85] Thus the likelihood is that judicial correction will for the most part be restricted to checking the expansion of strict liability[86] although some few judges may decide that it is necessary and proper to take a fundamental stand—that strict liability is opposed to sound principle and that such legislation is unreasonable.[87] At the

---

tinguishing the facts from *Lambert* in various technical ways (*id.* at 784-85) which, if sustained, will seriously limit the holding in *Lambert*.

[84] *Supra* note 81, at 260.

[85] *Supra* note 82, at 230-31. Frankfurter, J. used even stronger language in support of strict liability in United States v. Dotterweich, 320 U. S. 277, 88 L. Ed. 48, 64 S. Ct. 134 (1943). *Cf.* Hart, *op. cit. supra* note 2, at 430-35.

[86] In United States v. Dotterweich, *supra* note 85, at 277, Mr. Justice Murphy, who wrote the dissenting opinion, emphasized that: "There is no evidence in this case of any personal guilt on the part of the respondent. . . . It is a fundamental principle of Anglo-Saxon jurisprudence that guilt is personal and that it ought not lightly to be imputed to a citizen who, like the respondent, has no evil intention or consciousness of wrongdoing." *Id.* at 285-86.

[87] Apt judicial language is available: "If, therefore, a statute purporting to have been enacted to protect the public health, the public morals, or the public safety, has no real or substantial relation to those objects, or is a palpable invasion of rights secured by the fundamental law, it is the duty of the courts to so adjudge. . . ." Mugler v. Kansas, 123 U. S. 623, 661, 31 L. Ed. 205, 8 S. Ct. 273 (1887). "We can scarcely conceive of a valid penal law which would punish a man for . . . an act which the utmost care . . . would not enable him to avoid." State v. Laundy, 103 Or. 443, 204 P. 958, 976-7 (1922).

same time, there is no reason to minimize the difficulties of achieving major reforms by way of judicial decision. Legislation would provide a better, certainly a much faster, solution. A favorable prognostication in that regard is indicated by the fact that at least the national legislature has been critical of bills that would exclude *mens rea* from offenses subject to punitive sanctions.[88] Such legislative endeavors should be encouraged by the progress in administration and administrative law, in summary adjudication, specialized courts, and the like which now make available the instrumentalities needed not only for regulation in the field, but also for handling large numbers of cases efficiently in regular hearings and without violence to basic principles.

Attention should be directed, finally, to a recently proposed different solution of this problem. It will be recalled that, from the very beginning of the modern law of strict liability, many judges have suggested that the defendants were negligent and that, had they used due care, the violation would not have occurred. This need to rest penal liability on some semblance of rational support was again evidenced by the Supreme Court in *Morissette*, where Jackson, J. wrote: "The accused, if he does not will the violation, usually is in a position to prevent it with no more care than society might reasonably expect and no more exertion than it might reasonably exact from one who assumed his responsibilities."[89] But despite many similar judicial expressions, due care, indeed, even extraordinary care does not exculpate; and this seems also to be the situation in Britain.[90]

After a thorough study of the problem in Britain, Professor J. Ll. J. Edwards has proposed that negligence be

[88] *Cf. Hearings, before Committee on Banking and Currency,* 73d Cong., 1st Sess. (1933) S. Rec., Pt. 15 6508. This secured the inclusion of knowledge as a material element in the F. S. E. C. Act. Common carriers secured the inclusion of knowledge as a basis for liability in the receiving of stolen goods section of the Anti-Theft Act. 43 Stat. 793, 18 U. S. C. § 409 (1927), F.C.A. 18 §§ 659, 660, 2117.

[89] *Supra* note 81, at 256.

[90] "Formally, the choice still is between *mens rea* in the full sense of the term and absolute liability." Devlin, *supra* note 2, at 212.

accepted "as a sufficient degree of *mens rea*" in statutory offenses concerning traffic, food and drugs, weights and measures and public health.[91] The reader will at once be impelled to ask, if negligence is defensible there as a "minimal *mens rea*," why not employ that rule elsewhere or even generally in penal law?[92] This problem has been previously discussed, and the reasons for excluding negligence from penal law have been set out in detail.[93] It must, however, be recognized that legal scholars are sharply divided on this question and that a proposal like Professor Edwards', which has the merit of requiring a civil form of fault instead of current absolute liability, may for the various indicated reasons elicit wide support. Nonetheless, the fact remains that penal sanctions would be imposed for inadvertence.

Penal theory can elucidate this problem, draw the important distinctions, and supply investigators with a set of apt variables to be explored. But it cannot do the work of the legislature which requires the implementation of policy at particular points, *e.g.* regarding which petty offenses ignorance of the law should be a defense. At the same time, it is not the theorist's function to acquiesce in a proposed reform because public opinion demands some kind of legal sanction even though no rational support of those attitudes is discoverable.[94] In the writer's view of the relevant policy,

[91] Edwards, *supra* note 2, at 257. This has also been recommended by the draftsmen of the American Law Institute's Model Code, Tentative Draft No. 4, Sec. 2.05 (2) b. (1955).

[92] The tentative A. L. I. Model Code accepts negligence as a type of "culpability" and treats it as "a sufficient basis for imposing criminal liability." Tent. Draft No. 4, at 126; also Sec. 2.02 (2) d. at 13 (1955). This is to be contrasted with Professor Edwards' limitation of negligence to the public welfare offenses and the like.

[93] *Supra* chapters 4 and 5.

[94] In a significant Wisconsin study of the administration of food, drug, fish and game statutes, the authors emphasize the fact that for the most part only culpable offenders are arrested or prosecuted. But they believe that the strict liability provisions help the administration of these laws (1) by relieving the prosecution of the burden of proving criminal intent and (2) by deterring potential culpable violators "from relying on an innocent and reasonable-sounding story." *Op. cit. supra* note 65, at 653-55, 664-67 (1956). For reasons stated above and in the light of the actual policy regarding prosecution, this is not a

reform should proceed along the more defensible lines suggested above. In any event, the important agreement among students of the problem—that the public welfare and similar regulations be removed from the penal law—should not be forgotten. That auspicious beginning would render more persuasive, as an initial reform, the allocation of these rules to a separate code of "civil offenses" requiring negligence and tried by administrative tribunals or civil courts. If, at the same time, inspection, education and counsel were provided by regulatory boards, and the work of the criminal courts were restricted to violations involving *mens rea*, we might be well on the way to the solution of this problem.

The least consensus regarding the instant problem must certainly be that the entire structure of strict liability should be subjected to the most careful socio-legal investigation possible.[95] A principal goal of such endeavor would be the differentiation of problems, types of fact, instrumentalities and methods of control. A careful study of the various problems would no doubt reveal the particular areas where specialized courts could handle large numbers of cases. In other fields, investigatory boards and administrative tribunals could best contribute their special resources. As the totality of cases was sifted through the numerous and diverse instrumentalities of control, they would receive differential treatment in conformity with rational principles and available knowledge regarding actual implementation of the relevant policies.

---

persuasive reason for retaining strict liability. See Hart, *op. cit. supra* note 2, at 423-24, 428-29.

[95] The author of an interesting article, which challenges some of the positions taken above, argues for the retention of strict liability in food and drug laws. Rissman, *Criminal Intent Under the Federal Food, Drug, and Cosmetic Act,* 7 Food-Drug-Cosmetic Law 498 (1952). The issues raised are largely factual and much more data are required to resolve them. The author grants: "If such [consumer] protection can effectively be obtained through some means other than strict liability, continuation of strict liability would, of course, be unjustifiable." *Id.* at 503.

Doctrines

CHAPTER XI

IGNORANCE AND MISTAKE

AT the threshold of an inquiry into the criminal liability of persons who commit harms as the result of ignorance or mistake, one confronts an insistent perennial question — why should such persons be subjected to any criminal liability? *Ignorantia facti excusat* accords with the implied challenge. But *ignorantia juris neminem excusat* seems to oppose it and to require explanation. This problem has recently been re-examined by many European scholars[1] whose discussions suggest that further study of the Anglo-American law is desirable.[2] Certainly, the usual taking of numerous "exceptions" to *ignorantia juris neminem excusat* and *ignorantia facti excusat* leaves the law disorganized and obscures the significance of these doctrines.[3] It is easy to see that analysis may well begin with the insight that, while coercion directly concerns volition, ignorance and mistake immediately involve cognition. From there the trail leads plainly to *mens rea* and other principles of criminal liability;

[1] See the symposium in Rev. Intn'l de Droit Pénal, Nos. 3 and 4 (1955).

[2] Lambert v. California, 355 U. S. 225, 2 L. Ed. 2d 228, 78 S. Ct. 240 (1957), discussed *supra*, chapter 10 at note 82, indicates that the question, far from being a closed one in the United States, may in the near future be thoroughly re-examined by the courts.

[3] Several excellent articles are available, and the writer is indebted especially to the following: Keedy, *Ignorance and Mistake in the Criminal Law*, 22 Harv. L. Rev. 75 (1908); Stumberg, *Mistake of Law in Texas Criminal Cases*, 15 Tex. L. Rev. 287 (1937); Perkins, *Ignorance and Mistake in Criminal Law*, 88 U. of Pa. L. Rev. 35 (1939); L. Hall and Seligman, *Mistake of Law and Mens Rea*, 8 U. of Chi. L. Rev. 641 (1941).

and the indications are that a thorough elucidation of the two doctrines must deal especially with the formal foundation of penal law — the principle of legality.

IGNORANTIA FACTI EXCUSAT
Factual Error and the Ethics of the Doctrine

"Ignorance" and "mistake" are words of ancient mintage which have been discussed in all ages by the wise and the prudent, by realists and idealists, and many others. We need not here review this vast literature on the theories of human fallibility, but we may note certain widely accepted conclusions which are important in the present legal inquiry. Except for utter skeptics (who seem to claim knowledge of their negations), it is agreed that knowledge exists; and the contrary of that is ignorance. Likewise, except for those sophisticates who hold that factual errors are non-existent because all perception is "relative" to the given conditions, mistakes also occur. This is assumed in numerous studies which have shown that mistakes of perception are much more common than even trial lawyers suspect.[4] The existence of ignorance and mistake is also assumed in modern systems of penal law, and they are rarely distinguished. The distinction noted by Story that, "Mistake of facts always supposes some error of opinion as to the real facts; but ignorance of facts may be without any error, but result in mere want of knowledge or opinion,"[5] has had no appreciable effect on the law.

The meaning of "factual error," as defined in the criminal law, represents a common sense version of the philosopher's definition: "All error consists in taking for real what is mere appearance."[6] For example, a person looks at a far-off

[4] See Burtt, Legal Psychology, ch. 2 (1931); Spindler, The Sense of Sight 85 (1917); Wigmore, The Science of Judicial Proof 391-418 (1937).

[5] 1 Story, Equity Jurisprudence 158 (13th ed. 1886). *Cf.* "Ignorance implies a total want of knowledge in reference to the subject matter. Mistake admits a knowledge, but implies a wrong conclusion." Hutton v. Edgerton, 6 S. C. 485, 489 (1875).

[6] Stout, *Error*, in Studies in Philosophy and Psychology 271 (1930)

object and believes he sees a man; later, on closer approach, he decides it is a tree. The first opinion is then recognized as error. But the object may not actually be a tree; perhaps it is a dead stump or a bit of sculpture. Indeed, on examining it the next morning by aid of daylight and a clear head, our actor decides that he was mistaken in both judgments the night before. In this view he will be supported by all normal persons who, viewing the object under "adequate" conditions, agree: "It is a tree stump;" moreover, they would not concede the possibility of the slightest error in this opinion. Thus, an opinion (judgment or belief) is erroneous by reference to another opinion which corresponds to the facts. In sum, "error" implies:

1. That facts exist;

2. That sense *impressions* of facts, "sensa," are different from the facts;

3. That the sensa fit (correspond to, are congruent with) or do not fit the facts;[7]

4. That erroneous sensa (those that do not fit the facts) are for a time accepted as true, *i.e.* they are believed to be congruent with the facts;[8] and

5. That this is later recognized as erroneous, *i.e.* certain opinions become error when they are subjected to a broader experience, especially when relatively adequate conditions of correct perception obtain.

All mistakes of fact can be reduced to the above elements which are frequently directly applicable to the cases. There is, *e.g.* a mistake in identity, in believing that a pocket or drawer contains things, that a person is being attacked, that a dangerous weapon is in an assailant's hand, and so on. But while every case of mistake of fact can be stated in terms of the above criteria, it is also true that many such mistakes involve much more than perception. For example,

[7] Rogers, *The Problem of Error*, in Essays in Critical Realism 117, 119 (1920).

[8] "Error would not be error were we not convinced whilst erring that we were knowing the truth." Aron, The Nature of Knowing 57 (1930).

in situations relevant to libel, perjury, or bigamy, the defendant may never have sensed the phenomena which he erroneously interpreted. Someone may have told him that X served a term in the penitentiary for forgery; he may have heard X's employer discharge him, and read in the newspaper that forged checks had been found in the possession of a certain employee of that firm; or someone may have informed a woman that he had learned "on good authority" of the death of her husband. Thus, mistakes of fact often result not only from faulty perception but also from erroneous higher types of cognitive experience, *e.g.* the ideas already in the interpreter's mind, including his bias. In the case of an inventor who makes certain mistakes of fact, these ideas may include invalid theories of physics.

To understand the rationale of *ignorantia facti excusat*, it is necessary to recognize and take account of the relevant ethical principle, namely, moral obligation is determined not by the actual facts but by the actor's opinion regarding them. It is determined by the actor's error concerning a situation, not by the actual situation. This is implicit in the decisions, and occasionally it has been rather definitely expressed.[9] For example, the driver of an automobile who turned a corner very quickly, although he thought he would probably meet a car coming from the opposite direction, would certainly be culpable despite the fact that there was actually no car there. Again, it is often impossible to know the facts or to know that any act of ours will improve a situation. If the actual facts determined our duties, we would sometimes be under a moral obligation without knowing it, perhaps without being able to discover it. Accordingly, apart from questions of previous incapacitation, the morality of an act is determined by reference to the actor's opinion of the facts, including his erroneous beliefs.[10]

[9] Steinmeyer v. People, 95 Ill. 383, 389 (1880); Pond v. People, 8 Mich. 150 (1860); Thomas v. The King, 59 Comm. L.R. 279, 299-300 (Austr. 1937).

[10] See Prichard, *Duty and Ignorance of Fact*, XVIII Proc. British Academy 67 (1932). Prichard's essay is summarized and discussed by Ross, Foundations of Ethics 148-65 (1939).

Aristotle came to the same conclusion on the ground that behavior in ignorance of the facts is involuntary,[11] and that view was adopted by Hale.[12] With reference to the above analysis of the meaning of factual error and of the relevant ethical principle, certain guides are available to aid appraisal of the penal law.

Illustrative Cases

That the above ethical principle has long been expressed in the criminal law is apparent from an early seventeenth century case.[13] The defendant was awakened in the night by strange noises in his house; thinking he was attacking a burglar, he ran his sword through a cabinet where the intruder was hiding and killed a friend of his servant, present by the latter's invitation. This was held not to be manslaughter, "for he did it ignorantly without intention of hurt to the said Frances."[14] Perhaps the most frequent situation in the cases and certainly the least doubted instance of the recognized defense of mistake of fact concerns apparently necessary self-defense. Here the courts hold, "it is not necessary . . . that defendant should have been actually in danger of death or great bodily harm at the time he fired the fatal shot, or that retreat would have really increased his peril, in order for him to have been justified in shooting deceased."[15] So, too, if the mistake stimulates an attack, perpetrated in apparently necessary self-defense, the harm is privileged.[16] The doctrine has expanded far

[11] Ethica Nicomachea, bk. V.8, 1135a, 20-25 (Ross trans. 1925). See also note 41 *infra*.

[12] 1 Hale, Pleas of the Crown 42 (1736).

[13] Levett's Case (K.B. 1638), Cro. Car. 538, 79 Eng. Rep. 1064.

[14] *Ibid. Cf.* ". . . if this be ignorance of fact it excuses. . . ." The Mirror of Justices 137 (Seld. Soc'y ed. 1893).

[15] Williams v. State, 18 Ala. App. 473, 93 S. 57, 58 (1922). On the above ground the following instruction was reversed: ". . . the jury is told that the right of self-defense cannot be exercised 'in *any* case or to any degree NOT NECESSARY, and that the party making the defense is permitted to use no instrument and no power beyond what will prove simply effectual.'" People v. Anderson, 44 Cal. 65, 69 (1872).

[16] State v. Nash, 88 N. C. 618 (1883).

beyond such primary interests as those involved in the above cases. A railroad conductor "is justified in forcibly ejecting him [a passenger] from the car, because he, the conductor, honestly believes that the passenger has not paid his fare, but persistently refuses so to do."[17] The defense was also allowed where the defendant voted before he was twenty-one, believing he was of age;[18] in charges of uttering a forged instrument;[19] in larceny, where the defendant was mistaken as to the denomination of the bill handed him;[20] and in many other situations.[21] Thus, in a very large number of cases, the criminal law seems to be in complete accord with purely ethical appraisal of action in mistake of fact.

In the above cases the mistake of fact excluded any *mens rea*. This raises a question concerning harms which would not have been committed except for a mistake, but where the actor's intention was nonetheless criminal, *e.g.* a mistake in the identity of the intended victim of an assault. One who inflicted a mortal wound on an intimate friend, whom he mistook for a person who had attacked him earlier in the evening, could derive no advantage from his error. There is an ambiguity in the court's assertion that "he intended to kill the man at whom the knife was directed;"[22] but it is clear, in any event, that such a mistake is not legally significant since the defendant intended to kill or seriously injure a human being.[23] Thus, the doctrine must be qualified as follows: mistake of fact is a defense if, because of the

[17] State v. McDonald, 7 Mo. App. 510 (1879).

[18] Gordon v. State, 52 Ala. 308 (1875).

[19] United States v. Carll, 105 U. S. 611, 26 L. Ed. 1135 (1882).

[20] Regina v. Hehir, (1895) 2 Ir. R. 709.

[21] See Perkins, *supra* note 3, at 54-55, also Perkins, Criminal Law 826 (1957).

[22] McGehee v. State, 42 Miss. 747 (1885).

[23] See also Isham v. State, 38 Ala. 213 (1862) and Queen v. Lynch (1846), 1 Cox C.C. 361. In these cases the interest marked for destruction was of equal value to that actually destroyed. The writer's criticism concerns the terminology employed and the hypostatization of "general intent," "transferred intent" and the like. See *supra* chapter 4 at notes 10 and 11.

mistake, *mens rea* is lacking.[24] This qualification is quite consistent with the ethical principle represented in *ignorantia facti excusat*.

Restrictions: (a) Reasonableness of the Error

But Anglo-American criminal law restricts the scope of *ignorantia facti* in ways which constitute serious limitations and, sometimes, a complete repudiation of the underlying policy. These restrictions concern (a) the requirement that the mistake be a "reasonable" one (the civilian expression is that the ignorance be "invincible") and (b) certain sexual offenses, bigamy and other types of strict liability.

An actual mistake of fact is not sufficient. "The apprehension of danger must be bona fide and reasonable."[25] Not the defendant's erroneous perception of the facts, but the facts "as they reasonably appeared to him" determine whether he is criminally liable.[26] After the usual instruction to the jury that the "defendant was bound to act as a reasonably cautious and prudent person would," a court specified that "the excitement of the moment" (the deceased had followed the defendant's daughter and other children in a frightening manner) would not modify this rule.[27] So, too, intoxication is irrelevant,[28] and only rarely is there even a hint that a court will permit consideration of serious incapacities, falling short of insanity.[29] Nor is the require-

[24] In criminal attempt, the problem of impossibility concerns failure to actualize the intention because of a mistake of fact. See *infra* chapter 15. But the *mens rea* remains constant.

[25] Hill v. State, 194 Ala. 11, 23, 69 S. 941, 946 (1915), 2 A. L. R. 509, 518 (1915).

[26] Nalley v. State, 28 Tex. Ct. App. 387, 391, 13 S. W. 670, 671 (1890).

[27] State v. Towne, 180 Ia. 339, 160 N. W. 10 (1916).

[28] ". . . if the defendant by voluntarily putting himself under the influence of liquor incapacitated himself for taking such a view of the situation as a reasonably prudent man would have taken, under the circumstances, and, in consequence thereof, he acted upon an exaggerated or unjustifiable belief as to the necessity for taking the life of the deceased in defense of his own, such belief could not avail him as a defense to the charge in the indictment." Springfield v. State, 96 Ala. 81, 85-86, 11 S. 250, 252 (1892).

[29] In Yates v. People, 32 N. Y. 509 (1865) the court did take account of the defendant's "extreme infirmity of vision."

ment that the mistake be reasonable confined to the perception of facts. For example, where the defendant, charged with bigamy, mistakenly believed his wife was dead, his opinion was based on information which was acquired and evaluated in various ways. The prevailing restrictive interpretation of the doctrine requires that the whole cognitive process function reasonably.[30]

The plain consequence of this application of objective liability to *ignorantia facti* is that persons who commit harms solely because they are mistaken regarding the material facts are nonetheless criminally liable[31] despite the complete lack of criminal intent. Moreover, a person who has acted "unreasonably" seems occasionally to have been held just as culpable as he would have been if he had actually intended to commit the harm;[32] and we shall see that this is often done in convictions of bigamy and sexual offenses. There are surprisingly few reports of homicide cases which specifically discuss this question, but the indicated holding is that a killing by the defendant in the unreasonable mistake that his life was in danger is manslaughter.[33] Thus the requirement that a mistake of fact

---

[30] "No man can be acquitted of responsibility for a wrongful act, unless he employs 'the means at command to inform himself.' Not employing such means, though he may be mistaken, he must bear the consequences of his negligence." Dotson v. State, 62 Ala. 141, 144 (1878).

[31] Hill v. State, 194 Ala. 11, 69 S. 941 (1915), 2 A. L. R. 509, 518 (1915); State v. Terrell, 55 Utah 314, 186 P. 108 (1919), 25 A. L. R. 497, 525 (1919). The requirement of "reasonableness" does not apply to perjury, People v. Von Tiedeman, 120 Cal. 128, 52 P. 155 (1898), or to the various property offenses. See note 9 *infra*, referring to mistakes in property law in relation to *mens rea*. "If they [defendants] did so believe it is not material whether their belief was well founded or not." Lewis v. People, 99 Colo. 102, 117, 60 P. 2d 1089, 1096 (1936).

[32] In Regina v. Rose (1884), 15 Cox C. C. 540, the judge's instruction indicated that a verdict of murder could be returned against the defendant who unreasonably believed he was preventing a homicide. A. R. N. Cross suggests that this would now be manslaughter. 51 Law Soc'y Gaz. 515 (1954). *Cf.* Miles v. State, 52 Tex. Cr. R. 561, 108 S. W. 378 (1908).

[33] Allison v. State, 74 Ark. 444, 86 S. W. 409, 413 (1904); State v. Thomas, 184 N. C. 757, 761-62, 114 S. E. 834, 836 (1922); State v. Doherty, 72 Vt. 381, 48 A. 658 (1900); State v. Sorrentino, 31 Wyo. 129, 224 P. 420, 424 (1924).

be reasonable has very drastic consequences and in this respect the common law is harsher than civilian legal systems.[34] The meaning of "reasonableness," as an essential instrument of inquiry,[35] must be sharply distinguished from its application as an external standard of criminal liability represented in the substantive law on mistake of fact. It is the latter which is objectionable because some defendants are inexperienced or awkward or, for other causes, are not reasonable ("normal") persons; nor, on the other hand, do they fall within the definition of legally recognized incompetence.[36]

Negligent behavior implies inadvertence regarding the harm caused; while in action in ignorance of the facts, the actor "intended" to inflict a harm which, however, he would not have committed had he not been mistaken. Thus, it is the defendant's capacity (to know and to act with due care) which is often emphasized as the salient common element.

Invincible Ignorance

The defendant's capacity to acquire necessary knowledge is discussed in European law in terms of whether his ignorance was "vincible" or "invincible;"[37] and this has resulted in more searching inquiry than is customary with reference to "reasonableness." Aristotle, from whom that notion stems, attached culpability to harms committed "in ignorance," but he absolved the doer if the harm was done not only "in ignorance" but also "through ignorance."[38] The former is "vincible" ignorance, the latter, "invincible," *i.e.* the doer was competent to acquire the necessary knowledge

---

[34] *E.g.* Art. 19 of the Swiss Federal Penal Code provides "If the offender had been able to avoid the error by acting with due caution, he shall be punished for negligence, provided that the negligent commission of the act is punishable." Translation, 30 J. Crim. L., C. & P. S. Supp. 22 (1939).

[35] See *supra* pp. 152-58. *Cf. infra* pp. 370-71.

[36] *E.g.* Fisher v. United States, 328 U. S. 463, 90 L. Ed. 1382, 66 S. Ct. 1318 (1946).

[37] See *supra* note 1.

[38] Ethica Nichomachea, bk. III.5, 1113b-1114a; bk. V.8, 1136a, 5-10 (Ross trans. 1925); Magna Moralia bk. I.33, 1195a. 28-32 (Ross trans. 1915).

or he lacked that ability.[39] As regards the latter, Aristotle's position is more discriminating than the common law which holds that if a person is sane, he is conclusively presumed to have the necessary capacity. If that presumption is rejected, *e.g.* there are persons who, although sane, are so handicapped in certain respects that they lack normal skill[40] or knowledge, it follows that such persons are not morally culpable for harms resulting from their lack of competence and that they should not be held criminally liable.

Aristotle, however, had still another test to apply to such persons before he would exculpate them. With regard to persons who were invincibly ignorant or inefficient when they committed certain harms, *i.e.* they could not have done better at that time, Aristotle maintained that some of them might nevertheless be found culpable by reference to their past. While holding that morality concerns only voluntary conduct, he took an extremely rigorous position in this regard. He specifies an intoxicated person who cannot function properly and he finds him culpable on the ground that he need not have become intoxicated. In the past he "willed" in certain respects, which led to the habit of indulgence. According to Aristotle, moral culpability may be posited in such cases on the voluntary actions performed or omitted in the past which had the cumulative effect of incapacitation.

But there are serious difficulties with this subtle ethic as regards its application to criminal law. In order to implement that position, it would be necessary to survey the entire course of the defendant's life, to decide, *e.g.* whether one who was not competent to drive an automobile with due care had deliberately refrained from bicycle-riding, chosen not to learn about machinery, etc., including all his overt acts that had any bearing on the incompetence which now

---

[39] *Cf.* ". . . there is an ignorance that is superable, and that is no excuse; and there is an ignorance that is insuperable, and that is an excuse, whether it arises from nature, as from excessive age, or from a malady such as madness." The Mirror of Justices 138 (Seld. Soc'y ed. 1893).

[40] See Yates v. People, 32 N. Y. 509 (1865).

makes his lack of skill or ignorance invincible. If the driver were a woman who could not gauge a distance or the angle of a curve, it would be necessary to decide whether her present ignorance was determined by her own culpable acts and omissions or was always invincible. Thus, while there is no escape from the sheer logic of the Aristotelian thesis, the factual difficulties are so considerable as to preclude its use in criminal law. Here it is not only a question of ethical principle; the punishment of human beings within the limits and limitations of a legal system is also involved. Can any child or youth foresee that a series of petty transgressions may lead years in the future to a condition of ignorance or inefficiency that produces serious harms? Is there any feasible basis to impute present criminal liability for harms caused by voluntary lapses in the distant past? Accordingly, one would wish to delegate that kind of adjudication to an omniscient philosopher-king who had precise records and the wisdom to assess culpability for a major harm caused many years later by minor lapses that were completely unrelated, in human prescience, to any serious consequences.

On the other hand, if an historical inquiry, a "case-history," is limited to the determination of the defendant's present competence, it is feasible to apply certain phases of it to criminal liability. For example, as will be seen later with reference to *ignorantia juris*, if illness or absence from the country made it impossible to acquire necessary information, that should be a defense. But while it will be generally agreed that such invincible ignorance should bar penal liability, it by no means follows that vincible ignorance should incur it. For vincible ignorance may imply mere negligence ("unreasonableness").

For the purposes of ethical inquiry, persons who have the competence to acquire necessary information and fail to do that may be deemed culpable. But, it is submitted, if only voluntary harm-doing merits the severe blame implied in penal liability, it cannot be shown that either negligent behavior or the commission of a harm in ignorance of

material facts is culpable in that degree or in that sense.[41]
For there is a great difference between asserting that a
person must voluntarily commit a certain harm to be sufficiently culpable to merit penal sanctions and asserting
that he is thus culpable if he could have prevented himself
from involuntarily causing an unforeseen harm. Those who
support the present limitation of "reasonableness" on *ignorantia facti* might find it difficult to prove that a person
who had the capacity to acquire adequate knowledge or to
use due care is culpable in the above degree and sense even
though he acted in the absence of such knowledge and skill.

Much of the discussion of negligent and uninformed behavior by modern writers on ethics becomes tangled in the
quagmires of an ambiguous syllogism that is silent at the
crucial point. Thus it is said: *If* the actor had wanted to,
or *if* he had thought of it, he could have performed the act
properly. But voluntary harm-doing, *i.e.* in the knowledge
of at least the risk of that, is quite different from a lack of
sensitivity to the risk of injuring others or to the need for
knowledge of the likelihood of doing that. Thus, it is not
logical to assert that because a person is competent to do
an act properly *if* he thinks about it, *therefore* he is culpable
for doing harm inadvertently. If the argument is restated
to base culpability upon insensitivity (incapacity) regarding
the need for knowledge, it must also be rejected on.the
ground that what is required to support the kind or degree
of moral condemnation characteristic of, and defensible in,
modern penal law is voluntary action—at least reckless

[41] *Cf.* "If an Action be done without any malicious design, and not
with Ignorance voluntarily contracted, but such only as crept in by
Inconsideration and Inadvertency, the Imputation is not altogether
taken away, yet it is considerably diminished. Hither we may refer
the Case propos'd by *Aristotle* of a Woman that gave a Love-Potion
to her Gallant of which he died. Now the *Athenian* Judges absolv'd
the Woman from this Indictment, because she did the Fact unde-
signedly, and only miss'd the Effect of her Potion, and procur'd his
Death instead of his Love, which was her only Aim. But to make this
Sentence equitable, it must have been suppos'd as a Principle, that the
Woman never so much as thought the Potion she administered was
any way hurtful." Pufendorf, Of the Laws of Nature and of Nations,
bk. I, ch. V, at 40 (1703). See Aristotle, Ethics, bk. 3, ch. 1, 1110b,
18-22.

conduct. The chief conclusion to be drawn from the above analysis is that action in ignorance of material facts, where no more than negligence is shown, should not incur penal liability. But if the judgment proceeds from a finding of unreasonableness or vincibility to one of penal liability, it does not take account of the crucial difference between negligence and recklessness. Although the incompetence or ignorance may have been vincible or unreasonable, it does not follow that the harm in issue was committed voluntarily.

Harms resulting from inadvertence or ignorance signify incompetence and inefficiency rather than the voluntary misconduct that is the concern of penal law. Or, at most, those phases of such harms that are believed to connote fault are not of the grosser type of culpability that falls within the proper range of penal law. Moreover, as regards deterrence, it must be observed that efficiency and competence are probably not increased by punishment, certainly not, so far as is known, by rare, sporadic imprisonment.[42] This does not imply that the community should not be protected from dangerous inefficiency or ignorance. If we look about us for measures more likely than punitive ones to secure the required kind of protection, recent advances in the vocational training of handicapped persons, supervision, and revocation of licenses seem promising. The elimination of "reasonableness" as a substantive restriction of the doctrine of *ignorantia facti* would clarify the public mind regarding the nature of criminal conduct. It would facilitate analysis of the criminal law and stimulate a sounder administration of it.

Restrictions: (b) Strict Liability

The strict liability imposed for public welfare offenses[43]

---

[42] There is considerable psychological literature indicating that punishment has little influence on learning. See, *e.g.* Thorndike, The **Psychology** of Wants, Interests and Attitudes 149-52 (1935), and Estes, *An Experimental Study of Punishment*, 57 Psych. Monog. No. 3, 1 (1944). Practically all the data relied upon concern the acquisition of various skills and not of moral sensitivity. Hence the conclusions reached in such studies do not affect the function of punishment where the offender has committed morally culpable acts.

[43] See *supra* chapter 10.

excludes any consideration of mistake of fact even though the mistake was one which any reasonable person would have made. Thus, as regards many serious offenses, only "reasonable" mistakes exculpate—and we have seen the arbitrary import of that as it affects honestly mistaken harm-doers; and, as regards a large number of minor offenses, even a reasonable mistake of fact is no defense.[44] This strict liability has also been applied to various major crimes, especially sexual offenses and bigamy.

A leading illustrative case is *Regina v. Prince*,[45] where the defendant was charged with having taken an unmarried girl, under sixteen, from the possession and against the will of her father. The jury found that the girl told the defendant she was eighteen, that he believed her and that his belief was a reasonable one, *i.e.* all the usual requirements of exculpation on the ground of reasonable mistake of a material fact were met. Nonetheless, of the ten judges all but one upheld the conviction. Two theories were relied on: the legislature intended to exclude *mens rea;* and the defendant's conduct was immoral regardless of the girl's age, hence the mistake of that fact was irrelevant.

The first ground was persuasively challenged by Brett, J., in a detailed historical survey of the legislation. In the light of that, it is clear that the judges' own view of the relevant policy determined "the legislative intent." As regards the second ground, the judges' chief reliance was upon analogy from the misdemeanor-manslaughter rule. Brett, J., supported that rule[46] but refused to expand the analogy to

---

[44] *Ibid.* In Regina v. Bishop (1880), 14 Cox C. C. 404, where the defendant was convicted of receiving a "lunatic" into her house, such house not being an asylum, it was held no defense that there was an honest belief that the person received was not a lunatic. But *cf.* State v. Williams, 94 Oh. App. 249, 115 N. E. 2d 36 (1952).

[45] (1875) 13 Cox C. C. 138. The earlier English cases are there cited. Similar decisions in this country are: People v. Dolan, 96 Cal. 315, 31 P. 107 (1892); Heath v. State, 173 Ind. 296, 90 N. E. 310 (1909); State v. Ruhl, 8 Ia. 447 (1859); People v. Marks, 146 App. Div. 11, 130 N. Y. Supp. 524 (1st Dep't 1911).

[46] Regina v. Prince (1875), 13 Cox C. C. 138, 155-56. *Cf.* Regina v. McLeod (1954), 111 Can. Cr. C. 106.

the point accepted by the majority, namely, that the required *mens rea* could be posited on immoral conduct that was not illegal.[47] From convictions in cases of assault and illegal entry into a dwelling house, where the mistakes of fact were irrelevant because the intentions were nonetheless criminal, Bramwell, J., induced the wide *ratio* that liability could be supported on the ground that "the act [intended] was wrong in itself."[48]

With reference to the strict liability imposed,[49] it has been noted in the above discussion of that subject that no evidence supporting the assumed need for such arbitrariness is available. In these circumstances, one may certainly believe that application of the usual restriction of *ignorantia facti* to reasonable mistakes would result in convictions in the vast majority of such cases. Even without that unjustifiable limitation on the doctrine, judges and juries would not easily be persuaded that the defendants in such cases actually believed the girls were above the statutory age. Moreover, since recklessness is sufficient to support penal liability, it would be necessary only to find that the defendant was in doubt regarding the material facts.[50]

In addition to various sexual offenses, bigamy[51] and adultery,[52] strict liability, based on the exclusion of even reasonable mistakes of fact from the doctrine of *ignorantia facti*, has been applied to embezzlement, the sale of narcotics and in cases of persons defending others against apparent serious aggression.[53] Heavy penalties are imposed in such

---

[47] "I do not say illegal, but wrong." *Id.* at 141.

[48] *Id.* at 143. *Cf.* "And though the wrong intended was even not indictable, the defendant would still be liable. . . ." State v. Ruhl, 8 Ia. 447, 450 (1859).

[49] Rex v. Maughan (1934), 24 Cr. App. R. 130.

[50] "Consequently, doubt is not error, nor is suspension of judgment, for in such experiences there is no conviction that we now know." Aron, *op. cit. supra* note 8, at 57 note 1.

[51] See *infra* pp. 395-401.

[52] State v. Anderson, 140 Ia. 445, 118 N. W. 772 (1908); Commonwealth v. Elwell, 43 Mass. (2 Met.) 190 (1840).

[53] State v. Cook, 78 S. C. 253, 59 S. E. 862 1907), 15 L. R. A. (n. s.) 1013 (1908).

cases. Thus strict penal liability has swept over a vast terrain in the past century,[54] and the conclusions reached above in the context of mistake of fact support that previously emphasized:[55] This branch of our law is so thoroughly disorganized, rests so largely on conjecture and dubious psychology, and effects such gross injustice as to require major reform.

Mention must be made, finally, of a type of factual ignorance which is not usually discussed in relation to *ignorantia facti*, namely, ignorance of elementary science, *e.g.* regarding sickness, medicine and the use of physicians. The defendants in these cases are sometimes very stupid persons, unaware of the gravity of a child's illness and the availability of physicians.[56] In other cases the defendants are members of religious sects which believe, *e.g.* that the devout cannot be harmed even by the bite of a rattlesnake[57] or that it is sinful to use medicine. There are surprisingly few reports of such cases, apparently because prosecutors are reluctant to initiate proceedings and, when they do, juries are apt to acquit.[58] But there have been a number of convictions, and the relevant holdings imply that ignorance of ordinary factual knowledge, possessed by every "normal" adult in the community except such eccentrics as these defendants, is no defense. Although mitigation is undoubtedly frequent, it is assumed that the ignorance was "unreasonable," and the conduct is held criminal. Such

[54] But *cf.* the English Criminal Law Amendment Act, 1922, 12 & 13 Geo. 5, c. 56, § 2, which provides: "Reasonable cause to believe that a girl was of or above the age of sixteen years shall not be a defence to a charge under section five . . . of the Criminal Law Amendment Act, 1885. . . . Provided that in the case of a man of twenty-three years of age or under the presence of reasonable cause to believe that the girl was over the age of sixteen years shall be a valid defence on the first occasion on which he is charged with an offense under this section."

[55] See *supra* chapter 10.

[56] Stehr v. State, 92 Neb. 755, 139 N. W. 676 (1913).

[57] Kirk v. Commonwealth, 186 Va. 839, 44 S. E. 2d 409 (1947).

[58] Larson, *Child Neglect in the Exercise of Religious Freedom*, 32 Chi.-Kent L. Rev. 283 (1954).

decisions raise difficult questions regarding the application of objective *mens rea*[59] and the quality of legal justice.

IGNORANTIA JURIS NEMINEM EXCUSAT
Fact and Law

In current discussions of criminal law theory, it is sometimes argued that *ignorantia juris neminem excusat* is an archaism that should be discarded. This doctrine seems to hold morally innocent persons criminally liable, and to do so in reliance upon an obvious fiction—that everyone is presumed to know the law. But if the meaning of *ignorantia juris* differs greatly from that of *ignorantia facti*, their respective functions should also be very different. The first step toward the solution of this problem is to elucidate the terms that distinguish the two doctrines.

Certain differences between fact and law are easily recognized. Law is expressed in distinctive propositions, whereas facts are qualities or events occurring at definite places and times. Facts are particulars directly sensed in perception and introspection. Legal rules are generalizations; they are not sensed, but are understood in the process of cognition.[60] Law and fact are, of course, closely interrelated—law is "about" facts, it gives distinctive meaning to facts. For example, that A kills B is a fact; that this is murder is signified by certain legal propositions.[61] When practical questions must be decided, what is "fact" and what is "law" differ in various contexts, *e.g.* if the purpose is to determine the respective functions of judge and jury or if a question of foreign law is in issue.

[59] See *supra* chapter 3 and pp. 163-170.

[60] It is important to distinguish this meaning of "law" from its equally important sociological meaning, where it denotes a type of social fact, *i.e.* it is viewed as an external "thing" which influences behavior. This would fit the following definition of "fact": "No one doubts that there are coercive factors in general experience which certainly determine action, and also in some degree determine thought and will, though to an extent which is disputable. These existences, science, like common sense, calls facts." Barry, The Scientific Habit of Thought 93 (1927). *Cf.* Hall, Living Law of Democratic Society ch. 3 (1949).

[61] See Kelsen, *The Pure Theory of Law*, 50 L. Q. Rev. 474, 478 (1935).

Although the terms of the doctrines concerning *ignorantia* indicate that it is important to make the above distinctions, it will be seen later that the crucial difference is not between fact and law, but between what is and what is not morally significant. Indeed, we have already seen that fact is subordinated to a mistaken belief about fact, *i.e.* to what is relevant to morality. Again, the distinction of property and other non-penal law from penal law and treating the former as "fact," to be discussed later in relation to property crimes and bigamy, will also be seen to support the hypothesis that the two doctrines move in different directions because they function differently in relation to the moral significance of criminal law. But we must first relate the distinctions drawn above regarding law and fact to *ignorantia*.

"Ignorantia"

Of the various sources of difficulty encountered in analysis of *ignorantia juris,* the most serious one concerns the meaning of *"ignorantia."* Since that term suggests a negative condition, *i.e.* the absence of "knowledge," analysis of this problem must deal with the latter term. It may be inferred from the distinctions drawn above between fact and law, that perception is a primitive form of knowledge, and that knowledge of law, the cognition of legal propositions, is much more complex. More important is that perception of facts is relatively certain; given external objects, all normal persons who perceive them under "adequate" conditions arrive at uniform judgments, and errors are attributed to excitement, negligence, poor conditions of observation, intoxication, and the like. But with reference to knowledge of law, there can never be such certainty as that. Although it is true that one is sometimes just as certain that a particular situation is within a rule as he is that he sees an external object, much more is required to determine the meaning of the rule. To do that one must take account of the vagueness of legal rules at their periphery, the unavoidable attribute of all propositions that refer to facts. Hence, no one can say with certainty that a rule of law means precisely thus and so.

These differences regarding knowledge of law and knowledge of fact indicate that *ignorantia facti* is an apt expression because "mistake" implies the possibility of certitude but that *ignorantia juris* is not apt. In any case, whatever view of the two kinds of knowledge or *ignorantia* is preferred, the relatively much greater difficulty of knowing the law suggests that the two doctrines may implement very different policies. This preliminary insight into the nature of legal knowledge provides a perspective from which to gauge the significance of various theories of *ignorantia juris*.

Earlier Theories

The Roman theory—that the law is "definite and knowable"[62]—seems to have been interpreted quite literally. As Blackstone noted, "every person of discretion . . . may . . . know" it;[63] hence ignorance is culpable. It is stated by many writers that the rigor of the Roman doctrine, unlike Blackstone's version, was relieved by the exception of large classes of persons (minors, women, farmers and soldiers) from its operation.[64] But whatever may have been its original persuasiveness in small communities, this theory seems so far-fetched in modern conditions as to be quixotic. Its rationale must be found in a policy that can be justified otherwise than by mere reference to a fiction.

A modern theory, constructed with due appreciation of this, was presented by Austin who maintained that it rested on, and was required by, the impossibility of determining the relevant issue. "Whether the party was *really* ignorant of the law, and was *so* ignorant of the law that he had no *surmise* of its provisions, could scarcely be determined by any evidence accessible to others."[65] He also pointed out that even if the above problem were solved, it would be

[62] 1 Austin, Lectures on Jurisprudence 497 (4th ed. 1879). See Pufendorf, *op. cit. supra* note 41, bk. 1, ch. 3, at 10.

[63] 4 Blackstone, Commentaries *27.

[64] This general opinion was rejected by Binding, who limited the exceptional treatment to civil law. Ryu and Silving, *Error Juris—A Comparative Study*, 24 U. of Chi. L. Rev. 421, 425 (1957).

[65] Austin, *op. cit. supra* note 62, at 498.

impossible to determine whether the defendant had been negligent in failing to acquire the legal knowledge since it would be "incumbent upon the tribunal to unravel his previous history, and to search his whole life for the elements of a just solution."[66]

Austin's theory was rejected by Holmes who "doubted whether a man's knowledge of the law is any harder to investigate than many questions which are gone into. The difficulty, such as it is, would be met by throwing the burden of proving ignorance on the law breaker."[67] Unfortunately, Holmes did not discuss Austin's claim that the determination of parallel questions regarding fact was quite different and "soluble," that they "may be solved by looking at the circumstances of the case. The inquiry is limited to a given incident... and is, therefore, not interminable."[68] His own theory was that *ignorantia juris neminem excusat* was merely a phase of objective liability required by social utility: "to admit the excuse at all would be to encourage ignorance where the law-maker has determined to make men know and obey...."[69]

Austin's theory of *ignorantia juris*, it is submitted, has much to recommend it. If, *e.g.* a defendant claimed that he believed he had a right to kill a trespasser, how could his testimony be disproved? How could the prosecution establish that he actually believed he had no such legal right?[70] To hold, as did Holmes, that the difficulty could be met by placing the burden of proof upon the defendant does not meet Austin's position. If ignorance of the law is unprovable, how is the nature of that negative issue changed by requiring the defendant to establish his ignorance, *i.e.* by a technical rule of procedure? Thus, it must be concluded that, if his position is literally interpreted, Austin

---

[66] *Id.* at 499.
[67] Holmes, The Common Law 48 (1881).
[68] Austin, *op. cit. supra* note 62, at 499.
[69] Holmes, *op. cit. supra* note 67.
[70] See Gordon v. State, 52 Ala. 308 (1875).

stood on firm ground.[71] In addition, Austin's doubts regarding proof of negligence are certainly warranted.

On the other hand, however, it must be recognized that it is possible to prove that a person had an opportunity to acquire certain knowledge or *per contra*, that due, *e.g.* to illness, his ignorance in the above "operational" sense, was invincible. Thus, it might be shown that certain information had been brought to the defendant's attention, *e.g.* that he was handed a booklet containing certain laws, that an administrative board mailed him a set of regulations, or that certain rules governing his vocation were published in a newspaper to which he subscribed. From such facts, it might be presumed that he read the law in question; it might also be inferred that, being a normal adult, he understood it or enough of it to satisfy a relevant *mens rea*. But for reasons to be discussed below, the defense of invincible ignorance of the law, since it proceeds on the premise that knowledge of law is material, can have only a limited application, *i.e.* to certain petty offenses.

It is significant that both Austin and Holmes,[72] while they differed regarding the practical implementation of a defense of ignorance of the law, shared a common utilitarian viewpoint which, in addition, did not distinguish major crimes from petty offenses. Holmes' thesis, that to allow the defense would "encourage ignorance where the law-maker has determined to make men know and obey," is surely questionable. For this implies that knowledge of the penal law is important, whereas such knowledge is usually irrelevant. Moreover, it can hardly be established that a principal purpose of penal law is to stimulate legal education; even Bentham balked at punishment as a method of

[71] *Cf.* "But the proof of a belief in the existence of private rights, such as ownership, can be found in objective evidence of conduct, while belief in the existence of a general law generally would have no such objective manifestations." Note, 45 Harv. L. Rev. 336, note 19 (2) (1931). See Winfield, *Mistake of Law*, 59 L. Q. Rev. 327 (1943).

[72] Holmes' theory has been accepted by Williams, Criminal Law § 115 at 385 (1953).

making the law known.[73] In Holmes' theory, if a defendant who, *e.g.* had shot his wife's paramour in adultery, could show that he had studied the criminal law long and assiduously before doing that, he should be entitled at least to mitigation of the punishment.[74] But no one has ever sought mitigation on that ground; indeed, it would warrant aggravation of the punishment since the *mens rea* had long been entertained. This indicates that penal policy is not to make men know the law, as such, but to help them inhibit harmful conduct.[75] The influence of penal law results not from men's learning criminal law as amateur lawyers, but from the significance of the public condemnation of, and imposition of punishment for, certain highly immoral acts. Thus, despite a lawyer's predilection, there is not the slightest evidence that the generality of men study the criminal law in order "to know and obey it." The deterrent theory here, again, reflects an over-simple, intellectualistic psychology that hardly comes into contact with the actual springs of moral conduct and conformity with penal law.

As was suggested above, neither Austin's nor Holmes' theory cuts to the heart of the problem of *ignorantia juris*. The universality of the doctrine[76] alone suggests that it rests on extremely important, positive grounds. The frequent expression of the *necessity* of reliance upon it, of the *dependence* of any administration of justice upon it, and the like[77] also indicate that the doctrine is grounded in a

[73] 6 The Works of Jeremy Bentham 519-20 (Bowring ed. 1843).

[74] *Cf.* Holmes, J.,: "It may be assumed that he intended not to break the law . . . but if the conduct described crossed the line, the fact that he desired to keep within it will not help him. It means only that he misconceived the law." Horning v. District of Columbia, 254 U. S. 135, 137, 65 L. Ed. 185, 41 S. Ct. 53 (1920).

[75] Also *cf.* "If he knew that his representations were false, and if he intended to deceive by them, and by the help of the motives thus created to get Kearns's property, he had the only criminal intent which the statute requires." Holmes, J., in Commonwealth v. O'Brien, 172 Mass. 248, 256, 52 N. E. 77, 80 (1898).

[76] See Radulesco, De L'Influence de L'Erreur sur la Résponsibilité Pénale 15-17 (1923).

[77] "Without it justice could not be administered." 1 Bishop, Criminal Law 197 (9th ed. 1923); People v. O'Brien, 96 Cal. 171, 176, 31 P. 45, 47 (1892). The like views of Ortolan, Laborde, Garcon and

more fundamental rationale than was expressed by either
Austin or the Holmes of *The Common Law*.

The Rationale of Ignorantia Juris

A defensible theory of *ignorantia juris* must, it is suggested, find its origin in the central fact noted above, namely,
that the meaning of the rules of substantive penal law is
unavoidably vague, the degree of vagueness increasing as
one proceeds from the core of the rules to their periphery.
It is therefore possible to disagree indefinitely regarding the
meaning of these words. But in adjudication, such indefinite
disputation is barred because that is opposed to the character and requirements of a legal order, as is implied in the
principle of legality. Accordingly, a basic axiom of legal
semantics is that legal rules do or do not include certain
behavior; and the linguistic problem must be definitely solved
one way or the other, on that premise. These characteristics
of legal adjudication imply a degree of necessary reliance
upon authority. The debate must end and the court must
decide one way or the other within a reasonable time. The
various needs are met by prescribing a rational procedure
and acceptance of the decisions of the "competent" officials
as authoritative. Such official declaration of the meaning
of a law is what the law is, however circuitously that is
determined.

Now comes a defendant who truthfully pleads that he
did not know that his conduct was criminal, implying that
he thought it was legal. This may be because he did not
know that any relevant legal prohibition existed (ignorance) or, if he did know any potentially relevant rule, that
he decided it did not include his intended situation or
conduct (mistake). In either case, such defenses always
imply that the defendant thought he was acting legally. If
that plea were valid, the consequence would be: whenever

Garraud are summarized by Radulesco, *op. cit. supra* note 76, at 41-
43. "That ignorance of law does not exempt from obligation is a
principle which prevails in all legal orders and which must prevail,
since, otherwise, it would be almost impossible to apply the legal
order." Kelsen, General Theory of Law and State 72 (1945).

a defendant in a criminal case thought the law was thus and so, he is to be treated as though the law were thus and so, *i.e. the law actually is thus and so.* But such a doctrine would contradict the essential requisites of a legal system, the implications of the principle of legality.

This is apparent when we examine some necessary elements of a legal order, signified by the principle of legality, in greater detail. These are:

(1) that rules of law express objective meanings;

(2) that certain persons (the authorized "competent" officials) shall, after a prescribed procedure, declare what those meanings are. They shall say, *e.g.* that situations A, B,C but not X,Y,Z are included within certain rules; and

(3) that these, and only these, interpretations are binding, *i.e.* only these meanings of the rules are the law.

To permit an individual to plead successfully that he had a different opinion or interpretation of the law would contradict the above postulates of a legal order. For there is a basic incompatibility between asserting that the law is what certain officials declare it to be after a prescribed analysis, and asserting, also, that those officials *must* declare it to be, *i.e.* that the law is, what defendants or their lawyers believed it to be. A legal order implies the rejection of such contradiction. It opposes objectivity to subjectivity, judicial process to individual opinion, official to lay, and authoritative to non-authoritative declarations of what the law is. This is the rationale of *ignorantia juris neminem excusat.*

This rationale can also be expressed in terms of the ethical policy of *ignorantia juris neminem excusat,* namely, that the criminal law represents certain moral principles; to recognize ignorance or mistake of the law as a defense would contradict those values.[78]

---

[78] The same considerations do not apply to *ignorantia facti* because: (a) Such a mistake is particular, *i.e.* it concerns a unique experience which in no way opposes the meaning of rules of law. These meanings are generalizations; they can be and are fitted to mistakes of fact, while, as seen, a plea of mistake of law challenges the meaning of the

Reference to the criminal cases where a defense of ignorance was pleaded supports this insight. A plea of ignorance or mistake of law is rarely encountered in prosecutions for serious crimes; it is raised almost solely in relation to minor offenses. Thus no sane defendant has pleaded ignorance that the law forbids killing a human being or forced intercourse or taking another's property or burning another person's house. In such cases, which include the common law felonies and the more serious misdemeanors, instead of asserting that knowledge of law is presumed, it would be much more to the point to assert that knowledge of law (equally, ignorance or mistake of law) is wholly irrelevant. But many have and do plead ignorance of laws requiring them to supply certain reports or forbidding the manufacture or sale of intoxicating liquor, the possession of gambling appliances, conducting a lottery, betting on horse races, keeping a saloon open on election day, and the like.[79] In the relatively few cases of major crimes where ignorance of law was pleaded, no challenge was raised concerning the validity of the moral principle generally implied, but it was claimed that the situation in which the defendant acted was "exceptional." Thus, in a murder case, the defendant sought to justify his action on the ground that his victim was a willful trespasser;[80] in another homicide, on the ground that he was protecting his sister from one who was attempting to drug her to facilitate her rape.[81] There are kidnapping cases, defended by police officers, where suspected offenders were held *incommunicado* under a claim that the penal law permitted such conduct.[82] But none of the above defendants alleged that he was ignorant that the criminal law forbade murder or kidnapping. This problem

---

rules. (b) Behavior in ignorance of the facts is "involuntary"; it is not immoral while at least action violative of a major criminal law is immoral regardless of ignorance of the law.

[79] See notes 51 and 52 *infra.*

[80] Weston v. Commonwealth, 111 Pa. 251, 2 A. 191 (1886).

[81] People v. Cook, 39 Mich. 236 (1878).

[82] People v. Weiss, 276 N. Y. 384, 12 N. E. 2d 514 (1938).

is closely related to the valuation of harms in the criminal law, expressed in the principle of *mens rea.*

It is pertinent to recall here that the criminal law represents an objective ethics which must sometimes oppose individual convictions of right.[83] Accordingly, it will not permit a defendant to plead, in effect, that although he knew what the facts were, his moral judgment was different from that represented in the penal law. The only defensible method is to apply the established ethical judgments of the community; and the only relatively certain data evidencing them are the penal laws.

They may not validly be contrasted with individual ethics because the individual participates in the determination and development of the community's ethics, hence, in that sense these are, also, his ethics.[84] The process of legislation, viewed broadly to include discussion by the electorate, provides additional assurance that the legal valuations are soundly established.[85] Thus, as regards the homicide of a willful trespasser or of a spouse's paramour in adultery, it is clear that the defendant, though he may have acted in accordance with honest conviction, was mistaken in his moral judgment. Indeed, his action and judgment were undoubtedly influenced by his emotional disturbance; hence the probability is that he would, himself, take another view of his action if he considered the situation calmly. While a person who acts in accordance with his honest convictions is certainly not as culpable as one who commits a harm knowing it is wrong, it is also true that conscience sometimes leads one astray.[86] Penal liability based on *mens rea* implies the objective wrongness of the harms proscribed—regardless of motive or conviction.

[83] See *supra* chapter 3. *Cf.* Salmond, Jurisprudence 82 (1924).

[84] See Gurvitch, *Is the Antithesis of "Moral Man" and "Immoral Society" True?*, 52 Philos. Rev. 533 (1943).

[85] Special considerations relevant to petty offenses are discussed *infra* pp. 402-408.

[86] "If to act in accordance with one's conviction is always, in one sense, to do one's duty, it remains true that one's conscience may be very much mistaken and in need of improvement." Ross, Foundations of Ethics 165 (1939).

This is also required to preserve the principle of legality. As is widely believed, the principle of legality functions as a limitation on the authority of officials[87] and, thus, as a major protection of the individual. This aspect of the "rule of law" has been emphasized in political and legal literature on the subject. But, as a necessary corollary, the shield has its other side—certain conduct definitely *does* fall within the rules and is punishable. This often predominates in the popular view as the primary function of the criminal law—to locate and take control of certain harm-doers. These functions of the criminal law are interrelated and inseparable; neither can be modified without affecting the other. If a crime were defined in vague terms (*e.g.* by including bad motives) it would be easier to bring harm-doers and "anti-social" persons within its scope and under the State's control; but the protection of individuals, now assured by precise case-law implementation of legality, would also suffer proportionately. A sharply defined concept definitely excludes everything except the class it definitely includes; but if the concept is confused by setting up incompatible criteria, its vitality to carry out both functions becomes weakened. The survival of the principle of legality requires the preservation of the definiteness of the rules, which must not be dissolved by the incompatible recognition of the opinions of litigants and lawyers as authoritative.

There are, thus, two aspects of the rationale of *ignorantia juris neminem excusat.* The doctrine is an essential postulate of a legal order, a phase of the "rule of law." And, second, legality cannot be separated from morality in a sound system of penal law. In such a system, at least the penal law of the major crimes represents both the formal criteria of legality and sound values. It follows that the two theories discussed above, (1) that the principle of legality implies the doctrine of *ignorantia juris,* and (2) that the doctrine is necessary to the maintenance of the objective morality of the community, can be combined in a

---

[87] See *supra* chapter 2.

single rationale—the legally expressed values may not be ignored or contradicted. Thus, the direction of reform of the doctrine is also indicated, *e.g.* to take account of ignorance or mistake of property laws, other technical rules and certain petty penal laws. This will be discussed later.

With reference to the position presented above, it is possible, of course, to challenge the underlying premise—the desirability of having a legal system. Some may prefer decision by individuals who exercise completely unfettered power; and occasionally cases arise regarding which almost everyone wishes a decision could be rendered without restriction by existing laws. But this issue need not be discussed here.[88] For present purposes it is necessary to assume the existence of a legal system and the consequent implications of the principle of legality. The validity of the above theory of *ignorantia juris neminem excusat* must be tested by criteria which are relevant to that basic premise.

Application of the Rationale of Ignorantia Juris

In light of the above discussion we may consider certain problems raised in the literature and case-law on *ignorantia juris*. Two proposed exceptions to *ignorantia juris neminem excusat*—mistake based on the "advice of counsel" and the "indefiniteness" of a law—may be disposed of briefly. The above analysis reveals the reason for the uniform holding that the advice of counsel regarding the meaning of a criminal law is not a defense. It is not that the lawyer may be incompetent or corrupt,[89] but that lawyers are not law-declaring officials; it is not their function to interpret law authoritatively. Suppose that an opinion was obtained from the most distinguished lawyers, that the subject was not complicated, that numerous precedents were found, and that the law was clear and simple—in short, a situation where knowledge of law was easy to acquire. A person

---

[88] *Ibid.*

[89] Despite occasional assertions to that effect, the obvious fact is that, *e.g.* in England, where the Bar is held in very high esteem, the doctrine of *ignorantia juris* is also rigorously applied.

acts upon such advice, then a prosecution is instituted. His plea of ignorance would nonetheless be invalid because the court before whom the case is tried cannot substitute the opinion of counsel for its own "knowledge."[90]

This leads to a major conclusion previously suggested, namely, that "knowledge" of law (and thus ignorance or mistake of it) has not only the usual meaning discussed above but also a meaning that is distinctive and decisive as regards the doctrine of *ignorantia juris.* "Knowledge" of the law in this context means *coincidence with the subsequent interpretation of the authorized law-declaring official.* If there is coincidence, the defendant knew the law and his action is legal. If there is not coincidence, it can avail nothing that the defendant thought his conduct was legal.[91] This is the special meaning of *ignorantia,* which distinguishes it from the ordinary meaning of ignorance, expressed, *e.g.* in *ignorantia facti.*

The above analysis also indicates the invalidity of the other proposal, that indefiniteness in the meaning of a penal law should provide an exception to the doctrine of *ignorantia juris.* This problem is presently dealt with in terms of strict construction and "due process." If a criminal statute is ambiguous, its meaning is rendered "sufficiently" precise by excluding the disadvantageous sense of the words. And if a penal statute is vague, it is unconstitutional.[92] The survival of a rule, after being subjected to the tests of strict construction and due process, is an authoritative finding that it is sufficiently definite to constitute law.[93] Accord-

[90] To allow such a defense would make "the opinion of the attorney paramount to the law." People v. McCalla, 63 Cal. App. 783, 795, 220 P. 436, 441 (1923). So, too, in Needham v. State, 32 P. 2d 92, 93 (Okl. 1934), and Hopkins v. State, 193 Md. 489, 69 A. 2d 456 (1949).

[91] In the discussion of bigamy *infra* at note 35, advice of counsel is approved as a defense. This advice, however, concerns the law of marriage and divorce, not criminal law.

[92] Lanzetta v. New Jersey, 306 U. S. 451, 83 L. Ed. 888, 59 S. Ct. 618 (1939); United States v. Cohen Grocery Co., 255 U. S. 81, 89, 65 L. Ed. 516, 41 S. Ct. 298 (1921). See *supra* chapter 2.

[93] "If the right to collect depends upon the construction of various statutes, and is apparently doubtful, the officer should stop; for if he

ingly, the defendant cannot be permitted to raise the question of indefiniteness again under a plea of ignorance of the law and avoid liability by that procedure.[94]

But there are certain large areas of criminal law which are presently assumed to be within the scope of *ignorantia juris* although, actually, the doctrine is not relevant to them. If this can be shown, the presently wide range of the doctrine will be substantially narrowed and its meaning should become proportionately clearer. One of the most important of these situations concerns the effect of changes in the validity of a statute or regulation. For example, a statute forbidding the sale of intoxicants is held unconstitutional; then, this decision is overruled and the statute is held constitutional. The courts usually state that they are required to deal with *ignorantia juris* in cases involving, *e.g.* the sale of intoxicants after the first decision and prior to the second, the validating, one. They say this is an "exception" justified on the ground that it is "manifestly unfair" to hold the defendant to a greater knowledge of the law than that possessed by the State's Supreme Court. But when an individual's conduct conforms to the decisions of the highest court, the claim that he acted "in ignorance of the law" is almost fantastic. It is submitted that the above situation does not call for application of an exceptional rule because neither ignorance nor mistake of law is involved.

This is evident if the traditional theory of the unbroken validity of the statute in question is repudiated so far as penal law is concerned. The above situation would then

---

does not, he will proceed at his peril." Levar v. State, 103 Ga. 42, 49, 29 S. E. 467, 470 (1897).

[94] In the *Lewis* case, 124 Tex. Cr. R. 582, 64 S. W. 2d 972 (1933), although some *dicta* might so imply, the decision was not placed on "indefiniteness," but rather on the ground that "wilfully" required a *mens rea* that included knowledge of illegality. In Burns v. State, 123 Tex. Cr. R. 611, 61 S. W. 2d 512 (1933), both grounds were relied on; greater emphasis was placed on the fact that the statute was "obscure and confusing." Such holdings usually refer ultimately to Cutter v. State, 36 N. J. L. 125 (1873), which involved the taking of an illegal fee by a justice of the peace. But the language of that

be interpreted, in effect, as: enactment, repeal by judicial decision, and "re-enactment" by the later decision.[95] The traditional theory should not apply to criminal law because the policy prohibiting *ex post facto* enactment excludes the dependence of penal liability upon any subsequent law-making, such as a decision reversing a previous one that held a statute unconstitutional. The traditional theory implies that the law covers all possible situations and that it is certain in meaning. At the opposite extreme is the skepticism which asserts that the law is only what the judges in each particular case say it is—nothing more. Neither theory is persuasive. Law does pre-exist, but not in the degree of specificity required for all subsequent adjudications. It pre-exists "sufficiently" to bar arbitrariness and to limit the scope of judicial legislation, but judicial decision plays an essential role in its development. Without adding details, it may be concluded that when a court (certainly the highest court) holds the law to be thus and so, that is what the law is from that date on. Thus the correct *ratio* of the decisions dealing with the above type of situation is not that the defendant acted in ignorance of the law, that it is unfair to require him to know the law when the Supreme Court was ignorant of it, etc. It is, on the contrary, that the defendant is not criminally liable because the law at the time he acted was what the Supreme Court declared it to be; in short, his conduct conformed to the law.[96]

The above analysis can be applied to other problems which are presently confused in the same way.[97] In general, the

---

opinion shows that the "obscurity" of the statute was relatively unimportant. The decision emphasized *mens rea*, and did not purport to be an exception to *ignorantia juris*.

[95] This, however, does not explain how a void statute can be revived by the later decision. It is preferable, therefore, to speak of the unconstitutional statute as unenforceable rather than void.

[96] See Cardozo, J., in Great No. Ry. v. Sunburst Co., 287 U. S. 358, 364-65, 77 L. Ed. 360, 53 S. Ct. 145 (1932) and State v. O'Neil, 147 Ia. 513, 126 N. W. 454, and Annot., 33 L. R. A. (n.s.) 788, 794, 797 (1910).

[97] *E.g.* to a statute that repeals an older one, during which time the act in question occurs, then the repealing statute is declared un-

same conclusion arrived at above is applicable to lower courts[98] and to other law-declaring officials, *e.g.* administrative officials.[99] Hence, an individual who conforms to such declarations should be protected without invoking an "exception" to *ignorantia juris.* This seems equally applicable to the following cases: conforming to the interpretation of a conservator of game that dynamiting fish is permissible;[1] to that of officials of the State's corporation department, including the corporation commissioner, that certain instruments are not "securities," and that a permit to sell them is not needed;[2] and to a ruling by election judges that the defendant is privileged to vote.[3] Such opinions rendered by officials who are primarily responsible for the administration of the laws they interpret[4] are law-declarations within

constitutional. See Claybrook v. State, 164 Tenn. 440, 51 S. W. 2d 499 (1932).

[98] Reliance upon a decision of a county circuit court has been supported. Wilson v. Goodin, 291 Ky. 144, 150, 163 S. W. 2d 309, 313 (1942). See, also, State *ex rel.* Williams v. Whitman, 116 Fla. 196, 156 S. 705 (1934). But it has been held that reliance upon a decision of a municipal court is not a defense: ". . . we refuse to hold that the decisions of any court below, inferior to the Supreme Court, are available as a defense, under similar circumstances." State v. Striggles, 202 Ia. 1318, 1320, 210 N. W. 137, 138 (1926). And see note 4 *infra.*

[99] See United States v. 100 Barrels of Vinegar, 188 F. 471 (D. Minn. 1911) and, generally, Lee, *Legislative and Interpretive Regulations,* 29 Geo. L. J. 1, 25-29 (1940).

[1] State v. Freeland, 318 Mo. 560, 567, 300 S. W. 675, 677 (1927). The court cited the *Cutter* and *O'Neil* cases *supra* notes 94 and 96 and also noted that the regulation in issue was *malum prohibitum,* not *malum in se. Cf.* People v. McCalla, 63 Cal. App. 783, 793-94, 220 P. 436, 439-40 (1923) where, under similar facts, advice of counsel was rejected, and "knowingly" and "wilfully" were held not to require knowledge of the law.

[2] People v. Ferguson, 134 Cal. App. 41, 24 P. 2d 965 (1933).

[3] See State v. Pearson, 1 S. E. 914 (N. C. 1887), and State v. Boyett, 32 N. C. 336 (1849).

[4] In People v. Settles, 29 Cal. App. 2d 781, 78 P. 2d 274, 276 (1938) the California Superior Court refused to exculpate a defendant who had received a license to conduct a "game of skill" from the Los Angeles police department on the ground that the statute in issue (concerning lotteries) was part of the State's Penal Code, hence the city police had no authority to interpret it and grant licenses. The Court approved the *Ferguson* decision, *supra* note 2, on the ground that the official there "was directly charged with the duty of enforcing the law. . . ."

their competence. Conduct which conforms to them should be held legal.[5]

Closely related to the above are cases of officials charged with the violation of laws governing the exercise of their own duties. Since their office requires them to interpret these statutes, such interpretations are law-declarations if they are honestly made; and their conduct in conformity with them is not criminal. The relevant cases exculpating judicial officers, usually justices of the peace, are limited to interpretations of the very statutes which prescribe their official duties. Thus an official could not defend on the ground that he conformed to his interpretation of penal statutes when that was outside the scope of his duties.[6] Moreover, the defense might well be limited to ordinary interpretations of the law, which, e.g. would exclude opinions that the laws in question were unconstitutional.[7] Finally, the above defense, i.e. that the conduct was legal, need not be extended to ministerial officers who, in the discharge of their duties, acted upon their own interpretations of penal laws. There is another defense, however, that is sometimes available to such persons as well as to judicial officers, namely, that certain penal statutes require a knowing violation of the law.[8] This is part of the larger problem to be discussed next.

Knowledge of Illegality Included in Mens Rea

This problem arises chiefly in relation to larceny, embezzlement, malicious destruction of property, willful trespasses and other similar offenses where the defendant did not know that another person's legal rights were being violated. The uniform exculpation of the defendants in these cases[9] does not represent an exception to *ignorantia juris*

[5] See 22 Calif. L. Rev. 569, 570-71 (1934).

[6] State v. McLean, 121 N. C. 589, 28 S. E. 140 (1897); Skeen v. Craig, 31 Utah 20, 86 P. 487 (1906).

[7] Cf. Leeman v. State, 35 Ark. 438 (1880); Hunter v. State, 158 Tenn. 63, 12 S. W. 2d 361 (1928), 61 A. L. R. 1148, 1153 (1928).

[8] E.g. Lewis v. State, 124 Tex. Cr. R. 582, 64 S. W. 2d 972 (1933).

[9] Larceny—Rex v. Clayton (1920), 15 Crim. App. R. 45; Queen v.

neminem excusat. It is not because the defendants were ignorant of the law that they are not criminals, but because, being ignorant of certain law, they lacked the required *mens rea.* Can these cases be distinguished from criminal homicide and other crimes where ignorance of the illegality of the conduct is not relevant to the *mens rea*?

In the above cases, the defendants were mistaken regarding the law of property,[10] hence their exculpation would obviously not involve any exception to *ignorantia juris neminem excusat* if that doctrine, when employed in penal law, were interpreted to exclude property law. But no insight or elucidation is provided regarding the above problem by asserting that property crimes require a specific intent.[11]

If we compare (1) a situation where the defendant shoots a trespasser, thinking he has a legal right to do so, and (2) the typical property case, where the defendant takes a chattel, thinking he has a legal right to its possession, we note that both situations involve private and criminal law. In (1) the defendant's ignorance of the law is not a defense to a criminal charge, whereas in (2) it is. The reason is not merely that the mistake in (2) concerns property law but rather that in (1) we have facts that are directly characterized as criminal, *i.e.* there is a penal law that proscribes shooting a trespasser whereas in (2) we do not have such facts. In (1) no private law exists which can place any interpretation on the facts that would alter their meaning for penal law; in (2) no meaning can be ascribed to the facts

---

Reed, (1842) C. & M. 306, 174 Eng. Rep. 519; especially interesting is Rex v. Gilson and Cohen (1944), 29 Crim. App. R. 174; Embezzlement —Lewis v. People, 99 Colo. 102, 60 P. 2d 1089 (1936); Robbery—Barton v. State, 88 Tex. Cr. R. 368, 227 S. W. 317 (1921); Forgery— Regina v. Parish, (1837) 8 C. & P. 93, 173 Eng. Rep. 413; Malicious destruction of property—Regina v. Twose (1879), 14 Cox C. C. 327; Receiving stolen property—Robinson v. State, 84 Ind. 452, esp. 456 (1882); State v. Rountree, 80 S. C. 387, 61 S. E. 1072 (1908), 22 L. R. A. (n. s.) 833 (1909); State v. Alpert, 88 Vt. 191, esp. 204, 92 A. 32, esp. 37 (1914); unlawfully removing timber from Federal lands —Stone v. United States, 167 U. S. 178, 189, 42 L. Ed. 127, 17 S. Ct. 778 (1897). See note 31 *supra.* The legal mistakes need not be reasonable.

10 See Radulesco, *op. cit. supra* note 76, at 13-14.

11 See *supra* note 23.

that is relevant to the penal law until the defendant's opinion regarding the right of possession is determined. But this is little more than recognizing, somewhat more clearly, perhaps, that in some crimes an opinion regarding certain private law qualifies the criminal significance of the conduct. Such opinions function as facts, and such ignorance or mistake falls within the meaning and purpose of *ignorantia facti*. But is there an underlying reason for this?

It was suggested above that it is not the distinction between private and penal law or even the factual quality of the error regarding the former, but the moral significance of the respective norms, and consequently of the defendant's conduct, that is decisive. Accordingly, *"juris"* should not be restricted to criminal law nor should a plea of ignorance of all non-penal law be allowed. For example, parts of torts and family law, like the law defining the major crimes, also reflect simple moral values. The plea of lack of *mens rea*, resulting from ignorance of the above property law, is not inconsistent with the ethical principle that it is wrong to steal another's chattel. That value is not contradicted if the actor thinks he has a right to its possession. On the other hand, a defendant's plea of ignorance of the criminal law, *e.g.* in killing a trespasser, would contradict the ethics of the criminal law. This conclusion regarding ignorance of certain private law is consistent with *ignorantia facti excusat*. For there, too, the defendant does not challenge the moral norms represented in the criminal law. It may be noted, finally, that "knowledge" of certain private law is given its ordinary meaning, similar to "knowledge of fact" and that, so far as penal law is concerned, the principle of legality is compatible with the recognition, as a defense, of certain mistakes of law, indicated above.

In other areas of major crime, besides the property offenses, knowledge of the illegality of an act has been recognized as an essential element of the relevant *mens rea, e.g.* certain conspiracies[12] and serious income tax offenses. Thus

---

[12] Commonwealth v. Rudnick, 318 Mass. 45, 60 N. E. 2d 353 (1945); Commonwealth v. Benesch, 290 Mass. 125, 194 N. E. 905 (1935).

a charge of willful failure to report taxable income may be controverted by showing a mistaken interpretation of the relevant tax law. In *Hargrove*[13] the defendant was convicted of "willfully failing" to file a tax return for certain years and "willfully and knowingly" attempting to evade payment of taxes. Evidence that he had relied upon the advice of a tax expert was excluded by the trial judge who instructed the jury: "Ignorance of the law, of course, gentlemen, is not excused. The question of willfulness and intent rests, then and depends upon whether you find that the defendant willfully and knowingly did what he intended to do. . . . A man may have no intention to violate the law and yet if he willfully and knowingly does a thing which constitutes a violation of the law he has violated the law." On appeal, the conviction was reversed: Where a statute denounces "as criminal only [the] . . . willful doing [of an act] . . . a specific wrongful intent, that is, actual knowledge of the existence of obligation and a wrongful intent to evade it, is of the essence."[14]

The most serious failure to recognize that certain crimes require a belief in the illegality of the conduct is found in bigamy cases. Here the issues are clouded, partly by the assumption that the doctrine of *ignorantia juris* includes any law, private as well as penal, and partly by the dogma that bigamy does not require a criminal intent. In some States the problem has been avoided by express provisions, *e.g.* requiring knowledge of the continuance of the first marriage. But most of the statutes are silent as to that; they run in the traditional terms of "a person who, being mar-

[13] Hargrove v. United States, 67 F. 2d 820 (5th Cir. 1933); Yarborough v. United States, 230 F. 2d 56 (4th Cir. 1956).

[14] *Id.* at 823. So, too, held in Haigler v. United States, 172 F. 2d 986 (10th Cir. 1949) reversing the conviction where the trial judge, in addition to several correct instructions, instructed that ignorance of the law was no excuse. In United States v. Di Silvestro, 147 F. Supp. 300, 304 (E.D. Pa. 1957) the recognized rule regarding the required *mens rea* was thus stated: "Although that [ignorance of the law] is no defense to a crime in itself, it may be shown in a crime like the present where willfulness is an element in that it may negative willfulness in failure to perform the duty."

ried, goes through a form of marriage." These statutes have often been interpreted to exclude *mens rea, i.e.* just as strictly as petty "public welfare" regulations.[15] In this country, the chief influence has been the *Mash* case, decided more than a century ago, which held that even a reasonable mistake regarding the death of the spouse was no defense.[16] In some jurisdictions this is still the law, and the occasional judicial suggestion that the legislature ought to do something about it[17] is small comfort to honest persons serving long sentences in prison cells. Moreover, so long as reasonable mistake of a material fact is not recognized as a defense, it is practically impossible even to consider that a mistake of law may exclude *mens rea* in bigamy.

Whatever might have been said for such strict liability when *Mash* was decided, the continued exclusion of even reasonable mistakes of fact from *ignorantia facti excusat* after the *Tolson* case[18] is indefensible. A typical bigamy statute was carefully analyzed there by a very able court which held that a reasonable belief in a spouse's death was a defense despite the fact that the second marriage occurred prior to the expiration of the specified time, *i.e.* that the statute, although completely silent regarding *mens rea,* nonetheless required it. Ever since the *Tolson* decision, it has been widely recognized that *mens rea* is required in bigamy. But that decision or, at least, what was suggested there regarding *mens rea* was restricted by *Rex v. Wheat and Stocks*[19] to belief in the death of the spouse; elsewhere, it was held, *mens rea* is not required in bigamy.[20] Despite the

[15] "This rule has been applied in a great variety of cases, from breaches of police regulations to bigamy, adultery, and statutory rape." State v. Ackerly, 79 Vt. 69, 72, 64 A. 450, 451 (1906). So, too, Cornett v. Commonwealth, 134 Ky. 613, 121 S. W. 424 (1909).

[16] Commonwealth v. Mash, 48 Mass. (7 Met.) 472 (1844).

[17] Commonwealth v. Hayden, 163 Mass. 453, 40 N. E. 846 (1895).

[18] Queen v. Tolson, (1889) 23 Q. B. 168.

[19] (1921) 2 K. B. 119. For American cases, see Annot., 27 L. R. A. (n. s.) 1097 (1910).

[20] English law had previously indicated that reasonable mistake of law was a defense. Rex v. Connatty (1919), 83 J. P. 292; Rex v. Thompson (1905), 70 J. P. 6. R. v. Dolman (1949), 33 Cr. App. R. 130, 1 All E. R. 813 indicates that *Wheat* has been reversed in England

prestige of English law in the Commonwealth, however, various courts in the latter jurisdictions have followed the wider implications of *Tolson*. The emphasis is properly placed on the necessity of *mens rea* in bigamy.[21] Most courts which recognize reasonable mistake of fact as a defense still have difficulty in reaching sound decisions because it is assumed that wherever there is a mistake of law, there is no defense,[22] and many of the situations include mistaken opinions regarding both facts and law — the so-called "mixed" questions. If *ignorantia juris* were limited to penal law and simple aspects of tort, family law etc., or if at least technical rules of private law, unsupported by moral attitudes, were excluded from the doctrine, it would usually be superfluous to decide whether the mistake was one of law or fact. As was suggested above, the issue would concern what was relevant to an actual *mens rea*.

The issues in the bigamy cases parallel those involved in the property offenses discussed above, and *ignorantia juris neminem excusat* is no more relevant in the former than it is in larceny; conversely, it is equally relevant to require knowledge of the illegality in both. In bigamy there is no *mens rea* if the defendant believes the first marriage was legally dissolved, just as it is now recognized that an erroneous opinion that the defendant has a legal right to the possession of a chattel excludes the *animus furandi* of larceny. Accordingly, the defendant's ignorance of technical divorce law, *e.g.* rules of jurisdiction, should be a defense.[23] Although it may not be wise to restrict the doctrine of *ignor-*

---

and that the current law requires *mens rea* in bigamy. See Edwards, Mens Rea in Statutory Offences 73-4 (1955). See, also, Wilson v. Inyang (1951), 2 K. B. 799, 2 All E. R. 237.

[21] Thomas v. The King, 59 Commw. L. R. 279 (Austr. 1937); The King v. Carswell (1926), N. Z. L. R. 321 (C. A. 1926); *Cf.* Rex v. Sellars (1905), 9 Cox C. C. 153.

[22] See Dixon, J., in Thomas v. The King, 59 Commw. L. R. 279, 306-07 (Austr. 1931) and Weigall, *Mens Rea and Bigamy*, 16 Austr. L. J. 3, 5-6 (1942).

[23] But *cf.* Williams v. North Carolina, 325 U. S. 226, 89 L. Ed. 1577, 65 S. Ct. 1092 (1945).

*antia juris t*o penal law,[24] that is the most likely starting-point to achieve a sound perspective.[25] This is indicated in the exclusion of the *ius civile* from the scope of the doctrine by Roman jurisconsults,[26] in the commentaries of distinguished civilians, and in various codes of penal law.[27] In any case, it seems clear that strict liability in bigamy[28] is incompatible with the ethics of modern penal liability.

Nor does the claim that bigamy is a statutory offense warrant strict liability even if "legislative intention" and public welfare enactments suggest easy rationalizations. For, although it is true that a statute of James I gave the common law courts jurisdiction over what was previously an ecclesiastical concern, statutes of the vintage of James I have long been treated as part of the common law in this country. What is important is not that bigamy is a statutory offense, but the fact that the penalty is severe. This should definitely establish the position, supportable also on other grounds noted above, that bigamy requires a *mens rea, e.g.* entry into a marriage with knowledge of an existing one.

The tacit recognition of the validity of this position is reflected in the sentences imposed: in *Mash,*[29] a governor's

[24] For some of the difficulties that arose from such a sweeping restriction, see Mannheim, *Mens Rea in German and English Law,* 17 J. Comp. Leg. & Int'l L. at 248-49 (1935).

[25] The range of *ignorantia juris* in private law is not directly involved in the present problem but the same considerations would seem to apply. See Note: *Mistake of Law: A Suggested Rationale,* 45 Harv. L. Rev. 336 (1931). On the other hand, in agreements and in other transactions there is an autonomous sphere where the parties are, in effect, permitted to legislate for themselves. The intent of the parties is correspondingly important, *e.g.* in allowing reformation. The further relaxation of the doctrine in private law, *e.g.* as a defense to specific performance, suggests that some weight must be given to the principle implied in the Roman restriction of the maxim to *ius naturale.* See Radulesco, *op. cit. supra,* note 76, at 25.

[26] Radulesco, *op. cit. supra* note 76, at 25, 27.

[27] See *id.* at 13-15. *Cf.* Blackstone's statement, ". . . a mistake in point of law . . . is in criminal cases no sort of defence." 4 Blackstone Commentaries *27 follows a specific illustration of a mistake in criminal law. *Cf.* Lord Westbury in Cooper v. Phibbs (1867), 16 L. T. R. (n. s.) 678, 683; Lord King in Lansdown v. Lansdown (1730), Moseley 364, 365, 25 Eng. Rep. 441; Art. 5, Italian Penal Code of 1930.

[28] As regards strict liability in adultery, see State v. Woods, 107 Vt. 354, 179 A. 1 (1935).

[29] Commonwealth v. Mash, 48 Mass. (7 Met.) 472 (1844).

pardon; in *Wheat and Stocks,* imprisonment for one day "which means that they were immediately discharged;"[30] in two similar cases,[31] imprisonment for one week. This contrast between hard law and soft administration makes it pertinent to ask, as did a New Zealand judge, "Why then . . . should the Legislature be held to have wished to subject him to punishment at all?"[32] For the above reasons the continued interpretation of bigamy as a strict liability offense, the premise that this is required by *ignorantia juris,* and the imposition of severe penalties can only be characterized as both cruel and unenlightened.

A minority of American courts have recognized the unsoundness and injustice of treating bigamy as a strict liability offense. As long ago as 1874 the Indiana Supreme Court reversed a conviction of bigamy partly because the trial court refused to charge that "the honest belief that his former wife had been divorced from him" was a defense.[33] Subject to the qualification that the defendant "had used due care and made due inquiry to ascertain the truth," the Court held: "The same rule [*i.e.* acquittal] would apply to the dissolution of the marriage relation by divorce as by death."[34] In this case the defendant's error regarding the divorce was treated as a mistake of fact.

[30] Weigall, *supra* note 22, at 8.

[31] Cited *ibid.*

[32] Sim, J., In The King v. Carswell (1926), N. Z. L. R. 321, 339 (C. A. 1926). *Cf.* ". . . it is submitted that (a) it is illogical to allow prisoner's honest belief in death to be a defence and to reject the plea of honest belief that a divorce had been granted: (b) that the prisoner should be acquitted if he raises a doubt as to the validity of the first marriage: (c) that honest belief in the invalidity of the first marriage should be a defence." Paton, *Bigamy and Mens Rea,* 17 Can. B. Rev. 94, 101 (1939).

[33] Squire v. State, 46 Ind. 459, 461 (1874).

[34] *Id.* at 463. See, too, Baker v. State, 86 Neb. 775, 782-83, 126 N. W. 300, 302-03 (1910), following the Indiana decision *supra,* Robinson v. State, 6 Ga. App. 696, 65 S. E. 792, 795-96 (1909), State v. Cain, 106 La. 708, 31 S. 300 (1902). A defense was implied in Gillum v. State, 141 Tex. Cr. R. 162, 147 S. W. 2d 778 (1941) although the conviction was affirmed on the ground of lack of reasonable inquiry by the defendant.

It is only quite recently, however, that these issues have been carefully analyzed by American courts. In *Long*[35] a decree of divorce had been granted the defendant in Arkansas against his wife who continued to live in Delaware and testified that she had not been "served with any divorce papers" or had any notice by mail of the Arkansas action. The conviction of bigamy was set aside on the ground that the trial court erred in refusing to admit evidence that the defendant had in good faith followed the advice of a lawyer both before the Arkansas action and also after the decree of divorce and prior to the second marriage. Allowing the defense of mistake of law in the above circumstances (despite the invalidity of the Arkansas decree), the Supreme Court of Delaware emphasized that, "The defendant would have the burden of demonstrating that his efforts [to ascertain the relevant law] were well nigh exemplary."[36]

The New Jersey Supreme Court considered the same issue in *De Meo*[37] in 1955. De Meo had gotten a Mexican "mail-order divorce" which, the Court observed, is widely considered in this country to be "valueless" and, in addition, he had taken no "reasonable steps toward ascertaining the legal validity of the divorce; indeed, if such steps had been taken they would quickly have disclosed its utter worthlessness."[38] Although the conviction was affirmed, it is very significant that the Court states in the closing lines of the decision that they "expressly withhold determination as to the availability 'in situations not before us' . . . of a defense to a bigamy prosecution resting upon the defendant's honest belief, reasonably entertained, that he was legally free to remarry in New Jersey." Even more significant, from the viewpoint of criminal theory, is Justice Wachenfeld's vigorous dissent.

[35] Long v. State, 44 Del. (5 Terry) 262, 65 A. 2d 489 (1949).

[36] *Id*. at 282-83, 65 A. 2d at 499. "It would not be enough merely for him to say that he had relied on advice of an attorney, unless the circumstances indicated that his conduct throughout in seeking to ascertain the law and in relying on advice received manifested good faith and diligence beyond reproach." *Id*. at 283, 65 A. 2d at 499.

[37] State v. De Meo, 20 N. J. 1, 118 A. 2d 1 (1955).

[38] *Id*. at 14, 118 A. 2d at 8.

He insisted that a decree of divorce should be a defense even though it is void and widely known to be void "unless this general knowledge is imputed or brought home to the defendant. . . ."[39] De Meo had made a full disclosure of the facts on his application for the marriage license. "It must come as a distinct shock to an honest person who has made full disclosure to his sovereign state . . . to find that without wrongful or criminal intent he automatically becomes a convict on a criminal charge which he cannot even defend because the court refuses to accept the very evidence he relied upon and which was . . . approved by the state itself at the time he made his original intentions known."

The California Supreme Court recently dealt with similar issues in *Vogel*.[40] The defendant was not permitted by the trial court to introduce evidence that his wife had told him she was going to secure a divorce in a jurisdiction unknown to him so that he could not contest the custody of their children, that, during his absence in military service, she had lived with a certain man as his wife and that when she was injured in an automobile accident, she identified herself as that man's wife. Reversing the conviction and earlier decisions, the California Supreme Court held that "a bona fide and reasonable belief" that he was free to marry was a defense to a bigamy charge. The Court added that "reliance on a judgment of divorce or annulment that is subsequently found not to be the 'judgment of a competent Court' " is also a defense. "Since it is often difficult for laymen to know when a judgment is not that of a competent court, we cannot reasonably expect them always to have such knowledge and make them criminals if their bona fide belief proves to be erroneous."[41] These recent decisions strengthen the American minority position considerably and indicate that other jurisdictions may pursue a similar path.

[39] *Id.* at 15, 118 A. 2d at 9.
[40] People v. Vogel, 46 Cal. 2d 798, 299 P. 2d 850 (1956).
[41] *Id.* at 854-55.

PETTY OFFENSES

One result of the above discussion is to narrow the scope of *ignorantia juris neminem excusat* considerably since many situations presently treated as both within the meaning of, and also "exceptions" to, that doctrine were shown to be irrelevant to it. The correct *ratio decidendi* of the cases dealing with those situations is either that the requisite *mens rea* included knowledge that the act was illegal (larceny, bigamy) or that the act conformed to the law declared by the authorized officials. *Ignorantia juris*, as thus restricted, was defended in terms of its rationale — a fusion of the principle of legality and the ethics of criminal law. We shall now consider the implications of this theory of *ignorantia juris* with reference to the reform of that doctrine in relation to certain petty offenses.

In an ideal system, ancient laws, no longer useful, would be discarded by a rule of desuetude. The legislature would never enact laws favoring special interests; like Plato's ideal legislator, it would be influenced only by reason and science. And all normal persons would be sufficiently sensitive and informed to recognize even very minor offenses as immoral. In such circumstances, it could be said with complete persuasiveness that any person who intentionally or recklessly did anything forbidden by the criminal law, however small the penalty, acted immorally and merited penal liability.

But actual systems of penal law fall short of such perfection. In the absence of any principle of desuetude, there are instances of prosecutors' digging into ancient books to exhume and enforce long-forgotten statutes.[42] As regards some minor offenses, newly created ones, and those regulating certain businesses, there is frequently a gap between public opinion and the policy of the enactment, between mores and morality. These segments of existing criminal law raise serious questions concerning the reform of *ignorantia juris neminem excusat*.

The principle of *mens rea* requires the voluntary commission of a harm forbidden by penal law. Accordingly, if

[42] See Everhart v. People, 54 Colo. 272, 130 P. 1076 (1913).

there was conduct expressing a *mens rea* and the relevant penal law had been promulgated, the ethical conditions of modern penal liability are satisfied.[43] But as regards certain criminal offenses, indicated immediately above, *the knowledge that the relevant conduct is legally forbidden is an essential element of its immorality.*[44] This is quite different from the judicial distinction between *mala in se* and *mala prohibita.* For, on the one hand, it does not imply that the former (*i.e.* major offenses) are immoral "apart from positive law;" nor, as regards the latter, does it imply that an act becomes immoral because it is legally forbidden. How could the mere prohibition under sanction of force effect such a change? The distinction that should be made, it is submitted, is that some acts are immoral regardless of the actor's ignorance of their being legally forbidden (*e.g.* the felonies and principal misdemeanors) whereas other acts are immoral *only* because the actor knows they are legally forbidden.[45] This would reenforce the writer's criticism of strict liability.[46] If that judicial construction were abandoned, then, instead of saying that because an act is *malum prohibitum* it is unnecessary to find any criminal intent, the rule would be that, since the only rational basis for finding a criminal intent in these cases is knowledge that the act is legally forbidden, a finding of such knowledge is essential.

[43] Opportunity to examine and study the laws is implied in democratic theory which would not be satisfied if conflicts were adjudicated according to laws inaccessible to public inquiry. In addition, promulgation is a condition of valid determination of the law, *i.e.* the ground of adjudication must be public to permit criticism and appraisal. But these do not imply that knowledge of law is essential to the just imposition of criminal liability. The principle of legality functions primarily as a limitation on official conduct, not as a determinant of culpability. It rests on the wide ethical considerations that concern the legitimacy of a government. And see note 65 *infra*.

[44] "Knowingly and intentionally to break a statute must . . . always be morally wrong. . . ." Queen v. Tolson, (1889) 23 Q. B. 168, 172. *Cf.* United States v. Anthony, 24 Fed. Cas. 829, No. 14,459 (N. D. N. Y. 1873).

[45] *Cf.* "This rule, [*ignorantia juris*] essential to the orderly administration of justice, is harsh when applied to what is only *malum prohibitum.*" 1 Bishop, Criminal Law 198 (9th ed. 1923). See Glaser, *Ignorantia Juris dans le Droit Pénal*, Rev. Dr. Pénal et de Crim. et Arch. Intn'l Méd. Leg. 133 (1931).

[46] See *supra* chapter 10.

As was suggested above, ignorance of penal law, of itself, *i.e.* of sheer positivist illegality, presents no general ground for exculpation. But as regards certain petty offenses, where normal conscience (moral attitudes) and understanding cannot be relied upon to avoid the forbidden conduct, knowledge of the law is essential to culpability; hence the doctrine of *ignorantia juris* should not be applied there. This has recently been recognized to a limited but potentially very significant extent by the United States Supreme Court in *Lambert.*[47]

Since the questions requiring determination, in order to demark the exact area within which ignorance of the law is a defense, are beyond the province of the judicial function, the need for legislation is clear. A likely area would include recent misdemeanors punishable only by small fines, various ordinances and technical regulations of administrative boards.[48] Here actual knowledge of the illegality should be required.[49] It seems necessary to retain the presumption that there was such knowledge, allowing the defendant to introduce evidence tending to prove his ignorance or mistake of the law, but placing the final burden of proving *mens rea*, in the above sense, upon the State.[50]

The above general direction to be taken in reform of *ignorantia juris* seems defensible, but certain difficult ques-

[47] Lambert v. California, 355 U. S. 225, 2 L. Ed., 2d 228, 78 S. Ct. 240 (1957). This case is discussed *supra* chapter 10 at note 82. But *cf.* Reyes v. United States, 258 F. 2d 774 (9th Cir. 1958), and United States v. Juzwiak, 258 F. 2d 844 (2nd Cir. 1958).
"In our own law, 'ignorantia juris non excusat' seems to obtain without exception. I am not aware of a single instance in which ignorance of law (considered *per se*) exempts or discharges the party, civilly or criminally." Austin, *op. cit. supra*, note 26 at 499. *Cf.* note 20 *supra*.

[48] *Cf.* Radulesco, *op. cit. supra* note 76, at 74. He quotes Haus' proposal to include new laws that penalize what was formerly legal. *Id.* at 100. See Zakrasek v. State, 197 Ind. 249, 150 N. E. 615 (1926) and Rex v. Ross, (1945) B. C. Co. Ct., 3 D. L. R. 574.

[49] See Mannheim, *supra* note 24, at 247; L. Hall and Seligman, *supra* note 3, at 661-62.

[50] As was noted *supra*, the proof would be in "operational" terms, showing, *e.g.* that the necessary information had been brought to the defendant's attention or that he had avoided that.

tions need to be considered somewhat further. If we examine the petty offenses more closely, we find that there are different types of them. First, as noted, there are archaic, long forgotten offenses — the curiosities of the statute-book and, also, other obviously unsound enactments; and second, there are new, technical and regulative offenses, *e.g.* that it is criminal to drive an uninsured automobile, that land must be used in conformity with the purpose of a local authority, that it is criminal to sell eggs except on a prescribed grading system,[51] that minimum wages determined by certain classifications must be paid to certain employees,[52] that one who undertakes the care of a foster child for reward must give notice to the local welfare authorities, and so on. But third, some petty offenses, *e.g.* insults, minor assaults and others are neither new nor technical; instead, they are well known and many of them are of the same type of harm as major crimes, only less serious. And fourth, there are petty offenses which are not intuitively recognized as immoral,[53] but if the forbidden harm is considered, the correct evaluation will be made. As will appear, this category raises difficult questions.

Reform is also complicated by the fact that to some degree there is an unavoidable clash between the principles of criminal law and historical accretions. For example, if criminal theory[54] is based upon principles defining "harm" partly in terms of morality, the first class lies outside its range. So, too, if *mens rea* is defined in terms of objective morality, the law cannot admit, nor is it the judge's function to allow, nullification of any law on the ground that it is unsound. Reform can, of course, override such theoretical considerations and, on practical grounds, warrant the restriction of the doctrine of *ignorantia juris*.

[51] Witte, *A Break For the Citizen*, 9 State Government 73 (1936).

[52] Borderland Const. Co. v. State, 49 Ariz. 523, 68 P. 2d 207 (1937).

[53] *E.g.* carrying a pistol in public: Crain v. State, 69 Tex. Cr. R. 55, 153 S. W. 155 (1913). Travel interstate with intent to avoid testifying in a criminal case: Hemans v. United States, 163 F. 2d 228 (6th Cir. 1947). Tapping the wife's telephone wire: United States v. Gris, 247 F. 2d 860, 864 (2nd Cir. 1957).

[54] Hall, Studies in Jurisprudence and Criminal Theory, ch. 1 (1958).

In addition to a classification of petty offenses, perhaps along the lines of the criteria suggested above, there are other important questions to be decided with regard to reform of the doctrine. For example, should every kind of ignorance of the law defining the designated petty offenses be a defense or should only "invincible" ignorance be thus recognized? Should the prosecution be required to prove not only that the ignorance was vincible but also that it was the result of recklessness? And, still within the specified area of petty offenses, should mistake of the relevant penal law be distinguished and treated differently from ignorance of it?

A person who is ignorant of a law or regulation may have been on the high seas when it was adopted[55] or he may have been in a hospital or so distraught with serious troubles that he failed to read the newspaper or a bulletin of his Association, giving the pertinent information. These may be instances where definite use can be made of "invincible ignorance" consistently with the test of recklessness. Or, the defendant may be very inexperienced in the operation of his new business or merely stupid, but not to the point of legally recognized incompetence. On the other hand, the defendant may have received the necessary publication or other information but was indifferent to it or positively set against acquiring knowledge of the pertinent rules. Except for the last, the recklessly ignorant, there is no *mens rea* in the above cases. As has been urged with reference to negligence, education, not punishment, is indicated wherever ignorance is not the result of a voluntary indifference to the acquisition of the relevant legal knowledge. Such pleas of ignorance of the law do not contradict the principle of legality.

Mistake of law, however, raises more difficult problems.[56] The mistaken person is in a more meritorious position than

---

[55] Rex v. Bailey (1800), Russell and Ryan 1, 168 Eng. Rep. 651.

[56] Mistake of law is distinguished from ignorance of law and it is stated that the former should not be a defense, 2 Molinier, Traité Théorique et Pratique de Droit Pénal 210-11 (1894), citing 1 Carrara, Programme du Cours du Droit Criminel 209, note (trans. Baret).

the recklessly ignorant one since he has made an effort, perhaps to the extent of consulting a lawyer, to discover what his duty is under the criminal law. That certainly recommends mitigation; indeed, if knowledge of the illegality is the only ground for inferring a *mens rea*, there should be complete exculpation.[57] This would seem to apply rather clearly to the first two classes of petty offenses, noted above. On the other hand, the plea of mistake implies that the penal law in question was actually brought to the defendant's attention, that he examined the relevant words in the code, statute or decisions. This places the defendant in a much less favorable position than that of the invincibly ignorant person. For error implies acquaintance and opportunity to form a correct opinion and that might support a charge of recklessness.

But this estimate may be deemed too refined for everyday decision and an exaggeration of the sensitivity of normal conscience regarding the policy of petty offenses. It may be urged that all that is pertinent is analysis of the meaning of certain words and a lawyer's definite opinion of the scope of those words. As a practical matter, probably most persons would agree with Salmond, "That he who breaks the law of the land disregards at the same time the principles of justice and honesty is in many instances far from the truth. In a complex legal system a man requires other guidance than that of common sense and a good conscience."[58] The difficulty, however, so far as *ignorantia juris* is concerned, is that the defendant and his lawyer, in effect, are setting their interpretation of the words defining a penal law against that of the authorized officials.[59] From a theoretical viewpoint, this is precisely what a legal order cannot consistently admit. From that viewpoint, *i.e.* with reference to

[57] This would seem to contradict the requirement of "invincibility" since, on the usual premise regarding the meaning of "*ignorantia*," a lawyer has the competence to acquire the correct legal knowledge.

[58] Salmond, Jurisprudence 408 (10th ed. 1947). So, too, Lord Atkin in Proprietary Articles Trade Ass'n v. Atty. Gen. of Canada (1931), A. C. 310, 324.

[59] *Cf.* Holmes, J., in Horning v. District of Columbia, 254 U. S. 135, 65 L. Ed. 185, 41 S. Ct. 53 (1920), quoted *supra* note 74.

the principles of legality and *mens rea* (in its objective meaning), and on the assumption that only social harms are proscribed, mistake of penal law cannot be recognized as a defense.

Thus, the solution of this problem seems to be caught between two fires. On the one hand, a defendant's interpretation of the law cannot prevail over official declarations of it. On the other hand, where mistakes of non-penal law directly exclude *mens rea*, *e.g.* larceny, bigamy, etc., such mistakes are admitted as a defense. But penal law, presumably, is composed of moral norms, hence even the pettiest of penal laws, by definition, proscribes a social harm binding on normal conscience. And theory also recalls the objective meaning of *mens rea* and the judicial duty to assume that all penal laws are sound. But the voice of practical sense replies that, in fact, the accepted "penal" law contains many petty proscriptions of conduct which are not recognized by normal persons as having moral significance, and that when social harm becomes so diluted that it cannot be thus recognized, it is time in the sphere of positive criminal law to do justice in light of the facts.

This is the kind of problem where authority should step in to resolve the issues; and, as was suggested above, the proper authority is the legislature. Such practical resolution of a difficult problem should be respected in a branch of law that must represent thoughtful public attitudes. Legal systems survive and prosper despite the incompatibility of some of their rules, indeed, because they are able to tolerate such antinomies. How much of such incompatibility a legal system can and should tolerate is a question regarding which there are probably many opinions.

SUMMARY OF THE PRINCIPAL PROBLEMS

The principal difficulties encountered in analysis of *ignorantia juris* and the reasons, also, for the apparent divergence among writers on the subject, arise from several sources. First, is the failure to distinguish theory from reform.[60] It is the function of theory to elucidate a problem in the fullest

60 Hall, *op. cit. supra* note 54, and *supra* chapter 1.

measure, while sound reform includes an ideal element. Accordingly, there is bound to be some difference of opinion regarding proposed reforms, which cannot be resolved by theory. But theory can guide reform, and it can discover and elucidate the bases upon which proposed reforms rest.

A second, probably the greatest, source of difficulty is the assumption that ignorance or mistake of law concerns the same kind of questions as ignorance or mistake of fact, that they are phases of a single problem, specifically, that *"ignorantia"* in the two doctrines has substantially the same meaning. Actually, however, *"ignorantia"* in the doctrine *ignorantia juris* has two quite different meanings. One of these is the straightforward, generally assumed meaning — there is a subject matter (law) and there is knowledge of it derived from the study of codes, statutes, cases, treatises, dictionaries and experience. This is the meaning of "knowledge" of law and illegality, applied, accordingly, to *"ignorantia,"* which seems to appeal particularly to civilian scholars. But among common lawyers and, no doubt, for many civilians, "knowledge" of law also has a very different meaning which, so far as *ignorantia juris* is concerned, is the decisive one. In this sense, "knowledge" does not mean knowledge at all. As was seen above, it means an interpretation of a law which coincides with the later relevant interpretation by the authorized officials. This is central to an understanding of the doctrine of *ignorantia juris*.

Third, difficulties arise concerning the meaning of *"juris."* What needs to be known is whether a writer holds that at least the laws defining the major crimes have moral significance[61] or whether, on the contrary, the premise is that law and morals are separate spheres. From that latter (positivist) viewpoint, "law," including "penal law," means a command of the Sovereign or a hypothetical judgment that originated in and conforms to superior positive laws, in brief, the so-called "formal" criteria. But when a non-

[61] *Ibid.* and chapters 3 and 7.

positivist argues the question, his premise is that morality is expressed in penal law. Thus the two theorists may agree that "knowledge of penal law is essential to penal liability" when, actually, there is sharp conflict — the one is thinking of the sheer positivity, the formal criteria, of penal law while the other is thinking of its moral significance.

This issue can be clarified if it is agreed — as is usually implicit — that *"juris"* in *ignorantia juris* be limited to the formal meaning of the term. But this does not suffice since it is necessary to determine how much of positive law must be known. The apparent consensus is that *"juris"* in the doctrinal phrase has a wide meaning, *e.g.* at least all of penal law, except certain petty enactments, and probably, also, those simple aspects of torts, family law and other non-penal law which have obvious moral significance. With reference to this meaning, the position of those who insist on knowledge of the illegality as a condition of penal liability seems obviously untenable. For it collides with the universally recognized fact that it is *impossible* for anyone to know that law; and this is quite persuasive even from the viewpoint of the ordinary meaning of "knowledge" of the law. To insist on what is impossible as a condition of liability is to exclude liability entirely. Such a patent fallacy cannot be attributed to those who urge complete abandonment of the doctrine of *ignorantia juris*.

They attempt to secure their position by insistence that *"juris"* means or should mean not a specialized knowledge of the law of even the major crimes but only a "general" knowledge of it. Thus, they say, the differences between murder and manslaughter need not be known, but only that it is illegal to kill a human being,[62] and so on as regards the other major crimes. It is submitted, however, with deference, that this is not persuasive. This interpretation of *"juris"* departs drastically from its usual meaning; and if we are presented with a proposed change in the definition of that important term, restricting it to its simplest possible

---

[62] Busch, *L'Erreur de Droit*, Rev. Intn'l de Dr. Pénal 309, 312, Nos. 3 and 4 (1955).

sense, it can easily be shown that the new meaning is not relevant to the problems actually met in the application of *ignorantia juris,* in its present sense. For example, every normal person knows it is illegal to steal, but is it illegal to keep money one finds, knowing that the owner can be discovered? In some places a "finder's keepers" custom represents the common opinion. Everyone knows it is illegal to steal, but in certain American states it was the custom that anyone was privileged to take unbranded cattle.[63] Everyone knows it is illegal to kill a human being, but is it well-known that it is illegal to shoot a trespasser or to kill a wife's paramour apprehended in adultery? It is precisely these ramifications of the penal law, "exceptional" only in a formal sense, which require the principle of objective *mens rea* and the doctrine of *ignorantia juris* to support penal liability. Accordingly, since there is no escape from the fact that it is impossible to know this law regarding even the serious offenses, criminal liability imposed in the above "exceptional" areas must rest on grounds other than knowledge of the illegality.

The theory which posits criminal liability, in part, upon the principle of *mens rea* in its recognized objective sense not only provides a defensible ground of liability for the obviously immoral harms, it also provides a ground for liability in the more difficult "exceptional" situations. That ground may be criticized—legal justice is far from perfect individualized justice—but it does provide a rational basis for criminal liability which is certainly preferable to having no basis at all. Moreover, as regards the "exceptional" situations, the legal system and the methods of its interpretation by thoughtful disinterested persons improve upon lay opinion. They provide objective bases for discovering the better answers to serious moral problems.

Nor will it have escaped attention that to the extent that "knowledge" of law is given a vague, general meaning, *e.g.* that a mere feeling or intuition of illegality suffices, that

---

[63] Lawrence v. State, 20 Tex. Ct. App. 536 (1886).

position tends to approximate *mens rea*, the traditional requirement of moral culpability. Whatever plausibility the insistence upon knowledge of illegality achieves, results from the unconscious, hardly avoidable identification of the sheer illegality of the major harms with their known immorality. But it should not be assumed by those who advocate abandonment of the doctrine of *ignorantia juris* that the contents of even the major penal laws have a common quality or that there is any relation between morality or custom and that content or that the fact that the major harms are commonly forbidden by penal law supports their position. These factors concern non-legal matters (in the agreed positivist sense); to the extent that they are relied upon, the position approximates the traditional meaning of *mens rea* and criminal responsibility.

A fourth source of uncertainty in the literature is the failure of some writers to specify whether they are thinking of *ignorantia juris* in relation to the major crimes as well as to the petty offenses or whether they have only the latter in mind. They often generalize without limitation, and the impression given is that they are advocating a very sweeping reform, namely, that knowledge of the illegality, in the positivist sense, should be a required element in all crimes. Later, they are apt to concede — sometimes at the very end of their argument and almost as an aside — that, of course, no one will be permitted to plead that he did not know murder, robbery, etc. are legally forbidden.[64] Obviously, the failure to articulate the significance and implications of the concession unsettles the entire argument. If the concession were dealt with at the outset, it would be neces-

---

[64] This difficulty is aggravated in comparative studies. For example, in a recent case the German Supreme Court recognized ignorance of the law as a defense to a charge of "coercion" against a lawyer who demanded fees from a client on threat of ceasing to represent him in a pending action. In an article where it is asserted that German penal law by this decision completely abandoned the doctrine of *ignorantia juris*, the writers, concluding their advocacy of such a reform, assert: "Nor would any man — in legal systems which admit error of law as a defense — be heard to say that he did not know the killing of a human being to be unlawful." Ryu and Silving, *Error Juris: A Comparative Study*, 24 U. of Chi. L. Rev. 421, 470 (1957).

sary to elucidate *ignorantia juris* with reference to the serious crimes and to view the remaining problem against the bulking fact of that explanation. Indeed, unless one does elucidate the doctrine in relation to the major crimes, its rationale is simply ignored.

Finally, various ethical-political arguments against *ignorantia juris* are unclear because of the assumption that the moral significance of penal law is unimportant or that there are no significant differences in the content of the "commands of the State" regardless of whether they concern capital felonies or petty technical rules of property law. In this view the only defensible ground of criminal liability in any case is knowledge of the relevant illegality.[65] So, too, on the above premises, democratic "ideology," as it is called, requires the abandonment of the doctrine of *ignorantia juris.*

But if normal adults understand the simple morality that is relevant to criminal law, insistence on knowledge of the formal penal law (except as regards certain petty offenses discussed above) is not persuasive, even apart from the illusory nature of such a requirement. Although such insistence seems on the surface to exhibit greater concern for individual dignity and to afford greater protection, actually it does neither. For it depreciates the moral significance of the principle of *mens rea* (requiring the voluntary commission of a legally forbidden harm) as a ground of liability and, thus, the conception of man as a responsible moral agent, *i.e.* influenced by morality and not requiring to know, in addition, that harms are illegal. And, since the proposed abandonment of the doctrine of *ignorantia juris* implies the proportionate abandonment of the principle of legality (the "rule of law"), what remains is not the assured protection

---

[65] It is sometimes argued that the *ex post facto* prohibition implies that knowledge of the law is essential to the just imposition of penal liability. But see note 43 *supra*. This cannot be the rationale of *ex post facto* because "knowledge" of the promulgated laws, in the special sense discussed above, is impossible. The above argument confuses the principle of *mens rea* with that of legality. See *supra* chapter 2 at note 97.

of the individual, but unfettered authority.[66] Of course, it would be very nice to have all the advantages of the criminal law and, also, to apply its sanctions only to those who knew the law. Unfortunately, no one has shown how this can be done in an inevitably "second-best" world.

[66] See *supra* chapter 2.

CHAPTER XII

NECESSITY AND COERCION

THE law of penal responsibility expresses the considered ethics of the common man. It absolves the psychotic and the infantile; and it mitigates punishment in extenuating circumstances. But as regards normal adults and situations, the common law rests firmly on the proposition that, however it may be that such persons come by their thoughts and motives, it is possible for them to control their conduct—at least as regards the infliction of serious harms. The determinism that posits the inevitability of emotional states is deemed irrelevant to penal liability. Especially repudiated is that "hard determinism" which holds that conduct, also, is but a link in a fixed chain of events, the unavoidable product of what preceded. It is rejected as untrue and incompatible with rational punishment. It is opposed by a vivid awareness of one's organized self, initiating changes as it functions daily in hundreds of purposeful actions, *i.e.* by experience—against which the sophistication of determinist theory falls like snowflakes on a mountain.[1]

Equally ingrained in the criminal law is the judgment that normal persons sometimes commit serious harms justifiably, as in self-defense or in overcoming resistance to the service of legal process. But the major issues of the present chapter concern legal privileges claimed in other circumstances, in which the salient facts are harms to persons innocent of any wrong-doing, which were inflicted on them

---

[1] For excellent discussions, see Montague, *Free Will and Fate*, 24 The Personalist 178 (1943), Stout, *Free Will and Responsibility*, 37 Proc. Arist. Soc. (n. s.) 213 (1937), and Determinism and Freedom in the Age of Modern Science (Hook ed. 1958).

under extraordinary pressure. From ancient times, "necessity" and "coercion" have been the terms used to designate many of these situations. These terms were derived and took their meaning in the perennial struggles of a frail being against powerful, sometimes overpowering, forces. In these circumstances the law of crimes represents principles avowed bravely but without other-worldly idealism. The doctrines of "necessity" and "coercion" are a tacit admission of man's impotence against some of the greatest evils that assail him, as well as a measure of his moral obligation even *in extremis.*

The explication of these rules in English and American law, which has perforce dealt only piecemeal with peripheral aspects of the general problem, is disappointing. The difficulties encountered include serious linguistic problems, and they are accentuated by the failure of the courts to discuss the doctrines in relation to the relevant principles. Throughout the professional literature there is, nonetheless, a tacit assumption that their meanings are well-established. In such circumstances it becomes plain that we have to deal with terms and ideas which have been anciently woven into the fabric of our culture. To indicate the complexities of the problem more fully, it will be helpful to supplement the above remarks by a brief, historical survey.

The Laws of Alfred already provided that a homicide "of necessity . . . as God may have sent him into his hands, and for whom he has not lain in wait [shall] be worthy of his life;"[2] but the only clue to the meaning of the term is suggested by the exclusion of a particular intentional killing. Bracton lists "necessity" as a defense, providing the harm was not "avoidable."[3] The likelihood is that he was concerned with self-defense and was insisting on what we have come to call the "duty to retreat" before inflicting a fatal blow; or he may have meant simply, that to be exculpated, one must not have been an aggressor. In any event, from

[2] 1 Thorpe, Ancient Laws and Institutes of England s. 13, 47-49 (1840).

[3] 2 De Legibus, f. 121 at 277 (Twiss ed. 1879).

early times "necessity" has been associated with "self-defense."[4] Especially important in the early law was *Reninger v. Fogossa*[5] where Pollard, for the defendant, argues that "a man may break the words of the law, and yet not break the law itself...."[6] He may do this "where the words of them are broken to avoid greater inconveniences, or through necessity, or by compulsion...."[7] Pollard is already familiar with what he calls the "common proverb," *Quod necessitas non habet legem*; and he cites Scriptural approval of the eating of sacred bread "through necessity of hunger" and the taking of others' corn in the like situation.[8] Compulsion, he states, is also "a good excuse." But the illustration he gives—"So if a man's arm be drawn by compulsion, and the weapon in his hand kills another, it shall not be felony"[9]—reveals the confusion of that term with complete inaction. The treatment of many diverse problems as species of "necessity" reached its culmination in Dalton. His discussion of "homicide upon necessity"[10] includes capital punishment by officers executing a sentence of death, homicide in effecting the arrest of a fleeing felon or jail breaker, that committed to overcome resistance to lawful arrest,[11] killing another "in the necessary defence of himself or his,"[12] in appeals of felony or in a "turney in the presence of the King," coercion of a wife by her husband, and Act of God or of a stranger. Thus, by the seventeenth century there were already extensive, though vague and ambiguous, interpretations of "necessity" and "compulsion."

There was little advance in the analysis of these ideas in the succeeding treatises until Stephen's *History* appeared.

---

4 *Cf.* 1 Britton 113 (Nichols ed. 1865).

5 1 Plowd. 1 (1551).

6 *Id.* at 18.

7 *Ibid.*

8 Matthew, ch. 12, VI, 3, 4.

9 *Op. cit. supra* note 5, at 19.

10 The Countrey Justice, ch. 150 (1682).

11 "But in all these former cases," he writes, "there must be an inevitable necessity; *sc.* That the offender could not be taken, etc. without killing of him." *Id.* at 355.

12 *Id.* at 356.

The problem was viewed by him in terms of "compulsion"—
by a husband of his wife, by threat of death, and by necessity.[13] The first of these has become relatively unimportant.[14] As to a harm committed under threat of death,
Stephen, while conceding that moral guilt in such a case "is
less than that of a person who commits it freely,"[15] believed,
nonetheless, that even such extreme compulsion should not
be a defense. In his discussion of "compulsion by necessity"
he cites the classical case of two drowning men struggling
for a plank which can support only one, and that of ship-
wrecked persons in a boat which cannot carry all of them
as "the standing illustrations of this principle." He argues
that if a case should arise concerning a homicide in these
circumstances "it is impossible to suppose that the survivors
would be subjected to legal punishment."[16] Obviously,
Stephen believed that there was a very great difference
between "compulsion by threats" and "compulsion by necessity." But he nowhere provided an analysis of his theory
of penal responsibility regarding them. Nor have the issues
been greatly clarified in the subsequent case-law. The problems are glossed over in typical generalities, e.g. "there
must be, if not a physical, at least a moral necessity for the
act."[17] In another case, the defendant, charged with reckless

---

[13] 2 H. Cr. L. 105 (1883).

[14] For a brief summary, see 1 Burdick, The Law of Crime 210-213
(1946).

[15] Supra note 13 at 107.

[16] Id. at 108. The situation was apparently first noted by Cicero,
who credits a book of Hecaton's Moral Duties as the source. The case
has been discussed by many writers down to the present time, and
many diverse answers have been given to the specific questions raised
by the plank case. We need to note that they often confuse three
situations: the actor pushes off a person who is already on the
plank; or the actor is on the plank and he repulses one who seeks to
push him off; or, both persons reach the plank at the same time, and
one thrusts the other aside so that he may secure the plank for himself. See, e.g. (a) Cicero, De Officiis, bk. III, 23, 363-364 (Miller's trans.
1913); (b) 4 Bacon, Works 34 (1803); (c) Kant, The Philosophy of
Law 52-53 (Hastie ed. 1887); (d) Grotius, The Rights of War and
Peace 93 (Campbell ed. 1925); (e) 2 Pufendorf, De Jure Naturae et
Gentium 300 (Oxford ed. 1934); (f) 4 Bl. Comm. 186; (g) Fichte,
Science of Rights 336 (Kroeger trans. 1869).

[17] Ross v. State, 169 Ind. 388, 390, 82 N. E. 781 (1907).

driving, pleaded that he was trying to escape serious injury and illegal arrest by police officers who wished to ambush him. The driving was held justified because the act "was without free will upon his part"[18]—despite the fact that the defendant certainly wanted to escape and accelerated his automobile to that end.

The above cases and professional literature provide a fair index of the continuing uncertainty of the penal law on traditional and recurring problems of great theoretical significance. They also indicate the major questions to be investigated regarding "coercion" and "necessity."

BASIC DISTINCTIONS

In elucidating the meaning of these basic terms, it must be recognized that the relevant stock of ideas is a very limited one. We think in terms of human conduct and, at the opposite pole, of the happening of physical events—the operation of physical forces. We think of human conduct as more or less controlled or as free; and we think of the controls in terms of influence by other persons or as the pressure of physical conditions. This suggested figure indicates the general perspective from which "necessity" and "coercion" must be viewed. In order to understand those ancient terms which lawyers borrowed from contemporaneous non-legal thinking, it is especially helpful to consult Aristotle, who summarized the thought of preceding centuries, and whose discussion greatly influenced the interpretation of the relevant legal doctrines during the succeeding ages.[19]

For Aristotle, "necessity" is of two distinct types: absolute and hypothetical. " ... [A]bsolute necessity [is] manifested in eternal phenomena. ... "[20] "We may say that that

[18] Browning v. State, 244 Ala. 251, 13 S. 2d 51, 56 (1943).
[19] *E.g.* Aquinas, Summa, II-1, Q. 6, Art. 6; Hobbes, The Elements of Law 47-48 (1928); 2 Pufendorf, De Jure Naturae et Gentium 63-64 (Classics of Int'l Law ed. 1934); Moriaud, De La Justification Du Délit par L'État de Nécessité 45-46, 156-158 (1889); and Holmes in *The Eliza Lines*, 199 U. S. 119, 130-131 (1905).
[20] D. P. A. 639b, 25.

which cannot be otherwise is necessarily as it is."[21] Thus "demonstration is a necessary thing because the conclusion cannot be otherwise . . . and the causes of this necessity are the first premisses. . . ."[22] "The necessary in nature, then, is plainly what we call by the name of matter, and the changes in it."[23] He illustrates "hypothetical necessity" by noting that " . . . if a house or other such final object is to be realized, it is necessary that such and such material shall exist; and it is necessary that first this and then that shall be produced, and first this and then that set in motion, and so on in continuous succession, until the end and final result is reached, for the sake of which each prior thing is produced and exists."[24] Thus "drinking the medicine is necessary in order that we may be cured of disease. . . ."[25] "What is necessary then, is necessary *on a hypothesis*; it is not a result necessarily determined by antecedents."[26] To summarize: in "absolute" necessity, "the starting point is that which is;" in hypothetical necessity, it is "that which is to be."[27] Thus the latter may preferably be designated "teleological necessity," *i.e.* necessary to attain an end, while Aristotle's "absolute necessity" in modern thought means physical causation. "Necessity" in Greek tragedy and in early epistemology meant more than that—it implied absolute certainty.[28] But modern scholars agree that empirical science knows only probabilities. Modified in these ways, Aristotle provided a fundamental distinction of great importance in analysis of the legal problem—that between

[21] Metaphys. 1015a, 34.

[22] *Id.* at 1015b, 5.

[22] *Id.* at 1015b, 5.

[24] D. P. A. 639b, 27-31; *cf.* Bramhall in 5 Hobbes, English Works 248 (1841).

[25] Metaphys. 1015a, 25.

[26] Physics, bk. II, ch. 9, 200a, 14.

[27] D. P. A. 640a.

[28] "Powerless is everything against necessity" writes Euripides. Bellerophantes frag. 229; and Plato observes that "even God is said not to be able to fight against necessity." Laws, bk. V, 741a.

physical causation and human causation characterized as teleological necessity or, simply, as end-seeking.[29]

The difficulties in Aristotle and assuredly in later legal discussions begin when we relate "compulsion" to the above ideas. The Aristotelian view is that " . . . that is compulsory [and involuntary] of which the moving principle is outside . . . e.g. if he were to be carried somewhere by a wind, or by men who had him in their power,"[30] "when the cause is in the external circumstances and the agent contributes nothing."[31] Human conduct implies decision, initiative, action and not mere reaction, but at the same time, it is always more or less influenced by external conditions. Hence: "With regard to the things that are done from fear of greater evils . . . it may be debated whether such actions are involuntary or voluntary."[32] Aristotle notes the jettison of cargo of a ship in distress, and he remarks that "any sensible man does so" to secure the safety of himself and his crew.[33] "Such actions, then," he concludes, "are mixed, but are more like voluntary actions." They are also, in a sense, "involuntary; for no one would choose any such act in itself."[34] But what Aristotle previously designated as compulsion[35] and involuntary (e.g. "being carried somewhere by a wind") is but a form of physical causation, and therefore preferably designated as "non-voluntary." And since his "mixed action" implies a significant degree of voluntary conduct, it is a form of teleological necessity. With these modifications, there is available a set of basic ideas whose relationship to the instant legal problems must now be considered.

PHYSICAL CAUSATION

Of these conceptions, "physical causation" is the one most easily applied to the legal problem. It is significant in the

---

[29] See chapter 8, supra.
[30] Ethics, bk. III, 1110a.
[31] Id. at 1110b.
[32] Id. at 1110a.
[33] Ibid.
[34] Ibid.
[35] Cf. Metaphys. bk. V, ch. 5, 1015a.

case-law only as a reference to distinguish conduct in teleological necessity from non-voluntary behavior. For, as regards behavior where the cause is entirely outside the person, where his "self" does not participate in the slightest degree, the legal rules represent the traditional judgment that the defendant has not acted at all, *i.e.* "act" implies volition. Since officials do not prosecute in such circumstances, the relevant case-law is very scant, indeed, it is limited to situations where there was uncertainty regarding the facts. The courts sometimes confuse harms committed under teleological necessity with those produced solely by physical forces—probably because there must be exculpation on either determination. Thus in *The William Gray*,[36] the charge was violation of an embargo act by illegal entry of a port. Sailing from Alexandria to Boston with a cargo of flour, the ship was "driven by storms, tempests, stress of weather, and necessity, out of her course, and forced to proceed to Antigua, for the preservation of the vessel and cargo, and the lives of those on board."[37] Judge Livingston held that "the alleged necessity is sufficiently made out."[38] Despite his intimation of inevitability, it is plain that the conduct in issue, the illegal entry, was not caused by mechanical forces.[39] The captain might have persisted on his course or tried to do so, and gone down. Clearly he participated in effecting the entry; he chose to make port in order to save his ship.[40]

A more persuasive instance of physical causation seems to be represented in a case[41] where the defendant was indicted for failure to repair a road adjoining the sea. The

[36] 29 Fed. Cas. 1300, No. 17,694 (C. C. D. N. Y. 1810).

[37] *Id.* at 1301.

[38] *Id.* at 1302.

[39] *Cf.* "That is necessary . . . which is, or will be, notwithstanding all supposable opposition." Jonathan Edwards, Inquiry into the Freedom of Will 17 (1804).

[40] It is not, of course, implied that there should be penal liability here, but rather that the ground of decision is teleological necessity, which is discussed in the next section.

[41] R. v. Bamber (1843), 5 Q. B. 278, 286.

water had washed the road away with "all the materials of which a road could be made;" and Denman, J., instructed "not guilty because of the 'Act of God.'" It was not considered whether the building materials could be obtained elsewhere, hence the court's characterization of the omission was based upon a restricted interpretation of the statute. The only unequivocal instances of prosecution for harms caused solely by physical forces concern petty statutory infractions. Typical of these is a prosecution for illegally permitting a vehicle to remain in the street for twenty minutes. Although Judge Bray did not use the language of "necessity" (physical causation), he stressed the fact that "the defendant . . . was delayed by the crowding of other vehicles which he could not control."[42] His decision is in accord with French law that in such circumstances even a "public welfare regulation" is not violated.[43]

We can supplement the scant Anglo-American case-law on harms caused mechanically by illustrations taken from the professional literature, some of which represent decisions of foreign courts. Thus, if a ship is cast by a storm upon a shore, the entry is not illegal; hence a passenger on the boat, deported from the country, is not guilty of illegal re-entry in such a case. So, also, as to failure to be present at a required time and place (e.g. a juror, witness, or soldier on leave) because of a flood or a broken bridge, or any other physical force that makes locomotion impossible. If a juror or witness has been imprisoned, the fact that a human agency created the barriers makes such cases no less instances of physical causation so far as the above persons are

---

[42] Commonwealth v. Brooks, 99 Mass. 434, 437 (1868).

[43] Baudry, La Force Majeure en Droit Pénal 103 (1938). But cf. Commonwealth v. N. Y. Cent. & H. R. R., 202 Mass. 394, 398, 88 N. E. 764, 765 (1909) in which trains remained at a crossing more than 5 minutes because air-brake valves had been deliberately opened by unknown persons and the additional time was needed to close them. The court held that "in statutory offenses created in the exercise of the police power," . . . a wrongful intent is not required. ". . . the defendant was bound at its peril to know and obey the law. . . ." Cf. the exactly opposite reasoning in The William Gray, 29 Fed. Cas. No. 17,694, at 1302 (C. C. D. N. Y. 1810); and Chesapeake & O. R. R. v. Commonwealth, 119 Ky. 519, 84 S. W. 566 (1905).

concerned, *e.g.* a cafe owner whose establishment remained open beyond the fixed closing time because he was tied hand and foot by his patrons. Thus, also, a married woman who was raped did not commit adultery, according to Ulpian.[44] Where automobile lights are put out by electrical storms, this does not constitute a violation of the ordinance requiring them. But a swimmer whose clothes were stolen cannot plead physical necessity to a charge of nudeness since he had the alternative of remaining in the water until relieved. Illness does not always imply that the relevant ensuing wrongs were caused solely by physical forces; perhaps the legal duties could have been fulfilled at the cost of a minor hazard to health. But, of course, an illness may be so severe as to incapacitate and thus render it physically impossible to perform a duty. Thus, too, it may be physically impossible for an engineer or a passenger to avoid passing a station because he has been awake so long that sleep could not be resisted. Most of the above cases, it will be noted, are omissions to perform required affirmative acts. Illustrations of harms by overt movements caused by physical force are: being pushed or thrown against someone, being physically forced to trace another's signature or to pull the trigger of a gun, the hand being merely the coercer's instrument.[45]

Finally we must take note, in this connection, of epilepsy and hypnosis. Epilepsy is sometimes treated as a form of insanity,[46] but what needs emphasis in the present context is that movements in the course of an epileptic seizure no more constitute conduct than does slipping on an icy walk. In the epileptic the physical cause is not external, but lies within himself, seeming to provide an exception to the Aristotelian definition of involuntary behavior. This, however, is not a significant difference in the nature of the epileptic's (non-voluntary) behavior; indeed, the physical body may be viewed as external to the "self." As for hypnosis, penal

----

[44] D. 48. 5.

[45] Many of the above cases were suggested by Baudry, *op. cit. supra* note 43.

[46] Sauers v. Sack, 34 Ga. App. 748, 131 S. E. 98 (1925).

liability would also be excluded in the absence of prior knowledge of probable harmful behavior in the hypnotic state. For, again, such behavior would be entirely unrelated to volition. Thus the uniform test of physical causation is the lack of any volition. The mechanical force encountered is irresistible, and any consequent behavior is non-voluntary. "Ought" presupposes "can." Where physical forces so dominate as to exclude any capacity to alter their course, there is no moral responsibility and no penal liability.

TELEOLOGICAL NECESSITY

It has been indicated above that there is, in fact, an essential difference between harms caused solely by the operation of physical forces and harms which were inflicted under pressure of such forces. Teleological necessity concerns the latter. It does not exclude the operation of physical forces; on the contrary, it implies conduct in the face of serious danger threatened by the impact of physical forces. This is reflected in the decisions applying the "doctrine of necessity" which, in the case-law, designates not harms caused by natural forces but those inflicted in certain instances of teleological necessity. Here, in short, is the area not of non-voluntary behavior but of that "mixed action" which has been termed partly involuntary and partly voluntary.[47]

The records of the classical illustration of teleological necessity, the jettison of a cargo to save the lives of those on board, date at least from Biblical times when, on a perilous voyage "the mariners were afraid . . . and cast forth the wares that were in the ship into the sea, to lighten it of them."[48] Everyone agrees that the destruction of goods in such circumstances is privileged. In an early American case, sailors, charged with mutiny, justified their refusal to obey their captain on the grounds that the ship was leaky and that in this unseaworthy condition it encountered a gale, putting them in imminent danger of death unless they returned to port. The court held that if the ship was unsea-

---

[47] *Supra* p. 421.
[48] Jonah, ch. I.

worthy, it was "a case of justifiable self-defence against an undue exercise of power."[49] These cases, where an obviously lesser value is sacrificed to preserve life, represent the most persuasive illustrations of the validity of the legal doctrine of necessity. Less evident is the case of a father, charged with violation of a statute prescribing school attendance for children between eight and fourteen years of age unless excused by the school board for ill-health, who withdrew his sick daughter from school without first obtaining the board's permission. It was held that since delay might have been dangerous, he was not bound to comply with that part of the statute prescribing application to the board, the court stressing the "necessity" of a parent acting "in defense of a child's life."[50] It found that absence from school, without the board's consent, was the only means to preserve the child's health.

The above decisions suggest the following essential conditions of the doctrine of teleological necessity: (1) the harm, to be justified, must have been committed under pressure of physical forces; (2) it must have made possible the preservation of at least an equal value; and (3) the commission of the harm must have been the only means of conserving that value.[51]

The validity of these generalizations can be further supported by reference to cases where the plea of necessity was denied. In a prosecution for illegally having liquor near a church, it was shown that the defendant kept a bottle of liquor in his buggy, 200 yards from the church, to be used

[49] United States v. Ashton, 24 Fed. Cas. 873, 874, No. 14,470 (C. C. D. Mass. 1834). The decision is ambiguous as to whether reasonable belief in the ship's unseaworthiness is sufficient.

[50] State v. Johnson, 71 N. H. 552, 53 A. 1021 (1902); *cf.* Davies, *The Law of Abortion and Necessity*, 2 Mod. L. Rev. 126 (1938). In People v. Whipple, 207 Cal. 739, 279 P. 1008 (1929), on a charge of escape from prison, it was held that unsanitary conditions, vermin, lack of food, etc. were not justification in terms of the doctrine of necessity. *Cf.* Bacon's exculpation of felons who escape from a burning jail. 2 Works 34 (1803).

[51] See Hersey and Avins, *Compulsion as a Defense to Criminal Prosecution*, 11 Okl. L. Rev. 283, 292 (1958).

by his wife who had a heart disease, in accordance with the doctor's prescription in the event of an attack. The court held that the defendant "must either stay at home, or . . . take with him some other kind of medicine,"[52] *i.e.* endanger his wife's life. The wife's health could be protected by staying in any permitted place—with the liquor. Thus the decision underlines the third requirement of the doctrine of necessity, noted above. In another case, a large number of unemployed persons demonstrated before a Red Cross Commissary for a greater allowance of flour than the relief committee was providing. This being refused, they went to the committee's storehouse and took some groceries. The court held that such "economic necessity" was no defense.[53] It was not claimed that the defendants were in any danger of starvation or even that they were hungry,[54] nor did it appear that additional food could not be obtained elsewhere or by other means. The situation, therefore, lacked any of the requirements of a "state of necessity" noted above.

We can supplement and test the above criteria of "state of necessity" by a more intensive study of two very important cases, one, American, the other, English, which have become part of the international literature on this problem. The leading decision in this country on the doctrine of necessity is *Holmes*.[55] The case is unexcelled in its suggestiveness of the nature of the problem regarding action taken in a "state of necessity."[56]

In March of 1841 the American ship, *William Brown*, sailed from Liverpool, carrying a crew of seventeen and sixty-five emigrants bound for the United States. On April

---

[52] Bice v. State, 109 Ga. 117, 34 S. E. 202, 203 (1899). *Cf.* Butterfield v. Texas, 317 S. W. 2d 943 (1958), discussed in 13 Southwestern L. J. 265 (1959).

[53] State v. Moe, 174 Wash. 303, 24 P. 2d 638 (1933).

[54] See Hamilton, *Freedom and Economic Necessity*, pub. in Freedom in the Modern World 25 (Ed. Kallen, 1928).

[55] 26 Fed. Cas. 360, No. 15,383 (E. D. Pa. 1842). See, also, The Trial of William Holmes *et al.* on an Indictment for Murder on the High Seas (Boston, 1820).

[56] See Hicks, Human Jettison (1927) for a detailed description.

19th, after thirty-eight days at sea, it struck an iceberg late at night and began to fill rapidly. Thirty-two passengers, the first mate and eight seamen got into a "long-boat;" the captain, eight seamen and one passenger took to the smaller "jollyboat." In little more than an hour the *William Brown* sank, carrying with her thirty-one passengers, the majority of them children. "But not one of the officers or crew went down with the ship."[57] The two lifeboats parted the next morning, when it was apparent that the long-boat would be unmanageable, indeed, the first mate had already informed the captain that "it would be necessary to cast lots and throw some overboard." "Let it be the last resort,"[58] said the captain, ordering his crew to pull away. Almost immediately after being occupied, the long-boat had begun to take water through a hole in which the plug had become loosened. The boat was so crowded that the passengers were lying and sitting on one another; there was not sufficient room to bail out the water. For twenty-four hours they carried on in the icy waters off the coast of Labrador. Then it began to rain and it rained all the next day, and by night the sea had become very rough and the wind stronger than ever. The men bailed frantically but the boat seemed doomed. Someone cried, "we are sinking," and others, "we shall all be lost." "The plug is out. The boat is sinking. God have mercy on our poor souls."[59] The mate gave the order to cast overboard all the male passengers except two whose wives were present. Unheeded, he repeated the order; and fourteen men were thrown overboard,[60] and two young women, sisters of one of them, either met a like fate or chose to join their brother. The next morning two men who had hidden themselves were discovered, and the crew put both overboard. Almost immediately afterwards the long-boat was sighted

[57] *Id.* at 33.

[58] 26 Fed. Cas. No. 15,383, at 361 (E. D. Pa. 1842).

[59] Hicks, *op. cit. supra* note 56, at 64.

[60] In an eighteenth century civil suit, it was shown that numerous Negro slaves were cast overboard. Apparently no criminal action was brought. Gregson v. Gilbert (K. B. 1783), 3 Doug. 232.

by the *Crescent*; all survivors were transferred to it and later disembarked at Le Havre.

The American case cited above concerns the trial of Holmes, a member of the crew of the *William Brown*. The grand jury had refused to indict him for murder; the charge was manslaughter, punishable by a maximum of three years' imprisonment.[61] The arguments were resolved to three principal issues: necessity, self-defense, and the futility of punishment in such a case. The captain, in his deposition, insisted that "nothing was done on board the long-boat, but what inexorable necessity demanded."[62] This was affirmed in the report of the American and British consuls at Le Havre, who had interviewed the survivors, which concluded that there was only " . . . the alternative of either going down with all in her, or of saving her by sacrificing one part of those who were in her, to save the others."[63] This was the argument of "imperious necessity." Counsel relied, next, on various natural law writers to establish the privilege of "self-defence." "We contend, therefore," they asserted, "that what is honestly and reasonably believed to be certain death, will justify self-defence to the degree requisite for excuse."[64] Holmes "was driven by the impulse of self-preservation to do what we all might have done if placed in the same trying situation."[65] "The instinct of these men's hearts is our authority,—the best authority. Whoever opposes it must be wrong, for he opposes human nature. . . . Every man on board had a right to make law with his own right hand. . . ."[66] Finally, as regards deterrence, which had been much labored by the press, concerned with passenger traffic on American ships if it were held that "might

---

[61] After the *William Brown* had been abandoned, Holmes, at considerable risk to himself, returned to the sinking ship and saved a girl who had been left behind. He stripped himself of most of his clothes to aid the women passengers and it was he, too, who directed the maneuvers that led to the rescue.

[62] Hicks, *op. cit. supra* note 56, at 109.

[63] *Id.* at 89.

[64] *Id.* at 205-206.

[65] *Id.* at 191.

[66] 26 Fed. Cas. No. 15,383, at 366 (E. D. Pa. 1842).

is right,"[67] the defense argued that punishing Holmes would deter no one in such circumstances. The verdict would not "change the current of human nature and alter the first principles of action." Indeed, it might well have the opposite effect. Sailors in such circumstances would thenceforth be inclined to cast all overboard for fear that if they saved some, these might testify against them in a subsequent trial.[68]

Judge Baldwin, in his charge to the jury, distinguished mitigation from justification; necessity implies the latter. He illustrated this by reference to "self-defense against lawless violence" and to "other circumstances where the act is indispensably requisite to self-existence."[69] He held that passengers must be favored over seamen. "The sailor is bound, as before, to undergo whatever hazard is necessary to preserve the boat and the passengers."[70] The captain and enough seamen to navigate the boat must be saved. Then those passengers whom necessity requires to be cast over must be chosen by lot. That, he said, is not prescribed by law, but it is the fairest method, and it is "in some sort, as an appeal to God. . . ." "For ourselves, we can conceive of no mode so consonant both to humanity and to justice. . . ."[71] The jury brought in a verdict of guilty, with a recommendation of mercy. Holmes had been imprisoned for eight months awaiting trial, in view of which fact and the jury's recommendation, the court sentenced him to imprisonment at hard labor for six months.

The leading English decision on the doctrine of necessity was rendered in the case of *The Mignonette*, known professionally as *The Queen v. Dudley and Stephens.*[72] On

[67] Hicks, *op. cit. supra* note 56, at 102-103.

[68] *Id.* at 188.

[69] 26 Fed. Cas. No. 15,383, at 366 (E. D. Pa. 1842).

[70] *Id.* at 367.

[71] *Ibid. Cf.* Book of Jonah. There are other such instances in the Bible, and numerous Natural Law writers approve this method of selection.

[72] (1884) 14 Q. B. 273.

July 5, 1884, the crew of a yacht, consisting of three adult seamen and a boy of seventeen or eighteen, was compelled to abandon ship and take to an open boat. For twelve days they subsisted on pitiably small rations. On the eighteenth day in the boat, one thousand miles from land, without food and water for several days, the sacrifice of the boy was suggested by the defendants to Brooks, the third seaman, but he rejected it. Two days later, having been entirely without food for eight days, one of the defendants, with the assent of the other, killed the boy who was then in a quite helpless condition. The men, including Brooks, who had opposed the killing to the last, fed on the boy's body for four days when they were rescued by a passing ship. In the trial for murder of the boy, the jury found that the men would probably have perished from famine within the four days had they continued without food, that the boy would probably have died first, and that, at the time of the killing, there was no reasonable prospect of rescue, "there was no appreciable chance of saving life except by killing some one for the others to eat."[73]

Chief Justice Coleridge, speaking for a distinguished bench, entirely repudiated the defense of necessity. In a detailed review of the literature he found that most of the language concerning necessity, at least in English treatises, was written in the context of self-defense; it merely justified the killing of an assailant to avoid death. To apply the doctrine to such a case as this, where no wrongful act had been committed by the deceased, indeed, where he was only "the weakest, the youngest, the most unresisting," was preposterous. The doctrine of necessity was a notion which seemed to the judges "at once dangerous, immoral, and opposed to all legal principle and analogy."[74] Hale had correctly stated that hunger is no defense of larceny; how could it possibly justify murder?[75] The decision in *Holmes*

[73] *Id.* at 275.

[74] *Id.* at 281.

[75] But Hale also stated that the judges could reprieve in such cases.
[1] P. C. 54. Natural Law writers invariably held that taking another's

which approved the doctrine of necessity and, also, the selection by lot was dismissed as resting on a "somewhat strange ground" — an estimate which followed Stephen, who thought that method of selection "odd,"[76] indeed, "almost grotesque."[77] The Court was eloquent in its repudiation of the alleged "duty" of self-preservation: "the plainest and the highest duty" may sometimes be to sacrifice one's life, as had been done frequently in war and in shipwreck by the crew of many vessels. They stressed the hazards of approving the doctrine of necessity. In this very case, the men might have been picked up the next day, or they might never have been rescued — in either event the sacrifice would have been futile. Who is to judge of the necessity? How measure the comparative value of each life? How avoid tempting the strong to profit from such a rule? Matters of mitigation must not interfere with legal principle, specifically, with "the legal definition of the crime." If the law is too severe, the Sovereign may be merciful. The defendants were accordingly found guilty of murder and sentenced to death. But the Crown commuted the sentence to six months' imprisonment.

The facts in *Dudley and Stephens* were undoubtedly a great stimulus to repudiation of the doctrine of necessity. The harm was not perpetrated in such emotional stress as prevailed in *Holmes* or in fear of imminent drowning. It

---

food in case of famine was justified. The *Carolina* (art. 166) provided for justification in such cases, stipulating (1) the necessity must be so extreme as to threaten life, *e.g.* famine; (2) taking the property of another must be the only means available to obtain relief; (3) the doer, himself, or his family must be the persons endangered; (4) the situation must not have arisen through prodigality or other fault; (5) the person whose property is taken must not be in equal distress; (6) the taking must be with intent to restore or compensate and (7) actual restitution must be made as soon as possible. See Moriaud, *op. cit. supra* note 19, at 125-126. *Cf.* Aquinas, Summa, II-II, Q. 66, Art. 7. For a modern case exculpating taking bread by a famished woman, see Dalloz, Jurisprudence, 1899 II. 329, the *Note* by Josserand, *id.* at 329-331, and Garraud, Précis de Droit Criminel 313 (1934).

[76] Digest of the Criminal Law 25 n (1887).

[77] 2 H. Cr. L. 108 n (1883). But none of these critics proposed any alternative method except, presumably. that everyone must die unless self-sacrificing volunteers come forward.

was, instead, committed in calm determination, evidenced by the fact that the homicide was discussed several times, although, to be sure, in the firm conviction that death by starvation was not far off. In addition, there was the cannibalism which must have suggested that this was one of those cases where men ought to die rather than live by utterly repugnant means.[78] But however revolting facts may be, they do not invalidate the rationale of the doctrine of necessity—that it is better that some live than that all perish. They merely suggest certain esthetic limits as conditions of the application of the doctrine.

It is significant that in both cases the final sentence was six months' imprisonment, although Holmes actually served fourteen months. On a functional view of the penal law of both countries, one may therefore conclude that both in fact approved the doctrine of necessity. But the important difference is that whereas that doctrine is recognized in the substantive criminal law of the United States, English law is left in an unsatisfactory condition that is almost universally opposed.[79]

Yet the chief ground of the English decision was approved by no less a jurist than Cardozo. Emphasizing the crucial fact, he asked, "Who shall know when masts and sails of rescue may emerge out of the fog?"[80] This viewpoint, it will be recalled, was expressed in the unwillingness of the English bench to admit the necessity of the homicide, indicated by its remark that the men might have been picked up the

---

[78] Several other cases of cannibalism are cited by Moriaud, *op. cit. supra* note 19, at 9-11. *Cf.* Fuller, *The Case of the Speluncean Explorers*, 62 Harv. L. Rev. 616 (1949).

[79] For the anomalous effects of the decision on English criminal law, see Stallybrass in 14 J. Comp. Leg. & Int. L. 237 (1932); and *cf.* Davies, "Every student of the elements of the subject knows how unsatisfactory was the discussion of the matter in the leading case of *R. v. Dudley and Stephens.*" *Supra* note 50 at 135. But *cf.* Rex v. Bourne (1939), 1 K. B. 687, 693.

[80] Cardozo, Law and Literature 113 (1931). This view was also expressed by the contemporary *Philadelphia Public Ledger:* "They must consent to leave their fate together in the hands of events, and take what comes . . . while there is life, there is hope. . . ." Hicks, *op. cit. supra* note 56, at 113.

next day or might never have been rescued. It is therefore clear that neither the English court nor Cardozo considered the ethics of the doctrine of necessity. They rejected the doctrine because, in effect, they denied that a state of necessity could ever exist. Such repudiation of the doctrine of necessity amounts not to the invalidation of the principle to conserve the maximum value possible but to such a challenge of it on empirical grounds as to guarantee that it could never be applied. For factual knowledge neither is, nor can it ever attain, certainty. It has at best only a degree of probability. We can, therefore, never be certain that any emergency will not pass, that "masts and sails of rescue may [not] emerge out of the fog." In the lack of such certainty, it is wrong to sacrifice any life — so runs the Coleridge-Cardozo thesis.[81] Plainly, on this estimate, the doctrine of necessity becomes a mere speculation. Modern legal systems, however, do not require omniscience of human beings. The doctrine, on the contrary, is that a very high probability of complete destruction by physical forces is a justification for sacrifice of some to save some, provided the method of selection is fair. These judgments are embodied in the criminal law.[82]

Before appraising the policies underlying the doctrine of necessity, it is desirable to distinguish it from "self-defense," with which, as seen above, it is often confused.

To assert that a harm is privileged is to assert that it is not a legal harm. This implies that the individual whose interests were injured by another's exercise of his privilege had no right to protect them and, therefore, that any injury inflicted by such an individual is illegal. Failure to recognize these implications of legal privilege, together with a blurring of self-defense and state of necessity, confused Stephen's analysis of the latter. Thus, after commenting adversely on *Holmes*, he remarks: "Self-sacrifice may or may not be a

---

[81] See, also, Cahn, The Moral Decision 71 (1955).

[82] The legal issue is narrowed to complete exculpation or the imposition of some punishment that is slight as compared with that for usual homicide, as was actually done in the above cases.

moral duty, but it seems hard to make it a legal duty, and it is impossible to state its limits or the principle on which they can be determined. Suppose one of the party in the boat had a revolver and was able to use it . . . could anyone deny that he was acting in self-defence . . . and would he violate any legal duty in so doing?"[83] But if there is a duty to preserve the greatest possible value in situations where, due to the impact of physical forces, some value must be lost, then a guiding principle does exist. And, as regards the situation Stephen described, far from it being impossible to "deny that he was acting in self-defence," a correct statement of the legal import of such conduct is that not only was he not acting in self-defense (any more than does one who resists a legal arrest or self-defense, itself) but, also, that he was guilty of inflicting a proscribed harm. A wise exercise of discretion would, of course, suggest considerable mitigation of the penalty, but this does not alter the substantive law.

That the privilege of self-defense is closely related to the doctrine of necessity is apparent.[84] Sometimes, self-defense is indiscriminately treated as a form of action in teleological necessity in the sense that the defender's conduct is justified on the ground that the harm he inflicted was necessary to preserve his legally protected and thus, superior, interests. If "self-defense" is employed loosely to denote conduct stimulated by any danger, human or inanimate, to the instinct of self-preservation, this usage would include harms committed in states of necessity. Technically, the privilege of self-defense implies that there is a human assailant, one who is bound by a legal duty. In the exercise of the privilege of necessity, on the other hand, there was no violation of the actor's legal right. In self-defense, the defender injures the creator and embodiment of the evil situation; in necessity, he harms a person who was in no way responsible for the

[83] 2 H. Cr. L. 108-109 (1883).
[84] See Oliver v. State, 17 Ala. 587 (1850). Cf. "Self-defence naturally falleth under the Head of Homicide founded in Necessity. . . ." Foster, Of Homicide, in Trials of the Rebels of Scotland 273 (1762).

imminent danger, one who, indeed, might himself have been imperiled by it.[85]

COERCION

To elucidate the meaning of "coercion"[86] relevant to penal law, we need to note, first, that all human conduct is limited by the forces of physical and biological nature as well as by social conditions. Justifiable action taken in states of necessity is not regarded as coerced. Nor is bodily movement caused solely by physical forces (non-voluntary behavior) ordinarily opposed to free action.[87] Capacity to attain a desired objective under normal conditions is a major factor in the definition of freedom of action and, correspondingly, of coercion. However else we feel, we do not feel *unfree* because we are helpless in mid-ocean or because we cannot breathe under water. Nor are the limitations of the blind or lame, of children and sick persons regarded as coercive. The history of the struggle for freedom is concerned with oppression by human beings,[88] and it has given "freedom" a special significance which, as noted, excludes

[85] Some very nice problems arise in application of these distinctions. One of these is posed by an attack by an animal — beating it off is no more legally significant than is the control of an inanimate force. Hence such conduct is inaccurately termed self-defense. The animal's behavior cannot constitute a violation of a legal right. More complex is the case of protection against an attack by an insane person, which is sometimes treated as "self-defense." But since an insane person is not bound by duties of the penal law, it follows that he cannot violate any legal right conferred by that law. See *supra* chapter 7 at note 72. Accordingly the better solution is suggested by the fact that, although in attacks by animals or insane persons, the measures of protection are directed against the attacker, yet. in a truer sense they are directed against a natural force. *Cf.* Note, *Necessity as a Defense*, 21 Col. L. Rev. 71 (1921).

[86] See *supra* pp. 235-36.

[87] Whether we use the traditional terminology or, in the modern temper, reject "will" as a fictitious entity and think of "the organized self in function, the self in movement," (Hadfield, Psychology and Morals 93 (1936)), the central problem does not appear to be significantly altered. *Cf.* Ross, Foundations of Ethics 194 (1939).

[88] See, generally, Freedom, Its Meaning (Anshen ed. 1940). An excellent discussion is, Knight, *The Meaning of Freedom*, in The Philosophy of American Democracy 59 (1943). See Newman and Weitzer, *Duress, Free Will and the Criminal Law*, 30 So. Cal. L. Rev. 313 (1957).

both movement caused physically and action in states of necessity. This is the first step required to determine the meaning of "coercion" relevant to the legal doctrine. Coercion, in its special legal meaning, thus implies misconduct by human beings, *i.e.* limitations imposed by them on personal desires and capacities.

Even if the phenomena of coercion are viewed in this restricted sense, it is clear that they represent a great variety of controls, ranging from the threat of death, at one extreme, to those forms of duress and undue influence that are important in civil law, as intermediates, and extending at the opposite extreme to such influences as indifference, withholding of affection or praise, and relatively innocuous devices that also lie outside the legal orbit. Only the most serious form of coercion is relevant to criminal responsibility. "Duress" in civil transactions and "undue influence" in the law of wills include relatively subtle forces that operate by suggestion of which the victim is not aware. So, too, the forms of coercion that are disapproved in the law of industrial relations, monopoly, boycott and blacklisting, are relatively refined ones. Even in the criminal law, "coercion" is used much more extensively than the problem of responsibility requires, *e.g.* in connection with the admission of confessions. In Anglo - American law, the relevant meaning of "coercion" must be derived from a mere handful of cases.

The English cases on compulsion, with rare exception, concern treason and the coercion of a wife by her husband.[89] The law on the former is very uncertain, and the latter has become little more than a vestige of the medieval conception of marriage.[90] This almost *tabula rasa* as re-

---

[89] 2 Stephen, H. Cr. L. 106 (1883). In Att'y Gen. v. Whelan (1934), Ir. R. 518, a conviction for receiving stolen property was quashed because the act was committed under threat of death. The court noted Stephen's statement that he had never known of a case of compulsion, and that counsel had not been able to find any reported case in later years. The case was decided "from the standpoint of general principle." *Id.* at 525-6.

[90] In the literature, "coercion" has been limited to the marital relationship and "compulsion" has been employed in all other situa-

gards coercion is a curious phenomenon in English penal law, and the mystery is only heightened when it is recalled that in a murder case, tried over a century ago, where the defense was fear of violence, Justice Denman remarked to the jury: "You probably, gentlemen, never saw two men tried at a criminal bar for an offence which they had jointly committed, where one of them had not been to a certain extent in fear of the other . . . yet that circumstance has never been received by the law as an excuse for his crime . . . ." He instructed them that "the law is; that no man, from a fear of consequences to himself, has a right to make himself a party to committing mischief on mankind"[91] — a proposition which must be understood in relation to the facts in that case (murder).[92] In the treason cases[93] it was held that joining or aiding the rebels was excusable only on a well-grounded fear of death and if escape were effected as soon as possible. Unfortunately for legal doctrine, the cases of the regicides were so influenced by political expediency that very little aid can be derived from them that is relevant to the instant problem.[94] The general rule in this country

---

tions. They are here used interchangeably.

For discussions of the coercion of a married woman, see Burdick, *op. cit. supra* note 14, and Note: *The Doctrine of Martial Coercion*, 29 Temple L. Q. 190 (1956). The presumption was abolished in England by § 47 of the Criminal Justice Act, 1925 (15 & 16 Geo. V, ch. 86). See, also, Note, 71 A. L. R. 1116 (1931).

[91] Reg. v. Tyler and Price (1838), 8 C. & P. 616, 620.

[92] There was no reference to R. v. Crutchley (1831), 5 C. & P. 133, where, on an indictment for destroying a thrashing machine as a member of a mob, evidence was admitted to prove that the defendant was compelled by the mob to participate in the damage, and he was acquitted.

[93] The chief English decisions are Oldcastle's Case (1419), 1 Hale, P. C. 50; 1 East P. C. 70; Cook's Case (1660), 5 How. St. Tr. 1077; Axtel's Case (1660), 5 How. St. Tr. 1146; Vane's Case (1662), 6 How. St. Tr. 120; Rex v. McGrowther (1746), 18 How. St. Tr. 394; R. v. Stratton (1780), 21 How. St. Tr. 1045. But *cf.* Rex v. Steane (1947), K. B. 997, 1 All E. R. 813.

[94] The American cases on treason apply the same rules noted above concerning compulsion. Res. v. M'Carty, 2 Dallas 86 (U. S. 1781); United States v. Vigol, 2 Dallas 346 (U. S. 1795); United States v. Greiner, 4 Phila. 396 (1861). D'Aquino v. United States, 192 F. 2d 338 (9th Cir. 1951). There are many court martial cases, *e.g.* United States v. Olson, No. 8210, 7 U.S.C.M.A. 460, 22 C.M.R. 250 (1957).

is that a well-founded fear of immediate death or, occasionally, of serious injury is a defense to any criminal charge except murder.[95]

The rule that coercion is not a defense to a charge of murder would seem to call for summary disposition of such cases. In fact, the courts have usually placed their decisions on other grounds, as well. Thus a boy who committed a homicide at his father's order was not permitted to show that he was completely under the parent's control, that he never doubted him in the slightest degree, and that as a result of harsh discipline, he greatly feared him. The conviction was upheld on the grounds that the above facts would not establish "reasonable apprehension of imminent death," the crime was murder, and the defendant's plea did not constitute a claim of insanity.[96] In *Arp*, a leading case,[97] the court rested its affirmance of the conviction of murder on the ground that the defendant had an opportunity to escape from those who were threatening him, and that it was his culpable failure to do that which subjected him, later, to the compulsion under which he committed the offense. In a case where the defendant had held the deceased's hands while his accomplice killed the latter with an axe, the trial judge refused to instruct the jury that if the defendant aided the killing in fear of instant death by the accomplice, armed with the axe, he was guilty only of manslaughter.[98] The court affirmed the conviction of murder, holding that the requested instruction took "no account of opportunity to escape; to successfully defend himself; the reasonableness of the fear; or other matters which may properly be taken

[95] Note, 40 A. L. R. 2d 908 (1955); Hersey and Avins, *Compulsion as a Defense to Criminal Prosecution*, 11 Okl. L. Rev. 283 (1958). Texas and Georgia apparently include murder within the rule. Paris v. State, 35 Tex. Cr. R. 82, 31 S. W. 855 (1895). Jones v. State, 207 Ga. 379, 62 S. E. 2d 187 (1950) based on Ga. Code § 26-402. See note 26 *infra* regarding Canada.

[96] Rainey v. Commonwealth, 101 Ky. 257, 40 S. W. 682 (1897). *Cf.* People v. Martin, 13 Cal. App. 96, 108 P. 1034 (1910).

[97] Arp v. State, 97 Ala. 5, 12 S. 301 (1895).

[98] State v. Nargashian, 26 R. I. 299, 301, 58 A. 953 (1904).

into account." It rejected the analogy of reduction to manslaughter under legal provocation.

Even opinions which emphatically avow the rule excepting murder stress some other element in the situation to support the conviction. Thus, while emphasizing the rule, a Michigan court also stressed the fact that the threat of death was made three days prior to the murder.[99] In another decision affirming a conviction of murder, the court rejected the defense partly because there was only the defendant's confession to support the alleged compulsion[1] and, partly, because the court believed that the defendant, armed with a gun, could have turned the weapon on his assailant instead of killing an innocent person. Hence even if the defendant's testimony were true, he had a chance to escape; death was not imminent, with only the alternative of the ordered killing.[2] Not a single case of conviction for murder has been found where the decision rests squarely on facts signifying a plain choice between self-sacrifice and the killing of an innocent person, with a ruling that the former is required by law, even though in some of the cases there was reasonable fear of imminent death. Why have the courts not been content to rest their decisions on the exception of murder from the scope of the doctrine of compulsion? It might be thought that they shared the opinion of the Alabama Court in *Arp*, noted above, that a reasonable fear of imminent death should be a defense to murder as well as all other crimes. But they affirmed the convictions. Thus the judges seem to support the exception but they also indicate that the doctrine is not actually relevant.

---

[99] People v. Repke, 103 Mich. 459, 61 N. W. 861 (1895) ; so too, in State v. Moretti, 66 Wash. 537, 120 P. 102 (1912).

[1] In People v. Petro, 13 Cal. App. 2d 245, 56 P. 2d 984 (1936) the court, relying on Section 26 of the California Penal Code, rested its affirmance of the conviction on the enactment of the exception as to murder. But, again, the court found: "The evidence does not support this contention" of fear of his life induced by threats of his accomplice. *Ibid.*

[2] Brewer v. State, 72 Ark. 45, 78 S. W. 773 (1904). In Leach v. State, 99 Tenn. 584, 42 S. W. 195 (1897), the defendant testified that he was coerced by two armed men in his immediate presence. In such circumstances, resistance would probably have been fatal to him.

It is even more significant that in cases other than murder, insistence on "reasonable fear of imminent death" renders compulsion a defense of highly dubious value there, also, despite the expectations raised by opinions rendered in the homicide cases. On a charge of bigamy, *e.g.* it was shown that a Texas mob, intent on enforcement of its mores, demanded that the defendant marry a young girl with whom he was suspected of improper intimacy. Because this occurred the night preceding the marriage, the court held that no instruction on compulsion was required — there was no "immediate personal constraint" at the time of the marriage.[3] On this ground, also, the defense was disallowed in a robbery case where the defendant occupied and drove the escape car, and his accomplice had said, before going into the gasoline service station to commit the robbery, "Don't you dare go and leave me." The court decided that the defendant could have driven away, hence there was "no present and immediate" danger at the time the robbery was committed.[4] A serious beating subsequent to the commission of a crime clearly falls outside the required "present, active and imminent peril."[5] A woman charged with arson sought to introduce evidence to prove "that she was weak in will power, easily persuaded, timid, and shy," and also that a short time prior to the act, she was threatened with death. The conviction was affirmed — the coercion was not "instant and imminent," and the mental condition, not amounting to insanity, was irrelevant.[6] Still less considered were the command of a police official to an officer who took merchandise from a store he was assigned to guard[7] and an order by a superior to shield the keeper of a bawdy house from arrest.[8] In this type of case, the coercion is economic — at most, a threat of dismissal from employment — and this, of

[3] Burton v. State, 51 Tex. Cr. R. 196, 101 S. W. 226 (1907).

[4] People v. Villegas, 29 Cal. App. 2d 658, 85 P. 2d 480 (1938).

[5] People v. Sanders, 81 Cal. App. 778, 256 P. 251 (1927).

[6] Ross v. State, 169 Ind. 388, 82 N. E. 781 (1907).

[7] Hall v. State, 144 Fla. 333, 198 S. 60 (1940).

[8] State v. Ash, 33 Ore. 373, 54 P. 184 (1898).

course, falls far short of the extreme threat that is required. So, too, where the defendant embezzled a large sum of money through fear of a threatened exposure of his former embezzlement, the plea of coercion was dismissed as neither a threat of death nor serious injury.[9] In charges of perjury, the courts have obvious, if not always realistic, grounds for holding that there could be no reasonable fear of imminent death at the time of testifying, since the defendant was in the midst of officers of the law, ready and able to protect him.[10]

In *Nall*, the defendant, eighteen years old, was convicted of breaking and entering a storehouse with intent to steal.[11] He testified that he was compelled to do this by a woman who kept a pistol pointed at him up to the time he broke into the building. She had called for him in her automobile earlier in the evening and, while driving, told him what she wanted. She drew a pistol and threatened to kill him then, and she repeated this at the place of the burglary. It was held that the trial judge erred in refusing to instruct on the question of coercion, even though the defense might be "a mere sham or subterfuge."[12] There is also some sup-

---

[9] State v. Patterson, 117 Ore. 153, 241 P. 977 (1925).

[10] Bain v. State, 67 Miss. 557, 7 S. 408 (1890); but *cf.* Hall v. State, 136 Fla. 644, 187 S. 392, 409 (1939).

[11] Nall v. Commonwealth, 208 Ky. 700, 271 S. W. 1059 (1925).

[12] *Cf.* Paris v. State, 35 Tex. Cr. R. 82, 31 S. W. 855 (1895) and People v. Pantano, 239 N. Y. 416, 146 N. E. 646 (1925), State v. St. Clair, 262 S. W. 2d 25 (Mo. 1953) and White v. State, 150 Tex. Cr. R. 546, 203 S. W. 2d 223 (1947). An exceptional decision was rendered in a prosecution for selling pooled tobacco in violation of a statute. Commonwealth v. Reffitt, 149 Ky. 300, 148 S. W. 48 (1912). In the tobacco-growing belt, an organization of planters, known as the Society of Equity, had been perpetrating numerous acts of violence on persons who did not collaborate in their program. The court took cognizance of the fact that the civil authorities, even when aided by the military, were "wholly unable to preserve the peace and prevent acts of violence and lawlessness and the destruction of property. . . ." *Id.* at 301. The defendant, a tenant farmer, pooled his tobacco, as "requested" by the Society, and in violation of the statute. He was acquitted of the charge, and the State appealed, complaining especially of an instruction which defined "duress" as "a just fear of great injury, to person, reputation, or property. . . ." *Id.* at 304. The Appellate Court followed the trial judge in defining "duress" very broadly.

port for the view that fear for the safety of members of the family may support a defense of coercion.[13]

In sum, the fear must be of death or of "serious bodily injury." The fear must be a reasonable one; as Judge Washington put it in an early decision, it must be "such a fear as a man of ordinary fortitude and courage might justly yield to."[14] It must be imminent; and, as seen, since this excludes even situations where an attempt to escape would involve considerable risk of death, it too must function in great restriction of the privilege, although, on the basis of *Nall*, noted above, there is some ground for believing that in crimes other than murder such hazardous escape is not required. Finally, it should be noted that coercion is an affirmative defense, and the defendant has the burden of proving it by a preponderance of the evidence.[15]

Thus we must conclude that when the formally broad defense of coercion is examined in the context of actual ad-

[13] Rex v. Steane, *supra* note 93, a treason case; and Recreation Center, Inc. v. Aetna Casualty and Surety Co., 177 F. 2d 603 (1st Cir. 1949), a suit on an insurance policy covering a theft.

[14] United States v. Haskell, 26 Fed. Cas. No. 15,207 at 210 (E. D. Pa. 1823). See Hall v. State, 136 Fla. 644, 187 S. 392 (1939). Where the issue concerns the testimony of an alleged accomplice the rule is that if he acted under compulsion, the witness was not guilty of participating in the offense, hence he was not an accomplice, and his testimony is admissible for the prosecution. People v. Hart, 98 Cal. App. 2d 514, 220 P. 2d 595 (1950). But "compulsion" is here interpreted to require less than "reasonable fear of imminent death." Fear of "serious bodily injury" is stressed here. Beal v. State, 72 Ga. 200 (1883); Robinson v. State, 141 Tex. Cr. R. 380, 148 S. W. 2d 1118 (1941). A much more extensive meaning of coercion was given in the prosecution of an officer, in charge of a reformatory, for sodomy with three inmates. The evidence was that the boys were unwilling participants, that they were coerced by the defendant's position in the institution, and by his having said: "If you don't, I am going to make it hard for you; . . . I will slap you down every time I see you." Perryman v. State, 63 Ga. App. 819, 820, 12 S.E. 2d 389 (1940). This was obviously far from circumstances constituting "reasonable fear of imminent death" or even of "serious bodily injury," but a conviction was affirmed. The boys were held not to be accomplices and their testimony was therefore admitted for the State—the supporting citations being cases involving sex offenses or interpretations of coercion in civil suits, *e.g.* to invalidate a will, contract or sale.

[15] State v. Sappienza, 84 Oh. 63, 95 N.E. 381 (1911); *cf.* Hitchler, *Duress as a Defence in Criminal Cases*, 4 Va. L. Rev. 544 (1917).

ministration of the law, it all but disappears.[16] It has met a judicial hostility which has drastically reduced its potential effectiveness. It is not unlikely that, in part, this has resulted from the difficulty of assessing degrees of participation in joint criminal conduct, of influence and control, of passivity, suggestibility, and so on, indicating that these questions should be left mostly to judicial discretion in determining the sentence. But the paramount reason for drastic restriction of this defense is the reliance upon policies which have influenced the law on necessity and compulsion differently.

POLICY AND PUNISHMENT

In the extensive literature on the major policies relevant to necessity and coercion, various theories have been expressed in terms of Natural Law, moral coercion, inutility of penal law, and objective value. In Grotius and other Natural Law writers, "the compact" is presumed to exclude harms committed in states of necessity from the scope of positive law.[17] A version of this thesis is that positive law obtains only with regard to the coexistence of individuals; hence, it is irrelevant to situations where that is impossible. Again, it has been argued that since God implanted the instinct of self-preservation in man, it is right to act in conformity to it; or, as Pufendorf stated, the instinct is irresistible, which implies that behavior stimulated by the instinct of self-preservation is an instance of physical causation. In this regard, Pufendorf's position was substantially that espoused by the later positivists: A man cannot act in opposition to his instinct of self-preservation — hence appraisal is irrelevant.[18] These Natural Law interpretations merged with and gave way to the "free will"

---

[16] Cf. id. at 535. The defense is similarly rare in French jurisprudence. See Garraud, op. cit. supra note 75, at 313, and Baudry, op. cit. supra note 43, at 99-100.

[17] Grotius, Rights of War and Peace, bk. II, ch. 2, VI, 193 (Oxford ed. 1925).

[18] See generally, 2 Pufendorf, De Jure Naturae et Bentium, bk. II, ch. VI (Oxford ed. 1934). Cf. " . . . man cannot help avoiding and repelling whatever tends to his destruction." Id. at 296.

theory. Especially in the nineteenth century, Continental writers emphasized the thesis that a person acting under extreme necessity or compulsion was under "moral constraint." They also argued that positive law should fit the quality of average human nature, not heroism or martyrdom.[19]

While there is merit in some of the above arguments, they are not the ultimate factors in the positions they reflect. We come to closer grips with these elements in the theory of the inutility of punishment for action under extreme necessity or compulsion. Thus, it is asked, how can the fear of future legal punishment equal that of imminent death? As Hobbes put it: ". . . a man would reason thus, *If I doe it not, I die presently; if I doe it, I die afterwards; therefore by doing it, there is time of life gained;* Nature therefore compels him to the fact."[20] That this argument has been very persuasive may be inferred from its adoption by Kant—although he did distinguish the ethical condemnation of the harm-doer from his exculpation from punishment, approving only the latter.[21] The theory reached its culmination in Feuerbach whose principles of penal law were based on intimidation, deterrence by psychological constraint. It has been endorsed by distinguished writers on the common law.[22] The proponents of that theory could hardly be expected to distinguish between necessity and coercion. They rely on "the facts."

The chief "fact" commonly held by many of the proponents of the above theories is that action under extreme necessity or compulsion is uniformly selfish. But it certainly has not been, and probably cannot be, established that the drive of self-preservation is irresistible, that con-

---

[19] Filangieri, discussed in Marchand, De L'État de Nécessité en Droit Pénal 72-75 (1902).

[20] Leviathan pt. 2, ch. 27, at 157 (1651).

[21] Kant, Philosophy of Law 53 (Hastie ed. 1887).

[22] 1 Bentham, Works 397 (Bowring ed. 1843); Austin, Jurisprudence 515 (4th ed. 1879); Holmes, The Common Law at 47 (1881); Kenny, Outlines of Criminal Law 88 (15th ed. 1936); Salmond, Jurisprudence 406 (7th ed. 1924).

duct in such situations is inexorably fixed for all human beings. On the contrary, the complex processes of evaluation and control that enter into the choice made and the conduct pursued render such explanations over-simple and highly dubious. All human acts are "mixed" in the sense that they are more or less conditioned by forces beyond control. But this does not mean that there is no control of action in states of necessity or coercion, or that the degree of control is not "sufficient" to warrant relevant evaluation and legal liability.

That the above view of human nature is rejected in the principles of criminal law is clear, nowhere more so than in the rules dealing with voluntary manslaughter. Thus killing in a passionate fight or in sight of adultery is nowhere regarded as a mechanical, uniform reaction. It need not have been committed and, accordingly, mitigation, not exculpation, is the proper consequence. In many ordinary matters, it is a common experience to act against a very strong desire and to do so by a deliberate decision which, once taken, becomes integrated in a network of sentiments and ideals, reducing the formerly powerful desire to a relatively minor impulse. When the decision is translated into action, there is frequently an especially sharp realization that one is acting against his desires.[23]

In the light of such facts and experiences how much less persuasive is the dogma that men will always choose to live even though they must kill unoffending persons to preserve themselves! It is sufficient for the present argument to assume that the question of fact is debatable. What policy does a wise course then suggest? Surely it is to proceed on the hypothesis that a substantial percentage of persons

[23] See Ewing, *Can We Act Against Our Strongest Desire?*, 44 Monist 126 (1934).

Tragedies, such as those in the Boston night club (Commonwealth v. Welansky, 55 N. E. 2d 902 (Mass. 1944) *supra* and the circus fire in Hartford, where many deaths occurred and most of them were caused by panic-stricken patrons seeking to escape, were not followed by prosecution of the patrons. Their behavior was apparently regarded as entirely instinctive, *i.e.* as instances of physical causation.

in such situations will act against their instinctual desires, that human nature is sufficiently undetermined in this regard to warrant the adoption of legal policy accordingly.

There are valid grounds in support of the above noted differences between the doctrines of necessity and coercion. In the former the pressure which influences the action is physical nature, while in coercion it is the immoral and illegal conduct of a human being that creates the problem. Certain major consequences result. In coercion, the situation may be completely transformed in a split second by the malefactor's change of mind, and he is morally obligated to do that. There can hardly ever be any such very high probability that he will not change his mind as that no relief will come to alter imminent destructive physical forces. From the viewpoint of the coerced, there are usually far greater chances of removing the evil human coercion — by positive action or by flight; certainly the cases show that the courts take this view. Even if the execution of the coercer's threat were just as probable as the continuing impact of destructive, physical phenomena, there would frequently be a duty to resist the evil-doer — and that is the meaning of the policy which excludes murder and other serious crimes, as in Canada, from the scope of the rule.[24] In necessity, man bows to the inevitable; but in coercion there is no such inevitability.[25] Stephen would make no compromise whatever in this situation, and the law of Canada[26] limits coercion

[24] Cf. 3 Jeremy Taylor, Works 397 (1853).

[25] But there may be situations where the values involved are so unequal as to alter the above judgment—e.g. the lives of many persons may be lost if the command to kill one is disobeyed. Few would now uphold an absolutist position in such cases; and this suggests a modification of the rule excluding homicide from the scope of the defense. The point emphasized in the text is that the immorality of the coercion should be considered together with the other values involved. The text generalizes in terms of approaches to the solution of typical problems; where evaluation is very difficult or the opinions of thoughtful persons differ, the criminal law may well exclude liability. The major function of the criminal law, to implement morality, must be tempered by feasibility. This does not mean, however, that criminal law should enforce only "a minimum of morality," but rather that it should enforce as much of morality as is feasible.

[26] Sec. 20 of the Canadian Penal Code excludes from the scope of the

much more rigorously than does ours — unless one remembers the restrictions actually imposed in the decisions and discounts the formal rules accordingly. It would seem that sound policy might reflect a consensus at least at the extremes — that coercion should not exculpate in the most serious crimes but that it should be a defense where, *e.g.* it is a question of imminent death or the commission of a relatively minor harm. With regard to American law it follows that rape, kidnapping, treason, and very serious mayhem— perhaps all crimes punishable by death, life imprisonment or very long terms of imprisonment—should be added to murder and placed beyond the privilege of harm-doing under coercion.

The above noted ethical differences underlying the doctrines of necessity and coercion must be interpreted by reference to the principles of criminal law, previously discussed.[27] These differences concern causation, *e.g.* the motivation by the coercer, conduct, especially its volitional component, justification and excuse, and the respective relations of necessity and coercion to these notions, particularly to the relevant principles. The ethical differences emphasized in the present chapter are important determinants of relevant penal policy. But when the doctrines of necessity and coercion are placed in the wider context of the relevant principles, their basic similarities are also revealed.[28]

---

defense of coercion: murder, attempt to murder, piracy, assisting in rape, robbery, forcible abduction, arson, and serious battery.

[27] *Supra* especially chapters 3 and 7.

[28] *Supra* pp. 235-36.

CHAPTER XIII

MENTAL DISEASE

IF the defendant was insane at the time of the conduct in issue, the requisite *mens rea* was lacking and no crime was committed. Punishment presupposes normal competence and the relevant causing (authorship) of a proscribed harm; hence there can be no question of responsibility or punishment of insane persons. A psychotic harm-doer should, instead, be placed in a hospital.

The problem of mental disease and criminal responsibility has, therefore, the appearance of utter simplicity. It is merely a matter of finding out which harm-doers had a serious mental disease at the legally relevant time, and the experts in that kind of disease are psychiatrists. Accordingly, Judge, then Solicitor General, Soboloff suggested what seemed to be a rather obvious solution, noting that "We do not insist on a legal formula in diagnosing other diseases; why in this instance? It is a question of fact. . . ."[1] And the Circuit Court of Appeals of the District of Columbia said, "Mental 'disease' means mental illness . . . like physical illnesses, [they] are the subject matter of medical science."[2]

It happens, however, that a very large number, perhaps half, of the practicing psychiatrists in this country are not doctors of medicine; and this raises a doubt about the

---

[1] Soboloff, *Insanity and the Criminal Law: From McNaghten to Durham and Beyond*, 41 A. B. A. J. 793, 795 (1955). *Cf.* Hall, *Responsibility and Law: In Defense of the McNaghten Rules*, 42 A. B. A. J. 917 (1956).

[2] Carter v. United States, 252 F. 2d 608, 617 (C. A. D. C. 1957).

validity of the above solution. In fact, the difficulties run much deeper than that. They inhere in the vagueness of "disease" and in the assumption that mental disease is like physical disease.

A disease is said to be an abnormal condition, and if one therefore seeks the meaning of "normal," *i.e.* the condition or standard by reference to which "disease" must be defined, one encounters the greatest diversity imaginable. Even in biology, where it might be thought that "health" referred to a definite standard, that conception of "normality" is a moot issue. Not only is there an enormous range in the relevant standards of different societies, but differences in vocation, social status and cultural factors also qualify the meaning of "physical health." This is further complicated by the divergence between "normality" as a standard and statistical "normality," referring to what is usual.[3] The uncertainty of "disease" in biology is, however, restricted by the minimal norm of the functions required to survive.

But what is the norm by reference to which "mental disease" is to be determined? The criminal law answers this question in terms of ordinary rationality, especially as regards the valuation of serious personal harms. On the other hand, many psychiatrists believe that in their work they "cannot safely operate with ambiguous words and concepts, such as health and disease now are."[4]

The only point of relatively substantial agreement seems to be that it is possible and easy to recognize a mental disease which is a very great deviation from the ordinary standard of mental health in a particular culture. This

---

[3] Wegrocki, *A Critique of Cultural and Statistical Concepts of Abnormality*, 34 J. of Abnor. & Soc. Psych. 166 (1939).

[4] Lewis, *Health as a Social Concept*, 4 Brit. J. Sociol. 109 (1953). *Cf.* "The opinions of medical witnesses vary greatly as to what is meant by '*mental illness*'. Some would extend it to neurosis and some to psychopathic condition without psychosis, which would make for elaborate forensic debate beyond the comprehension of a lay jury." Rep't of the Royal Comm'n on the Law of Insanity as a Defence in Criminal Cases (Canada, 1956).

implies that any intelligent person, given the facts, can recognize seriously disordered persons — the conclusion reached by a leading psychiatrist after careful study of the question. "I think," he said, "we [psychiatrists] know what the seriously ill person in a given culture is. That we do know. In this respect we agree, incidentally, with policemen, with the clerk in the drug store. Our crude diagnostic criteria are reasonably similar."[5] He finds that there are only "operational criteria" to guide psychiatrists in this regard, especially that seriously disordered persons create difficult social situations. There is an "urgency" to have them treated: "society responds to this by legalizing removal of the seriously ill."[6] Thus, it is ordinary social judgment which determines who is psychotic, not any "medical science" that is even remotely like the knowledge used to determine that a person has tuberculosis or malaria.[7]

This, however, does not prevent psychiatrists from having their individual, very definite ideas about "mental disease." Exactly what a psychiatrist has in mind when he uses that term in other than the above noted common meaning is one

[5] Redlich, in Interrelations Between the Social Environment and Psychiatric Disorders 120 (Milbank Mem. Fund, 1953). See also, Redlich, *The Concept of Normality*, 6 Am. J. Psychotherapy 551 (1952).

[6] Redlich, *id.* at 121.

[7] "The analogy between medicine and psychiatry is dangerously misleading." Szasz, *Psychiatry, Ethics, and the Criminal Law*, 58 Col. L. Rev. 187 (1958). ". . . the notions of 'normal,' 'abnormal,' 'symptom,' 'disease' and the like are social conventions." Szasz, *A Contribution to the Philosophy of Medicine*, 97 A. M. A. Arch. Int. Med. 5 (1956).

"But outside of this inner core, there is a vast fringe area of conditions which may, or may not, be considered to be diseases of the mind. Are psychopathies, psychoneuroses (like kleptomania) or perversions (like exhibitionism) diseases of the mind? The definition of the term becomes arbitrary, and the above questions will be answered differently by different psychiatrists. Whether or not a psychiatrist is willing to classify any one of these conditions as disease of the mind depends more on his philosophy than on any factual question that can be settled by observation and reasoning." Waelder, *Psychiatry and the Problem of Criminal Responsibility*, 101 U. of Pa. L. Rev. 384 (1952).

"[I]f psychiatry seems not a little vague about what mental health and disease are, scientific medicine does not actually fare much better." Zilboorg, *The Struggle For and Against the Individual in Psychotherapy*, 104 Am. J. Psychiatry 524 (1948).

of the most difficult questions to answer. Some of them, *e.g.*
say that all criminals are mentally diseased, while others say
that only a small percent of criminals are mentally diseased.[8]
An eminent psychiatrist has even suggested that normality
is a mental disease,[9] which, at least to an uninitiated reader,
renders everything on the subject *boule versé.* Thus, too,
the psychiatrists on the staff of an excellent hospital, having
previously agreed that psychopathy (sociopathy) was not a
mental disease, changed their position and they now hold,
and will testify, that it is a mental disease.[10] The least effect
of this uncertainty of expert views of "mental disease" is to
dissolve the plain path leading to the apparently simple solution of an easy problem. Instead, we are plunged into the
extremely complicated task of trying to establish the conditions of intelligible inter-communication among lawyers and
psychiatrists.

In the course of pursuing that objective, one learns that
much more than the vagueness of "mental disease" is involved. One learns, *e.g.* that approaches to the entire
problem of crime and punishment differ vastly among psychiatrists and that there are many psychiatries, some of
which are compatible with legal principles while others are
diametrically opposed to them. This is the inevitable result
of the fact that theories of mental disease are not restricted
by psychiatrists to the cases recognizable by laymen, but

---

[8] ". . . criminals differ from mentally ill people only in the manner
we choose to deal with them." Roche, The Criminal Mind 29 (1958).
See also, Banay, We Call Them Criminals 6 (1957); Menninger,
Medicolegal Proposals of the American Psychiatric Association, 19
J. Cr. L. & Criminol. 373 (1928); Karpman, The Sexual Offender and
His Offenses 218 (1954).
Cf. "It is well to keep in mind that the majority of criminals are
neither neurotic nor psychotic." Schilder, Psychoanalysis, Man, and
Society 237 (1951). See also, *id.* at 236, 242. Guttmacher holds a simi-
lar view in *The Psychiatric Approach to Crime and Correction,* 23
L. & Contemp. Prob. 635-36 (1958). "Only one and a half to two per-
cent of criminals are definitely psychotic." *Id.* at 640.

[9] ". . . normality may be a form of madness which goes unrecognized because it happens to be a good adaptation to reality." Glover,
Medico-psychological Aspects of Normality, 23 Brit. J. Psychol. 165
(1932).

[10] See notes 7 *supra* and 13 *infra.*

are expanded by some of them to include almost every imaginable mental condition expressed in any "deviation." This, of course, involves the law of criminal responsibility and the entire structure of morality upon which that depends.

There is also a very insidious aspect of this expansion of "disease," resulting from the fact that persons who are found to have a "mental disease" on the basis of a psychiatrist's opinion can be incarcerated indefinitely. What this may mean has already been seen in the operation of "sexual psychopath" laws in states where no conviction is required to incarcerate.[11] Thus, on the one hand, the expansion of "mental disease" is made the basis of avoidance of criminal responsibility; while, on the other hand, a "mentally diseased" person may not only have his property taken from him, he may also be locked up indefinitely in a place called a "hospital" which, in fact, is sometimes a place of terror, more punitive than any penitentiary.[12] This impelled a thoughtful student of the problem to suggest that ". . . any state of mind which our masters choose to call 'disease' can be treated as crime, and compulsorily cured."[13] It is, there-

---

[11] See Ludwig, *Control of the Sex Criminal*, 25 St. John's L. Rev. 203, 212-13 (1951); Sutherland, *The Sexual Psychopath Laws*, 40 J. Crim. L., C. & P. S. 543 (1950).

It should be added that although the number of persons incarcerated under these statutes is relatively small, very serious abuse of fundamental rights is prevalent. See Mihm, *A Re-examination of the Validity of Our Sex Psychopath Statutes in the Light of Recent Appeal Cases and Experience*, 44 J. Crim. L., C. & P. S. 716 (1954).

[12] In Miller v. Overholser, 206 F. 2d 415 (C. A. D. C. 1952), habeas corpus proceedings were brought to secure the petitioner's release, as a sexual psychopath, from St. Elizabeth's Hospital in Washington. The petitioner alleged that he was confined with the criminally insane, many of them "wild and violent insane persons;" that he had been assaulted by mentally deranged persons, etc. "He described noisome, unnatural and violent acts by inmates. . . ." *Id.* at 418.

See note 44 *infra*.

[13] Lewis, *The Humanitarian Theory of Punishment*, 6 Res Judicatae 229 (1953). *Cf.* ". . . until a few weeks ago, members of the medical staff of an outstanding mental hospital were in the habit of testifying that a psychopathic or sociopathic personality did not constitute a mental disease. Recently, however, a formal announcement was made by the acting head of that institution that thereafter members of the staff would express the opinion that such a mental state is in fact a

fore, hardly self-evident that the grant of unfettered authority to psychiatrists to control the lives of human beings is more humane than control limited by the rule of law.[14]

At the same time, in the writer's opinion, psychiatry has much to offer in the improvement of criminal law and its administration. The problem is to establish the basis on which a sound psychiatry, law, and legal science can co-operate. That this is not insuperable should be apparent if the question is viewed as essentially a problem of inter-disciplinary knowledge.[15] The principal barrier to such progress in forensic psychology is lack of understanding of the grounds on which psychiatry and law can meet. It is the purpose of this chapter to explore these grounds and then to re-examine the central questions concerning the law of criminal responsibility in the context of relevant psychiatric theories.

---

mental disease. In other words, the concept was changed overnight by the psychiatrists themselves." Holtzoff, J., *In re* Rosenfield, 157 F. Supp. 18, 21 (1957). "The definition of the term 'psychopathic personality' changes from author to author." Schilder, *op. cit. supra* note 8, at 238.

In Briscoe v. United States, 248 F. 2d 640, at 644 note 6 (C. A. D. C. 1957) the Assistant Superintendent of St. Elizabeth's Hospital is reported as having said that "the hospital staff agreed that socio-pathic or psychopathic personality (which may include pyromania . . .) should not be regarded as 'mental disease' within the meaning of the new rule."

[14] After describing the sympathetic attitude of doctors towards suffering and unfortunate people, the late Dr. G. Zilboorg said, "Imagine a lawyer learning to see and feel everything his clients, or the defendants who will appear before him, will see and feel . . . the lawyer . . . is taught emotionally, sociologically. and profession-ally to be estranged from the people. . . ." Zilboorg, The Psychology of the Criminal Act and Punishment 40, 41 (1954). *Cf.* notes 28 and 72 *infra*.

Cf. An English psychiatrist, describing his efforts in the past century to improve the extremely wretched condition of asylums for mental patients and his struggle to achieve that very worthy goal, states: ". . . I had the whole medical world against me . . . At length Mr. Sergeant Adams came to the rescue as my advocate, and by his powerful aid . . . the system [reform] was no longer a dream but a success." Hill, Lunacy 43, 44 (1870).

[15] *E.g.* Berle & Means, The Modern Corporation and Private Property (1932); Llewellyn & Hoebel, The Cheyenne Way (1941); Moore & Callahan, Law and Learning Theory (1943); Hall, Theft, Law and Society (2nd ed. 1952).

THE UNDERLYING ISSUES
The Conflict of Perspectives

The most important fact in the current polemics regarding psychiatry and criminal responsibility is the clash of elementary philosophical perspectives. Every science rests upon distinctive axioms or postulates that are accepted by the scientists as "given," while philosophers remain curious about them. Without describing the postulates of current psychiatry, we can perceive the general perspective that it, especially psychoanalysis, draws from them. It purports to be rigorously scientific and therefore takes a determinist position. Its view of human nature is expressed in terms of drives and dispositions which, like mechanical forces, operate in accordance with universal laws of causation.[16]

On the other hand, criminal law, while it is also a science in a wide sense of the term, is not a theoretical science whose sole concern is to understand and describe what goes on. It is, instead, a practical, normative science which, while it draws upon the empirical sciences, is also concerned to pass judgment on human conduct, entailing serious consequences for both individuals and the community. Its view of human nature asserts the reality of a "significant" degree of free choice, and that is incompatible with the thesis that the conduct of normal adults is merely a manifestation of imperious psychological necessity. Given the scientific purpose to understand conduct, determinism is a necessary, although by no means the only helpful, postulate. Given the additional purpose to evaluate conduct, some degree of autonomy is a necessary postulate.

Accordingly, there is no more validity in a scientific psychiatrist's criticism of the ethical perspective of the criminal law than there would be in a lawyer's criticism of the determinist perspective of theoretical science. It is not implied that psychiatrists have no business criticizing law; on the contrary, they have important contributions to offer. But

---

[16] It will be suggested below that the determinist perspective in psychiatry is supplemented by the problem-solving viewpoint, especially in therapy. See text at notes 51, 52 and 56 *infra*.

whatever contribution they can and should make to criminal law will not result from the substitution of the perspective of empirical science for that of a normative one.

Unfortunately, this has often not been recognized. For example, a prominent psychiatrist denies the responsibility of any criminal since every crime is a "pathological phenomenon."[17] In explaining this position, it was said: " 'The phenomena of the will like other natural phenomena are subject to natural laws and are determined by antecedents; . . . responsibility, therefore, . . . does not exist scientifically in any case, sane or insane. . . . The scientific point of view presupposes an irrevocable commitment to the concept of determinism in nature, as an article of faith.' " And he concluded: "The determinist can make no distinction between the killing of a human being through criminal violence or through toxines of a tubercle bacillus."[18] This represents the position of many psychiatrist-critics of criminal responsibility. In their view and terms, the instinctual drives, the pleasure-pain principle, the conflict between *id* and *super-ego*, repression and sublimation, etc., are conceived as operating in accordance with universal laws of causation.

The question thus raised concerns not only the substitution of a scientific for a normative perspective but also and beyond that, the utility of a rigorously scientific perspective in psychiatry. Many psychologists take a larger view of that discipline,[19] one which takes account of the distinctive phenomena of decision-making, problem-solving, and evaluation; and this suggests that postulates other than that of

[17] Zilboorg, Mind, Medicine, and Man 282 (1943). *Cf.* "Man is pre-destined by anthropological, social, and physical causes to violate the law. . . ." Belbey, *Psychoanalysis and Crime*, 4 J. Crim. Psychopath. 639, 647 (1943).

[18] Brill, *Determinism in Psychiatry and Psychoanalysis*, 95 Am. J. Psychiatry 597, 600, 609 (1938), quoting Rosanoff.

Cf. "The more sage leaders of American psychiatry, however, have accepted the fact that man is not without freedom of choice." Guttmacher, *The Psychiatric Approach to Crime and Correction*, 23 L. & Contemp. Prob. 635 (1959), quoting Whitehorn and Alexander.

[19] Allport, Becoming — Basic Considerations for a Psychology of Personality (1955).

physical science may also be fruitful in psychiatry. So, too, sociologists and other scholars present very different theories of human nature from that which dominates current scientific psychiatry.[20] An increasingly large number of psychiatrists also express serious doubts regarding scientific psychiatry. They disagree especially with the Freudian disparagement of evaluation,[21] *e.g.* Jung stresses the paramount importance of moral attitudes in a sound psychiatry.[22] Another critic writes that "Freud's causal interpretation of the analytic situation . . . amounts to a denial of all personal autonomy in favor of the strictest possible determinism, that is to say, to a negation of life itself."[23] Many other scholarly psychiatrists censure Freud "for having attempted to swallow up morality in psychotherapy. . . ."[24]

Although Freud insisted on absolute adherence to the "scientific outlook on the world"[25] and expressed the

[20] "The model of man that most sociologists find congenial is profoundly different [from that of psychoanalysis] . . . Man is taken as first and foremost a social, not an instinctual, being . . . Although man's impulses are acknowledged to be a great force, his intellect is hardly written off as a 'feeble and dependent thing.' On the contrary, his rational strivings and purposeful behavior to achieve social goals are taken to be the chief key to an understanding of social behavior." Inkeles, *Psychoanalysis and Sociology*, pub. in Psychoanalysis, Scientific Method and Philosophy 117, 125-26 (Hook ed. 1959).

[21] For a presentation of this naturalistic viewpoint, see Schroeder, *Attitude of One Amoral Psychologist*, 31 Psychoanal. Rev. 329-333 (1944).

[22] Jung gives as a specific reason for breaking with Freud, his (Jung's) perception that "behind the confused deceptive intricacies of neurotic phantasies, there stands a *conflict*, which may be best described as a *moral* one." Jung, Analytical Psychology 242 (trans. Long 1916).

[23] Rank, Beyond Psychology 278 (1941); *cf. id.* at 34. *Cf.* "As a matter of fact, when he calls psychoanalysis a re-education Freud contradicts his own ideal, succumbing to the illusion that education is conceivable without at least implicit moral measuring rods and goals." Horney, New Ways in Psychoanalysis 297 (1939); *cf. id.* at 10-11, 237, 292-293.

[24] 2 Dalbiez, Psychoanalytical Method and the Doctrine of Freud 265 (1941). And he adds, ". . . we may search in vain for the will in the picture of the psychism which he has sketched for us. . . . The end of treatment is the return to normality, to the possibility of using the will." *Id.* at 295.

[25] Introductory Lectures on Psychoanalysis 38 (1920).

"sharpest opposition" to the "illusion of psychic freedom,"[26] he realized that this postulate could not be employed rigorously even in diagnosis. "So long," he wrote, "as we trace the development from its final stage backwards, the connection appears continuous. . . . But if we proceed the reverse way, if we start from the premises inferred from the analysis and try to follow these up to the final result, then we no longer get the impression of an inevitable sequence of events which could not be otherwise determined. We notice at once that there might have been another result . . . ."[27] This, however, presents the precise question of fact upon which decisions regarding legal responsibility turn, namely, the mental condition of the defendant prior to and at the time he committed the harm in issue.

Punishment

It is when they concern themselves with punishment that the psychiatrist-critics of the law disclose their philosophical predilections most definitely, making it abundantly clear that the issue is a clash of philosophies, not that of science versus common sense. The avowal of scientific indifference to responsibility and justice[28] is forgotten, and the psychiatrist of this persuasion sallies forth as the most confident of positivists: The criminal law represents "vengeance [which] still functions but under a disguise, namely, the disguise of deterrence. . . ."[29] All crime is a "pathological

[26] Id. at 37-38.

[27] Quoted in 2 Dalbiez, op. cit. supra note 24, at 299-300.

[28] ". . . the psychiatrist is not in the least interested in justice, and perhaps even doubts its existence. . . ." Menninger, op. cit. supra note 8, at 372.
Cf. "The law enforcement agencies and the legal profession did their duty in the Fish case by arresting him and sending him to psychiatric hospitals for observation. The psychiatrists whom the author [Dr. Zilboorg] considers so far ahead of the lawyers first failed the community, then tried later deliberately to deceive it." Wertham, Review, Zilboorg, The Psychology of the Criminal Act and Punishment, 22 U. of Chi. L. Rev. 569, 574 (1955).

[29] White, The Need for Cooperation Between the Legal Profession and the Psychiatrist in Dealing with the Crime Problem, 7 Am. J. Psychiatry 502 (1927).

phenomenon ;"[30] hence, "the time will come when stealing
or murder will be thought of as a symptom, indicating the
presence of a disease. . . ."[31] The corollary is that "all moral
issues should be discharged from consideration . . . anti-
social conduct should be considered as dispassionately as a
broken leg. . . ."[32] Lombroso is hailed for his "epoch-making
work," especially for his substitution of "social defense" for
punishment.[33] "Dangerousness" must replace "the vague
concept of the magnitude of the guilt;" it "alone should be
the standard for the kind, and duration of the treatment."[34]

This view of punishment has been previously discussed ;[35]
and it need only be added, since the polemic rests upon the
efficacy of treatment, that psychoanalysis has been conspicuously weak in therapy.[36] Its position regarding the treatment of criminals is contradicted by many experts who have

[30] Zilboorg, *op. cit. supra* note 17, at 282.

[31] Menninger, *op. cit. supra* note 8, at 373.
Cf. "Leaving to one side such uninformed judgments as those pro-
claiming that all criminals are insane or feebleminded, or that criminality is a diseased condition of the human character, or that the
criminal is a psychopath whose dominant passion is to commit a
crime, it has been found that some of those who commit crimes are
mentally disordered." Lowrey, *Delinquent and Criminal Personalities*, pub. in 2 Personality and the Behavior Disorders 805 (Hunt ed.
1944).

[32] White, *supra* note 29 at 503.

[33] Overholser, *The Role of Psychiatry in the Administration of
Criminal Justice*, 93 J. A. M. A. 830, 834 (1925).

[34] Brill, *supra* note 18 at 609-10.

[35] *Supra* chapter 9. *E.g.* in the above discussion, it was emphasized
that treatment designed solely to reform is unjust if the innocent
are not excluded, if it frees those who have committed major crimes
or if it incarcerates for long periods those who have committed only
petty transgressions. It also involves the untenable assumption that
adequate empirical knowledge is available to rehabilitate or even to
recognize with assurance those who can and those who cannot be
reformed. See note 36 *infra*.

[36] "If we discover a substantial improvement in the patients who
have undergone analysis, we have by no means shown that this is
due to their treatment. . . . This is a matter of extreme urgency, and
one concerning which we are wholly ignorant. I repeat *wholly* ignorant. . . ." Scriven, *The Experimental Investigation of Psychoanalysis*, pub. in Psychoanalysis, Scientific Method and Philosophy 228
(Hook ed. 1958).
Myerson, *Error in Psychiatry*, pub. in The Story of Human Error
412 (Jastrow ed. 1936); *cf.* Kessel and Hyman, *The Value of Psychoanalysis as a Therapeutic Procedure*, 101 J. A. M. A. 1612 (1933).

had experience in the administration of the criminal law.[37] Of greater theoretical pertinence is the fact that from the viewpoint of an empirical science, punishment may be seen as emotional reaction, the vengeance of an angry group, a condition which must be included among the causal factors of behavior, and finally, as Alexander and other Freudians have emphasized,[38] as a vicarious experience which keeps a purely factual "sense of justice" in precarious equilibrium.[39]

In the perspective of penal law, however, punishment must be interpreted consistently with a view of human nature that takes account of problem-solving and available empirical knowledge as well as of valuation. The key to this interpretation is the meaning of responsibility, which includes normal competence, authorship of a proscribed harm and accountability.[40] In sum, punishment is a corollary of responsibility, based upon the concept of man as capable, within limits, of making free choices and putting them into effect. To do nothing to a normal adult who has killed or tortured someone or taken his property is the negation of responsibility in its social and legal significance. And a dogma that equates normal adults with helpless victims of disease is incompatible with respect for personality. On the other hand, since incarceration in a mental hospital not only entails the loss of freedom but is often extremely painful, the final result may be that punitive treatment is imposed without the benefit of, or control by, law.

The Rule of Law

The issues resulting from the conflict of philosophical perspectives, psychologies of human nature, and attitudes toward punishment must be resolved for practical as well as

---

[37] See note 61 *infra* and the criticism of "official" psychiatrists *e.g.* note 28 *supra*.

[38] Alexander & Staub, The Criminal, The Judge and The Public 207-25 (1931).

[39] Campbell, *Crime and Punishment from the Point of View of the Psychopathologist*, 19 J. Cr. L. & Criminol. 244, 251 (1928). See also, Alexander & Staub, *supra* note 38 at 210-221.

[40] See *supra* chapter 9.

theoretical purposes. And the practical resolution involves another issue which also has far-ranging significance: the issue of the rule of law versus the unlimited power of officials over the lives and freedom of human beings.

We have previously considered this problem[41] and may confine this discussion to the instant question. The issue thus narrowed is usually stated as a conflict between the lawyer's interest in society and the doctor's concern for his patient — which can run to insistence upon complete individualization of therapy.[42] As to this, it need only be recalled that the sovereignty of law protects even the worst type of convicted criminal from being coercively subjected to sanctions that are not prescribed by law. From a medical viewpoint, it may be absurd to release an offender at a fixed time that has no relation to his rehabilitation. But if no law fixes an upper limit, there is no protection for anyone.

The issue of the rule of law is involved in the criticism of the legal classification of defendants as either "sane" or "insane." This "black or white" business, say some psychiatrists, flies in the face of the known facts — the intermediate grays, the hardly perceptible differences forming an unbroken continuum between the ideal extremes. But a legal order, unlike the specific findings of unfettered experts, requires generalizations describing *classes* of persons, conduct, harms, and sanctions. Given such a class, it follows inexorably that any "item," *e.g.* a mental condition, falls within the class or it falls outside it, if only by a hair's breadth. The same holds equally for the classes of data defined in any science or discipline, and the difficulties encountered by psychiatrists in reaching agreement on a sound classification of the psychoses[43] aptly illustrate the limita-

---

[41] *Supra* chapter 2.

[42] *Cf.* Zilboorg, *The Struggle for and Against the Individual in Psychotherapy*, 104 Am. J. Psychiatry 524 (1948).

[43] "There is growing recognition of the inadequacies of our present psychiatric classification based on rigid 'all or nothing' diagnostic labels. These inadequacies have caused some to go so far as to stress individual case studies and not even make a diagnostic evaluation. This appears to be giving up scientific methodology in the fields of

tions that are inherent as well in legal systems. These limitations, as regards legal classification, could not be met by adding a class of the "partially responsible," for there would still be intermediates between the three classes. And so it would continue, no matter how many classes were provided.

Substantive penal law is constructed to determine the basic questions, who shall be subjected to the control of the state, and who shall remain free of that. The social interpretation of punishment qualifies the meaning of the relevant substantive classification — determines, that is, what kind of control shall be exercised by the state. It assumes, therefore, that there are important differences between hospitals and prisons, even though the criminal law does not prevent wardens from using the services of psychiatrists or transferring sick inmates to hospitals or, for that matter, unfortunately, from converting hospitals into penitentiaries.[44]

If some of the critics have ignored or misunderstood the function of legal classification and the relation of that to the rule of law, still their criticisms are not devoid of substance. It is a fact that among those who are sane and legally responsible there are appreciable degrees

---

psychiatry and abnormal psychology before it has been given a fair trial. It not only gives up classification but in effect says that these fields can never be developed into a science. For if there is no agreement on classification there can be no discovery of truths or laws." Wittman & Sheldon, *A Proposed Classification of Psychotic Behavior Reactions*, 105 Am. J. Psychiatry 124 (1948).

[44] ". . . if men who violate the laws are to be confined for various periods in institutions, what reasons have we to believe that they will be more humanely treated in buildings officially labeled 'hospitals' than in those called 'jails'? . . .

"As matters now stand, some 'jails' . . . are less restrictive and punitive and more therapeutic than are some 'hospitals'. . . ." Szasz, *Psychiatry, Ethics, and the Criminal Law*, 58 Col. L. Rev. 189, 197 note 21 (1958).

"Shock treatment induces convulsions. They have been described as 'terrifying in the extreme'. . . . It is the psychiatrist who would incarcerate even the minor offender for life unless cured." De Grazia, *The Distinction of Being Mad*, 22 U. of Chi. L. Rev. 351, 352 (1955).

of mental impairment,[45] and it is unjust to ignore that and impose uniform sentences. Within the rule of law there can and should be a substantial measure of individualization. For example, the definition of criminal conduct can be more directly guided by differences in types of offenders, social problems and pertinent situations. Again, the disorganized mass of penal sanctions has long required thorough, systematic study. A more flexible but still legally controlled plan might be adopted, establishing sharply reduced prison terms, with added provisions for taking aggravating and mitigating circumstances into account in proper cases.[46] Indeed, perhaps the entire initial sentencing function should be returned to the judge. The pre-sentence hearing, making use of evidence of impaired personality, motivation, and so on, could then be widely adopted. To such individualization of treatment within the rule of law, psychiatrists can make important contributions.[47]

There is a further characteristic of the legal order that must be taken into account. The application of the principles of criminal law in a concrete situation is presently placed to a large extent in the hands of lay juries. Whether they should be replaced by experts as the triers of criminal responsibility is a separate question which will be examined shortly; but so long as we have juries performing that function, it is necessary to help the jurors understand what they are to do so that they may reach sound results.[48] This

[45] Fisher v. United States, 328 U. S. 463, 90 L. Ed. 1382, 66 S. Ct. 1318 (1946). Compare Wilson v. Inyang (1951), 2 K. B. 799 and the provision regarding "diminished responsibility" in the English Homicide Act (1957). For adverse criticism of "partial responsibility," see Note, 43 Cornell L. Q. 283 (1957).

[46] See the recommendations in the ALI's current draft of a Model Penal Code 10-57 (Tent. Draft No. 2, May 3, 1954).

[47] Dession, *Psychiatry and the Conditioning of Criminal Justice*, 47 Yale L. J. 319 (1938).

[48] See Report of the Royal Commission on Capital Punishment [hereinafter cited as Royal Comm'n Report] 287 (1953) (minority recommendation).
Cf. "If a general question is to be left to them, why restrict it to sanity or insanity? Why not ask them in a general way whether the accused was responsible at all? Under our system the prosecution

necessitates, and is a principal function of, the "rule of law." While the law must adapt to a changing world and the increased knowledge of that world, the need for stability, certainty and predictability in the law must also be remembered.

THE EXPERT AND THE JURY

It is obvious that psychiatrists know far more about mental disease than do judges and jurors. Indeed, would anyone deny that if he were seeking knowledge about mental disease, he would consult psychiatrists rather than jurors, lawyers and judges? Notwithstanding the obvious answer to this question, there are many reasons for not allocating the final authoritative fact-finding function to psychiatrists.

In the first place, a criminal trial, while it ought to use the best available knowledge, is not a scientific inquiry or an experiment in a clinic. For reasons which have long been persuasive, it is an adversarial investigation. The psychiatrists' work does not call upon them to decide whether their patients should or could have acted differently than they did, whether, *i.e.* they had the capacity to conform. But it is precisely this question which does make sense in everyday life; and it is the central issue in the trial. In many scientific inquiries a preponderance of the evidence suffices, and majority opinion among the élite prevails. In a criminal trial, because of the human values at stake, the jury must be convinced beyond any reasonable doubt, and they must be unanimous in their verdict. It is also rather widely believed that experts are prone to decide not on the evidence but "almost always on their own private

---

must allege and prove a definite crime. No one would suggest that the jury should be left with a general question whether the law has been broken or whether the prisoner should be punished or not. I believe that a general question on insanity would be just as objectionable. I think there is great force in the observation of the minority of the Commission on this point at p. 286 where they say: 'It is the traditional duty of our criminal law to lay down by definition, as clearly as possible, the essential elements of liability to conviction and punishment.' " Devlin, *Criminal Responsibility and Punishment: Functions of Judge and Jury*, 1 Crim. L. Rev. 661, 683 (1954).

opinion of the subject-matter."[49] Disagreement is frequent even among experts in well-established sciences. [50] Disagreement among psychiatrists is to be expected; indeed, a lack of disagreement would raise doubts regarding their integrity or competence. [51] Psychiatrists can defer their acceptance of any proffered theory or interpretation indefinitely and the thorough diagnosis of a single patient may take a year or longer; in a criminal trial definite decisions must be reached within a short time.

Moreover, the question of mental disease, viewed as a legal issue, cannot be separated from other legally material issues; hence, unless the entire body of relevant law were completely abandoned, it would still be necessary to have a jury or judge to interpret what the experts found and how that affected *mens rea* and the other issues. The criminal trial seeks to ascertain whether the accused had the normal competence to make a moral decision; many psychiatrists insist that they know nothing about this sort of question. There are also sound reasons of policy, implemented by constitutional guarantees, for the retention of trial by judge or jury; and a basic postulate in a democratic society is the avoidance of government by experts in crucial areas of law-making and adjudication.[52]

Finally, it must also be recalled that "mental disease" is not disease in the ordinary sense, and that psychiatry cannot

---

[49] Stephen, General View of the Criminal Law of England 216 (1863).

[50] Palmer's Trial, discussed in Wigmore, The Principles of Judicial Proof § 231 (2nd ed. 1931).

[51] Davidson, *Psychiatrists in Administration of Criminal Justice*, 45 J. Crim. L., C. & P. S. 12, 13-14 (1954).
"Nor can we go to the other extreme and completely abandon all idea of legal formulation for this would result in a chaos of unpredictability and complete lack of stability. Each succeeding issue of the psychiatric journals that brought forth a new theory or a varied concept would then become the law. And the law would vary from journal to journal and from article to article." Polsky, *Application and Limits of Diminished Responsibility as a Legal and Medical Concept*, pub. in Psychiatry and the Law 196, 198 (Hoch & Zubin eds. 1955).

[52] With reference to this question, there is a thoughtful essay by Harold J. Laski on the limitations of the expert which merits careful

provide expert knowledge that a person's conduct is so far from normal as to be labeled "psychotic." In sum, the initial, apparently easy solution of the problem, *i.e.* simply to ask a "doctor" to diagnose a "disease," gives way, in the light of the various considerations discussed above, to the defensible conclusion that the prevailing methods of fact-finding are to be preferred.[53]

THE STATUS OF PSYCHIATRY AMONG THE SCIENCES

We have previously discussed the scientific perspective of the psychiatry based upon a determinist cause-effect postulate (long regarded as outmoded among physicists). But a perspective is an approach; it is not a science. Nor is the "status" of a body of knowledge in the hierarchy of the sciences an arbitrary matter; there are definite criteria which determine that. Thus, it could easily be shown that psychiatry is far from being a science in a rigorous sense.[54] A science, such as physics, has a highly systematized struc-

---

reading. Recognizing that in modern complex society the use of expert knowledge is essential, Laski insists that although the expert is "an invaluable servant," he is also "an impossible master." Laski, The Limitations of the Expert 10 (Fabian Tract No. 235, 1931). Laski also writes:

"The expert tends . . . to make his subject the measure of life, instead of making life the measure of his subject. . . . For your great chemist, or doctor, or engineer, or mathematician is not an expert about life. . . . He does not co-ordinate his knowledge of a part with an attempt at wisdom about the whole . . . Such [expert] analytic comprehension is purchased at the cost of the kind of wisdom essential to the conduct of affairs. The doctor tends to think of men as patients; the teacher sees them as pupils; the statistician as units in a table. . . . Because a man is a brilliant prison doctor, that does not make him the person who ought to determine the principles of a penal code. . . ." *Id.* at 9. See also Frank, *The Place of the Expert in a Democratic Society*, 16 Philosophy of Sci. 3 (1949).

[53] "I think it would be a calamity if the disposition of criminal cases would be taken out of the hands of judges and given into the hands of psychiatric and other experts." Wertham, *A Psychiatrist Looks at Psychiatry and the Law*, 3 Buffalo L. Rev. 41, 48 (1953).

"Even if it were on other grounds desirable to do so, it would, in the present state of medical knowledge, be out of the question to remove the issue of criminal responsibility from the courts and entrust its determination to a panel of medical experts, as has sometimes been suggested." Royal Comm'n Report 100.

[54] *Cf.* Michael and Adler, *Crime, Law and Social Science* 55-65 (1933).

ture composed of empirically verified generalizations that express a co-variation of variables and, most important, these empirical laws are logically interrelated, allowing deductive manipulation. Even judged by other, more lax criteria, *e.g.* of taxonomic sciences, psychiatry is not scientific.[55]

Important advances have undoubtedly been made, but dissension among psychiatrists is more acute than anywhere else in psychology. "The best psychiatry is still more of art than of science," states one authority.[56] "There are, in fact, many methods, standpoints, views and convictions which are all at war with one another," writes Jung;[57] and these limitations are regularly reflected in enormous divergencies in diagnosis.[58] A competent practitioner admits "the debatable character of many theories,"[59] while a forthright investigator concludes that "no critically-minded person practiced in scientific research or in disciplined

[55] That psychoanalysis has very few rules linking constructs to each other and to observables, that its terms are unclear, its distinctions vague and contradictory, that it is not predictive, has been inadequately tested and, for other reasons, is unscientific, see Nagel, *Psychoanalysis and Scientific Method*, pub. in Psychoanalysis, Scientific Method and Philosophy 38 (Hook ed. 1959). Among several other noteworthy papers in that volume, those by Silverman and Scriven are especially relevant.

[56] Sullivan, *Psychiatry*, 12 Encyc. Soc. Sci. 580 (1934).
". . . psychiatry cannot be formalized either as a clinical system or as a method of treatment. When a formalistic clinical attitude is assumed in psychiatry, the psychiatrist loses his usefulness as a healer; but strange as it may seem, he may gain in stature as a psychiatric expert." Zilboorg, The Psychology of the Criminal Act and Punishment 118 (1954).

[57] Modern Man in Search of a Soul 33 (1939). *Cf.* "Psychopathology is a speculative subject, whose limits remain undefined. . . . There is much division of opinion among psychopathologists on basic principles." Coleman, *Psychopathology*, 90 J. Ment. Sci. 152 (1944).

[58] *E.g.* "Whereas Dr. Adler finds only twelve cases of 'mental disease' . . . out of 413 individuals examined at the Pontiac Reformatory, Dr. Hickson finds 240 cases of mental disease . . . out of 464 cases examined in the Chicago morals court. About the same time that Dr. Hickson was finding 50% of his street-walkers afflicted with dementia praecox, Dr. Leopold, in Philadelphia, could unearth less than ½ of 1% from his 1924 examinations." Hussey, *Psychiatrists in Court*, 22 Am. Mercury 342, 346 (1931). See note 8 *supra*.

[59] Horney, New Ways in Psychoanalysis 8 (1939).

speculation can accept psychoanalysis on the basis of the writings of Freud or of any of his followers. The presentation of facts is inadequate; the speculation is irresponsible; verifications are lacking; conclusions are hastily arrived at, and concepts are hypostatized."[60] It has been admitted by a specialist in the field that, "there has been no real psychiatric insight into criminalistic behavior."[61]

In the principal lecture at a recent annual meeting of the American Psychiatric Association,[62] Dr. Percival Bailey, the director of the Illinois State Psychopathic Institute, said that after years of studying psychiatry he finds himself in a state of grievous bewilderment. He examined the results of shock therapy and finds there is nothing in that. Lately, he says, "the crowd" (of psychiatrists) has rushed to use a new series of drugs. But that has had no appreciable effect which a scientific doctor can discover. Psychiatry is "largely a matter of faith" and many of Freud's speculations have been "severely battered." He concludes that the attempts to prove that psychiatry is a science have not convinced him and have convinced very few careful observers. Freud neglected the social nature of man, especially his disinterested curiosity. He over-emphasized the unconscious as contrasted with G. H. Mead's study of the intelligent conduct that is peculiarly characteristic of the higher forms of life. Additional voluminous criticism of psychiatry could be reported,[63] but perhaps enough has been adduced to allow a pertinent question to be raised.

[60] Murray, *Psychology and the University*, 34 Arch. Neurol. and Psychiat. 803, 809 (1935).

[61] Abrahamsen, Crime and the Human Mind 26 (1944).

"Some authors compensate for prevailing ignorance by overoptimism, some by overpessimism, concerning the future possibilities of the therapy of criminosis. *The simple fact is that we just don't know.*" Bergler, *Crime and Punishment*, 21 Psychiatric Q. Supp. 37-38 (1947).

[62] Bailey, *The Great Psychiatric Revolution*, 113 Am. J. Psychiatry 387 (1956).

[63] See *supra* note 55, for revelant articles.

Cf. "Psychiatric testimony should not be admissible in court. . . . It should be unmistakably clear on the basis of the evidence adduced here . . . that psychiatrists have not attained the level of competence

Since there is better and worse psychiatry, who is to decide which is the best psychiatry as regards the soundest solution of the problems of criminal law? If many able experts, after much study, came to the above conclusions about current "scientific" psychiatry, what is the lawyer, legislator or judge expected to do? Is he to say that he understands psychiatry better than these expert critics, that they are mistaken in their appraisal of the present state of psychiatric knowledge? Is he to accept the claim of the psychiatrist-critics of criminal law, that their knowledge is scientific? Or is he to appraise the various theories from the viewpoint of common sense, experience and compatibility with the psychology and ethics of the criminal law? It is submitted that the last is both valid and necessary in a democratic society.

---

and scientific reliability and validity necessary to make their testimony eligible for serious consideration by the courts." Hakeem, *A Critique of the Psychiatric Approach to Crime and Correction*, 23 L. & Contemp. Prob. 681 (1958); and Hakeem, *A Critique of the Psychiatric Approach to the Prevention of Juvenile Delinquency*, 5 Soc. Prob. 194 (1957-58).

"[A]t the present time, coming closest to the phrenology and animal magnetism of another age, both from the standpoint of cult value and in success in erecting an imposing scientific facade, is that discipline which has come to be known as psychoanalysis." Johnson, *Psychoanalysis—A Critique*, 22 Psychiatric Q. 321 (1948).

"So many and so flagrant have been the unscientific theorizing and practices of psychoanalysts during the past 50 years that many critics of analysis have become quite disillusioned and have begun to see science and analysis as antithetical." Ellis, *An Introduction to the Principles of Scientific Psychoanalysis*, 41 Genetic Psychol. Monographs 149, 195 (Murchison ed. 1950). Dr. Ellis also concludes that:

"[O]rthodox analytic theory is itself so formulated that a premium is often set on preconception and prejudice, while objectivity and open-mindedness on the part of analytic interpreters is made most difficult to achieve and retain." *Id.* at 155.

"Analytic theory has frequently managed to get so far away from factual referents that analysts easily fall into the habit of evolving such clever, complex, and almost fiendishly astute hypotheses that they neglect entirely to look for objective data with which to support them." *Id.* at 157.

Commenting on Ellis' monograph, Dr. Hilgard states:

"Anyone who tries to give an honest appraisal of psychoanalysis as a science must be ready to admit that as it is stated it is mostly very bad science, that the bulk of the articles in its journals cannot be defended as research publications at all." Hilgard, *Psychological Science and Psychoanalysis*, in Psychoanalysis As Science 44 (Pumpian-Mindlin ed. 1952).

Psychiatry is said to be superior to common sense psychology, to have outmoded this living psychology of the thoughtful layman. This, however, apart from any comparison of specific point by point issues, ignores the respective perspectives and the diverse functions of the two types of psychology, *i.e.* the relevance of knowledge. Given the purpose to cure neurotic patients and, at the same time, construct a science, psychiatry provides relevant knowledge. By like token, given its perspective and purposes, common sense psychology is both relevant and valid in daily life. It is not suggested that psychiatry is irrelevant to the problems of daily life. Psychiatry has already contributed very much to the common sense psychology of intelligent laymen, and it is important in the trial of the insanity issue. But it has thus far largely been oriented to individual therapy and scientific theories, not to the type of competence and the social problems that are of particular concern in law. The present point concerns especially those elementary psychological truths that intelligent persons acquire regarding their daily decisions, appraisals and actions. This psychology, while it may be enlightened, is not supplanted by, nor should it be supinely subordinated to, the "authoritative" tenets of a presumed scientific psychiatry. Perhaps the point can be further clarified by contrasting modern physics and common sense perception. Physics is highly abstract and some of its findings, *e.g.* that matter is non-existent or is reducible to energy, are both relevant to and significant for the high-level generalizations of physical theory. But that science does not exorcise tables and chairs from daily life or prove that the relevant common knowledge is outmoded. In the common sense perspective, guns, broken heads and dead bodies are very real and very meaningful. Neither physics nor psychiatry invalidates these truths.

It may be concluded that current psychiatry is far from having reached the scientific status of chemistry or biology. Neither in using expert witnesses nor in developing the legal formulas that govern the determination of socially harmful conduct should it be assumed that the psychology of modern penal law needs to give way to unassailable psychiatric authority based on relevant demonstrable truth.[64] That psychiatry has much to offer to penal law is not disputed; but that knowledge must be carefully appraised, selected and fitted into the framework in which it can function usefully. The elements of this structure have been indicated in the above discussion: first, a view of human nature that recognizes a significant degree of free choice; second, corresponding legal principles that make punishment a corollary of responsibility; third, within this order of law, stable and workable classifications permitting consistency of treatment appropriately tempered to the needs of individual cases; fourth, effective application of these classifications through rules that can be understood and employed by the agencies of justice, the judge and the jury; and finally, a corresponding maximum use of empirical knowledge, including psychiatry that is compatible with the above requirements of the legal order.[65]

[64] Some legal champions of psychiatry have, in effect, said: how inconsistent for a lawyer to criticize psychiatry on that ground when the law itself is full of uncertainty and disagreement! The plain answer is that lawyers do not claim that law is an exact science. Accordingly, the obvious way to terminate the criticism that psychiatry is not a science in a rigorous sense is to stop making that extravagant claim. Unfortunately, the claim of scientific status is used as a weapon to abolish law and norms of personal responsibility.

Cf. The legal scholar must "throw himself into psychology completely enough to become his own competent critic on matters of psychological theory." Robinson, Law and the Lawyers 111 (1935).

"Dealing as it does mainly with human behavior, the law very likely has more to teach psychology than to learn from it. The law has had a long history and very able students and practitioners." Thorndike, Man and His Works 133 (1943).

[65] *Cf.* ". . . the [M'Naghten] 'rule' intends to apply purely moralistic criteria to a clinical or scientific problem. . . ." Zilboorg, The Psychology of the Criminal Act and Punishment 17 (1954). See Wertham's review of the above book in 22 U. of Chi. L. Rev. 569 (1955).

It is possible, of course, to challenge the writer's formulation of the problem in other ways, *e.g.* to maintain that there are no objectively valid valuations which penal law expresses but only subjective preferences, that the ethics implicit in the tolerant *tout comprendre* attitude of some psychiatrists are superior to the ethics of penal law, and so on. This is a large problem, some aspects of which have been discussed *supra* in chapters 2 and 9, and in the writer's Living Law of Democratic Society, ch. 2 (1949).

With this framework in mind, we can turn to a considera-tion of the M'Naghten Rules, the criticism that has been leveled against them, and the substitutes that have been proposed.

THE M'NAGHTEN RULES

With minor modifications, the M'Naghten Rules have continued from 1843 to this day to comprise the most sig-nificant part of the law on insanity in relation to criminal responsibility. Of the several rules then published, the most important one is the following:

" . . . to establish a defence on the ground of insanity, it must be clearly proved that, at the time of the committing of the act, the party accused was labouring under such a defect of reason, from disease of the mind, as not to know the nature and quality of the act he was doing; or, if he did know it, that he did not know he was doing what was wrong."[66]

The judges who formulated the M'Naghten Rules did not regard them as innovations; they were published as "restatements" to clarify the law long in vogue in England as well as in this country.[67] To laymen as well as to the vast majority of lawyers and experienced forensic psychi-atrists, the Rules have seemed sound and efficient instru-ments in determining the important issues involved. Their survival for more than a century in many countries is a further index of their validity. Yet, almost from the day they were published the Rules have been subjected to the insistent criticism of psychiatrists, reaching its peak in the United States as a phase of the remarkable rise of psy-choanalytic theory.

One of these psychiatrist-critics of the criminal law, who was one of Freud's first American disciples, set the temper

---

[66] (1843) 10 Cl. and F. 200, 210, 8 Eng. Rep. 718, 722.

[67] The M'Naghten Rules were a synthesis of Rex v. Arnold (1724), 16 How. St. Tr. 695; Ferrers' Case (1760), 19 How. St. Tr. 886; Hadfield's Case (1800), 27 How. St. Tr. 1282; and Bellingham's Case (1812) in 1 Collinson, A Treatise on the Law Concerning Idiots, Lunaticks and Other Persons Non Compotes Mentis 636 (1812). In

of the campaign against the M'Naghten Rules. "Here," he wrote, "it [psychiatry] meets with antiquated, outworn, archaic ways of thinking that have been crystallized in the statutory law. . . ."[68] The right and wrong test . . . represent antiquated and outworn medical and ethical concepts, . . . responsibility carries with it a metaphysical implication . . . the remedies [especially punishment] upon which the law seems to repose its faith are hangovers, as it were, from old theological and moral ideas that have survived their period of usefulness in this twentieth century civilization."[69] Another prominent psychiatrist of the same persuasion attacked "that hoary old legal dogma, the presumption of sanity;"[70] and he concluded that "the framework of the criminal law still savors too much of the medieval to be brought readily into rapport with psychiatric

---

Ferrers' Case the Solicitor General, purporting to summarize Hale, stressed: "a faculty to distinguish the nature of actions; to discern the difference between moral good and evil. . . ." *Supra* at 948. In Hadfield's Case, Erskine minimized the "right and wrong" test and emphasized knowledge of the nature of the act. In Bellingham's Case, Mansfield said: "If a man were deprived of all power of reasoning, so as not to be able to distinguish whether it was right or wrong to commit the most wicked transaction, he could not certainly do an act against the law." 1 Collinson, *op. cit. supra* at 671. It will be noted that the M'Naghten Rules modified this by focusing the test on the particular harm committed, rather than on knowledge of right and wrong "in general." *Cf.* "To excuse a man in the commission of a crime, he must at the period when he committed the offense, have been wholly incapable of distinguishing between good and evil, or of comprehending the nature of what he was doing. . . ." *Id.* at 474. Cockburn's argument in defense of M'Naghten contains an excellent summary of the earlier leading cases and of the medico-legal treatises. 4 St. Tr. (n. s.) 872-892. Shortly after the M'Naghten Rules were announced, and apparently without having seen them, Shaw, C. J., held: "In order to be responsible, he must have sufficient power of memory to recollect the relation in which he stands to others, and in which others stand to him; that the act he is doing is contrary to the plain dictates of justice and right, injurious to others, and a violation of the dictates of duty." Commonwealth v. Rogers, 7 Metc. 500, 502 (Mass. 1844).

[68] White, Twentieth Century Psychiatry 110 (1936).

[69] White, *op. cit. supra* note 29, at 493, 494, 495.

[70] Overholser, *The Place of Psychiatry in the Criminal Law*, 16 B. U. L. Rev. 322, 329 (1936).

concepts of the present day."[71] These criticisms have been often repeated.[72]

To this criticism of the psychology and ethics of the M'Naghten Rules was added the equally confident criticism of its terms on the ground that they do not refer to the data and theories with which the psychiatrist deals and are therefore incomprehensible. Thus a leading psychiatrist insisted that the "rules are unintelligible to me. . . ."[73] The sophistry of this criticism is demonstrated in the practice of psychiatrists who have participated effectively in the trial of many insanity cases.

But language is only the vehicle of thought, and the actual reason for criticizing the terms of the M'Naghten Rules is that they express a psychology and ethics which scientific psychiatrists reject. For example, some years ago, a committee of psychiatrists announced: "Various curious tests then had to be decided upon to determine the 'responsibility' of persons suspected of 'insanity' . . . Once they were compared in appearance and conduct with wild beasts, later with the mentality of a 14-year-old child. This was actually the criterion of 'responsibility' in use in courts

---

[71] *Id.* at 343.

[72] Zilboorg, *op. cit. supra* note 17, at 279. This writer, in his History of Medical Psychology (with Henry) (1941), devoted many pages to conflicts between physicians and "the law" in which the latter is invariably cast in the role of an evil, malicious spirit barring the psychiatrists' road to progress. But if one reads this book carefully, it appears that not only lawyers but the vast majority of medical men were also opposed to the new discoveries. Thus the criticism is reduced to strident complaint of the Bar because it did not lead the medical profession on questions in the latter's own special field. *Cf.* note 14 *supra. Cf.* ". . . as doctors we have been needlessly unjust, and have not sufficiently taken into consideration the fact that the lawyers in stating their case and opinion have based it on the medical knowledge of the period." Henderson, *Psychiatry and the Criminal Law*, 4 Psychiatric Q. 103, 104-5 (1930). Also see *id.* at 109, and note 28 *supra.*

[73] Zilboorg, *op. cit. supra* note 17, at 274.
Cf. "One of the greatest difficulties in psychiatry is its esoteric vocabulary." Guttmacher, *op. cit. supra* note 8, at 636.
"Freudian doctrine, for example, provides a language for saying silly things in an impressive way." Frankel, *The Status of Freud's Ideas*, pub. in Psychoanalysis, Scientific Method and Philosophy 327 (Hook ed. 1959).

not so many years ago. Current even today in many states
is the slightly less hoary 'right and wrong' test. . . ."[74]

The first "curious test" of insanity, the so-called "wild
beast test," harks back to language employed by Bracton
in the thirteenth century. "A madman," he said, "is one
who does not know what he is doing, who is lacking in
mind and reason, and who is not far removed from the
brutes." In dealing with the civil obligations of such persons, he said, "a madman [is] not of sane mind, so that he
cannot discern or has no discretion at all. For such persons
do not differ much from brutes who are without reason. . . ."[75]
A psychotic person is certainly not a wild beast; but neither
did Bracton say he was. He was merely repeating, in a
metaphor, the ancient doctrine that man is distinguishable
from other animals by his reason. The above caricature
of Bracton's meaning is typical of the distortion of the
history of forensic psychology.[76] As a matter of fact,
from at least the thirteenth century onwards, there was
considerable knowledge of mental disease represented in
the criminal law, as is apparent in *The Mirror*,[77] the statute
Praerogativa Regis[78] and the classical law writers.[79] This
is especially true of Hale, whose discussion is both well-

[74] Menninger, *op. cit. supra* note 8, at 374. *Cf.* Menninger, The
Human Mind 450 (3rd ed. 1945).

[75] 6 Bracton, De Legibus f. 420b, 321 (Twiss ed.).

[76] Some fair insight into the bizarre historicism of the contemporary critics of the criminal law may be attained in a brief glance
at the contributions of a contemporary of Bracton—the Monk, Bar-
tholemeus Anglicius, who wrote *De Proprietatibus Rerum* about 1240.
Concerning his discussion of mental disease, an American psychiatrist, who took pains to inform himself, writes: "One is struck by
the modernity of his viewpoint. . . . If one transposes some of the
words into modern terms, there results a statement which reads like
a discussion encountered in a modern textbook of psychiatry. . . .
The treatment the Monk Bartholomew prescribed was equally rational. . . . His portrayal of the depressive patient is quite accurate
according to present-day clinical standards." Bromberg, The Mind
of Man 39-40, 41 (1937).

[77] Selden Soc. 136 (1895).

[78] *Circa* 1324. See 1 Pollock and Maitland, H. E. L. 481.

[79] See, generally, Crotty, *The History of Insanity as a Defense to
Crime in English Criminal Law*, 12 Cal. L. Rev. 105 (1924).

informed and critical.[80] He also wrote that insane persons cannot be guilty of a crime "for they have not the use of understanding, and act not as reasonable creatures, but their actions are in effect in the condition of brutes." The metaphor became common.[81]

Disregarding the actual meaning of the phrase, the current psychiatrist-critics of the M'Naghten Rules read the "wild beast test" literally and lay it at the door of Justice Tracy's decision.[82] In that early eighteenth century case, the defendant, without any rational motive, shot a man, and although there was testimony strongly indicating that he suffered from a serious mental disease, there was also evidence to support a contrary finding. Justice Tracy made a careful summary of the law and evidence, in the course of which he said: ". . . that is the question; whether this man hath the use of his reason and sense? If he . . . could not distinguish between good and evil, and did not know what he did, . . . he could not be guilty of any offence against any law whatsoever; . . . On the other side . . . it is not every kind of frantic humour or something unaccountable in a man's actions, that [exculpates] . . . ; it must be a man that is totally deprived of his understanding and memory, and doth not know what he is doing, no more than an infant, than a brute, or a wild beast, such a one is never the object of punishment; therefore I must leave it to your consideration, whether [the defendant] . . . knew what he was doing,

---

[80] *E.g.* after noting Fitzherbert's tests of idiocy (inability to count to 20 or recognize parents or tell one's age) he adds circumspectly, "These, tho they may be evidences, yet they are too narrow and conclude not always; . . ." 1 Hale, P. C. 29.

[81] *Id.* at 31-32. Cockburn, in his defense of M'Naghten, spoke of "that disease . . . which deprives man of reason, and converts him into the similitude of the lower animal. . . ." Queen v. M'Naghten, (1843) 4 St. Tr. (n. s.) at 874. In a small treatise on the subject published in 1700 (Braydall, Non Compos Mentis) the professional literature up to that time is well reviewed. The author discusses the now familiar grounds for exculpation: that the punishment of an insane person "cannot be an example to other;" and, also, on legal principle, the harm was committed "without a felonious intent or purpose." *Id.* at 75.

[82] Rex v. Arnold (1724), 16 How. St. Tr. 695.

and was able to distinguish whether he was doing good or evil, and understood what he did. . . ."[83]

It would not be difficult to give an accurate account of the judicial use of the other "curious tests," such as the "14-year-old test;" but the facts established would be cumulative. They reveal a clear recognition of serious mental disease, that the feeble-minded were long ago distinguished from the psychotic, and that symptoms persuasive to intelligent laymen and supported by the contemporary medical psychology guided judgment.

The M'Naghten Rules were characterized in the above report as "the slightly less hoary right and wrong test." That the "right and wrong" test[84] is a superstition, that psychiatrists "do not believe it helps to call an act . . . bad . . .,"[85] that "such knowledge [of morality] is not an important factor in deciding a question of mental illness . . ." are representative opinions of these critics. On the other hand, we must set against this, the sharp dissent by other psychiatrists. A leader of modern psychiatry insists that, "The moral attitude is a real factor in life with which the psychologist must reckon if he is not to commit the gravest errors."[86] In this position, he is supported by a steadily increasing number of psychiatrists;[87] and even the notion of responsibility is taken by some of them as the most cogent index of normality.

The above criticism of the "right and wrong" test parallels the psychology of "moral insanity" introduced in England

---

[83] *Id.* at 764-765.

[84] This test is commonly said to have been originated by Hawkins who wrote of "a natural disability of distinguishing between good and evil, as infants under the age of discretion, ideots and lunaticks" (1 P. C. 2), but it is evident that Hawkins merely received this from Hale (1 P. C. 25) who, himself, probably took it from much older literature. See notes 76-80 *supra*.

[85] White, *supra* note 29 at 502.

[86] Jung, *op. cit. supra* note 57, at 224.

[87] *E.g.* Kahn, Psychological and Neurological Definitions and the Unconscious 65 (1940). See *infra* final notes 50, 51, 52 and 56.

by Prichard,[88] and in the United States by Ray.[89] The
theory was that some individuals were completely lacking
in normal conscience, although they were otherwise unimpaired; and a very extensive literature was devoted to the
analysis of these "amoral" persons. After careful research,
however, Dr. William Healy concluded, "We have been
constantly on the look-out for a moral imbecile, that is,
a person not subnormal and otherwise intact in mental
powers, who shows himself devoid of moral feeling. We
have not found one . . . the person who failed to appreciate
his moral duties was the person who had not intelligence
enough to realize what was best for even himself as a social
being . . . if the 'moral imbecile' exists who is free from
all other forms of intellectual defect, he must indeed be a
rara avis."[90] Dr. Healy's findings accord with the theory
of the integration of the self;[91] and in that psychology a
person's moral judgment ("knowledge of right and wrong")
is not reified as an outside, icy spectator of a moving self.
On the contrary, the corollary is that such valuing is permeated with the color and warmth of emotion. Indeed, in
the integrative view of personality, all normal conduct,
especially that relevant to penal law, involves a unified
operation of the various functions of personality, *e.g.* a
normal person who saw someone committing a serious battery on a child would understand and condemn the immorality of that and at the same time feel the surge of emotion
and be disposed to take appropriate action.[92] It is that kind

[88] A Treatise on Insanity and Other Disorders Affecting the Mind
(1835).

[89] A Treatise on the Medical Jurisprudence of Insanity (1838).
Cockburn, in his defense of M'Naghten drew heavily on Ray, pro-
nouncing his book ". . . the most scientific treatise that the age has
produced upon the subject of insanity in relation to jurisprudence.
. . ." Queen v. M'Naghten (1843), 4 St. Tr. (n. s.) 878.

[90] Healy, The Individual Delinquent 783, 788 (1927). So, also,
Lowrey, *op. cit. supra* note 31, at 801.

[91] See *infra* pp. 494-95.

[92] *Cf.* Karpman, *Criteria for Knowing Right from Wrong,* 2 J.
Crim. Psycopath. 377, 379, 386 (1941); Prideaux, *The Criminal Re-
sponsibility of the Alleged Insane,* 1 Camb. L. J. 319, 320-21 (1923).
Also, see citations in footnotes 13-18 and 66 *infra.*

of moral knowledge which many judicial interpretations of
the M'Naghten Rules require. In sum, as an Australian
jurist stated, "We are not dealing with right or wrong in
the abstract. The question is whether he was able to appreciate the wrongness of the particular act he was doing at
the particular time. . . . What is meant by wrong is wrong
having regard to the everyday standards of reasonable
people."[93]

The decision of the English Court of Criminal Appeal in
Windle[94] has raised some doubt about this widely recognized
meaning because it apparently held that "wrong," as used
in the M'Naghten Rules, means legally, not morally, wrong.
Windle was a man of weak character, married to a psychotic woman 18 years older than himself and constantly
talking about suicide. Windle gave her 100 aspirins, ending
her earthly travail, but found himself charged with
murder. On a plea of insanity, a psychiatrist testified that
Windle had "a form of communicated insanity known as
folie a deux," which he contracted from his wife. It was
admitted by the defense that Windle knew what he was
doing and that it was illegal. Justice Devlin ruled that there
was no evidence of insanity to be submitted to the jury;
and the conviction was affirmed in the Court of Criminal
Appeal.

On appeal, an argument was made regarding the meaning
of "wrong" in the M'Naghten Rules, and most of the decision
is devoted to that question. Lord Goddard, who wrote the
opinion, said that the defendant "may have thought it was
a kindly act to put her out of her sufferings or imagined
sufferings, but the law does not permit such an act as
that."[95] Here, and in similar language,[96] the court was

[93] Dixon, J., in The King v. Porter, 55 C. L. R. 182, 189-90 (1933).
So, too, Cardozo, J., in People v. Schmidt, 216 N. Y. 324, 340, 110 N. E.
945 (1915).

[94] (1952), 36 Cr. App. R. 85.

[95] *Id.* at 89.

[96] ". . . it would be an unfortunate thing if it were left to juries
to consider whether some particular act was morally right or wrong."
From the report of *Windle* in (1952) 2 Q. B. at 833.

only insisting on the objective meaning of the principle of *mens rea.*[97]

It is the language in the opinion defining "wrong," *i.e.* the dicta, which stirred criticism, especially the statement, ". . . there is no doubt that the word 'wrong' in the M'Naghten Rules means contrary to law and does not have some vague meaning which may vary according to the opinion of different persons whether a particular act might not be justified."[98] If the first clause in this statement is interpreted apart from its context, especially that it was contrasted with an individual's uncommon ethics, the adverse criticism which has been directed against it seems amply warranted. That definition of "wrong" is clearly opposed to the prevailing view in this country;[99] and it has been thoroughly criticized in Australia.[1] In any event, in view of the principal issue in *Windle*, noted above, that decision does not seriously challenge the prevailing view that "wrong" in the M'Naghten Rules means morally wrong.

The polemical character of much of the current criticism of this part of the M'Naghten Rules is revealed in the fact that incompatible positions are urged. Thus, on the one hand, it is asserted that the Rules require an ordinary person to do what philosophers through the ages have with very

---

[97] See *supra*, especially chapters 3 and 5.

[98] Windle, *supra* note 94, at 90. The latter clause in the above statement again reveals the issue.

[99] *Supra* note 93.

[1] Stapleton v. the Queen (1952), 82 Comm. L. R. 358. See also, Morris, *"Wrong" in the M'Naghten Rules*, 16 Mod. L. Rev. 435 (1953). It is very doubtful that Codere (1916), 12 Cr. App. R. 21, the principal English case on the subject, supports Windle. In Codere, while there was language which, literally interpreted, might support Windle, it was also said, "There may be minor cases before a court of summary jurisdiction where that view may be open to doubt, but in cases such as these [homicide], the true view is what we have just said." *Id.* at 28. Reading, L. C. J., also said, ". . . once it is clear that the appellant knew that the act was wrong in law, then he was doing an act which he was conscious he *ought not* to do, *and* as it was against the law, it was punishable. . . ." *Id.* at 27-28 (italics added). It is submitted that instead of separating the illegality of the forbidden conduct from its immorality, the two were treated together in Codere, at least as regards felonies.

dubious success been trying to do, namely, to distinguish right from wrong. If the Rules actually required such competence in abstract thinking, as a test of normality, most persons would be held insane, but the attendant complaint is that because of the M'Naghten Rules many psychotics are held to be sane. On the other hand, it is charged that the Rules require such elementary valuations that only a "drooling idiot" could not "pass" that test of normality. But while it is easy for any normal person to "pass" the M'Naghten test, psychotic defendants fail to do that because they seriously lack the competence to realize the wrongfulness of their conduct. This has been recognized in recent decisions and it is stipulated in the Canadian Penal Code[2] as *appreciation* of the wrongness of the act.

In sum, what the clause requires is incapacity, due to serious mental disease, to make the relevant valuations of a normal adult—to realize, for instance, that it is wrong to kill a human being or take his property. When psychiatrists attack this criterion of normality as outmoded "metaphysics" they are saying nothing more than that valuation is irrelevant in the perspective of scientific psychiatry.[3] Obviously, if conscience is no more than the sub-

[2] Criminal Code of Canada, 1955, Sec. 16 (2). "There is . . . a great weight of opinion from judges, lawyers and doctors in favour of no substantial change." Rept. Royal Comm'n on the Law of Insanity as a Defence in Criminal Cases 29 (1956).

[3] "A second assumption of the Rules is that the existence or absence of such 'knowledge' is readily determinable by the methods of psychiatry. This assumption is unwarranted. There is no developed scientific method of determining the existence of such 'knowledge' of the nature and quality or the right and wrong as related to an act, or the lack of it. Nevertheless, the law in effect compels answers to invalid questions of 'knowledge,' which cannot be met." Committee on Psychiatry and Law of the Group for the Advancement of Psychiatry, Criminal Responsibility and Psychiatric Expert Testimony 6 (1954).
When the members of this same Group for the Advancement of Psychiatry were asked in a questionnaire, "Are there cases where a person, suffering from mental derangement, knows that it is wrong to inflict bodily harm (killing, maiming, ravishing) upon another person, but owing to the mental derangement is incapable of controlling (resisting) the impulse to commit such bodily harm?," 93 of 102 who answered replied "yes." Keedy, *Irresistible Impulse as a Defense in the Criminal Law*, 100 U. Pa. L. Rev. 957, 989 (1952).

limation of instinct, there is no room for moral blame or responsibility. On the other hand, it is highly significant, as regards the present problem, that many, probably a large majority of, experienced forensic psychiatrists believe the M'Naghten Rules function very well in practice, without the miscarriage of justice attributable to the use of the Rules, and that no better substitute has been proposed.[4] It must therefore be concluded that this clause of the M'Naghten Rules represents neither a "hoary superstition" nor a legal technicality. It expresses in plain words an abiding insight into what is paramount in human nature.

The other major clause of the M'Naghten Rules includes the terms "know," "nature," and "quality" of the act. These words "in the abstract" represent ultimate ideas of epistemology; pertinently and actually, they designate common sense notions of daily life. While philosophers have discussed these ideas with vast erudition and in technical vocabularies, the judges have talked about them very simply. Their analysis has been clarified by specific illustrations based on the facts in issue, e.g. Justice Darling's observation, "He knew the nature and quality of the act; for he knew that he was shooting, and that this shooting would kill her."[5] The judges have also substituted synonyms, e.g. for "know": "appreciate," "comprehend rationally," "judge," "understand," "perceive," "be aware of," "conscious of," and the like.

The judicial opinions have dealt more fully with the terms "nature" and "quality,"[6] the chief questions being

---

Replying to a similar inquiry, 84 of 86 Canadian psychiatrists expressed their disapproval of the M'Naghten Rule with "irresistible impulse" as an added feature. Stevenson, *Insanity as a Defense for Crime: An Analysis of Replies to a Questionnaire*, 25 Can. B. Rev. 871 (1947).

[4] East, An Introduction to Forensic Psychiatry in the Criminal Courts 73-74 (1927); East, *Delinquency and Crime*, 90 J. Mental Sci. 382, 391 (1944); cf. Royal Comm'n Report 86.

[5] Rex v. Pank, London Times, May 22, 1919, p. 9, col. 3, quoted by Davis and Wilshire, Mentality and the Criminal Law 95-96 (1935).

[6] Weihofen, Insanity as a Defense in Criminal Law 43-44 (1933); Glueck, Mental Disorder and the Criminal Law 215-216 (1925).

whether they are synonyms[7] and whether this clause must be distinguished from the other principal one, discussed above. It has been held that "in using the language 'nature and quality' the judges were only dealing with the physical character of the act, and were not intending to distinguish between the physical and moral aspects of the act."[8] Some American courts, however, have so distinguished the two terms.[9] In support of this view, it has been argued that the judges who formulated the M'Naghten Rules "could not have intended two different words to mean exactly the same thing."[10] But for most judges, elucidation has been largely confined to the substitution of synonyms, such as "consequences," "character and consequences," "effect," "implications," or "significance." This treatment of "quality" and "nature" as synonymous is defensible inasmuch as the other principal clause of the Rules, discussed above, deals explicitly with the moral aspect of criminal conduct. The Rule is not limited to perception of external objects; it also includes the various other characteristics of intelligent functioning,[11] e.g. understanding ordinary relationships and the usual non-physical consequences of simple actions.

Psychiatrists who profess their inability to understand what is meant by "knowledge of the nature and quality of the act" accept, as a criterion of normality, the "correctness of the reality-testing,"[12] suggested by the Freudian "reality-

---

Barnes, *A Century of the McNaghten Rules*, 8 Camb. L. J. 300, 303 (1944).

[7] Oppenheimer argued that neither word ought "to be rejected as mere surplusage." He distinguished the terms on the ground that "nature" refers to the physical character; "quality" to the "social and legal character;" "wrong" or "criminality," to the "legal significance of the act." The Criminal Responsibility of Lunatics 142-148 (1909). *Cf.* Foote, K. C., for the appellant in Rex v. Codere, *supra* note 1, at 21, 24-25.

[8] Reading, J., in Rex v. Codere, *supra* note 1 at 27.

[9] *E.g.* Schwartz v. State, 65 Neb. 196, 91 N. W. 190 (1902); *cf.* Davis and Wilshire, *op. cit. supra* note 5, at 113.

[10] *Id.* at 95-96.

[11] Stoddard, The Meaning of Intelligence 4 (1943).

[12] See Hacker, *The Concept of Normality and Its Practical Significance*, 15 Am. J. Orthopsychiatry 47, 52 (1945).

principle."[13]   It is possible to equate this principle with the prevailing legal test.   Thus both the M'Naghten Rule and the "reality-principle" assume the existence of an outer world.[14]   Both assume "nature-events" and "social events" which occur in that world.[15]   Both assume the possibility of knowledge of that world.[16]   Both correlate changes in functioning in that regard with "mental abnormality."[17]   Both imply that there are methods by which the "knowledge of the outer world" can be tested[18] and that this is the

[13] "This more far-seeing attitude of controlling intelligently the instinctual demands in accordance with the requirements of the given external situation is the reality principle." Alexander and Healy, Roots of Crime 276 (1935). *Cf.* "A loss of reality must be an inherent element in psychosis; . . . the new phantastic outer world of a psychosis attempts to set itself in place of external reality." 2 Freud, Collected Papers 277, 282 (1925).

[14] "Let us, moreover, bear in mind the great practical importance there is in the capacity to distinguish perceptions from mental images. . . . Our whole attitude toward the outer world, to reality, depends on this capacity so to distinguish." 4 Freud, Collected Papers 147 (1925); See also, Brill, Freud's Contribution to Psychiatry 139 (1944); Hinsie & Shatsky, Psychiatric Dictionary 460 (1940).

[15] For the recognition given to the social event as distinguished from the nature event, see, *e.g.* Sterba, *Introduction to the Psychoanalytic Theory of the Libido*, 68 Nervous and Mental Disease Monograph Series 69 (1942); Alexander, *The Psychoanalysis of the Total Personality*, 52 Nervous and Mental Disease Monograph Review 125-126 (1930); Laforgue, *The Relativity of Reality*, 66 Nervous and Mental Disease Monograph Series 4, 37, 39, 49-50 (1940). "In a way, the ego pursues the same aims as the id, but by virtue of its knowledge of the outer world, it takes account of its lawfulness and regularity, and instead of permitting the id to run blindly into dangerous situations, the ego interposes reason between the desire and the act." Brill, *op. cit. supra* note 14, at 155; *cf.* 2 Stephen, H. Cr. L. of Eng. 174 (1883). See also, 4 Freud, Collected Papers 18 (1934).

[16] See Brill, *op. cit. supra* note 14. ". . . we use the term *ego* where is commonly meant the intellect." Laforgue, *supra* note 15 at 37. Similarly, Ferenczi, *Stages in the Development of the Sense of Reality* in Contributions to Psycho-Analysis 233-234 (1916).

[17] "Schizophrenics see the world differently; our notion of reality is not theirs. We call them 'crazy' because they see and perceive things we do not see and which to us appear absurd." Laforgue, *supra* note 15 at 40; ". . . neurosis does not deny the existence of reality, it merely tries to ignore it; psychosis denies it and tries to substitute something else for it." 2 Freud, Collected Papers 279 (1934). See also, *id.* at 250-251, 277.

[18] ". . . the ego takes a perception for real if its reality is vouched for by the mental faculty which ordinarily discharges the duty of

function of the intelligence.[19] Indeed, the "reality-principle" has been defined in almost the very words of the legal Rule, as "the apprehension of the true nature of an object . . . ;"[20] and Erskine's argument in *Hadfield* long ago revealed the close approximation of the legal and psychiatric principles.[21] The suggestion may be ventured, however, that even a slight acquaintance with the literature of philosophy indicates that the authors of the M'Naghten Rules achieved a vast improvement over both Erskine and Freud in avoiding the use of the term which has as good a claim as any to being the vaguest of all words, namely, "reality." Whatever the criteria of scientific psychiatry may require, it is not unlikely that those who know that term to be pregnant with the limitless equivocations of hundreds of years of speculation prefer the simpler language of the M'Naghten Rules.

Viewed historically, there can be little doubt that the M'Naghten Rules represented an intellectualistic psychology.[22] A fallacious "faculty psychology," expounded by Cockburn,[23] the defendant's counsel, was also reflected in

---

testing the reality of things." Freud, Group Psychology 77 (1922). See also, Schilder, *Introduction to a Psychoanalytic Psychiatry*, 50 Nervous and Mental Disease Monograph Series 19 (1928).

[19] ". . . intelligence is the capacity for acquiring, absorbing and using knowledge of reality. " Podolsky, *Psychoanalytical Views of Intelligence*, 28 Psychoanal. Rev. 359 (1941).

"Now conscious thought by means of speech signs is the highest accomplishment of psychical apparatus, and alone makes adjustment to reality possible. . . ." Ferenczi, Contributions to Psycho-Analysis 195 (1916). The quotation in the text is from Alexander, Fundamentals of Psychoanalysis 85 (1948).

[20] Wälder, in 20 Imago 467 (1934).

[21] *E.g.* The disease consists "in the delusive sources of thought; all their deductions within the scope of the malady, being founded upon the *immoveable* assumption of matters as *realities*, either without any foundation whatsoever, or so distorted and disfigured by fancy. . . ." He spoke of delusions as "where imagination . . . holds the most uncontrollable dominion over reality and fact. . . ." (1800) How. St. Tr. 1281, 1313. He distinguished Hadfield from Ferrer's Case (1760), 19 How. St. Tr. 886—the latter exhibited "violent passions and malignant resentments, *acting upon real circumstances.* . . ." *Id.* at 1314; *cf.* Pope, A Treatise on the Law and Practices of Lunacy 2 (2nd ed. 1890).

[22] The dominant general psychology was represented by Mill, Analysis of the Phenomena of the Human Mind (1829).

[23] (1843) 4 St. Tr. (n. s.) 847, 887.

the disjunctive statement of the two principal clauses of the Rules. Psychiatrist-critics of the law who, of course, have not studied the processes and techniques whereby the legal system changes and is improved, are prone to assume that the Rules are literally interpreted by the courts in terms of the older outmoded psychology. Actually, modern psychology and psychiatry have greatly influenced adjudication, and the M'Naghten Rules have been widely interpreted in recent years[24]—hence their approval by psychiatrists who have had considerable experience with their actual operation.[25]

THE "IRRESISTIBLE IMPULSE" HYPOTHESIS

The major corollary of the criticism of the Rules has long been expressed in the hypothesis of "irresistible impulse," with accompanying demands for legal recognition of it. That hypothesis did not coincide with the rise of modern psychiatry; it is said to have been "fully and clearly stated by Weyer" in the sixteenth century.[26] The psychological foundation of the present controversy was laid by certain French physicians in the early nineteenth century. Pinel, one of the pioneers of modern psychiatry, diagnosed cases of *manie sans delire* and reported that he found no loss in the functioning of perception or intelligence, but did find a compulsion to violence, even homicide. His

[24] "It seems true to say that in cases where there is evidence of real mental disease, antecedent to the commission of the alleged crime, and there is no evidence of a motive which might influence a sane person, juries have no difficulty in finding either that the prisoner did not appreciate the nature of his act, or that he did not know that it was wrong." Hewart, 57 H. L. Deb. 468 (5th ser. 1924). See H. M. Advocate v. Sharp, S. C. (J.) 66 (1927).

[25] "Various attempts have been made to modify in some way or other the M'Naghten rules, but I do not believe that any better criterion has ever been formulated, provided these rules are interpreted in a broad and liberal spirit, as is mostly the case today." Henderson, *Psychiatry and the Criminal Law*, 4 Psychiat. Q. 115 (1930). So, too, East, *Delinquency and Crime*, 90 J. Ment. Sci. 391 (1944); East, Introduction to Forensic Psychiatry 73-74 (1927); MacNiven, *Psychoses and Criminal Responsibility* in Mental Abnormality and Crime, 9, 70 (Radzinowicz and Turner eds. 1944); for a like view by American psychiatrists, see McCarthy and Maeder, *Insanity and the Law*, 136 The Annals 132 (1928), and Cleckley, The Mask of Insanity 495-501 (1950) and note 47 *infra*.

[26] Zilboorg and Henry, A History of Medical Psychology 243 (1941).

theory was first repudiated in England, Dr. Burrows characterizing it as "both absurd and dangerous . . . absurd, because he who can perpetrate such acts, and yet be in possession of all these faculties, is neither in a delirium nor mad. . . ."[27] But the "irresistible impulse" hypothesis gained ground, aided in England by Prichard's diagnosis of "moral insanity" which, he reported, left the reasoning faculties unimpaired[28] and, in the United States, by Ray's similar views.[29] Thus, shortly after the M'Naghten Rules were published, and long before the rise of modern psychiatry, it was insisted that ". . . this should be the test of irresponsibility—not whether the individual be conscious of right and wrong—not whether he had a knowledge of the consequences of his act—but whether he can properly control his action!"[30] Especially influential in this regard was the work of Maudsley who presented the hypothesis of "impulsive insanity" so persuasively as to enlist wide support.[31] The adoption of the "irresistible impulse" test in a number of American states in the early part and middle of the past century reflects the influence of this outmoded psychiatry, not the advance of modern clinical psychiatry— a fact that is ignored by present advocates of that test.

To understand what is involved in the "irresistible impulse" hypothesis, it is essential to keep in mind that it asserts that persons of normal intelligence, who therefore understand what they are doing and realize, *e.g.* that it is wrong to kill, rob or rape, are nonetheless so diseased in their volitional function as to be unable to keep from committing these harms. This thesis has some appeal because of common, but erroneous, beliefs that kleptomaniacs and pyromaniacs are psychotics who fit the above descrip-

---

[27] Burrows, Commentaries on Insanity 267 (1828).

[28] *Op. cit. supra* note 88.

[29] *Op. cit. supra* note 89.

[30] Knaggs, Responsibility in Criminal Lunacy 69 (1854).

[31] Maudsley, Responsibility in Mental Disease 133 *et seq.* (1874). After one of the cases described by him, he concluded: "In face of this example of uncontrollable morbid impulse, with clear intellect and keen moral sense, what becomes of the legal criterion of responsibility?" *Id.* at 136.

tion and also because everyone has sometime in his life succumbed to a desire to do something against his better judgment. With reference to the latter, what must be stated emphatically is that the "irresistible impulse" hypothesis is not at all involved in such common experiences. Genuinely compulsive acts, supported by clinical evidence, are limited to harmless matters like excessive handwashing, counting windows and the like.[32] The legal issue of "irresistible impulse" concerns the commission of serious harms, and it is insisted by very competent psychiatrists that there are no clinical data which support the hypothesis that a person's intelligence may be quite normal but that he may nonetheless be unable to keep from killing or robbing or committing some other serious harm.[33] The assumption that kleptomania and pyromania are psychoses expressing irresistible impulses is also untenable. Recent studies have shown that they are usually neuroses, and also that the claim of concomitant unimpaired intelligence is fallacious. Thus, a psychiatrist reporting on his study of kleptomaniacs states, "One thing is certain. Every patient who has ever been investigated extensively showed some faults in the critical appreciation of the factors of reality."[34]

It is futile to attempt to decide the validity of the "irresistible impulse" and related hypotheses by authority, for the specialists disagree;[35] besides, only a very small

[32] Wertham, *The Psychiatry of Criminal Guilt*, pub. in Social Meaning of Legal Concepts, No. 2, Criminal Guilt 164-65 (N. Y. U. Law School, 1950); Davidson, *Irresistible Impulse and Criminal Responsibility*, 1 J. of Forensic Sciences 1 (1956).

[33] *Ibid.* See, also, Rep't of the Royal Comm. on Capital Punishment 1949-1953 at 95, 96 (1953), and note 71 *infra*.

[34] Lorand, *Compulsive Stealing*, 1 J. Cr. Psychopath. 247 (1940); *cf.* ". . . compulsion neurosis is an intellectual disease *par excellence* . . . ." Gutheil, *The Criminal Complex in Compulsion Neurosis*, 3 J.

[35] *E.g.* Zilboorg, *op. cit. supra* note 17, at 273. But *cf.* this same psychiatrist's discussion of "knowledge," citation in note 66 *infra*.
"It is impossible to say, in any particular case, that an impulse was irresistible; all that can be said is that the impulse did not appear to have been successfully resisted." Hamblin Smith, Psychology of the Criminal 179 (2nd ed. 1933). *Cf.* ". . . the difficulty of distinguishing between uncontrollable impulse and the impulse which is not controlled would make too fertile a dialectic field." Henderson, *supra* note 25 at 114.

portion of practicing psychiatrists have given their opinion in the matter. Some of those who have commented on the subject said that the problem lies outside the scope of their discipline or their competence. They are concerned with what happened, not with what could or could not have been resisted. Any effort to determine the validity of the hypothesis also encounters the difficulty that "there appears to be no clear-cut agreement as to its exact meaning."[36] A theory has only that degree of validity which supporting facts confer upon it, and the writer must acknowledge that he knows of no book, article or report of clinical data which even makes a serious effort to establish the validity of the "irresistible impulse" hypothesis. If the like question were raised regarding, e.g. immunization or diabetes, a vast amount of supporting fact would be immediately adduced. No reason appears why psychiatrists should claim an exemption from the ordinary canons of scientific proof.

Although the "irresistible impulse" test is assumed to be the law of a number of jurisdictions in this country, it is not easy to discover just where that test is actually recognized; nor, if the fragile precedents of early nineteenth century decisions are examined, together with the outmoded psychology upon which they rest, is it easy to predict what a future decision in those jurisdictions will be if the issues are thoroughly investigated. Another reason to question the statement that twelve or fourteen or seventeen jurisdictions, as is variously stated, recognize the "irresistible impulse" test is provided by the early decisions mainly relied upon,[37] especially *Rogers*.[38] In *Rogers*, Chief Justice Shaw

For other summaries of, and citations to, expert opinion opposed to the "irresistible impulse" theory, see Waite, *Irresistible Impulse and Criminal Liability*, 23 Mich. L. Rev. 443, 445-456, 466 fn., 468 (1925); and Whitman, *Capital Punishment and Irresistible Impulse as a Defense*, 5 Notre Dame Lawyer 188, 195 (1929).

[36] Spier, *The Psychology of Irresistible Impulse*, 33 J. Cr. L. & Criminol. 458 (1943).

[37] In the United States, the "irresistible impulse" test "was first accepted in Ohio as long ago as 1834." Rep't of Royal Comm on Capital Punishment 1949-1953 at 105 (1953). But *cf.* note 49 *infra*.

[38] Commonwealth v. Rogers, 7 Metc. 500, 11 Am. Dec. 458 (Mass. 1844).

stressed both the intellectual and the volitional aspects of conduct; hence, while some of his language, clipped from its context, is ambiguous,[39] the opinion definitely indicates that he believed control and intelligence are interdependent.[40] The Chief Justice not only emphasized disorder of reasoning and knowledge of right and wrong but, in addition, when he did speak of impulsive, non-controllable action, it was always *in its relation to the disease of the intelligence*.[41] For example, in the passage which is especially relied upon to support the assertion that the "irresistible impulse" test was adopted in that case, he said, "the question will be, whether the disease existed to so high a degree, that for the time being it overwhelmed the reason, conscience, and judgment, *and* whether the prisoner, in committing the homicide, acted from an irresistible and uncontrollable impulse. . . ."[42] If the meaning of the "irresistible impulse" test, stated above, is kept in view, (*i.e.* that it is an independent, sufficient *substitute* for the M'Naghten Rules), it is reasonably clear that this passage, set in the broader context of the opinion, did not adopt it.

Mosler,[43] however, did adopt the "irresistible impulse" test. In his decision, Judge Gibson strongly approved the then attractive psychology of separate faculties, including the theory of "moral insanity" that had recently been expounded by Ray.[44] Nevertheless, he cautioned the jury so emphatically regarding it—that it is "dangerous" and "can be recognized only in the clearest cases"[45]—that a

---

[39] See Professor Keedy's analysis of it in *Insanity and Criminal Responsibility*, 30 Harv. L. Rev. 724, 725-729 (1917).

[40] Glueck recognizes that the decision "might therefore, be distinguished from the usual version of the irresistible impulse test. . . ." Glueck, *Psychiatry and the Criminal Law*, 14 Va. L. Rev. 155, 163 (1928).

[41] *E.g.* ". . . if his reason and mental powers are either so deficient that he has no will . . . ," *supra* note 38 at 501. See also his general statement of the test at 508.

[42] *Id.* at 502. Italics added. This same theory of integration is repeated. *Id.* at 503.

[43] Commonwealth v. Mosler, 4 Pa. 264 (1846).

[44] "Insanity is *mental* or *moral;* the latter being sometimes called homicidal mania. . . . But there is a *moral* or *homicidal* insanity,

conviction of murder in the first degree was returned. A full, official imprimatur of the "irresistible impulse" test in this country was given in Judge Somerville's opinion in *Parsons*.[46]

Accordingly, at least the claim that seventeen states have adopted the "irresistible impulse" test[47] is highly questionable[48] because many of the cases relied upon are of the same type as *Rogers*. They reveal not the adoption of the "irresistible impulse" test, an alternative to the M'Naghten Rules, but, instead, the holding that ability to control one's conduct is a concomitant of normal intelligence.[49] It is also sometimes asserted that most European penal codes recognize the "irresistible impulse" test. But, this, too, is very doubtful despite the fact that the literal language of some codes can be interpreted to support that view.[50] For the hypothesis

---

consisting of an irresistible inclination to kill, or to commit some other particular offence. There may be an unseen ligament pressing on the mind, drawing it to consequences which it sees, but cannot avoid, and placing it under a coercion, which, while its results are clearly perceived, is incapable of resistance." 4 Pa. 264, 266-267 (1846).

[45] *Id.* at 267.

[46] 81 Ala. 577 (1886). So, too, State v. Green, 78 Utah 580, 6 P. 2d 177 (1931).

[47] Weihofen, *op. cit. supra* note 6, at 44.

[48] *Ibid.* The states are listed *id.* at 16 note 6.

[49] *E.g.*, the earliest cases cited (*id.* at 46-47) as adoptions of the "irresistible impulse" test: State v. Thompson, 90 Wright Ohio Rep. 622 (1834) and State v. Clark, 12 Ohio Rep. 483, 495 (1843). In the former, Judge Wright's instruction identified "the power of discriminating" good from evil with the power to control. In the latter case, there is language which, taken from its context, could support the claim. But, interpreted in its context, it is clear that Judge Birchhard's views were in accord with his predecessor's. The plain implication again was that the answer to the question regarding control by the defendant was included in the answer to the question, did the defendant know right from wrong? It is clear that his instruction did not contemplate an affirmative answer to the latter question and a negative one to the question on control. If there were any doubt regarding the meaning of his instruction, the questions he asked the witnesses would be conclusive as to this interpretation. State v. Clark, *supra* at 485. (In 70 A. L. R. 659 at 676, Ohio is classified with states which do not recognize the "irresistible impulse" test, the Clark Case cited.)

[50] See Oppenheimer, *op. cit. supra* note 7, ch. 2.

that a seriously disordered volition may co-exist with normal rational functions has not been as insistently urged in Europe as it has in the United States. What seems to express the "irresistible impulse" test is probably interpreted, as in *Rogers*, to be an implicate of seriously diseased intelligence.[51] In addition, it should be recognized that the word "or" sometimes means "and;" indeed, there is ample support among logicians that that is the usual meaning of "or."[52] Finally, it should be recalled that many European penal codes were enacted in the early nineteenth century when faculty psychology and theories of "moral insanity" and the like prevailed. In sum, the literal wording of European penal codes is hardly relevant to the current psychiatric claims made in this country. Here, the tremendous impact and far-ranging implications of twentieth century scientific psychiatry give the legal issues a unique meaning.

The English experience regarding the "irresistible impulse" test has paralleled the American—with the striking difference that that test is not law in England and proposals to adopt it have invariably been rejected.[53] A clear adoption of the "irresistible impulse" test is found in Justice McCardie's instruction in *True*[54] but this was disapproved on

[51] *Id.* at 88. Thus Mannheim, who apparently supports the "irresistible impulse" test, reports that in 1929, the German Supreme Court quoted: "The free determination of the will is excluded when, as a consequence of mental disturbances, certain ideas and feelings or influences dominate the will to such a degree as to exclude the possibility of determining the will through reasonable considerations." Mannheim, *The Treatment of Mental Disorders and Mental Deficiency in Continental Criminal Law*, 84 J. Ment. Sci. 526 (1938).

[52] ". . . the *onus probandi* lies on those who assert that the *logical* interpretation of 'or' should be exclusive. It cannot be maintained the common use is exclusive . . . It is not to be denied that it is sometimes clear that two alternatives exclude each other. But the exclusion is due to the nature of the alternatives, not to the form of the proposition." Stebbing, A Modern Introduction to Logic 70-71 (6th ed. 1948). The following writers hold that usage supports the inclusive meaning of "or": Burtt, Right Thinking 134 N. (3rd. ed. 1946), 1 Coffey, Science of Logic 285 (1918), Frye and Levi, Rational Belief 178 (1941), Mace, Principles of Logic 61 (1933). and Quine, Methods of Logic 4 (1950). See Dickerson, in 46 A. B. A. J. 310 (1960).

[53] MacNiven, *op. cit. supra* note 25, at 71, and Henderson, *op. cit. supra* note 25.

[54] Quoted in Barnes, *A Century of the McNaghten Rules*, 8 Camb.

appeal[55] and was shortly afterwards repudiated as utterly "fantastic."[56]

In contrast to the judiciary, several Commissions have recommended the adoption of an "irresistible impulse" test.[57] Thus, Lord Atkin's Committee[58] recommended an addition to the M'Naghten Rules recognizing that an act may be "committed under an impulse which the prisoner was by mental disease in substance deprived of any power to resist."[59] An appropriate bill was introduced and argued in the House of Lords,[60] where it was shortly withdrawn. In the debate, participated in by such notable judges as Haldane, Hewart, Darling and Dunedin, the arguments against the "irresistible impulse" test were vigorously put: An "irresistible impulse" does not and cannot co-exist with unimpaired knowledge of right and wrong.[61] Even if it were assumed that there could be such an impulse, it could not be distinguished from a resistible, but unresisted impulse.[62] Important questions of policy were also stressed,

---

L. J. 317 (1944). Another like instance is Judge Bray's decision in Rex v. Fryer (1915), 24 Cox C. C. 403, 405. Oppenheimer quotes from two unreported English cases where, apparently, the "irresistible impulse" test was adopted. *Op. cit. supra* note 7, at 27.

[55] (1922) 16 Cr. App. R. 164.

[56] Hewart, C. J., in Rex v. Kopsch (1925), 19 Cr. App. R. 50.

[57] The history and recommendations of these commissions are summarized by Davies, *Irresistible Impulse in English Law*, 17 Can. B. Rev. 147 (1939).

[58] (1923) Cmd. 2005.

[59] *Id.* at 21.

[60] 57 H. L. Deb. 443 (5th ser. 1924).

[61] *Cf.* "For myself I cannot see how a person who rationally comprehends the nature and quality of an act, and knows that it is wrong and criminal, can act through irresistible innocent impulse." Brannon, J., in State v. Harrison, 36 W. Va. 729, 742, 15 S. E. 982 at 990 (1892).

[62] Scientific psychiatrists who conform to the implications of their theory are apt to assert that all actions are irresistible in the sense that given "sufficient" cause, the action follows. In this view, the distinction posited by the "irresistible impulse" test is invalid. See note 35 *supra*.

Cf. "The majority of witnesses were, however, opposed to proposals of this kind, either on the ground that a genuine irresistible impulse due to disease of the mind was already covered by the M'Naghten Rules, or on the ground that such a test would be impossible to apply and would inevitably lead to abuses, or on both these grounds." Royal Comm'n Report 95.

e.g. "insanity" was characterized as a rich man's defense. "Almost invariably" an expert could be found who would testify that an impulse was irresistible. Finally, it was urged, "If you pass this . . . you will make irresistible an impulse which now is resistible and resisted because of the penal law."[63]

Opposed to the psychological hypothesis of "irresistible impulse" and its current equivalents is the theory of the integration of the self, the coalescence of the various functions of the normal personality.[64] Although it is possible and it may sometimes be useful to distinguish them, the fact is that in normal persons the emotional, the cognitive, and the conative functions interpenetrate one another. Unlike the analysis of mathematical problems or the verbal recognition of rules, knowing, *i.e.* understanding, moral situations, problems and duties fuses with tendencies to action and it is permeated also by the warmth of the emotions. Inevitably, therefore, serious mental disease is a drastic impairment of all the principal aspects of the personality. In psychotic persons, there may be calculation of a high order; but it is unsupported by the affect and sensitivity that in normal adults stimulates an identification with a prospective victim or a realistic imaging of the meaning and consequences of a serious attack on him. In short, a psychotic person does not actually understand the moral significance of his conduct.[65] The above statements are the evident implicates of the theory of personality that is accepted by

---

[63] Cave, 57 H. L. Deb. 476 (5th ser. 1924). *Cf.* Keedy's summary of the reasons for American courts' opposition to the "irresistible impulse" test in 30 Harv. L. Rev. 536, 546-548 (1917).

[64] It begins with the reference to Aristotle's "unitary" theory of the soul.

The range of the integration theory is very extensive in modern thought. Those phases of it that are immediately relevant to the instant problem include, of course, Gestalt psychology. See, A Source Book of Gestalt Psychology (Ellis ed. 1938), and the works of Sherrington, Child and Lashley; and Goldstein, The Organism (1939). Of special interest, also, is Commins, *Some Early Holistic Psychologists*, 29 J. of Philos. 208 (1932).

[65] See Zilboorg's discussion in *Misconceptions of Legal Insanity*, 9 Am. J. Orthopsychiat. 552-53 (1939).

everybody including the psychiatrist-critics of the present Rules.[66] The upshot is that the "irresistible impulse" hypothesis cannot be maintained consistently with the theory of the integration of the functions of the personality.

This was basically Stephen's position: "the absence of the power of self-control would involve an incapacity of knowing right from wrong. . . . It is as true that a man who cannot control himself does not know the nature of his acts as that a man who does not know the nature of his acts is incapable of self-control."[67] This implies the relevance of the M'Naghten Rules;[68] and a number of recent opinions have emphasized that, *e.g.* Justice Greer's statement in *True*: "What I really told the jury was that the definition of insanity in criminal cases was the one laid down by the judges in *McNaughton's Case*, but that men's minds were not divided into separate compartments, and that if a man's will power was destroyed by mental disease it might well be that the disease would so affect his mental powers as to destroy his power of knowing what he was doing, or of knowing that it was wrong."[69]

Unlike the Group for the Advancement of Psychiatry,[70] the *Royal Commission on Capital Punishment (1949-1953)*

[66] *E.g.* Overholser, *supra* note 33 at 831. Zilboorg gives an excellent interpretation of this viewpoint in his discussion of "knowledge," "understanding" and "defect of reason" in terms that are directly important for the criminal law. Zilboorg, *supra* note 65 at 552-53. So, too, Prideaux, *supra* note 92 at 320-21.

[67] 2 H. Cr. L. 171 (1883). Oppenheimer regarded "Stephen's attempt to read the latter faculty into the term 'knowledge' . . . a hopeless failure." Oppenheimer, *op. cit. supra* note 7, at 142, 33. But Stephen nowhere equates "knowledge" with "control," nor does he say that the latter is a form of the former. His argument was that the two powers were integrated, so that one could not be essentially disturbed without impairment of the other.

[68] 2 H. Cr. L. 149 (1883); Digest of the Criminal Law, Art. 27 (1887).

[69] Rex v. True (1922), 16 Cr. App. R. 164, 167. Similar views were well expressed in a recent Australian case, Sodeman v. The King (1936), 55 C. L. R. 192, among them, Evatt, J.: "It is quite out of accord with modern research in psychology to assert an absolute gap between cognition and conation." *Id.* at 227. See Barry, *Insanity in the Criminal Law in Australia*, 21 Can. B. Rev. 427, 435, 437 (1943).

[70] Of the 350 members of the American Psychiatric Ass'n who

concluded that: "[T]he concept of the 'irresistible impulse' has been largely discredited . . . it is inherently inadequate and unsatisfactory."[71] Yet the Commission itself made a recommendation that on the surface, at least, goes much farther than the "irresistible impulse" hypothesis. A majority of the Commission recommended as its second preference[72] (and the minority's primary recommendation) retention of the M'Naghten Rules, with an additional independent alternative clause exculpating the accused if he "was incapable of preventing himself from committing [the act]."[73] A similar proposal is made in a tentative draft of the American Law Institute, which would exculpate any defendant who, although he had the capacity "to appreciate the criminality of his conduct," was unable "to conform his conduct to the requirements of law."[74] It is submitted that these proposals are merely verbal reformulations of the "irresistible impulse" test and that they amount to the abolition of the relevant rules of law.

This is apparent on examination of the Commission's argument. First, it avows the integrative view that mental disease affects *both* cognition and volition: "insanity does

---

answered the question, "Do you believe the concept of the irresistible impulse test is psychiatrically and legally sound?" 60% answered in the negative, 40% in the affirmative. Guttmacher, in ALI Model Penal Code, Tent. Draft No. 4, 174 (April 25, 1955).
"In a poll taken of the members of the Group for the Advancement of Psychiatry [who are also members of the American Psychiatric Association] more than 90% were of the opinion that the existence of the irresistible impulse is a psychiatrically valid concept." Guttmacher, *The Quest for a Test of Criminal Responsibility*, 111 Am. J. Psychiatry 430 (1954).

[71] Royal Comm'n Report 109. "Sir Norwood East said that in fifty years he had never met a murder due to irresistible impulse unconnected with mental disease." *Id.* at 96. "The Medical Superintendent of Broadmoor . . . emphasized that he had never known an irresistible impulse leading to a crime of violence except in association with other signs of insanity." *Id.* at 95. Compare Hoedemaker, *"Irresistible Impulse" as a Defense in Criminal Law*, 23 Wash. L. Rev. 1, 7 (1948): "Every tenet of modern psychiatry points toward the acceptance of the 'irresistible impulse' plea as a proper defense in criminal law."

[72] The first preference is discussed in the text *infra* 499.

[73] Royal Comm'n Report 111, 287.

[74] Model Penal Code 27 (Tent. Draft No. 4, 1955).

not only, or primarily, affect the cognitive or intellectual faculties, but affects the whole personality of the patient, including both the will and the emotions."[75] Then, however, the inference is drawn that, "An insane person may therefore often know the nature and quality of his act and that it is wrong and forbidden by law, but yet commit it as a result of the mental disease."[76] But this is a clear *non sequitur*— the premise that both A and B are syndromes of serious mental disease does not imply that A but not B is a syndrome. Unfortunately, this sort of analysis is typical of the current criticism of the M'Naghten Rules. It utilizes the theory of integration to insist that a psychotic's volition is diseased — a fact that is not disputed. But it passes over and, in other contexts, opposes the equal corollary that a psychotic's intelligence is also greatly impaired. What therefore emerges is identical in significance with the "irresistible impulse" hypothesis in the essential respect of hypothesizing a mental disorder which, it is said, is so severe as to be a psychosis while, at the same time, the intelligence is normal.[77]

The Commission distinguished its proposal from the "irresistible impulse" hypothesis on the ground that the former

[75] Royal Comm'n Report 80.

[76] *Ibid. Cf.* "One of the greatest dangers now confronting analysts, and standing stalwartly in the way of their founding a truly scientific theory and practice of psychoanalysis is their utilization of what seems to be an outdated, unscientific, compartmentalized notion of personality: namely, Freud's concept of the ego, super-ego and id.
"Obviously, to anyone who has imbibed deeply at the well of modern psychological and psychiatric knowledge a person's ego, id or superego cannot do, under it's own power, anything whatever. It is, in the case of any normal adult human being, the whole *person*, or *individual*, or *organism* who thinks, emotes, and acts." Ellis, *supra* note 63, at 169-70.

[77] In this analysis, it has been inferred that the proposed alternative, "or was incapable of preventing himself from committing it," was intended to provide for volitional and emotional disorder, since the entire approach of the Commission, as is evident from the context, was to take account of those phases of personality. See, *e.g. id.* at 107-08. If the context were different, another interpretation, much closer to the valid implication of the premise of integration, might obtain, namely that the "or" clause refers to and includes *all*

is not restricted to impulsive action. The facts, states the Commission, do not support the notion of sudden impulsive action but reveal, instead, the lapse of considerable time during which a psychotic person may be "brooding" or "reflecting" on the harm he subsequently commits.[78] The pertinent question as regards legal responsibility is whether the Commission's proposal has a different legal effect than that of the "irresistible impulse" test. That test is law in some American states; and the cases there do not exhibit its restriction to impulsive action. The facts in the cases examined by the writer reveal "the lapse of considerable time;" the test in practice apparently purports to determine "inability to conform" or "to prevent himself," and so on.[79] In sum, the proposed alternative to the "irresistible impulse" test does not make any appreciable change in the substance of that test;[80] nor does it resolve the incompatibility of the proposed formula with the psychology of the integration of the personality.

The "irresistible impulse" test is not law in England, of course, and it is possible that the Commission's recommendation was intended to go beyond what has been recognized in American states as the "irresistible impulse" test. This raises the second major question: Is the proposed alternative so vague that it neither provides nor allows any legal rule of criminal responsibility? In support of its recommendation to add the alternative clause ("or was incapable of preventing himself from committing it"), the Commission

---

the essential criteria concerning cognition, will and emotion. See note 52 *supra*.

[78] Royal Comm'n Report 110. It was urged a century ago that "The use of 'impulse' . . . has been particularly unfortunate." Bucknill, Unsoundness of Mind in Relation to Criminal Acts 84 (1856).

[79] Professor Weihofen's valuable book, Mental Disorder as a Criminal Defense 81-103 (1954), unfortunately provides very little description of the facts in the cases involving "irresistible impulse."

[80] "The real criticism that is now directed against the rule is that although a man may know what he is doing is wrong, he may be unable to help himself doing it. This is what used to be called irresistible impulse." Devlin, *Criminal Responsibility and Punishment: Functions of Judge and Jury*, 1 Crim. L. Rev. 661, 682 (1954). See note 36 *infra*.

describes the *Ley* case as illustrative of its meaning. But its interpretation of the facts in that case refers to criteria that fall directly within the orbit of the M'Naghten Rules; and whatever there may be in addition is so vague as to provide no guidance to any jury — if, indeed, it has any definite meaning for psychiatrists.[81] This was substantially the conclusion reached by Justice Devlin who rejected both of the Commission's principal recommendations.[82]

In fact, the Commission's primary recommendation, and the central thrust of its Report, was "to abrogate the [M'Naghten] Rules and to leave the jury to determine whether at the time of the act the accused was suffering from disease of the mind (or mental deficiency) to such a degree that he ought not to be held responsible."[83] This total exclusion of any legal test of criminal responsibility would, no doubt, satisfy the demands of those few psychiatrists who claim to be unable to testify under the M'Naghten Rules. It would allow them to testify in any terms they pleased and in support of any of the extant theories, opinions, guesses and predilections about "mental disease," in-

---

[81] "Ley, because of his insanity, lived in a twilight world of distorted values which resulted not so much in his being 'incapable of preventing himself' from committing his crime, in the strict sense of those words, as in his being incapable of appreciating, as a sane man would, why he should try to prevent himself from committing it. It seems to us reasonable to argue that the words 'incapable of preventing himself' should be construed so as to cover such states of mind; that they should be interpreted as meaning not merely that the accused was incapable of preventing himself if he had tried to do so, but that he was incapable of wishing or of trying to prevent himself, or incapable of realising or attending to considerations which might have prevented him if he had been capable of realising or attending to them. If each of Ley's acts is considered separately, it would be difficult to maintain that he could not have prevented himself from committing them. Yet if his course of conduct is looked at as a whole, it might well be argued that, as a result of his insanity, he was incapable of preventing himself from conceiving the murderous scheme, incapable of judging it by other than an insane scale of ethical values, and, in that sense, incapable of preventing himself from carrying it out. If the addition to the M'Naghten Rules were construed in this way, it would serve its purpose well, and the Rules thus amended should cover most of the cases where a defence of insanity ought to be admitted." Royal Comm'n Report 111.

[82] Devlin, *supra* note 80, at 683.

[83] Royal Comm'n Report 116.

cluding the notion that all criminals are mentally diseased. But what use would the testimony be to the jury? How could there be any certainty at all of conforming to the social purposes of the rule of law and the community's understanding of disease and responsibility?

These difficulties inhere equally in the American Law Institute's tentative draft, aggravated by the fact that "criminality" is there substituted for "wrong," thus raising the issue of *Windle*.[84] The American Law Institute's proposed rule places the lack of substantial capacity to conform upon an alternative, coordinate basis with the capacity to appreciate. It therefore makes its version of the "irresistible impulse" test the independent autonomous substitute for the M'Naghten Rule. The proposal must therefore be judged in that light, *i.e.* on the supposition that every defendant will plead that although he understood perfectly well what he was doing and thoroughly appreciated its wrongfulness ("criminality"?), he was nonetheless unable to keep from homicide, rape, etc. The fact that a defendant may, if he chooses, also rely on the amended M'Naghten clause does not alter the above crucial meaning of the Institute's proposal. In sum, as will shortly appear more fully, the Institute's proposed formula, like that of the Royal Commission, is, in substance, the equivalent of the Durham rule, to be discussed next. All of them represent the ideological position of extremist, "scientific" psychiatry with reference to criminal responsibility.

THE DURHAM "PRODUCT" RULE

In *Durham*, the United States Circuit Court of Appeals of the District of Columbia, claiming authority to legislate

---

[84] See notes 94-99 *supra*. *Cf.* ". . . . the A.L.I. suggestion . . . would seem to restrict the concept to legal, not moral, wrong. Thus to restrict the concept . . . is a step backward." Hofstadter and Levittan, *The McNaghten Rules—A Reappraisal and a Proposal*, 140 N. Y. L. J. 4 note 55 (Sept. 17, 1958).

Cf. "The Guilt of offending against any Law whatsoever, necessarily supposing a wilful Disobedience can never justly be imputed to those, who are either uncapable of understanding it, or of conforming themselves to it. . . ." Hawkins, Pleas of the Crown 1 (2nd ed. 1724).

regarding the test of criminal responsibility, adopted what it regarded as a new rule.[85] Durham, pleading insanity, was convicted of housebreaking, and although a procedural issue regarding the prosecution's burden of proof was also involved, the principal point, argued in reversal and accepted by the Circuit Court, was that the "existing tests of criminal responsibility are obsolete and should be superceded."[86]

The existing tests were assumed to include both the M'Naghten Rule and the "irresistible impulse" test. The former was found "fallacious" and "discredited" because, in the words of the *Royal Commission on Capital Punishment (1949-1953)*, it is "based on an entirely obsolete and misleading conception of the nature of insanity."[87] The "irresistible impulse" test was held, again in reliance upon the authority of the Royal Commission, to be "also inadequate in that it gives no recognition to mental illness characterized by brooding and reflection. . . ."[88] "We conclude," said the Court, "that a broader test should be adopted," namely, "simply that an accused is not criminally responsible if his unlawful act was the product of mental disease or mental defect."[89]

The new test was then explained in the following respects: (1) "mental disease" and "mental defect" were defined. (2) It was emphasized that the fact that the accused was suffering from a mental disease or mental defect at the time he committed the act in issue would not suffice. "He would still be responsible for his unlawful act if there was no causal connection between such mental abnormality and the act." (3) The prosecution has the burden of proving "beyond reasonable doubt . . . that the act was not the product of such abnormality."[90] (4) The M'Naghten Rule

[85] Durham v. United States, 214 F. 2d 862, 874 (C. A. D. C. 1954).
[86] *Id.* at 864.
[87] *Id.* at 871.
[88] *Id.* at 874.
[89] *Id.* at 874-75.
[90] *Id.* at 875.

and the "irresistible impulse" test could still be employed. The new test was to be used in addition to those tests.[91]

Before considering the *Durham* "product test" attention should be directed to the assumption made not only in that decision but also by the District of Columbia courts generally that the prior law on the subject included the "irresistible impulse" test. This assumption is based on *Smith*[92] and ultimately on the Supreme Court's decision in *Davis*, upon which the decision in *Smith* relied.[93] *Davis* followed an earlier, much more detailed decision concerning the defendant's first conviction,[94] and the earlier *Davis* decision clarifies the later one. The plain fact is that neither of the *Davis* decisions nor both of them combined adopted the "irresistible impulse" test. That test had been included in the instruction of the Arkansas trial judge, in addition to the M'Naghten Rule. The Supreme Court merely held in the later *Davis* case that the instruction given in Arkansas regarding the test of insanity "was in no degree prejudicial to the rights of the defendant. . . ."[95] The only references to any legal tests in the first *Davis* opinion, which give any indication of the Supreme Court's views on the subject, are references to the M'Naghten test: "These extracts from the charge of the [trial] court present this important question: . . . if upon the whole evidence from whatever side it comes they [the jury] have a reasonable doubt whether at the time of killing the accused was mentally competent to distinguish between right and wrong or to understand the nature of the act he was committing?"[96] Again, the Supreme Court stated that "the crime of murder involves sufficient capacity to distinguish between right and wrong . . .;" and there are other indubitable references to the M'Naghten test.[97]

---

[91] *Id.* at 876.

[92] 36 F. 2d 548 (C. A. D. C. 1929).

[93] Davis v. United States, 165 U. S. 373, 41 L. Ed. 750, 17 S. Ct. 360, 362 (1897).

[94] Davis v. United States, 160 U. S. 469, 40 L. Ed. 499 (1895).

[95] 165 U. S. 373 at 378.

[96] 160 U. S. 469 at 478. See also the excerpts from the cases cited by the Supreme Court, *id.* at 485.

[97] *Id.* at 488. Also see 489.

The issue in *Davis* concerned the burden of proof and the first conviction was set aside because of a faulty instruction in that regard;[98] and the second *Davis* decision, which affirmed the second conviction, contains nothing which alters the meaning of the earlier lengthy opinion or in any way suggests that the Supreme Court approved the "irresistible impulse" test. The only reference in that decision to the test of mental disease was to the testimony of the psychiatrist, and the Court's language is wholly in terms of the M'Naghten Rule. Recently, in *Leland v. Oregon*, the Supreme Court held, " . . . it is clear that adoption of the irresistible impulse test is not 'implicit in the concept of ordered liberty.' "[99] And in *Fisher*, which arose in the District of Columbia, the Supreme Court stated that the accused "was then sane in the usual legal sense. He knew right from wrong. See M'Naghten's Case. . . ."[1]

The decision in *Smith*[2] did approve the "irresistible impulse" test, but in an extremely loose manner and with obviously inadequate support. The Court referred to "the modern well-established doctrine of 'irresistible impulse' "[3] which, at that time (1929) was centuries old and had won recognition in very few of the states. The opinion asserted

---

[98] The jury should have been instructed that in order to convict, they must believe beyond reasonable doubt that the defendant was sane, and that the burden of proving that rested on the prosecution. This is implied in the burden to prove the *mens rea* beyond reasonable doubt. "In *Davis v. United States*, we adopted a rule of procedure for the federal courts which is contrary to that of Oregon." Leland v. Oregon, 343 U. S. 798-99, 96 L. Ed. 1309, 72 S. Ct. 1002 (1952).

[99] Leland v. Oregon, 343 U. S. 800-801, 96 L. Ed. 1309, 72 S. Ct. 1002 (1952).

[1] 328 U. S. 463, 466, 90 L. Ed. 1382, 66 S. Ct. 1318, 1330 (1946). *Cf.* " . . . the test established in M'Naghten's case . . . approved by the Supreme Court in Davis v. United States, 160 U. S. 469, 476-477, 480, 492-493, 40 L. Ed. 499 (1895) . . .; Davis v. United States, 165 U. S. 373, 378, 41 L. Ed. 750 (1897) . . .; and Hotema v. United States, 186 U. S. 413, 421, 46 L. Ed. 1225 (1902). . . ." Dusky v. United States, 271 F. 2d 385, 394 (8th Cir. 1959).

[2] Smith v. United States, 36 F. 2d 548 (C. A. D. C. 1929).

[3] *Id.* at 549.

that the M'Naghten Rule "is no longer followed by the federal courts or by most of the state courts."[4] And the Court relied upon two civil actions involving insurance, neither of which represents the "irresistible impulse" test since they imply or assume that seriously impaired reason accompanied and caused the irresistibility of the impulse. Finally, the Court cited the second *Davis* decision, quoting in full the instruction of the Arkansas trial court but omitting to state that the issue there concerned the burden of proof. Ignoring, also, the important statement that the Arkansas instruction was "not prejudicial to the rights of the defendant," the Court asserted that the Supreme Court "adopted and followed" the "doctrine of irresistible impulse."[5] It can only be concluded that in the District of Columbia the "irresistible impulse" test rests upon a very frail foundation, if indeed it can be said to have any support in precedent. Both the M'Naghten Rule and the "irresistible impulse" test were, however, assumed to be the law there when *Durham* was decided and, as stated, both tests combined were found inadequate for the reasons noted above.

A sufficient number of decisions have been rendered in the District of Columbia since 1954 to show very definitely that *Durham* has greatly confused the law on mental disease and criminal responsibility. It is important to determine the reasons for this and to discover, if possible, what can be learned from this costly legal experience.

The opinion in *Durham* defined "disease" as "a condition which is considered capable of either improving or deteriorating." This seems to include almost any condition, indeed, it is regretfully submitted, almost anything in the universe that is subject to change. "Defect" was defined in

---

[4] *Ibid. Cf.* "The present test of criminal responsibility as adopted by forty-seven states, Hawaii, the federal circuits, the Supreme Court of the United States and many foreign jurisdictions is the now famous *M'Naghten* rule." Note, 43 Cornell L. J. 283 (1957), citing Annot., 45 A. L. R. 2d 1447 (1956) and an opinion of the Superior Court of Zurich, Switzerland, of March 22, 1950, 47 Schweiserisch Juristerzeitrag (1951).

[5] *Id.* at 550.

terms negating the above condition, which raises the additional troublesome notion that defects somehow defy the law of change. Both terms are included coordinately in the new rule, joined by the disjunctive—"if his unlawful [sic!] act was the product of mental disease or mental defect."

In addition to the problems thus raised regarding what the jury is to look for and find as "mental disease" or "mental defect," the same Circuit Court in *Stewart*[6] seems to have suggested that "psychopathy"—perhaps the vaguest and most disputed notion in the entire vast domain of psychiatry[7]—might be recognized as a mental disease or mental defect and thus as a defense under a plea of insanity, available, presumably, to the hundreds of thousands of offenders who are said to be psychopaths or "sociopaths," the presently preferred term.[8] It is difficult to avoid the conclusion that any mental condition which any psychiatrist believes to be a "mental disease" or "mental defect" will satisfy this phase of *Durham*.[9] In sum, the product in issue, *i.e.* the conduct, must be caused by a condition which is *"considered capable of either improving or deteriorating"* or is *"considered"* not able to do that; and that condition is the subject matter of "medical science."

[6] 214 F. 2d 878, 881-2 (C. A. D. C. 1954) ; see Overholser v. Leach, 257 F. 2d 667 (C. A. D. C. 1958) and 248 F. 2d 641 n 2 (1957).

[7] "The only conclusion that seems warrantable is that, at some time or other and by some reputable authority, the term psychopathic personality has been used to designate every conceivable type of abnormal character." Curran and Mallinson, *Psychopathic Personality*, 90 J. Ment. Sci. 278 (1944). See notes, 7 *supra* and 8 *infra*.

[8] "In view of Durham, the psychopath would be relieved of criminal responsibility if his behavior were regarded as a product of mental illness." Roche, The Criminal Mind 258 (1958).
Cf. "The definition of the term 'psychopathic personality' changes from author to author." Schilder, *op. cit. supra* note 9, at 238.

[9] The Circuit Court recognized that there is a problem in this regard: "The terms 'disease' and 'defect' are not so self-explanatory and our definition of them in Durham is not so definitive as to make elucidation always superfluous." Wright v. United States, 250 F. 2d 4, 11 (C. A. D. C. 1957). In Carter v. United States, 252 F. 2d 608, 617 (C. A. D. C. 1957), the Court said: " 'Mental disease' means mental illness. Mental illnesses are of many sorts and have many characteristics. They, like physical illnesses, are the subject matter of medical science." See the text at first note 2 *supra*.

After the *Durham* decision, it was suggested by several writers[10] that, instead of assisting defendants who pleaded insanity, the new formula might actually handicap them. This might happen because, lacking any definite tests, any psychiatrist could testify, on any ground, that the defendant was not suffering from a mental disease or mental defect. It now appears in subsequent decisions that *Durham* invites additional difficulty by requiring proof not only that there was a mental disease, which might be a very severe psychosis, but also that the act in issue was the product of that disease. It had previously been assumed, as no doubt continues to be the opinion of psychiatrists and others, that if the defendant had a psychosis at the time of the act in issue, that fact *ipso facto* excluded the required causal connection. The opinion in *Durham* suggests that additional proof must now be given in the District of Columbia to establish the causal connection between the disease and the act. In the writer's view, however, the hazard thus added to the problem of a psychotic defendant was certainly not intended by the Court, but resulted from the confusion produced by the *Durham* decision. In a goodly number of other jurisdictions, after evidence of insanity is introduced by the defendant, the prosecution has the burden of proving him sane. Proof that the defendant did or did not have a psychosis settles the causal question. But that is not decisive in the District of Columbia, as the cases show.

The emphasis by the Circuit Court, in reversing repeated convictions, is on the failure of the prosecution to establish beyond a reasonable doubt that the act was *not* the product of the disease. In view of the amorphous meaning of "mental disease" and "mental defect," it is not difficult to see why controversy has concentrated on the required negative causal connection. For by reference to the Court's definition of those terms, there can be some evidence of "mental disease" or "mental defect" in any case; and if psychopathy or socio-

---

[10] Note, 30 Ind. L. J. 194, 204 note 59 (1955); Hall, *Responsibility and Law: In Defense of the McNaghten Rules*, 42 A. B. A. J. 988-89 (1956); McGee, *Defense Problems Under the Durham Rule*, 5 Catholic Lawyer 35 (1959).

pathy, neurosis and other mild deviations from "normality" qualify, the prosecutors' burden must in practice center on the negative causal requirement.

That this requirement cannot be met by anyone under present circumstances is the inevitable result of the fact that psychiatry lacks the relevant knowledge. Just as psychiatry does not know the cause of psychosis, which is as mysterious as the cause of cancer, so, too, there is no knowledge of causal connection between psychoses and harmful conduct and, even more plainly between such conduct and sociopathy, neurosis, etc. No psychiatrist or group of psychiatrists can now establish that a mental disease is the *cause* of a subsequent act in the intended sense of that term. They simply do not know.[11] If that kind of causal connection cannot be established, how can anyone prove beyond any reasonable doubt that no such connection exists?[12]

Suppose, *e.g.* one were asked to prove that drinking unclean water does not cause typhoid fever. He could do this by showing (1) that some people who drink such water do not contract that disease and, much more persuasively, by showing (2) that people who drink only very clean water do contract typhoid when they are inoculated with typhoid germs, *i.e.* by proving the real cause. But if one set out to prove that inhaling gasoline fumes is not a cause of cancer, he could not support his effort by showing what was the cause of cancer, since that is unknown. If, in addition, it were assumed, erroneously, that the cause of cancer was known and one were then required to prove that X was not the cause of cancer, he would have a very difficult assign-

---

[11] ". . . if mental illness causes some to commit crimes, and not others, do we have a reliable method of discriminating those crimes which have no causal nexus with mental illness? . . . the answer is that psychiatry has yet to discover a method."
"I would submit that if the product question is withheld from the expert and confined to the triers, psychiatry can function properly."
"I have stated my belief that the 'product' question can be answered only affirmatively by the psychiatrist or not at all." Roche, The Criminal Mind 260, 266, 270 (1958).

[12] The logic of negative demonstration is a difficult subject which cannot be discussed here. Some of the relevant problems are noted in the following text.

ment, indeed. In *Durham*, the burden to disprove a causal relation between a "mental disease" or a "mental defect" and a particular act implies that knowledge of the cause exists. Since no such knowledge does exist, that is all that anyone can show. But showing that is not proof that there was no causal connection between a mental disease or mental defect and the act in issue.

In order to convey the fuller implications of the above, it is necessary to refer to the meaning of "cause" previously discussed.[13] It was found there that there are three aspects of causation, each one of which must be proved to establish a cause in criminal law, namely, (1) *sine qua non*—the "but for" test which requires that an antecedent be *necessary*; (2) the substantiality of that, which requires that the necessary antecedent be the sufficient (efficient, adequate) cause; and (3) the *mens rea* expressed in the conduct, in sum, the means-end causation required in penal liability. This type of causation was contrasted with the scientific view of causation, namely, that of co-variance of variables, the recurrent pattern of co-variation.

In Anglo-American law, criminal liability is imposed for the intentional or reckless commission of forbidden harms. Accordingly, to make sense of "causation" in penal law is to take account of the actor as a rational being. A harm is imputed to, *i.e.* is *caused* by, a normal actor *because* he voluntarily brought it about. And to say that he voluntarily brought it about is to say also that normal intelligence was involved in the conduct. This is how the problem of causation must be dealt with in analysis of criminal conduct; this is the logic and psychology of the plea of insanity, where only the *mens rea* factor in causation is in issue. The relevant psychology has been elucidated by many writers. "The power to act intelligently is volition," writes Professor H. G. Wyatt, "and the degree of volition expressed in any act is in direct ratio to the degree in which intelligence outweighs impulse. . . . [I]n no sense is volition

[13] *Supra* chapter 8.

random or arbitrary; for it is only so far as intelligence, the power of principle or order, participates, that volition participates also." In sum, "volition is the active aspect of intelligence."[14]

Under the *Durham* holding, the jury may be asked to assume that the defendant had normal intelligence, but exclude that from its consideration of the facts in issue, determine whether the defendant had a mental "disease" or "defect" according to the criteria specified by the court and reach a verdict as to whether the harm he committed was "the product" of the disease or defect. Since *Durham* also allows the "irresistible impulse" test, it is doubly certain that this non-teleological view of causation will be urged. In sum, what *Durham* attempted was to omit normal intelligence, accept the "irresistible impulse" hypothesis, which severs the bond between such intelligence and control of conduct, and thus define causation not in terms of its central means-end meaning in criminal law but in terms signifying a popular version of the scientific view of cause-in-fact—recurrent co-variation.

The District of Columbia judges assumed that the "product test" was "simple."[15] But for the reasons indicated above, the subsequent history of the test in the courts of the District of Columbia shows that it is anything but simple. In *Douglas,*[16] there had been two convictions for robbery. Both juries found the defendant sane at the time of the act, but the convictions were set aside on the ground that "the evidence affords no legal support for a finding beyond a reasonable doubt that mental disease did not cause the in-

[14] Wyatt, The Psychology of Intelligence and Will 153, 156 (1930). *Cf.* "If a crime is really the product, the result, the symptom of a psychosis, it is inevitable that the person who committed it cannot sufficiently distinguish between right and wrong and/or sufficiently know the nature and quality of his act." Wertham, *Psychoauthoritarianism and the Law,* 22 U. of Chi. L. Rev. 337 (1955).
"Irrationality is still accepted as a criterion of severe mental illness. . . ." Zilboorg, *The Sense of Reality,* 10 Psychoanal. Q. 183, 184 (1941).

[15] Durham v. United States, 214 F. 2d 862, 874 and again at 876 (C. A. D. C. 1954).

[16] Douglas v. United States, 239 F. 2d 52 (C. A. D. C. 1956).

dicted conduct. . . ." "Each case," the court added, "must be decided upon its own facts. No uniform legal principle is available to lead to a like appraisal of different factual situations."[17]

In *Carter*,[18] a conviction of first degree murder was reversed. In accordance with *Durham*, the trial court had instructed that it is not enough, to support an acquittal, to find that the defendant " 'was suffering from a diseased or defective mental condition. . . . You must find that the act was the result, the product of the mental abnormality.' " It was held that this did not make it clear that the government must establish beyond any reasonable doubt "that the alleged criminal act was not the product of a mental disease or defect. We spelled this out in detail in Durham supra." The trial judge in *Carter* had instructed the jury in terms of "the consequence, a growth, natural result or substantive end of a mental abnormality. . . ." But this was held "not adequate or sufficiently accurate."[19]

The Circuit Court then explained the meaning of the "product test:" "The simple fact that a person has a mental disease or defect is not enough to relieve him of responsibility for a crime. There must be a relationship between the disease and the criminal act . . . such . . . that the act would not have been committed if the person had not been suffering from the disease."[20] It was emphasized that this relationship is "a critical relationship." It does not mean "a direct emission, or a proximate creation, or an immediate issue of the disease. . . ."[21] It does mean "that the accused would not have committed the act he did commit if he had not been diseased as he was." By "critical relationship" the court also means "decisive, determinative, causal; we mean to convey the idea inherent in the phrases 'because of,' 'except for' . . . 'effect of,' 'result of,' 'causative factor'; the

---

[17] *Id.* at 58, 59.
[18] Carter v. United States, 252 F. 2d 608 (C. A. D. C. 1957).
[19] *Id.* at 614, 615.
[20] *Id.* at 615-16.
[21] *Id.* at 616.

disease made the effective or decisive difference between
doing and not doing the act. . . . But for this disease the act
would not have been committed."[22] The trial judge should
have made it clear that in order to convict "the jury must
find (1) that beyond reasonable doubt the accused is free of
mental disease; or if the finding is 'No, he may have a mental
disease,' then (2) that beyond reasonable doubt no relationship existed between the disease and the alleged criminal act
which would justify a conclusion that but for the disease
the act would not have been committed."[23]

In *Wright*,[24] a conviction of second degree murder was
set aside, three of the nine judges dissenting. Eleven psychiatrists had testified, five of them for the defense. Of four
of these, asked whether the act was the product of the
disease, one answered, "Yes;" another, "Could very well
be;" a third, "Likely;" a fourth, "Surely possible." Two
other psychiatrists who testified, "when asked the causation
question, replied that they had insufficient data to support
an opinion, Dr. Cushard noting that the causal connection
between an individual's mental illness and his act 'requires
very intensive investigation and examination of the person.' "[25] From the expert testimony the majority drew the
inference that several of the psychiatrists stated "with
varying degrees of certainty, that the shooting was the
product of the illness."[26] The minority, reading the same
record of the testimony, found that only five of the psychiatrists thought the defendant was insane at the time of the
killing "and only one of the five thought the criminal act
was the 'product' of the postulated insanity. The other six
psychiatrists, who had had equal opportunity for observation, said they could not diagnose Wright's mental condition
as of the morning of the murder."[27] The majority held:
"None of the eleven witnesses [psychiatrists] said that he
was not ill at the time of the shooting or that the shooting

[22] *Id.* at 617.
[23] *Id.* at 618.
[24] Wright v. United States, 250 F. 2d 4 (C. A. D. C. 1957).
[25] *Id.* at 8.
[26] *Ibid.*
[27] *Id.* at 15.

was not the product of the illness."[28] Several other decisions further reveal the causal difficulties produced by *Durham*.[29] In *Fielding*, *e.g.* a conviction of second degree murder was reversed "because the Government had failed to sustain its burden of proving beyond a reasonable doubt that the shooting was not the product of appellant's mental illness."[30]

By reference to the meaning of causation in law, summarized above,[31] it is evident that the emphasis on "but for" was unfortunate because that only connotes that an antecedent must be *necessary*. In that wide sense, a headache can be a cause of a homicide. It would include every temporary aberration, however slight, because it would be true that "but for" that condition, the act would not have been committed. There is, indeed, the additional language quoted above, especially in *Carter* and *Wright*, requiring not only that the mental disease or mental defect be a necessary antecedent, but also that it be efficient or substantial in producing the act.

Nonetheless, for the reasons stated above, the "product test" is fallacious in several respects: (1) It is so vague in

[28] *Id.* at 8. With reference to the causal problem, the court raised the question, may the jury convict "if it finds that . . . the illness was *one of the causes* of the act, *but not the exclusive cause?*" *Id.* at 12. It answered that question by referring to *Carter*. It then quoted from that decision, noted above, and repeated the formula from *Douglas:* "Without which [the crime] would not have occurred." *Id.* at 13.

In the dissenting opinion it was stated that the "product test" "is made more vague by what the majority says here. I am sure the District Court judges, who have heretofore found it difficult to understand and apply the rule, will now find it even more difficult." *Id.* at 19. See also the comment by Miller, J. in Catlin v. United States, 251 F. 2d 368, 372 (C. A. D. C. 1957). The minority stressed the fact that a clearly controverted issue had been presented for decision by the jury. See Dusky v. United States, 271 F. 2d 385 (8th Cir. 1959).

[29] Bradley v. United States, 249 F. 2d 922 (C. A. D. C. 1957). In Catlin v. United States, 251 F. 2d 368, 373 (C. A. D. C. 1957), a concurring judge referred to "a long and widely felt need for an explanation of the basis of the so-called 'product test.'" See also United States v. Fielding, 148 F. Supp. 46 (C. A. D. C. 1957).

[30] 251 F. 2d 878, 879 (C. A. D. C. 1957).

[31] *Supra*, also chapter 8.

its definition of "mental disease" and "mental defect"—and it must be remembered that not only psychiatrists but laymen also testify regarding the defendant's mental condition, and that lay juries decide the issue—that it does not provide the slightest clue regarding what the jury is to look for and find as the cause. (2) By making the *Durham* test independent of the M'Naghten test, the Court postulated a view of "product" which, while necessary to the determination of cause in law, is both insufficient and misleading as a sufficient alternative to the voluntary causing that is essential in penal law. All conduct is the expression of a mental state; and if a mind is seriously disordered, congruent conduct is not criminal. Nor did the inclusion of the M'Naghten Rule, as a retained, possible test, alter the significance of *Durham* because that Rule was discredited and the entire emphasis of the decision was upon the "product test." (3) There is no relevant psychiatric knowledge of causal connection in that sense. As the cautious statements of the expert witnesses in the District of Columbia cases indicate,[32] psychiatry is very far from having discovered valid factual generalizations correlating the relevant causes and effects.[33] Psychiatry is unable, *e.g.* to show any correlation between schizophrenia and harmful conduct; indeed, most psychotics are quite harmless and 80 per cent of the criminals are normal. To assume that psychiatry can say that a particular act was the product of a particular person's specific mental illness or defect is to require a kind of knowledge which cannot even analogously be supplied by physics. (4) The Court's formulation of the causal problem casts doubt upon the prevailing assumption that if a person was psychotic at the time he committed a harm, his psychosis was the substantial, sufficient cause of the harm in issue. The fact that this was stated in a way which technically places

---

[32] "In our experience psychiatrists generally are unwilling or unable to give testimony on the absence of causality, particularly to the extent required by the Government." Gasch, *Prosecution Problems Under the Durham Rule*, 5 Catholic Lawyer 21 (1959). See also *id.* at 26.

[33] See Nagel, *op. cit. supra* note 55.

an impossible burden on the prosecution is not appreciated by juries who appear in the cases following *Durham* to have been impressed by the surface meaning of the formula, especially the emphasis upon the causal connection that must exist in addition to the mental disease. At the same time, the door was opened wide to the sheerest speculation about "sociopathy."

The judges of the District of Columbia Court who formulated the *Durham* rule stated there and in succeeding decisions that the rule was "new" in relation to the existing law.[34] The only explicit indication of the novelty of the *Durham* rule is contained in the criticism of the "irresistible impulse" hypothesis, taken from the Report of the Royal Commission,[35] *i.e.* "irresistible" suggests impulsive, but what (some) psychiatrists now support is conduct, accompanied by brooding and reflection, which could not be prevented because of mental illness. Unfortunately, the Circuit Court apparently made no study of the interpretation of the "irresistible impulse" test in the jurisdictions where it is recognized; in any event, no citations are given to cases showing the restriction of the test to impulsive acts.

It is little wonder, therefore, that several judges have queried the claim that the *Durham* "product rule" added anything substantially new to the existing law of the District of Columbia, assumed to include the "irresistible impulse" test. In an American case which also accepted a recommendation of the Royal Commission, a New Mexico court, without deciding the moot issue—whether the "irresistible impulse" test was law in that State—adopted the formula, "incapable of preventing himself from committing it."[36]

---

[34] It was said to be "not unlike" the New Hampshire rule adopted in State v. Pike, 49 N. H. 399, 6 Am. Rep. 533 (1870). See Reid. *Understanding the New Hampshire Doctrine of Criminal Insanity*, 69 Yale L. J. 367 (1960).

[35] Quoted in Durham v. United States, 214 F. 2d 862 at 873.

[36] State v. White, 58 N. M. 324, 270 P. 2d 727, 731 (1954). See note 80 *supra*. It is noteworthy that while the Circuit Court of the District of Columbia and the New Mexico Supreme Court adopted the recommendation of the Royal Commission on Capital Punishment (1949-1953), that Report, as regards the instant question, has been ignored in Parliament, rejected as regards both of the principal

The majority made no inquiry into any actual difference between that formula and the "irresistible impulse" test. But the dissenting judge did raise that question, and he concluded that "the majority . . . have for all practical purposes embraced the doctrine of 'irresistible impulse' as a defence in criminal cases."[37] In *Fielding*, a District Court judge in the District of Columbia, after a careful study of the cases, also came to the conclusion that *Durham* added nothing to the law of the District. Is not *Durham*, he asked, only "a new manner of stating what may be called the test of 'inability to adhere to the right'?"[38] Again, in *Catlin*, one of the Circuit Court judges, in a dissenting opinion, came to the conclusion: "If the jury believed Catlin could distinguish between right and wrong and did not act under an impulse he could not resist, there was no basis for concluding that the criminal act, which was therefore knowingly, consciously and deliberately done, was the product of a mental defect or disorder. . . ."[39] If the facts to which the "irresistible impulse" test has been applied include not only impulsive acts but also "irresistible" acts accompanied by periods of "brooding" and "reflection," the avowed ground of novelty will not bear scrutiny.

There is a second, a ready and more persuasive, ground for concluding that the "product rule" adds nothing to the

---

recommendations by Justice Devlin, *Criminal Responsibility and Punishment: Functions of Judge and Jury*, 1 Crim. L. Rev. 661, 682 (1954), and similarly treated in Canada. See the Canadian Commission on the Law of Insanity as a Defence in Criminal Cases (1956).

[37] *Id.* at 270 P. 2d 737 (1954). To like effect, see the New Mexico Criminal Law Study Committee, Proposed Criminal Code 75 (Mimeo. Feb. 3, 1959).

[38] 148 F. Supp. 46, 52 (1957). ". . . an act committed by a person who though suffering from some mental abnormality is, nevertheless, able to distinguish between right and wrong, and whose will has not been so over-powered as to prevent him from adhering to the right, can hardly be deemed the product of a mental disease or a mental defect. In one sense it may be argued that the two tests are interchangeable. The basic difference between them is that the Pike and Durham formula is couched as an abstract, indefinite generality, which accords a greater freedom and range to scientific speculation and inquiry, and does not impose on expert witnesses a duty of precision of thought or statement; . . ." *Ibid.*

[39] 251 F. 2d 368, 372 (C. A. D. C. 1957).

"irresistible impulse" test, namely, the fact that both formulas take what significance they have from the scientific view of "cause." In the "product test," as in the other current versions of the "irresistible impulse" test—"inability to prevent himself" from committing the act and "inability to conform" to the law—the hypothesis is the same. Causing in the legal sense of means-end causing is irrelevant; what is pertinent and decisive is causing in the lay version of the scientific sense. It follows unavoidably, despite the fact that current polemics on the subject have taken a different course, that there is no substantial difference between the *Durham* rule and the proposed rule of the American Law Institute. Both include the M'Naghten Rule and "irresistible impulse" or its equivalent, the inability to prevent or conform. And, as Judge Samuel H. Hofstadter and S. R. Levittan, after criticizing the American Law Institute's tentatively proposed rule because, "like Durham, it goes too far toward permitting a medical diagnosis to supplant the concept of responsibility," state: "the term 'result' used in the [American Law Institute's] proposal is as nebulous as the expression 'product' used in Durham."[40]

A causal requirement, far from being new in penal law, is a *principle* of penal law, *i.e.* in every crime the conduct of the defendant must have caused the harm in issue. Thus, the immediate reaction of an experienced forensic psychiatrist to the *Durham* rule was that he had always interpreted the M'Naghten Rule as requiring that the conduct in issue must be the product of the mental illness.[41] In the M'Naghten view, a proscribed harm is caused in the sense of being an end sought by a rational person; and if the personality is seriously disordered, the harm that occurred is an event—it cannot be a harm caused, *i.e.* voluntarily committed, in the above sense. When that kind of causation

[40] *The McNaghten Rules—A Reappraisal and a Proposal*, 140 N. Y. L. J. 4 (Sept. 17, 1958).
[41] "If he had had better psychiatric advice, Judge Bazelon would have known that this [that the crime was the product of mental disease] is precisely how the *M'Naghten* rule has been interpreted in practice by experienced psychiatrists." Wertham, *op. cit. supra* note 14, at 336.

is excluded from penal law, only boundless uncertainty and pretense are introduced to confuse the problem of mental disease and criminal responsibility.

The ironical and unhappy consequence of such adjudication is to defeat the valid purpose which is sought. There is a sound core of psychiatric truth which, applied and explained by a competent practitioner, can be very helpful in the trial of the insanity issue. It is a body of truth that includes many valuable insights and resembles intensive case-history description. An able psychiatrist, given ample time and facilities, can tell the jury a great deal about the personality of diseased defendants, which would otherwise escape their notice. While this kind of knowledge can shed much light on the mental competence of a defendant, his understanding of the social and moral quality of his conduct, the integration or dissociation of his intelligence and the other basic functions of his personality, it is not the kind of knowledge that can be expressed in generalizations to answer the causal question of the correlation of a specific illness (with normal intelligence ignored!) and a specific act or even with classes of mental illnesses and classes of harmful acts. Psychiatrists in their clinical work do not even investigate whether a patient "could have" resisted his temptations.[42]

It is the lawyer's task to formulate a rule which reflects psychological-psychiatric theories that are compatible with criminal responsibility, not because lawyers may claim knowledge of psychiatry superior to that of opposed psychiatrists but because any rule necessarily reflects their opinion about the relevant psychiatry — as *Durham* abundantly reveals[43] — and also because in making their selection

[42] "Psychiatry can provide valuable aid to the criminal law if psychiatry remains on the periphery in a purely advisory capacity on medical matters: If psychiatry remains 'on tap'." Roche, The Criminal Mind 271 (1958).

For the specific areas and types of aid that psychiatry can thus render, see Dr. Roche's suggestions, *ibid.*

[43] "Medico-legal writers in large number . . . present convincing evidence that the right-and-wrong test is 'based on an entirely obsolete and misleading conception of the nature of insanity.'" Durham

among competing rules, they are bound to adhere to the foundations of the legal order. In the criminal law, this is expressed primarily in the law of criminal responsibility, especially the principle of *mens rea* and, of course, in the attendant exculpation of seriously diseased harm-doers. It is little wonder that in the dozen or more jurisdictions, including several federal circuits, where the *Durham* rule has been submitted, it has been invariably repudiated.[44] There is no reason why the like holding should not apply to the "irresistible impulse" and the "inability to prevent" or "conform" formulas.

If there is no novelty in the "product," "inability to conform" test, it by no means follows that these formulas can have no new effect. That *Durham* has been tremendously effective in raising difficult problems for the judges of the District of Columbia and in reversing repeated convictions is already evident. Equally clear is the abandonment of the principle of legality that such formulas produce. The experience of thoughtful laymen, guided by centuries of case-law, regarding what is normal must give way to the unfettered power of the expert to influence the jury by whatever conception of mental disease or mental defect he may entertain, and the Circuit Court decisions following *Durham* in the District of Columbia reveal that the expert testimony prevails.

---

v. United States, 214 F. 2d 862, 870-71 (C. A. D. C. 1954).

Cf. "To the extent that it relies on and quotes current psychiatric authorities, it is on shaky ground. The publications cited contain serious errors. . . . Judge Bazelon's final conclusion is unfortunately based on the psychiatric vagaries found in some of these publications." Wertham, *op. cit. supra* note 14, at 336.

". . . the language of the *Durham* decision . . . reifies some of the shakiest and most controversial aspects of contemporary psychiatry (*i.e.* those pertaining to what is 'mental disease' and the classification of such alleged diseases) and by legal fiat seeks to transform inadequate theory into 'judicial fact.'" Szasz, *Psychiatry, Ethics, and the Criminal Law,* 58 Col. L. Rev. 190 (1958).

[44] Some of the numerous decisions rejecting the Durham rule are cited in State v. Lucas, 30 N. J. 37, 152 A. 2d 50, 67 (1959); and see, also, the concurring opinion of Weintraub, C. J. in this case; Sauer v. United States, 241 F. 2d 640 (9th Cir. 1957) and United States v. Pollard, 171 F. Supp. 474 (D. C. E. D. Mich. 1959).

AMENDMENT OF THE M'NAGHTEN RULES

If we set aside the philosophical implications of psychiatric scientism, especially regarding the ethics of criminal responsibility, and attend to what has impressed many thoughtful lawyers and psychiatrists, it is essentially this—that the M'Naghten Rules are intellectualistic, that they test only the rational function but leave untouched the volitional and the emotional facets of the personality. Unfortunately, as the above discussion shows, the issues run much deeper and are far more complicated than that, as is evident from the fact that all parties in the current polemics accept the psychological theory of the integration of the functions of personality. If that were the only issue involved, there would be no problem except that of formulating rules to implement this common viewpoint. There is, however, a very critical problem because certain psychiatrists are seeking not to implement the psychology of integration but to put an end to criminal responsibility and all that that implies.[45] That is why they wish to terminate the test of rationality—the M'Naghten Rule—despite the fact that it stipulates an essential function of integrated personality.

It is a commonplace that a rule of law means what the courts say it means. And there is ample evidence that the vast majority of the courts take a very liberal view of the qualifications of experts, that the widest latitude is allowed psychiatrists in their testimony[46] and that, in effect, the

---

[45] "To the layman, the controversy over the M'Naghten Rules might seem something of an academic tempest in a legalistic teapot. But it is in fact the focus of a strenuous and socially significant struggle for power. The underlying issue is whether the courts shall retain their traditional right to determine . . . the issue of criminal responsibility or whether that right shall, under some guise or other, be transferred to members of the medical profession specializing in psychiatry." LaPiere, The Freudian Ethic 176-77 (1959).

[46] "No American case has been found where a trial court excluded evidence or refused to charge on the defense of insanity merely because the evidence in support of the defense related to neurosis or psychopathic personality or other mental disturbance rather than a psychosis." ALI Model Penal Code, Tent. Draft No. 4, 162 (April 25, 1955).

Cf. "Our conclusion is that . . . some other test must be added to those contained in the present formula. . . ." Royal Comm'n Report 108-109.

M'Naghten Rules have in recent years been interpreted to include the volitional and affective aspects of the personality. Considerable testimony could be adduced in support of the opinion of experienced forensic psychiatrists that the M'Naghten Rules function very well, especially that they do not result in holding psychotic persons criminally responsible,[47] although it is possible, of course, to find instances where trial courts have taken a restrictive view. In any event, it can hardly be expected that a rule, however formulated, will always be interpreted and applied in all courts in the best possible way.

There is a much more important point to be considered. Although it would be both interesting and important to have precise information regarding the actual functioning of the M'Naghten Rules, the fact that some courts or even that many courts interpreted them narrowly and unduly restricted the testimony of psychiatrists—assuming that this could be established—would not in the least signify that the M'Naghten Rules should be *abandoned*. Since it is agreed that such restrictive interpretation of the Rules is unwarranted, it is only necessary to give the word "know" in the Rules a wider definition so that it means the kind of knowing that is relevant, *i.e.* realization or appreciation of the wrongness of seriously harming a human being, as has been done by statute in Canada. The logic of reform is thus rigorously determined. There can be no question of abandoning the M'Naghten Rule of rationality but only of adding to it. As was suggested above, the word "know" in the M'Naghten Rules is the crux of the issue; and it is recognized by some critics of the Rules that a wide interpretation of that term would meet the current criticism.[48]

[47] The M'Naghten Rule "protects the mentally ill defendant, since he is not a free moral agent. Here is a direction in which psychiatrists can shape the application of the M'Naghten Rule without ripping it out of the statute books . . . I know of no workable rule that *is* any better." Davidson, *Criminal Responsibility: The Quest for a Formula*, reprinted from Psychiatry and the Law 61-70 (1955).

See *supra* notes 24 and 25.

[48] ". . . most of the legal witnesses . . . favoured the retention of the [M'Naghten] Rules unchanged." Royal Comm'n Report 86.

In sum, a sound rule of criminal responsibility must (1) retain irrationality as a criterion of insanity; (2) be consistent with the theory of the integration of all the principal functions of personality; (3) be stated in terms that are understandable to laymen; and (4) facilitate psychiatric testimony. Accordingly, the following is suggested:

A crime is not committed by anyone who, because of a mental disease, is unable to understand what he is doing and to control his conduct at the time he commits a harm forbidden by criminal law. In deciding this question with reference to the criminal conduct with which a defendant is charged, the trier of the facts should decide (1) whether, because of mental disease, the defendant lacked the capacity to understand the nature and consequences of his conduct; and (2) whether, because of such disease, the defendant lacked the capacity to realize that it was morally wrong to commit the harm in question.[49]

The proposed rule focuses attention upon the defendant's control of his conduct, thus taking full account of the voli-

---

Cf. "If the word 'know' were given this broader interpretation, so as to require knowledge 'fused with affect' and assimilated by the whole personality—so that, for example, the killer was capable of identifying with his prospective victim—much of the criticism of the knowledge test would be met." Weihofen, Mental Disorder as a Criminal Defense 77 (1954).

"When no longer dismembered and falsified in one-dimensional aspect, but considered in all that we sometimes imply by 'appreciation,' 'realization,' 'normal evaluation,' 'adequate feeling,' 'significant and appropriate experiencing,' etc. the term 'knowing' does not restrict us solely to a discussion of the patient's reasoning abilities in the abstract." Cleckley & Bromberg, *The Medico-Legal Dilemma*, 42 J. Crim. L., C. & P. S. 729, 737 (1952). See also Cleckley, Mask of Sanity 495-501 (2nd ed. 1950); Hall, *Psychiatry and the Law—A Dual Review*, 38 Iowa L. Rev. 686, 696 (1953).

"In many of the above cases the individual's mind is sufficiently clear to know what he is doing, but at the same time the true significance of his conduct is not appreciated either in relation to himself or others." Sir David Henderson, Royal Comm'n Report 87.

[49] A logical analysis of this formulation was made by Allen, *Symbolic Logic: A Razor-Edged Tool for Drafting and Interpreting Legal Documents*, 66 Yale L. J. 864-872 (1957). Some of Mr. Allen's assumptions, leading to the conclusion that the writer's proposed rule is ambiguous in certain respects, failed to take account of the preceding text, especially that the theory of integration is to be applied. The implications of this theory limit the postulates upon which verdicts could be rendered.

tional function of personality. The emotional facet is not specified because that is significant and relevant in its effect on the volitional function or as evidence of irrationality;[50] but the words "control his conduct" would make it easy for the expert witness to discuss the emotional result of dissociation and the like. The present allegedly restrictive word "know" gives way to the wider terms "understand" and "realize." These terms—the latter in association with the words "morally wrong"—should also facilitate interpretations that take account of the affective quality of personality. In short, the proposed rule, in conformity with the theory of integration, joins the rational and the volitional functions. Finally, it might be desirable, in instructing juries, to supplement the above rule by a longer statement, explaining in very simple terms the theory of the integration of the mental functions, preferably in relation to the facts in issue.

Since the capacity to make ordinary relevant valuations is retained in the proposed rule, it is necessary to consider the assertion that psychiatry cannot contribute to the adjudication of that issue. This assertion, it is submitted, is far from reflecting what is implied in psychiatric therapy. "Cure" implies a standard,[51] as does the psychiatrist's painstaking effort to confront his patient with the truth about himself.[52] Moreover, despite occasional assertions

[50] "The value of the 'right and wrong' concept is that it is a more easily measurable aspect of the mind than any other except intelligence. One cannot measure affect, or imagination, or will, but we can measure ethical values, and we can measure the accuracy of the individual's subjective evaluation of reality." Cavanagh, *The Responsibility of the Mentally Ill For Criminal Offenses*, 4 Catholic Lawyer 325 (1958).

[51] See *supra* notes 4 and 5. "Some philosophers and psychiatrists believe that the alleged moral neutrality of the psychotherapist is a fiction. If this is so, as the present writer believes, the psychiatrists need to be acutely aware of their value orientations." Crockett, *Misunderstanding One Another*, pub. in Psychoanalysis, Scientific Method and Philosophy 362 (Hook ed. 1959). See also, Hospers, *Philosophy and Psychoanalysis*, id. at 350-52.

[52] ". . . the analyst's job . . . is essentially one of encouraging and facilitating the growth of the patient's own spontaneous ethical standard. . . ." French, *Psychoanalysis and Ethics* 10 (U. of Chi. Round Table, 1950).

regarding the scientific rigor of psychiatry, clinical analysis consists largely of case-history and a reconstruction of the patient's experiences in terms of various theories. The essence of the principal method of diagnosis is the use of empathy, the sensitive re-living of the patient's experience. While the causal postulate and genetic explanation are employed, it is also widely recognized that such analysis would be both incomplete and inaccurate if the analyst did not attain considerable insight into the patient's scheme of values.[53] This requires a vicarious experience of his moral conflicts and a diagnosis which, if it is meaningful, implies an ethical appraisal.[54] The psychiatrist's purpose, as a physician, is to marshal the patient's potentialities to help him overcome his difficulties.[55] Therapy looks to the future, and it assumes that at least some patients can assist their own recovery; and that, to a very large extent, requires them to cope with moral problems.[56] Thus, it seems arbitrary to insist that psychiatrists can tell a jury nothing about the

[53] Whitehorn, *Psychiatry and Human Values*, in Psychiatry and the Law 152-56 (Hoch & Zubin ed. 1955).

[54] See Hall, Theft, Law and Society xvi (2nd ed. 1952).

[55] Whitehorn, *The Concepts of "Meaning" and "Cause" in Psychodynamics*, 104 Am. J. Psychiatry 289 (1947).

[56] Dr. Harry Stack Sullivan writes:
"[T]he therapist functions by rectifying impractical evaluational systems. Personal evaluations—those things that we call good and bad, right and wrong . . . are momentary manifestations in a given personal situation—momentary presenting features, if you please— of highly integrated, interpenetrative systems of evaluation. And, therefore, the therapist in attempting to alter the value that a patient puts upon a certain act, or a certain belief, is not dealing with a little atom but is actually undertaking to change a very large integrated system in the person. These systems of evaluations, these very large integrations, all of which combine in various ways to form the personality itself are very intimately connected with what we may call the feeling of personal worth which the particular individual has. This feeling of personal worth is most intimately tied up with the evaluational systems which apply to one's acts and the acts of other people, and thereby forms the channels by which are expressed most of the positive movements of the personality and most of the negative, hostile, or destructive movements of the personality." Sullivan, *The Theory of Anxiety and the Nature of Psychotherapy*, 12 Psychiatry 4-5 (1949). See also Wertham, *A Psychiatrist Looks at Psychiatry and the Law*, 3 Buffalo L. Rev. 41, 49-50 (1953), and Fingarette, *Moral Guilt and Responsibility*, 4 Psychoanalysis 46 (1955-56).

capacity of the defendant to appreciate the ordinary moral significance of his conduct.

Finally, insofar as it is true that some psychiatrists are not qualified to testify about such problems, it may be suggested that they have neglected the societal milieu in which mental disease occurs. A distinguished forensic psychiatrist has made this point very persuasively, concluding that "an asocial psychiatry becomes inevitably an anti-social psychiatry."[57] If more clinical psychiatrists could be persuaded to study the social environment in which mental diseases occur, they would be able to co-operate fully in the interpretation of the proposed rule, and they would also accelerate the development of forensic psychiatry. Fortunately, there are indications that many psychiatrists have recently been alerted to the pertinent issues, and they are giving increased attention to the social aspects of psychiatry, its interrelations with other disciplines, and the cogency of valuation in the study of human conduct.

The presently rudimentary character of forensic psychiatry is evident in the fact that it has hardly been noticed that the use of psychiatry in the administration of rules of law[58] presents quite different problems than does the interrelation of psychiatry and an empirical legal discipline.[59] The construction of interdisciplinary knowledge[60] is also handicapped by the fact that psychiatry is based upon di-

[57] Wertham, Book Review, *op. cit. supra* note 28, at 572. Dr. Wertham also writes, "The whole overemphasis on psychology as the basic consideration is misleading, and serves to divert attention from the social environment in which all psychological forces operate." *Id.* at 569. See Szasz, *Some Observations on the Relationship Between Psychiatry and the Law,* 75 Arch. Neur. & Psych. 297 (1956).

[58] "The purpose of expert testimony is to communicate to this body of ordinary persons [the jury] the wisdom and understanding necessary for the triers to exercise sound judgment in determining the issues in controversy." Ladd, *Expert Testimony,* 5 Vand. L. Rev. 414, 428 (1952).

[59] See Lasswell, *Legislative Policy, Conformity and Psychiatry,* in Psychiatry and the Law 13 (Hoch & Zubin ed. 1955).

[60] "One of the greatest difficulties connected with cooperation between representatives of different sciences is the lack of a common terminology." Linton, *Foreword* to Kardiner, The Individual and His Society V (1939).

verse conflicting theories and employs vague, strange words;[61] and the day of a uniform terminology among psychiatrists, such as is found in biology, is remote. The difficulties in the way of constructing a forensic psychiatry are by no means due only to the limitations of psychiatry. They arise equally from the limitations of legal theory where it is necessary to clarify many fundamental problems, including, even, the difference between motive and *mens rea* and the exclusion of the former from the legal definition of criminal conduct.

One of the most difficult barriers to the progress of forensic psychiatry is the thesis advanced by judges and lawyers, and accepted by many psychiatrists, that criminal responsibility is a strictly legal question. In 1883, Stephen, *e.g.* wrote, "The question, 'What are the mental elements of responsibility?' is, and must be, a legal question."[62] And in 1923 Lord Atkin's Committee said, "much of the criticism directed from the Medical side at the M'Naghten Rules is based upon a misconception. It appears to assume that the rules contain a definition of insanity. . . ."[63] Since it is customary to emphasize the formal meaning of law, the inference is that lawyers are raising a "no trespassing" sign, that they are, in effect, saying, "insanity is a purely legal, technical matter which has nothing to do with psychiatry." But the plain fact is that psychiatry is very closely involved in the meaning of the legal tests of responsibility.

[61] "Psychoanalytic language has been . . . ultra-complex and involved, derived from Greek and other esoteric terminology, usually idiosyncratic, and frequently vague and meaningless. There has been a notable lack, in analytic writings, of sticking to concepts and terms which have clear-cut factual referents and avoiding the coining of terms and abstractions which have a dubious existence." Ellis, *An Introduction to the Principles of Scientific Psychoanalysis*, 41 Genetic Psychol. Monographs 149, 193 (Murchison ed. 1950). See note 73 *supra*.

[62] 2 Stephen, A History of the Criminal Law of England 183 (1883).

[63] Committee on Insanity and Crime, Report 6 (1923). So, too, Lord Hewart: "The law does not purport or presume to define insanity. That is a medical question." Essays and Observations 216 (1930). And see Wechsler, *The Criteria of Criminal Responsibility*, 22 U. Chi. L. Rev. 373 (1955).

Stephen himself gave the clue to that when, after making the above quoted statement, he said, "the mental elements of responsibility . . . are knowledge that an act is wrong and power to abstain from doing it"[64]—in which statement not a single word is a legally technical one. Nonetheless, it is often asserted that the tests laid down in the M'Naghten Rules were not intended to, nor do they, specify any criteria of serious mental disease. Instead, it is said that mental disease is a psychiatric question, and that the legal question is, which mentally diseased harm-doers shall be held "insane," *i.e.* not legally responsible? But the facts of adjudication show that "psychosis" and "insanity" are far from being unrelated.

The definitions of "psychosis" that psychiatrists formulate in their classifications and for purposes of clinical work reflect their professional objectives. When a trial concerns the defendant's legal responsibility, certain questions are asked regarding "insanity," but they do not express peculiarly legal criteria or anything technical or arbitrary regarding the symptoms of serious mental disease. They specify characteristics of psychosis that are relevant to legally significant conduct. If those questions or tests had no foundations in fact, the testimony of psychiatrists would not be relevant to the issue of responsibility. But, of course, it is relevant;[65] and the reason for its relevance is revealed in the application of the tests of responsibility. The facts of adjudication are that, given the case of a psychotic defendant, as determined by legally recognized methods, exculpation follows because a defensible, relevant meaning of "psychosis" is incapacity to understand the wrongness of

---

[64] 2 Stephen, *op. cit. supra* note 62.

[65] "The criteria that an offender, to be held not responsible, must be in such a state of disorder 'as not to know the nature and quality of the acts for which he is indicted and not to know the acts are wrong,' are valuable ones." Cleckley, Mask of Sanity 289 (1941). See Cleckley, *id.* at 495-501 (2nd ed. 1950).

"The word 'psychosis' is a synonym for insanity and the adjective 'psychotic' is a synonym for insane." Davidson, *The Psychiatrist's Role in the Administration of Criminal Justice*, 4 Rutgers L. Rev. 578, 580 (1950).

one's extremely harmful conduct and to control oneself in that regard. Indeed, it is assumed or granted that the defendants excluded from responsibility by the M'Naghten Rules were psychotic. Does not this imply that the tests specify valid criteria of psychoses?[66]

The triers of the facts do not first listen to the expert's testimony, decide that it signifies that the defendant was psychotic and then later ask themselves, as an independent question, whether he was insane, knew what he was doing, and so on. On the contrary, not only are the experts asked to testify in direct relation to the terms of the tests, but every statement they make is also interpreted as telling the triers of the facts something about the accused's competence to understand and control his conduct. The inquiry proceeds upon the assumption that to have a psychosis means to be incompetent in the ways the tests designate. There is no requirement of science or language that there be only one correct or one scientific definition of "psychosis." A definition reflects a point of view and certain objectives, and all descriptive definitions, apart from an inevitable degree of vagueness, must find verification in the facts. In sum, the so-called "legal" definition of "insanity" is a *social* definition of "psychosis," relevant to the criteria of criminal responsibility. The notion has spread that "insanity" is a technical legal term because clinical psychiatrists have not been interested in the social aspects of psychiatry. Since the definitions they use reflect their special clinical needs, they are bound to differ from the definitions of "psychosis" which they would propose if they studied the social incidence and meaning of mental disease.

In the present situation, the principal clue to a sound resolution of many issues concerning mental disease and criminal responsibility is that recognized by Stephen—the psy-

[66] "The criterion [M'Naghten Rules] is therefore sound as far as it goes." Royal Comm'n Report 108. See also Wertham, *A Psychiatrist Looks at Psychiatry and the Law*, 3 Buffalo L. Rev. 41, 49-50 (1953).

chology of the integration of the functions of personality. This is the common ground upon which lawyers and psychiatrists can collaborate.

CHAPTER XIV

INTOXICATION

THE penal liability of grossly intoxicated harm-doers raises difficult theoretical questions, involving the principles of *mens rea* and concurrence. The case-law also reflects traditional attitudes of marked hostility toward drunken offenders,[1] which renders sound adjudication harder to achieve than in insanity cases.[2] And recent research on alcoholism supports the impression that where gross intoxication and serious harm-doing concur, the criminal law is severe and indiscriminate.

The following discussion of the criminal liability of inebriate harm-doers is restricted to the substantive law. In such an analysis it is necessary to draw definite distinctions in legally significant terms, *e.g.* between the normal habitual drunkard and the addict. A full discussion of the problem would, of course, take account of the administration of the law and of impairments in personality which, while they do not lie beyond the range of "normality," are sufficiently serious to require mitigation and special treatment in peno-correctional institutions; and it would also deal with relevant aspects of alcoholism and the far-ranging problem of hospitalization and therapy. The elucidation and reform of the substantive penal law is, however, a prerequisite to the improvement of administrative and therapeutic facilities.

THE COMMON LAW AND THE EXCULPATORY RULE

The early common law apparently made no concession be-

[1] See People v. Townsend, 214 Mich. 267, 183 N. W. 177 (1921).
[2] East, *Murder, From the Point of View of the Psychiatrist,* 3 Medico-Legal & Criminol. Rev. 61, 92 (1935).

cause of intoxication,[3] although the contemporaneous records indicate mild treatment of insane homicides[4] and medieval canon law recommended indulgence to inebriate harm-doers.[5] The earliest relevant English report,[6] dated 1551, approved the death sentence for a homicide committed in extreme intoxication. This, however, was typical of the era of the greatest severity in the entire history of English criminal law rather than indicative of harshness regarding intoxication in particular. In any event, from that time to the early part of the nineteenth century, rigorous law prevailed, although the efforts by Coke and Blackstone to hold drunkenness an aggravation met with no success.

Hale supported this law "partly from the easiness of counterfeiting the disability."[7] Even two centuries later, Wharton said, "There could rarely be a conviction for homicide if drunkenness avoided responsibility,"[8] and he also feared it would be deliberately resorted to "as a shield." Other thoughtful observers, Stephen included, believed most homicides and many other crimes were caused by intoxication and that it would not do to recognize it as a defense. Story, apparently influenced by Coke's somber righteousness, stressed the merit of "the law not permitting a man to avail himself of the excuse of his own gross vice and misconduct, to shelter himself from the legal consequences of such crime."[9] These opinions of classical writers reflect the psychological foundation of the current penal law.[10]

---

[3] See Singh, *History of the Defense of Drunkenness in English Criminal Law*, 49 L. Q. Rev. 528, 530 (1933).

[4] *Ibid.* In 1330 a lunatic homicide was pardoned by the king. Fitz. Abr. No. 351, cited *id.* at 530 note 9.

[5] Mittermaier, *On the Effect of Drunkenness upon Criminal Responsibility and the Application of Punishment*, 23 Amer. Jurist 294 (1840).

[6] Reninger v. Fogossa (1551, K. B.), 1 Plowd. 1, 75 Eng. Rep. 1.

[7] Hale, Pleas of the Crown 32 (1736).

[8] 1 Wharton, Criminal Law 95 (1932); *cf.* H. M. Commissioners' Seventh Report on Criminal Law 19 (1843).

[9] United States v. Drew, 25 Fed. Cas. No. 14, 993 (C. C. D. Mass. 1828). Note his premise that the crime charged was committed, that the intoxication was merely superadded.

[10] For a summary of the law of various countries, see Lee, *Drunkenness and Crime*, 27 Law Mag. & Rev. (5th ser.) 144, 157, 308 (1902);

One of the grounds put forth, that drunkenness can be readily feigned, may be disposed of at once. No reason has been advanced why determination of this fact presents any greater difficulty than do those raised, *e.g.* by mistake, legal provocation or fraud; indeed, the contrary seems more probable when it is considered that the history of the defendant and the events preceding his harm-doing are examined in greater than usual detail in the drunkenness cases. In addition, the burden of proving intoxication was, and usually is, placed on the defendant.[11] Moreover, simulation of intoxication to avoid liability for a crime presupposes high intelligence, histrionic ability and careful calculation. Even a superficial survey of the reported cases shows that inebriate offenders have the very opposite qualities — they are weak, impulsive, and frequently subnormal. In light of these considerations, the persistently voiced fear of deception suggests the presence of influences other than the expressed reasons. Since a normal person who planned to commit a crime would not wish to incapacitate himself by becoming grossly intoxicated (and that is the degree relevant to the moot issues of penal liability), the argument that prospective offenders would actually become intoxicated "as a shield" is even less persuasive. Such professed grounds of decision indicate bias against inebriate harmdoers and lack of knowledge of alcoholism rather than rational support of the rule.

There is, moreover, internal evidence in Anglo-American cases that the supporters of the rigorous law experienced serious doubts, misgivings that were expressed in a mitigating rule, at odds with various other laws, but, nonetheless, a step in a wiser, more humane direction. It seems to have been suggested first by Justice Holroyd in a murder case in 1819 that, while, of course, voluntary drunkenness could not be an excuse, it should be considered in deter-

---

Mittermaier, *op. cit. supra* note 5; Barbier, Le Délit Alcoolique 56 ff., 99 ff. (1930).

11 Wilson v. State, 60 N. J. L. 171, 37 A. 954 (1897); Gustavenson v. State, 68 P. 1006 (Wyo. 1902); see Underhill, Criminal Evidence 625 (4th ed. 1935).

mining the issue of premeditation.[12] The prescient Justice
is said to have later retracted this view; in any event,
Justice Park confidently asserted that "there would be no
safety for human life if it were to be considered as law,"[13]
and the defendant in that case was executed. There was
some tendency to relax the rule in a later case of aggravated
assault but this was largely negatived by the instruction
that if a stick was used, then the drunkenness was relevant,
"but where a dangerous instrument is used, which, if used,
must produce grievous bodily harm, drunkenness can have
no effect on the consideration of the malicious intent of the
party."[14] In 1838, however, in a case of assault with intent
to murder, the jury was instructed that gross intoxication
might disprove the intention required for the aggravated
offense.[15] The exception, slow to take root,[16] was stated by
Stephen in language which became accepted as the major
exculpatory rule, establishing the most important change
in the law of the criminal liability of inebriates.   "[A]l-
though," said Stephen, "you cannot take drunkenness as any
excuse for crime, yet when the crime is such that the intention of the party committing it is one of its constituent
elements, you may look at the fact that a man was in drink
in considering whether he formed the intention necessary
to constitute the crime."[17] Stephen's formulation definitely

[12] Rex v. Grindley, quoted in Rex v. Carroll (N. P. 1835), 7 C. & P.
145, 173 Eng. Rep. 64.

[13] *Id.* at 147, 173 Eng. Rep. at 65.

[14] Rex v. Meakin (N. P. 1836), 7 C. & P. 297, 173 Eng. Rep. 131;
cf. State v. Kale, 124 N. C. 816, 32 S. E. 892 (1899), where a conviction of murder in the first degree was affirmed. "Drunkenness . . . does
not repel malice nor lower the grade of the crime." *Id.* at 819, 32 S. E.
at 896.

[15] Regina v. Cruse (N. P. 1838), 8 C. & P. 541, 173 Eng. Rep. 710.

[16] It was stated in Regina v. Monkhouse (N. P. 1849), 4 Cox C. C. 55.

[17] Regina v. Doherty (N. P. 1887), 16 Cox C. C. 306, 308. In his
Digest of the Criminal Law 22 (5th ed. 1894), Stephen used the term
"specific intention." In Regina v. Baines (Lancs. Assizes, 1886), Justice Day said: "I have ruled that if a man were in such a state of intoxication that he did not know the nature of his act or that his act
was wrongful, his act would be excusable." London Times, Jan. 25,
1886, p. 10, col. 4. No English case has gone to that extent despite a
similar dictum in D. P. P. v. Beard (H. L. 1920), 14 Cr. App. R. 197.

established the emerging rationale of the long-desired mitigation of punishment of grossly inebriated homicides. It
was technically persuasive; it has been applied and reiterated in hundreds of cases. The judges straight-facedly
insist that this rule is quite consistent with the traditional
one that voluntary drunkenness never excuses; it is simply
that a material element, the required *mens rea*, is lacking in
the commission of a homicide under gross intoxication.
Logic and law, not sentiment for drunkards, prevail.

One might have imagined that the exculpatory rule would
have completely undermined the rigorous traditional liability, since *mens rea* is the requirement of a fundamental
principle. But major limitations persist,[18] enmeshed in a
structure of inherited unsound rules which complicate
matters. These complexities are, of course, not found in the
few states which simply reject the exculpatory rule *in toto*.[19]
So, too, the rule is sometimes ignored in cases that outrage
public sensibilities,[20] as in a Texas decision where the defendant failed to stop his automobile after injuring a
woman. His plea that he was "crazy drunk" and did not
know what had happened was rejected, the defendant's
"lack of knowledge having arisen because of his voluntary
intoxication."[21] Even when lip-service is paid the exculpatory rule, it is sometimes sharply curtailed, even rendered
entirely ineffective, by the insistence that "the intoxication
must be, in order to be available, of that degree and extent
as renders the defendant practically an automaton. . . ."[22]
And, as noted, the burden of proof of lack of capacity to entertain the required criminal intent is upon the defendant.[23]
Thus there is avowed resistance to the exculpatory rule in

[18] See *infra* pp. 532, 536-37, 541.

[19] See Note, 26 U. of Mo. Bull. L. Ser. 32, 59 (1925).

[20] *E.g.* assault with intent to rape. See Note, 25 J. Crim. L. 457, 458
(1934) ; *cf.* State v. Comer, 296 Mo. 1, 247 S. W. 179 (1922).

[21] Martinez v. State, 137 Tex. Cr. App. 434, 441, 128 S. W. 2d 398,
401 (1939).

[22] Tate v. Commonwealth, 258 Ky. 685, 695, 80 S. W. 2d 817, 821
(1935).

[23] See note 11 *supra*.

some quarters and in aggravating circumstances. But the rule permitting disproof of the relevant *mens rea* has been widely accepted and, no doubt, it has functioned to ameliorate the older law in most jurisdictions. It is in these jurisdictions that interesting problems of penal theory arise.

Bishop, summarizing the prevailing law, states: "Evidence of intoxication therefore is admissible for the purpose of ascertaining ... whether he was incapable of entertaining the specific intent charged, where such intent, under the law, is an essential ingredient of the particular crime alleged to have been committed."[24] The application of this rule in homicide cases has been limited to the exclusion of premeditation in most states, and thus results in liability for second degree murder. In a minority of the states and in England, where murder is not divided into degrees, the liability is for manslaughter.[25] This diversity in the United States might be expected to result from differences in statutes as to the requirement of *mens rea* in murder of the second degree.[26] But there are other much more potent influences. In a Pennsylvania case,[27] *e.g.* the court held that intoxication would not avail unless the defendant was "incapable of conceiving any intent," in which event "his grade of offense is reduced to murder in the second degree."[28] The premise of the majority view is that: "As between the two offenses of murder in the second degree and manslaughter, voluntary intoxication cannot be a legitimate subject of inquiry. What constitutes murder in the second degree by a

---

[24] 1 Bishop, Criminal Law 299 (9th ed. 1923). *Cf.* ". . . where a particular intent is charged, and such intent forms the gist of the offense, as contradistinguished from the intent necessarily entering into every crime. . . ." Crosby v. People, 137 Ill. 325, 342, 27 N. E. 49, 52 (1891).

[25] For a collection of cases, see Notes, 12 A. L. R. 861, 875 (1921); 79 A. L. R. 897, 904 (1932). See also Note, 29 Yale L. J. 928 (1920).
Some doubt is cast on the English law by Rex v. Scholey (1909), 3 Cr. App. R. 183.

[26] See Borland v. State, 249 S. W. 591 (Ark. 1923).

[27] Commonwealth v. Lehman, 309 Pa. 486, 164 A. 526 (1932).

[28] *Id.* at 499, 164 A. at 530.

sober man is equally murder in the second degree if committed by a drunken man."[29]

While the courts do not explain why intoxication cannot be "a legitimate subject of inquiry" in the above regard, the reasons may be surmised. The proximate analogy is "legal provocation," and intoxication is presumed to be unacceptable as an equivalent of that.[30] The presence of influences other than the statutes is further revealed in the majority's reiteration of the old dictum that, regardless of gross intoxication, "Where a homicide results from the use of a dangerous and deadly weapon, the law implies malice, and an intention to kill from the effective use of the weapon, and, therefore, the crime is presumably murder in the second degree."[31] It is apparent, also, that although the minority view[32] reaches results that are defensible, i.e. manslaughter, the analysis employed is often fallacious. Frequently the decisions rest upon the erroneous assumption that intention is invariably excluded from manslaughter;[33] and this suggests that "criminal negligence" (recklessness)[34] is the ground of liability. But this is not discussed. Both majority and minority interpretations are further confused by the notion that murder requires no "specific intent," that "general intent" is sufficient.[35]

[29] Wilson v. State, 60 N. J. L. 171, 184, 37 A. 954, 958 (1897). See Gustavenson v. State, 68 P. 1006, 1010 (Wyo. 1902). In this case, the court cites as an authority, Upstone v. People, 109 Ill. 169 (1883), and 2 Bishop, Criminal Law § 400 (8th ed. 1892). Cf. Johnson v. Commonwealth, 135 Va. 524, 115 S. E. 673 (1923), and note 69 infra.

[30] See State v. Aragon, 35 N. M. 198, 292 P. 225 (1930).

[31] Aszman v. State, 123 Ind. 356 (1889); cf. People v. Leonardi, 135 N. Y. 360, 38 N. E. 372 (1894). "He may be perfectly unconscious of what he does and yet be responsible. He may be incapable of express malice; but the court imputes malice in such a case. . . ." Johnson v. Commonwealth, 135 Va. 524, 527, 115 S. E. 673, 674 (1923).

[32] Laws v. State, 144 Ala. 118, 42 S. 40 (1905); State v. Rumble, 105 P. 1 (Kan. 1909); State v. Corrivau, 93 Minn. 38, 100 N. W. 638 (1904).

[33] In these instances, no special statutes are involved, nor is the manslaughter classed as "involuntary."

[34] See Note, 6 Cornell L. Q. 193 (1921).

[35] See supra pp. 142-43.

There is not the least admission anywhere that drunkenness may be treated as the equivalent of "legal provocation." On the contrary, so far as their utterances are concerned, it is clear that the courts do not relax the rules on legal provocation to include homicides committed in gross intoxication.[36] They deny legal effect to the admitted fact that drunken persons are more easily aroused and lose self-control more quickly than do sober ones. Nor will they allow intoxication to enter the jury's determination of "cooling-time." Indeed, some judges do not hesitate to color the jury's calculation by instructing that: "The question is, was there time for a reasonable man, in like circumstances, to have cooled, not a drunkard or a madman,"[37] even suggesting that no indulgence should be granted to one who had "taken the quantity of liquor requisite to make him a savage. . . ."[38]

The alleged reason for refusing to equate drunkenness with legal provocation, namely, that since "drunkenness does not excuse homicide, so by the same token it may not be available as a factor contributing to heat of passion,"[39] is hardly persuasive, especially in the light of the exculpatory rule that is simultaneously avowed.

[36] But *cf.* "where what the law deems sufficient provocation has been given," drunkenness may be considered because "passion is more easily excitable. . . ." Rex v. Thomas (N. P. 1820), 7 C. & P. 817, 173 Eng. Rep. 356, 358. This rather ambiguously suggests modification of the usual rule, but no English case appears to have adopted the implication. *Cf.* Rex v. Birchall (1913), 9 Cr. App. R. 91; Rex v. Letenock (1917), 12 Cr. App. R. 221; State v. Hurley, 1 Houst. Cr. Rep. 28 (Del. 1858).

[37] State v. McCants, 1 Speers 391 (S. C. 1843).

[38] *Id.* at 395.

[39] State v. Aragon, 35 N. M. 198, 200, 292 P. 225, 227 (1930). *Cf.* Bishop v. United States, 107 F. 2d 297 (C. A. D. C. 1939); McGaffin v. State, 178 Ala. 40, 59 S. 635 (1912); Commonwealth v. Hawkins, 3 Gray 463 (Mass. 1855); Keenan v. Commonwealth, 44 Pa. 55 (1862); Pirtle v. State, 9 Humph. 663 (Tenn. 1849).
Similarly when mistake is pleaded, the courts generally refuse to permit drunkenness to be considered. Springfield v. State, 11 S. 250 (Ala. 1892); State v. Davis, 43 S. E. 99 (W. Va. 1903). But *cf.* Rex v. Letenock (1917), 12 Cr. App. 221. And in a prosecution for negligent homicide, a court held the defendant subject to the same degree of care as a sober person. Haynes v. State, 224 S. W. 1100 (Tex. Cr. App. 1920).

When it is recalled that the law on recognized legal provocation "indulgeth human frailty,"[40] the import of the refusal to relax the rules on account of drunkenness is apparent. The meaning must be that different evaluations apply, *e.g.* that it is right to reduce a killing to voluntary manslaughter if committed in a fight or in sight of adultery, whereas a person who "voluntarily gets drunk"[41] merits no like extenuation. We shall shortly consider the "voluntariness" of intoxication, and note here that the above judicial view does not take account of the fact that the grossly intoxicated harm-doer behaved without normal understanding or control of his conduct. Rather obviously, harms committed by such persons do not reveal wild aimless movement, but conduct adapted to attain specific goals.[42] But this is far from signifying that the defendant actually had the required *mens rea, e.g.* the behavior of a psychotic homicide is also end-directed. The fact that the state of mind and lack of inhibition of a grossly intoxicated person closely approximate that of a psychotic person should be the paramount datum in the determination of the relevant penal liability.

The policy of the prevailing law represents a compromise between the imposition of liability upon inebriate homicides in complete disregard of their condition, on the alleged ground that it was brought on voluntarily, and the total exculpation required by the defendant's actual state of mind at the time he committed the harm in issue. A balance, in other words, has been compounded from the realization, on the one hand, that the mental state and culpability of a drunken homicide should be distinguished from that of a sober homicide, and from a persistence of the judgment, on the other hand, that a person who voluntarily indulges in alcohol should not escape the consequences. The question to

[40] *Discourses* in Foster, Crown Cases 291 (1762).

[41] This is discussed *infra* pp. 438-43.

[42] See Johnson v. State, 129 Wis. 146, 160, 108 N. W. 55, 61 (1906). See also, H. M. Commissioners' Seventh Report on Criminal Law 20 (1843), and People v. Decina, 2 N. Y. 2d 133, 138 N. E. 2d 799 (1956).

be considered next is whether this policy has been made effective in the penal law.

"VOLUNTARY INTOXICATION"

The initial difficulty of ascertaining the meaning of "voluntary" intoxication results from the failure of the courts to define the term. In the first English report on a drunken homicide[43] which expressed the above rationale, it was said that although the defendant "did it through ignorance . . . that ignorance was occasioned by his own act and folly, and he might have avoided it. . . ."[44] The rigorous rule, as formulated by Baron Parke, was that "voluntary drunkenness is no excuse for crime."[45] The chief judicial method of elucidating the meaning of "voluntary" has been by way of generalizing the exceptions from liability, *e.g.* Baron Parke's remark in *Pearson's Case:* "If a party be made drunk by stratagem, or the fraud of another, he is not responsible."[46] The courts interpret "coercion," also used in this connection, to mean that one was "forced . . . to drink"[47] by overt, physical means. "Fraud," which is often equated with force in the criminal law, is also so rigorously restricted as to exclude, *e.g.* imposition upon the young and inexperienced by calculating adults. A boy of sixteen was admitted to a gambling house where the proprietor plied him with whiskey in order to cheat him in the play. In a fight, the boy, drunk to the point of "temporary insanity," killed the calloused operator. Holding that "involuntary intoxication is a very rare thing, and can never exist where the person intoxicated knows what he is drinking, and drinks the intoxicant voluntarily, and without being made to do so by force or coercion," the court affirmed a conviction and sentence of twelve years' imprisonment.[48] In a tragic case of patricide, the son

---

[43] Reninger v. Fogossa, *supra* note 6. See 8 Holdsworth, H. E. L. 441 (1937).

[44] 1 Plowd. at 19, 75 Eng. Rep. at 31.

[45] Pearson's Case (N. P. 1835), 2 Lew. C. C. 144, 168 Eng. Rep. 1108.

[46] 2 Lew. C. C. at 145, 168 Eng. Rep. at 1108.

[47] Borland v. State, 249 S. W. 591, 594 (Ark. 1923).

[48] Perryman v. State, 12 Okl. Cr. App. 500, 159 P. 937-38 (1916).

showed that his father supplied the liquor and urged him to drink it; but again, the intoxication was held "voluntary."[49] A college student under eighteen, who had never before tasted intoxicating liquor, was given a ride by the deceased in his automobile. The latter had been drinking heavily and insisted that the boy participate, became abusive and threatened to put him off in the Arizona desert if he refused. The court, noting that the "defendant, being alone, penniless, and fearing that he might be ejected and left on the desert did drink some beer and whiskey," nonetheless held that involuntary intoxication "must be induced by acts amounting in effect to duress."[50] So, finally, although it has been stated that "taking liquor prescribed by a physician" is a defense,[51] a court was unwilling to entertain the plea that the defendant drank to obtain relief from an acute pain.[52]

These cases are not selected specimens of extreme adjudication. The surprising thing about the factual situations in the relevant cases is that *involuntary intoxication is simply and completely non-existent.* It is hazardous to generalize so unqualifiedly concerning such an enormous body of law as that on crimes committed by inebriates; but the reports known to the writer record hardly a single decision holding that the defendant was involuntarily intoxicated.[53]

[49] State v. Sopher, 30 N. W. 917 (Ia. 1886).

[50] Burrows v. State, 38 Ariz. 99, 116, 297 P. 1029, 1036 (1921).

[51] Choate v. State, 19 Okl. Cr. App. 169, 197 P. 1060 (1921); Johnson v. Commonwealth, 135 Va. 524, 115 S. E. 673 (1923).

[52] Johnson v. Commonwealth, *ibid.*

[53] The reason for the slight qualification is the apparently unreported case of Regina v. M. R., quoted in Lee, *Drunkenness and Crime,* 27 Law Mag. & Rev. (5th ser.) 147 (1902). And in a case decided more than one hundred years ago, the complainant sold the defendant, a child of twelve, a cigar and a strong alcoholic drink. Later the boy took the complainant's watch, and on a charge of larceny, the court instructed the jury: "This case essentially differs from that where a crime is committed by a person, who by a free indulgence of strong liquors, has at the time voluntarily deprived himself of his reason." Commonwealth v. French, Thacher's Cr. C. 163, 165 (Mun. Ct. Boston, 1827). But the court also intimated that the child might have been temporarily insane, which diminished the force of the instruction as to the lack of volition.

The opinions invariably hold that the intoxication was "voluntary," but with equal uniformity they state that fraud or coercion is a defense. The encyclopedias and treatises give the dicta equal status with the holdings, perpetuating the myth that the matter has been adjudicated and that there exists an actual rule. But the contrary import of the huge volume of relevant case-law and of the enormous diversity of situations represented is plain: "fraud," narrowly interpreted in these cases to require complete innocence of the effect of alcoholic drink, cannot be perpetrated even on normal children of the age of any legal capacity. And as regards "coercion," the case-law implies that a person would need to be bound hand and foot and the liquor literally poured down his throat or, possibly, that he would have to be threatened with immediate serious injury before the exception, so universally voiced, would have any effect.

The suspicion of bias raised by the narrow construction of "fraud" and "coercion," when the courts deal with the "voluntary intoxication" of normal defendants, is further supported by typical cases that involve sick persons. A rather frequent defense is that a serious injury predisposed the defendant to alcoholic addiction. It is claimed that a fracture of the skull,[54] a blow on the head,[55] an injury to the brain,[56] or some other serious accident[57] stimulated indulgence or resulted in great impairment of understanding and capacity to control conduct. These claims are usually rejected by the courts, and the defendants are treated as normal. But a recognized student of these problems reports that persons "having had severe head injuries and sunstrokes, are particularly predisposed" to mental disease when under the influence of alcohol.[58] Without considering

[54] Choice v. State, 31 Ga. 424 (1860).

[55] State v. Wilson, 104 N. C. 868, 10 S. E. 315 (1889).

[56] State v. Kavanaugh, 4 Penne. 131, 53 A. 335 (Del. Ct. Gen. Sess. 1902).

[57] H. M. Advocate v. Campbell (1921), Session Cases 1 (Ct. Just. 1920).

[58] Lewis, *Psychiatric Resultants of Alcoholism: Alcoholism and Mental Disease*, 2 Q. J. Stu. Alc. 293, 296 (1941).

the merits of the issue, courts insist that "this is in law no excuse whatever. . . ."[59] On the contrary, such a person is held even more culpable because, so it is argued, knowing his weakness, he should have put forth greater efforts to abstain; and convictions, even of murder, are upheld in such cases.

Despite the fact that the defendant is believed to have been temporarily insane at the time of the behavior in issue, he is held punishable because, in Blackstone's phrase, it is "an artificial voluntarily contracted madness."[60] In many cases it seems very probable that the defendant was mentally ill while sober. These are often homicides where the motive for killing was obviously irrational. A grossly intoxicated defendant who "cruelly shot down the deceased, when he was performing neighborly and kindly acts for him"[61] was found guilty of murder and the capital penalty was imposed. A drunken blacksmith killed a dear friend.[62] There was considerable evidence of insanity; testimony that liquor made the defendant "crazy wild;" that his conduct at the time of the killing was of a "very strange, wild and irrational character;" that his mother, a sister, and three brothers were insane, the mother, sister and one brother dying in insane asylums; and the superintendent of the state insane asylum testified that in his opinion the defendant was insane. In this case the intoxication might have been merely a symptom of a psychosis. But the court assumed that the defendant's mental condition was merely the temporary result of voluntary drunkenness, and he was held guilty of murder. In a case where the defendant killed a theatre cashier in an attempted robbery, there was considerable

[59] Concerning drug addiction, see Note, 17 Notre Dame Lawyer 145 (1942).

[60] "A man may have partial or general insanity, and that, too, from blows on the head, yet if he drink, and bring on temporary fits of drunkenness, and, while under the influence of spirits, takes life, he is responsible." Choice v. State, 31 Ga. 424, 480 (1860).

[61] Buckhannon v. Commonwealth, 86 Ky. 110, 111, 5 S. W. 358 (1887).

[62] Upstone v. People, 109 Ill. 169 (1883).

testimony of mental abnormality, accompanied by long excessive drinking. The defendant's eyes were described as "wild and stormy and froth was running out of his mouth." He kept talking to himself, refused to eat, and had to be carried into his home in a helpless drunken condition. On the night of the killing, his mother had called the police, asking them to take her son to a hospital. Here again, the intoxication might have been merely symptomatic of a psychosis, but it stimulated the bias against "voluntary" inebriates, and the defendant was found guilty of murder and hanged.[63] The temper of prevailing adjudication is indicated in a case where the defendant killed a clerk over a petty argument about being served, and the court held, "Temporary insanity, occasioned immediately by drunkenness, does not destroy responsibility for crime where the defendant, when sane and responsible, voluntarily makes himself drunk."[64] The theory is that unless the defendant is "permanently" insane, his abnormal mental condition should be ignored in homicide, except as regards premeditation, on the inhibiting premise that the intoxication was "voluntary." As a Michigan court stated, "he must be held to have intended this extraordinary derangement . . . and the other results produced by it."[65]

The rigor of the prevailing interpretation of "voluntary" would be considerably lessened if the courts recognized that addiction to alcohol is sometimes a disease. But it has been held that dipsomania is not a defense.[66] A conviction of murder in the second degree was affirmed where the defendant, who had become a morphine addict five years previously, following the death of his wife, also had consumed a quart of liquor a day for several years preceding the killing.[67] A like decision was upheld where the evidence

---

[63] People v. Brislane, 295 Ill. 241 (1920).

[64] Collier v. State, 17 Okl. Cr. App. 139, 151, 186 P. 963, 966 (1920), quoting from Cheadle v. State, 11 Okl. Cr. App. 566, 571, 149 P. 919, 921 (1915).

[65] Roberts v. People, 19 Mich. 401, 422 (1870).

[66] State v. Kidwell, 62 W. Va. 466, 59 S. E. 494 (1907).

[67] State v. English, 164 N. C. 497, 80 S. E. 72 (1913).

showed that the defendant for ten years preceding the homicide, "had been addicted to strong drink, including whiskey, brandy, absinthe, and every other kind of drink sold in saloons; that he . . . suffered from delirium tremens, and . . . with a chronic disease which deeply impaired his nervous system; that on the night in question he was suffering from a recent surgical operation which gave him great pain," and so on.[68] There are many similar cases which bear unmistakable marks of severe mental abnormality. A court which heard credible evidence that the defendant was from boyhood known as "crazy Nick," that drinking "put him in a frenzy," that he was "a steady drinker," that after a night's absence, he came home "terribly intoxicated," took his Sunday clothes and chopped them into little pieces, still found that the intoxication was "voluntary;" and there was no reduction in liability "even when the intoxication is so extreme as to make the person unconscious of what he is doing, or to create a temporary insanity."[69] The court summarily dismissed the claim of delirium tremens, asserting there was "nothing more or less than the condition of mind usually resulting from a condition of thorough drunkenness."[70] "It would be utterly impossible to distinguish between the two conditions of mind, if in reality there be a difference between the two."[71] In a California case, the defendant had been taken from an old men's home and given employment doing odd chores. After a trivial dispute, the deceased pushed the defendant who shortly thereafter became intoxicated and killed him. The defendant was syphilitic, had hardening of the arteries, was quite susceptible to the alcohol, "was definitely confused and reacted emotionally and almost instinctively." The court held that his condition at the time of the homicide "was a state voluntarily brought about, and therefore was no excuse for the crime." It affirmed the conviction of

[68] Atkins v. State, 119 Tenn. 458, 462, 105 S. W. 353, 354 (1907).
[69] State v. Kraemer, 49 La. 766, 22 S. 254, 255 (1897).
[70] *Id.* at 774, 22 S. at 257.
[71] *Ibid.*

murder in the first degree and the death sentence.[72]

It must, unfortunately, be concluded that many courts ignore serious physical injuries, addiction, chronic alcoholism, delirium tremens, psychoses accompanied by intoxication and, in general, adhere to a course of adjudication that can only be regarded as unenlightened. The combined result of narrowing "fraud" and "coercion" to the vanishing point when dealing with normal persons and of failing to recognize that many defendants are diseased, implemented by traditional disapproval of drunkards, makes harsh law that adds cruelty to misfortune. Yet it is clear that at least since Stephen, able judges have tried to alleviate the rigor of the criminal liability of grossly intoxicated harmdoers. But serious legal barriers have joined the traditional bias to frustrate the substantial attainment of this objective.

LEGAL OBSTACLES TO REFORM

It is easy to understand the motivation that led Stephen and other judges to rely on "specific intent" as the most likely technique to achieve mitigation, and thus to formulate the exculpatory rule by reference to it. The solid unavoidable fact was that an injury committed under gross intoxication ought to be clearly distinguished from a like harm by a sober person. On the other hand, the commission of a serious injury by a person who was normal when sober, combined with traditional attitudes stigmatizing intoxication as a vice, indicated with equal clarity the impropriety of complete exculpation. The rules on criminal intent lay closest at hand to suggest a plausible mediation. Most of the harms met in these cases were homicides and aggravated assaults,[73] and here the accepted distinction concerning "general" and "specific" intent could operate to produce the desired end in England and a minority of American

---

[72] People v. Smith, 14 Cal. 2d 451, 95 P. 2d 453 (1939). See also, Commonwealth v. Chapman, 359 Pa. 164, 58 A. 2d 433 (1948).

[73] See Gray and Moore, *The Incidence and Significance of Alcoholism in the History of Criminals*, 3 J. Crim. Psychopath. 289, 294 (1941); Lewis, *Personality Factors in Alcoholic Addiction*, 1 Q. J. Stu. Alc. 21, 29-30 (1940).

states where the resulting liability for the homicide was manslaughter. So, too, since the exculpatory rule requires that wherever a "specific" intent is an essential element of a crime, the inebriate defendant must be acquitted, it has sweeping effect as regards numerous crimes. For example, in cases of assault with intent to murder,[74] assault with intent to rape,[75] burglary,[76] attempted burglary,[77] larceny,[78] and passing counterfeit notes,[79] the defendant was acquitted.

But, as noted, in homicide and serious assault, drunkenness is usually admitted in the United States only to exclude murder in the first degree and aggravation of the assault. In these situations it is emphasized that "of course . . . voluntary intoxication furnishes no excuse for crime. . . ."[80] The juxtaposition of the decisions on burglary, larceny, etc. and those on homicide and aggravated assault therefore produces an incongruous mixture since the former seem to contradict the rule regarding voluntary intoxication, while the latter raise insistent questions concerning the imposition of penal liability there in contrast to the complete exculpation of the other inebriate harm-doers. Only rarely does a court note the incongruity.[81] As has been suggested, these diverse results reflect the incidence of certain invalid rules and distinctions in current penal law.

[74] Roberts v. People, 19 Mich. 401 (1870), held that this crime was not like murder, which requires no specific intent.

[75] State v. Donovan, 61 Ia. 369, 16 N. W. 206 (1883).

[76] Schwabacher v. People, 165 Ill. 618, 46 N. E. 809 (1897) ; State v. Bell, 29 Ia. 316 (1870).

[77] People v. Jones, 263 Ill. 564, 105 N. E. 744 (1914).

[78] Chatham v. State, 9 S. 607 (Ala. 1891), citing Regina v. Moore (N. P. 1852), 3 C. & K. 319, 175 Eng. Rep. 571; State v. Kavanaugh, 4 Penne. 131, 53 A. 335 (Del. Ct. Gen. Sess. 1902) ; Bartholomew v. People, 104 Ill. 601 (1882) ; People v. Walker, 38 Mich. 156 (1878).

[79] United States v. Roudenbush, 27 Fed. Cas. No. 16, 198 (C. C. E. D. Pa. 1832) ; O'Grady v. State, 36 Neb. 320, 54 N. W. 556 (1893) ; Pigman v. State, 14 Oh. 555 (1846). But cf. Clinton v. State, 132 Tex. Cr. App. 303, 104 S. W. 2d 39 (1937) (burglary).

[80] State v. Bell, 29 Ia. 316, 319 (1870).

[81] "We confess that the doctrine touching cases of this character is not placed upon the clearest ground in the books." Id. at 320.

We have previously considered one of these problems, namely, the current distinction of "specific" and "general" intent,[82] and it will be recalled that one of the conclusions reached was that all *mentes reae* are specific. This implies various possible determinations, *e.g.* that there should be complete exculpation in the inebriate homicide and aggravated assault cases or that complete exculpation in burglary, larceny, etc. is invalid, and so on. The former solution is indicated if liability is imposed solely upon the basis of the defendant's mental condition at the time the harm was committed.[83] For, at that time, a grossly intoxicated homicide no more has the *mens rea* of criminal homicide than does a grossly intoxicated housebreaker or utterer of a counterfeit coin have the *mens rea* required in those crimes. On the other hand, if liability is validly posited on the prior voluntary intoxication, why should not that also be applied to the housebreaking, etc.?

As regards the homicide, the salient facts are (a) the requisite *mens rea* was lacking at the time of the homicide; (b) there was never an intention to kill or seriously injure formed by a sober person and (c) in some cases the dangerous condition of the intoxicated harm-doer was culpably induced. If these facts, which can be generalized to apply to all cases of harm-doing by grossly intoxicated persons, constitute the central problem of the relevant penal liability, the inaptness and inadequacy of the exculpatory rule are apparent. It is arbitrarily limited in the extent of its application to homicide and aggravated assault, and the consequent confusion has been increased by acceptance of the distinction between "general" and "specific" intents.

Equally potent in obscuring the instant problem are the rules concerning negligence, felony-murder and misdemeanor-manslaughter and, as noted, "cooling-time" and legal provocation. This results from reliance upon these rules as a fixed valid structure within which the liability

---

[82] *Supra* pp. 142-43.
[83] See People v. Decina, *supra* note 42.

of inebriate harm-doers must be determined. So long as ordinary negligence suffices to incur penal liability for homicide, any grossly intoxicated homicide may be found negligent, because behavior, not any positive state of mind, determines that; and the objective definition of provocation and cooling-time facilitates analogous findings. If these rules were excluded, only when an inebriate homicide was at least reckless could he be held criminally liable. Equally effective in sustaining the present law on the penal liability of inebriates are analogies insinuated by the prevailing felony-murder, misdemeanor-manslaughter rules.[84] "Voluntary intoxication" is the prior "wrong," and as regards some of the cases, e.g. Prince,[85] it conforms very closely to the logic and policy of those outmoded rules.

The felony-murder rule was well on its way to oblivion in England[86] forty years ago, when the House of Lords decided Beard.[87] Beard, under the influence of liquor, committed a rape on a young girl; and in the course of violent resistance by the girl, he seized her by the throat, causing her death. He was convicted of murder but this was reversed by the Court of Criminal Appeal[88] which substituted manslaughter on the ground that the trial judge should have instructed, according to Meade,[89] that if the defendant was so intoxicated "that he was incapable of knowing that what he was doing was dangerous, i.e. likely to inflict serious injury," he should be convicted of manslaughter.[90] The

---

[84] "This is the first time, that I ever remember it to have been contended, that the commission of one crime was an excuse for another. Drunkenness is a gross vice, and, in contemplation of some of our laws is a crime; and I learned in my earliest studies that so far from its being in law an excuse for murder, it is rather an aggravation of its malignity." Justice Story, in United States v. Cornell, 25 Fed. Cas. No. 14,868 at 657-58 (C. C. D. R. I. 1820). Such a statement by so great a judge reveals the complexity, if not the hopelessness, of the problem. The fact is that drunkenness was rarely a crime at common law, and it was never an aggravation.

[85] Regina v. Prince (1875), 13 Cox C. C. 138, supra p. 373-74.

[86] It was abolished by the English Homicide Act, 1957.

[87] (H. L. 1920), 14 Cr. App. R. 159.

[88] (1919), 14 Cr. App. R. 110.

[89] (1909), 1 K. B. 895.

[90] (1909), 1 K. B. at 899.

conviction of murder was, however, reinstated in the House of Lords, and their decision was based squarely on the felony-murder rule, thus sharply limiting, if not overruling, both *Meade* and *Serné*.[91] The decision, in effect, denied the possibility that Beard might have been so drunk as not to have understood the dangerousness of his act. He was attempting rape and he consummated it; therefore, held the judges, with the impeccable logic of gentlemen, the defendant was not too intoxicated to realize that he was seriously injuring the girl. The holding that a person who can commit rape is competent to, and actually did, have an intent to kill or seriously injure thus substituted a presumption for the determination of moot facts. This also imposed a sharp limitation on the exculpatory rule[92] for, under that rule, a charge of murder could be met by disproof of "specific" intent.[93] Since the abolition of the felony-murder rule in England in 1957, the authority of *Beard* is presumably terminated. In the United States, unfortunately, the notion of the felony-murder rule continues to obstruct the reform of penal law, including that on the liability of inebriate harm-doers.

It joins the survival of negligence and other objective standards and the arbitrary restriction of the exculpatory rule to premeditation and certain other "specific" intents to form a structure of fallacious analogy within which the problem of the penal liability of intoxicated harm-doers is obscurely formulated. The attendant unfortunate interpretation of "voluntary intoxication"[94] may be further appraised by reference to current research on alcoholism.

[91] "The result of *Beard's Case* . . . nullified all the progress in improving the law of murder which had been achieved during the past century." Turner, *The Mental Element in Crimes at Common Law*, 6 Camb. L. J. 31, 64 (1936).

[92] A more hopeful handling of the felony-murder doctrine, in the decision reached, was indicated in People v. Koerber, 244 N. Y. 147, 155 N. E. 79 (1926).

[93] In light of the decision it is rather surprising to find a dictum to the effect that drunkenness which rendered a person incapable of wrongful intent should be a complete defense. 14 Cr. App. R. at 197.

[94] Aristotle apparently approved double penalization of intoxicated harm-doers. Ethics, bk. III, ch. 5, 1113b, 31.

FINDINGS OF RESEARCH ON ALCOHOLISM

In stressing the discoveries of twentieth century research on alcoholism, it is not suggested that little was known about intoxication in past times. Seneca's *Epistle on Drunkenness, e.g.* abounds in many shrewd observations;[95] and skipping centuries of like sophistication, even experts can hardly improve on Kant's definition of drunkenness as "the unnatural state of inability to organize sense impressions according to the laws of experience."[96] Dr. Kerr's book,[97] originally published in 1888, may still be read with much profit. But there has been great progress during the past quarter of a century which may fairly be said to mark the emergence of sustained research on the problems of alcoholism.

Among the definitely established facts of great importance for the criminal liability of inebriates is that "some people find it impossible to refrain from drinking alcohol in spite of repeated experiences which prove to them that its use always leads to very unpleasant situations."[98] There is abundant uniform expert opinion to the effect that this disease is no more difficult to diagnose than many others which are commonly recognized, and it is clearly distinguishable from habitual intoxication.[99] Delirium tremens has

---

[95] See Note, 3 Q. J. Stu. Alc. 302, 303 (1943).

[96] See Note, 1 Q. J. Stu. Alc. 777 (1941).

[97] Inebriety or Narcomania (3rd ed. 1894). *Cf.* Crothers, *The Scientific Study of Inebriate Criminals,* pub. in The Medical Jurisprudence of Inebriety 57 (1888).

[98] He continues: "These unfortunate persons know that if they yield to the temptation of the first drink, all power of inhibition is lost. They know that they will go on and on with a spree of intoxication ending only when the flesh rebels. Such people drink in spite of losing their standing in society, their ability to hold positions and their physical health. The suffering of dependents is no deterrent. During periods of sobriety they grieve and repent but in a short time they are off on another debauch." Darling, *Inebriety: A Classification,* 2 Q. J. Stu. Alc. 677, 678 (1942).

[99] For a diagnosis of the dipsomaniac and the differences between him and the habitual drinker, see Krafft-Ebing, Text Book of Insanity 434-36 (Chaddock trans. 1904); Haggard and Jellinek, Alcohol Explored 156-57 (1942).

also long been definitely diagnosed as a disease in medical classifications everywhere;[1] and many courts have recognized that.[2] But some courts think this disease can be simulated, and others insist that it is nothing more than the ordinary result of extreme intoxication.[3] Also dubious is the position that temporary insanity in these cases is caused by intoxication and is, therefore, no defense. This, too, runs counter to generally held expert opinion,[4] and the rationale that the defendant "voluntarily" became intoxicated[5] is least persuasive here. For this presupposes that the defendant has correctly diagnosed his illness and that, although diseased, he is able to act like a healthy person.[6] There is also a widely held expert opinion that excessive drinking is frequently symptomatic of serious mental disease,[7] and this indicates that the cur-

[1] Wortis, *Delirium Tremens*, 1 Q. J. Stu. Alc. 251 (1940).

[2] For a collection of cases, see Note, 12 A. L. R. 895-900 (1921).

[3] See 1 Wharton and Stilles, Medical Jurisprudence 209 (3rd ed. 1873).

[4] *Cf.* "One of the popular conceptions of insanity is that the condition usually lasts for a considerable time and cannot be transient. This is not the case, and some forms of insanity, notably those associated with acute infections, may be of very short duration." Davis, *Drunkenness and the Criminal Law*, 5 J. Crim. L. 166, 181 (1941).

[5] *Cf.* "If insanity follows immediately upon the drunken state, the mere fact that it assumes the form of·*delirium tremens* rather than some other form can make no difference in principle and should not excuse. Such a result seems to violate neither logic nor sound policy. The decisive question should simply be whether in a given case the temporary frenzy can fairly be said to be voluntary." Book Review, 15 Harv. L. Rev. 755-56 (1902).

[6] Various abnormalities which are entirely controlled during sobriety are manifested in drunkenness, *e.g.* homosexual acts, the setting of fires "without ever having shown in a state of sobriety any pyromanic tendencies." Kinberg, *Alcohol and Criminality*, 5 J. Crim. L. & Criminol. 569, 573 (1914). He cites various other harms committed by persons in a drunken state who never did any of them while sober. *Ibid.* These manifestations are sometimes followed by complete amnesia as to the conduct during the drunken condition.

[7] ". . . there is a great agreement among present-day psychiatrists on the question of alcohol addiction as symptomatic of many psychoses rather than as their primary cause." Bowman and Jellinek, *Alcoholic Mental Disorders*, 2 Q. J. Stu. Alc. 312, 315 (1941).
"Alcohol sometimes precipitates mental disorders, in other instances its use modifies the picture and course of mental disorder and in still other cases it is merely one of its symptoms." Lewis, *Psychiatric Resultants of Alcoholism: Alcoholism and Mental Disease*, 2 Q. J. Stu. Alc. 293, 295 (1941).

rent assumption regarding temporary psychoses immediately induced by gross intoxication is superficial. Instead of assuming that only "voluntary intoxication" is involved, the courts should be alerted to the likelihood of a serious underlying mental disorder.[8] Dipsomania and delirium tremens are commonly known diseases which involve inebriety in some form. There are various others, equally recognizable, and rather uniformly diagnosed.[9] It is indubitable also that many inebriates who commit crimes are impaired both physically and psychically,[10] even though they do not exhibit well-marked psychoses.[11]

Much of the literature on alcoholism is quite discriminating in terms of the great diversity in personality and etiology involved.[12] The fact is that "the progress of . . . research . . . has been impeded by two misconceptions: the first that *all* habitual excessive drinking is a disease, and the second, that it is the same disease."[13] And "it must be stressed that mere drunkenness is not regarded in the scientific literature as evidence of either addiction or chronic alco-

---

[8] *Ibid.*

[9] For classification and description, see Blair, *Alcoholism — A Medico-Legal Survey,* 9 Medico-Legal & Criminol. Rev. 211, 215-18 (1941); Bowman and Jellinek, *op. cit. supra* note 7, at 312, 314, 315; Lewis, *op. cit. supra* note 7, at 293. The *Quarterly Journal of Studies on Alcohol* is an invaluable source of information on the entire problem.

[10] See Lewis, *Personality Factors in Alcoholic Addiction,* 1 Q. J. Stu. Alc. 21, 29 (1940).

[11] See Haggard and Jellinek, Alcohol Explored 8-16 (1942). The authors classify inebriates as "*normal excessive drinkers, symptomatic drinkers, stupid drinkers, and addicts.*" *Id.* at 13. In symptomatic drinkers, "drinking is a symptom of their psychotic state." *Id.* at 14. Stupid drinkers are feeble-minded. The most confused term is "chronic alcoholic." "Chronic alcoholism is not the habitual drinking of large amounts of alcohol but definite disease conditions resulting from such habits . . . an addict is not necessarily a chronic alcoholic. . . . An alcohol addict is a person with an 'uncontrollable craving for alcohol. The outstanding criterion is the inability to break with the habit.' " *Id.* at 15.

[12] See Jellinek and Jolliffe, *Effects of Alcohol on the Individual: Review of the Literature of 1939,* 1 Q. J. Stu. Alc. 110, 135 (1940); *cf.* Haggard and Jellinek, Alcohol Explored (1942).

[13] Haggard and Jellinek, *supra* note 12 at 143.

holism. . . ."[14] Able experts in this field emphasize the futility of generalizing about inebriates "as if the term denoted a well-defined individual."[15] They believe that about "50.0 per cent of inebriates have definite nervous and mental abnormalities," but that "30.0 per cent of the inebriates show no abnormalities at all. . . . The true addicts constitute at present the smallest group of inebriates."[16] "Delirium tremens is a mental disorder of brief duration which occurs only in some 4.0 per cent of heavy drinkers."[17] "There are many excessive drinkers who by all appearances have normal personalities."[18] These findings, which should influence the penal liability of inebriates,[19] also support the thesis that "false sentimentality should not be permitted to enter into the situation. It must be recognized that many inebriates are simply criminals who drink excessively, not victims of drink driven to crime, and such individuals are properly the wards of penal institutions."[20]

PROPOSED LEGAL REFORMS

In appraising the law on the penal liability of inebriates, one must bear in mind that the harm charged was committed during gross intoxication. The usual fact is that the defendant, while sober, had no intention to injure anyone and, when he did commit a harm, he did not realize the

[14] Bowman and Jellinek, *Alcohol Addiction and Its Treatment*, 2 Q. J. Stu. Alc. 98, 100-101 (1941); *cf.* Kerr, Inebriety or Narcomania 12-14 (3rd ed. 1894).

[15] Haggard and Jellinek, Alcohol Explored 153 (1942).

[16] *Id.* at 151, 157.

[17] *Id.* at 230.

[18] *Id.* at 163-64.

[19] Banay, *Alcoholism and Crime*, 2 Q. J. Stu. Alc. 686 (1942), controverts the general impression that the majority of crimes are caused by drunkenness. Commenting on Dr. Banay's findings, Drs. Jellinek and Haggard say: "This study differs from others in that the prisoners are classified according to the role of inebriety in their crimes. It appears from Dr. Banay's analysis that the usual estimate of crimes caused by inebriety, given as 60.0 per cent, must be lowered to 25.0 per cent. This is, however, still a formidable proportion." Haggard and Jellinek, Alcohol Explored 163 (1942).

[20] *Id.* at 273. See East, *Alcoholism and Crime in Relation to Manic-Depressive Disorder*, 230 Lancet 161, 163 (1936). But *cf.* Kinberg, *Alcohol and Criminality*, 5 J. Crim. L. & Criminol. 569, 584, 587-88 (1914).

dangerousness of his conduct and was unable to restrain
his impulses. Certain astute critics, influenced by these
facts, have argued that a solution of the problem requires
penalization for the voluntary intoxication and complete
exculpation for the harm committed under gross intoxication.[21] But voluntary intoxication in itself was, with rare
exception, no crime at all at common law, and under modern
statutes the penalties for the accompanying "disorderly
conduct" are small. Their indiscriminate imposition for
ordinary drunken conduct and drunkenness followed by the
commission of a serious harm would seem socially incongruous, however logical. And although there is an important
suggestion in the view that under certain conditions, serious
penalties should be attached to voluntary intoxication,[22]
the instant problem concerns the commission of a major
harm under gross intoxication.

A persuasive theory in support of penal liability for
harms committed by such inebriates was advanced by
Austin, who argued that a person who voluntarily became
intoxicated acted recklessly since he made himself dangerous, in disregard of public safety.[23] Austin, naturally,
took no cognizance of facts which have since become of
paramount importance, e.g. that the inebriate might be an
alcohol addict or mentally diseased. Nor did Austin or
Stroud, who followed him,[24] distinguish the normal habitual
drunkard from the inexperienced inebriate. The present
need, therefore, is to supplement Austin's theory in the
light of available knowledge concerning alcoholism and to
classify inebriates and drunken harm-doing in a way that
is defensible empirically and is also significant as regards
penal liability. We must, for the present purpose, eliminate
the two extremes, i.e. slight intoxication, which would have

[21] Markby, Elements of the Law 363 (6th ed. 1905) ; cf. 1 Le Sellyer,
Traité de la Criminalité, de la Pénalité et de la Résponsabilité 140
(1874).

[22] Analogous crimes are "reckless driving" and "possession of
burglars' tools."

[23] Austin, Lectures on Jurisprudence 512-13 (1879).

[24] See Stroud, Mens Rea 115 (1914).

only the effect of mitigation, and intoxication so gross as to induce complete loss of control or even stupor, in which condition motor activity of any kind is simply impossible. In the cases relevant to the present problem, the defendant is in a state of intoxication between these extremes. What we have to deal with is not incapacity to perform simple acts or such an obliteration of cognitive functions as to exclude any degree of purposive conduct,[25] but instead a severe blunting of the capacity to understand the moral quality of the act in issue, combined with a drastic lapse of inhibition. As has been suggested, this closely resembles, if it is not identical with, insanity.[26]

Certain very important distinctions must next be drawn between two types of normal offenders, i.e. those who had no previous experience with intoxication that rendered them dangerous, and those with such experience. As regards the inexperienced inebriate, it is submitted that on principle he cannot be held criminally liable for a harm committed under gross intoxication. For such persons, there can be no valid reliance on the drinking, to support liability, because, though "voluntary," it was quite innocent. Complete exculpation in such cases might offend public opinion. But there are certain practical considerations that render the indicated reform palatable. First, is the likelihood that serious injuries are very rarely, if ever, committed by inexperienced inebriates.[27] The reported cases, where such

[25] See East, *Murder, From the Point of View of the Psychiatrist,* 3 Medico-Legal & Criminol. Rev. 61, 78 (1935).

[26] "Writing in 1877, Sir Arthur Mitchell put the matter thus: 'It should be at once understood that alcoholic intoxication, *i.e.* ordinary drunkenness, *is really a state of insanity.*'" Quoted in Christie, *Intoxication in Relation to Criminal Responsibility,* Scots L. T. News 75, 80 (1920). "'In reality the acute alcoholic intoxication is a poisoning of the brain and can be placed side by side with the severest mental disturbances which are known to us.' (Meggendorfer)." Bowman and Jellinek, *Alcoholic Mental Disorders,* 2 Q. J. Stu. Alc. 312, 319 (1941). "There is no question but that the higher degrees of alcohol intoxication impair perception, judgment and motor function." Schilder, Psychoanalysis, Man and Society 133-34 (1951).

[27] "The acute alcoholic intoxication is different in persons who are chronic alcoholics than in those who are intoxicated for the first time. It seems that in the chronic alcoholic the acute intoxication brings for-

injuries were committed, exhibit addiction or long histories
of repeated dangerous intoxication. In addition, non-punitive treatment of the inexperienced inebriate may be indicated and should be available.

Experienced normal inebriates, who should be subjected
to penal liability, range from persons who have been intoxicated and dangerous in that condition at least once
prior to the harm in issue, to persons whose behavior exhibits such a regular pattern of these occurrences as to be
habitual. It is the combination of experience of prior
intoxication and of dangerousness while in that condition
that must have been in the mind of the inebriate harm-doer
when he was sober and indulged his desire, that is legally
significant. For this group, it is apparent that the drinking
was a serious matter; indeed, as suggested, quite apart
from any harmful consequences, it should itself be made
criminal and punished much more severely than the "disorderly conduct" associated with ordinary intoxication.

As regards inexperienced and habitual drunkards, some
writers[28] have posed this problem: the habitual drunkard
knows the effect of alcohol on him, whereas the inexperienced drinker lacks such knowledge. This factor emphasizes the greater culpability of the habitual inebriate.
On the other hand, he is assailed by much greater temptation and his self-control is impaired. This implies less culpability. The dilemma thus raised rests, however, on two
fallacies: it confuses the habitual drunkard (who is normal)
with the addict (who is diseased); and it assumes that because the drinking was voluntary, the intoxication of the
uninitiated inebriate is also culpable, indeed that it may be
more so than that of the habitual drunkard. The difference,
however, is that only the habitual drunkard had sufficient
fore-knowledge of the dangerousness of his indulgence to
warrant his being held criminally liable.

---

ward more primitive material." Schilder, *The Psychogenesis of Alcoholism*, 2 Q. J. Stu. Alc. 277, 290 (1941).

   [28] See, *e.g.* Tarde, Penal Philosophy 190-91 (Howell trans. 1912).

Thus, we may conclude that although the exculpatory rule represented sound insight and the beginning of a valid policy concerning the penal liability of inebriates, its formulation in terms of, and its restriction to, the negation of "specific" intent is unfortunate. The problem cannot be solved by ignoring the actual state of mind of inebriate harm-doers. The principal facts to be taken into account are: (a) the inebriate's serious lack of understanding and capacity to control his impulses at the time the harm was committed and (b) circumstances which signify that drinking intoxicating liquor by certain persons is criminally reckless. In summary:

1. The medical literature on alcoholism does not purport to invalidate the principles of penal law but, instead, it clarifies the need to re-examine the penal liability imposed for harms committed during gross intoxication by adducing relevant facts and knowledge of the personality of inebriate harm-doers.

2. The principle of *mens rea* limits penal liability to normal persons who intentionally or recklessly commit harms forbidden by penal law. But since drinking alcoholic liquor is not usually followed by gross intoxication and such intoxication does not usually lead to the commission of serious injuries, it follows that persons who commit them while grossly intoxicated should not be punished unless, at the time of sobriety and the voluntary drinking, they had such prior experience as to anticipate their intoxication and that they would become dangerous in that condition. This would require a major change in the existing rules regarding inexperienced inebriate harm-doers,[29] which, however, the available data indicate would be very rarely invoked. This change in the law is an implication of valid rules which impose liability upon culpable offenders.

[29] The author of a Note in 55 Col. L. Rev. 1210 (1955) dismisses the suggestion that gross intoxication should be a complete defense in the above type of case, but he does not present any reasons for imposing liability in such cases. He accepts the notion of "general" and "specific" intentions and admits negligence as a valid basis of penal liability. Moreover, he asserts that "nearly all drunken offenders in-

In addition, the need for treatment, perhaps hospitalization, may be indicated for inebriate harm-doers beyond the reach of penal law.

3. Voluntary intoxication, realistically defined, should not be a defense if the defendant is a normal person whose previous experience forewarns him that he will probably become intoxicated if he drinks, and that he is dangerous when intoxicated.[30] Such a person acts recklessly when he drinks intoxicating liquor, and if he kills a human being while grossly intoxicated, he is guilty of manslaughter.[31]

---

tend their criminal acts in a manner similar to sober men. Thus under alcoholic influence the person's intent remains unchanged; only the inhibitory influences normally restraining him are removed." *Id.* at 1211; see also, *id.* at 1217. For the reasons discussed in the text above, this misses the central problem concerning the penal liability of grossly intoxicated harm-doers. With reference to his statement that if there were exculpation, "any effect criminal sanctions have on inhibiting alcoholic conduct would be lost," (*Id.* at 1217) *cf.* "What is the object of inflicting any punishment at all? It cannot seriously be thought the risk of such punishment will deter people in general from getting drunk. The most it can do is to deter the particular offender from getting drunk another time. Yet for this purpose it might be equally efficacious to have a rule confining punishment to a man who commits a *second* misdeed when in drink." Williams, Criminal Law: The General Part 375 (1953).

30 This conclusion is supported by many writers. See, *e.g.* 1 Bentham, Works 79 (Bowring ed. 1843); Gilson, Moral Values and the Moral Life 293-94 (Ward trans. 1931); Paley, The Principles of Moral and Political Philosophy 171 (1817); Mill, On Liberty 175 (2nd ed. 1859).

31 For a discussion of the above proposed reforms, see Baird, *Science and the Legal Responsibility of the Drunkard*, 5 Q. J. Stu. Alc. 629, 634-646 (1945).

CHAPTER XV

CRIMINAL ATTEMPT

WHOEVER has speculated on criminal attempt will agree that the problem is as intriguing as it is intricate.[1] Its solution, like *la belle dame sans merci*, has eluded many a zealous pursuer. Perhaps, the principal reason for this is that its history has been neglected. For example, social and psychological factors have had great influence upon the law of criminal attempt, especially in determining the relevant harm or, at least, what was regarded as sufficiently harmful to warrant penalization. The legal history also discloses that there is an irreducible element of experience in law that cannot be persuasively dissolved in logical analysis and which penal theory must somehow take into account. The notions employed in various places, in the formulation of this problem, are also helpful in suggesting the underlying policies.

HISTORY

Plato speaks of "one [who] has a purpose and intention to slay another who is not his enemy, and whom the law does not permit him to slay, and he wounds him, but is unable to kill him. . . ."[2] Such a person "should be regarded as a murderer and be tried for murder."[3] But from respect for

---

[1] Criminal attempt "is more intricate and difficult of comprehension than any other branch of the criminal law." Hicks v. Commonwealth. 86 Va. 223, 9 S. E. 1024, 1025 (1889).

[2] Plato, Laws 876d-877a (Jowett ed. 1892).

[3] *Ibid. Cf.* "To him whose feelings are tempered by thought, 'a man,' as Seneca says, 'is no less a brigand, because his sword becomes entangled in his victim's clothes, and misses its mark.'" 1 Westermarck, Origin and Development of the Moral Ideas 247 (2nd ed. 1912).

"fortune" and "providence" and "as a thank-offering to this deity, and in order not to oppose his will," the death penalty should be remitted and banishment for life, together with compensation for the injury, substituted. Thus, the philosopher posed a simple case and suggested a solution which represents the present law of many jurisdictions.

The Romans punished attempts to commit ordinary crimes only occasionally and by a smaller penalty. As regards "atrocious" crimes, they emphasized the intent rather than the actual harm;[4] yet it is uncertain whether they punished the attempt equally with the intended crime.[5] A distinction between remote and proximate acts was made: in the former there was greater room for repentance, hence a less severe penalty was imposed.[6] These fragmentary notes of ancient law[7] indicate that the problems involved in analysis of criminal attempts are perennial ones. The nature of these problems accounts for their appeal to the speculative temperament of medieval legal scholars, although it seems that they were thoroughly explored only in Italy.[8] In any event, when we come to the beginning of the modern era, we find

[4] In the case of William of Essex, for Treason (1619), ". . . Doddridge said that the rule is *in atrocioribus delictis, punitur affectus, licet non sequatur effectus*. . . ." 2 How. St. Tr. 1086-1087 (1816).

[5] Garraud says they did. Précis de Droit Criminel 192-193 (1934).

[6] Chamcommunal, *Étude critique de législation comparée sur la tentative*, 24 Rev. Crit. 43-46 (1895).

[7] *Cf.* " 'The general impression,' says Dr. Richey, 'produced by the rules in the commentary is that the attempt to commit an act was treated as equivalent to its commission, unless the results of the attempt were very insignificant.' " Introduction to Book of Aicill, quoted by Cherry, Lectures on the Growth of Criminal Law in Ancient Communities 32 (1890).
Cf. "If any attempt is made to deprive in any wise a man in orders, or a stranger, of either his goods or his life. . . ." Edward and Guthrum; Attenborough, The Laws of the Earliest English Kings 109, cap. 12 (1922). "If, where men are drinking, a man draws his weapon, but no harm is done there. . . ." Hlothhere and Eadric; *id.* at 21, cap. 13.

[8] See Ullmann, *Reasons for Punishing Attempted Crimes*, 51 Jurid. Rev. 353 (1939). *Cf.* "But one may search in vain in the Custumals of the Middle Ages for a theory of attempt; the texts . . . dwell only on the accomplished act, without inquiring whether the offender had purposed to commit a greater offense." von Bar, A History of Continental Criminal Law 157 (1916). *Cf.* note 13 *infra*.

that in the sixteenth century provisions regarding criminal attempts are already included in the most important codes: the *Carolina* in 1532 and the *Ordonnance de Blois* in 1579 are notable instances.[9]

Criminal attempts are conspicuously absent in early English law.[10] There is little more than a handful of specific findings of liability for wrong-doing which fell short of the major crimes.[11] Apparently in those forthright days, a miss was as good as a mile. And this Bracton tells us in almost so many words, quoting an apparently established maxim, " 'For what harm did the attempt cause, since the injury took no effect?' "[12]

But what of *voluntas reputabitur pro facto*[12] and of Maitland's observation "that the adoption, even for one limited purpose, of this perilous saying was but a momentary aberration" stimulated by excessive leniency in "murderous assaults which did not cause death"?[14] Two or three cases are generally stated to evidence the maxim: the mid-fourteenth century case[15] in which Shardlowe, J., is reported to have said, "one who is taken in the act of robbery or burglary even though he does not carry it out, will be hanged according to the law."[16] The other cases are those of at-

[9] Champcommunal, *supra* note 6 at 47 note 3.

[10] "It [the old English law] had started from the principle that an attempt to do harm is no offence." 2 Pollock and Maitland, H. E. L. 508 note 4 (2nd ed. 1923). "Ancient law has as a general rule no punishment for those who have tried to do harm but have not done it." *Id.* at 509.

[11] "Likewise if a person has employed force to the womb of a woman, in order to produce abortion, he is liable." 2 Bracton, Legibus 465, f. 144b, 3 (Twiss ed. 1878).

[12] *Id.* at 337, f. 128, 13.
Westermarck states that among primitive peoples, criminal attempt is either not punished at all or is "punished less severely than the accomplished act." *Op. cit. supra* note 3, at 241.

[13] A capitulary of Charlemagne provided: "Qui hominem voluntarie occidere voluerit et perpetrare non potuerit homicida tamen habeatur. liv. 7, ch. 151." Quoted by Champcommunal, *supra* note 6 at 47 note 3.

[14] 2 Pollock and Maitland, *op. cit. supra* note 10, at 477n.

[15] 27 Ass. pl. 38 (1353); see Sayre, *Criminal Attempts*, 41 Harv. L. Rev. 821, 823 note 10 (1928).

[16] Brooke adds: "query for at that time a man would not be hanged except for an act committed except in treason." Ab. 1573, Corone 106.

tempted murder — one by a servant who cut his master's throat and fled with his goods, the other by a wife's paramour who attacked the husband and left him for dead. The death sentence was imposed on the ground that felonies had been committed since *voluntas reputabitur pro facto*.[17]

It is apparent, however, on the face of the reports that intent alone was not penalized;[18] there was also conduct and very serious harm. Hence, the maxim served not to extend culpability to mere intent[19] but rather to preserve an appearance of legality in the application of the extreme sanction to lesser harms than those covered in the current rules.[20] The significant fact is that the perpetrators of what we should consider "criminal attempts" were punished as if they had committed the intended more serious crimes. The conclusions as to this phase of the problem of criminal attempts in the early law are that *mens rea* is necessary to criminal liability,[21] but *mens rea* is not sufficient. At least in the medieval law there was insistence on conduct.[22]

And Fitzherbert reports Stoufford as having objected: "he did not put anything into practice, merely because his intent was such." Ab. 1565, Corone 202. The case is discussed by Dalton, Countrey Justice 363 (1619), who accepts the voluntas maxim as law "in former times."

Cf. "But it seemth, Ass. 27. Pl. 38, that he which is taken in the attempt (onely) of a Burglary, shall be hanged for it, although he have not put anything in execution thoroughly, Lamb. page 267." Young, A Vade Mecum and Cornu Copia, an Epitome of Mr. Stamfords Plea of the Crown 89 (1663).

17 See Sayre, *supra* note 15 at 824-825.

18 "Our old law started from the other extreme: — *Factum reputabitur pro voluntate*." 2 Pollock and Maitland, *op. cit. supra* note 10, at 477n.

19 See Eden, Principles of Penal Law 77-78 (1771).

20 Dalton suggests another possible use of the *voluntas* formula. After citing cases of a man who carried his sick father from town to town in cold weather, a harlot who placed her newly born child in an orchard, and an owner of a dangerous animal which killed a man, all of which were held murder, he states: "And in these three last cases, *voluntas reputabitur pro facto*, death ensuing thereupon: For it may plainely appeare, that they had a wil and meaning of that harme which followed, which will in them doth amount to malice, and so maketh their offences to be Murder. . . ." *Op. cit. supra* note 16, at 219.

21 2 Pollock and Maitland, *op. cit. supra* note 10 at 476-477.

22 *Id.* at 474-475. " 'The thought of man shall not be tried, for the devil himself knoweth not the thought of man': — thus at the end of the middle ages spoke Brian C. J. in words that might well be the

Although early English law lacked rules in terms of criminal attempts, there were many other ways to check criminal conduct, *e.g.* the system of frankpledge and surety for the peace.[23] There were also the vagrancy laws and laws dealing broadly with the crime of being a nightwalker, rogue or vagabond, or simply "without a livelihood." The closest parallel to the later attempt was the law of unlawful assembly, rout and riot. It is a rout if three or more persons assemble for an illegal purpose and act toward its accomplishment "whether they put their intended purpose in execution, or not."[24] It is riot if they accomplish their purpose. And if they simply meet in such circumstances even though "they depart by their owne consent, upon some feare conceived, or other cause," it is unlawful assembly.[25] The presence of three or more persons was a material fact in the above offenses; the conceptual proximity of rout and unlawful assembly to attempt is otherwise apparent.

Finally, we must note the early treatment of certain recognized misconduct such as going armed, carrying "pistolls that be charged,"[26] keeping guns or cross bows in the house,[27] lying in wait, drawing a sword "to strike a justice,"[28] witchcraft "to hurt or distroy any person in his or her body, although the same be not effected," and so on.[29] As the legal system matured, reliance was increasingly

motto for the early history of criminal law . . . where there is no harm done, no crime is committed; an attempt to commit a crime is no crime." *Ibid.* But the last statement is too broad as is shown in the text above.

[23] Pulton, De Pace Regis et Regni, 22b No. 384 (1609). *Cf.* Dalton, *op. cit. supra* note 16, at 141, 143, 171. "Also against such as shall lye in wait to rob, or shall be suspected to lye in wait to rob, or shall assault, or attempt to rob another. . . ." *Id.* at 171.
"But if one man do threaten another to beate him, the partie threatened may have the suertie of peace against him: for that beating may tend to maiheming or killing of him, which the suertie of peace might have prevented." *Id.* at 19 No. 72.

[24] *Id.* at 25.

[25] *Ibid. Cf.* Dalton, *op. cit. supra* note 16, at 199, 200.

[26] *Id.* at 31.

[27] *Id.* at 56.

[28] *Id.* at 211.

[29] Pulton, *op. cit. supra* note 23, at 11 No. 36.

placed upon the development of the doctrines implied in the emerging law on these offenses rather than upon the older administrative devices and police organization.[30] But it was not until well into the sixteenth century that the law of criminal attempts received unmistakable and intensive development in the decisions of the Court of Star Chamber. Before we discuss those cases, we must note the most important preceding influence on the development of the law on criminal attempts, namely, the law of treason.

The fount of the English law of treason, as well as the basis of its modern development, is the statute of 25 Edward III (1352).[31] The most severe statute on the subject was that of 21 Richard II (1397) which made "compassing" the death of the king treason, and said "nothing of any overt act."[32] The subsequent statutes are too numerous for even brief description here.[33] They included such conduct as ". . . to wish, will, or desire by words or writing . . . or attempt any bodily harm to the King, queen, or their heirs apparent;"[34] to riot [if twelve or more persons were involved] with intent to kill or imprison any of the Privy

[30] Another important factor was legislation which, though not employing the word "attempt" or a synonym, yet made many types of incipient wrong-doing criminal. See 2 Edw. III, cap. 3 (1328); 12 Rich. II, cap. 6 (1388); 33 Hen. VIII, cap. 6 (1541); 3 & 4 Edw. VI, cap. 5 (1549), 5 & 6 Edw. VI, cap. 4 (1552).

[31] This statute made it treason "(1) to compass or imagine the death of the king, his queen, or eldest son; (2) to defile the king's wife or his eldest unmarried daughter or his eldest son's wife; (3) to levy war against the king in his realm; (4) to be adherent to his enemies, giving them aid and comfort; (5) to counterfeit the king's great or privy seal or money; (6) to bring false money into the realm; (7) to slay certain officers or justices being in their places doing their offices." *Op. cit. supra* note 10, at 502 note 6.

[32] "It is difficult to understand the object of this statute, unless it was to convert into treason mere words, or indeed anything whatever which could be considered to indicate in any way hostility to the king." 2 Stephen, H. Cr. L. 253 (1883).

[33] See, 2 Stephen, *id.* at ch. 23. After listing several statutes of Henry VIII, Stephen states: "Each of these statutes . . . made it high treason to attempt to alter the settlement. . . ." *Id.* at 258.

For the history of American Colonial legislation on treason, in which proscription of various "attempts" is frequent, see Hurst, *Treason in the United States*, 58 Harv. L. Rev. 226 (1944).

[34] 6 Hen. VIII, ch. 13 (1514); 26 Hen. VIII, ch. 13 (1534).

Council;[35] to "pray . . . God would shorten the queen's life;"[36] to absolve any person from obedience to the Queen, or to attempt to do so;[37] to "compass, imagine, invent, devise, or intend death or destruction . . . of the person of the king;"[38] or attempt to prevent the succession as established by Act of Settlement.[39] Even more than the statutes, the vocabulary of the treason trials and indictments was frequently that of "attempt."[40]

We have seen that early English law did not propose to "try the thought of man" and that even in treason, the notable exception (the statute of 21 Richard II) was short-lived. The treason statutes spoke of "compassing and imagining;"[41] but the statute of 25 Edward III and its successors, save the above instance, required an overt act as evidence of the intention,[42] although it need not have operated in the least to effectuate the harm sought.[43] It is

[35] *Op. cit. supra* note 32, at 259.

[36] 1 & 2 Ph. & M., ch. 9.

[37] 23 Eliz., ch. 1 (1581).

[38] 13 Charles II, ch. 1 (1662).

[39] (1702) I Anne, ch. 17. See *supra* note 32 at 262n; and Foster, Discourse on Treason, in Crown Law 195 (1762).

[40] Thus, if an almost random selection is examined, we read that " . . . the Prisoner at the Bar stands indicted for no less than for an intention and endeavour to murther the King; For an endeavour and attempt to change the Government of the Nation, so well settled and instituted, and to bring us all to ruin and slaughter of one another, and for an endeavour to alter the Protestant religion. . . ." The Tryal of Edward Coleman, Gent. 7 (1678); the Trial of Robert Earl of Essex, and Henry Earl of Southampton, for High Treason (1600), 1 How. St. Tr. at 1334, 1355.

[41] "These words, at this day, do not convey the proper meaning of the original 'compasser ou imaginer.' . . . I believe they would be justly rendered by the words 'attempt or contrive.' Many passages contemporary with the statute, could be brought to shew that this was the meaning of the law-makers. . . . What has occurred in my reading, would lead me to derive it from 'machinari,' not from 'imaginatio.' Glanville and Bracton and M. Paris use that verb. where those who came after them, writing in French, use 'ymaginer.' " Note, by Luders, 7 How. St. Tr. at 961-962.

[42] 1 Hale P. C. 107, 2 (1736).

[43] But *cf.* Lord Chief Justice Abbott: "I have already intimated, that any act manifesting the criminal intention, and tending towards the accomplishment of the criminal object is, in the language of the law, an *overt act.*" Trial of Arthur Thistlewood, for High Treason

harm to the king, his family and his business, and what his courts, his law and his army do about it that is involved. Attempt is criminal in treason; statutes and cases emphasize the exceptional liability.

The contribution of the Court of Star Chamber, viewed in this perspective, was almost routine. It required no inventive genius to provide a new kind of legal control. The Chamber needed only to recognize that the interests of the general public were of sufficient importance to merit a protection similar to that which had for centuries shielded the king. The situations dealt with exhibit all stages of accomplishment of intended crimes. Threats, challenges[44] and words "tending to a challenge" were the most incipient wrongs held punishable. Nip violence in the bud and do that without hindrance from existing law — that was the salient objective. The times were quarrelsome; and there were many cases of "lying in wait" with intent to assault, beat, murder and the like.[45]

Extending beyond such incipient misconduct are cases which still fall short of assault: the defendant only "set his hand upon his dagger;"[46] but the wrong-doers were nonetheless convicted in the Chamber. Thus, in an interrogatory addressed to certain defendants, it was asked "whether they or any of them had not purposed to slay or at least to hurt

---

(1820), 33 How. St. Tr. at 685.

[44] Henry Peterche v. John and Abbone Prior (1562), Burn, The Star Chamber 61 (1870).

"Mr. Attorney shewed that this Theodore Kelly had written a letter to Sir Arthur Gorge, tending to a challenge. . . ." Att'y-Gen. v. Kelly (1632), Gardiner, Reports of Cases in the Courts of Star Chamber and High Commission 112 (1886).

For cases of threats, see Wymark v. Fynes (Hen. VII), 16 Sussex Record Society, Court of Star Chamber 2 (1913); Mutton v. Coke (Ph. & M.), *id.* at 88; and for "threat and menace," Saxbeers v. Spilman (Ph. & M.), *id.* at 91.

[45] Complaint of George Dukkett and others, 10 Collections for a History of Staffordshire 171 (Salt ed. 1907). Also Feners v. Aston (1533), Collections for a History of Staffordshire 27 (Salt ed. 1910). "Waylaying a man to assault or beat him, is an offence ever held worthy of the sentence of this court. . . ." Hudson, *A Treatise on the Court of Star Chamber* in 2 Hargrave, Collectanea Juridica 64 (1791).

[46] Grosvenour v. Leveson (1537), Collections for a History of Staffordshire 66-67 (1910).

the said Richard Alkyn? and how many times have they gone as well through the said park as abo . . . in other places with bows and arrows and other unlawful weapons to the intent to have brought to pass that their ungracious purpose?"[47] There were also cases concerning conduct which fell short of assault but constituted attempts rendered ineffective by timely intervention.[48] Beyond that were situations that fit snugly into modern definitions of assault, *e.g.* "the Lord Viscount Savill strooke at Sir John with his drawn sword, and followed after him and drove him into a plush of water. . . . That thereupon divers swords were drawn, and one of my Lords men struck at Sir John Jackson with his sword but missed him narowlie. . . ."[49]

Related to the above cases, and almost invariably charging riot, assault and battery, were complaints alleging attempted forcible ejectment.[50] In a number of the cases, one surmises that the more criminal purpose of the defendant was alleged in order to enlist the court's assistance and that the attack on the complainant was, in fact, slight, *e.g.* the defendants did come "supposing that your orator had been there, for that intent and purpose only to have murdered

[47] (Hen. VIII) 10 Collections for a History of Staffordshire 84 (Salt ed. 1907). *Cf.* Dean of Wells v. Hardwich and others (Hen. VII) (1493-1498), Proceedings in the Court of Star Chamber 56 (Bradford ed. 1911); Cappis v. Cappis (1548), *id.* at 265.

[48] Complaint of Edw. Aston, 10 Collections for a History of Staffordshire 108 (Salt ed. 1907). The complaint (*id.* at 106) illustrates the composite character of the typical charge. In a similar complaint strongly suggestive of the later recognized attempt, the complainant asserts: "the said Ralph Agard and the other mysruled persons began to draw their bows with arrows in them, and would have shot at your said subject if the servants of your said subject had not quietly cut the bow strings of the said 'misruled persons'." Longford v. Bykley (1540) Collections for a History of Staffordshire 45 (1910).

[49] Att'y-Gen. v. Savile and others in the Star Chamber (1632), Gardiner, *op. cit. supra* note 44, at 145. *Cf.* Kenneth v. Gawen and others (1606), Hawarde, Les Reportes del Cases, in Camera Stellata, 1593 to 1609, 264-66 (Baildon ed. 1894); and Henry Peterche v. John and Abbone Prior (1562), Burn, *op. cit. supra* note 44, at 61. See Proceedings in the Court of Star Chamber 21 (Bradford ed. 1911) and *cf.* Cheyney in 18 Am Hist. Rev. 727, 734 (1913).

[50] Best, a pauper v. Neale and Winter and others (1632), Burn, *op. cit. supra* note 44, at 122.

and slain your orator, who at that time was absent."[51] Such cases suggest a basis for later distinctions between attempt and aggravated assault.

In the reports, the occasional use of "attempt," "endeavor," or a synonym heralded the later doctrine. Hudson represents the transition: "Attempts to coin money, to commit burglary, or poison or murder, are in ordinary example. . . ."[52] He also stated that duelling was "a preparation to murder" and "if a man endeavour to murder or poison a man, that endeavour is punishable in this court, although it never came in act."[53] In one case, after the usual allegations of riot, assault, and battery, it was asserted that the defendant "attempted to strike up his heels."[54] The loose use of the word is apparent;[55] but occasionally the language ran precisely in terms of the later established crime, *e.g.* the defendant "attempted to set fire to his house."[56]

As one surveys the array of complaints entertained by the Star Chamber, especially the numerous cases of assault, riot, attempts to kill and various breaches of the peace, all disturbing and potentially serious, one sees a growing recognition of a great variety of relatively lesser harms which ought to be put down. Within the sphere of its wide jurisdiction, anti-social conduct which fell short of the traditional categories was regularly held criminal, and of these, various efforts to commit serious harms stimulated decisions of great significance for the later doctrine.

[51] Complaint of Richard Cruse, Collections for a History of Staffordshire 169 (Salt ed. 1907). Also Hill v. Corbette (1597), Hawarde, *op. cit. supra* note 49, at 69.

[52] Hudson, *op. cit. supra* note 45, at 79.

[53] *Id.* at 64.

[54] Vane v. Morgan (1626), 3 Rushworth, Historical Collections app. 10.

[55] So we find it reported that "Pledall, for attempting to cloke and colour the murder of one Headart, and attempting to discredit the proceedings of the Justices of Assize, is sent to the Tower, and recognizance of 1000 marks estreated." (4 & 5 Ph. & M.), Burn, *op. cit. supra* note 44, at 56.

[56] Praty v. Midmore (Hen. VIII), 16 Sussex Record Society, Court of Star Chamber 76, 77 (1913).

But although the opinions of the Star Chamber are re-
plete with common-sense observations on the seriousness
of the relevant harms, they did not, with one exception,
express any doctrine of criminal attempt. This exception,
whose significance has apparently escaped notice, is the
Case of Duels, prosecuted in the Star Chamber in 1615 by
Francis Bacon, the Attorney General.[57] Bacon described the
prevalent evil of duelling and suggested that the wisest
method of prevention was to nip the practice "in the
bud" by punishing "all the acts of preparation."[58] He
said: "For the Capacity of this Court, I take this to be a
ground infallible: that wheresoever an offence is capital, or
matter of felony, though it be not acted, there the combination or practice tending to that offence is punishable in
this court as a high misdemeanor. So practice to impoison,
though it took no effect; waylaying to murder, though it took
no effect; and the like; have been adjudged heinous misdemeanours punishable in this court. Nay, inceptions and
preparations in inferior crimes, that are not capital, as
suborning and preparing of witnesses that were never deposed, or deposed nothing material, have likewise been
censured in this court. . . ."[59]

Thus the author of *Novum Organon* anticipated the common law courts and the treatises[60] by almost two centuries.
The Chamber adopted Bacon's analysis almost verbatim.
But, except for this product of Bacon's genius, we see no
theorizing about criminal attempts, no formulation of the
attempt doctrine by the Court of Star Chamber.[61]

[57] 2 How. St. Tr. at 1033. The court included the Archbishop of
Canterbury, Lord Chancellor Ellesmere, Lord Chief Justice Edward
Coke, and Hobart.

[58] *Id.* at 1041, 1044.

[59] *Id.* at 1041.

[60] Scottish law was far ahead of the English, *e.g.*: "I shall form
these conclusions, first, that all endeavour, is an offence against the
Common-wealth: though nothing follow thereupon." Mackenzie, The
Laws and Customs of Scotland in Matters Criminal 5-6 (2nd ed. 1699).

[61] "The law as to . . . attempts to commit crimes, was there developed." 4 Holdsworth, H. E. L. 273 (3rd ed. 1924). *Cf.* 2 Stephen, *op.
cit. supra* note 32, at 223.

Sayre apparently accepted the view, suggested by Stephen, that "the

Nevertheless, the influence of the Chamber decisions upon the subsequent common law courts seems obvious.[62] Its rejection by Professor Sayre is difficult to understand except as the result of certain ambiguities.[63] There is explicit reference to the Chamber in an early common law decision.[64] Other cases clearly represent the treading of a well-worn path.[65] The very assumption by later courts that relevant rules exist for which authority need not be cited is not without significance. Although the evidence supports the view that the Chamber's influence on the common law courts was considerable, it is also true that a good many years elapsed after its abolition before a doctrine of criminal attempt was formulated.

Mansfield's opinion in *Scofield* has been said to be the origin of the doctrine of criminal attempt.[66] But much as one is tempted to honor the "just and intrepid" judge with

---

modern doctrine" of criminal attempt originated in the Star Chamber. *Supra* note 15 at 828. Except for Bacon's formulation, no doctrine was expressed in the Chamber.

[62] "The doctrine of the court of Star Chamber was so obviously necessary to any reasonable system of criminal law that it was adopted by the common law courts." 5 Holdsworth, H. E. L. 201 (3rd ed. 1945). So, too, 2 Stephen, *op. cit. supra* note 32, at 224.

[63] Sayre rejects the view that the Star Chamber doctrine was "taken over by the common law courts." Since he assumes there was a "doctrine" he is literally correct in saying "there is not a ripple in the calm surface to indicate that a new doctrine of criminal attempts has been suggested." (*Supra* note 15 at 829). But, if not "doctrine" but the decisions of the Chamber with reference to attempt situations are regarded, the influence is clear.
Cf. "In fact, the manner in which the common law courts adopted the Star Chamber's view as to the criminality of attempts to commit crimes, and treated these attempts as common law misdemeanours, removed the chief reason for reviving the dangerous doctrine that a mere intent to commit a crime entailed liability." 8 Holdsworth, H. E. L. 434 (3rd ed. 1945).

[64] Rex v. Sidley (1664), 1 Sid. 168, 82 Eng. Rep. 1036, quoted by Sayre, *supra* note 15 at 829.

[65] Holt, C. J.: "Words that directly tend to the breach of the peace, as if one man challenge another, are indictable. . . ." Reg. v. Langley (1703), 2 Salk. 697, 91 Eng. Rep. 590. In Rex v. Pigot, the defendant "was convicted upon an indictment for a misdemeanor in attempting forcibly to carry away one Mrs. Hescot, a woman of great fortune." (1707) Holt 758, 90 Eng. Rep. 1317.

[66] Sayre, *supra* note 15 at 834, 835. See his discussion of the case at 834-836.

yet another wreath, that opinion is questionable. Scofield, in possession of a house as tenant, was indicted for having placed a candle and matches in the house with intent to set fire to it; the house did not burn. Scofield's counsel admitted that if the purpose had been accomplished, the offense would have been a misdemeanor. He also admitted that an attempt to commit a felony was criminal,[67] but he insisted that "an attempt to commit a misdemeanor [was] not a misdemeanor."[68] The defendant was convicted.[69]

The cases cited by the prosecution and relied upon by Mansfield included: an attempt at subornation,[70] giving a bribe for a vote, an attempt to bribe an official to secure an office, and an attempt by an attorney to bribe a witness. But such bribery and subornation meant interference with public business, and they were long regarded as exceptional. Additional cases cited by Mansfield concerned transportation of wool, a misdemeanor by statute, keeping gunpowder, a nuisance of long standing, and words tending directly to breach of the peace. On the other hand, *Pedley*,[71] decided only two years previously by the identical bench, stood directly in the way. When Scofield's counsel stated that the *Pedley Case* had established that "to set fire to one's own

[67] "It is no argument to say, that because the defendant is not guilty of the highest offence, therefore he is guilty of none, for there are graduations in law which vary the offences of men, and proportion their punishments to their crimes." The King v. Cowper (1696), 5 Mod. 206, 208, 87 Eng. Rep. 611, 612.
Cf. "Thomas Sylvester was indicted for a Misdemeanor, in attempting to commit the unnatural Sin of Sodomy." Rex v. Thomas Sylvester (1732), Old Bailey Sessions, No. 51, at 171; Rex v. Harris (1784), Old Bailey Trials, No. 513, at 643-644. In Rex v. Ingleton it was assumed that "an attempt to commit a felony" was criminal. (1746) 1 Wils. 139, 95 Eng. Rep. 537.

[68] (1784) Cald. Mag. Rep. 399.

[69] The influence of the law of treason on Mansfield's contribution to attempt is evident. "If a man endeavours to do an act of treason, and that act of treason fails through some intervening accident or occurrence, the party so endeavouring and acting to the best of his ability and power is deemed to be guilty of an overt-act, as though he had done the thing he had proposed and intended." The Trial of Florence Hensey, M. D., for High Treason (1758), 19 How. St. Tr. at 1372.

[70] This and the succeeding cases are cited by Sayre, *supra* note 15 at 835 note 56.

[71] (1782) Cald. Mag. Rep. 218.

house is not a felony," Mansfield retorted, "But on wretched reasoning." Mansfield stressed *Holmes' Case*,[72] decided in 1634,[73] and said: "It was objected that an attempt to commit a misdemeanor was no offence: but no authority for that is cited, and there are many on the other side. Nor is the completion of an act, criminal in itself, necessary to constitute criminality."[74] This can hardly be called the formulation of the doctrine of criminal attempt.[75]

That doctrine was no doubt "in the air" since the first quarter of the eighteenth century, but it was not formulated in the common law courts until 1801, when *Higgins* was decided.[76] The indictment charged that the defendant did "solicit and incite" a servant to steal a quantity of twist from his master. The servant did not take the merchandise. The defense was that under these circumstances "a bare solicitation . . . is not indictable;" and an imposing array

[72] (1634) Cro. Car. 376, 79 Eng. Rep. 928. In this case the charge, like Pedley's, included an "intent to burn the houses of others adjoining." Holmes was found not guilty of felony since he burnt a house in his possession, but he was found guilty of "an exorbitant offense," fined £ 500, imprisoned, pilloried and put under bond.

[73] In Gordon's Case, Mansfield had charged the jury that: "an attempt, by intimidation and violence, to force the repeal of a law, was . . . high treason." 21 How. St. Tr. at 486, 649 (1781).
Numerous statutes were enacted in the eighteenth century punishing such behavior as: attempting to kill or unlawfully attempting to strike or wound any member of the privy counsel, 9 Anne, cap. 16 (1710); shooting at any person while having face blacked, or being otherwise disguised, 9 Geo. I, cap. 22 (1722); ripping, cutting or breaking with intent to steal any lead, iron bar or iron-gate, 4 Geo. II, cap. 32 (1731); going from door to door attempting to gather alms, 17 Geo. II, cap. 5, § 1 (1744); attempting to rescue or set at liberty any person, etc., 25 Geo. II, cap. 37, § 9 (1752); attempting to take, kill, or destroy any fish, etc., 5 Geo. III, cap. 14, § 3 (1765); and attempting to kill, wound or destroy any red or fallow deer, 15 Geo. III, cap. 30 (1776).

[74] (1784) Cald. Mag. Rep. 400, 402. Presumably Mansfield was familiar with MacKenzie and other Scottish treatises, *supra* note 60.

[75] *Cf.* Justice Lawrence's contribution toward the formulation of the doctrine of criminal attempt. Lawrence had prosecuted both Pedley and Scofield. Later, as judge, he decided the Higgins Case (discussed *infra* p. 573).

[76] 2 East 5, 102 Eng. Rep. 269 (1801).
East (1803), almost twenty years after the Scofield decision, has no discussion of criminal attempt. Farrell's Case, a clear case of attempted robbery, was decided in 1787, but East made no comment whatever on the attempt phase. 2 East 557. *Cf. id.* at 411. He treats

of authority was cited.[77] The defendant was nonetheless found guilty and the modern law of solicitation was established.[78] It is the treatment of the offense as a criminal attempt that is especially significant: "On the part of the Crown it was contended, that every attempt to commit a crime, whether felony or misdemeanor, is itself a misdemeanor and indictable. . . ."[79] And Grose, J., said: "it must be admitted that an attempt to commit a felony is in many cases at least a misdemeanor; to instance the common cases of an attempt to rob or to ravish, which are indictable offences in every day's practice. But further, an attempt to commit even a misdemeanor has been shewn in many cases to be itself a misdemeanor."[80] *Scofield*, a true attempt case, can hardly be said to have expressed the doctrine of criminal

---

the Scofield Case as a phase of arson, and does not even use the word "attempt" in connection with it. *Id.* at 1029-1030. It is in Russell that the first recognition of a new doctrine is discussed. 1 Russell, Crimes and Misdemeanors 61 (1819).

For a summary of the treatises and a digest of cases, see Curran, *Criminal and Non-Criminal Attempts*, 19 Geo. L. J. 185 (1931).

[77] The defense argued: "In none of the books is there any case or precedent to be found of an indictment for a bare solicitation to commit an offence without an act done in pursuance of it: and the silence of all the writers on the Crown law on this subject is of itself a strong argument that no such offence is known to the law. The general principle of our penal code is to punish the act, and not the intent; with the single exception of high treason, where the traiterous intent constitutes the crime; but even there it must be manifested by some overt act." The King v. Higgins (1801), 2 East 5, 102 Eng. Rep. 269, 271. To which, Lawrence, J., replied: "The whole argument for the defendant turns upon a fallacy in assuming that no act is charged to have been done by him; for a solicitation is an act." *Id.* at 19, 102 Eng. Rep. 275.

[78] The law on solicitation has fallen into disuse because of difficulty of proof where nothing more occurred, because, where the crime solicited was committed, the offense becomes that of complicity (accessory) before the fact, and because of the expansion of the law of conspiracy.

[79] *Id.* at 11, 102 Eng. Rep. at 272 (1801).

[80] *Id.* at 274-275. Subsequently the formula was frequently reiterated. Thus, in 1837, on a charge of attempt unlawfully to know a child under twelve, Parke, B., said: "There are many cases in which an attempt to commit a misdemeanor has been held to be a misdemeanor; and an attempt to commit a misdemeanor is a misdemeanor, whether the offence is created by statute, or was an offence at common law." Rex v. Roderick (1837), 7 C. & P. 795, 173 Eng. Rep. 347. So, too, Regina v. Eagleton (1885), 1 Dears. 515.

attempt. *Higgins,* a solicitation case, relied directly upon *Scofield* and practically formulated the doctrine of criminal attempt in language which generalized as to both situations.[81] The terms of *Higgins,* while they comprised neither a full nor a precise statement of the attempt doctrine, went sufficiently far in that direction to be the immediate origin of the modern doctrine.

In concluding the above historical sketch, it may be noted that the early reliance on frankpledge, suretyship, justices, unlawful assembly, rout and the like retarded the formulation of the doctrine of criminal attempt. More direct factors in delaying the appearance of that doctrine were the rules on "aggravated assault," itself a species of attempt which, for psychological reasons, was regarded as a "consummated" crime. The accelerated growth of aggravated assaults in the period just prior to that of the formulation of the attempt doctrine is highly significant. Blackstone's discussion of such assaults is brief, but in East (1803), the subject was for the first time fully treated. Here we find an array of such specific offenses as assault on privy counsellors, members of Parliament, revenue officers, persons wrecked, woolcombers, in churches, with intent to murder, with intent to rob, with intent to spoil cloth, and so on. The analogous development of the even greater variety of aggravated larcenies suggests the common method thus employed in the expansion of the criminal law: utilize the concept at hand, build upon it, retain the familiar word, and extend the new rule to all situations where the common denominator, *i.e.* the minimum cognate offense, is present.

Why did attempt appear despite the above legal method and the social organization to prevent crime? From the point of view of doctrinal development, the significant facts

---

[81] The following historical sequence may be observed: (1) Talk, unless the harm urged is effected, is not criminal. (2) But as regards the King, treason was deemed to require no such discrimination. Here talk alone is enough to merit torture and execution. (3) Next, as to bribery of officials, subornation of witnesses and the like, talk is criminal. But here the talk is thought of independently, and not, as with solicitation, related to other criminality. So, also, conspiracy is

are that *Scofield* concerned attempted arson and *Higgins*, solicitation to steal certain goods. These situations provide a very important clue to the necessity for the development of the law of criminal attempts, namely, the standard technique of "assault plus aggravation" could not be literally applied.

RULES AND DOCTRINE

For centuries, as was seen in the above legal history, there were rules defining specific criminal attempts before there was a doctrine of criminal attempt, *i.e.* any generalization of the common features of those rules.[82] Typical statute books contain a number of rules defining criminal attempts and providing penalties; and, in addition, there is often a residuary provision to the effect that anyone guilty of any attempt, other than those specified, shall be punished by a stated penalty. Sometimes the statutes include a doctrinal statement: "An act, done with intent to commit a crime, and tending but failing to effect its commission, is 'an attempt to commit that crime.' "[83] An attempt to

---

regarded exceptionally. *E.g.* The Poulterers' Case (1610), 9 Co. 55b., 77 Eng. Rep. 813, and Regina v. Best (1705), 2 Ld. Raym. 1167, 92 Eng. Rep. 272. Also, the interests involved concern public justice— hence, in principle, the King. In Bacon's Case (1664), 1 Sid. 230, the solicitation was to murder the Master of the Rolls. In Rex v. Vaughn (1769), Mansfield said: " . . . in many cases, especially in bribery at elections to Parliament, the attempt is a crime. . . ." 4 Burr. 2494, 98 Eng. Rep. 308, 311. (4) Then in Scofield's Case (1784) overt behavior is held a criminal attempt though purely individual interests are involved. (5) Finally, The King v. Higgins, dealing with like interests, established the criminality not of overt behavior but of talk—solicitation here subsumed under attempt. *Cf.* Holt, J.: " . . . advising one to rob or kill, without something be done thereupon, is not indictable . . . a conspiracy to . . . is indictable." The Queen v. Daniell (1703), 6 Mod. 99, 100, 87 Eng. Rep. 856, 857.

[82] See chapter 1.

[83] N. Y. Penal Law Art. 1, § 2. This provision is found at the beginning of the Code, under "Definitions." This part of American compilations of statutes corresponds somewhat to the General Part of European penal codes. *Cf.* chapter 1 *supra*.

Perjury is a crime concerning which it would usually seem impossible to have an attempt because an incomplete utterance is incomprehensible. But *cf.* where one thinks he is lying, but actually tells the truth. Stephen adds treason, riot, libel, offering bad money and assault. 2 Stephen, *op. cit. supra* note 32, at 227.

Cf. State v. Latiolais, 225 La. 878, 74 S. 2d 148 (1954) where a

commit a proscribed harm is no less criminal than the intended harm. Instead of using the problematical term "inchoate," it seems preferable, therefore, to designate criminal attempts, solicitations and conspiracies as "relational" crimes which are defined by reference to the intended "ultimate" crimes.

So far as the conduct is concerned, there is no essential difference between some criminal attempts, *e.g.* shooting which misses the intended victim, and the "ultimate" crimes; it follows that those material elements are not distinctive in the doctrine.[84] What is distinctive in the doctrine of criminal attempt concerns the harm. The doctrine of criminal attempt emphasizes the common features of all of the harms described in the rules defining specific criminal attempts; and these descriptions are particular instances of the doctrine. On the other hand, the doctrine of criminal attempt is only one of the doctrines included in the principle of harm. The principle subsumes the harms of all crimes, while the doctrine of criminal attempt does that only with regard to criminal attempts.

The vagueness of the relational crimes, as compared with "ultimate" crimes, is not an essential characteristic of them.

---

conviction of attempt to commit perjury was upheld. The facts are not stated, but the opinion indicates that D swore falsely before one not qualified to give the oath. On those facts the conviction should have been reversed on the ground of "legal impossibility." See *infra* at notes 45-48.

Cf. Prof. J. Edwards' criticism of R. v. Moran (1952), 1 All E. R. **803,** holding that there is no such crime as an attempt to demand money with menaces, etc. Goddard, C. J., said there: "But the court cannot see how you are guilty of an attempt to demand: you either demand or you do not." Prof. Edwards, in criticism, notes the case of a person with a speech defect who begins to threaten X, and that of an accomplice who puts his hand over his confederate's mouth just when the latter is about to demand. Edwards, Note. 15 Mod. L. Rev. 345, 347 (1952). *Cf.* Mann, *Attempted Perjury*, 33 No. Car. L. R. 641 (1955).

[84] See Thacker v. Commonwealth, 134 Va. 767, 114 S. E. 504 (1922). For a discussion of cases where recklessness enters into the *mens rea* in certain criminal attempts, see Williams, Criminal Law 475 (1953) and Smith, *Two Problems in Criminal Attempts*, 70 Harv. L. Rev. 429-432 (1957). In these cases recklessness is also a part of the *mens rea* of the intended ultimate crime, *e.g.* obtaining property by false pretenses where D is reckless regarding the truth of the representation which he intentionally expressed.

It could be provided, *e.g.* that in an attempt to commit arson, a lighted match must have reached the distance of two inches from combustible materials in a dwellinghouse. The lack of such specificity probably reflects the policy that it is desirable and practicable to maintain an area of vagueness because of the great number and variety of relevant fact-situations. The major qualification of that policy is the principle of legality. An indictment charging a criminal attempt can, if necessary, be supplemented by a bill of the particulars, stating the precise time, place, instrument used, and so on. The law of criminal pleading must therefore be considered in appraising the definiteness of the relational crimes.

PREPARATION AND ATTEMPT

In the analysis of criminal conduct, one may distinguish the following stages: (1) conceiving the idea of committing a legally proscribed harm, (2) deliberation, (3) the *mens rea,* (4) preparation, (5) attempt stopped before the necessary conduct was completed, and (6) completion of that conduct, with or without attainment of the end sought.[85] We may dismiss the first two stages out of hand because, although they may be relevant to ethical evaluation, they

---

[85] These are the stages substantially set forth by Vidal, building on Carrara. See Vidal, Cour De Droit Criminel 128 (1916). The French differentiate attempts as indicated in stages 5 and 6, 5 being *tentative,* while 6 is *délit manqué* rather than *délit consommé*.

Cf. in a case of *felo de se*: "And Walsh [for defendant] said, that the act consists of three parts. The first is the imagination, which is a reflection or meditation of the mind, whether or no it is convenient for him to destroy himself, and what way it can be done. The second is the resolution, which is a determination of the mind to destroy himself, and to do it in this or that particular way. The third is the perfection, which is the execution of what the mind has resolved to do. And this perfection consists of two parts, viz. the beginning and the end. The beginning is the doing of the act which causes the death, and the end is the death, which is only a sequel to the act. And of all the parts the doing of the act is the greatest in the judgment of our law, and it is in effect the whole, and the only part that the law looks upon to be material. For the imagination of the mind to do wrong, without an act done, is not punishable in our law, neither is the resolution to do that wrong, which he does not, punishable, but the doing of the act is the only point which the law regards; for until the act is done it cannot be an offence to the world, and when the act is done it is punishable." Hales v. Petit (1562), 1 Plowd. 253, 259, 259a, 75 Eng. Rep. 387, 397.

are not legally significant. And as regards the *mens rea*, we have seen[86] that while that is material, it is not sufficient to incur penal liability. Since attempt implies failure,[87] one must also exclude attainment of the objective. This leaves preparation and attempt, the latter including interrupted conduct which extends beyond preparation and completion of the conduct but failure to commit the intended harm.

That any criminal attempt is essentially different from the intended "ultimate" crime is self-evident. This is simply a matter of immediate perception or intuition and an application of the "law of identity." The pertinent question is whether the same holds true for preparations and criminal attempts. It is agreed that there must be some conduct to constitute preparation and there must be some falling short of the intended "ultimate" crime to constitute a criminal attempt. It is equally clear that if the notion of attempt were extended sufficiently, it would include preparatory conduct. It follows also that if *all* conduct "in the direction" of certain harms were penalized, which is the rule in some legal systems, the above problem would disappear. But in other legal systems, only the criminal attempt, not the preparation, is punishable. This raises the difficult question of distinguishing them on tenable grounds.

In the decisions on the subject, the one point of universal agreement is that no definite line can be drawn between criminal attempts and states of preparation. "[E]ach case," we are informed, "must be determined upon its own facts."[88] Yet trial judges instruct juries; appellate courts

---

[86] *Supra* chapter 6.

[87] Professor Perkins points out that many attempts succeed and he argues that the usual assumption that attempts fail is a fallacy. Perkins, *Criminal Attempt and Related Problems*, 2 U. C. L. A. 319 (1955). It is submitted, with deference, that the problem of criminal attempt is the problem of the failure of the attempt. Where it succeeded, the law of procedure, *e.g.* concerning verdicts for an included cognate offense, may be relevant.

[88] State v. McCarthy, 115 Kan. 583, 224 P. 44, 45 (1924), noted in 24 Col. L. Rev. 790. *Cf.* Clark, An Analysis of Criminal Liability 17 (1880).

Garraud points out that the question whether the distinction between

reverse convictions, and alas! they must give reasons why
the conduct in issue constituted "mere preparation." Among
these reasons, we are told that in order to have a criminal
attempt, there must be an act "moving directly toward the
commission of the offense"[89] or "the commencement of
consummation"[90] or "direct movement, tending immediately" or "proximately,"[91] and so on.[92] Holmes held that
"the act done must come pretty near to accomplishing that
result . . . ;"[93] "very near to the accomplishment of the act
. . . ."[94] After stating that "Every question of proximity
must be determined by its own circumstances," he concluded
that "analogy is too imperfect to give much help."[95]

It is apparent that the above formulas refer to the doctrine of criminal attempt and assume that there are substantial factual differences between states of preparation
and criminal attempts. It is also clear that the decisions
imply that there are valid criteria to determine the above

---

preparation and attempt is one of law or fact has been variously decided by the Cour de Cassation, the last view being that it is a question
of law. Whether the defendant did such and such is a question of fact;
whether such conduct constitutes a criminal attempt is a question of
law. Nonetheless under French procedure the jury decides both questions and the courts cannot control the results. See 1 Garraud, Traité
Théorique et Pratique de Droit Pénal 488-489, 494, 501 (3rd ed. 1935).

[89] Milner v. State, 18 Ala. App. 157, 89 S. 306 (1921). See Miller,
Criminal Law 103 note 49 (1934).

[90] Lee v. Commonwealth, 144 Va. 594, 131 S. E. 212 (1926) ; Andrews
v. Commonwealth, 135 Va. 451, 115 S. E. 558 (1923).
This approximates the requirement of the French Code Pénal, Art. 2.
The 1934 *Projet* for revision of the Code Pénal requires the beginning
of the execution or acts tending directly towards the beginning. Vidal.
op. cit. supra note 85, at 138. For excellent illustrations of the Cour de
Cassation, see *id.* at 137. *Cf.* Garraud and Laborde-Lacoste, Précis
Elémentaire de Droit Pénal 45 (12th ed. 1936).

[91] Skilton, *The Requisite Act in a Criminal Attempt*, 3 U. of Pitt. L.
Rev. 308, 313 (1937).

[92] 1 Bishop, Criminal Law 519, § 729 (2) (9th ed. 1923); State v.
Dumas, 118 Minn. 77, 136 N. W. 311 (1912) ; People v. Lanzit, 70 Cal.
App. 498, 233 P. 816 (1925) ; People v. Rizzo, 246 N. Y. 334, 158 N. E.
888 (1927).

[93] Commonwealth v. Kennedy, 170 Mass. 18, 48 N. E. 770 (1897).

[94] Commonwealth v. Peaslee, 177 Mass. 267, 59 N. E. 55, 56 (1901).
Cf. "it must come, dangerously near to success." Beale, *Criminal Attempts*, 16 Harv. L. Rev. 492 (1903).

[95] Commonwealth v. Kennedy, *supra* note 93, at 771.

issue objectively. If we do not dismiss that as a mere formality, we must account for the widespread criticism of the law distinguishing criminal attempts from preparations. As was suggested above, some of the criticism results from the confusion of the doctrine of criminal attempt with the rules defining specific criminal attempts. Some of it results from a confusion of the *distinction* between preparation and attempt with the *application* of the distinction to the facts in the cases.

COMPETING THEORIES

One theory is that when the offender, moving toward his objective, has committed some crime (not, of course, the intended one) he has also committed a criminal attempt. But there is no necessary connection between these two crimes nor any support of that theory in the cases. One may be guilty, *e.g.* of an attempt to steal money from a drawer or of an attempt to poison although at no point preceding the criminal attempt was there a violation of any penal law. Nor does that theory hold conversely, *e.g.* stealing a gun for the purpose of killing someone would not be an attempt to kill him.[96] If the above theory is modified by being limited to prior crimes which are causally related to the intended harm, it has, in effect, been abandoned; for what is then relied upon is the factual relationship, not the prior criminality.

A somewhat similar theory is that the greater the intended offense, the less "immediate" or "proximate" need conduct be to constitute the relevant criminal attempt. This has some plausibility in explanation of the psychology of certain decisions.[97] But the writers who present it as a theory of criminal attempt have relied on Holmes rather

[96] Cf. Commonwealth v. Eagan, 190 Pa. 10, 42 A. 374 (1899).

[97] *E.g.* Lewis v. State, 35 Ala. 380 (1860), where the defendant, a Negro, who had chased a white woman for more than a mile, was found guilty of attempted rape, although he had not come within ten steps of her.
Cf. People v. Petros, 25 Cal. App. 236, 143 P. 540 (1914), a conviction for attempted pandering; and People v. Lombard, 131 Cal. App. 525, 21 P. 2d 94 (1933), an attempt to kidnap.

than on any thorough testing of it in the cases.[98] That it will not bear scrutiny is apparent on reference to many cases where serious criminal attempts were charged and the prosecution failed because the situations amounted merely to states of preparation.[99]

Another theory, suggested by a remark of Baron Parke,[1] is that the criminal attempt begins when the offender no longer controls the agency he has set in motion, when the outcome has become a matter of physics, not volition. But this theory, too, finds no support in the cases. Liability attaches although the offender is still in charge of his forces and needs to perform additional acts before the intended harm can be effected. Indeed, nothing is more definitely settled than that the last "proximate" act need not have been done.[2]

More persuasive than any of the above theories is the "unequivocality theory," presented originally by Carrara, which denies that there is any factual difference between states of preparation and criminal attempts, and rests wholly on the proof of the *mens rea*. The gist of this theory, as modified by Salmond, is that: "An attempt is an act of such a nature that it is itself evidence of the criminal intent with which it is done. A criminal attempt bears criminal intent upon its face. *Res ipsa loquitur*. An act, on the other hand, which is in itself and on the face of it innocent, is not a criminal attempt, and cannot be made punishable by evidence *aliunde* as to the purpose with which it is

---

[98] Sayre, *supra* note 15 at 821, 845. Skilton, *op. cit. supra* note 91, at 313.

[99] See, *e.g.* State v. Rains, 53 Mont. 424, 164 P. 540 (1917); People v. Miller, 2 Cal. 2d 527, 42 P. 2d 308 (1935); People v. Rizzo, *supra* note 92.

[1] In Regina v. Eagleton (1855), Dears. 515, 538, 169 Eng. Rep. 826, 836, on a charge of attempting to obtain money from guardians of the poor by false representation, etc., Parke, B. said: " . . . no other act on the part of the defendant would have been required. It was the last act, *depending on himself*, towards the payment of the money, and *therefore* it ought to be considered as an attempt. (Italics supplied).

[2] People v. Lanzit, *supra* note 92; The King v. Barker (1924), N. Z. L. R. 865.

done . . . the ground of the distinction between preparation and attempt is evidential merely."[3]

Despite the initial persuasiveness of this thesis, it can readily be shown that the unequivocality theory is fallacious. That it is impossible or less possible to prove the requisite *mens rea* in criminal attempts by a confession than elsewhere can certainly not be established; nor is there any reason to support such an exceptional rule.[4] Moreover, as was previously seen,[5] isolated behavior is always ambiguous so far as *mens rea* is concerned. Thus, it will be recalled, every rule is qualified by the doctrines, *e.g.* sometimes killing a human being is privileged. An individual is arrested just after he has unlatched a window in a dwelling-house. Is that *res ipsa loquitur* in a charge of burglary? Not at all, for his intention may have been to take a nap, or to make a gift anonymously. Any valid judgment on the issue must take into consideration not only the defendant's immediate conduct but also the surrounding conditions, preceding circumstances, the relation of the parties, and any other matters relevant to *mens rea*.[6]

If it is asserted that in the "nature of the facts" there cannot be sufficient evidence of the necessary *mens rea* unless the defendant proceeds to the point of attempting to inflict a criminal harm, it must be noted that that is not the rationale of the decisions. On the contrary, despite absolute

[3] Salmond, Jurisprudence 404 (7th ed. 1924). He discussed this theory in The King v. Barker (1924), N. Z. L. R. 865, 875-876.
Cf. Turner, *Attempts to Commit Crimes*, 5 Camb. L. J. 230, 234-235 (1934).

[4] With reference to Salmond's argument that because a confession will not transform an act of preparation into a criminal attempt (The King v. Barker (1924), N. Z. L. R. 865, 876), therefore a confession cannot supply the proof of the *mens rea* in an otherwise innocent attempt, *cf.* "When a man puts sugar into his wife's tea, this is in its true manner a perfectly innocent act; but if he believes that it was arsenic he is guilty of attempted murder." *Id.* at 877.

[5] *Supra* pp. 230-31.

[6] This is further discussed *infra* with reference to cases of factual impossibility. If decision were rigorously confined to the defendant's immediate act, it would be impossible to pass any valid judgment on his conduct.

certainty as to the required *mens rea*, the defendant must be acquitted if his conduct did not go "far enough," *i.e.* if it was only "preparatory."[7]

In sum, the unequivocality theory is fallacious in maintaining that in states of preparation there is merely a lack of sufficient evidence to support a finding that the required *mens rea* was present. Because it arbitrarily confines judgment regarding *mens rea* to a narrowly circumscribed "act," it would frequently impose liability for non-criminal acts by barring evidence *aliunde* which, if introduced, would show that the intent was anything but criminal. This, fortunately, is not the law. On the other hand, the unequivocality theory would sometimes exclude liability in clear cases of criminal attempt, *e.g.* taking possession of harmless powder, believing it is narcotics or administering such powder, believing it is poison.[8] Thus, the unequivocality

---

[7] Among the many cases where it was held that, despite the definite existence of the required *mens rea*, the defendant had not committed a criminal attempt, the following are especially significant: In State v. Hurley, 79 Vt. 28, 64 A. 78 (1906), a confederate had thrown some hack-saws up to the defendant's cell window and the latter caught them, when he was seen and ordered to drop them. It could hardly be imagined that he wanted the saws for any other purpose than to break jail; yet a conviction for attempting to break jail was reversed.

In People v. Rizzo, *supra* note 92, Crane, J., said: "There is no doubt that he had the intention to commit robbery if he got the chance." See People v. Youngs, 122 Mich. 292, 81 N. W. 114 (1899).

In The King v. Robinson (1915), 2 K. B. 342, the defendant was charged with an attempt to obtain money from an insurance company by false pretenses. The month after he had taken out the insurance on his stock of jewelry, he hid the jewelry, had himself tied up, and shouted out to a passing policeman whom he told that he had been robbed the previous night. Suspicious of his statement, the police searched the place and found the jewelry, whereupon he confessed. Despite the fact that "it was not disputed that the appellant had arranged a fraudulent scheme" (*id.* at 348) and had gone so far as to misrepresent the facts to the police, it was held that, inasmuch as the police were not agents of the insurance company, ". . . what the appellant did was preparation for the commission of a crime, not a step in the commission of it. . . . But there must be some act beyond mere preparation if a person is to be charged with an attempt." *Id.* at 349. So, too, in Hope v. Brown (1954), 1 All E. R. 333.

[8] "Lading wool is lawful, but if it be done with an intent to transport it, that makes it an offence. . . ." Rex v. Sutton (1736), 2 Strange 1074, 93 Eng. Rep. 1041. *Cf.* The case of Henry Sampson Woodfall (1770), 20 How. St. Tr. at 914, 919, and Ellenborough's remarks in The King v. Philipps (1805), 6 East 464, 471, 102 Eng. Rep. 1365, 1368,

theory is only an instance of an unvarying rule of procedure: to convict a person of any crime, there must be sufficient evidence proving each material element of the crime beyond any reasonable doubt.

THE COMMON LAW THEORY

The common law theory, implicit in the case-law and opposed to the above theories, is that criminal attempts differ factually from states of preparation; specifically, that the former are harms of sufficient gravity to require penalization, whereas the latter are not such harms.[9] As was previously noted, the relevant harm is defined in terms of its "proximateness" to the intended ultimate harm, the beginning of the execution of the intended harm, the discharge of the collected forces, and so on.[10] The substantive law restricts and guides judgment concerning the determination of the required harm by constructing, at one pole, the state of preparation and, at the other, the relevant ultimate harm, and describing the criminal attempt as intermediate. The case-law supplies numerous instances of apt analogies. The trial judge must decide the factual issue in the first instance; there is the consensus of the jury, and review by the appellate court.

From a critical viewpoint, however, it can be maintained that *any* conduct directed toward the commission of a crime endangers social interests and is therefore harmful, *i.e.* that there is no essential difference between states of preparation and criminal attempts. Accordingly, the distinction be-

---

administering a harmless substance which is believed to be poisonous— State v. Glover, 27 S. C. 602, 4 S. E. 564 (1888); and see *supra* note 4.

[9] *Cf.* ". . . the *corpus delicti* of a criminal attempt might be stated as a *substantial* but incomplete impairment of some interest. . . ." Strahorn, *The Effect of Impossibility on Criminal Attempts*, 78 U. of Pa. L. Rev. 962, 970 (1930); "An attempt . . . causes a sufficient social harm to be deemed criminal." Hitchler, *Criminal Attempts*, 43 Dick. L. Rev. 211 (1939); ". . . societal harm. . . ." Curran, *Criminal and Non-Criminal Attempts*, 19 Geo. L. J. 185, 316 (1930). See, especially, Strahorn, *Preparation for Crime as a Criminal Attempt*, 1 Wash. & Lee L. Rev. 1 (1939).

[10] See Roux, Traité élémentaire de Droit Pénal 119 (2nd ed. 1927). Professor Roux also suggests that there is a criminal attempt when the offender's conduct penetrates "the sphere of legally protected interests of another person." *Id.* at 105-106.

tween "proximate" and "remote," the fact that the attempt "must come dangerously close to succeeding," etc., indicate only a difference in degree, not in kind. This implies that preparations expressing *mentes reae* are harms essentially like those of criminal attempts and ultimate crimes.

This view, however, is not accepted in the penal law of some countries, including the common law jurisdictions. On the side of feasibility, the difficulties concern the insignificance of the harms produced by the very first steps taken to commit an "ultimate" crime. On the factual side, what is most important is the state of public opinion regarding punishable harms. For although a critical estimate, guided by principle and logic, finds only a difference in degree in preparations and criminal attempts, this identity in the kind of harm is not supported by ordinary experience. From that viewpoint, "mere" preparation is no harm whatever. It is too remote from its target; it has not actually threatened any person's "sphere of interest."

As was seen in the above historical survey, the proscription of harms was largely determined by psychological factors. There had to be not any antisocial conduct, but conduct which was plainly harmful, injuries that stimulated resentment and the like. Historical influences and social experience condition all penal codes. Thus, early English law did not penalize overt attempts to commit major harms, except in treason, and the relative simplicity of even Bracton's time, as regards such conduct, is far removed from the modern attitude. The ample law on criminal assaults is an index of the distance from that primitive appraisal. The rise of the law on solicitation, conspiracies and, indeed, practically the entire law on misdemeanors represent the inclusion of a vast array of harms which were formerly beyond the range of penal law. So, too, in the future, various states of preparation may be considered sufficiently harmful to be penalized.

With reference to the current penalized states of preparation, *e.g.* possession of counterfeit money or dies or burglars' tools or stolen property, the social insight is that we confront a pattern of conduct where the probability of *using* the burglar's tools, *uttering* the counterfeit coin, etc., is very high. This is opposed by the lack of any corresponding, equally assured attitude regarding "ordinary" states of preparation. The pertinent fact as to these is not that the *mens rea* is lacking or that the *mens rea* cannot be proved. It is the much greater likelihood that the criminal design will be abandoned and, also, that, in any event, it has not proceeded far enough to constitute a definite harm. On the other hand, abandonment of a criminal plan is not likely as regards the possessor of burglars' tools or counterfeit money — here, recurrent or professional criminality must be considered. In addition, there is the relative uniformity and simplicity of these offenders' conduct, which facilitates their being regarded as penal harms. There is also the greater ease of proof.

That is the factual side of the question, reflected in a judgment which depends on cultural influences and experience. If, *e.g.* one who sees a person holding a lighted match to combustible materials in a dwelling-house insists that that is not harmful (the requisite *mens rea* being assumed), it is as impossible to *demonstrate* the difference between that situation and a related state of preparation as it is to demonstrate the difference between murder and rape.[11] It is a matter of direct perception and experience, influenced by elementary notions of the significance of the respective situations. We have previously discussed the question of what is involved in the contention[12] that there is no harm in any criminal attempt.[13] It may be added here

[11] See *supra* chapter 7.

[12] See Turner, *supra* note 3.

Cf. "There is again another exceptional class of events . . . which *do* ground criminal proceedings although not *directly* injurious to any individual or the community, but only so in their tendency." Clark, *op. cit. supra* note 88, at 14-15.

Cf. "Generally, attempts are perfectly innocuous, and the party is punished, not in respect of the attempt, but in respect of what he intended to do." 1 Austin, Jurisprudence 523 (4th ed. 1873).

[13] *Supra* pp. 217-220.

that the above appraisal should also apply to assault; but few would think that having an assailant's bullet pass 1/64 of an inch from one's head was no harm at all. On the premise that criminal attempts are not harms, it would seem necessary to hold likewise regarding many other crimes: *e.g.* the possession of burglars' tools, counterfeit dies or money, solicitations, the conspiracies, burglary, reckless driving, bribery, subornation, and other offenses which "tend toward" the commission of various ultimate crimes. Indeed, since there is nothing in nature which distinguishes the presently designated "ultimate" crimes as actually ultimate, it is possible to arrange the entire catalogue of crimes in a series in which only a very few crimes would be "ultimate" harms and all the rest would "merely" tend toward the commission of those harms. As was previously suggested, however, the question of penal harm concerns practical valuation, not physical effect. The above considerations apply equally to states of preparation and the harm of criminal attempts.

IMPOSSIBILITY

Of the various problems in the law of criminal attempt, that concerning "impossibility" presents the major difficulties. The rules attach liability to attempts which failed because of "factual impossibility" but they exculpate where the attempt failed because of "legal impossibility." The rationale of the latter is that since the defendant would not have committed any crime even though he had done everything he intended to do, *a fortiori* he cannot be guilty of a criminal attempt if he did less than that. In a literal sense, there is no such thing as "legal impossibility" because any behavior and any conduct can be made criminal. What is meant is the distinction between conduct which has been forbidden in penal law and conduct which is legal. "Legal impossibility" is therefore only an awkward expression of the principle of legality. In sum: (1) unless the intended end is a legally proscribed harm, causing it is not criminal, hence any conduct falling short of that is not a criminal attempt (*i.e.* the principle of legality); and (2) if the intended end is a legally proscribed harm, the failure to effect it because of the lack of a factual condition necessary to its occurrence, is no defense (*i.e.* factual impossibility).

In sharp contrast to this apparently simple rationale, the dialectics of the case-law on impossibility are ingenious. They begin with *Collins* and result from the failure to appreciate the rationale of the decisions rejecting *Collins*. Collins tried to pick a woman's pocket, which turned out to be empty; and a policeman arrested and charged him with an attempt to commit a felony. But Collins' fortune soon changed for the better. Instead of being tried by a Mansfield or a Lawrence, he fell into the hands of a metaphysician. At first it seemed "plausible" to Baron Bramwell "that a man putting his hand into an empty pocket might be convicted of attempting to steal. . . ." Then, the Baron, having reached a sensible result, began to speculate, and in the course of doing so he suggested two hypothetical cases which, alone, must assure his academic immortality: "You may put this case: Suppose a man takes away an umbrella from a stand with intent to steal it, believing it not to be his own, but it turns out to be his own, could he be convicted for attempting to steal?"[14] And he recalled that in *M'Pherson* he had asked: "suppose a man, believing a block of wood to be a man who was his deadly enemy, struck it a blow intending to murder, could he be convicted of attempting to murder the man he took it to be?"[15] The prosecutor's insistence that he had proved both *mens rea* and an act well designed to effect it was not persuasive. The judges were convinced that the conviction (note the jury's attitude) was wrong. "We are all of opinion," said Cockburn, C. J., "that this conviction cannot be sustained. . . . This case is governed by that of *Reg. v. M'Pherson*, and we think that an attempt to commit a felony can only be made out when, if no interruption had taken place, the attempt could have been carried

[14] Regina v. Collins (1865), 9 Cox C. C. 497, 498, 169 Eng. Rep. 1477.
[15] Regina v. McPherson (1857), 7 Cox C. C. 281, 169 Eng. Rep. 975.

out successfully, and the felony completed of the attempt
to commit which the party is charged."[16] He said it was
like going into an empty room to steal. "[N]o attempt to
commit larceny could be committed."[17] There was authority
to support *M'Pherson,* upon which this remark was based.[18]

But the jury's rather than the judges' view prevailed.
The *Collins* decision was rejected by the Criminal Code
Commission in 1879,[19] by judicial implication in 1889,[20]
despite Stephen's criticism of the Draft Code on the ground
that "there is no danger to the public,"[21] and expressly in
1892.[22] The French courts came to the same conclusion
after a similar history of exculpation in such cases.[23] The
present difficulties in the analysis of criminal attempts are
the direct result of ignoring these decisions which imposed
liability in cases where the facts made it impossible to
commit the intended harm.

The difficulties were facilitated because, side by side with
these decisions, conflicting rules persisted. In some, *e.g.*
attempts to procure abortions or to poison, there were
statutes that were interpreted to require sufficient conditions

---

[16] See *supra* note 14, at 498, 499.

[17] *Id.* at 499, 169 Eng. Rep. at 1477.

[18] Rex v. Scudder (1828), 3 C. & P. 605, 606, 172 Eng. Rep. 565, 566,
was a prosecution for administering a drug to procure an abortion. It
appeared that there was no pregnancy. The twelve judges reversed
the conviction because "it was necessary that the woman should be
with child." *Cf.* Anonymous (1811), 3 Campb. 73, 170 Eng. Rep. 1310,
where a harmless draught had been given under the belief that it could
procure an abortion. Lawrence, J., charged: "It is immaterial whether
. . . it was capable of procuring abortion, or even whether the woman
was actually with child. If the prisoner believed at the time that it
would procure abortion, and administered it with that intent, the case
is within the statute. . . ." *Id.* at 1311.
See also Rex v. Empson, Old Bailey Trials, April 25, 1781, at 240;
stated by East, P. C. 412. In Regina v. St. George (1839), 9 C. & P.
483, 173 Eng. Rep. 921, the defendant was found guilty of an assault
though his gun was not properly cocked and could not be discharged.

[19] Section 74, Draft Code of the Royal Commission on the Law Relating to Indictable Offenses (1879). *Cf.* Lewis, A Draft Code of
Criminal Law and Procedure 251, §§ 474 and 252, n. (1879).

[20] Regina v. Brown (1889), 24 Q. B. 357.

[21] 2 Stephen, H. Cr. L. 225 (1883).

[22] Regina v. Ring (1892), 17 Cox C. C. 491, L. T. (N. S.) 300.

[23] D. 1896 1. 21; S. 1895. 1. 108.

(pregnancy, poisonous substance) to commit the intended harm.[24] The attempt provision in the French Code[25] was interpreted, like *Collins,* to require the possible commission of the intended "ultimate" harms. French theory first sought to reconcile the empty pocket and similar decisions with these holdings by distinguishing "absolute" from "relative" impossibility, only the latter being held punishable. This was presented as an intermediate position that rejected not only subjectivist theories which held that all attemptors should be liable but, also, the older objective theory which would never punish impossible attempts because, following the Code, "they do not constitute the beginning of a crime."[26] The intermediate view held that there might be absolute impossibility either as to means (an unloaded gun) or as to the external conditions (the intended victim was dead; this corpse case is the French counterpart of Bramwell's block of wood). Instances alleged to be typical of relative impossibility were: the intended victim was alive but not in the expected place, *e.g.* he did not sleep in his usual bed that night;[27] the gun was properly loaded but the doer's aim was deflected, and so on.

The above distinction was vigorously attacked. If a pocket is empty, larceny is just as impossible as is killing with an unloaded gun. Shooting into an empty bed cannot kill a human being any more than it is possible to procure an abortion on a woman who is not enceinte. There are no degrees of impossibility and no sound basis for distinguishing among the conditions necessary for the commission of the intended harm. The one is as "absolutely" impossible of accomplishment as the other.[28] The judicial decisions

[24] In People v. Cummings, 296 P. 2d 610 (Cal. Dist. Ct. App. 1956) the defendant was held guilty of an attempt to commit an abortion although the P. W., who was a police investigator, was not pregnant.

[25] Code Pénal, Art. 2.

[26] Garraud and Laborde-Lacoste, *op. cit. supra* note 90, at 49-50.

[27] After some differences in French decisions, the Cour de Cassation held this a criminal attempt. D. 78. 1. 35; S. 77. 2. 329 (Apr. 12, 1877).

[28] Besson, *Le Délit Impossible,* Rev. Crit. 353-354 (1929).

went far to support this criticism,[29] and the theory of "absolute impossibility" gave way to the only tenable position, that based upon the difference between factual impossibility and "legal impossibility." French jurisprudence on this question now closely parallels Anglo-American criminal law[30] — the issue is focused on "legal impossibility."

But, for the reason indicated above, the rule of "legal impossibility" was said to govern when the external conditions lacked a material fact, e.g. murder presupposes a human being; larceny, another's property; and criminal receiving, stolen goods. When those material facts were absent, it was said by some writers to be "legally impossible" to commit either the intended crimes or to attempt to do so. But this view of "legal impossibility" has no greater validity than the earlier theory of "absolute impossibility;" indeed, it is only a restatement of it. For the logic of liability in the empty pocket and unoccupied bed cases is inexorable. It is precisely that the absence of a

[29] In 1928 the Cour de Cassation upheld a conviction for attempt to procure an abortion by use of eau de cologne, an "absolutely" impossible means. D. 1929.97 (Nov. 9, 1928). An excellent discussion of the various theories by Prof. A. Henry is appended, id. at 97-99.

See R. v. Davies (1956), (3) S. A. 52 (A. D.) for a discussion of "relative" and "absolute" impossibility.

Where the means employed have been inadequate, there has been a general tendency to impose liability on the ground that they were in the doer's control, that the consequent impossibility should not therefore aid him. But it is apparent that capacity to control will not account for the liability imposed in such cases as the harmless powder mistaken for arsenic or of an unloaded gun.

[30] Where poison was administered, but not in sufficient quantity to kill, conviction was sustained. State v. Glover, supra note 8. Held, likewise, where the intended victim did not take any of the poison. No allegation that the dose was large enough to kill was required. Commonwealth v. Kennedy, supra note 93. There are occasional decisions holding that if the substance administered was not poisonous, though the defendant believed so, there was no criminal attempt. These are early decisions that hark back to the era when unsuccessful pickpockets were held not guilty. Maudsley's Case (1830), 1 Lewin 51, 168 Eng. Rep. 955; State v. Clarissa, 11 Ala. 57 (1847); Anthony v. State, 29 Ala. 27 (1856). Upholding conviction for attempted rape though the defendant was impotent are Hunt v. State, 114 Ark. 239, 169 S. W. 773 (1914); State v. Ballamak, 28 N. M. 212, 210 P. 391 (1922).

fact that is material in the intended ultimate crime does not exclude liability for the relevant attempt. There is no difference between the proposition: murder is the killing of a human being, X is a corpse or a tree stump, therefore it is "legally impossible" to commit murder; and the proposition: larceny is the taking and asportation of a chattel in another's possession, X is not such a chattel (but is nothing), therefore it is "legally impossible" to commit larceny. The fallacy underlying the above interpretation of "legal impossibility" is in the failure to observe that what is legally material depends on the crime charged and the more serious failure to recognize the meaning of the empty pocket and like decisions — that there is a criminal attempt regardless of the fact that external conditions render it impossible to commit the intended crime. Once it is granted that liability for criminal attempt may attach despite the absence of a material element of the intended ultimate crime, "legal impossibility" in the above sense becomes untenable.

But is there not some validity in opinions which distinguish the tree stump from the empty pocket case? As regards shooting a corpse and "stealing" one's own goods, *e.g.* Professor Garraud asked, "Whose right or sphere of interest has been violated?"[31] And Professor Roux, one of the most acute writers on this problem, asserted that in such cases no right whatever has been menaced but only "phantoms of rights."[32] But metaphors do not resolve inconsistencies nor do they dissolve the inexorable logic of the empty pocket decisions. They do, however, suggest the importance of the apparent objective risk of harm as a qualification of the relevant rules.

OBJECTIVE RISK

In considering this question, we may start with the fact that in the pickpocket case, the emptiness of the pocket was fortuitous; usually it contained things. So, too, as regards the person who decided to kill his roommate and shot into

[31] 1 Garraud, *op. cit. supra* note 88, at 516-518.

[32] "But penal sanctions are too real to serve for the protection of phantoms." Roux, *op. cit. supra* note 10, at 118-119.

the bed where the latter usually slept[33] — it was sheer accident that he slept elsewhere on that particular night. To state that such failures were caused by fortuitous circumstances implies that, at the time of the conduct in issue, the probability of success seemed high. This suggests that the reasonableness of the effort provides a limitation; and in the absence of case-law on this subject, one may hazard the suggestion that any rational effort to commit a proscribed harm falls within the legal prohibition. As regards the simple situations met in the criminal cases, extreme mistakes regarding the external world would be symptomatic of severe mental disorder[34] — the Freudian "reality principle." This would certainly be true of a person who, while sober and in daylight, etc., shot a tree stump, thinking it was a human being, or of one who furtively went about "stealing" his own property. The indicated limitation on penal liability cannot be invalidated on the ground that a psychiatrist might regard such "mistaken" persons as dangerous[35] since segregation of dangerous psychotics is quite different from punishment for a criminal attempt.

There are no American decisions on attempts by "hexing," voodoo or other superstitious or irrational means used to commit legally forbidden harms.[36] In dealing with this problem, Professor Sayre suggested, "If from the point of view of a reasonable man in the same circumstances as the defendant the desired criminal consequence could not be expected to result from the defendant's acts, it cannot endanger social interests to allow the defendant to go unpunished, no matter how evil may have been his intentions."[37] This, however, seems to overstate the limitation on criminal attempt. It is only necessary to point to cases

[33] State v. Mitchell, 170 Mo. 633, 71 S. W. 175 (1902).

[34] See *supra* chapter 13 at note 13 for a discussion of "the reality principle" in relation to mental disease.

[35] Arnold, *Criminal Attempts—The Rise and Fall of an Abstraction*, 40 Yale L. J. 70 (1930).

[36] *Cf.* 2 Gardiner and Lansdown, South African Criminal Law and Procedure 1499-1500 (1946).

[37] Sayre, *supra* note 15 at 851; also at 859.

where normal persons take an extremely marginal chance of successfully committing a harm, *e.g.* shooting at someone 1000 feet away with a bow and arrow, to indicate the untenability of using "reasonable man" in the above way to limit the law of criminal attempt.[38] What seems defensible is not the "reasonable man's" expectation in particular cases, but the "reasonable man's" expectation (informed by expert opinion in certain cases) in *all cases of that type.* But to state the rule in this manner implies that irrational attempts are not criminal and that if a plea of insanity were filed the defendant should be adjudged insane.[39]

As regards the hypothetical cases stated by Bramwell, it seems to havé been assumed that no risk to any person was involved and that this was known to the actor. An apt hypothetical case would assume that the actor believed he was attacking an interest protected by law, and it would determine or present the risk factor in the above indicated way. Specifically, in the above cases, it would be necessary to ask: given the totality of sense-data in those cases, what is the likelihood of the imagined corresponding reality being present? If we assume "normal" perception and conditions of observation, the answer would be almost 100 per cent — deduction being made for "normal" error. For if we have sense-data that signify a human being to normal perception, the likelihood of congruence between them and the actual person they represent is very great.[40] If, given sense-data which normally mean "a pocket containing things," the external requirement of a criminal attempt is satisfied, there is no reason why that should not also be the judgment in the above hypothetical cases. The intriguing difficulty of Bramwell's illustrations results from the fact that they are cases from Never-Never Land and it is covertly assumed that the facts are known to the attemptor. But the fact

[38] See also, R. v. Davies, *supra* note 29 at 64.

[39] But *cf. supra* chapters 3 and 5.

[40] The French 1934 *projet* provided that "Attempt is punishable even though the end sought could not be attained because of a circumstance of fact unknown to the actor." Vidal, *op. cit. supra* note 85, at 147-48.

that these cases did not happen and may never occur must not confuse the analysis of the problem. Is there, *e.g.* any difference, as regards the criminal attempt, between the case of shooting a bullet into an unoccupied bed and Col. Moran's doing the like to an effigy of Sherlock Holmes by Madame Tussaud, the intent being to kill a human being in each instance? The problem is obscured by the premise that there is no harm in any criminal attempt. In the alternative view, a harm has been committed because the reasonable (rational) *appearance* of the external facts is material, not the actual facts in those particular situations where an attempt must fail.

FACTUAL IMPOSSIBILITY AND THE PRINCIPLE OF LEGALITY

In *Jaffe*,[41] it was held that the defendant was not, indeed, could not be, guilty of a criminal attempt to receive stolen goods because the goods had been recovered and were therefore no longer "stolen." It is submitted that this decision confused the external situation and the defendant's *mens rea*, which included his belief regarding that situation. An intention is mental;[42] and the fact that someone is mistaken regarding the external facts does not alter his state of mind, but merely makes it impossible for him to effectuate it. This problem should not be confused with that of mistake of law — the fact that a person erroneously believes that his conduct is illegal does not make it illegal any more than a belief in the legality of his conduct is a defense.[43] In *Jaffe*, to be sure, the characterization of the goods received as "stolen" is a legal conclusion or a "mixed" one of fact and law, not a physical fact. But the decision was not rested on the indicated distinction,[44] and it may

---

[41] People v. Jaffe, 185 N. Y. 497, 78 N. E. 169 (1906).

[42] The court's assertion that "belief [that the goods were stolen] is not enough under this statute" finds no support in New York cases, and it is everywhere recognized that such belief is sufficient. See, *e.g.* U. S. v. Werner et al., 160 F. 2d 438 (C. C. A. 2d 1947).

[43] Relevant questions concerning mistake in attempt are discussed *supra* chapter 11.

[44] *Cf.* People v. Gardner, 144 N. Y. 119, 38 N. E. 1003 (1894);

be assumed that "stolen" was properly treated as purely factual. The absence of that material element excludes the criminal receiving but not the criminal attempt. This concerns the crucial point in the analysis of "impossibility" and some further discussion of it seems warranted.

The principle of legality implies that when certain injuries or effects are not criminal, an attempt to cause them is not criminal. For example, it is not a crime to throw even a Kansas steak into a garbage can, and if a foolish person took his steak and started towards the can, but was prevented from accomplishing his purpose, he is not guilty of a criminal attempt. Since it is not forgery to raise the figures on a check from 2.50 to 12.50, because that is not a material alteration, doing that or trying to do that is not an attempt to forge.[45] Since a husband cannot rape his wife, his violent effort to have forced intercourse is not an assault with intent to rape.[46] In a Missouri case,[47] the defendant offered money to a city official to secure his favorable vote regarding a contract with the city. The official, however, had no authority to vote for or against such a contract. It was held that there was no criminal attempt to bribe. The same result was reached where the bribery of a tax assessor was in issue and the indictment failed to allege that the property in question was located inside the city limits and thus within the sphere of the assessor's authority.[48] In these cases, it should be noted, there was no mistake about the facts; and it is this kind of situation

Commonwealth v. Johnson, 312 Pa. 140, 167 A. 344 (1933).

Cf. State v. Guffey et al., 262 S. W. 2d 152 (Mo. 1953) where the court reversed D's conviction of violating a hunting statute by shooting a stuffed deer which a Conservation agent had set up. That the statute included "attempt" was held immaterial, citing Jaffe and *dicta* in State v. Taylor, 133 S. W. 2d 336 (Mo. 1939), that "it is no crime to attempt to murder a corpse."

[45] Wilson v. State, 85 Miss. 687, 38 S. 46 (1905).

[46] Frazier v. State, 48 Tex. Cr. R. 142, 86 S. W. 754 (1905); Duckett v. State, 191 S. W. 2d 879 (1946). So, too, of a boy legally incompetent because of his age, to commit rape. State v. Fisk, 15 N. D. 589, 108 N. W. 485 (1906).

[47] State v. Butler, 178 Mo. 272, 77 S. W. 560 (1903).

[48] Gunning v. People, 189 Ill. 165, 59 N. E. 494 (1901).

which judges have in mind when they say, in effect, that if doing something is not criminal, doing part of that is not a crime, *i.e.* it is "legally impossible" to commit a criminal attempt.

In the universally accepted decisions regarding the empty pocket, the administration of sugar thought-to-be-arsenic case, and shooting into an empty bed where the intended victim usually slept, criminal attempts were committed despite the lack of a material element of the intended, ultimate crime. It follows that here the principle of legality regarding criminal attempt, *i.e.* the legal definition of criminal attempt, *is not determined by reference to the actual facts in the external situation.* That principle is "satisfied," *i.e.* a criminal attempt can be committed, regardless of the absence of facts that are essential to the commission of the intended ultimate crime. The legal definition of criminal attempt must, accordingly, in that regard (*i.e.* apart from the required act) be based on the only other relevant material factor — the *mens rea*, including the belief in the existence of all the material elements specified in the definition of the intended ultimate crime. In sum, the material facts referred to in the definition of criminal attempt are those *supposed* to exist by a person manifesting the requisite *mens rea*.[49] Here, unlike the above situations, there was a mistake of fact, and the crucial issue concerns *mens rea*.

There is, *e.g.* nothing harmful in eating a spoonful of sugar, but intentionally administering what is believed to be arsenic radically transforms the meaning of the situation.

[49] In commenting upon the writer's analysis of *Jaffe*, Mr. J. C. Smith quotes the writer's statement: "Intent is in the mind . . . The fact that the defendant was mistaken regarding the external realities did not alter his intention. . . ." In criticism of this, Mr. Smith states, "This seems to suggest that the only thing that mattered in the case was whether Jaffe had *mens rea*. . . ." Smith, *supra* note 84, at 442. It is submitted, with deference, that this was not suggested. The sufficiency of the defendant's conduct was not in issue since it had gone far beyond preparation: Jaffe took possession of the cloth from the employee who had previously sold him stolen cloth, and he paid him about half the value of it. The intention of the defendant is the decisive factor, not in the sense that conduct beyond preparation is immaterial, but in the sense that the intention determines the meaning of the conduct.

The actualization of that *mens rea* would result in a crime — therefore the effort to do that, going beyond preparation, is a criminal attempt. In *Siu*,[50] the defendant, a police officer, proposed to a fellow officer that the latter provide him with narcotics for illegal sale. After consultation with superior officers, a package of talcum powder was handed the defendant, and he was later convicted of attempting illegally to take possession of narcotics. Thus, the *mens rea* reveals the character of the conduct, *i.e.* conduct is criminal because it expresses a *mens rea*.[51]

Analysis of these cases[52] has sometimes failed to take account of the ambiguity of "intention." "Intention" sometimes means *mens rea*, while in other contexts, *e.g.* that of strict liability, it means only the consciousness of an act, that the doer was awake, etc.[53] If D shoots X, mistakenly believing X is his mortal enemy Y, he is liable for the homicide of X; and in their opinions, judges sometimes say D intended to shoot X, the man he shot. On the other hand, if D utters a coin, believing it is genuine but, in fact, the coin is counterfeit, he is not guilty of uttering counterfeit money although it is true, in a sense, that he intended to utter the particular coin he did hand over. In both cases *mens rea*, not the narrower innocent "intention," is the decisive legal factor, and this must also be true of attempts to commit crimes in which *mens rea* is a material element. This interpretation of the two "intentions" is inferentially

[50] People v. Siu, 126 Cal. App. 2d 41, 271 P. 2d 575 (1954).

[51] *Cf.* ". . . the intent alleged would convert what on their face might be no more than ordinary acts of competition or the small dishonesties of trade into a conspiracy of wider scope, as has been explained more than once." Holmes, J., in Nash v. U. S., 229 U. S. 373, 57 L. Ed. 1232, 33 S. Ct. 780 (1913).

[52] *Cf.* R. v. Percy Dalton, Ltd. (1949), 33 Crim. App. R. 102, where the defendant, who sold pears, believing they weighed less than, in fact, they did weigh, was acquitted of violating a price regulation, but was convicted of a criminal attempt. Conviction reversed: " . . . the completed transaction was no offence . . . steps on the way to the doing of something, which is thereafter done, and which is no crime, cannot be regarded as attempts to commit a crime." *Id.* at 110. See notes 54 to 56 *infra*.

[53] See generally the discussion of this problem by Edwards, *Mens Rea in Statutory Offences* (1955).

supported by the judicial construction of statutes imposing strict liability, where it is said that the defendant intended to do what he did (in the sense that he was not physically pushed into doing it, was not a somnambulist, etc.) ; and it is well established that such an intention is not a *mens rea* since that is not material in strict liability offenses.

In criminal attempts (excluding strict liability), one must take account of the defendant's *mens rea*, and if it is said that the defendant "did everything he intended" to do, that must therefore be understood to mean the actualization (realization or fulfillment) of his *mens rea*.[54] In *Jaffe, Siu* and *Dalton*,[55] the defendants did not actualize their *mentes reae*. In *Jaffe*, there was lacking the quality ("stolen") of the assumed merchandise, in *Siu*, the nature of the desired powder, and in *Dalton*, the weight of the imagined merchandise sold. Accordingly, none of these defendants did what he intended to do in the relevant legal sense of that term, *i.e. mens rea*. What, therefore, is implied in saying that no criminal attempt was possible in *Dalton* and *Jaffe* is that a criminal attempt can be committed only where it is factually possible to commit the intended ultimate crime. That, however, is untenable because of well-established law, *e.g.* the empty pocket, empty bed, and the sugar-"arsenic" cases.

That the present law of New York accords with this conclusion is indicated in *Boord*.[56] There, a hotel "runner" was convicted of an attempt to divert a "traveller or

---

[54] *Cf.* "The defendants in *Dalton* . . . achieved all the consequences which they intended: the boxes of pears were sold." Smith, *op. cit. supra* note 84, at 437.

[55] In *Dalton, supra*, note 52, which was similar to an O. P. A. violation, the court did not decide whether *mens rea* was a material element of the intended crime. Dalton intended to sell for more than the allowed legal price. If *mens rea* was material, the case is indistinguishable from *Jaffe*. If *mens rea* is not material in the completed offense, it is presumably not material in the relevant criminal attempt. That problem should be definitely distinguished from the problem of impossibility with reference to ultimate crimes, like receiving stolen property, where *mens rea* is required. The thesis of chapter 10 *supra* would, of course, apply to innocent conduct which fell short of the proscribed behavior.

[56] 260 App. Div. 681, 23 N. Y. S. 2d 792 (1940).

other person to another hotel. . . ." The prosecuting witnesses were policewomen who pretended to be strangers in New York en route to a hotel near the Fair Grounds. The defendant urged them to stop at a different hotel and, later, they registered there and occupied a room. The policewomen had been assigned the duty of obtaining evidence against violators of the statute and, in stopping at the hotel recommended by the defendant, they did not rely upon his representations, hence they were not actually diverted. The conviction of a criminal attempt to divert was affirmed by the Supreme Court (which, in New York, is subordinate to the Court of Appeals). The dissenting justice relied heavily on *Jaffe*, insisting that the policewomen were not travellers and that therefore the "completed" transaction, summarized above, was neither a violation of the statute nor an attempt to violate it: "An attempt to violate the statute would indeed have been committed if the detectives had in fact been travellers. . . ." The majority opinion, in evident deference to the higher Court, did not refer to *Jaffe*! Instead, earlier decisions of that Court were cited. "To sustain a conviction for an attempted crime," held the majority, "it is not necessary that every element constituting the crime be present."[57] This is the rationale of the empty pocket decision. Once it is decided that the defendant had the required *mens rea*, the remaining question concerns his conduct in relation to the preparation-attempt distinction—the premise being that the external situation was what the defendant believed it to be.

[57] The Court of Appeals affirmed the decision without opinion. 285 N. Y. 806, 38 N. E. 2d 195 (1941). But *cf.* People v. Jelke, 1 N. Y. 2d 31, 135 N. E. 2d 213 at 218 (1956).

CHAPTER XVI

CRIMINOLOGY AND PENAL THEORY

THAT the elucidation of the meaning of legal rules and doctrines depends upon empirical knowledge was seen, *e.g.* in the discussion of "insanity," "gross intoxication," "disease," and other terms. This was also indicated with regard to normal mental processes, *e.g. mens rea*, the fusion of cognitive and volitional functions. Thus, penal law refers to data which are the subject matter of psychology. That it also refers to social data is apparent in the study of crimes against property. The external facts of "property," the business of dealing in stolen property as contrasted with the occasional purchase of a stolen chattel for the buyer's consumption, indeed, all the facts, sometimes designated in penal theory as the "external situation," also fix the meaning of legal norms.[1] This is the sociological reference of penal law. It seems evident that the greater the empirical knowledge, the better is the elucidation provided by penal theory.

While this dependence of penal theory upon criminology seems indubitable, its contributions to criminology are not generally recognized. Moreover, the problem of the inter-relations of criminology and penal theory raises many difficulties which are aggravated by the prevalent specialization. For example, in the United States and, perhaps, in other countries, penal theory is the province of legal scholars while criminology is viewed as a branch of sociology or psychiatry or even of political science. In the uni-

[1] See Hall, Studies in Jurisprudence and Criminal Theory, ch. 1 (1958).

versities, each of these disciplines is studied in a separate department or school, and penal theory is regarded as an independent, technical body of knowledge.

The specialization, characteristic of our times, is manifested in criminology not only in the narrowing of the subject matter to psychological or to sociological factors but also, within these, to criminal behavior isolated from penal laws and values. Thus, the work of criminologists and lawyers sometimes suggests that their disciplines have only casual contacts. A criminologist who never sees a criminal statute may spend a life-time studying the relationship of economic or biological factors to a particular type of criminal conduct, while a lawyer may completely ignore such studies. In the short time available for the trial of a case, narrow issues are formulated and the practical business of adjudication proceeds apace in order that the community may survive and carry on its diverse activities.

Notwithstanding the current specialization, it is submitted that criminology and penal theory are actually inter-dependent phases of a single body of knowledge.[2] Their relationship is much more complex than is suggested by the usual interpretation of Aristotle's distinction between theoretical and practical knowledge. Interpreted in that way, criminologists would seek disinterestedly to discover the causes of crime, the effects of punishment and the like, while penal theorists would be concerned to influence action, such as adjudication and other decision-making, i.e. penal theory would be the application of criminology to practical uses. But criminology is also employed in the solution of practical problems, e.g. the prevention of juvenile delinquency and the rehabilitation of criminals. In addition, it depends upon knowledge of penal law, e.g. to locate "criminals" and in other important respects, as will more fully appear; hence, it must look to penal theory to elucidate the meaning of that law. At the same time, as was previously noted, the meaning of penal laws is largely

---

[2] Id. ch. 4, and Hall, Theft, Law and Society, Introduction (2nd ed. 1952).

derived from their reference to facts, the intensive study of which is the province of criminology. Thus, the suggestion that penal theory is "only" the practical application of criminology is not a very significant clue to their inter-relations.

The indicated inter-dependence of criminology and penal theory presupposes a criminal science in which both penal law and the congruent conduct form the principal subject matter. This insight, however, encounters considerable difficulty *vis à vis* the dominant theory in recent and, perhaps, current criminology. In order to understand the reasons for this and to appreciate the present position of criminology, it is necessary to take account of the historical influences which have molded that discipline.

Without engaging in a detailed analysis of the literature of criminology, and with full recognition of the very important contributions of individual scholars, it may be suggested that the expectations of the founders of the school of scientific criminology are very far from having been realized. The most salient fact about current criminology, if a wide generalization is permitted, is that it is a congeries of unresolved conflicts—the result of failure to bring the diverse streams of thought known as Classical and Positivist criminology into compatible inter-relationship. This does not represent a mere neglect of interesting professional literature; no less than the basic postulates and theories of a sound criminology are involved. The issues can be stated in a brief comparison of the origin and principal motifs of the above Schools.

Beccaria wrote in 1764, while Ferri's most important book appeared in 1884. Beccaria's essay is a severe criticism of the contemporaneous criminal law and its administration, a plea for the rational correspondence of the gravity of the crime and the severity of the punishment, and an eloquent denunciation of torture, secret accusation and indiscriminate capital punishment. Beccaria was very much

---

3 Beccaria, An Essay on Crimes and Punishments 164, 174 (3rd ed. 1770).

interested in the prevention of crimes which, he held, "is the fundamental principle of good legislation. . . ." And he also insisted that "the most certain method of preventing crimes is, to perfect the system of education."[3] His essay led not only to the greatest penal reforms in modern history, it also stimulated acceptance of the Humean philosophy of "a moral [*i.e.* social] science" modeled after physics and based on the precise application of the pleasure-pain principle and "the greatest good to the greatest number" axiom. Relevant questions of fact were not explored by Beccaria, but he was far from being the conceptualist of the "Classicism" conjured up by the Positive School of criminology.[4]

An historian of social ideas would take account of the distinctive cultural situations from which the schools emerged. He would note, *e.g.* that in eighteenth century revolutionary liberalism, a criminologist would be deeply concerned with the *ancien régime* whose unrestricted power dispensed not equal justice but punishment according to rank, facilitated by vague laws which provided ample range for indiscriminate death sentences. In a broader configuration, he would note the rising tide of rationalism, the Encyclopaedists, and the intellectual revolt against authoritarian government which shortly found violent expression in the American and French revolutions. He would thus find many reasons why the founders of the Classical School emphasized the values of the emerging penal law of the modern democratic State.[5] In contrast, Ferri wrote in the halcyon days of an established liberalism, the issue of indi-

---

[4] It was none other than Beccaria who wrote ". . . the good, or bad logic of the judge . . . will depend on his good or bad digestion; on the violence of his passions; on the rank, and condition of the accused, or on his connections with the judge; and on all those little circumstances, which change the appearance of objects in the fluctuating mind of man. Hence we see the fate of a delinquent changed many times in passing through the different courts of judicature, and his life and liberty, victims to the false ideas, or ill humour of the judge; who mistakes the vague result of his own confused reasoning, for the just interpretation of the laws." *Id.* at 15.

[5] "*Every member of society should know when he is criminal, and when innocent. . . .* The uncertainty of crimes hath sacrificed more victims to secret tyranny, than have ever suffered by public and solemn cruelty." *Id.* at 41.

vidual protection against political tyranny apparently resolved forever. He wrote well after Comte, in the heyday
of Evolution, and after Socialism had taken root and the
social legislation of the latter nineteenth century had
ushered in a new age.

Another major influence on current criminology, that was
no less effective because its force was a negative one, was
the rise of Legal Positivism in the early nineteenth century.
This School, oriented to the practice of the law, expounded
an Imperative Theory in which the origin of law—the
"command of the Sovereign"—was the central thesis. The
principal motif of this School was the separation of rules
of positive law from morality and fact, *i.e.* the clear, definite
identification of the State's rules of law. Viewed, however,
in relation to an empirical discipline, it culminated in the
tautology that "crime is a violation of criminal law."[6] But
it developed many precise ideas and contributed much to the
elucidation of legal terms.

The polemic of the Positive School of criminology, influenced by Comte's sociology, was understandably directed
against such formalism. Its confusion of the theories of the
two schools can be accounted for on the ground that both
the Classical School and Legal Positivism preceded the
Positive School of criminology and both had emphasized
the "rule of law." One has only to contrast Beccaria's thesis
that crime is an "injury done to society,"[7] which is "destructive of the public safety and happiness,"[8] with the above
positivist legal definition of "crime" to apprehend the critical difference between formalism and a theory which had
descriptive reference. The bias against ideas ("metaphysics"), stimulated by Comte, joined one against valuation,
and both were directed against the Classical School. This
was facilitated by the fact that the founder of the Positive
School of criminology, Lombroso, was a physician little in-

---

[6] *Cf.* Ruml, *Crime, Law and Social Science: A Symposium,* 34 Col.
L. Rev. 274 (1934).

[7] Beccaria, *op. cit. supra* note 3, at 26, 29.

[8] *Id.* at 21.

terested in theory.[9] He was all the more certain that he knew a criminal when he saw one or read his anatomical measurements.[10] Yet, it must be granted, Lombroso brought to the study of criminals all the advantages that a crude empiricism not infrequently contributes to scientific experiment.

The first theoretician of the School was Baron Garofalo, a judge and scholar of definitely speculative bent. He argued that to determine "the boundaries of criminality, the sociologist cannot turn to the man of law . . . we must arrive at the notion of the *natural crime*," i.e. "those acts which no civilized society can refuse to recognize as criminal and repress by means of punishment."[11] The decisive criterion was "the average moral sense of the whole community."[12] Specifically, the natural crime was "injury to . . . the elementary altruistic sentiments of *pity* and *probity*."[13] He later added that the act "must, in addition, be *harmful to society*."[14] And he concluded that "the legal notion of crime must be laid aside as valueless for our purposes."[15]

If Lombroso provided the scientific ideology and Garofalo the theoretical framework, it was Ferri who supplied the zeal and eloquence (he was one of Italy's greatest trial lawyers) which established the Positive School as a vital force in criminology. Ferri criticized the "doctrines of criminal law developed to the highest degree of metaphysical pedantry,"[16] insisting that the Classical School "had and

[9] The meanings given the term "crime" parallel the entire history of human thought. One might classify them as theological, ethical, classical, utilitarian, positivistic, formal, pragmatist, eclectic, and the various neo-modifications of these. See Saldana, L'Évolution Du Crime (1930).

[10] He found the equivalents of criminal behavior in animals and even in certain plants.

[11] Garofalo, Criminology 4-5 (trans. Millar, 1914).

[12] *Id.* at 10.

[13] *Id.* at 33.

[14] *Id.* at 51.

[15] *Id.* at 60.

[16] Ferri, Criminal Sociology 2 (trans. Kelly and Lisle, 1917).

preserves a theoretical method, the 'a priori' study of crime as an abstract juridical being."[17] "To the classical criminologist, the person of the criminal is an entirely secondary element, as the patient formerly was to the physician. . . . He was concerned with the crime and not with the criminal. . . ."[18] Diametrically opposed to this was the school of Positive Criminology which, he said, "proposes the complete study of crime, not as a juridical abstraction, but as a human act, as a natural and social fact. . . ."[19] He rejected Tarde's thesis that "crime is always 'a wilful violation of law,'" asserting that "this is remaining in the old circle where crime is what the legislator punishes. . . ."[20] Instead, " . . . the fact remains that the proper subject of criminal anthropology is the *anti-social individual* in his *tendencies* and in his *activity*."[21] He regarded Garofalo's definition of crime as "original and happy" but incomplete;[22] and he finally accepted Colajanni's definition of the "natural crime": "Punishable acts (delicts) are those which, determined by individual and anti-social motives, disturb the conditions of existence and shock the average morality of a given people at a given moment."[23]

Ferri's polemics gained wide acceptance of the non-legal "natural crime"[24] as the ultimate conception of the Positive School. In the first third of this century, it became the

[17] *Id.* at 3. "Criminal law, also, has until now consisted in the study of crimes considered as abstract entities. Until now the criminologist has studied robbery, homicide, and forgery, in and for themselves, as 'juridical entities,'—as abstractions." *Id.* at 12.

[18] *Id.* at 13. In a footnote he adds that "before studying crime as a juridical fact, it should be studied as a natural and social phenomenon." *Ibid.*

[19] *Id.* at 18.

[20] *Id.* at 78.

[21] *Id.* at 79.

[22] *Id.* at 80.

[23] *Id.* at 81. He repeated this frequently. *Cf.* La Justice Pénale, Résumé Du Cours De Sociologie Criminelle 11 (1898).

[24] For a number of sociological (non-legal) definitions of "crime" see Crocq, *Compte Rendu*, Congress International D'Anthropologie Criminelle 408, 412 (1901). *Cf.* Hamon, *De la Définition du Crime*, 8 Arch. Anthr. Crim. 242 (1893), and Maxwell, Le Concept Social Du

dominant criminology,[25] although it was not taken up in England as in America, and the dissent of Tarde and Saleilles as well as the influence of Durkheim's sociology considerably moderated the movement in France, and that despite Comte.[26] We know of course that the School's vast pretensions of originality have been thoroughly exposed.[27] Its basic theory, which excluded criminal law from the subject matter of criminology, raised the most important issue in social science.

Before discussing this, it should be recognized that each of the above Schools concentrated upon an essential aspect of crime. There is the emphasis upon values, including legality, of the Classical School, the elucidation of legal concepts by the Imperative School,[28] and the Sociological School's concentration on facts and empirical knowledge. The present problem may be said to require the sound integration of these theories in the construction of an adequate criminal science. What this consists of and the rele-

---

Crime (1914).

[25] Ferri wrote much of "the illusion of the free human will" and of that "dangerous malady, which we call crime." The Positive School of Criminology 21, 45 (1913). For criticism of this, see Saleilles, Les Nouvelles Écoles De Droit Pénal 22-23 (1901). In 1926 Ferri came to admit the punitive nature of penal sanctions as necessary. See the quotation by Saldana, La Nouvelle Philosophie Pénale 6 (1927).

[26] See *supra* chapter 10 at notes 28-32.

[27] See Lindesmith and Levin, *The Lombrosian Myth in Criminology*, 42 Am. J. Soc. 653 (1937); *English Ecology and Criminology of the Past Century*, 27 J. Cr. L. & Crim. 801 (1937). *Cf.* "I have no more doubt of every crime having its cure in moral and physical influence, than I have of the efficacy of the Peruvian bark in curing the intermitting fever." Rush, *An Enquiry into the Effects of Public Punishments upon Criminals, and upon Society* (1787), in Essays 155 (1798).

See, too, 3 Rossi, Traité De Droit Pénal 310 (1829); Roscoe, Observations on Penal Jurisprudence and the Reformation of Criminals (1819); Turnbull, A Visit to the Philadelphia Prison 2, 61-62, 81-83 (1797); Ahrens, Cours De Droit Naturel 230-1 (1868); Thonissen, Le Droit Pénal De La République Athénienne 453 (1875); Quincy, Charge to the Grand Jury 4, 10 (1822).

"A prison thus regulated becomes a hospital for the treatment of moral diseases." Draft Proposal on the Principles of Punishment (1847). *Cf.* Radzinowicz and Turner, quotation from Hencke (1823), *The Language of Criminal Science*, 7 Camb. L. J. 233 (1940).

[28] See chapters 4 and 6 *supra*.

vance of the above crucial issue must now engage our attention.

Penal theory and criminology (here viewed as inclusive of all the social disciplines, especially psychology and sociology, relevant to crime) can be brought into sound rapport only by recognizing and building upon their reference to a common subject matter. The first step in that direction is to show that at least the more important penal laws are social norms and thus within the province of a criminology which does not cleave to the dogma that only observable behavior is the proper subject matter of a social science.

It is now widely accepted among social scientists that all groups exhibit evidence not merely of patterns of habitual behavior but also, and more significantly, of conduct more or less consciously directed by norms that imply socially approved goals (values). It is clear that there is invariably some tension between the standards of the imperatives and the relevant behavior; and it may also be taken, as generally agreed, that the norms are distinguishable from the values which they express and implement.

As a result of the dominance of Legal Positivism, however, it is often assumed that the State's rules are quite different from the norms of sub-groups, *i.e.* associations less extensive than "the great society." If one asks, in what respects these rules differ, the answers received depend upon the perspective of the answerer.[29] If the question is answered from the viewpoint of the practicing lawyer, the source of the State's rules, *i.e.* the "command of the Sovereign," is essential. If it is answered from the viewpoint of political obligation, *i.e.* of "right" problem-solving, the ethical validity of those commands is equally emphasized. And, if the social scientist seeks an answer, he wants a solution which will include a subject matter that is observable; but if he avoids the positivist dogma, he also recognizes that this requirement is not incompatible with, indeed that it is enlightened by, the inclusion of social norms.

[29] Hall, *Reason and Reality in Jurisprudence*, 7 Buffalo L. Rev. 353-54 (1958).

In dealing with this problem, political scientists have maintained that courts and a professional official personnel provide the distinctive mark which sets positive law apart from other norms. From an historical and evolutionary point of view, the highly developed structure of a modern legal order, including the specialized functions of a class of experts in adjudication and law enforcement, stands out in contrast to the amorphous reciprocity and retaliation that characterized primitive social control. Nevertheless, it is submitted, the specialization of official personnel is a problematical differentia. In most primitive societies, perhaps in all of them, there was (or is) some degree of authority and organization; indeed, society and order seem to be correlative notions. And beyond the simplest type of social organization lie only speculation and verbal problems regarding "society." In any event, the above criterion represents a difference in degree rather than one in kind. While it may serve as a convenient datum in current research, it dissolves into the similarity of lesser degrees of specialization and finally into a very diffuse organization which represents a parallel, if very simple, structure. In sum, specialization implies a development of what previously existed in an unspecialized form.

We must turn, therefore, to other criteria to determine whether the State's rules differ in essential respects from the norms of sub-groups. The principal subject that has been widely discussed in this regard concerns the sanction. Many scholars hold that legal sanctions consist of the use of physical force, that this distinguishes them from other sanctions, and thus distinguishes positive laws from other norms. Kelsen, *e.g.* maintains that the legal sanction "has the character of a measure of coercion;"[30] and it is clear that by this he means physical force which, of course, is not always applied since resistance is unusual.[31] He often speaks of law as "an organization of force" and of "forcible

[30] Kelsen, General Theory of Law and State 18 (1945).
[31] *Ibid.*

deprivation;"[32] and he sometimes explicitly distinguishes the legal from other sanctions by reference to "the employment of physical force."[33] He concludes that the State has a monopoly of physical force.[34]

It must be granted that this restrictive view of the State's legal sanctions supplies a criterion that is simple and manifest. It is initially persuasive by reference to the most commonly applied sanctions, such as imprisonment and the seizure of a debtor's assets, where there is physical handling of the body or the chattels. And the externality and physical character of legal sanctions might facilitate the demarcation of a definite field of distinctive data.

There are, however, several difficulties in the way of this theory of legal sanctions.[35] Where intangible property is "transferred," it is metaphorical or the exaggeration of the significance of a superficial datum, e.g. a certificate of stock, to say that the sanction is physical. Even when tangible property is taken from a debtor's possession and delivered to his judgment-creditor, that sanction is not a physical force in the implied sense of being directed against the defendant's body. Legal sanctions are evidently more complex than what "measure of physical force" implies.

More directly pertinent is the fact that some legal sanctions are obviously not measures of physical force. For example, in a Washington case, a lawyer was censured by the governors of a State bar association, pursuant to a judgment of the supreme court, for his refusal to file income tax re-

[32] *Id.* at 21.

[33] *Id.* at 19.

[34] *Id.* at 21, 190, 339. An excellent discussion of the entire problem is presented by Recasens Siches, *Les Usages Sociaux et leur Differenciation D'Avec les Norms Juridiques*, pub. in Droit, Morale, Moeurs 145 (Paris, 1936).

[35] They apply to both forms of that thesis — that physical force distinguishes legal from other sanctions, although other attributes, *e.g.* their moral validity, are also essential, and that physical force is the only substantive characteristic of legal sanctions.

turns and pay taxes.[36] In the United States' military law, which is part of the law of the country, reprimand and admonition are regular legal sanctions.[37] There is also the sanction of discharge from military service and public employment for serious violation of statutes or regulations; and the United States' Internal Revenue Code of 1954 provides that for certain breaches of duty, *e.g.* extortion, officers "shall be dismissed."[38] Again, there is the sanction of adverse publicity which, *e.g.* the United States' Securities Exchange Commission imposes for violation of the duty to provide required information regarding securities.[39] It may also strike the names of national security exchanges, persons and stocks from the registration lists.[40] Similarly, the Federal Food and Drug Act permits publication of violations, including the names of the offenders and the dispositions made, a further instance of the use of adverse publicity as a legal sanction.[41] Thus, it must be concluded that some legal sanctions are not measures of physical coercion; and this alone invalidates the above theory regarding the distinctiveness of legal rules.

The corollary of that theory is that the sanctions of non-State norms are not measures of physical coercion. But in the family, there is the "inexorable imposition" of some rules (which may also be quite definite), and their violation is sometimes sanctioned by physical force. The evidence of

---

[36] *In re* Molthan, 327 P. 2d 427 (Wash. 1958). In Kentucky Bar Association v. McAfee, Ky., 301 S.W. 2d 899 (1957) the defendant in a similar case was reprimanded in the opinion of the State Supreme Court.

[37] See Winthrop, Military Law and Precedents 414-416 (2nd ed. 1920). Winthrop refers to similar provisions in the British Army Acts, s. 44. Sometimes the sentence designates the official who will administer the reprimand, *e.g.* "the general commanding" or "the Secretary of War." *Id.* 415. See also Manual for Courts-Martial of the United States ch. 25, § 126f (1951).

[38] Section 7214.

[39] 48 Stat. 899, 15 U.S.C. § 78u.

[40] 48 Stat. 898, 15 U.S.C. § 78s.

[41] 52 Stat. 1057, 21 U.S.C. § 375. Similar sanctions are used in the states, *e.g.* the discontinuance of "Certified Seed" marking of standardized products.

criminal gangs is perhaps more persuasive since no question of infancy is involved. In the Mafia and Camorra, *e.g.* rules are adopted and orders are issued, there are regular modes of hearing charges of violation, formal judgments are rendered by the Grand Council,[42] followed by the action of designated agents who impose very severe physical sanctions, including death, razor slashes across the face, severe beatings, etc.[43] There have also been various minority groups, *e.g.* gypsies, Chinese in New York and San Francisco, Vigilante Committees in California during the Gold Rush, utopian communities, revolutionary parties and others which enforced their rules by measures of physical compulsion. Moreover, these sanctions were (or are) imposed on non-members as well as on members; hence, the voluntariness of membership cannot be adduced to distinguish these norms from legal ones.

In sum, whether we scrutinize the laws of the State and discover reprimands, adverse publicity, etc., among their sanctions or whether we observe the norms of certain subgroups and find inexorable imposition[44] and physical compulsion[45] among their sanctions, the thesis that the sanctions of the State's laws are distinctive, as measures of physical compulsion, becomes untenable.[46] It is necessary

---

[42] *The Camorra in Modern Italy*, 214 Edinburgh Rev. 390 (Oct. 1911).

[43] Reid, Mafia 30, 38-39 (1952). See Petrazycki, Law and Morality 73 (Twentieth Century Legal Philosophy Series, VII, 1955).

[44] Bentham, writing of the "moral sanction" of social norms, states: "It admits of no evasion; it comes upon a man from all quarters: he can see no end to its duration, nor limits to its effects." The Rationale of Punishment 210 (1830).

[45] It is not clear in the literature whether "inexorable imposition" is always to be taken as the equivalent of "physical compulsion." In any case, the theory is that the state's sanctions are distinctive.

[46] *Cf.* "Such an order will be called *law* when conformity with it is upheld by the probability that deviant action will be met by physical or psychic sanctions aimed to compel conformity or to punish disobedience, and applied by a group of men especially impowered to carry out this function." Weber, The Theory of Social and Economic Organization 127 (trans. Henderson and Parsons, 1947). "It is thus naturally just as much a case of 'law' whether an order is upheld by ecclesiastical or by a political organization, whether in conformity with the rules of an association or by the authority of the head of a house-

to conclude that in none of the above substantive respects do the State's laws differ from sub-group norms.

Is it possible, however, that a combination of significant criteria distinguish the State's laws from all other norms? Such a combination might include the following: (1) the origin of the State's rules in the maximum power center of the society; (2) the inclusiveness of the public interests, *i.e.* they are interests of the entire society; (3) the organization of the State's laws as a system; (4) the highly formal procedures of adjudication; and (5) a specialized corps of officials—legislators, judges and enforcement officers. It will be granted at once that this combination of criteria might be helpful in current research. But for the reasons stated above, it may be hazarded that this would not lead to the discovery of major substantive differences among the various norms. The ultimate push of presently available theory and the logic of the selected criteria oppose the separation of the State's laws from those of sub-groups except, of course, for practical purposes.

The literature of cultural anthropology provides abundant evidence that rules of criminal law are among the most important social norms. This implies the spontaneity of making or discovering the norms defining the major crimes, the "naturalness" of the core of penal law. The laws on homicide, theft, treason and incest, *e.g.* have not been arbitrarily imposed, nor are they fortuitous. Not only are they among the norms which appear to be practically universal, they also have rational, normal inter-relations with economic and political institutions and changes.[47] Once this is recognized, other rules of penal law which share those characteristics are also proper candidates for admission into the province of criminology. The same is true of the doctrines of penal law, *e.g.* the literature of anthropology also reveals the recognition of mental disease among primitive people, and there are similar data concerning intoxication, infancy,

---

hold." *Id.* 129. Accordingly, Weber's inclusive meaning of "law" must be distinguished from that of political scientists, discussed above.

[47] Hall, *op. cit. supra*, note 2.

and other conditions which are the subject of doctrinal references. If such evidence is not presently available regarding coercion, mistake and other doctrines, this is probably due to the neglect of specialists rather than to the lack of significant data.

If the "really" penal laws, or some of them, are also social norms, the implication for criminology is decisive, and the issue raised by the Positivist School is resolved by the inclusion of at least those penal laws within the subject matter of criminology. With reference to this crucial issue, there is an increasing affirmative consensus among criminologists, which is of the greatest importance for the future progress of that discipline.[48] A corollary of that position, supported in the above discussion, is that penal norms of sub-groups are also within the subject matter of criminology. This is true even though, in the present state of criminology, it may be highly desirable, as a practical matter, to confine research to violations of some of the State's penal laws, as established by convictions. That question, however, should be distinguished from the theoretical demarcation of the subject matter of criminology. Another corollary is that the fact that a penal law satisfies certain formal requirements does not exclude the possibility that it is substantively fortuitous.[49]

The penal laws which are within the subject matter of criminology have been described as "actual penal laws," suggesting supporting public attitudes (mores, *représentations collectives*). What this may imply and, in any case, what is posited here as the subject matter of criminal science, is distinctive conduct and relevant norms that are

[48] Jeffery, *The Structure of American Criminological Thinking*, 46 J. of Cr. L. Crim. & P.S. 658 (1956) ; Jeffery, *Crime, Law and Social Structure*, 47 J. of Cr. L. Crim. & P.S. 424 (1956) ; Tappan, *Who Is the Criminal?* 12 Amer. Soc. Rev. 96 (1947) and see notes 51 and 52.

[49] While penal theory shares this viewpoint, its practical purpose requires it to deal with formal penal laws, which it elucidates by reference to the knowledge of penal law that conforms to the principles of that law. As was suggested in the text *supra*, apart from authoritative technicality, the ultimate basis of elucidation is derived from knowledge of the penal laws which are expressed in conformity and violated in deviation. See note 50.

oriented towards the implementation of the community's values. This is not incompatible with the recognition of certain differences in criminology and penal theory.

One of these concerns the fact that rules are recognized in penal theory as rules of penal law regardless of public attitudes and congruent conduct. Public attitudes (mores) and conduct are essential factual criteria in the subject matter of a social science; and they limit the subject matter of criminology. But in the perspective of penal theory, rules of penal law are either merely formal or they are also true or "real" penal laws, *i.e.* they conform to the principles of penal law. Given the perspective and purposes of the practice of penal law and the corresponding tasks of penal theory, its subject matter is determined in the above direction. On the other hand, while criminology narrows its field by reference to mores and conduct, it enlarges its field by inclusion of the penal laws of sub-groups, which penal theory ignores.

In penal theory, conduct is regarded as separate and apart from the rules of penal law. The premise is that there are rules of penal law, there is criminal conduct violative of those rules, and there are the sanctions. That has also been the perspective of many criminologists, while sociologists speak of the "internalization" of norms. This implies that norms are expressed in certain conduct and that that distinctive conduct is the subject matter of an inclusive socio-legal discipline.[50]

An unavoidable consequence of the current specialization is that serious problems of terminology arise, *e.g.* many legal terms do not suit the requirements of criminological research. In the United States, where fifty legislatures define crimes, it is inevitable that a variety of legal terms is used. "Theft" may be far too inclusive for the purposes of social research. On the other hand, a single social norm may be sub-divided for legislative purposes, *e.g.* embezzlement and larceny by bailee. Again, larceny by trick and

50 See *op. cit. supra*, note 29, note 1, ch. 2, and Hall, Living Law of Democratic Society, ch. 3 (1949).

obtaining property by false pretenses may be viewed by criminologists as references to a single type of criminal conduct. So, too, through inertia or because available knowledge is ignored, penal law may cleave to rules that are indiscriminate in their empirical reference, *e.g.* in most American states the law on receiving stolen property does not distinguish the professional criminal receiver from the occasional one who buys for his own consumption. There are, accordingly, various adjustments in terminology which a social scientist must make to denote relevant social processes and to indicate important differences, where current penal law is indiscriminate, oblique, or vague.[51]

But neither the above tasks of penal theory nor the reformulation of terms by social scientists imply that the latter are working in an utterly different field than that of the penal theorist. If allowance is made for unavoidable technicality, the "distinctively" legal is for the most part only a combination of non-legal data, *i.e.* the various parts of the legal structure are assembled from a non-legal realm of fact, value and meaning. In any event, while the above indicated criminological re-definition of terms requires analogous uses of the findings by penal theorists *vis à vis* the practice of law, their relevance is clearly indicated. In sum, criminology, by providing such factual knowledge, contributes to the elucidation of legal terms, while penal theory contributes to criminology essential meanings which guide the social scientist in his empirical research.

In addition to the instances noted above, there are other contributions which penal theory makes, or can make, to criminology that are equally significant but remain unrecognized because lay scholars have been habituated to assume that "law is technical." The analysis of criminal conduct in terms of the fusion ("concurrence") of cognition and effort, the elucidation of intention, recklessness and inadvertence, the distinction of conduct and behavior and so on could contribute at least precision to the current social

---

[51] See Cressey, *Criminological Research and the Definition of Crimes*, 56 Amer. J. of Soc. 546 (1951).

inquiries. No less important are the distinctions drawn in legal theory among various sanctions, the analysis of their relation to harm and conduct, etc. In these and other respects, there is an imbalance between penal theory and much of current criminology.

This is shown even in some of the work of the late Edwin Sutherland. At the peak of his distinguished career, Sutherland engaged in extensive research on "white collar crime." He studied many violations of law by corporations and businessmen, including false advertising, breaches of trust, and adulteration; and he raised many important questions regarding accepted theories of crime. But Sutherland's research met with sharp criticism among criminologists, and it is especially significant that this criticism relied largely, if unavowedly, upon penal theory. For example, Sutherland assumed that strict liability "penal law" was penal law in the same sense as the law of felonies. He sought to meet criticism on this point by saying that he was not concerned with the reform of the penal law. But the criticism directed against the research on this score did not imply that criminologists should try to improve the law. It meant, instead, that there are important differences in the respective conduct, attitudes and valuations and, also, that the imposition of a punitive sanction for innocent careful conduct which violated a regulation was a very different datum from punishment for murder or robbery. Sutherland, *i.e.* ignored the social significance of *mens rea*. Among criminologists, it was emphasized that his theory of "white collar crime" did not take account of the mores, *e.g.* the public attitudes which support the law on felonies but not that on petty economic offenses. Because of the neglect of penal theory, much of Sutherland's research was also indiscriminate regarding legal sanctions.[52] This, in turn, ob-

---

[52] "In addition, the stipulation, the desist order, and the injunction . . . have the attributes of punishment." Sutherland, *Is "White Collar Crime" Crime?*, 10 Amer. Soc. Rev. 132, 135 (1945). In his book, where he reprinted the above article, the qualification, "in a limited manner," was added to the above sentence. Sutherland, White Collar Crime 38-39 (1949). *Cf.* Caldwell, *A Re-examination of the Concept of White Collar Crime*, 22 Fed. Prob. 30 (1958) and see note 48 *supra*.

scured the differences among various harms, *e.g.* the notion of "social injury" was used by Sutherland to include all violations of law, thus blurring important distinctions among torts, crimes, breaches of contract, and so on.[53]

Penal theory and criminology are directly concerned with proscribed harms, *i.e.* deviation. But deviation, as was seen in determining the meaning of "mental disease" by reference to "normality," implies conformity. The fact that conformity is ignored in penal theory does not alter its relation to the problem of understanding penal law; nor does the equal neglect of conformity by some criminologists and psychiatrists make it any less relevant to social abnormality. Statistically, conformity looms far more importantly than does deviation; indeed, it is axiomatic that the "weight" of conformity must prevail over that of deviation if a society is to retain its identity and survive.

Conformity includes much more than the acts of fulfilling contracts, paying taxes, driving carefully, refraining from the commission of criminal harms, and the like. "Conformity" implies all the positive values whose violation is proscribed, as well as the actions that express those values. In this wide meaning, conformity implies the various processes and actions that, together with the relevant norms and values, constitute a social, legal order. It is that order which sets the standards for appraisal of the disvalues (harms, deviations). That order is an essential part of the subject matter of a socio-legal discipline in which criminal science would be included.

This inclusive socio-legal discipline involves some fundamental questions concerning "social science," where the moot issues in the present inquiry will become evident. Since it is impossible to discuss here the many different

[53] The unfortunate consequence of this neglect of penal theory has been that extremely important parts of Sutherland's researches have been overlooked, *e.g.* his studies of embezzlement, fraud and other criminal conduct; and he also showed that many of these offenders receive relatively lenient treatment. By directing attention to these offenses and offenders, he achieved his purpose to challenge prevailing theories of the causes of crimes, especially the over-emphasis on economics.

meanings given to "social science," it seems preferable to state directly the conclusions reached by this writer and how they concern the subject of the present chapter. Simplified for this purpose, the two "extreme" positions regarding "social science" are: (a) that there are no differences between the physical sciences and the social sciences as regards subject matter, methods of inquiry and type of knowledge; and (b) that human beings and inter-personal relations are unique, and that the methods of social science and the knowledge derived from employing them are distinctive.

, In taking a defensible position with reference to these questions, certain facts seem compelling. If attention is fixed upon present knowledge, not upon future hopes or prospects, it is undeniable that there is very little social science which exhibits the rigorous structure of the physical sciences or provides the consequent type of knowledge of causes. At the same time, however, it is possible to discover significant recurrent patterns among inter-personal relations. These generalizations express a co-variation of variables, they extend beyond merely statistical statements, and they are verifiable by determinate empirical proof.[54] In addition to this type of knowledge, detailed case-histories and similar inquiries, while they do not find expression in the above sort of generalization, add considerably to our knowledge of human action in relation to certain variables, including the State's laws. This type of knowledge reflects the methods of history and art in the reconstruction of life-situations; and it is derived from "participation" in specific instances of problem-solving.[55] In sum, social science is a composite kind of knowledge whose subject matter exhibits both unique characteristics and also common recurrent properties that can be classified and expressed in generalizations which approximate scientific laws.

The above conclusions apply to the inter-relations of penal theory and criminology, viewed as divisions of a

[54] Hall, Theft, Law and Society, chs. 6 and 7 (2nd ed. 1952).
[55] *Id.* Introduction and ch. 1.

criminal science, and, to a large extent, they can be referred
to the question of causation and values. Criminologists are
apt to emphasize a scientific view of causation, while penal
theory, as seen in preceding chapters, emphasizes the autonomy of normal adults. But, in fact, as was also shown,
both disciplines are concerned with both types of causation.
There may seem to be a theoretical incompatibility between
causal explanation proceeding on premises of universal determinism and that derived from sympathetic participation
in the dynamic functioning of the human personality, motivated and end-seeking. Actually, however, these two types
of explanation supplement each other, and both are regularly relied upon unless one of them is barred arbitrarily.
We wish to know the general conditions, physical, biological
and social, that influence the problem-solving exemplified in
criminal conduct; and we wish, also, to know the internal
processes of reasoning, decision, and evaluation that precede
and accompany such conduct, which are the particular concern of penal theory. The fact is that we remain unsatisfied
with explanation that ignores the internal states, the reasoning and rationalizations, the way in which the problems
were presented and in which various motives and intentions
came into being—in short, the dynamism of the thinking,
problem-solving personality. We cannot apprehend this
process by rigorous scientific investigation alone, for such
knowledge of it as we have shows that the process is not
limited by preceding or accompanying conditions—else we
could not say that anyone ever *solved* any problem.

In addition, if it be granted that the various "solutions"
reached by offenders, manifested in their criminal conduct, can be significantly criticized by reference to other
possible ones, it becomes both relevant and necessary to
make such appraisals. The underlying premise is that more
or less "correct" answers to human problems are discoverable. Thus, as was previously suggested,[56] evaluation is
implicit in the diagnosis of the personality of deviators
since an understanding of moral conflict and of the de-

[56] *Supra*, chapter 13, at notes 51-57.

cisions made by problem-solvers implies the cogency of ethical criticism. Penal theory provides that critique; and criminology can make much use of it in understanding the values of deviators.

In sum, since the principles of penal law subsume the rules and doctrines of penal law, they refer ultimately to facts and valuations which are indistinguishable from those denoted by the norms of sub-groups. Penal theory and criminology therefore share a common interest in principles, doctrines and rules of penal law as well as in the concomitant criminal conduct. This should not be obscured by the fact that penal theorists concentrate upon the elucidation of legal terms while criminologists study the causes of crime. Knowledge of causes of criminal conduct, in the two principal senses discussed above, is knowledge of the nature of criminal conduct. When the criminologist generalizes descriptively, he does so with regard to the empirical references of certain prescriptions. When the penal theorist elucidates these prescriptions, he does so in reliance upon the knowledge of relevant facts which the empirical discipline provides. Accordingly, the various disciplines concerned with criminal conduct, law and punishment should be viewed as a single inquiry in which naming and the elucidation of the terms proceed coordinately with empirical investigation and ethical criticism. There is an inter-penetration of these branches of knowledge when they are focused upon the solution of practical problems.

TABLE OF CASES

References are to Pages.

References are to Pages.

SUBJECT INDEX

References are to Pages.

CAUSATION—Continued
  direct, 257-61
  explanatory, 285-86
  Hart-Honoré theory, 284-94
  homicide, 257-60, 279
  instinctive movements, 271
  instrument, 270
  intervening, 261-70, 273
  legal, 196, 250, 251-54, 256, 258,
    283
  means-end, 252-53, 425-35
  medical negligence, 262-64
  mens rea, relation, 258, 261,
    282-83, 292
  mental disease, 506-09, 512-13
  motivation, 251, 270-80
  negligence, 255-56
  omission, 195-97, 287-88
  Pennsylvania cases, 275-81
  perspective, 247-48
  physical, 421-25
  policy, 284-95
  proximate, 277-80
  scientific, 251, 252
  simultaneous, 268
  sine qua non, 267-68, 282
  subsequent act, 265-67, 273
  substantial, 283
  suicide, 273
  teleological, 252-53, 256, 258,
    425-35
  tort and crime, 254-57

CIRCUMSTANCES, 171, 172,
    237-40
      See *Actus Reus*
  "extenuating" and
    "aggravating," 101
  "material," 240
  principles, allocated to, 238
  Salmond, 239
  Smith, J. C., 239

CODES
  criticism, 17-18
  European, general part, 16
  specific part, 17

COERCION, 436-48
      See NECESSITY
  accomplice, 443
  Canadian law, 447-48
  cases, 437-42
  compulsion, 417, 418, 421
  defined, 436-37

  duress, 437
  excuse, justification, 235-36
  limitations on defense, 440-43
  murder, 438-40
  necessity, distinguished, 447-48
  phenomena of, 437
  policy, 445-48
  treason, 437

CONCURRENCE
  cases illustrating, 186-90
  conduct, 179
  homicide, 189
  larceny, 187
  omission, 188-89
  principle, 179, 186-90

CONDUCT, 177-79
      See ACT; OMISSION
  analysis of, 181
  case-law, logic, 180-82
  concurrence, 179
  dimensions, 219
  harm, condition of, 183-84
  manifested effort, 179
  "privileged," 272

CONSTRUCTION OF
STATUTES
      See INTERPRETATION
        OF STATUTES

CONSTRUCTIVE HOMICIDE
  felony-murder, 129, 259-60,
    547-48
  misdemeanor-manslaughter,
    259-60

CORPUS DELICTI, 225-27, 230
      See *Actus Reus*

CRIME
  defined, 17-22
  legal definition, 35-55, 157
  means-end, 228, 236
  Stephen's definition, 157

CRIMINAL ATTEMPT
      See ATTEMPT

CRIMINAL THEORY
      See PENAL THEORY
  Blackstone, 9-10
  Bracton, 6-7
  classification, 17
  defined, 1-2

F

FELONY-MURDER RULE
    See CONSTRUCTIVE HOMICIDE
limitation of liability, 129

G

GUILT
    See CULPABILITY; *Mens Rea*

H

HARM
       See *Actus Reus*
  attempt, 214, 217-18
  attitudes, 214, 216
  constitutionality, 212-13
  conduct, condition of, 183-84
  conduct, relation, 213
  culpability, element, 242
  formal, 214
  gravity, 216-17
  ignorance, 372
  inchoate crimes, 214, 217-18
  incorporeal in nature, 217-19
  mistake, 372
  penal, 217
  penal and tort, 240-46
  practical problems, 212
  punishment, relation to, 213
  role in theory, 221-22
  sociological, 216
  tort and crime, 243-46, 317-18
  values, implied, 215-16

**HOLMES' THEORY OF
PENAL LIABILITY, 147-64**

I

IGNORANCE AND MISTAKE
  advice of counsel, 387-88
  Aristotle, 368-70
  Austin's theory, 378-79, 381
  bigamy, 395-401
  doctrines of, 360

ethical principle, mistake of
  fact, 363-64, 366-68
fact and law, distinguished,
  376-77, 382
Holmes' theory, 379-80, 381
ignorance, defined, 361
income tax, 395
indefiniteness of statute, 388-89
invalidating decision, reversed,
  389-90
interpretations, official, 391-92
invincible, 368-70
"juris," 409-10
law, 376 ff., 383
negligence, 368, 370-71
objective liability, 367
petty offenses, 402-08
policy, 413-14
property crimes, 392-94
rationale of doctrine of fact,
  383-84, 386-87
reasonableness, 366-68, 371-72
reform of current law, 402-08
restrictions, 366-75
Roman law, 378
sexual offenses, 373-74
strict liability, 372-75
types of problem, 408-13
vincible, 368-70

*IGNORANTIA FACTI
EXCUSAT*
  See IGNORANCE AND MISTAKE;
  Mens Rea; OBJECTIVE LIABILITY
  act, relation to, 185
  defined, 360-61
  doctrine of, 231, 235, 238, 360
  involuntary, Aristotle, 364
  "knowledge of fact," 361, 394

*IGNORANTIA JURIS
NEMINEM EXCUSAT*
  See IGNORANCE AND MISTAKE;
  Mens Rea
  aptness of, 378
  ethical policy of, 383
  exception to, 391-93, 404
  ex post facto, 390
  "ignorantia," 377
    special meaning of, 388, 409
  "knowledge" of the law, 388, 409
  legal order, elements of, 383
  mens rea, 393, 396
  mistake of law, 406-07
  non-retroactivity, relation to, 63

References are to Pages.

*IGNORANTIA JURIS
NEMINEM EXCUSAT*—
Continued
  omissions, relation to, 200
  rationale of, 382-84
  application of, 387-89

INSANITY
  See MENTAL DISEASE

INTEGRATION OF MENTAL
FUNCTIONS, 478, 494-95

INTENTION
  See *Mens Rea*
  ambiguity, 597-98
  Austin's view, 108-11
  "constructive intent," 142
  desire, 111
  expectation, 108-10
    Salmond's criticism, 110
  "general," 142-44
  meaning, 113-14
  objective risk, 117-19
  proof of, 119
  "specific," 142
  "transferred," 145

INTERPRETATION OF
PENAL STATUTES
  See LEGALITY
  ambiguity, 41, 43-44
  analogy, 35-38, 48, 50-51
  canons, 38-40
  genuine, 38, 40-42, 44-45
  judicial attitudes, 38, 47
  liberal, 38, 48
  Marshall, 40
  strict, 39-40, 45
  theory of, 41, 44, 46, 47
  vagueness, 41-42, 44-45, 53-54

INTOXICATION
  See *Mens Rea*
  addiction, 549
  alcoholism, research on, 549-52
  classes of inebriates, 551
  delirium tremens, 544, 549-50
  dipsomania, 542
  exculpatory rule, 531-34
  felony-murder, 547-48
  grounds for early law, 530-31
  history, common law, 530
  manslaughter, 535-37
  mens rea, 107
  murder, 534-35, 546
  policy, 537

reform of the law, 552-56
  Austin, 553
  experienced, normal
    inebriates, 555-56
  inexperienced inebriate
    harm-doers, 555-56
  "specific intent," 532-34, 544-46
  temporary insanity, 541-42, 550
  "voluntary intoxication,"
    538-40, 550-51
  coercion, 538-39
  fraud, 538
  sickness, 540, 542-43

"IRRESISTIBLE IMPULSE"
  See MENTAL DISEASE

J

JUSTIFICATION AND
EXCUSE, 227-37
  arrest, 228-29
  coercion, 235-36
  common law, 232-34
  criticism, 234-35
  distinguished, 233-34
  legality, principle, 237
  logic of, **233**
  procedure, 231-32
  Radbruch, 233-35
  self-defense, 229

L

LEGALITY
  analogy, 35-38, 66-67
  Anglo-American, 52
  case-law, 52
  definition of crime, 35-55
  divergence, German, 48-49, 50,
    65, 67
    Russian, 48-49, 66, 67
  ex post facto, 60
  extraordinaria judicia, 29, 30
  historical meaning, 28
  history, 28-35
    American colonial, 33
    Continental, 32-34
    English, 31-32, 52-53
    Feuerbach, 34
    Greek, 30
    medieval, 30

References are to Pages.

References are to Pages.

NECESSITY—Continued
  history, 416-17
  hypothetical, 419-20
  involuntary action, relation of,
    421, 422
  physical causation, 421-25
  policy, 445-48
  self-defense, distinguished,
    434-35
  state of, defined, 426
  Stephen, 418
  teleological, 420-22, 425-34
  types of, 419-21
  volition, mixed, 421
  voluntary action, relation of,
    421-22

NEGLIGENCE
        See *Mens Rea*
  correction, 141
  criminal, 127
  defined, 114, 116, 120
  degrees, 116
  ethical rationale, 133-34
  ethics, 135-39
  exclusion from penal law, 3-4,
    135-39
  factual ignorance, 375
  history, 122-24, 126
  homicide, 130-33
  invincible error, 368-72
  logic of ethics, 371-72
  policy, 135-39
  proof, 120
  punishment, 135-37
  recklessness, 115, 122-24,
    128, 130
  tort, rationale, 136

NON-MORAL LIABILITY
        See Liability
  Holmes' theory, 147-64
  "external" liability, 151, 153

NON-RETROACTIVITY OF
PENAL STATUTES
        See Legality
  case-law, 61
  defined, 60
  English history, 59
  policy, 61-62
  U. S. Constitution, 59-60

NORMAL
  standard, 289
  statistical, 289

NULLA POENA SINE LEGE
        See Legality

*NULLUM CRIMEN SINE
LEGE*

        See Legality

O

OBJECTIVE LIABILITY
        See Negligence
  "cooling time," 160, 162
  evidence, distinguished, 163
  murder, 160-61
  policy, 167
  provocation, 160, 162
  recklessness, 120
  restriction of, 166
  subjective, distinguished, 163

OBJECTIVE RISK, 117-19

OMISSION, 190-206
        See Act
  Bentham, 191
  case-law, 201-05
  causation, 195-97, 201
  commission par omission, 199
  concurrence, 188-89
  difficulty in analysis, 200-01
  direct and indirect, 198-99
  ignorantia juris, relation, 200,
    201
  legal duty, 193-94, 204
  Macaulay, 190-92
  mens rea, 200-01, 204-05
  movement of will, modern view,
    198
  physical aspect, 198
  policy, 208-11
  possession, 206-07
  reform proposed, 210-11
  theories, 200, 208
  voluntary, 197

P

PENAL THEORY
        See Criminal Theory;
            Criminology
  criminal science, 607-08

CPSIA information can be obtained at www.ICGtesting.com
Printed in the USA
LVOW092046260213

321729LV00005B/50/P